IBN TAYMIYYA

Studies in Islamic Philosophy

Studies in Islamic Philosophy

General Editor: S. Nomanul Haq
VOLUME IV

IBN TAYMIYYA AND HIS TIMES

editors
YOSSEF RAPOPORT
and
SHAHAB AHMED

OXFORD
UNIVERSITY PRESS

OXFORD
UNIVERSITY PRESS

Oxford University Press is a department of the University of Oxford. It furthers the University's objective of excellence in research, scholarship, and education by publishing worldwide. Oxford is a registered trade mark of Oxford University Press in the UK and in certain other countries

Published in Pakistan by
Ameena Saiyid, Oxford University Press
No.38, Sector 15, Korangi Industrial Area,
PO Box 8214, Karachi-74900, Pakistan

First Edition published in 2010

This edition in Oxford Pakistan Paperbacks 2015

ISBN 978-0-19-940206-9

Printed on 68gsm Local Offset paper

Printed by Mushtaq Packages, Karachi

CONTENTS

FOREWORD BY THE GENERAL EDITOR

It is hard to imagine a meaningful discourse on contemporary Muslim political thought and activism without reference to Ibn Taymiyya. An eminently energetic and bold thinker, often appearing as harsh and overbearing, this northern Syrian witness of the thirteenth-century Mongolian devastations has been appropriated by the major modern-day radical 'Islamist' movements as their revered fountainhead. Of course, this activist invocation of Ibn Taymiyya is common knowledge. And yet, though he looms large on the horizons of our times, he 'is more often cited than understood, constantly evoked and not sufficiently studied,' as the editors of this volume ruefully report. In modern scholarship Ibn Taymiyya has been examined only in bits and pieces—and while these bits and pieces may be fascinating in their own isolated rigor, they give us no coherent synthesis of his legacy that has dramatically risen into prominence in the Islamic world since the eighteenth century, after a long period of relative obscurity.

This re-emergence of a largely overlooked medieval thinker in a particular ideological posture, and at a particular later time in Islamic history, is in itself an intriguing question, especially perhaps because it is a pre-colonial phenomenon. Then, as the essays in this book take us closer and closer to the totality of Ibn Taymiyya's intellectual and functional worlds, we see how complex and variegated these worlds are, both philosophically and historically. After reading these essays, which are conceived in a way so as to arrange individual units of research into some kind of a coherent whole, as atoms of a gravitational field of force, we begin to imagine now a formidable personage who defies neat and easy classification—is Ibn Taymiyya a traditionalist or an iconoclast? A puritan or a pragmatist? A philosopher or a neo-mutakallim? Is his *salafism* a reactionary formula or a liberating act? Is his dislike of tomb visitations a dismissal of sufi practices or an attempt to re-claim spiritualism for his own system? Or is he simply a zealot who embodies an exclusivist Muslim bigotry?

So the studies gathered here problematize Ibn Taymiyya—and this is a big gain, since they open for us new vistas of theoretical and historical enquiry rather than closing them up. Besides, this volume also leads us to appreciate the fact that the subject of these studies is not simply of a fleeting, topical interest, subject to political winds; no, it would now seem that Ibn Taymiyya is of interest in his own right, given the sheer philosophical worth and acumen of his ideas, and given that he provides us with the means to explain the trends of political appropriations of our times, enabling us also to recognize the dangers of all those selective expositions of medieval Muslim figures that are employed in the service of naïve criticisms and essentializing journalistic rhetoric.

I ought to congratulate my colleague and friend Michael Cook for his generous financial support of the Princeton University Ibn Taymiyya conference whose edited papers constitute the bulk of this book. Professor Cook paid for the conference out of his research funds, and this is a gesture that is to be cherished gratefully by the whole world of scholarship. A special word of thanks need to be placed on record for Everett Rowson too: like Professor Cook, he is also a member of our editorial committee, but he has performed more than a ceremonial function. Professor Rowson read each of the essays that follow, practically line by line, meticulously, painstakingly, and at a relatively short notice. He made numerous corrections, gave the editors erudite suggestions, and what we have ended up with is so much better due to his expert involvement in the work. I am very grateful to him. Here I must also acknowledge Robert Wisnovsky's editorial role in the *Studies in Islamic Philosophy* series.

Once again, I have exercised the patience of the editors, particularly of Yossi Rappoport, and I am thankful to them for bearing with me. And as always, I remain obliged to Ghousia Gofran Ali, Academic Editor of Oxford University Press, and Ameena Saiyid, Managing Director, for their elegant encouragement and efficient support throughout the process.

Syed Nomanul Haq
School of Humanities, Social Sciences, and Law
Lahore University of Management Sciences
August, 2009

ACKNOWLEDGEMENTS

This project originated with Michael Cook, who invited us to join the Department of Near Eastern Studies at Princeton University as Visiting Scholars, co-teach a graduate seminar on Ibn Taymiyya and organize a conference on Ibn Taymiyya's thought and legacy. Thus, this volume is in many ways his brain-child.

The conference, entitled "Ibn Taymiyya and His Times," was held at Princeton University from 8 to 10 April 2005. All the papers in this volume, apart from Yossef Rapoport's contribution, were presented at that conference. We would like to thank all the participants, some of whom presented papers that are not included in this volume: Zayde Antrim, Felicitas Opwis, Aron Zysow, Tamer el-Leithy, Baber Johansen, Giovanni Schallenbergh and Yudian Wahyudi.

Our students at Princeton shared our enthusiasm and admiration for the Shaykh, and they influenced our interpretation of his work in many ways. They are Sibtain S. Abidi, John-Paul Ghobrial, Suzanne Gunasti, George Hatke, Naseem Surhio, Mairaj Syed and Jack Tannous. We would like to especially thank John-Paul Ghobrial, who has been involved in the preparation of this volume by casting a careful eye over all the contributions.

During the editing of this volume, we have benefited from the collaboration and input of Ahmad Dallal, Geneviève Gobillot, Adam Sabra, Mark Swanson and Stefan Winter. Yahya Michot has generously shared with us his intimate knowledge of Ibn Taymiyya's writings.

Finally, our stay in Princeton and the conference were generously funded by the Mellon Foundation. At the final stages of editing, we received financial support from the History Department at Queen Mary, University of London.

LIST OF CONTRIBUTORS

Shahab Ahmed is Assistant Professor of Islamic Studies at Harvard University. He has also been Assistant Professor of Classical Arabic Literature at the American University in Cairo, Junior Fellow of the Harvard Society of Fellows, Visiting Scholar in the Department of Near Eastern Studies at Princeton University, and Higher Education Commission of Pakistan Visiting Scholar in the Islamic Research Institute, Islamabad.

Tariq al-Jamil is Assistant Professor of Religion and Islamic Studies at Swarthmore College. His research focuses on Shiʿism and intercommunal violence, religious dissimulation, and the transmission of knowledge in medieval Islam. He is currently completing a monograph on Sunni-Shiʿi relations in Baghdad during the 13th and 14th centuries.

Caterina Bori teaches Islamic studies at the Gregorian Pontifical University in Rome and at the University of Perugia. She is also a Research Associate in the Department of History at the School of Oriental and African Studies, London, and the author of *Ibn Taymiyya: una vita esemplare* (2003).

Racha el Omari is Assistant Professor of Arabic at the University of California Santa Barbara. She works on Islamic theology and intellectual history, and is completing a monograph on the theology of Abu al-Qāsim al-Balkhī (d. 319/931).

Khaled El-Rouayheb is Assistant Professor of Islamic Intellectual History in the Department of Near Eastern Languages & Civilizations at Harvard University. He works on the history of logic and other aspects of Arabic-Islamic intellectual history from 1200 to 1800. He is the author of *Before Homosexuality in the Arab-Islamic World, 1500–1800* (2005).

Mona Hassan is Assistant Professor of Islamic Studies and History at Duke University. Her PhD dissertation is entitled "Loss of Caliphate: The Trauma and Aftermath of 1258 and 1924" (Princeton University, 2009).

Jon Hoover is Assistant Professor of Islamic Studies at the Near East School of Theology in Beirut. He is the author of *Ibn Taymiyya's Theodicy of Perpetual Optimism* (2007) and other studies on Taymiyyan thought.

Livnat Holtzman is a Lecturer in the Department of Arabic at Bar Ilan University. Her fields of research include Ḥanbalī and Ash'ari theology, Qur'ān exegesis and didactic poetry, and she has published articles on Ibn Qayyim al-Jawziyya and Aḥmad Ibn Ḥanbal.

M. Sait Özervarli is a fellow at the Research Centre of Anatolian Civilizations at Koç University in Istanbul and also teaches at Marmara University. He has published (in Turkish) "Ibn Taymiyya's Methodology of Thought and his Criticisms of the *mutakallimūn*" (2008), and "The Revitalization of Muslim Theology in Modern Times" (1998).

Yossef Rapoport is a Lecturer in the Department of History at Queen Mary University of London. He has published on Islamic law, gender, cartography and the economic history of medieval Islam. He is the author of *Marriage, Money and Divorce in Medieval Islamic Society* (2005), and co-editor of *The Book of Curiosities: A critical edition* (Internet publication, 2007).

Walid A. Saleh is Associate Professor in the Department and Centre for the Study of Religion at the University of Toronto. His research interests are the Qur'ān and its exegesis. He is the author of *The Formation of the Classical* Tafsīr *Tradition* (2004).

David Thomas is Professor of Christianity and Islam in the School of Philosophy, Theology and Religion at the University of Birmingham. He works on Islamic religious thought and on the history and theology of Christian-Muslim relations. His recent publications have centred on polemical exchanges between the two faiths.

Raquel Ukeles is Assistant Professor of Religious Studies at Fairfield University. Her PhD dissertation is entitled "Innovation or Deviation: Exploring the Boundaries of Islamic Devotional Law" (Harvard University, 2006).

Introduction

Ibn Taymiyya and His Times

Yossef Rapoport and *Shahab Ahmed*

On 22 May 2003, ten days after a series of suicide bombings in Riyadh, a leading Saudi newspaper published an article entitled 'The Individual and the Homeland are more valuable than Ibn Taymiyya'. The author, Khaled al-Ghanami, placed ultimate responsibility for the terrorist attacks on the medieval theologian and jurist Taqī al-Dīn Ibn Taymiyya (1263–1328). For al-Ghanamī, it was the blind adherence to Ibn Taymiyya, and his long posthumous shadow, that stimulated violence and intolerance:

> How did these murderers justify the shedding of the blood of Muslims and children? They did this based on a *fatwā* of Ibn Taymiyya on jihad, in which he rules that if infidels take shelter behind Muslims, and these Muslims become a shield for the infidels, it is permitted to kill the Muslims in order to get at the infidels. Ibn Taymiyya did not base his *fatwā* on any verse in the Qur'ān, nor on any saying of the Prophet. I don't see this *fatwā* as bringing about the ultimate goals of the Sharī'a, but rather it is a mistaken legal opinion, that goes against the way of the Prophet.... Let us say this honestly: Our problem today is with Ibn Taymiyya himself. Some of our jurists have taken Ibn Taymiyya to be their sole yardstick, and elevated him to a position he never enjoyed in his own lifetime, in his own land.[1]

Not for the first time, Ibn Taymiyya had been identified as the ultimate trouble-maker. A refugee from a city in northern Syria that had been devastated by the Mongols, and a member of the minority Ḥanbalī community in Damascus, Ibn Taymiyya rose to public prominence during the brief Mongol occupation of Syria in 1300 CE. While most of the civilian and military elite fled, Ibn Taymiyya stayed put, bravely representing the ravaged city in front of the Mongol generals. When the Mongols withdrew and the authority of the Cairo-based Mamluk sultans was restored, he set out to preach an increasingly radicalized program of religious reform. Committed to direct action, on a few occasions he even led bands of disciples against what he perceived to be un-Islamic practices.

But it was mostly his words that his contemporaries found inspiring or, more often, unsettling. He was put on trial three times, first for supporting a literal interpretation of God's attributes, then for undermining the power of legal oaths, and finally for denouncing the popular practice of tomb visitation. Criticism also came from the direction of fellow scholars. His disciple and colleague al-Dhahabī thought he was cantankerous, arrogant and tactless, and the Moroccan traveller Ibn Baṭṭūṭa, when passing in Damascus, noted in his journal that Ibn Taymiyya 'had a screw loose'.

Today, few figures from the medieval Islamic period can claim such a hold on modern Islamic discourses. Revered by the eighteenth-century Wahhabi movement in the Arabian Peninsula, Ibn Taymiyya also inspired like-minded reformers, as near as Iraq and as far away as Indonesia. Later on, Ibn Taymiyya was hailed as the architect of Salafism, the concept espoused by revivalist movements calling for a return to the pristine golden age of the Prophet. For these modern groups, Ibn Taymiyya stands out not only because he claimed to be following the footsteps of the *salaf*, the first three generations of Islam, but also because of his active involvement in society and his defiant stand against foreign occupation. In the last few decades Ibn Taymiyya's name has become associated with political violence and terror, especially since his works were cited by the radical group responsible for the assassination of the Egyptian President Anwar Sadat in 1981. A recent book on Islamic extremism, *The Age of Sacred Terror*, treats the entire history of modern Islamic movements, from the Syrian reformer Rashid Rida (d. 1935), through the Pakistani al-Mawdudi (d. 1979), the radicalism of the Egyptian Sayyid Qutb (d. 1966) and, eventually, al-Qa'ida, in a single narrative improbably, yet significantly, entitled 'Ibn Taymiyya and His Children'.[2]

Yet Ibn Taymiyya is more often cited than understood, constantly evoked and not sufficiently studied. This is partly due to the wide scope of his interests and his immense scholarly output—the modern incomplete edition of his works spans 35 volumes, which are written in a characteristically digressive, disjointed style that bears the marks of brilliant insights hastily jotted down. Both friends and foes acknowledged that Ibn Taymiyya had a breathtaking mastery of the Islamic intellectual tradition. Much of his early writing is theological, with its main thrust focused on the interpretation of divine attributes and the role of reason in interpreting revelation. His later writing is oriented towards questions of practice, such as the visitation of tombs. In between he wrote—to take a few examples—the most detailed anti-Christian and anti-Shiʿi polemics to come from the medieval Sunni tradition; an unprecedented empiricist critique of Greek logic; and a revisionist reappraisal of the Satanic Verses incident, which allows for the Prophet to be temporarily tempted by the Devil.

The sheer scale of Ibn Taymiyya's writings, the diversity of subjects and disciplines, and the different contexts in which he was and is invoked, require, almost by necessity, a collective effort of interpretation. Over the last few years there have appeared in western languages up-to-date and scholarly monographs on central aspects of Ibn Taymiyya's thought, such as his theodicy and legal thought, as well as a new biography.[3] As yet, however, there has emerged no coherent synthesis that could serve as a standard introduction to the study of Ibn Taymiyya's work and legacy. As several contributors to this volume note, Laoust's ground-breaking and monumental scholarship is by now mostly surpassed, but has not yet been replaced.[4]

The present volume has its origins in a conference entitled "Ibn Taymiyya and His Times", sponsored by Michael Cook and funded by the Mellon Foundation, which was held at Princeton University from 8–10 April 2005. The conference set out to bring together leading authorities on medieval Islamic theology, philosophy and jurisprudence, as well as students of modern Islamic movements, in order to offer a multi-disciplinary, historically contextualised perspective on Ibn Taymiyya's life, work and legacy. All the papers in this volume, apart from Yossef Rapoport's contribution, were presented at that conference.

Like the conference from which it originates, the present volume seeks to answer three interrelated sets of questions. The first is to identify a common approach underpinning Ibn Taymiyya's prolific and diverse contributions to the discourses of law, theology, philosophy, Qur'ānic exegesis, Hadith, law, mysticism, political theory and inter-faith polemics. Is there a discernible "Taymiyyan" method, and, if so, what are its characteristics? The second course of inquiry concerns Ibn Taymiyya's historical context. In what ways were Ibn Taymiyya's career and thought expressive and illustrative of the social, political and intellectual context in which he lived? What aspects of his personal biography, social network and communal allegiances informed the development of his ideas? Finally, the volume is concerned with the nature of Ibn Taymiyya's legacy in the centuries that followed his death. How have Ibn Taymiyya's ideas been received and rendered by modern Muslims? Why and in what ways have his ideas commanded such an apparently powerful influence during the past century? Has Ibn Taymiyya really dominated the history of Islamic thought in the 20th century, or has he in fact been dominated by modern concerns?

The following introductory essay will draw on the contributions in this volume in order to address these questions of a 'Taymiyyan' methodology, historical context and contemporary resonance. Although the papers cover very diverse aspects of Islamic thought and history, they are far short of a comprehensive account of Ibn Taymiyya's work and legacy. Still, the proceedings of the conference do converge on several key points, which, when viewed in their entirety, challenge much of the popular image of Ibn Taymiyya today. First, several papers highlight the central importance of reason to Ibn Taymiyya's theology and jurisprudence, and the degree to which he has broken ranks with his traditionalist, Ḥanbalī training. Second, the papers offer a critical examination of Ibn Taymiyya's reliance on the model of the early Islamic community (the *salaf*), suggesting that his Salafism is instrumental to his reform agenda. Thirdly, the image of Ibn Taymiyya as staunch puritan is undermined by several contributors who highlight a pervasive pragmatism in his approach to questions of practice. Finally, Ibn Taymiyya emerges from this volume as a minority, un-representative figure in his own times and in the centuries that followed. The reasons for his astonishing modern appeal are yet to be fully explained. However, it is clear that his modern popularity stands in stark opposition to his pre-modern marginality.

Ibn Taymiyya and Contemporary Traditionalism

In her study of Ibn Taymiyya's intellectual milieu, which opens this volume, Caterina Bori illustrates his break with the traditionalist, Ḥanbalī circles in which he had been brought up. Contemporary scholars with a traditionalist outlook, who emphasized revelation as the sole guide to religious truth, were not necessarily supportive of Ibn Taymiyya. We have noted above the famous criticism by the

Shāfiʿī historian and scholar of Hadith al-Dhahabī (d. 1348), a one-time disciple and colleague who expressed exasperation with Ibn Taymiyya's constant polemics, his contempt for fellow scholars and his sense of superiority. Ibn Taymiyya, however, did not even receive much support from within his own Ḥanbalī community. His views were regarded as a challenge to Ḥanbalī orthodoxy, and his *ijtihād*, especially in matters of law, was rarely welcomed. There is no evidence that Ibn Taymiyya had a large following among the Ḥanbalī community. In fact, Bori demonstrates that Ibn Taymiyya led a small group of devout followers, maybe no more than a dozen, who were not all Ḥanbalī but rather were attracted to his cause from outside the established boundaries of the schools of law.

Rather than a leader of a mass movement, Ibn Taymiyya was the spiritual guide of a small circle of radical scholars. Bori examines closely the internal correspondence between the members of this tightly knit group, the *jamāʿa* of disciples who studied with him, transmitted his texts, and shared his taste for activism and religious reform. Far from being populist, the group's correspondence resonates with the sort of pride and self-righteousness of the elect few. Towards the end of his life, even the cohesion of this small radical group appears to have been tested, as it was faced with increasing opposition to the perceived erratic behaviour of their *shaykh*. The popular appeal of Ibn Taymiyya, most evident in the mass attendance at his funeral, was partly based on admiration for his courage during the Mongol occupation of Damascus in 1300[5], partly on reverence for his moral ideals.

Bori suggests that the opposition of the office-holding scholarly elite to Ibn Taymiyya had only little to do with his admittedly difficult personality. Ibn Taymiyya was indeed tactless and arrogant, a man with little time for pleasantries and small talk. Bori, however, sees Ibn Taymiyya's increasing isolation primarily as a result of the radicalization of his doctrines. One watershed may be his first trial in Damascus, during which he refused to seek shelter under his Ḥanbalī credentials, and insisted that his famous creed, entitled *al-ʿAqīda al-Wāsiṭiyya*, was not merely a variation on Ḥanbalī doctrine. Another watershed may have been the issue of divorce, in which his legal opinions stood in direct opposition to the orthodox position of all the Sunni schools. More generally, however, traditionalist criticisms of Ibn Taymiyya seem to concentrate on his overall methodology of bringing philosophical methods into the fold of traditionalist scholarship, and his combination of rational and traditional sciences.

Reason and Revelation in Ibn Taymiyya's Thought

The combination of rationalism and traditionalism is perhaps the most distinctive trait of Ibn Taymiyya's religious thought, and it is the focus of the contribution of Mehmet Sait Özervarli, who terms Ibn Taymiyya's theology 'Qur'ānic rationalism'. For Ibn Taymiyya, rational and traditional proofs exist together as two complementary components of knowledge that are not truly separate from each other. Reason (*'aql*) does not and could not contradict revelation (*naql*), because revelation, all-inclusive and faultless, contains within itself perfect and complete rational foundations. The most obvious example of supposed contradiction between revelation and rationalism concerns the attributes of God. The theologians believed that the attributes of God that appeared in the Qur'ān contradicted reason, and need to be interpreted away metaphorically. But Ibn Taymiyya argued that if reason endorses all revelation as reliable, then it is impossible to reject specific parts of it—i.e., the attributes of God—as unreliable. Doing so would invalidate the status of reason as a source of knowledge. Rather, the apparent contradictions arose because the theologians followed a flawed kind of rationalism. The most perfect rational method is provided in the Qur'ān and the Sunna, and it is this Qur'ānic rationalism which needs to be followed.

Ibn Taymiyya never denied the authority of reason and its role in demonstrating the truthfulness of the revealed and transmitted sources. Unlike earlier traditionalist scholars, Ibn Taymiyya discusses the topics of philosophical theology at length, and is in constant dialogue with philosophical writings. Özervarli argues that Ibn Taymiyya's thought should be seen against the background of the increasing influence of philosophy in theological discourses, which Ibn Taymiyya then counters by reviving traditionalism in a philosophical manner. The end result is that reason becomes as essential as revelation, a seamless complementarity beautifully summed up in the image opening Özervarli's contribution—"reason with faith and the Qur'ān is like eyes with light and the Sun".

The impossibility of contradiction between revealed and rational knowledge is also the foundation of Ibn Taymiyya's legal theory. Yossef Rapoport demonstrates how Ibn Taymiyya applies the principle of complete congruence between reason and revelation to the sources of Islamic law, and therefore rejects the possibility that analogy—the primary tool of legal rationalism—could ever contradict a revealed text. Similarly, Ibn Taymiyya believes that any perceived contradiction between the revealed sources and the legal principle of *maṣlaḥa*, or public good, necessarily stems from restrictive or deficient application of notions of utility. The mental process by which one correctly weighs benefit and harm, or arrives at a correct analogy, is in itself derived from the revealed sources. Thus, the Qur'ān and the Sunna serve not only as a repository of reports (*khabar*), but also as a guide to correct rational legal interpretation.

Jon Hoover also argues that the image of Ibn Taymiyya as an anti-rationalist needs to be corrected. Hoover sees Ibn Taymiyya as an apologist for the coherence and rationality of the theological data found in the tradition, offering "a philosophical interpretation and defence of tradition". His theology of a personal God is informed by his ordinary language reading of the Qur'ān and the Hadith and represents an attempt to explain and protect that reading through rational means. Focusing on Ibn Taymiyya's treatise on God's "voluntary attributes", Hoover shows how Ibn Taymiyya, far from rejecting rational arguments per se, rather offers an alternative reasoning of his own. In the *kalām* tradition the perfection of God is associated with eternity because eternity is assumed, rationally, to be perfect. This leads al-Ash'arī (d. 935) and his followers to maintain that God's attribute of speech, for example, is eternal and therefore independent of God's will. But Ibn Taymiyya turns this rational argument on its head. For Ibn Taymiyya rational perfection dictates that speech (and other similar attributes) is not timelessly eternal but truly volitional. A being who acts by will is more perfect than a being whose attributes are timeless. At the same time, Ibn Taymiyya acknowledges that God's attributes must be eternal, and that it is impossible that God became a Creator or a Speaker after he was not one. The ingenious Taymiyyan solution is that God has been perpetually creating and speaking by His will and power since eternity. God's speech, like God's attribute of creation, is thus ongoing. He keeps on speaking and creating, has always been a

Speaker and a Creator, and yet his actions have occurred in time and are also "personal" in the sense that they are enacted by an exercise of will in time.

The Meaning of the *Salaf* in Ibn Taymiyya's Thought

Several papers in this volume address the significance and meaning of the authority of the *salaf*, the early generations of the Muslim community, in Ibn Taymiyya's theology, hermeneutics and law. All agree that the concept of the *salaf* is central to Ibn Taymiyya's thought; yet they also point out that it has an instrumental quality directly related to Ibn Taymiyya's challenge to the dominant doctrines of the theological and legal schools. It is in the face of charges of contempt towards the established authorities that Ibn Taymiyya often appeals to the authority of the *salaf*.

The clearest articulation of Ibn Taymiyya's Salafism is found in his *Introduction to the Foundations of Qur'ānic Exegesis*, studied in this volume by Walid Saleh. Saleh examines Ibn Taymiyya's *salaf*-based epistemology as an alternative to the dominant tradition of Qur'ānic exegesis, which was guided by philology. Instead of an encyclopedic search for the possible meanings of the Divine word, Ibn Taymiyya suggests that one should only look at the interpretations of the Qur'ān transmitted by the members of the early community. As the *salaf*'s understanding of the Prophetic message was by necessity superior to that of later generations, one need only verify that the report attributed to the *salaf* is indeed authentic for it to become authoritative. The implication is that the science of exegesis is merely an off-shoot of the science of Hadith, where Prophetic traditions are assessed, at least in theory, not according to content but rather according to the strength of the chain of transmission. In this manner, the authentic views of the *salaf* on the interpretation of the Qur'ān are raised to the level of Prophetic traditions, to be given precedence over later interpretations.

The focus of the *Introduction to the Foundations of Qur'ānic Exegesis* is on epistemology, not on details of theology or law. The thrust of the treatise is that the views of the *salaf* are necessarily more correct than those of later generations, and, as Saleh notes, this is presented less as an argument than as an axiomatic principle. But one should not view this treatise in isolation from the wider context of Ibn

Taymiyya's writing, and specifically his views on Divine attributes. Ibn Taymiyya was prepared to go to jail for his views on the non-metaphorical interpretation of the Divine attributes in the Qur'ān, and his reliance on the Companions of the Prophet in rejecting metaphorical interpretations was part of a larger body of anti-Ash'arī polemics. Moreover, Ibn Taymiyya's Salafism was iconoclastic—as much as it was about revering the members of the early Islamic community, it was about undermining the binding authority of later interpretations. The anecdote opening Saleh's contribution, where Ibn Taymiyya mocks the achievement of the renowned grammarian Sibawayh (d. 793), illustrates his lack of reverence towards much of what contemporary Muslims thought was sound knowledge.

In Ibn Taymiyya's mind there was a complete identity between the views of the *salaf* and his own. In her examination of Ibn Taymiyya's polemics with the Ash'arī theologians Racha el-Omari formulates Ibn Taymiyya's premises as being simultaneously theological and epistemological. One Taymiyyan premise, noted above, is that reason and revelation are always in agreement; the other, epistemological, premise is that the *salaf* understood this agreement of reason and revelation better than any later scholars. Therefore, by necessity, Ibn Taymiyya's central theological tenet of the agreement of reason and revelation is identical with the original message by the Prophet, as understood by the early generations. Although Ibn Taymiyya's views represent a radical break from the theological traditions of his time, he does not see them as novel. Rather, he sees his role as that of retrieving the unity of reason and revelation advocated by the *salaf*, thereby peeling off the obscuring layers of interpretation added on in later centuries, often by well-meaning theologians and jurists. The closer one is to the original Prophetic message, the closer one gets to the truth.

Being loyal to the *salaf* exempts Ibn Taymiyya from maintaining allegiance to any one theological camp, or from ingrained animosity towards another. When under attack from followers of the theological school of al-Ash'arī during his Damascus trial of 1305, he appeals to the authority of al-Ash'arī himself as a representative of the Salafi rejection of metaphorical interpretation.[6] But when Ibn Taymiyya considers al-Ash'arī's views on the proof of the existence of God and on divine attributes in other contexts, he is unrelentingly critical. Ibn Taymiyya can view al-Ash'arī in this ambivalent way—

he can cross the lines, so to speak—because he does not bind himself to any of the existing theological schools. Ashʿarī doctrines contain correct and incorrect views, to be judged according to their distance from what he perceived to be the views of the *salaf*.

The same ambivalent attitude may even be shown towards the revered founder of his school, Aḥmad Ibn Ḥanbal (d. 855), a point made both by el-Omari and by Rapoport. Although his admiration for Ibn Ḥanbal is evident, Ibn Taymiyya does not view him as having a monopoly on correct theological or legal interpretations. He does not consider the doctrine of the school of law, expressed by the opinions of the major Ḥanbalī jurists, as a legal proof in and of itself. Moreover, even though Ibn Ḥanbal and the other school founders were very knowledgeable jurists, they were not infallible, and anyone who possesses the relevant knowledge should subject their opinions to scrutiny. As long as one is capable, one should study the evidence and form one's own opinion.

Ibn Taymiyya identifies his own doctrines with those of the *salaf*. But what happens if the one appears to contradict the other? Livnat Holtzman's study of Ibn Taymiyya's interpretation of the term *fiṭra* (man's inborn belief in God, or Islam) is a case in point. The dominant Sunni interpretation of Q 30:30, 'the *fiṭra* of God with which He created humankind', and the relevant Prophetic traditions, is that humankind was divided into believers and apostates at the moment of its creation. This view is opposed to the rationalism of the Muʿtazila, who emphasized free will and the ability of men to choose between belief and unbelief. The novelty and ingenuity in Ibn Taymiyya's approach is to use the same Hadith material, which is generally deterministic or even fatalistic in tone, in order to assert that human free will exists by all means when it comes to belief and disbelief. This non-deterministic interpretation, however, goes against the plain view of the *salaf*, who, as Ibn Taymiyya himself admits, appear to have understood the traditions on *fiṭra* in a deterministic way. Although Ibn Taymiyya does not blame them for this apparent mistake (they are excused, partly because they wished to overstate predetermination in their eagerness to combat the Muʿtazilī theories of free will), it is evident that Ibn Taymiyya interprets the traditions from the *salaf* in ways that would fit his own brand of philosophical traditionalism. The same is also true for Ibn Taymiyya's understanding of the Divine attributes of creation and speech, where the elaborate Taymiyyan theories of perpetual action discussed by Jon Hoover could not have stemmed directly from a reading of the simple theological formulae cited from the *salaf*. Salafism on its own simply cannot express the distinctiveness of the Taymiyyan method. Rather, the invocation of the *salaf* often occurred only at a secondary stage, as a way of legitimating and justifying a methodology that encountered opposition from the majority of his contemporaries.

Puritan or Pragmatist?

Another epithet that is usually associated with Ibn Taymiyya is that of a 'Sunni zealot'. He was, according to both sympathetic and unsympathetic modern accounts, an uncompromising enemy of any deviation from the way of the Sunna, a rigid purist who refused to accept any form of innovation. But, as several contributors to this volume suggest, his idealism is fused with pragmatism, and even with what Raquel Ukeles describes as an 'empathy' towards the motives of those who err. In her contribution, Ukeles tries to explain Ibn Taymiyya's ambivalent approach towards the celebration of the Prophet's Birthday (*mawlid*). On the one hand, Ibn Taymiyya regarded the celebration of the *mawlid* as a reprehensible innovation. Since the *salaf* did not observe the festival, the festival is not lawful. On the other hand, Ibn Taymiyya is also aware of the pious motives behind the celebration of the *mawlid*, motives that are rooted in the spiritual needs of the Muslim community. The *mawlid* is thus a mistaken, yet pious, response to deeper spiritual callings, and therefore cannot be corrected by any amount of condescending disapproval. Rather than merely condemning the innovation, the pious impulses of the public should be recognized and redirected towards permitted forms of worship through a program of religious reform.

In his study of Ibn Taymiyya as a jurist, Rapoport suggests that this pragmatic streak permeates much of his legal thought. Ibn Taymiyya criticises excessive application of the concept of *wara'*, i.e., pious caution in cases of disagreement or doubt, and applies a lenient approach with regard to several questions of ritual purity and agricultural contracts. Moreover, although Ibn Taymiyya is a fierce opponent of legal stratagems—i.e., a contract where the parties aim to achieve an illegal objective through means that are outwardly permissible—he does more than merely lament their use. As with his attitude towards the popular celebrations of the Prophet's Birthday, he shows empathy towards the pious motives of those who resort to legal trickery. He therefore seeks to amend relevant aspects of the law, in particular the law of oaths and of divorce, so that the need for legal stratagems will not arise in the first place.

Ukeles sums up Ibn Taymiyya's position towards popular religion as a pragmatic examination of its positive and negative elements, without ever relinquishing the ideal for which he strives. Mona Hassan identifies a similar Taymiyyan approach to political theory in her revisionist contribution on his concept of the Caliphate. Hassan questions much of modern scholarship on the political thought of Ibn Taymiyya, beginning with Laoust, who has wrongly claimed that Ibn Taymiyya regards the Caliphate as obsolete. In fact, Hassan shows that Ibn Taymiyya considers the institution of the caliphate, in the way it was practiced under the four rightly-guided Caliphs, as a moral and legal ideal that should not be relinquished in favour of secular kingship (*mulk*). Ibn Taymiyya does object, however, to the excessively pious purists who distance themselves from political life because the ideal of the just caliphate does not obtain. In his view, the inevitable shortcomings of the later generations mean that rulers may have to diverge from the ideal standard of governance. Yet he equally objects to wanton disregard for this ideal; as with popular religion, one should assess the positives and negatives in the conduct of the rulers in a pragmatic manner, without ever losing sight of the model of the Sunna.[7]

Ibn Taymiyya's extensive polemics against Shiʿis and Christians, by contrast, show no trace of his pragmatism, let alone empathy. In his study of the anti-Shiʿi polemical treatise *Minhāj al-sunna*, Tariq al-Jamil finds an uncompromising, and sometimes even undiscerning, aspect of Ibn Taymiyya's thought. Al-Jamil points out that while Ibn Taymiyya's objection to the Shiʿa was part of his overall criticism of innovation, falling under the same category as the visitation of tombs and the celebration of the Prophet's Birthday, the ferocity of his attacks on the Shiʿa could also be explained by intellectual and political contexts. Ibn Taymiyya may have been concerned about the increasing participation of Shiʿi scholars in Sunni academic circles, and their perceived influence—a phenomenon also noted by Walid Saleh in his contribution on Ibn Taymiyya's hermeneutics. In the political sphere, moreover, Ibn Taymiyya was definitely alarmed by the Shi'i sway over the Mongol Īlkhāns, specifically in light of Öljeitü's conversion to Shi'ism in 1310 under the guidance of al-'Allāma al-Ḥillī (d. 1325), who was Ibn Taymiyya's principal Shi'i intellectual adversary.

Ibn Taymiyya's attacks on the Shi'a focus on their similarities to Christians and Jews, and the corruption of the Muslim community by non-Muslim minorities is very much present in *al-Jawāb al-ṣaḥīḥ*, the extensive anti-Christian polemical treatise studied here by David Thomas. The *Jawāb* is ostensibly a response to an epistle written in Cyprus and sent to Muslim scholars in Damascus, in which a Christian author makes an unusual attempt to invite Muslims to see that the truth of Christianity is endorsed in the Qur'ān. Seen against the backdrop of a still vibrant Crusader movement operating through the Latin outpost of Cyprus, it is tempting to see Ibn Taymiyya's anti-Christian polemics as part of a struggle against an imminent external threat. Thomas points out, however, that the treatise gives no indication that Ibn Taymiyya was responding to acute political difficulties. The purpose of the *Jawāb* is not so much a refutation, but rather to utilise the Christian epistle in order to warn fellow Muslims against errors which resemble those of the non-believers. Rather than a polemical rejoinder in a tradition of Christian-Muslim debate, the *Jawāb* can be compared with Islamic theological treatises, with their blend of positive exposition of the teachings of the faith and of negative polemics. The dissociation of the anti-Christian polemics from the immediate context of the Crusades is a reminder that Ibn Taymiyya's thought and legacy cannot be reduced to a knee-jerk response to the Crusades or to the Mongol invasions. The defeat of the last remnants of the Latin kingdoms in 1291, as well as the retreat of the Mongol Īlkhāns from Syria, suggests that Ibn Taymiyya lived through a period in which, if anything, Islamic self-confidence was regained rather than lost.

The Modern Appeal of Ibn Taymiyya

In our own days, at the beginning of the 21st century, Ibn Taymiyya's writings are of central importance for several contemporary political and intellectual movements in the Muslim world. At the very least, he is one of the most cited medieval authors. But, as

Khaled el-Rouayheb demonstrates in his extensive study, Ibn Taymiyya's current reputation and influence should not obscure his pre-modern notoriety and marginality. El-Rouayheb's examination of the intellectual world of Sunni Islam, from just after the death of Ibn Taymiyya in the 14th century and up to the 19th century, shows that Ibn Taymiyya's works were castigated by the vast majority of leading Sunni theologians and jurists. Their criticism, often voiced in quite unequivocal terms of disparagement, concerned two tenets of the Taymiyyan outlook. One was his denial of allegorical interpretation of Divine attributes, a denial which most mainstream Sunni scholars took to be anthropomorphic literalism. The other was his objection to the visitation of tombs, and specifically to the visitation of the Prophet's tomb in Medina.

But mostly, Ibn Taymiyya was not simply criticised and disparaged; worse, he was often overlooked. Through a close examination of the lists of works studied in the major centres of learning in the Ottoman world, El-Rouayheb demonstrates that Ibn Taymiyya's writings were very rarely read or studied. All in all, Ibn Taymiyya was considered an eccentric marginal figure, of minor interest to the majority of Sunni scholars who paid no attention to Ibn Taymiyya's attacks on Ash'arī theology, logic, and the philosophical mysticism of Ibn 'Arabī. In many ways, this marginality is a direct continuation of his minority position during his own lifetime, as depicted by Caterina Bori. His break with traditionalism meant that he was not even seen as a representative of the theological and legal outlook of the Ḥanbalī school.[8] While some 17th- and 18th-century authors, such as the Indian reformer Shāh Walī Allāh al-Dihlawī (d. 1762), do express admiration for Ibn Taymiyya, El-Rouayheb argues that very few outside the Wahhabi movement in Arabia embraced the Taymiyyan outlook as a whole.

The sudden discovery of Ibn Taymiyya by non-Wahhabi intellectuals came about around the turn of the 20th century. The defence of Ibn Taymiyya by the Iraqi scholar al-Ālūsī (d. 1899), and, most importantly, the revisionist introduction of Ibn Taymiyya as a central and heroic figure of medieval Islam by Rashid Rida, are obvious milestones in this quite abrupt transformation of Ibn Taymiyya's image. As far away as Kazan, Musa Jarullah Bigiev (d. 1949) consciously followed in Ibn Taymiyya's footsteps by attacking the influence of Muslim philosophical writings. Ibn Taymiyya's radical hermeneutical method, discussed by Walid Saleh, was rescued from relative marginality by modern conservative Muslim intellectuals, who saw it as the foundation of a tradition-based exegesis. In the legal sphere, Ibn Taymiyya's views on divorce, declared weak and irregular by a consensus of Ottoman jurists of all schools, have been incorporated wholesale into the legal codes of almost all modern Muslim nation-states.

Over the last few decades of the 20th century, the authority of Ibn Taymiyya in all fields of Islamic discourse has increased manifold, so much so that he has become an indispensable peg on which contradicting programs of Islamic reform are suspended. Raquel Ukeles examines modern, web-based debates over the celebration of the Prophet's Birthday, in which both Salafis and Sufis summon Ibn Taymiyya in support of their position. Mona Hassan demonstrates that the legacy of Ibn Taymiyya among the Islamist movements is even more contested. Within the ranks of political Islam, his authority is hardly in doubt; both moderates and radicals call upon Ibn Taymiyya to authenticate their positions. Yet they do so with widely divergent agendas. Yūsuf al-Qaraḍāwī, a leading figure in the Muslim Brotherhood, cites Ibn Taymiyya in support of peaceful participation in the political life of an unjust, non-Islamic state. He taps into the pragmatism of Ibn Taymiyya in order to overcome puritan abhorrence of corrupt regimes in favour of political involvement, alliances with non-Islamist groups and respect for the legitimacy of the state. Al-Qaraḍāwī's pragmatist interpretation of Ibn Taymiyya contrasts sharply with the way his legacy has been invoked by radical Islamist groups as a platform for violent confrontation and indiscriminate attacks. It is in this garb of the 'spiritual father of Islamic terrorists' that Ibn Taymiyya is now most often portrayed in the West.

Ibn Taymiyya's current notoriety owes much to the way his writings were used by 'Abd al-Salām Faraj, the leader of the radical group responsible for the assassination of the Egyptian president Anwar Sadat in 1981. Faraj's work *al-Farīḍa al-ghā'iba* (The Neglected Duty) consists of long strings of quotations from Ibn Taymiyya, which are made to justify and legitimate the use of violence against tyrannical and non-Islamic regimes.[9] The citations are invariably taken from a series of legal opinions Ibn Taymiyya issued with regard to the Mongol invasions of Syria at the beginning of the 14th century. As Hassan argues, Faraj's work purposefully disregards the socio-historical context of Ibn Taymiyya's *fatwā*s and even distorts its juridical integrity. The question put before Ibn Taymiyya was whether the local civilian population of Damascus should assist the Mamluk sultans of Cairo against the invading Mongols, who had recently converted to Islam. Since both armies profess Islam, should the ordinary Muslim care about the result of the military encounter? In his reply, Ibn Taymiyya subsumes the Mongols under the legal category of rebels against the legitimate Islamic state, which for him was represented by the Mamluk regime. Because of the Mongols' continuous atrocities and obstinate pagan beliefs, their formal conversion to Islam has little legal effect, and one should fight them as one fights infidels. In Faraj's selective reading, the Egyptian regime is identified with the invading Mongols of Ibn Taymiyya's time in order to justify rebellion and assassination. Yet, as Hassan demonstrates, this particular *fatwā* actually reveals Ibn Taymiyya's pragmatic support for the imperfect Mamluk regime in its fight against foreign invaders. Such wilful ignorance of the historical and juridical context of the writings of Ibn Taymiyya is typical of the leaders of militant Islamic groups, as recently shown by Yahya Michot.[10]

Whatever one thinks of the current conflicting interpretations of Ibn Taymiyya's legacy, his transformation from a little-read marginal figure to a widely-cited religious authority raises the question of the appeal of his work to modern Muslims. El-Rouayheb suggests that the political, military and technological superiority of the West has promoted a call for a reassertion of pristine, uncorrupted Islam in the manner offered by Ibn Taymiyya. This is undoubtedly part of the answer, yet it needs to be qualified. Both for Ibn Taymiyya and for modern Salafis, the reliance on the *salaf* has an instrumental value. What is at stake, of course, is not so much a return to the values of the early Islamic community, but rather a rejection of the layers of interpretation and exegesis, which are seen as obstructing an Islamic revival. We have said above that Ibn Taymiyya's Salafism was iconoclastic; this is also true for the Salafis of our own days. It is noteworthy that, judging by the number of editions and translations, Ibn Taymiyya is known today more for treatises that discuss the epistemological superiority of the *salaf* (*The Principles of the Medinese*, *Introduction to the Foundations of Exegesis*), and less for the actual theological and legal conclusions he drew by this method. We hope that this volume will begin to alter this imbalance.

Ibn Taymiyya was, by almost universal consensus, one of the most original and systematic thinkers in the history of Islam. As Fazlur Rahman observed, Ibn Taymiyya brought a fresh new perspective and applied a singularly Taymiyyan approach to every question he wrote about, from the attributes of God to the creation of the world, from a refutation of the mystical union with God to the regulation of prices in the market place. Reading Ibn Taymiyya is intellectually satisfying, as he is such a challenging and original thinker. His extraordinary gift for distilling and lucidly presenting the most crucial and fundamental elements of any Islamic discipline makes him one of the most useful guides to Islamic intellectual history. But, he is also more than that. Because of his current standing in modern Islamic discourses, a faithful reading of his corpus matters for the future of Islam and of its relations with non-Muslims. Whether we like him or not, Ibn Taymiyya appears to be more relevant today than ever.

Notes

1. The publication of the article, with its criticism of Ibn Taymiyya, was seen as the main reason for the subsequent dismissal of the newspaper editor-in-chief, Jamal Khashoggi, by order of the Saudi Information Ministry. On the incident, see special dispatch no. 535 by the Middle East Media Research Institute in www.memri.org (includes extracts of the article in English translation). For the Arabic text, see www.alwatan.com.sa.
2. Daniel Benjamin and Steven Simon, *The Age of Sacred Terror* (New York: Random House, 2002), 38–52. See also the influential essay of Emmanuel Sivan, "Ibn Taymiyya: Father of the Islamic Revolution, Medieval Theology & Modern Politics," *Encounter* 60, no. 3 (1983): 41–4.
3. Jon Hoover, *Ibn Taymiyya's Theodicy of Perpetual Optimism* (Leiden: Brill, 2007); Abdul Hakim I. al-Matroudi, *The Ḥanbalī school of law and Ibn Taymiyyah* (London: Routledge, 2006); C. Bori, *Ibn Taymiyya: una vita esemplare.* Analisi delle fonti classiche della sua biografia, Supplemento monografico n. 1 alla Rivista degli Studi Orientali LXXVI (2003) (Roma—Pisa: Istituti Poligrafici Internazionali, 2003); M. Sait Özervarli, *İbn Teymiyye'nin Düşünce Metodolojisi ve Kelâmcılara Eleştirisi* ("Ibn Taymiyya's Methodology of Thought and His Criticisms of the Mutakallimun") (Istanbul: ISAM, 2008).
4. For the most comprehensive work, see H. Laoust, *Essai sur les doctrines sociales et politiques de Taḳī-d-Dīn Aḥmad b. Taimīya, canoniste ḥanbalite né à Ḥarrān en 661/1262, mort à Damas en 728/1328* (Cairo: Imprimerie de l'institut français d'archéologie orientale, 1939). For English readers, the most reliable introduction to the study of Ibn Taymiyya's thought is probably Thomas Michel's introductory chapters in *A Muslim theologian's response to Christianity: Ibn Taymiyya's* al-Jawab al-Sahih, edited and translated by Thomas F. Michel (Delmar, N.Y.: Caravan Books, 1984).

Yahya Michot is producing a growing corpus of annotated scholarly translations of Ibn Taymiyya's works, and has made several of them easily accessible on the world-wide-web. See Yahya Michot, "Pages spirituelles" and "Textes spirituelles" on www.muslimphilosophy.com/it.

5. For a recent study of Ibn Taymiyya's role in the events of that year, see Reuven Amitai, "The Mongol Occupation of Damascus in 1300: A Study of Mamluk Loyalties", in A. Levanoni and M. Winter (eds.), *The Mamluks in Egyptian and Syrian Politics and Society* (Leiden: Brill, 2004), 21–41.
6. On the Damascus trial and Ibn Taymiyya's innovative interpretation of Divine attributes, see also Sherman A. Jackson's "Ibn Taymiyya on Trial in Damascus," *Journal of Semitic Studies* 39 (1994): 41–85.
7. On the utilitarian aspects of Ibn Taymiyya's political thought, see also Michael Cook, *Commanding right and forbidding wrong in Islamic thought* (Cambridge: Cambridge University Press, 2000), 149–57.
8. On the limited influence of Ibn Taymiyya on the Ḥanbalī school, see also al-Matroudi, *The Ḥanbalī school of law and Ibn Taymiyyah*, chapter 5.
9. Muḥammad 'Abd al-Salām Faraj, *al-Jihād, al-farīḍa al-ghā'iba* (n.p., 1990). For an English translation, see Johannes Jansen, *The Neglected Duty: The Creed of Sadat's Assassins and Islamic Resurgence in the Middle East* (New York: Macmillan Publishing Company, 1986), 159–234.
10. Yahya Michot, *Mardin: Hégire, fuite de péché et « demeure de l'Islam »* (Beirut: Les Éditions Albouraq, 2004); English translation as Yahya Michot, *Muslims under non-Muslim Rule* (Oxford: Interface Publications, 2007).

I
Biography

Ibn Taymiyya *wa-Jamāʿatuhu*: Authority, Conflict and Consensus in Ibn Taymiyya's Circle*

Caterina Bori

The association of the Ḥanbalī school of law with Taqī al-Dīn Aḥmad Ibn Taymiyya is immediate. Ibn Taymiyya was, without a doubt, the most original, vocal and controversial Ḥanbalī scholar of the Mamluk period, and the most famous Ḥanbalī after the school's eponym. Yet, the image of Ibn Taymiyya as the representative of the Ḥanbalī community of his time owes much to Henri Laoust's work on the Ḥanbalīs in the early period of the Mamluk Sultanate, and to his still classic *Essai sur les doctrines sociales et politiques de Taḳī-d-Dīn Aḥmad ibn Taymīya*. In these two surveys, Laoust depicts the Ḥanbalī community as a cohesive unit gravitating around its charismatic centre, Ibn Taymiyya.[1] As a consequence, Hanbalism in the Mamluk period is now commonly identified with Ibn Taymiyya's thoughts and deeds.

The present paper seeks to re-examine this generally accepted representation of Ibn Taymiyya. To what extent did the Ḥanbalīs of Damascus in general, and the Damascene Ḥanbalī *ʿulamāʾ* in particular, actually identify with Ibn Taymiyya? What was Ibn Taymiyya's relationship with the larger group of traditionalist scholars, not necessarily Ḥanbalīs?[2] A close reading of the extensive biographical literature on Ibn Taymiyya strongly calls for a reconsideration of Ibn Taymiyya's authority among his own "community" of scholars.[3] Even internal Ḥanbalī or pro-Ḥanbalī sources reflect a plurality of voices that are interwoven with and conditioned by the nature of the author's relationship with Ibn Taymiyya and by his *madhhab* affiliation.

This essay is mostly concerned with the perception of Ibn Taymiyya by his Ḥanbalī and traditionalist contemporaries, and with the way he was viewed by his close disciples in their biographical narratives. These narratives are examined here for their role in constructing moral and religious authority. Thus, biographies are conceived not only as a means of establishing the historicity of individuals, but also as a way of transmitting a moral paradigm and a pattern of authority around which consensus is built.[4]

The intellectual world of Ibn Taymiyya was characterized by competition over knowledge and the social, religious, and political authority engendered by monopoly over it.[5] This competition was often negotiated through membership in a "group" (*ṭā'ifa*), which, for jurists, primarily meant the school of law (*madhhab*).[6] The institution of the *madhhab* was both a legal institution offering its members normative rules, but also, and more broadly, the focus of social and professional networks, as well as of a strong collective ideological identity. Thus, competition would often take the form of inter-*madhhab* polemics, in which loyalty to the law school and its representatives was the expected norm. These polemics would occasionally turn into violent civil disturbances (*fitan*), as exemplified by several incidents in Ibn Taymiyya's biography.[7]

Yet, lines were not always drawn according to *madhhab* identity.[8] A *madhhab* provided a framework, within which sub-groups of scholars sharing a common intellectual identity and cultural inclinations co-existed, albeit not always peacefully. In this regard, intra-*madhhab* polemics within a single school of law were no less important. As George Makdisi observes with regard to the Shāfi'ī school, the real theological debates often occurred between rationalists and traditionalists within the *madhhab*.[9] Thus, while the polemics surrounding Ibn Taymiyya's legal and theological doctrines can be partially explained through *madhhab* competition, or at least were couched in such terms, they often tended to go beyond the boundaries of the *madhhab*.

In order to challenge the commonly accepted identification of Ibn Taymiyya with 14th-century Syrian Hanbalism, I shall first draw attention to the close circle of followers around the Shaykh, frequently referred to as his *jamā'a*, and discuss the characteristics of this group on the basis of letters written by members of the group to each other. Next, by identifying some of the individuals in this group, I will show how their association to Ibn Taymiyya and his understanding of Islam went beyond the *madhhab* boundaries. I will then examine the attitudes towards Ibn Taymiyya among the Ḥanbalī and traditionalist scholarly communities, highlighting voices of dissent, even from within his own *jamā'a*, against aspects of Ibn Taymiyya's scholarship and public conduct. Finally, the narratives regarding Ibn Taymiyya's funeral will be examined against the background of this internal opposition.

Ibn Taymiyya *wa-Jamā'atuhu*: Exclusivity and Activism

Ibn Taymiyya, like other scholars, had his own "circle" (*jamā'a*) of faithful associates who honoured him, obeyed him and who at times were subject to public humiliation on his behalf. Contemporary sources use the term *jamā'a* (lit., a collection, an assemblage) to indicate the group of people who most closely affiliated with Ibn Taymiyya. This collective term refers both to intellectual association with Ibn Taymiyya (i.e., disciples who studied with him, shared his doctrines and were involved in the transmission of his works), and to those individuals who accompanied the Shaykh in public and shared his penchant for activism, especially on his excursions against popular religion.[10]

The term *jamā'a* is also used by Ibn Taymiyya and his brothers when writing letters to each other or to his disciples. After Ibn Taymiyya was transferred to a prison in Alexandria in 709/1309, his brother Sharaf al-Dīn (d. 727/1327) wrote from Egypt to another brother, Badr al-Dīn (d. 717/1318), that, "We and the *jamā'a* are in the complete favour of God".[11] At the end of another letter written in 706/1307 from his Cairo prison, Ibn Taymiyya sent his regards to the rest of his *jamā'a* in Damascus, and to his brother Badr al-Dīn in particular.[12] In yet another letter, this time from Alexandria, Ibn Taymiyya refers to his *jamā'a* more than once.[13] In the course of the letter, he states that what he misses most is the company of his *jamā'a* (*wa-akthar mā yanquṣu 'alayya al-jamā'a*).[14] He tells his companions that, while he cannot serve the *jamā'a* by way of meeting (*in lam yumkin khidmat al-jamā'a bi-al-liqā'*), he will serve them by constant prayer, performing in this way at least some of the obligation that is due to them. This letter demonstrates the intimacy of Ibn Taymiyya's relationship with his group of disciples, the reciprocity which characterized their relationship (*khidma* is not only from the pupil towards the master, but also the other way round) as well as his leadership. It is Ibn Taymiyya who guides the group: "The point here is to inform the *jamā'a*...that what I instruct (*āmuru*) each of them is to fear God and act for Him, seeking His help, fighting on His path...".[15]

Internal correspondence between Ibn Taymiyya's inner circle of scholars and followers sheds light on the meaning of membership in this *jamāʿa*. A particularly instructive example, which has not received much attention in secondary literature, is a letter from ʿImād al-Dīn Aḥmad ibn Ibrāhīm al-Wāsiṭī (d. 711/1311), who was one of Ibn Taymiyya's most intimate disciples.[16] Al-Wāsiṭī was of a Sufi background, his father being a Shaykh of the Aḥmadiyya Rifāʿiyya in Wāsiṭ in Iraq. While in Egypt, al-Wāsiṭī joined the Shādhiliyya order, but after arriving in Damascus he came under the influence of Ibn Taymiyya. Al-Wāsiṭī's Sufi background is evident in his letter, which can also be read as a broad articulation of Ibn Taymiyya's relationship to Sufism, a relationship that did not necessarily entail his affiliation with a specific Sufi order.[17]

Al-Wāsiṭī's letter is preserved by Ibn ʿAbd al-Hādī, who introduces it as follows: "He [al-Wāsiṭī] wrote a letter and sent it to some of the Shaykh's companions. In it he urged them to stand by the Shaykh constantly and inseparably (*mulāzamat al-shaykh*) and exhorted them to follow his way (*ṭarīqatihi*)".[18] The letter is addressed to seven of al-Wāsiṭī's "brothers" and is written in a highly rhetorical style. The recipients are supposedly close associates not only of the author, but also of Ibn Taymiyya.[19] The letter is not dated, but its urgent tone suggests that it may have been written during a time of crisis, probably after the Damascus trials of 705/1306 but before al-Wāsiṭī's death in 711/1311.[20] Ibn Taymiyya's trials would often entail persecutions of his *jamāʿa*, and al-Wāsiṭī may have felt a need for an outspoken endorsement of Ibn Taymiyya's authority as a spiritual leader of the group.

The text opens with introductory epistolary formulas, the names of addressees and an exhortation to perform religious practices.[21] The author encourages his companions to free themselves of any mundane activities and preoccupations for an hour a day so that they can get to know their spiritual state (*ḥāl*) with God. Al-Wāsiṭī uses the term *nufūdh* to express the final destination of the spiritual path at the end of which the believer's heart is led to contemplate the spiritual realities "from behind a fine veil" and to experience by means of intuitive knowledge (*maʿrifa*) the time of the Prophet "as if he was with him in his days, striving for his religion."[22] Further on, the author clarifies the meaning of *nufūdh* as reaching, through religious knowledge, to the Messenger of God and to the foundations of God's religion, the Book and the Sunna.[23] The *imitatio prophetae* is first of all conceived as an interior cognitive experience which finds its correspondence in the outer world through adherence to prophetic practice and observance of God's precepts.[24] According to al-Wāsiṭī, the superiority of Ibn Taymiyya (and his disciples) derives from his rank as the most perceptive of the jurists (*al-nāfidh min al-fuqahāʿ*), the one who has "complete knowledge" (*maʿrifa tāmma*).[25]

Then al-Wāsiṭī moves on to emphatically present a *summa* of Ibn Taymiyya's polemics, with a vigour rivalling that of the *Shaykh al-Islām* himself.[26] Al-Wāsiṭī calls for confrontation with those jurists who have obscured the attributes of God, otherwise classified pejoratively as *al-jahmiyya,* a term frequently used by Ibn Taymiyya to target the Ashʿarīs of his time.[27] One should also confront those who passively imitate the school eponyms (*taqlīd al-aʾimma*) without resorting to the primary foundations of religion, the Book and the Sunna.[28] He calls for opposition to the mystics (*fuqarāʾ*) who blindly follow the superstitions and deviations of their masters,[29] as well as to "the Sufis and scholars of convention" (*rasmiyyat al-ṣūfiyya wa-al-fuqahāʾ*) who have innovated conventional rules (*al-rusūm al-waḍʿiyya*), but are merely concerned with dress, flattery and material gains.[30] Those groups professing the indwelling of God in his creatures (*al-ḥulūl*), the union between them (*al-ittiḥād*) and the deification (*al-taʾalluh*) of created beings, such as al-Yūnusiyya, al-Sabʿīniyya, al-Tilmisāniyya and so forth, are labelled *zanādiqa* (heretics).[31] The celebration of non-Muslim festivals by the commoners, as well as their veneration of tombs and stones, is also condemned, as are the amirs and the soldiers whose injustice originates from their ignorance of the religion of God.[32] For al-Wāsiṭī, the project of Ibn Taymiyya and his followers is explicitly one of renewal (*tajdīd*).[33]

Further on, the author identifies the mission entrusted to Ibn Taymiyya by God, namely to unveil the true meaning of his religion (*ḥaqīqat dīnihi*) and to rectify the corruption of religious life. Ibn Taymiyya is presented as the master who synthesizes the outer dimension of revelation (*al-amr al-sharʿī al-ẓāhir*) with the inner one (*al-amr al-bāṭin*); those who acknowledge him admit both dimensions, for Ibn Taymiyya leads:

> to the intuitive knowledge (*ma'rifa*) of God's Names and Attributes, to the sublimity of His essence, to the spiritual conjunction (*ittiṣāl*) of his heart with the rays of His essence, to the enjoyment (*iḥtiẓā'*) of His special qualities and His most sublime experiences (*a'lā adhwāqihā*), to the penetration from the outer to the inner, from the visible (*al-shahāda*) to the invisible (*al-ghayb*), and from the invisible to the visible, and from the world of creation (*'ālam al-khalq*) to that of the divine command (*'ālam al-amr*).[34]

The disciple—very much a Sufi *murīd*—is strongly encouraged to look for his master's love and affection so that he may obtain a portion of the special Prophetic share (*naṣībihi al-khāṣṣ al-muḥammadī*)[35] that Ibn Taymiyya enjoys, and which constitutes his privileged status (*al-khuṣūṣiyya*).

The final part of the letter regards the relationship between master and disciple and the position that should be taken towards the pupil who criticizes his Shaykh.[36] This last section suggests that the letter as a whole was written in response to criticism of the Shaykh from within his circle of followers. Al-Wāsiṭī warns against a disciple who has turned against the master, and calls upon the recipients of the letter to treat the matter with care.[37] Sound criticism on the part of the sincere pupil is desirable, but false and malicious words can be a cause of corruption. Love for the Shaykh is essential. If the Shaykh's reputation is sullied, his pupils will desert him, change their attitude towards him and see in him faults which will deny them the benefits they are meant to take from him. When this happens, one fears for them first the aversion of God, then that of the Shaykh. Furthermore, if his reputation is harmed by one of his own companions, this will play into the hands of the innovators.[38] Hence, a careful examination of the dissenting disciple's intellect, his discernment, veracity, and age is to be carried out in order to verify his credibility. If he turns out to be deficient in one of these faculties, then he is to be tactfully warned and kept away.[39]

On the whole, the letter demonstrates al-Wāsiṭī's perception of the relationship between Ibn Taymiyya and his *jamā'a* as one similar to that of the Sufi master and his disciples. As a preamble to his call for activism, al-Wāsiṭī urges the recipients of the letter to thank God since "He has made you, among all the people of this time, like the white mark on the black animal".[40] The source of their uniqueness is specified a little further on:

> You have become my brothers under the banner of the Messenger of God (pbuh), God willing, together with your Shaykh, your Imam, our Shaykh, our Imam, with whose mention we have begun [this letter]. Verily you have distinguished yourselves from the whole of the people on earth, jurists and ascetics, Sufis and common people, by the authentic religion (*al-dīn al-ṣaḥīḥ*).[41]

These words reveal the remarkable sense of exclusivity and privilege which people like al-Wāsiṭī felt they were invested with, thanks to their affiliation with Ibn Taymiyya. The source of this elitism lies in a shared way of understanding Islam expressed by the all-encompassing formula of 'the authentic religion' as put to practice by Ibn Taymiyya. Accordingly, it is clear that the text is addressed to self-elected and restricted spiritual and intellectual elite that endowed itself with a universal mission of renewal: correcting deviation by eliminating ignorance of the religion of God, and by bridging the (spiritual) distance from the time of the Prophet.

The devotion and elitism of the *jamāʿa* can also be seen in a letter of another devoted admirer of Ibn Taymiyya, the Ḥanbalī scholar Shihāb al-Dīn Ibn Murrī. Ibn Murrī is mainly known for having been put on trial in 725/1324–25 for preaching in support of Ibn Taymiyya's ideas on intercession. He was eventually expelled from Cairo along with his family.[42] Ibn Murrī's letter was apparently written shortly after the Shaykh's death, and, like al-Wāsiṭī's, is addressed to Ibn Taymiyya's close followers.[43] Moreover, Ibn Murrī echoes al-Wāsiṭī's concern for a lack of cohesion and cooperation among the late Shaykh's disciples, and he is especially worried that such a situation might result in the dispersal of his books and, with them, of his knowledge.[44] For instance, he bemoans the existence of only one complete copy of a work entitled *Reply to the Beliefs of the Philosophers* (*al-Radd ʿalā ʿaqāʾid al-falāsifa),* a work whose value he praises highly.[45] He therefore strongly recommends the concerted collection of Ibn Taymiyya's works for which purpose he sets out an editorial strategy. He suggests that Ibn Taymiyya's writings be gathered for authentication by Ibn Rushayyiq, whom he considers the most competent of the group.[46] The manuscripts should then be checked by the best (*aṣlaḥ*) of the *jamāʿa,* and collated with the original copy. A further review should be carried out by al-Mizzī, Ibn al-Qayyim and the most authoritative members of Ibn Taymiyya's circle of pupils in order to avoid misreading and alteration of meaning.[47]

Ibn Murrī's concern for the preservation of Ibn Taymiyya's writings is striking. His call for a collective effort is aimed at providing the necessary tools for those who support and want to transmit the path of the *salaf* (*al-ṭarīqa al-salafiyya*) as conceived by Ibn Taymiyya.[48] Clearly, it is not only Ibn Taymiyya's legacy that is at stake, but a whole way of understanding Islam. Like al-Wāsiṭī, Ibn Murrī too is addressing a small circle of dedicated scholars, and both reveal a concern for the status of their Shaykh—the one in his lifetime, the other after his death. Significantly, both call for a collective effort to uphold the Shaykh's authority which, for some reason, they must have perceived as being under threat.

In many cases, association with the Shaykh seems to have implied not only loyalty to his teachings, but also a dynamic sharing of his commitment to public, direct action in the name of religion.[49] Some well-known instances include Ibn Taymiyya and his *jamāʿa* attacking Damascus wine shops, breaking wine jars, pouring wine on the floor, and censuring wine sellers.[50] On another occasion, he set out with his followers to destroy a rock which had become the object of popular devotion.[51] At the time of the Mongol invasion, the Shaykh and his companions toured the city walls with Ibn Taymiyya reciting Qur'ānic verses to stir up the spirit of holy war.[52] A short epistle composed by another of Ibn Taymiyya's disciples, al-Ghayyānī, is specifically devoted to Ibn Taymiyya's activities against places of popular devotion. Al-Ghayyānī, who expresses his own attachment to Ibn Taymiyya in terms of "service" (*khidma*), regards such actions as one of the precious rarities that set Ibn Taymiyya apart from past and contemporary *ʿulamā'*.[53] In his lively and anecdotal narratives, al-Ghayyānī makes frequent references to the Shaykh's brother Sharaf al-Dīn and, more generally, to his *jamāʿa*.[54]

The *Jamāʿa* and Its Members

The names of those disciples who were considered members of the *jamāʿa* are not systematically mentioned in the sources. Usually, contemporary accounts convey an image of a small circle of disciples sharing doctrines, time, action, and affection with its leader (*huwa wa-jamāʿatuhu* is in fact the recurrent expression), but do not dwell on the identity of the individuals who form this "community". Yet, when one attempts to count the names that do appear, they add up to a surprisingly limited number. All in all, the group that emerges from the list of individuals who are known to have been closely affiliated with Ibn Taymiyya is rather small, or at least not as numerous as one would expect given the popularity Ibn Taymiyya seems to have enjoyed in his lifetime.

An examination of the biographical dictionary of Ibn Rajab (d. 795/1393) demonstrates that only few Ḥanbalīs were seen as being closely attached to Ibn Taymiyya. Ibn Rajab describes only nine Ḥanbalī scholars as being companions or direct disciples of Ibn Taymiyya, including his brother ʿAbd Allāh, his biographer Ibn ʿAbd al-Hādī, the famous disciple Ibn Qayyim al-Jawziyya, the Sufi al-Wāsiṭī, Sharaf al-Dīn ibn al-Munajjā (d. 724/1324) and a few others.[55] Their relationship to Ibn Taymiyya is expressed in terms of a constant physical intimacy (*lāzama, ṣaḥiba/ṣāḥaba*) that carried with it close intellectual affiliation.[56]

Apart from this inner circle of disciples, Ibn Rajab also lists eight Ḥanbalī scholars who studied with Ibn Taymiyya in some form or another.[57] These individuals met the Shaykh (*laqiya al-shaykh*), sat in his company and studied with him (*jālasa al-shaykh...wa-akhadha ʿanhu*),[58] travelled to visit him (*sāfara...li-ziyārat al-shaykh*),[59] studied jurisprudence with him (*wa-tafaqqaha ʿalā al-shaykh*),[60] or, more simply, benefited from him (*wa-intafaʿa bi-ibn Taymiyya*).[61] Ibn Rajab also mentions a scholar who composed a poem in praise of the Shaykh[62] and another one who was put on trial in Baghdad for espousing Ibn Taymiyya's doctrines on visitation.[63] In each case, we can certainly assume a relationship to Ibn Taymiyya, but we have little idea of the degree of intimacy between pupil and master.

The limited influence of Ibn Taymiyya among the Ḥanbalī community is corroborated by the later author al-Nuʿaymī (d. 927/1521), who offers an overview of Ḥanbalī learning during Ibn Taymiyya's time, and provides information on the history of individual *madrasas*, their founders, and details of the scholars who taught in them.[64] Significantly, while the traditional centre of Hanbalism in Damascus was located in the neighbourhood of al-Ṣāliḥiyya, on the slope of Mount Qāsyūn outside the walls of the city,[65] the teaching activity of the Banū Taymiyya took place inside the walls, on the periphery of the main Ḥanbalī institutions. Al-Nuʿaymī correctly reports that Ibn Taymiyya inherited his father's position at the Dār al-Ḥadīth al-Sukkariyya[66] and that he also taught for some time at the Madrasa al-Ḥanbaliyya.[67] But he fails to mention his Friday lectures on Qur'ānic exegesis at the Ḥanbalī Zāwiya of the Ummayyad Mosque, and on the whole, al-Nu'aymī does not dedicate much attention to Ibn Taymiyya's teaching activity, perhaps an indication that it was of marginal importance for the Ḥanbalī community of his time.

Other sources, such as laudatory biographies and chronicles, do add a few names to the list of individuals who comprised Ibn Taymiyya's *jamā'a*. As noted above, al-Wāsiṭī's letter is addressed to seven named individuals. These were the Ḥanbalīs Ibn Shuqayr (d. 744/1343) who hosted Ibn Taymiyya in Cairo after his release from prison in 707/1307,[68] Sharaf al-Dīn ibn al-Munajjā, Muḥammad ibn 'Abīdān al-Ba'lbakkī (d. 734/1334), one of al-Wāsiṭī's followers who was put on trial in 718/1318–19 for a treatise in which he reported witnessing an ecstatic vision,[69] the Ḥanbalī scholar Ibn Nujayḥ (d. 723/1323),[70] as well as two brothers of the Ibn al-Ṣā'igh family[71] and the convert al-Āmidi (d. 798/1397).[72] A list of the most faithful disciples is also reported by the historians al-Nuwayrī and al-Jazarī in their account of the charges brought against these disciples and the public punishment to which they were subjected over the issue of visitation. The list includes the Shāfi'īs Ibn Kathīr and Ibn Shākir al-Kutubī (d. 764/1362), Ibn Qayyim al-Jawziyya and 'Abd Allāh b. Ya'qūb al-Iskandarī (d. 749/1348–49 or 754/1354–55).[73]

Beyond the inner circle of disciples there were others who formed a looser association with the Shaykh, or whose names do not come up so often in the sources. Ibn Kathīr, a zealous supporter of Ibn Taymiyya, reports the names of a few Mamluk amirs who were attached to the Shaykh. They included the vice-regent Sayf al-Dīn Arghūn (d. 731/1330),[74] the Chief Chamberlain of Damascus Kitbughā al-Manṣūrī (d. 721/1321),[75] and a few others.[76] He also mentions several minor Ḥanbalī followers of Ibn Taymiyya that, for whatever reason, are not included in Ibn Rajab's collection. These are Umm Zaynab al-Baghdādiyya (d. 714/1314–15),[77] 'Alī al-Maghribī (d. 749/1348)[78] and 'Imād al-Dīn al-Khashshāb (d. 744/1343).[79] The aforementioned Ibn Rushayyiq, who was a Mālikī, is also presented by Ibn Kathīr as very close to the *Shaykh al-Islām*.[80] Al-Bazzār, the author of a laudatory biography about Ibn Taymiyya, provides a unique list of names of friends (*aṣḥāb, a'wān, muḥibbūhu*) and foes (*a'dā'uhu wa-al-mu'tariḍūn 'alayhi*), a division that reflects a dichotomous vision of Ibn Taymiyya's world.[81] Roughly a century later, the Shāfiʿī Ibn Nāṣir al-Dīn (d. 842/1438) compiled a biographical collection of eighty-nine scholars who expressed favourable views of Ibn Taymiyya. The collection, entitled *al-Radd al-wāfir*, was produced in a polemical context, and includes very few names of actual disciples.[82]

Interestingly, these sources often fail to mention *madhhab* affiliation at all. For instance, Ibn Kathīr, who is evidently proud of his personal bond with Ibn Taymiyya, often overlooks the *madhhab* affiliation of those mentioned as followers of the Shaykh. Al-Bazzār, another disciple and biographer, makes similar omissions. All in all, the biographical material on the members of Ibn Taymiyya's *jamāʿa* demonstrates that *madhahb* affiliation mattered little to those who were close to Ibn Taymiyya and his group. Moreover, a close reading of these biographies also suggests that membership in the circle of close disciples was quite restricted. Ibn Rajab mentions surprisingly few Ḥanbalī followers, and while additional names are mentioned in other sources, it is rarely possible to determine whether their relationship with Ibn Taymiyya was one of occasional learning, cautious admiration or longstanding companionship.

Ḥanbalī Opposition to Ibn Taymiyya

The materials explored so far confirm the presence of a rather small group of loyal disciples around Ibn Taymiyya whose ties transcended that of the *madhhab*. The sources also draw attention to the bonds of loyalty that tied the group closely to the Shaykh, as well as the exclusive and elitist nature of the group and its activism. At the same time, the preoccupation with Ibn Taymiyya's authority and with his posthumous reputation, evident in the texts by al-Wāsiṭī or Ibn Murrī, reveals breaches in the group cohesion, possibly a reflection of internal friction within the circle of close disciples.

What, then, of the attitudes towards Ibn Taymiyya within the larger Ḥanbalī community? Rather than offering unqualified support, the position of the Ḥanbalīs of Damascus towards Ibn Taymiyya can be described as one of fluctuating scepticism, as is evident from an examination of Ibn Rajab's biographical collection of contemporary Ḥanbalī jurists.[83] Ibn Rajab was the foremost biographer of the Ḥanbalīs and the leading expert in the history of his school. He was a traditionalist Ḥanbalī himself, indeed very loyal to his own scholarly community and its intellectual tradition.[84] In his work, he dedicates a long biographical entry to Ibn Taymiyya, an entry that contains more than a note of disapproval.[85] Following the biographical literary conventions, Ibn Rajab quotes several passionate eulogies of Ibn Taymiyya from the pen of contemporary eminent scholars. Among them, we again encounter al-Wāsiṭī whom Ibn Rajab introduces as one of the most faithful disciples of Ibn Taymiyya, a disciple who had studied with him even though he was Ibn Taymiyya's senior.[86]

It is at this point, however, that Ibn Rajab brings to the fore voices of criticism of Ibn Taymiyya from within the Ḥanbalī and traditionalist community. He quotes a passage from al-Wāsiṭī's letter (the same letter discussed above) which was written, says Ibn Rajab, to recommend to Ibn Taymiyya's close disciples respect and veneration for their master.[87] Inspite of this, Ibn Rajab claims that al-Wāsiṭī, had reservations about the attitude of Ibn Taymiyya towards Sufi and other figures of authority. In this regard, he remarks:

> Yet, he [al-Wāsiṭī] and a group of the most intimate followers sometimes disapproved of what the Shaykh said about some of the great and prominent imams, or about the people of seclusion and extreme devotion (*ahl al-takhallī wa-al-inqiṭā'*) and the like. By this the Shaykh—may God be merciful with him—only meant good things and support for the truth.[88]

Elaborating on this internal opposition to Ibn Taymiyya, Ibn Rajab continues:

> A number of traditionalist scholars, including the most learned among them (*al-ḥuffāẓ*) and the jurists, loved and venerated the Shaykh, but did not like his excessive preoccupation with the speculative theologians and the philosophers. In this they followed the way of the early traditionalist Imams, such as al-Shāfi'ī, Aḥmad [ibn Ḥanbal], Isḥāq [ibn Rāhwayh], Abī 'Ubayd [al-Qāsim ibn Sallām al-Harawī] and the like.
>
> Similarly, many scholars, jurists, traditionalists and virtuous men disliked his taking isolated and irregular positions in questions of law, something which the Pious Ancestors (*salaf*) had abhorred. This was to the point where one of the judges of our school of law (*min aṣḥābinā*) prohibited him from issuing *fatwā*s on some of these issues.[89]

Thus, according to Ibn Rajab, Ibn Taymiyya was criticized from within the Ḥanbalī community with regard to his views on Sufism, *kalām*, philosophy and law. His legal opinions were censured by a Ḥanbalī *qāḍī*, who can be identified as Shams al-Dīn ibn Musallim al-Ḥanbalī (d. 726/1326), who in 718/1318 prohibited Ibn Taymiyya from issuing legal opinions on divorce and other aspects of Ḥanbalī doctrine.[90] Sources sympathetic to Ibn Taymiyya tell us that the Ḥanbalī judge bowed to pressure from a group of powerful men.[91] Yet, it is likely that since Ibn Taymiyya's innovative views on divorce contradicted the traditional Ḥanbalī doctrine, they were also a matter of concern for the local Ḥanbalī elite.[92] At least, this is what Ibn Rajab seems to suggest.

Another indication of Ḥanbalī opposition to Ibn Taymiyya's legal opinions is the verdict issued by the four Chief Qāḍīs of Cairo condemning Ibn Taymiyya's *fatwā* on visitation. It is again significant that the Ḥanbalī judge Aḥmad ibn ʿUmar al-Maqdisī was one of the signatories of the document, declaring Ibn Taymiyya's *fatāwā* as vain, odd and unacceptable (*al-bāṭina al-gharība al-mardūda*).[93] Although Ibn Taymiyya was literally a *mujtahid*, his *ijtihād* was not always welcomed. It was interpreted as an act of non-conformity that challenged the existing legal consensus, including that of the Ḥanbalī *madhhab* and its official representatives.[94]

Ibn Rajab also composed a separate treatise in defence of the authority of the four Sunni schools of law, in which he directs criticism at scholars who claim for themselves the rank of a *mujtahid* while departing from the doctrines of the four schools.[95] Although Ibn Taymiyya is never mentioned by name, he may well have been the object of this attack. In the treatise, Ibn Rajab upholds the superiority of Ibn Ḥanbal's religious knowledge and methodology.[96] One section of the treatise is in the form of an advice to a young Ḥanbalī student who is admonished never to depart from the path set by Ibn Ḥanbal.[97] On the one hand, Ibn Rajab's claims that the authentic Ḥanbalī methodology demands adherence to the Qur'ān, the Sunna of the Prophet and the Pious Ancestors (*salaf*); on the other hand he ultimately insists on full comprehension of Ibn Ḥanbal's works without need of "independence" from it, for the door of *ijtihād* has fortunately been closed (*insadda hādha al-bāb*).[98]

As recommended by Ibn Ḥanbal, Ibn Rajab also advocates non-participation in contentious and theoretical disputes (*al-khiṣām wa-al-jidāl*).[99] In fact:

> Imam Aḥmad and the leaders of the *ahl al-ḥadīth* [...] detested refuting the innovators (*ahl al-bida'*) by partaking in their opponents' discourse (*bi-jins kalāmihim*), that is the use of analogy in matters of theology (*al-aqyisa al-kalāmiyya*) and rational proofs (*adillat al-'uqūl*). They deemed refutation appropriate only by the texts of the Qur'ān, of the Sunna and by the words of the Pious Ancestors (*salaf*), if such were to be found. Otherwise they believed reticence (*al-sukūt*) to be safer.[100]

But non-participation and reticence were not among the characteristics of Ibn Taymiyya, and although he is never mentioned in this treatise, one could suppose a connection between this passage and the "excessive preoccupation with speculative theologians and philosophers" that Ibn Rajab mentions as a cause of internal criticism to Ibn Taymiyya. In fact, as has been recently shown, Ibn Taymiyya often did articulate his positions in a manner that owed much to the philosophical and *kalām* methods of argumentation.[101]

Clearly, Ibn Taymiyya and Ibn Rajab, two prominent members of the Damascene Ḥanbalī community, had some significant differences. It is especially interesting to note how the same premises, i.e., emulation of Ibn Ḥanbal and loyalty to the Book and the Sunna, led the two scholars to opposite conclusions. The absolute priority that Ibn Taymiyya grants to the revealed texts over the opinions of the school eponyms allows him to distance himself from his own law school by resorting directly to these very texts, a methodology he adopted when it came to the question of divorce. For Ibn Rajab, this was inconceivable.

Two other episodes betray tensions between Ibn Taymiyya's circle and other Ḥanbalī scholars. For instance, al-Zar'ī (d. 741/1340–41) is said to have been appointed at the Madrasa al-Ḥanbaliyya after Ibn Taymiyya's imprisonment in 726/1326. The matter greatly displeased and troubled Ibn Taymiyya's companions.[102] The Ḥanbalī al-Ṭūfī (d. 716/1316), he himself a controversial figure, is cited in later sources as making pejorative comments about Ibn Taymiyya. Ibn 'Abd al-Hādī, on the other hand, merely mentions al-Ṭūfī as Ibn Taymiyya's teacher of Arabic.[103]

Ibn Taymiyya and the Traditionalist Shāfiʻīs

Beyond the inner circle of his close disciples, Ibn Taymiyya was closely associated with a group of traditionalist Shāfiʻī scholars, such as the historian al-Birzālī, the traditionist al-Mizzī (d. 742/1341–1342), and the younger Ibn Kathīr (d. 774/1373). The most well-known member of this group, however, was Shams al-Dīn al-Dhahabī (d. 748/1348), who had been one of the most explicit critics of Ibn Taymiyya.[104] Al-Dhahabī was an authoritative Shāfiʻī scholar, a respected historian, a reliable traditionist as well as a copious writer but, above all, a very committed traditionalist.[105] The respect he enjoyed in Ḥanbalī circles is evident from the frequency with which his name is quoted in Ibn Rajab's biographical collection. His writings about the life and scholarship of Ibn Taymiyya are quite extensive, and he is often cited by later biographers.

Al-Dhahabī's attitude to Ibn Taymiyya vacillates between unqualified praise of his intellect and sharp criticism of his public conduct.[106] He condemns what he saw as the most excessive features of Ibn Taymiyya's personality: his choleric moods, his fondness of supremacy (*riyāsa*), his contempt for his fellow *ʻulamā*' and his rough manners. Sometimes, al-Dhahabī seems simply exasperated by the futility of Ibn Taymiyya's never-ending polemical skirmishes: "By Allah! Give us a break from talking about the 'Thursday innovation' and about 'eating the grains',[107] and make a serious effort to remember innovation which we used to consider the principle of misguidance and which has now become the pure *sunna* and the foundation of *tawḥīd*".[108]

Yet, mostly, he finds fault with Ibn Taymiyya's preoccupation with theological polemics. In *Bayān zaghal al-ʻilm wa-al-ṭalab*, a critique of the different disciplines of knowledge, al-Dhahabī highlights the defects of each of the disciplines. Ibn Taymiyya is mentioned in this work three times. First, under the heading "The Science of Prophetic Tradition (*ʻilm al-ḥadīth*)", he is listed among the most skilful traditionists of his time.[109] Second, in a chapter dealing with the Shāfiʻī school of law, al-Dhahabī warns against approaching knowledge in pursuit of prestige and money, while also condemning displays of arrogance such as those of Ibn Taymiyya, who, al-Dhahabī explains, was widely acknowledged as a scholar but despised by his fellow *ʻulamā*' for his pretensions and love for leadership.[110] Finally, in the chapter dealing with theology (*ʻilm uṣūl al-dīn*), al-Dhahabī contrasts the theological principles of the early generations with those of the later generations. Among the first Muslims, the principles of theology relied directly on revelation: "Belief in God the Highest, in His books, His messengers, in His angels and attributes, in the divine decree and in the revealed Qur'ān as the uncreated word of God the Highest, as well as full acceptance of every Companion, and other principles of the Sunna". The theology of the later generations, on the other hand, is based on reason (*al-'aql*) and logic (*al-manṭiq*), and they are in constant disagreement among themselves. In this regard he writes:

> War reigns among the theologians (*al-uṣūliyya*). They declare each other unbelievers or misguided. The theologian who sticks to the plain meaning of the words and traditions is declared by his adversaries to be an anthropomorphist, a *ḥashwī*, and an innovator. In turn, the theologian who promotes [allegoric] interpretation will be declared by the others a Jahmī and a Mu'tazilī and to be in error. [The theologian] who admits [the existence of] some [positive] attributes in God and rejects others and also permits [allegoric] interpretation in certain cases [and not in other cases] is called a person who contradicts himself. It would be better to go slow.
>
> You may excel in the basic principles [of religion] and its subordinated sciences (*tawābi'uhā*), such as logic, wisdom (*al-ḥikma*), philosophy, and opinions of the ancients, and the speculative ideas connected with [those] principles. You may, further, hold to the Qur'ān, the Sunna, and the basic principles of the early generations. You may, moreover, combine the rational and traditional sciences (*al-'aql wa-al-naql*). Yet, I do not think that in this respect,[111] you will reach the degree of Ibn Taymiyya. Indeed, you will not even come near to it. And you have seen how he was degraded, abandoned and considered to be in error, to be an unbeliever, and to be a liar, rightly or wrongly. Before he embarked upon this, he was brilliant and shining, with the mark of those early Muslims on his face. Then, he was wronged and exposed [to disgrace]. His face was blackened (*'alayhi quṭma*) in the opinion of some people, he was an impostor, fraud, and unbeliever in the opinion of his enemies; an excellent, correct, and outstanding innovator (*mubtadi'an*) in the opinion of many intelligent and excellent men; and the bearer of the banner of Islam, the guardian of the realm of religion, and the reviver of the Sunna in the opinion of the great majority of his followers.[112]

Al-Dhahabī appears to identify Ibn Taymiyya's combination of reason and revelation in theological speculation as the cause of much of the criticism to which he was subjected.[113] Al-Dhahabī's view is in line with that of Ibn Rajab's, as well as with the following account by the close disciple Ibn Murrī:

> He [Ibn Taymiyya] took correct tradition (*al-naql al-ṣaḥīḥ*) to be the base and the foundation for all that he built thereon, and he would then buttress this with sound reasoning (*bi-al-'aqliyyāt al-ṣaḥīḥa*) that agreed with it and with other supports, and exerted his *ijtihād* to reject all the pseudo-rational arguments (*shubah al-ma'qūlāt*) that contradicted this. He firmly committed himself to solve any theological or philosophical ambiguity in the way indicated above, and to combine correct tradition with clear reason (*ṣarīḥ al-ma'qūl*).[114]

The disagreement over Ibn Taymiyya's methods among the traditionalist scholars of his time was caused by Ibn Taymiyya's use of rationalism. These rationalist aspects of Ibn Taymiyya's thought have been indeed highlighted in recent scholarship.[115]

In the case of al-Dhahabī, there were perhaps also material considerations at stake. Al-Dhahabī, as well as his fellow traditionist al-Mizzī, were subject to public humiliation in 718/1318 because of their Taymiyyan sympathies. Al-Dhahabī says:

> The Shaykh is the one who strove for [the assignment of] the direction of the Dār al-Ḥadīth al-Ashrafiyya to al-Mizzī and that of the Turba al-Ṣāliḥiyya to me. And on that occasion some events occurred, the Shaykh was molested by his opponents and we were interrogated about our creed. As a result, al-Mizzī wrote for them a number of statements while I was exempted from writing.[116]

While Ibn Taymiyya did succeed in obtaining the two prestigious posts (the former more than the latter) for his disciples, they were to pay a price. When al-Mizzī showed up to deliver his inaugural lecture, he was faced with an empty hall—as witnessed with glee by his rival al-Subkī.[117] As for al-Dhahabī, his first day of teaching was spoiled by the arrest of a Ḥanbalī scholar who turned up in support, but was then put on trial by the Shāfi'ī Chief Qāḍī for a mystical vision he reported in one of his writings.[118]

There are two further examples of scholars whose sympathies for Ibn Taymiyya were ultimately transformed into public criticism. The Shāfi'ī Kamāl al-Dīn Ibn al-Zamlakānī (d. 727/1326–27), usually listed as one of Ibn Taymiyya's enemies, was not always one.[119] On several occasions he was suspected of close relationship to Ibn Taymiyya. In 702/1302–3 he was accused, along with Ibn Taymiyya and the Ḥanafī judge Ibn al-Ḥarīrī, of plotting with the Mongols to bring the ex-governor Qibjaq back to Damascus.[120] Following Ibn Taymiyya's trial in Cairo, Ibn al-Zamlakānī was also summoned to Egypt for questioning with regard to his Taymiyyan sympathies.[121] In the year 709/1309–10 he was dismissed from his position as supervisor of the Nūrī hospital.[122]

A final example of a friend who turned into a foe comes from beyond the boundaries of the Shāfiʿī school of law. The Ḥanafī jurist Ibn al-Ḥarīrī[123] lost his teaching position after writing an epistle in support of Ibn Taymiyya in 705/1306, and at the time was regarded as a zealous supporter.[124] But, with time, Ibn Taymiyya appears to have become more isolated, and companionship with him a matter of increasing inconvenience. During the Shaykh's last trial, concerning the issue of visitation, Ibn al-Ḥarīrī is reported to have co-signed, together with the Ḥanbalī judge in Cairo, a verdict declaring Ibn Taymiyya an unbeliever (*kāfir*).[125] Both Ibn al-Zamlākanī and Ibn al-Ḥarīrī had also previously criticized Ibn Taymiyya for his position on divorce oaths.[126]

How can we explain this shift from public support to a position of open criticism and hostility? Al-Dhahabī again proves helpful when he writes:

> He supported the pure Sunna and the way of the Pious Ancestors (*salaf*) which he vindicated with unprecedented proofs, premises and cases using expressions which men of former and recent times refrained from and feared. He was so daring in this that a group of scholars from Egypt and Syria turned against him in an unprecedented way. They accused him of being an innovator, they confronted him and treated him with contempt.[127]

And later in the text:

> His followers weakened and he involved himself in weighty questions that neither the intellects of his contemporaries nor their learning could bear, such as: the question of the expiation of the oath of repudiation, the opinion that repudiation uttered three times is valid only once, and the opinion that repudiation during menstruation is not valid. He composed writings about these topics in the order of some forty quires.

> Because of this, he was forbidden to issue legal opinions. He controlled himself in a strange way and held firm to his own opinion.[128]

Ibn Taymiyya's dynamic vision of Islam was upheld by an elitist minority. For the majority of traditionalist scholars, Ḥanbalīs and Shāfiʿīs alike, he appears to have been somewhat of an embarrassment. How then can we account for his popularity among the general population of Damascus?

Popular Support: Crowds

The preceding discussion would appear to be at odds with the popular support that Ibn Taymiyya seems to have enjoyed. Emotional crowds always accompanied Ibn Taymiyya wherever he went. When summoned to Cairo, a great mass of people (*khalq kathīr*) gathered to salute him. They stretched from the door of his house to al-Jasūra, and they cried and feared for him.[129] A similar crowd rejoiced when he was released from prison.[130] A vast crowd (*khalq ʿaẓīm*) gathered to listen to his sermon in the al-Ḥākim Mosque on Friday.[131] When imprisoned again, the jail was transformed into a place of devotion, a *madrasa* whose students, the detainees, were unwilling to leave even when set free. His visitors in prison were so many that he was moved to Alexandria.[132] There too the notables visited him, while scholars studied and benefited from his presence.[133] His support came from every segment of society: "There are people who love him from among the scholars and the pious, the soldiers and the amirs, the tradesmen and the authorities. The rest of the common people love him because he stands up for their benefit, day and night, in his words and his writings."[134]

The most striking example of popular support for Ibn Taymiyya comes from his funeral procession when thousands of people, men and women alike, mourned his death in loud despair.[135] These are said to have numbered fifteen or sixteen thousand women and up to two hundred thousand men.[136] The emphasis on multitudes highlights Ibn Taymiyya's irresistible popularity and charisma. Despite his trials and tribulations, people—and all sorts of people—loved him and supported him until his death. In the Islamic tradition, wide popular attendance at funerals was a mark of public reverence, a demonstration of the deceased's rectitude, and a sign of divine approbation. The scholar whose funeral enjoyed wide participation was confirmed as an authoritative figure.[137] Yet, the narratives of Ibn Taymiyya's funeral do more than affirm the authority of the Shaykh. Rather, they make explicit and meaningful references to the funeral of Aḥmad Ibn Ḥanbal; in fact, two of the most faithful supporters of Ibn Taymiyya, Ibn Kathīr and Ibn 'Abd al-Hādī, both report that, in the history of Islam, only the funeral of Aḥmad ibn Ḥanbal attracted wider participation.[138] Ibn Kathīr compares the two funerals, claiming that Ibn Taymiyya's procession had less attendance only because the population of Damascus was smaller than that of Baghdad of Ibn Ḥanbal's time. Moreover, he was denied visitors in his prison and few were aware of his illness, whereas Ibn Ḥanbal received numerous visits on his deathbed.

Ibn Kathīr quotes a saying of Ibn Ḥanbal to his son 'Abd Allāh (d. 290/903): "Say to the people of innovations: between us and you let there be funerals, when they pass by".[139] In these narratives, wide participation in a funeral procession marks the people of the Sunna from the innovators, the truthful from the erroneous. A direct line is here established between Ibn Ḥanbal and Ibn Taymiyya, who is placed one rank below the school founder. While this is a clear device for consolidating authority around Ibn Taymiyya (and the group who identified with him), it also suggests, as does the latter of al-Wāsiṭī, that the Shaykh's authority had to be emphatically demonstrated. Ibn Kathīr's explicit invocations of the founder of the Ḥanbalī *madhhab* were aimed not only at Ibn Taymiyya's opponents, but also—perhaps even in particular—directed against those critical and sceptical traditionalists who questioned his manners and methodology. Ibn Kathīr's narrative of Ibn Taymiyya's funeral procession should therefore be understood against the background of this entrenched Ḥanbalī and and traditionalist opposition.

Conclusion

This essay has tried to illustrate the nature of the group associated with Ibn Taymiyya. This was a zealous circle of individuals (which the sources usually refer to as *al-jamā'a* or *jamā'atuhu*) who considered themselves Ibn Taymiyya's disciples and shared his understanding of Islam and his taste for activism. The internal correspondence of this group displays strong bonds of loyalty, as well as a sense of a distinctive exclusivity and elitism. Examination of contemporary biographical collections reveals that his immediate Ḥanbalī disciples were not particularly numerous. At the same time, it is also clear that many of his followers were not Ḥanbalīs. This suggests that both support and hostility towards Ibn Taymiyya should be read in a framework that goes beyond the *madhhab*, a framework that also reflects Ibn Taymiyya's own quite indifferent attitude towards the authority of the schools of law.

Moreover, we have also seen evidence of explicit criticism of Ibn Taymiyya from within the traditionalist circles close to him, even from within the close circle of his disciples. It seems that support of Ibn Taymiyya waned with time, as his doctrines moved more radically away from Ḥanbalī tradition. His combination of reason and revelation in matters of theology was a particular cause for concern among some of his fellow traditionalists, while his views on divorce have been perceived as being at odds with current legal consensus and with the dominant opinion within the Ḥanbalī school of law. Hence, Ibn Taymiyya was far from being the undisputed representative of later Hanbalism as he has been characterized by modern historians. Rather, the sources portray a charismatic leader of a radical minority group with whom the majority of Ḥanbalī and traditionalist *'ulamā'* did not necessarily identify.

As for the popular support he seems to have enjoyed, the *topos* of acclaiming and emotional crowds has been highlighted as part of the construction of Ibn Taymiyya's authority. But, while we will never be able to determine the historicity of these accounts, we should not assume that elitism and mass support were by necessity mutually exclusive. His political commitment and high public profile during the Mongol invasions of Syria may well have won him real respect in the eyes of the people of Damascus. Moreover, the coexistence of conflicting elements in Ibn Taymiyya's biography reflects his vast, multi-layered intellectual production, the accessibility of which differed according to his audience and to the subject matter in question. The manner in which these elements stand together reveals the complexity of Ibn Taymiyya's scholarship and its impact on the society he belonged to, as well as the multifaceted nature of biographical construction and transmission, which are central to the continuing debates over the Shaykh's authority and his legacy

Notes

* This paper benefited from the careful reading and helpful comments of Shahab Ahmed, Yossef Rapoport and an anonymous reader. I am grateful to them and to the conference participants for their valuable remarks.

1. H. Laoust, "Le Hanbalisme sous les Mamlouks Bahrides (658/784–1260/1382)", *Revue des Études Islamiques* 28 (1960): 1–71, and idem, *Essai sur les doctrines sociales et politiques de Taḳī-d-Dīn Aḥmad b. Taimīya, canoniste ḥanbalite né à Ḥarrān en 661/1262, mort à Damas en 728/1328* (Cairo: Imprimerie de l'institut français d'archéologie orientale, 1939), 488ff. On the Ḥanbalī communities of Damascus and Syria, see also D. Talmon-Heller, "The Shaykh and the Community: Popular Hanbalite Islam in the 12th–13th Century in Nablus and Jabal Qasyūn," *Studia Islamica* 79 (1994): 103–20; D. Sourdel, "Deux documents relatifs à la communauté hanbalite de Damas", *Bulletin d'Etudes Orientales* 25 (1972): 141–50; W. Madelung, "The spread of Māturīdism and the Turks," Actas do IV congresso de estudos árabes e Islâmicos, *Biblos* 46 (1970), esp. 159–60; L. Pouzet, *Damas au VIIe/XIIIe s. Vie et structure religieuses dans une métropole islamique* (Beirut: Dār al-Mashriq, 1991), 80–96; M. Cook, *Commanding Right and Forbidding Wrong in Islamic Thought* (Cambridge: Cambridge University Press, 2000), 145–164.
2. Here and in what follows the word "traditionalist" is used to connote a Hadith-oriented scholar or group.
3. See the collections of Ibn Taymiyya's biographical material in Ṣalāḥ al-Dīn al Munajjid (ed.), *Shaykh al-Islām Ibn Taymiyya: sīratu-hu wa-akhbāru-hu 'inda al-mu'arrikhīn* (Beirut: Dār al-Kutub al-'Ilmiyya, 1976); Muḥammad 'Uzayr Shams and 'Alī ibn Muḥammad al-'Umrān, *al-Jāmi' li-sīrat Shaykh al-Islām Ibn Taymiyya khilāla sab'a qurūn* (Mecca: Dār 'Ālam al-Fawā'id, 1420H) [hereafter *Jāmi'*]. For assessment of the biographical tradition, see Hasan Q. Murad, "Miḥan of Ibn Taymiyya. A Narrative Account based on a Comparative Analysis of the Sources", MA dissertation (Montreal: Institute of Islamic Studies, McGill, 1968), 1–73; and C. Bori, *Ibn Taymiyya: una vita esemplare. Analisi delle fonti classiche della sua biografia*, Supplemento monografico n. 1 alla *Rivista degli Studi Orientali* LXXVI (2003) (Roma—Pisa: Istituti Poligrafici Internazionali, 2003), 29–59 and 177–81.
4. See N. Hurvitz, "Biographies and mild asceticism: a study of Islamic moral imagination", *Studia Islamica* 85/1 (1997): 41–65; A. Hourani, "Islamic History, Middle Eastern History, Modern History," in Malcolm H. Kerr (ed.), *Islamic Studies: A Tradition and its Problems* (Malibu, CA: Undena Publications, 1980), 5–26.
5. For the social uses of knowledge, see Michael Chamberlain, *Knowledge and Social Practice in Medieval Damascus, 1190–1350* (Cambridge: Cambridge University Press, 1994), especially 92–107 and 163–74, where he discusses knowledge as a major source of social power. See also J. P. Berkey, *The Transmission of Knowledge in Medieval Cairo: a Social History of Education* (Princeton: Princeton University Press, 1992); and idem, *Popular Preaching and Religious Authority in the Medieval Islamic Near East* (London and Seattle: University of Washington Press, 2001), esp. 70–87.
6. The term *ṭā'ifa* (pl. *ṭawā'if*) is employed by Michael Cooperson who defines it as: "a group of persons possessing the same expertise, holding the same office, or otherwise engaged in common and characteristic activity" (*Classical Arabic*

Biography. The Heirs of the Prophets in the Age of al-Maʾmūn [Cambridge: Cambridge University Press, 2000], xxi). Cooperson uses the word specifically to point out the criterion around which biographical dictionaries were collected.

7. For inter-*madhhab* competition, see M. Winter, "Inter-*madhhab* competition in Mamlūk Damascus: al-Ṭarsūsī's counsel for the Turkish Sultans," *Jerusalem Studies in Arabic and Islam* 25 (2001): 195–211; Y. Rapoport, "Legal diversity in the age of *taqlīd*: the four chief *qāḍīs* under the Mamlūks," *Islamic Law and Society* 10/2 (2003): 210–28.
8. See examples in J. Berkey, *Popular Preaching and Religious Authority*; idem, "Storytelling, Preaching and Power in Mamluk Cairo", *Mamlūk Studies Review* IV (2000): 53–73; and idem, "Tradition, Innovation and the Social Construction of Knowledge in the Medieval Islamic Near East", *Past&Present* 146 (1995): 38–65.
9. G. Makdisi, "L'Islam hanbalisant", *Revue des Études Islamiques* 42 (1974): 241–44.
10. See, for instance, Ibn Murrī, *Risāla min al-Shaykh Aḥmad ibn Muḥammad ibn Murrī al-Ḥanbalī (baʿd 728) ilā talāmīdh Shaykh al-islām Ibn Taymiyya*, in *Jāmiʿ*, 98, 100; al-Ghayyānī, *Nāḥiya min ḥayāt Shaykh al-islām Ibn Taymiyya*, ed. Muḥibb al-Dīn al-Khaṭīb (Cairo: al-Maṭbaʿa al-Salafiyya, 1352H.), 13, 14 and passim.
11. Ibn ʿAbd al-Hādī (d. 744/1343), *al-ʿUqūd al-durriyya min manāqib Shaykh al-islām Ibn Taymiyya*, ed. Muḥammad Ḥāmid al-Fiqī (Cairo: Maṭbaʿat Ḥijāzī, 1938), 273.
12. Ibn Taymiyya, *Majmūʿ fatāwā Shaykh al-islām Aḥmad ibn Taymiyya*, ed. ʿAbd al-Raḥmān ibn Muḥammad ibn Qāsim al-Najdī al-Ḥanbalī, 37 vols. (Rabat: Maktabat al-Maʿārif, 1981) [hereafter *MF*], 3:246. Excerpts from this long epistle (*MF*, 3:211–47) have been translated by Y. Michot, "Je ne suis dans cette affaire qu'un musulman parmi d'autres...", Textes Spirituels d'Ibn Taymiyya, x. *Le Musulman* 23 (Mai 1994): 27–32.
13. Ibn Taymiyya, *MF*, 27: 30–46, quotation from p. 30.
14. Ibn Taymiyya, *MF*, 27: 41.
15. Ibn Taymiyya, *MF*, 27: 44. For the meaning of *khidma* as a way to express loyalty by dependence and subordination, see Chamberlain, *Knowledge and Practice*, 116–18.
16. Al-Wāsiṭi, *al-Tadhkira wa-al-iʿtibār wa-al-intiṣār li-al-abrār fī al-thanāʾ ʿalā Shaykh al-Islām wa-al-wiṣāya bi-hi*, in Ibn ʿAbd al-Hādī, *ʿUqūd*, 193–212; also as a separate treatise edited by ʿAbd al-Jabbār al-Furaywāʿī (Riyadh: Dār al-ʿĀṣima, 1415/1994). I thank Shahab Ahmed for supplying a copy of the text. The letter is quoted in Y. Michot, *Ibn Taymiyya. Les saints du Mont Liban: absence, Jihad, et spiritualité entre la montagne et la cité* (Beirut: Editions Albouraq, 2007), 1. I am indebted to Frank Griffel for this reference. For the biography of al-Wasiṭī, see Ibn Rajab (d. 795/1393), *Dhayl ʿalā ṭabaqāt al-ḥanābila*, 2 vols., ed. M. Ḥ. Fiqī (Cairo: Maṭbaʿat al-Sunna al-Muḥammadiyya, 1952–53), 2:358–360; al-Ṣafadī, *al-Wāfī bi-al-wafayāt*, ed. H. Ritter at al. (Leipzig: Deutsche Morgenländische Gesellschaft, 1931–2004), 6:221; Ibn al-ʿImād (d. 1080/1670), *Shadharāt al-dhahab fī akhbār man dhahab* (Cairo: al-Maktaba al-Tijāriyya, 1350–51H., reprint ed. in Beirut, 1979), 6:24–25; Laoust, "Le Hanbalisme sous les Mamlouks Bahrides", 61–62; Pouzet, *Damas au VII*[e]*/XIII*[e] *s.*, 234–35; E. Geoffroy, "Le Traité de soufisme d'un disciple d'Ibn Taymiyya: Aḥmad ʿImād al-Dīn al-Wāsiṭī (d. 711/1311)," *Studia Islamica* 82/2 (1995): 83–101 (a study of *al-Sulūk wa al-sayr ilā Allāh*, a treatise on Sufism still in manuscript form).

17. See G. Makdisi, "Ibn Taymiyya: a ṣūfī of the Qadariyya order," *American Journal of Arabic Studies* 1 (1973): 119–29; and idem, "The Hanbali school and Sufism," *Humaniora Islamica* 2 (1974): 61–72. Makdisi's conclusions have been qualified by Thomas Michel, "Ibn Taymiyya's Sharḥ on the *Futūḥ al-Ghayb* of 'Abd al-Qādir al-Jīlānī," *Hamdard Islamicus* 4/2 (1981): 3–12; F. Meier, "Das Sauberste über die Vorberstimmung. Ein Stuck Ibn Taymiyya," *Speculum* 32 (1981): 74–89; and A. Knysh, *Ibn 'Arabi in the Later Islamic Tradition. The Making of a Polemical Image in Medieval Islam* (Albany: State of New York Press, 1999), 314 n5.
18. Ibn 'Abd al-Hādī, *'Uqūd*, 290.
19. For discussion of these individuals, see below.
20. In two other works, al-Wāsiṭī makes no mention of his attachment to Ibn Taymiyya. See al-Wāsiṭī, *al-Naṣīḥa fī al-ṣifāt* and *Madkhal ahl al-fiqh wa-al-lisān ilā maydān al-maḥabba wa-al-'irfān*, ed. Muḥammad 'Abd Allāh al-'Alī in *Liqā' al-'ashr al-awākhir bi-al-masjid al-ḥarām* (Beirut: Shirkat Dār al-Bashā'ir al-Islāmiyya, 2005), vol. 4, no. 39. The second work expands on ideas also found in the letter under discussion, such as the importance of the master's guidance for the disciple's path, the necessity of respecting one's Shaykh and strict adherence to the Book and the Sunna.
21. Al-Wāsiṭī, *Tadhkira*, in *'Uqūd*, 294–300.
22. Al-Wāsiṭī, *Tadhkira*, in *'Uqūd*, 299.
23. Al-Wāsiṭī, *Tadhkira*, in *'Uqūd*, 301.
24. See Geoffroy, "Le traité de soufisme," 88–91.
25. Al-Wāsiṭī, *Tadhkira*, in *'Uqūd*, 298, 301, 313–14.
26. On al-Wāsiṭī as a polemicist, see Geoffroy, "Le traité de soufisme," 93–96.
27. On the Jahmiyya as Ash'arīs, see *MF*, 4:148 et passim; Thomas Michel, *A Muslim Theologian's Response to Christianity. Ibn Taymiyya's* al-Jawāb al-Ṣaḥīḥ (Delmar-New York: Caravan Books, 1984), 43–44.
28. Al-Wāsiṭī, *Tadhkira*, in *'Uqūd*, 301.
29. Al-Wāsiṭī, *Tadhkira*, in *'Uqūd*, 302.
30. Al-Wāsiṭī, *Tadhkira*, in *'Uqūd*, 303. Al-Wāsiṭī clearly refers here to the same category of Sufis labelled by Ibn Taymiyya as *ṣūfiyyat al-rasm* in *MF*, 11:19–20 (*Risālat fī al-ṣūfiyya wa-al-fuqarā'*). For an English translation of the text, see T. Homerin, "Ibn Taymīya's *al-Ṣūfīya wa'l-fuqarā'*," *Arabica* 32 (1985), 233.
31. Al-Wāsiṭī, *Tadhkira*, in *'Uqūd*, 303–04.
32. Al-Wāsiṭī, *Tadhkira*, in *'Uqūd*, 305.
33. Al-Wāsiṭī, *Tadhkira*, in *'Uqūd*, 305, 309–10. For a critical discussion of the notion of *tajdīd* in the Sufi and Sunni tradition, see S. Pagani, *Il rinnovamento mistico dell'Islam. Un commento di 'Abd al-Ghanī al-Nābulusī a Aḥmad Sirhindī* (Napoli: Università di Napoli l'Orientale, Disserationes 3:2003), 95–115.
34. Al-Wāsiṭī, *Tadhkira*, in *'Uqūd*, 309–13. The quotation is from p. 310.
35. For discussion of the meaning of the word *naṣīb* in al-Wāsiṭī, see Geoffroy, "Le traité de soufisme", 92 and fn. 67.
36. Al-Wāsiṭī, *Tadhkira*, in *'Uqūd*, 313–21.
37. Al-Wāsiṭī, *Tadhkira*, in *'Uqūd*, 317–18. In several passages al-Wāsiṭī seems to refer to a particular individual whose name he chooses not to mention (al-Wāsiṭī, *Tadhkira*, in *'Uqūd*, 314–17, 320).
38. Al-Wāsiṭī, *Tadhkira*, in *'Uqūd*, 316.
39. Ibid., 317–18.
40. Al-Wāsiṭī, *Tadhkira*, in *'Uqūd*, 300: "*...ja'alakum bayna jamī' ahl hādhā al-'aṣr ka-al-shāma al-bayḍā' fī al-ḥayawān al-aswad.*"

41. Ibid., 301.
42. For the biography of Ibn Murrī, see Ibn Ḥajar (d. 836/1432), *al-Durar al-kāmina fī aʿyān al-miʾa al-thāmina*, ed. ʿAbd al-Wārith Muḥammad ʿAlī (Beirut: Dār al-Kutub al-ʿIlmiyya, 1997), 1:178–79. For an account of his trial, see al-Jazarī (d. 739/1338–39), *Taʾrīkh ḥawādith al-zamān wa-anbāʾi-hi wa-wafayāt al-akābir wa-al-aʿyān min abnāʾi-hi al-maʿrūf bi-Taʾrīkh Ibn al-Jazarī*, ed. ʿUmar al-Tadmurī (Beirut: al-Maktaba al-ʿAṣriyya, 1998), 2:61–62; Ibn Kathīr, *al-Bidāya wa-al-nihāya fī al-taʾrīkh*, ed. F.A. al-Kurdī (Cairo: Maṭbaʿat al-Saʿāda, 1932–39), 14:117; al-Maqrīzī (d. 845/1441), *Kitāb al-sulūk li-maʿrifat duwal al-mulūk*, ed. Muṣṭafā Ziyāda (Cairo: Maṭbaʿat al-Taʾlīf wa-al-Tarjama wa-al-Nashr, 1971), 2/1:263; H. Q. Murad, "Ibn Taymiyya on trial", 24–25 and his *Miḥan of Ibn Taymiyya*, 110–11; J. H. Escovitz, *The office of qâḍî al-quḍât in Cairo under the Baḥrî Mamlûks* (Berlin: K. Schwarz, 1984), 141–43.
43. Ibn Murrī, *Risāla*, in *Jāmiʿ*, 97–104.
44. Ibn Murrī, *Risāla*, in *Jāmiʿ*, 98–99.
45. Ibn Murrī, *Risāla*, in *Jāmiʿ*, 99.
46. Ibn Rushayyiq (d. 749/1348) was a Mālikī disciple of Ibn Taymiyya and, apparently, also his copyist. Ibn Kathīr confirms Ibn Murrī's view: "He copied the works of our Shaykh whose writings he knew in most depth, and if there was something lacking, it was this Abū ʿAbd Allāh who would elicit it" (*Bidāya*, 14:229). Ibn ʿAbd al-Hādī describes Ibn Rushayyiq as the one who wrote down Ibn Taymiyya's works and who strove for collecting it (*ʿUqūd*, 27). See also *Jāmiʿ*, 8–13, 98 n1 and 220–239 for the text of *Asmāʾ muʾallafāt Shaykh al-Islām Ibn Taymiyya*.
47. Ibn Murrī, *Risāla* in *Jāmiʿ*, 100.
48. The expression *ʿal-ṭarīqa al-salafiyya*ʾ is Ibn Murrī's: "*li-man yuʾallifu minhā wa-yanqulu wa-yanṣuru al-ṭarīqa al-salafiyya ʿalā qawāʿidihā*" (*Risāla* in *Jāmiʿ*, 101).
49. For the different ways in which Ibn Taymiyya's activism is understood in his biographical tradition, see Bori, *Ibn Taymiyya: una vita esemplare*, 111–40.
50. See al-Yūnīnī, *Dhayl Mirʾāt al-Zamān*, ed. Li Guo (Leiden: E. J. Brill, 1998), 1:165–6 (English translation)—2:126 (Arabic text); al-Nuwayrī (d. 733/1333), *Nihāyat al-arab fī funūn al-adab*, ed. M. ʿUlwī Shaltūt et al. (Cairo: Dār al-Kutub al-Miṣriyya, 1992), 31:401; al-Dhahabī, *Taʾrīkh al-Islām wa-wafayāt al-mashāhīr wa-al-aʿlām*, ed. ʿUmar al-Tadmurī (Beirut: Dār al-Kitāb al-ʿArabī, 2000), 41:95, for which also see the imprecise English translation of J. De Somogyi, "Adh-Dhahabī record of the destruction of Damascus by the Mongols in 699–700/1300–1301", in S. Löwinger and J. Somogyi (eds.), *Goldziher Memorial Volume* (Budapest, 1948), 1:380; al-Birzālī, *al-Muqtafā li-taʾrīkh Abī Shāma*, in *Jāmiʿ*, 150; Ibn Kathīr, *Bidāya*, 14:11; al-Maqrīzī, *Kitāb al-muqaffā al-kabīr*, ed. M. Yaʿlāwī (Beirut: Dār al-Gharb al-Islāmī, 1991), 1:459.
51. Al-Birzālī, *Muqtafā*, in *Jāmiʿ*, 156; Ibn Kathīr, *Bidāya*, 14:34. The episode is later quoted by al-Maqrīzī, *Sulūk*, 2/1: 8–9 and al-ʿAynī (d. 855/1451), *ʿIqd al-jumān fī taʾrīkh ahl al-zamān*, ed. M. M. Amīn (Cairo: al-Hayʾa al-Miṣriyya al-ʿĀmma li-al-Kitāb, 1992), 4:357–58.
52. Al-Birzālī, *Muqtafā*, in *Jāmiʿ*, 150; al-Yūnīnī, *Dhayl Mirʾāt al-Zamān*, 1:166 (English translation)—2:126 (Arabic text); Anonymus, *Beiträge zur Geschichte der Mamlūkensultane in der Jahren 690–741 der Hijra nach arabischen Handschriften*, ed. K. V. Zetterstéen (Leiden: E. J. Brill, 1919), 79; Ibn Kathīr, *Bidāya*, 14:11.

53. Ibrāhīm ibn Aḥmad al-Ghayyānī, *Nāḥiya.* The text is also in *Jāmiʿ*, 78–96. I have been unable to identify the author, who describes himself as "the servant of the *shaykh*" (*khādim al-shaykh*). Cf. al-Ghayyānī, *Nāḥiya*, 33, 34, 44. Internal evidence suggests that he was in Cairo when Ibn Taymiyya was imprisoned in the *Qāʿat al-tarsīm* (707–709). Some of the episodes related by al-Ghayyānī are not found in any other biographical source (*Nāḥiya*, 4). The text may be identical to a work entitled a 'Treatise on Breaking Rocks' in Ibn al-Rushayyiq's list of Ibn Taymiyya's works (Ibn Rushayyiq, *Asmāʾ muʿallafāt shaykh al-islām Ibn Taymiyya*, in *Jāmiʿ*, 239). The source awaits a more critical assessment.
54. Ibid., 10, 11, 13, 14, 17, 18.
55. Ibn Rajab, *Dhayl*, 2:359–60, 362, 376, 377, 383, 436, 439, 443, 448.
56. This is how al-Bazzār describes his own attachment to Ibn Taymiyya: "*wa-kuntu muddat iqāmatī bi-dimashq mulāzimahu jull al-nahār wa-kathīran min al-layl*" (*Aʿlām*, 38 and also 53).
57. These are al-Ṭūfī (d. 716/1316), al-Bazzār (d. 749/1349–50), Ibn Rabāṭir al-Ḥarrānī (d. 718/1318), Maḥmūd ibn ʿUbayd al-Baʿlī (d. 734/1334), Ibn ʿAbāda al-Ḥarrānī (d. 739/1338–39), Sirāj al-Dīn ʿUmar (d. ?), Ṣafī al-Dīn al-Baghdādī (d. 739/1338) and Aḥmad ibn al-Ḥasan al-Maqdisī (d. 771/1369–70).
58. Ibn Rajab, *Dhayl*, 2:366 and 444.
59. Ibid., 2:373.
60. Ibid., 2:423 and 432.
61. Ibid., 2:425.
62. Ibid., 2:414 (Najm al-Dīn Abū al-Faḍl al-Turkī, d. ?).
63. Ibid., 2:379. It seems that a whole group of scholars in Baghdad was actually jailed for prescribing Ibn Taymiyya's position on visitation (Ibid., 2:379, 430). Demonstrations of solidarity with Ibn Taymiyya in Baghdad are also reported by Ibn ʿAbd al-Hādī, *ʿUqūd*, 342ff.
64. Al-Nuʿaymī, *al-Dāris fī taʾrīkh al-madāris*, ed. Ibrāhīm Shams al-Dīn (Beirut: Dār al-Kutub al-ʿIlmiyya, 1990), 2:23–94.
65. On al-Ṣāliḥiyya, see Pouzet, *Damas au VIIe/XIIIe s.*, 82–83; D. Talmon-Heller, "The *Shaykh* and the Community"; A. Sayeed, "Women and *Ḥadīth* Transmission. Two Case Studies from Mamlūk Damascus," *Studia Islamica* 95 (2002): 73–74.
66. Al-Nuʿaymī, *Dāris*, 1:56–60. On Ibn Taymiyya's teaching there, 1:57.
67. Al-Nuʿaymī, *Dāris*, 2:50–624. On Ibn Taymiyya's teaching there, 1:57–58.
68. Ibn ʿAbd al-Hādī, *ʿUqūd*, 253. For short biographical entries, see al-Ṣafadī, *Wāfī*, 22:503 and Ibn Ḥajar, *Durar*, 3:102.
69. Cf. Ibn Rajab, *Dhayl*, 2:423–25.
70. Ibn Rajab, *Dhayl*, 2:376; Ibn Kathīr, *Bidāya*, 14:84.
71. Nūr al-Dīn Muḥammad and Fakhr al-Dīn Muḥammad Ibn al-Ṣāʾigh. The former was appointed *qāḍī al-ʿasākir* in Damascus, then Chief Shāfiʿī Qāḍī in Aleppo in 744/1343–4 (Cf. Ṣafadī, *Aʿyān al-ʿaṣr wa-aʿwān al-naṣr*, ed. ʿA. Abū Zayd et al. [Damascus: Dār al-Fikr, 1998], 5: 199–200). The latter was appointed *qāḍī al-ʿasākir* in 742/1341–2. Ibn Kathīr reports that Ibn Taymiyya's followers rejoiced at the news of this appointment because "he had once been one of his most intimate disciples" (Ibn Kathīr, *Bidāya*, 14:197).
72. A Christian who converted to Islam at the hands of Ibn Taymiyya. He lived in Cairo and was a Shāfiʿī follower of Ibn Taymiyya and of his disciples: "*wa-ṣaḥibahu thumma ṣaḥiba aṣḥābahu*" (Ibn Ḥajar, *Durar*, 1:22).

73. Al-Jazarī, *Ḥawādith*, 2:112–13; al-Nuwayrī, *Nihāya* in *Jāmi'*, 130–31. Not much is known about al-Iskandarī, except that he copied many *fatāwā* of the *Shaykh* (cf. Ibn Ḥajar, *Durar*, 2:187).
74. Ibn Kathīr, *Bidāya*, 14:155; al-Bazzār, *A'lām*, 82.
75. Ibn Kathīr, *Bidāya*, 14:101: "*wa kāna mulāziman li-shaykhinā Abī al-'Abbās Ibn Taymiyya kathīran*"; al-Bazzār, *A'lām*, 81.
76. Of particular importance is Sayf al-Dīn Quṭlubughā al-Fakhrī (d. 744/1343), who took the trouble of retrieving Ibn Taymiyya's writings some time after his death (*Bidāya*, 14:197–98; Laoust, "Le Hanbalisme sous les Mamlouks Bahrides", 59–60). The other Mamluk amirs who supported Ibn Taymiyya were: al-Amīr Ṣalāḥ al-Dīn Yūsuf al-Tikrītī (d. 744/1343): "*wa-fīhā...tuwuffiya ṣāḥibunā al-amīr...wa-kāna kathīr al-maḥabba ilā al-Shaykh Taqī al-Dīn ibn Taymiyya*" (*Bidāya*, 14:211; al-Bazzār, *A'lām*, 84); al-Amīr Sayf al-Dīn al-Burāq (d. 757/1356): "*wa-kāna min akbar aṣḥāb al-Shaykh Taqī al-Dīn ibn Taymiyya*" (*Bidāya*, 14:254; al-Bazzār, *A'lām*, 81; Laoust, "Le Hanbalisme sous les Mamlouks Bahrides", 59–61, reads al-Burāq rather than al-Barrāq).
77. Ibn Kathīr, *Bidāya*, 14:72; al-Bazzār, *A'lām*, 80; Laoust, "Le Hanbalisme sous le Mamluk Bahrides", 61; al-Ṣafadī, *A'yān al-'aṣr*, 4:28–29.
78. Ibn Kathīr, *Bidāya*, 14:227 (his *madhhab* is not specified). See Laoust, "Le Hanbalisme sous le Mamluk Bahrides", 65.
79. Ibn Kathīr, *Bidāya*, 14:209; al-Bazzār, *A'lām*, 81; Laoust, "Le Hanbalisme sous le Mamluk Bahrides", 65. For a few other names, see al-Bazzār, *A'lām*, 80, 82 and *Bidāya*, 14:127, 117.
80. Ibn Kathīr, *Bidāya*, 14:229; al-Bazzār, *A'lām*, 80; Laoust, "Le Hanbalisme sous le Mamluk Bahrides", 65.
81. Al-Bazzār, *A'lām*, 79–87.
82. Ibn Nāṣir al-Dīn, *al-Radd al-wāfir 'alā man za'ama anna man sammā Ibn Taymiyya shaykh al-islām huwa kāfir*, ed. Z. al-Shāwīsh (Damascus: al-Maktab al-Islāmī, 1973).
83. For Ibn Rajab's biography, see Ibn Ḥajar al-'Asqalānī, *Durar*, 2:195; Ibn al-'Imād, *Shadharāt*, 6:339–40; G. Makdisi, "Ibn Radjab", *Encyclopedia of Islam*, new ed.; Laoust, "Le Hanbalisme sous les Mamlouks bahrides", 70.
84. G. Makdisi, "L'Islam hanbalisante", 227–28.
85. Ibn Rajab, *Dhayl*, 2:387–96.
86. Ibid., 2:393.
87. Ibid., 2:393, ll. 18–23. Ibn Rajab quotes almost verbatim al-Wāsiṭī's *Tadhkira* (*'Uqūd*, 311, l.13–312, l.3).
88. Ibid., 2:394.
89. Ibid., 2:394, ll. 1–10.
90. Ibid., 2:381. For the episode mentioned, see also al-Nuwayrī, *Nihāya*, 32:328–29; al-Birzālī, *Ta'rīkh al-Birzālī*, Ms Leiden Or 309b, p. 181 (the MS folios are numbered by page), cited by Ibn Kathīr, *Bidāya*, 14:87 and Ibn 'Abd al-Hādī, *'Uqūd*, 325–27; al-Mar'ī, *Kawākib*, 145–48. For the reading of Musallim rather than Muslim I follow al-Nu'aymī, *Dāris*, 2:30, l.1.
91. Ibn 'Abd al-Hādī, *'Uqūd*, 325: "*jamā'a min al-kibār*". Ibn Kathīr specifies that they were legal scholars (*Bidāya*, 14:87).
92. Ibn Taymiyya refuses to accept the validity of triple divorce (*al-ṭalāq al-thalāth*) when pronounced in one session, and of a divorce uttered in the form of an oath. See Laoust, *Essai*, 422–34; Bori, *Ibn Taymiyya: una vita esemplare*, 157–60; Y. Rapoport, "Ibn Taymiyya on Divorce Oaths", in M. Winter and A. Levanoni

(eds.), *The Mamluks in Egyptian Syrian and Society* (Leiden: Brill, 2004), 191–217 and idem, *Marriage, Money and Divorce in Medieval Islamic Society* (Cambridge: Cambridge University Press, 2005) 101–10.

93. Ibn Taymiyya, *MF*, 27:289.

94. See al-Subkī, *al-Rasā'il al-subkiyya fī al-radd 'alā Ibn Taymiyya wa-tilmīdhi-hi Ibn Qayyim al-Jawziyya*, ed. K. Abū al-Mūnā (Beirut: 'Ālam al-Kutub, 1983), 157. For negative perceptions of Ibn Taymiyya's *ijtihād*, see also Bori, *Ibn Taymiyya: una vita esemplare*, 72–77 and 166–67.

95. Ibn Rajab, *al-Radd 'alā man ittaba'a ghayr al-madhāhib al-arba'a*, printed as an introduction to Ibn Hubayra al-Baghdādī al-Ḥanbalī (d. 560/1165), *al-Fiqh 'alā madhāhib al-a'imma al-arba'a*, eds. I. I. al-Qāḍī and 'I. al-Mursī (Cairo: Dār al-Ḥaramayn, 2000), 67–89, 67.

96. Ibid., 88.

97. Ibid., 81ff.

98. Ibid., 77–85.

99. Ibid., 85–89.

100. Ibid., 88.

101. On Ibn Taymiyya's method, see S. Ahmed, "Ibn Taymiyya and the Satanic Verses," *Studia Islamica* 87 (1998): 67–124 (esp. 112); J. Hoover, "Perpetual Creativity in the Perfection of God: Ibn Taymiyya's Hadith Comentary on the Creation of this World," *Journal of Islamic Studies* 15.3 (Sept. 2004): 287–329 (esp. 295); and idem, *Ibn Taymiyya's Theodicy of Perpetual Optimism* (Leiden: E.J. Brill, 2007), 19–69.

102. Al-Ṣafadī, *Wafī*, 5:309, Ibn Rajab, *Dhayl*, 2:434: "*fa-sā'a dhālika aṣḥāb al-Shaykh wa-muḥibbīhi wa-shaqqa dhālika 'alayhim kathīran.*"

103. Ibn Ḥajar, *Durar*, 1:92–93; Ibn 'Abd al-Hādī, *'Uqūd*, 3. Ibn Rajab does not mention his criticism of Ibn Taymiyya (*Dhayl*, 2:366–70). Cf. also W. P. Heinrichs, "al-Ṭūfī," *Encyclopedia of Islam*, 2nd ed.

104. Al-Dhahabī's criticisms of Ibn Taymiyya have received some scholarly attention. See Laoust, "Le Hanbalisme sous les Mamlouks bahrides", 58; Ṣalāḥ al-Dīn al-Munajjid's introduction to al-Dhahabī, *Siyar a'lām al-nubalā'* (Cairo: Dār al-Ma'ārif bi-Miṣr, 1957), 1:19; D. P. Little, "Did Ibn Taymiyya have a screw loose?," *Studia Islamica* 41 (1975), 93–111; Bori, *Ibn Taymiyya: una vita esemplare*, 142–48; idem, "A new source for the biography of Ibn Taymiyya," *Bulletin of the School of Oriental and African Studies* 67.3 (2004):321–348.

105. He is often reported to have studied with Ḥanbalī *Shaykhs*: Ibn Rajab, *Dhayl*, 2:346, 348, 350, 353, 354, 356 and *passim*.

106. Al-Dhahabī's criticism of Ibn Taymiyya is found in *Bayān zaghal al-'ilm wa-al-ṭalab*, ed. M. Z. al-Kawtharī (Damascus: Maṭba'at al-Tawfīq, 1928–29), 17–18 and 21–24. These passages are quoted also by al-Sakhāwī (d. 853/1449–50), *al-I'lān bi-al-tawbīkh li-man dhamma al-ta'rīkh* (Damascus: al-Maktabat al-Qudsī, 1930–31), 77–78. For an English translation see F. Rosenthal, *A History of Muslim Historiography* (Leiden: E. J. Brill, 1968), 376–78. In addition, the following texts by al-Dhahabī are all critical of Ibn Taymiyya: *al-Naṣīḥa al-dhahabiyya li-Ibn Taymiyya*, in *Bayān*, 32–34; idem, *Thalāth tarājim nafīsa li-al-a'imma al-a'lām: Shaykh al-Islām Ibn Taymiyya, al-ḥāfiẓ 'Alam al-Dīn al-Birzālī, al-ḥāfiẓ Ǧamāl al-Dīn al-Mizzī: min kitāb Dhayl Tārīkh al-Islām*, ed. M. Nāṣir al-'Ajamī (Kuwayt: Dār Ibn al-Athīr, 1995), 23–24, 26–27; idem, *Nubdha min sīrat Shaykh al-Islām*, in Bori, "A New Source", 334, 335, 337.

107. Al-Dhahabī alludes to Christian practices such as that of eating grains on the Thursday preceding Easter (or Maundy Thursday, *Yawm al-khamīs al-kabīr*), which attracted Muslim participation and therefore became the object of Ibn Taymiyya's polemics. See Ibn Taymiyya, *Kitāb iqtiḍā' al-ṣirāṭ al-mustaqīm mukhālafat aṣḥāb al-jaḥīm* (Cairo: al-Maṭba'a al-Sharīfa, 1907), 100–103; T. Michel, *A Muslim Theologian's Response to Christianity. Ibn Taymiyya's* Al-Jawab al-Sahih (Delmar NY: Caravan Books, 1984), 82–83.
108. Al-Dhahabī, *al-Naṣīḥa al-dhahabiyya*, in *Bayān zaghal al-'ilm*, 33.
109. Al-Dhahabī, *Bayān zaghal al-'ilm*, 11.
110. Ibid., 17–18.
111. Rosenthal (*Muslim Historiography*, 378) translates: "in the science of the principles of religion, nobody has ever reached the degree of Ibn Taymiyya". I believe al-Dhahabī refers to what he has stated immediately before, i.e., the combination of rational and speculative sciences.
112. The following passage is from al-Dhahabī, *Bayān zaghal al-'ilm*, 23–24, quoted by al-Sakhāwī, *al-I'lān*, 77–78. I have used Rosenthal's translation (*Muslim Historiography*, 377–78) with minor modifications.
113. For al-Dhahabī's attitude towards speculative theology, read C. Gilliot, "Al-Dhahabī contre la «pensée speculative»," *Zeitschrift der Deutschen Morgenländischen Gesellschaft* 150.1 (2000): 69–106 (concerning his relationship to Ibn Taymiyya, esp. 103–05). In his own abridgement of Ibn Taymiyya's *Minhāj al-sunna*, al-Dhahabī fails to mention the Shaykh's radical position on the Satanic verses (S. Ahmed, "Ibn Taymiyya and the Satanic Verses", 113–14).
114. Ibn Murrī, *Risāla*, 103.
115. See Yahya Michot, "Vanités intellectuelles...L'impasse de rationalistes selon le *Rejet de la contradiction* d'Ibn Taymiyya," *Oriente Moderno* 19 (2000): 597–617, especially 597–601; Hoover, "Perpetual Creativity in the Perfection of God," and idem, *Ibn Taymiyya's Theodicy of Perpetual Optimism.*
116. Al-Dhahabī, *Thalāth tarājim nafīsa*, 56.
117. Al-Subkī, *al-Ṭabaqāt al-Shāfi'īyya*, 6:252–53; Ibn Kathīr, *Bidaya*, 14:89; al-Nu'aymī, *Dāris*, 1:26. The charge that traditionalist Shāfi'īs were corrupted by association with Ibn Taymiyya is made by al-Subkī, *al-Rasā'il al-subkiyya*, 84–85; and his son Tāj al-Dīn (d. 771/1369), *al-Ṭabaqāt al-Shāfi'īyya*, 6:254 (quoted by G. Makdisi, "Ash'arī and the Ash'arites in Islamic Religious History", *Studia Islamica* 17 [1962]: 79).
118. This was Ibn 'Abīdān al-Ḥanbalī al-Ba'albakkī, mentioned above as a disciple of Ibn Taymiyya. Cf. Ibn Kathīr, *Bidāya*, 4:88 and al-Nuwayrī, *Nihāya*, 32:287.
119. For his biography see Ibn Kathīr, *Bidāya*, 14:35–38 and 131–32; al-Subkī, *al-Ṭabaqāt al-Shāfi'iyya*, 5:251–56; al-Ṣafadī, *Wāfī*, 4:214–221; Ibn al-'Imād, *Shadharāt*, 6:78–80. Sherman A. Jackson argues that Ibn al-Zamlakānī "appears to have had strong traditionalist leanings, but to have also been bound by an intense loyalty to the Shāfi'ī school, home of the leading Ash'arīs" ("Ibn Taymiyyah on trial in Damascus," *Journal of Semitic Studies*, 39/1 [1994]: 48–49). He was among the Shāfi'īs who conducted Ibn Taymiyya's trial.
120. Al-Nuwayrī, *Nihāya*, 32:22–23; Ibn Kathīr, *Bidāya*, 14:22.
121. Ibn Kathīr (*Bidāya*, 14:41) places the event in Rabī' II 706 whereas Ibn Dawādārī (*Kanz*, 9:136) places it in Ramaḍān 705.
122. See Ibn Kathīr, *Bidāya*, 14:50.
123. Muḥammad ibn al-Ḥarīrī (d. 728/1328) was Chief Ḥanafī Qaḍī in Damascus, between 699 and 705 (1299–1305), then in Cairo from 710 until his death. See

al-Ṣafadī, *Wāfī*, 4:90; Ibn Ḥajar, *Durar*, 4:25–26; Ibn al-ʿImād, *Shadharāt*, 6:88; Escovitz, *The office of qâḍî al-quḍât*, 55.

124. Al-Nuwayrī, *Nihāya*, 32:115.
125. Al-Jazarī, *Ḥawādith*, 2:112. Al-Jazarī does not mention them by name, but he does report that: "the Chief [Shāfiʿī] Qāḍī Badr al-Dīn Ibn Jamāʿa took the *fatwā* and wrote on its back: 'the person who pronounced these words is a misled and misleading innovator', and the Ḥanafī and the Ḥanbalī (judges) agreed". See *MF*, 27:288–89, for the names of the four judges.
126. See Rapoport, *Marriage, Money and Divorce*, 103–04. It is worth noting that Ibn al-Ḥarīrī is included by al-Bazzār in the list of Ibn Taymiyya supporters, whereas al-Zamlakānī is listed among his opponents (al-Bazzar, *Aʿlām*, 80 and 86).
127. Al-Dhahabī, *Nubdha* in Bori, "A New Source", 333, (Arabic text)—342 (English translation).
128. Al-Dhahabī, *Nubdha* in Bori, "A New Source", 336 (Arabic text)—346 (English translation).
129. Ibn ʿAbd al-Hādī, *ʿUqūd*, 249. Al-Jasūra is probably to be read as al-Shaḥūra, a locality not far from al-Kiswa, on the road from Damascus to the south. Cf. N. Elisséeff, *La Description de Damas d'Ibn ʿAsākir* (Damas: IFEAD, 1956), 242 (note 5), 243 (note 3).
130. Ibid., 253.
131. Ibid., 255.
132. Ibid., 269.
133. Ibid., 272, 277. See also the letter sent from Alexandria by his brother Sharaf al-Dīn ʿAbd Allāh to his other brother Badr al-Dīn in *ʿUqūd*, 272–76, found also in *MF*, 28:31–46.
134. Ibn ʿAbd al-Hādī, *ʿUqūd*, 118, quotes al-Dhahabī, *Nubdha*, in Bori, "A new source", 334 (Arabic text)—343 (English translation).
135. Al-Jazarī, *Ḥawādith*, 2:306–9; Ibn ʿAbd al-Hādī, *ʿUqūd*, 369–75; Ibn Kathīr, *Bidāya*, 14:135–39: Ibn Rajab, *Dhayl*, 2:405–8.
136. Ibn ʿAbd al-Hādī, *ʿUqūd*, 371; Ibn Kathīr, *Bidāya*, 14:135.
137. For the significance of funerals in early Islamic tradition, see M. Qasim Zaman, "Death, Funeral Processions, and the Articulation of Religious Authority in Islam," *Studia Islamica* 93 (2001): 27–58.
138. Ibn ʿAbd al-Hādī, *ʿUqūd*, 374; Ibn Kathīr, *Bidāya*, 14:138. Both Ibn ʿAbd al-Hādī and Ibn Kathīr cite al-Birzālī as their source.
139. Ibn Kathīr, *Bidāya*, 14:138–39. For the saying, see Ibn al-Jawzī (d. 597/1256), *Manāqib al-Imām Aḥmad ibn Ḥanbal*, ed. ʿA. M. al-Turkī- ʿA. M. ʿUmar (Cairo: Maktabat al-Khānjī, 1979), 505; al-Dhahabī, *Taʾrīkh al-Islām*, ed. al-Tadmurī (Beirut: Dār al-Kitāb al-ʿArabī, 1991) 25:142; Ibn Kathīr, *Bidāya*, 10:342; Qasim Zaman, "Death, funeral, processions", 47–48.

II
Theology

God Acts by His Will and Power: Ibn Taymiyya's Theology of a Personal God in his Treatise on the Voluntary Attributes

Jon Hoover

Introduction

Ibn Taymiyya's corpus presents peculiar difficulties for the study of Islamic theology in the medieval period. One obstacle is the character of the texts. Other Muslim theologians of the time wrote reasonably complete and well organized treatises in which we can easily locate what they thought on one question or another. So far as I know, however, Ibn Taymiyya did not write a major or definitive work of theology on the model of the traditional *kalām* treatises. Rather, he is at home in the genres of the *fatwā*, the commentary, and the refutation, with his writings varying widely in length, depth, and comprehensiveness and responding to a great diversity of questions, texts, and theological claims. The result is a very large universe of theological writings with the Shaykh's reflections on any one theological question scattered about in numerous places and often treated from a number of different angles.[1] Although significant attempts have been made to map this universe,[2] the study of Ibn Taymiyya's theology is still in its infancy, and it will be some time before its full import is understood.

A second difficulty, perhaps one that has discouraged research, is the old but enduring image of Ibn Taymiyya as the anti-rationalist polemicist who vigorously deconstructs the intellectual edifices of the likes of Ibn al-ʿArabī, Ibn Sīnā, and the *kalām* theologians while offering no theological vision of his own except obdurate adherence to the foundational texts of Islam. As Goldziher puts it, "He relied on the *sunna* and on the *sunna* alone."[3] Slowly eroding this portrayal is a growing body of research showing both that Ibn Taymiyya holds distinctive views of interest for the historical study of Islamic theology[4] and that he is much more the rationalist than earlier scholars recognized.[5]

In a recent translation article treating Ibn Taymiyya's Hadith commentary on the creation of the world, I observe that the Shaykh claims that reason and revelation are in agreement and that his critique of Avicennan philosophy and *kalām* theology on creation derives not from opposition to reason as such but from an alternative vision of God. Instead of God's eternal emanation of the world (Ibn Sīnā) or God's creation in time out of nothing (*kalām* theology), Ibn Taymiyya, much like Ibn Rushd, envisions a God who in His perfection perpetually creates one thing or another from eternity. Furthermore, I explain that the Shaykh believes this theological model to accord with revelation and that his aim is "to elucidate the rationality underlying the data on creation found in the Qur'ān and the Hadith." I then characterize his method in his Hadith commentary as "a philosophical interpretation and defence of tradition" or "a kind of philosophical theology."[6] Put another way, Ibn Taymiyya is more fundamentally an apologist for the rationality of the tradition in this treatise than a polemicist against alleged theological innovations, which, of course, he also is.

The present study expounds a 41-page treatise in Ibn Taymiyya's *Majmū' al-fatāwā* on God's "voluntary attributes" *(al-ṣifāt al-ikhtiyāriyya)* in order to make new data available for the wider project of understanding Ibn Taymiyya's theology.[7] This text, which I will call *Ikhtiyāriyya*, corroborates my characterization of the Shaykh's method as rational apologetic, and it shows him situating certain aspects of his view of God's speech outlined in my translation article within a wider frame. Whereas the Ash'arī *kalām* tradition maintains that God's attribute of speech is eternal and independent of God's will, the Shaykh consistently maintains that God has been speaking by His will and power from eternity. God's speech is thus perpetually dynamic like God's attribute of creation, and it is also "personal" in the sense that it is enacted by an exercise of will in time.[8] In *Ikhtiyāriyya*, Ibn Taymiyya subsumes God's speech, God's creativity and a number of other divine attributes like hearing, mercy, and sitting under the more general rubric of God's voluntary attributes. He then argues that rational perfection dictates that these attributes not be timelessly eternal but truly volitional by subsisting in God by His will and power. This gives God a distinctly personal character in that God's voluntary attributes interact with the world within its own sequential vicissitudes of time.

As in many of Ibn Taymiyya's writings, his style in *Ikhtiyāriyya* is discursive and prone to digression rather than systematic. While my exposition will follow the course of the text closely and include some translation, it will leave aside his comments on the *kalām* proof for God and numerous other matters of elaboration and detail. Page references to *Ikhtiyāriyya* in Volume 6 of Ibn Taymiyya's *Majmūʿ al-fatāwā* will be given in parentheses in the text.

Defining God's Voluntary Attributes

Ibn Taymiyya defines the "voluntary attributes" most concisely toward the end of *Ikhtiyāriyya* as those attributes of God "linked to will," that is, those attributes that God manifests via an act of His will (262). The introduction to the treatise, translated below, provides a more elaborate definition. Here the Shaykh links the voluntary attributes to both God's will and God's power and maintains that these attributes subsist in God's essence. He then outlines the two opposing views which he criticizes throughout the treatise, that of the Jahmīs and the Muʿtazilīs on one hand and that of the Kullābīs on the other.[9] For the former, attributes cannot subsist in God's essence.[10] For the latter, the Kullābīs, and, we may add, the Ashʿarīs, God's attributes subsist in God's essence, but eternally without any link to God's power and will. At the end of the introduction, Ibn Taymiyya identifies his own definition of voluntary attributes as that of the early Muslims, that is, the *salaf*, and, perhaps with some exaggeration, as that of most of the *kalām* theologians and philosophers.

> [The voluntary attributes] are affairs by which the Lord is qualified—He is Almighty and Great—which subsist in His essence (*taqūmu bi-dhātihi*) by His will (*mashīʾa*) and His power (*qudra*), such as His speech, His hearing, His sight, His will, His love, His good pleasure, His mercy, His anger, and His wrath, and such as His creating, His beneficence, His justice, and such as His sitting, His coming, His arriving, and His descending. And such like from among the attributes of which the precious Book and the Sunna speak.
>
> The Jahmīs and those who agree with them from among the Muʿtazilīs and others say, "Not one of these attributes or anything else subsists in His essence."

> The Kullābīs and those who agree with them from among the Sālimīs[11] and others say, "The attributes subsist [in God] apart from His will and His power. As for that which comes to be (*yakūnu*) by His will and His power, it comes to be only as a created thing (*makhlūq*), disjoined from Him (*munfaṣilan 'anhu*)."
>
> As for the *salaf* and the Imams of the Sunna and the Hadith, they say, "He is qualified by that [i.e. the voluntary attributes]," as the Book and Sunna speak of it, and this is the view of many among the *kalām* theologians and the philosophers, or most of them (217–18).

Following this introduction, Ibn Taymiyya illustrates these three positions with God's attribute of speech (*kalām*). In the view of the *salaf*, "[God] speaks by His will and His power. His speech is not a created thing. On the contrary, His speech is an attribute of His, subsisting in His essence (*qā'ima bi-dhātihi*)" (218). The Shaykh makes a strong appeal to traditional authority for the correctness of this view. He cites a long list of early Sunni scholars, among them Aḥmad Ibn Ḥanbal, al-Bukhārī, and al-Dārimī, noting that they "are agreed that [God] speaks by His will and that He has been speaking from eternity when He willed (*idhā shā'a*) and in the manner He willed (*kayfa shā'a*)" (218).

As for the two opposing views on God's speech, Ibn Taymiyya reports that the Jahmīs and the Mu'tazilīs say that even though God does speak by virtue of His will, God "has no speech subsisting in His essence. On the contrary, His speech is disjoined from Him, created by Him" (219). The Kullābīs and the Sālimīs, for their part, affirm that God's speech subsists in God's essence but independently of God's will and power. The Shaykh expands on this by introducing the distinction between an attribute of essence (*ṣifat dhāt*) and an attribute of action (*ṣifat fi'l*). For the Kullābīs, "Speech is an attribute of essence, not an attribute of action linked to [God's] will and His power." For the Mu'tazilīs, however, "It is an attribute of action, but the act, according to them, is something enacted and created by His will and His power" (219), which is to say that, even though God's speech occurs by God's will and power, it is a created entity and does not then subsist in God's essence.

Having outlined these three views of God's speech, Ibn Taymiyya briefly reports rational arguments for each. He supplies two reasons for the notion ascribed to the *salaf*, as well as to the Karrāmī *kalām* theologians and others, that God's speech is an attribute of both action and essence. The first argument runs:

> [God] speaks by His will and His power a speech which subsists in His essence. This is what is rational (*maʿqūl*) with respect to the attribute of speech for every speaker. As for everyone qualified by speech—like the angels, humankind, the jinn, etc.—their speech must inevitably subsist in their essences, and they speak by their wills and their powers (219).

In other words, each act of speaking is not disjoined from the speaker but subsists in the essence of the speaker to whom it is attributed. The foundational notion here is that an act or an attribute qualifying an essence necessarily subsists in that very essence. This "attribution principle" precludes the Jahmī/Muʿtazilī location of the act, which is identical to what is enacted, outside God's essence.

The second reason that Ibn Taymiyya gives for God's speech being an attribute of both action and essence appeals to God's *a fortiori* right to creaturely perfections. He advances the following argument: "Speech is an attribute of perfection (*kamāl*), not an attribute of imperfection (*naqṣ*), and whoever speaks by his will is more perfect than one who does not speak by his will. So, how can the creature be qualified by attributes of perfection, but not the Creator?!" (219). This argument departs from the *kalām* tradition by privileging volition over timeless eternity in the hierarchy of perfections.

More will be said about the pre-eminence of volition as a perfection later in the treatise, but this and the attribution principle constitute two key features of Ibn Taymiyya's theology of God's voluntary attributes. Closely linked to the perfection of volition is the notion that God interacts with creatures in sequential time. I call this the "sequence principle," and it also receives attention later in *Ikhtiyāriyya*.

Continuing on in the early pages of the treatise, Ibn Taymiyya examines basic arguments supporting the other two points of view. The Jahmīs and Muʿtazilīs maintain that "the attribute is an accident (*ʿaraḍ*), and the accident subsists only in a body (*jism*)" (220). Now, attributes defined as accidents cannot subsist in God's essence lest God be subject to corporealism (*tajsīm*) and assimilation to creatures (*tashbīh*). Quite simply, accidents construed as attributes cannot subsist in God because God is not a body.

As for the Kullābīs and the Ashʿārīs, the Shaykh observes that they subsume the voluntary attributes under the rubric of "the occurrence of temporally originating events (*ḥulūl al-ḥawādith*)" and insist that originating events cannot subsist in God. Ibn Taymiyya provides the basic "event-denier" arguments here in highly compressed form. First, "If originating events subsisted in [God], He would not be devoid of them, and whatever is not devoid of originating events is [itself] an originating event." It is understood of course that God is not an originating event. The second argument maintains that the possibility of originating events in God's essence opens the door to temporal events originating in pre-eternity (*al-azal*). However, the argument continues, there are no originating events in pre-eternity, and, if there were, they would regress infinitely, which is absurd (220).

Of the several *kalām* arguments mentioned here, Ibn Taymiyya sets out rational counter arguments only against the denial of originating events in pre-eternity, and this later in the treatise (247–49). For his purposes in *Ikhtiyāriyya*, it appears sufficient to dismiss the other arguments merely by noting that theologians such as Fakhr al-Dīn al-Rāzī (d. 606/1209) and Sayf al-Dīn al-Āmidī (d. 631/1233), as well as Naṣīr al-Dīn al-Ṭūsī (d. 672/1274), Ibn al-Muṭahhar al-Ḥillī (d. 726/1325) and others, have already shown that the earlier Mu'tazilī and Ash'arī *kalām* theologians had no rational argument for their view. Ibn Taymiyya also criticizes the *kalām* theologian al-Juwaynī (d. 478/1085) for ignoring the *salaf* and denying events in God's essence for no better reason than exposing Karrāmī contradictions (221–22).

Moreover, according to the Shaykh, al-Rāzī in his late work *al-Maṭālib al-'āliyya* asserts that the doctrine of originating events in the essence of God "follows necessarily for all groups" (221). Al-Rāzī does indeed say this. Even though al-Rāzī upholds the traditional Ash'arī event-denier position in earlier works such as *al-Arba'īn fī uṣūl al-dīn*,[12] he argues in *al-Maṭālib al-'āliyya* that the Ash'arīs, the Mu'tazilīs and the philosophers, notwithstanding their respective denials, cannot escape this doctrine. In closing his discussion of these groups, al-Rāzī asserts, "It is established through this investigation, which we have mentioned, that speaking of the temporal origination of attributes in the essence of God is the view that all sects speak of."[13]

Indicating the Voluntary Attributes from the Qur'ān and the Hadith

After delineating his position in the opening pages of *Ikhtiyāriyya*, Ibn Taymiyya assembles Qur'ānic verses and Hadith that indicate God's voluntary attributes. The Shaykh supplies a number of verses speaking of God doing one thing after another to undermine the Kullābī and Ash'arī notion that God's attributes are eternal. An example is the verse, "Surely We created you. Then (*thumma*) we formed you. Then we said to the angels, 'Prostrate to Adam', and they prostrated" (Q. 7:11). The Shaykh comments, "This is clear that [God] commanded the angels to prostrate only after creating Adam. He did not command them in pre-eternity" (222). Thus, God's command cannot be eternal. For Ibn Taymiyya, a timelessly eternal attribute cannot intersect meaningfully with the temporal creation. Rather, God in His voluntary attributes interacts with the world on its own terms of temporal sequence. This is the "sequence principle" that I mentioned earlier.

Ibn Taymiyya also cites verses to support the sequence principle in God's attributes of will, love (*maḥabba*), good pleasure (*riḍā*), and anger (*sukhṭ*). Concerning God's anger, the Shaykh quotes, "This [punishment] is because they followed what angered God, and they hated His good pleasure" (Q. 47:28). He then observes, "This indicates that their deeds angered Him. This is the cause of His anger. His anger with them is after the deeds, not before them" (226). The Shaykh also marshals verses to prove the sequential character of God's hearing (*sam'*), seeing (*baṣar*) and looking (*naẓar*). For example, he explains that, "Say, 'Perform deeds.' God will see your deeds" (Q. 9:105), means that God would see the deeds in question after this verse was revealed (227).

To support his assertion that God acts by means of His will, Ibn Taymiyya cites the following verse, "O you who believe! Fulfill your obligations. Lawful to you are the beast of the flocks except that which is recited to you.... Truly, God pronounces (*yaḥkum*) what He wills" (Q. 5:1). The Shaykh observes that God's making lawful and unlawful is linked to God's will. He adds polemically that the Kullābīs deny that God does these things by means of His will. Rather, for them such divine acts are "eternal, necessarily concomitant to His essence, not willed by Him and not an object of power." As for the Jahmīs and Mu'tazilīs, "All of that is created, disjoined from [God]. He has no speech subsisting in Him, neither by His will nor by other than His will" (224). Ibn Taymiyya maintains likewise that God's acts of creation, provision, beneficence and justice occur by His will and power, and he sharply distinguishes the very acts, which subsist in God's essence, from the objects of these acts which are outside God: "Creation is the act of the Creator, while what is created is the object of His act" (229).

The Shaykh brings his treatment of Qur'ānic texts verifying God's voluntary attributes to a close by commenting, "The point here is that the Qur'ān indicates this principle in more than one hundred places" (233). He then turns to Hadith reports substantiating God's voluntary attributes. One example will suffice. Ibn Taymiyya quotes the Hadith *qudsī*, "I am in the thought of My servant of Me, and I am with him when he remembers Me. If (*in*) he remembers Me in himself, I remember him in Myself. If (*in*) he remembers Me in a group, I remember him in a group that is better than them."[14] The Shaykh explains the conditional function of the Arabic particle *in* and then observes that recompense only ensues once the condition has been met: God remembers the servant only after the servant remembers God either in himself or in a group. Ibn Taymiyya remarks that opponents of this "say that [God] never ceases remembering him from eternity to eternity" (235).

Arguing that Volition is More Perfect than Timeless Eternity

After this survey of material from the Qur'ān and the Hadith, Ibn Taymiyya rehearses the basic positions of his opponents, clarifies that God's power extends both to that which subsists in His essence and to that which is distinct from Him, and digresses into polemics against the *kalām* proof for God (237–240). He then returns to his topic and signals a transition in *Ikhtiyāriyya* toward more sustained attention to the rational arguments of his opponents. He writes:

> The point here is only that it be known that [the *kalām* theologians] have no rational proof (*dalīl 'aqlī*) for their denial of the voluntary attributes, which they designate the occurrence of originating events (*ḥawādith*). The most intelligent of them acknowledge that. As for tradition (*sam'*),

> there is no doubt that it is filled with what contradicts it, and reason also indicates what contradicts it (240).

In the first sentence of this quotation, the subordination of the clause, "which they designate the occurrence of originating events (*ḥawādith*)," reveals Ibn Taymiyya's preference for the expression "voluntary attributes" over the *kalām* language of *ḥawādith* occurring in God.[15] While the Shaykh perceives the *kalām* denial of *ḥawādith* in God to be equivalent to the denial of God's "voluntary attributes," he does no more than refute or dismiss the *kalām* event-denying arguments. In *Ikhtiyāriyya*, he does not adopt the term *ḥawādith* to articulate his own position, and he does not explain why he avoids this expression. Elsewhere, however, he notes that some Sunnī scholars maintain the sense of *ḥawādith* in God but choose to speak of this only with expressions found in revelation.[16] Presumably, Ibn Taymiyya counts himself part of this group.

Two stages are apparent in the history of *kalām* treatments of originating events occurring in God. Early Mu'tazilī and Ash'arī *kalām* theologians argue that events cannot subsist in God's essence, but later theologians like Fakhr al-Dīn al-Rāzī and Sayf al-Dīn al-Āmidī find the event-denier case wanting. As mentioned previously, al-Rāzī abandons his early event-denying stance and argues in *al-Maṭālib al-'āliyya* that all Muslim groups, despite their disavowals, must admit originating events in God. Al-Āmidī, in his major *kalām* work *Abkār al-afkār*, also refutes the early *kalām* arguments. Nonetheless, he retains the event-denier position on the strength of two additional sets of arguments. The first set is called "establishing" (*taqrīriyya*), while the second set is called "reductive" (*ilzāmiyya*) and shows the absurdity of the Karrāmī arguments for events in God.[17] Without mentioning al-Āmidī by name, Ibn Taymiyya addresses the foundations of his "establishing" arguments first in *Ikhtiyāriyya*. Only after refuting these does he treat the event-denier arguments of the earlier tradition. The Shaykh does not respond to al-Āmidī's eight "reductive" arguments in *Ikhtiyāriyya*, although he does comment on the first seven of them in his vast *Dar' ta'āruḍ al-'aql wa al-naql*.[18]

Ibn Taymiyya observes in *Ikhtiyāriyya* that later event-deniers confess to having no rational proof for their position and so resort to arguing from consensus (*ijmā'*), or, in the terms of al-Āmidī's "establishing" arguments, from "the agreement of rational thinkers and the followers of [diverse] confessions."[19] Here is how Ibn Taymiyya sums up these arguments:

> If these [voluntary] attributes are attributes of imperfection (*naqṣ*), it is necessary to exonerate the Lord from them. If they are attributes of perfection (*kamāl*), then He was devoid of them before their origination. The nonexistence of perfection is imperfection. So, it follows necessarily that He was imperfect, and exonerating Him from imperfection is obligatory by consensus (240–41).

Ibn Taymiyya calls this one of the event-deniers most corrupt arguments and sets out a refutation with six aspects. In the first, the Shaykh gives short shrift to the appeal to consensus. He retorts that arguing from consensus is of no value in a disputed issue; the very presence of a dispute means that no consensus exists on the matter in question (241).

The remaining five aspects undermine the *kalām* notion of perfection embedded in the above argument, namely, that the perfection of God's attributes necessarily entails their timeless eternity. In the second aspect, Ibn Taymiyya asserts that the existence of something before its time is an imperfection. Things occur in their time according to God's wisdom (*ḥikma*). Perfection is the occurrence of things when wisdom dictates, not the eternal existence of a particular perfection.

> An example of this is God's speaking to Moses—Peace be upon him—and His call to him. His call when He called him is an attribute of perfection. If He had called him before he had come, that would have been an imperfection. Each of [these affairs] is a perfection at the time of its existence. It is not a perfection before its existence. On the contrary, its existence before the time at which wisdom requires its existence is an imperfection (241).

The third aspect maintains similarly that the absence of a particular manifestation of a voluntary attribute is not in itself an imperfection. For, "It is impossible for an originating event to be eternal, and the non-existence of the impossible is not an imperfection" (241–42). Imperfection is the absence of possible perfections, not the absence of what is impossible. Ibn Taymiyya does not make the full import of this argument clear, but it is apparent that the operation of voluntary attributes cannot be eternal by definition because these attributes are linked to God's will, which operates in time.

In the fourth aspect, Ibn Taymiyya notes that what God does and creates can be qualified neither as perfection nor as imperfection if judgments of perfection and imperfection are confined to God's eternal attributes. In other words, limiting judgments of perfection to the realm of the eternal renders discussion of perfection and imperfection in creation meaningless. The Shaykh's fifth aspect states that an essence speaking by its will and power is known by clear reason (*al-ʿaql al-ṣarīḥ*) to be more perfect than an essence that cannot do so. In the sixth and last aspect, Ibn Taymiyya argues that clear reason dictates that one who is able to do something step-by-step (*shay'an fa-shay'an*) is more perfect than one who is not able to act in this way (242–43).[20]

With these arguments, Ibn Taymiyya stands the *kalām*, not to mention Greek, identification of perfection and timeless eternity on its head. Perfection is found not in eternal stasis but in volition and the ability to interact with creatures and events in time. For Ibn Taymiyya, a being who acts sequentially by will and power in accord with wisdom is more perfect than a being whose attributes are timeless.

Reconciling God's Will with God's Prior Decree

Before tackling the event-denying arguments of the earlier *kalām* tradition, Ibn Taymiyya wraps up discussion of the later arguments by harping on the vanity of *kalām* theology, dealing with an objection, and reaffirming the congruity of tradition and reason. Of particular interest is the objection, which questions whether God's so-called "voluntary attributes" truly involve God's choice or volition (*ikhtiyār*). If the exercise of some of God's attributes follows necessarily from what is prior, then it would seem that these attributes no longer qualify as voluntary. As Ibn Taymiyya puts the problem, "If [God]—Glory be to Him—creates whom He loves like the Friend [Abraham], He loves Him, and He loves the believers and they love Him. Likewise, if people commit deeds, he sees them. This follows necessarily; it is inevitable (*lā budda min dhālika*)" (244). In other words, how can God's seeing and loving be called voluntary when God inevitably sees what He makes and loves what He wills?

What is the content of God's choice in the face of this inevitability? Ibn Taymiyya responds:

> It is not impossible that something, which is necessary of occurrence because the decree (*qaḍā'*) that it must inevitably be has preceded it, occur by His will (*mashī'a*) and His power and His will (*irāda*), even if it is among the necessary concomitants of His essence like His life and His knowledge. His willing of future events is preceded by His willing of the past. "His command when He wills something is only that He says to it, 'Be! ' And it is" (Q. 36:82). He wills that second [thing] only after having willed before it what His will required. The subsequent will occurs by the preceding will (245).

Rather than seeing contradiction between the necessity of God's prior decree and the freedom of God's own volition, Ibn Taymiyya maintains the compatibility of the two. While God does not have absolute freedom in the sense of facing a radically open spectrum of choices at each step in the course of creation, God's volition remains the instrument by which God works out the divine decree, and its exercise depends upon what has come before it. In short, for Ibn Taymiyya, God wills to do what God has beforehand decreed by means of God's preceding acts of will. Put passively, God's acts of volition are intrinsic to the course of events made necessary by God's prior decree.

Refuting Some Event-denying Arguments of the Early *kalām* Tradition

To this point in *Ikhtiyāriyya*, Ibn Taymiyya has not given serious attention to any of the event-denying arguments of the early *kalām* tradition. In the latter part of the treatise, however, Ibn Taymiyya provides a synopsis of four arguments against the occurrence of temporally originating events (*ḥulūl al-ḥawādith*) in God that he finds mentioned and refuted by "the stallions of the thinkers" (*fuḥūl al-nuẓẓār*) such as al-Rāzī and al-Āmidī (247).

The first, which Ibn Taymiyya calls the event-deniers' "famous argument" and which we have already met earlier, proceeds, "If [originating events] subsisted in [God], He would not be devoid of them and of their opposites, and whatever is not devoid of originating events is a temporally originating event (*ḥādith*)" (247). The implication is that events cannot subsist in God lest God Himself originate temporally. Ibn Taymiyya states that al-Rāzī and others deny the premises of this argument, but he explains no further, indicating only that "this has been elaborated in another place" (247).

The second early *kalām* argument against events in God's essence runs, "If God were receptive (*qābil*) to [originating events] in pre-eternity, the receptivity (*qubūl*) would be among the necessary concomitants of His essence, and the receptivity would require the possibility of the object received (*al-maqbūl*). And the existence of temporally originating events in pre-eternity is absurd" (247).[21] In short, God could not have been receptive to events in pre-eternity because it was impossible for events to exist in pre-eternity.

Ibn Taymiyya says that the later theologians counter this with the following: "[God] has power to originate events, and power (*qudra*) requires the possibility of an object upon which power is exercised (*al-maqdūr*). And the existence of the object upon which power is exercised, that is, the originating events, in pre-eternity is absurd" (247). Ibn Taymiyya's explanation is spare, but what we have here is a *reductio ad absurdum*. The later theologians are making the following argument. If, with the event-denying *kalām* theologians, God's receptivity entails the possibility of originating events to which God is receptive in pre-eternity, God's power likewise entails the possibility of events over which God's power is exercised in pre-eternity. Now, if the impossibility of originating events in pre-eternity precludes God being receptive to events in pre-eternity, it also precludes God's power in pre-eternity. So, in the eyes of later *kalām* theologians, the argument of the event-deniers entails the absurdity of denying not only God's receptivity to events in pre-eternity but also God's pre-eternal power.

Ibn Taymiyya offers his own refutation of this early *kalām* event-denying proof with four aspects. The first aspect is a disjunctive syllogism showing that it must be possible for the genus of originating events to exist in pre-eternity from the simple fact that events exist now.

> The existence of originating events is either [a] impossible or [b] possible. If it is [b] possible, it is possible that receptivity to them and power over them are perpetual (*dā'iman*). This being so, the existence of

> their genus in pre-eternity is not impossible. On the contrary, it is possible that their genus is an object upon which power and receptivity are exercised (*maqdūran maqbūlan*). If it is [a] impossible, the existence of originating events without end is impossible. This being so, they are not possible in pre-eternity, neither as objects upon which power is exercised nor as objects upon which receptivity is exercised. This being so, it follows necessarily that they are impossible after that [as well]. But originating events exist! Thus, it is not permissible to say that their impossibility is perpetual (247–48).

In the second aspect, Ibn Taymiyya maintains that God's power is pre-eternal. To show this, the Shaykh posits another disjunction, this time between a God who is powerful from eternity and one who only became powerful at some later point. Concerning the first view, which Ibn Taymiyya deems correct: "If [God] is powerful from eternity and if the object upon which power is exercised is possible from eternity, the perpetuity of the existence of possibles is possible. So, the perpetuity of the existence of originating events is possible. This being so, it is not impossible that He is receptive to them in pre-eternity" (248). Ibn Taymiyya then reduces to absurdity the notion that God changed from being unable to act to being able: "This is combining two contradictories. Indeed, the Powerful is not able to do something impossible. So how then does He have power over the fact that the object of power is impossible?" (248). In simpler terms, a God unable to act is trapped in this inability and cannot suddenly begin exercising power. Ibn Taymiyya affirms instead that God from eternity is both powerful over and receptive to whatever is possible in eternity (248).

The third and fourth aspects are brief. In the third, Ibn Taymiyya clarifies that God's pre-eternal receptivity is limited to what can possibly exist and to what God has power to do; God is not receptive to or able to do the impossible. Then, in the fourth aspect, the Shaykh argues that if God is able to originate created things distinct from Him, then God is *a fortiori* able to commit acts which subsist in His essence (248–49). With this fourfold refutation, Ibn Taymiyya undermines the event-denier claim that originating events cannot subsist in God because events themselves cannot exist in pre-eternity.

Following this, Ibn Taymiyya devotes considerable space to a third argument put forward by the event deniers. Their argument runs, "If originating events subsisted in [God], change (*taghayyur*) in

Him would follow necessarily, and change being incumbent upon God is absurd" (249). The Shaykh notes that the likes of al-Rāzī see nothing more in this than a tautology. "Change" can mean nothing but originating events, and yet, if it does mean this, it is tantamount to saying, "If originating events subsisted in [God], originating events would subsist in Him" (249).[22]

Ibn Taymiyya himself takes a somewhat different course in responding to this argument. He explains that the expression "change" is equivocal (*mujmal*) and that ordinary language (*al-lugha al-ma'rūfa*) does not apply this term to all temporally originating events. The sun and the moon move and human beings speak and pray, but, as this is their custom, they are not said to change. Rather, the word "change" applies only when attributes alter, as when someone falls ill or suffers a change in character and is no longer righteous but immoral. Ibn Taymiyya argues that God in His perfection is not subject to change in this sense. God's "perfection is among the concomitants of His essence" and God's attributes of perfection do not deteriorate into imperfection. The Shaykh continues, "On this foundation rests the view of the *salaf* and the People of the Sunna: '[God] has been speaking from eternity when He willed. He is powerful from eternity. He has been qualified with the attributes of perfection from eternity and He is still thus. He has not changed'" (250). Ibn Taymiyya then turns the tables on the event-deniers and accuses them of introducing change into God by positing a transition from the pre-eternal state of God's inaction to a later state when God did act (251–52).

The Shaykh further suggests that attributing change to God may not be as problematic as it first appears. This is because certain authentic Hadith reports qualify God with "jealousy" (*ghayra*), which is derived from the same Arabic root—*gh-y-r*—as the word "change" (*taghayyur*). The Shaykh cites three such traditions: "No one is more jealous (*aghyar*) than God that His slave, male or female, should commit adultery,"[23] "There is no one more jealous (*aghyar*) than God. Therefore, he forbade abominations, whether open or secret,"[24] and, "Do you marvel at the jealousy of Sa'd?! Indeed, I am more jealous than him, and God is more jealous than me" (252–53).[25]

Whereas the first three event-denier arguments are based on reason, the fourth that Ibn Taymiyya presents is founded on a Qur'ānic statement of Abraham, "I do not love things that set (*lā uḥibbu al-āfilīn*)" (Q 6:76). For the event-deniers, temporally originating events subsist in that which moves and sets, and such is what Abraham refused to love as a lord (252).[26] To counter this argument, Ibn Taymiyya first quotes the full Qur'ānic context of Abraham's statement:

> When the night grew dark upon him, he saw a celestial body. He said, "This is my lord." When it set, he said, "I do not love things that set." When he saw the moon rising, he said, "This is my lord." When it set, he said, "If my Lord does not guide me, I will surely be among the people who go astray." When he saw the sun rising, he said, "This is my lord; this is greater!" When it set, he said, "O people! I am innocent of that which you associate [with God]. I have turned my face to Him who constituted the heavens and the earth, as one upright. I am not one of the associaters" (Q. 6:76–79) (253).

Concerning these verses, Ibn Taymiyya first observes that Abraham says nothing about the celestial body, the moon or the sun while they are still visible. He does not, for example, say that he does not love things that rise, things that move, or things in which originating events subsist. Rather, he explains, the linguistic sense of "setting" (*ufūl*) is "absence" (*ghayb*) and "veiledness" (*iḥtijāb*). Thus, Abraham rejects only things that are absent and veiled as lords; he says nothing about things that move (253–54).

Beyond this, Ibn Taymiyya argues that the Lord of the Worlds, that is, God the Creator of all things, is not at issue in this text. The Shaykh asserts that both Abraham and his people acknowledge the Lord as Creator. At issue instead is the status of lower lords (*arbāb*), such as celestial bodies, which Abraham's people worship alongside the Lord of the Worlds. So, for Ibn Taymiyya, the point of the passage is to show that Abraham gives no regard to the lords that his people associate with the Lord, and it offers no support to those who deny originating events subsisting in God's essence (254–55).

Moreover, adds Ibn Taymiyya, the Qur'ān actually undermines the event-deniers. To cite only one example he provides here, Abraham said, "Truly, my Lord hears invocation" (Q. 14:39). Ibn Taymiyya notes, "What is meant by this is that [God] responds to invocation, as one performing the ritual prayer says, 'God hears those who praise Him'. He hears the invocation and responds to it only after it comes into existence, not before it comes into existence" (256). The Shaykh clarifies that God's hearing, as well as His vision, is an existent thing (*amr wujūdī*) by which God is qualified, and "It is necessary that this hearing and this vision subsist in Him after [human] deeds and statements are created" (257). So, God's hearing can be neither eternal in God nor subsist outside of God.

With this, Ibn Taymiyya ends his refutation of *kalām* event-denier arguments in *Ikhtiyāriyya*, and he wraps up his discussion by affirming the congruence of reason and tradition. The Shaykh could well have ended *Ikhtiyāriyya* here. The remainder of the treatise does not advance anything new theologically. However, he continues on with a very curious confession and an examination of the Fātiḥa.

Converting to the Correct View of the Voluntary Attributes

Just before this confession, Ibn Taymiyya injects the subject of *ziyāra* into his discussion for the first time in *Ikhtiyāriyya*. I translate *ziyāra* as "calling" as in "calling on someone" in order to capture both the sense of "visitation" that *ziyāra* typically brings to mind and the sense of entreaty and supplication of God that is at the fore in the current context. Here then is Ibn Taymiyya's confession that he formerly held different positions on both calling and the voluntary attributes:

> This issue [of the voluntary attributes], the issue of calling, and other [issues] originated among the later [theologians]. In them are obscurities. I and others used to adhere to the doctrine of the fathers (*madhhab al-ābā'*) in this. In these two fundamentals [of calling and the voluntary attributes], we used to uphold the views of the innovators (*ahl al-bid'a*). When what the Messenger brought became clear to us, the affair vacillated between our following what God sent down and following what we found our fathers adhering to. It was obligatory to follow the Messenger (258).

I know of no other reference to or evidence for the conversion mentioned here, whether in Ibn Taymiyya's own writings or in other sources. Yet, it might be tempting to link this to the Shaykh's mid-life turn against Ibn al-'Arabī, of which the historian Ibn al-Dawādārī provides the following account:

> One of Shaykh Taqī al-Dīn Ibn al-Taymiyya's [*sic*] friends once presented him a book by Shaykh Muḥyī al-Dīn Ibn al-'Arabī called *Fuṣūṣ al-ḥikam*. This was in the year 703 [1303–4]. Shaykh Taqī al-Dīn studied it and saw that it contained matters opposing his doctrine. So, he began to curse Ibn al-'Arabī and insult those who believed his doctrine. In the month of Ramadan, Taqī al-Dīn applied himself assiduously, compiled a refutation of it, and called it *Al-Nuṣūṣ 'alā al-Fuṣūṣ*....[27]

Ibn Dawādārī reports additionally that Ibn Taymiyya wrote letters to two prominent Sufi Shaykhs in Cairo—Karīm al-Dīn and Naṣr al-Manbijī—cursing Ibn al-'Arabī and warning of the danger in his teachings. Ibn al-Dawādārī tells us that this infuriated Naṣr al-Manbijī so much that he began to agitate with Baybars al-Jāshnakīr, who later became sultan, for Ibn Taymiyya's demise.[28] There is no reason to doubt that Ibn Taymiyya's extant letter to Naṣr al-Manbijī concerning Sufism and Ibn al-'Arabī is the letter al-Dawādārī mentions.[29] This letter is more paternalistic than inflammatory, and in it Ibn Taymiyya admits that he used to think well of Ibn al-'Arabī and found much of use in his books. When, however, he read *Fuṣūṣ al-ḥikam* and grasped the full import of his teaching, he saw need to reveal Ibn al-'Arabī's error.[30] The bulk of the letter sets out Ibn Taymiyya's vision of true Islamic spirituality and criticizes Ibn al-'Arabī's metaphysics and Sufi antinomianism. However, neither God's voluntary attributes nor the question of "calling" arises in this letter, and, more generally, neither is at issue in his polemic against Ibn al-'Arabī.[31] It thus appears unlikely that the conversion Ibn Taymiyya mentions in *Ikhtiyāriyya* is connected to his turn against Ibn al-'Arabī. Further research is required if we are to pinpoint the circumstances of Ibn Taymiyya's change of position on the voluntary attributes. However, my guess is that whatever conversion may have occurred took place early in the Shaykh's life because I have not encountered his alleged earlier views in primary or secondary sources.

Indicating the Voluntary Attributes from the Fātiḥa

The point that Ibn Taymiyya wishes to make in the last several pages of *Ikhtiyāriyya* is that the first sura of the Qur'ān, the Fātiḥa, speaks to both the issue of God's voluntary attributes and the question of calling. After admitting that he and his colleagues had had to change their doctrine on these two issues, he works through the first several verses of the Fātiḥa, showing how they indicate what is correct. I will note only the most essential points of the argument here.

On the question of calling, Ibn Taymiyya observes that the verse "You alone we worship, and you alone we ask for help" (Q. 1:5) distinguishes the "legislated calling" (*al-ziyāra al-shar'iyya*) of worshipping God alone from the "innovated calling" (*al-ziyāra al-bid'iyya*) of seeking the aid of others besides God. In this light, a correct prayer for the dead will call on God to forgive and have mercy upon the dead person. An incorrect prayer will call on the dead person himself for help and aid, and this is giving God an associate in worship (263–4).

With respect to the voluntary attributes, Ibn Taymiyya highlights the "praise" in "Praise be to God, Lord of the Worlds" (Q. 1:2) and contends that only voluntary acts bring into existence anything worthy of praise, or, for that matter, anything at all. He argues, "If [God] enacts good by His will and His power, He has a right to praise (*ḥamd*). Whoever does not have a voluntary act subsisting in him, or is not even able to do that, is neither the Creator nor the Lord of the Worlds" (259). Similarly, the Shaykh asserts, God can neither create the world nor send down the Qur'ān "if He has no act subsisting in Him by His volition." Without the exercise of God's will, no act occurs, nothing is created, and nothing originates (260). The Shaykh then moves on to "The Merciful, The Compassionate (*al-Raḥmān al-Raḥīm*)" (Q. 1:3) and asserts that God "is merciful to servants by His will and His Power" (260). If God's mercy were an eternal attribute, God could not then be said to "show mercy to whomever He wills" as He is said to do in the Qur'ān (Q. 29:21). In the same vein, Ibn Taymiyya invokes the sequence principle with the Hadith "My mercy precedes My anger,"[32] commenting, "Whatever precedes that which comes after it comes to be only by the will of the Lord and His power." If mercy were eternal, it could not precede God's anger (261). With respect to "Owner (*mālik*) of the Day of Judgment" (Q. 1:4), Ibn Taymiyya argues that someone who cannot act freely by his will is worthier to be called "owned" (*mamlūk*) than "owner." Thus, those who deny voluntary acts in God cannot truly speak of God owning anything (262–63). In the last few pages of *Ikhtiyāriyya*, Ibn Taymiyya reviews the virtues of the Fātiḥa in indicating correct doctrine in both calling and the voluntary attributes, and he ends, "God—Glory be to Him, and exalted is He—knows better" (267).

Conclusion

In *Ikhtiyāriyya*, Ibn Taymiyya does not offer a comprehensive treatment of the issues entailed in God's voluntary attributes. For example, he never refutes the most fundamental of the early *kalām* event-denying arguments, namely, that positing originating events in God turns God Himself into an originating event; later *kalām* theologians have already done that for him. Nonetheless, Ibn Taymiyya's theology in *Ikhtiyāriyya* is clear and reasonably well developed. He rejects the *kalām* notion that God's perfection consists in timeless eternity and places the perfection of volition in its stead. He envisions a perpetually dynamic and personal God whose voluntary attributes of speech, creation, mercy, sitting and such like subsist in God's essence and depend upon God's will and power for their exercise, which occurs within the temporal sequences of history. God Himself is actively and personally involved in time. Ibn Taymiyya would say that his theological formulation is what clear reason requires, quite apart from its confirmation in tradition. However, it seems apparent from his extensive exegesis that this theology of a personal God that he defends as rational is informed by his ordinary language reading of the Qur'ān and the Hadith and represents an attempt to explain and protect that reading. In this light, what we find in *Ikhtiyāriyya* is further evidence for regarding Ibn Taymiyya as an apologist for the coherence and rationality of the theological data found in the tradition.

Notes

1. Almost half of the material in the 37-volume *Majmū' fatāwā shaykh al-Islām Aḥmad b. Taymiyya* [hereafter *MF*], ed. 'Abd al-Raḥmān b. Muḥammad b. Qāsim and Muḥammad b. 'Abd al-Raḥmān b. Muḥammad (Cairo: Dār al-Raḥma, n.d.), may be classified as theology broadly conceived. Major theological works not found in MF include *Dar' ta'āruḍ al-'aql wa al-naql* (hereafter *Dar'*), ed. Muḥammad Rashād Sālim, 11 vols. (Riyadh: Dar al-Kunūz al-Adabiyya, 1979); *Minhāj al-sunna al-nabawiyya fī naqḍ kalām al-Shī'a al-Qadariyya* (hereafter *Minhāj*), ed. Muḥammad

Rashād Sālim, 9 vols. (Riyadh: Jāmi'at al-Imām Muḥammad b. Su'ūd al-Islāmiyya, 1406/1986); *Bayān talbīs al-Jahmiyya fī ta'sīs bida'ihim al-kalāmiyya aw Naqḍ ta'sīs al-Jahmiyya*, ed. Muḥammad b. 'Abd al-Raḥmān b. Qāsim, 2 vols. (n.pl.: Mu'assasat Qurṭuba, n.d.); and *Kitāb al-nubuwwāt* (Beirut: Dār al-Qalam, n.d.).

2. Broad ranging but preliminary accounts of Ibn Taymiyya's theology are found in Henri Laoust, *Essai sur les doctrines sociales et politiques de Takī-d-Dīn Aḥmad b. Taimīya, canoniste ḥanbalite né à Ḥarrān en 661/1262, mort à Damas en 728/1328* (Cairo: Imprimerie de l'institut français d'archéologie orientale, 1939), 154–78, and Victor E. Makari, *Ibn Taymiyyah's Ethics: The Social Factor* (Chico, CA: Scholars Press, 1983), 33–81.
3. Ignaz Goldziher, *Introduction to Islamic Theology and Law*, trans. of *Vorlesungen über den Islam* (Heidelberg, 1910) by Andras and Ruth Hamori (Princeton, NJ: Princeton University Press, 1981), 240. For an even more severe portrayal, see Majid Fakhry, *A History of Islamic Philosophy*, 2nd ed. (New York: Columbia University Press, 1983), 315–18.
4. Among the many pertinent studies are Daniel Gimaret, "Théories de l'acte humain dans l'école Ḥanbalite," *Bulletin d'études orientales* 29 (1977): 156–78; Joseph Normant Bell, *Love Theory in Later Ḥanbalite Islam* (Albany, NY: State University of New York, 1979), 46–91; Sherman A. Jackson, "Ibn Taymiyyah on Trial in Damascus," *Journal of Semitic Studies* 39 (Spring 1994): 41–85; Shahab Ahmed, "Ibn Taymiyyah and the Satanic verses," *Studia Islamica* 87 (1998): 67–124.
5. Yahya Michot, "Vanités intellectuelles...L'impasse des rationalismes selon le *Rejet de la contradiction* d'Ibn Taymiyyah," *Oriente Moderno* 19 (2000): 597–617, especially 599–601; Jean R. Michot, *Ibn Taymiyya: Lettre à Abû l-Fidâ'* (Louvain-la-Neuve: Institut Orientaliste de l'Université Catholique de Louvain, 1994), 17–19; and Binyamin Abrahamov, *Islamic Theology: Traditionalism and Rationalism* (Edinburgh: Edinburgh University Press, 1998), 51.
6. Jon Hoover, "Perpetual Creativity in the Perfection of God: Ibn Taymiyya's Hadith Commentary on God's Creation of this World," *Journal of Islamic Studies* 15:3 (Sept. 2004): 287–329, quotes on page 295.
7. "Faṣl fī al-ṣifāt al-ikhtiyāriyya," *MF* 6:217–67.
8. "Perpetual Creativity," 296–99, where I provide Ibn Taymiyya's full typology of views on God's speech.
9. The term "Jahmī" derives from Jahm b. Ṣafwān (d. 128/746) and was used by early Ḥanbalīs to cast aspersion upon Mu'tazilīs and Ḥanafīs who believed that the Qur'an was created. See W. Montgomery Watt, *The Formative Period of Islam* (Edinburgh: Edinburgh University Press, 1973), 143–48, for a discussion of "The alleged sect of the Jahmiyya." Ibn Kullāb (d. 241/855?), after whom the generic term "Kullābī" was coined, argued that God's attribute of speech was eternal. See J. van Ess, "Ibn Kullāb," *Encyclopedia of Islam*, new edition, Supplement, 391–92.
10. Ibn Taymiyya does not comment in this treatise on the diverse Mu'tazilī attempts to conceive God's attributes in some kind of nominal—as opposed to substantive or ontologically real—sense. For discussion of both Mu'tazilī and early Ash'arī approaches to the divine attributes, see D. Gimaret, "Mu'tazila," *Encyclopedia of Islam*, new ed., 7:783–93, especially 787–89.
11. A tenth-century Basran theological and mystical movement. See L. Massignon and B. Radtke, "Sālimiyya," *Encyclopedia of Islam*, new ed., 8:993–94.

12. Fakhr al-Dīn al-Rāzī, *al-Arbaʿīn fī uṣūl al-dīn*, ed. Aḥmad Ḥijāzī al-Saqā, 2 parts in 1 vol. (Cairo: Maktabat al-Kulliyyāt al-Azhariyya, n.d.), 1:168–73.
13. Fakhr al-Dīn al-Rāzī, *al-Maṭālib al-ʿāliyya min al-ʿilm al-ilāhī*, ed. Aḥmad Ḥijāzī al-Saqā, 9 parts in 5 vols. (Beirut: Dār al-Kitāb al-ʿArabī, 1407/1987), 2:106–7 (quote on 107). For a discussion of al-Rāzī's sundry treatments of temporal origination in God's essence, see Muḥammad Ṣāliḥ al-Zarkān, *Fakhr al-Dīn al-Rāzī wa ārāʾuhu al-kalāmiyya wa al-falsafiyya* (Cairo: Dār al-Fikr, 1963), 228–31. In *Ikhtiyāriyya*, Ibn Taymiyya also mentions al-Rāzī's *Nihāyat al-ʿuqūl*, but in a way that appears to identify it with *al-Maṭālib al-ʿāliyya*: "[Al-Rāzī] supports [the statement that all sects must admit events in God] in the last of his books, such as *al-Maṭālib al-ʿāliyya*, which is one of his largest *kalām* theology books, which he named *Nihāyat al-ʿuqūl fī dirāyat al-uṣūl*" (221). It could also be that this text is corrupt.
14. Bukhārī 6856, al-Tawḥīd: Qawl Allāh taʿālā wa yuḥadhdhirukum Allāh nafsahu; Muslim 4832, al-Dhikr wa al-duʿāʾ wa al-tawba wa al-istighfār, al-Ḥathth ʿalā dhikr Allāh taʿālā. Hadith references are given by the name of the collector, the Hadith number according to the *tarqīm al ʿālamiyya* system used on the CD-ROM *Mawsūʿat al-ḥadīth al-sharīf*, Version 2.0 (Cairo: Sakhr, 1997), and the Kitāb and Bāb location. The same numbering system is used at http://hadith.al-islam.com/. The Bukhārī text noted here is also found in Muḥammad Muḥsin Khān, trans., *Ṣaḥīḥ al-Bukhārī: Arabic-English* (Medina: Dār al-Fikr, n.d.), 9:369.
15. Earlier in *Ikhtiyāriyya* Ibn Taymiyya begins his discussion of Qurʾānic and Hadith texts supporting his position: "Moreover, the verses that indicate the voluntary attributes, which [the *kalām* theologians] call 'the occurrence of originating events (*ḥawādith*) ', are very many" (222).
16. *Minhāj* 1:422. In another text, however, Ibn Taymiyya attributes the doctrine that "originating events subsist in [God]" to the *salaf* without qualification ("Risālat al-furqān bayna al-ḥaqq wa al-bāṭil," *MF* 13:156). I am grateful to Khaled El-Rouayheb for this reference.
17. Sayf al-Dīn al-Āmidī, *Abkār al-afkār fī uṣūl al-dīn*, ed. Aḥmad Muḥammad al-Mahdī, 5 vols. (Cairo: Maṭbaʿat Dār al-Kutub wa al-Wathāʾiq al-Qawmiyya, 1423/2002), 2:20–33.
18. Ibn Taymiyya copies and comments upon all but the last few pages of al-Āmidī's discussion of "the impossibility of the occurrence of originating events in the essence of the Lord" in the fourth volume of *Darʾ*. The quotes in *Darʾ* are given here with the corresponding pages from *Abkār* in parentheses: 4:18–22 (2:20–22); 4:27–31 (2:22–23); 4:41–43 (2:23–25); 4:62–63 (2:25); 4:71–72 (2:26); 4:78–79 (2:26–27); 4:82–84 (2:27–28); 4:96–97 (2:28); 4:98–99 (2:28–29); 4:102–3 (2:29); 4:104–5 (2:29); 4:106–7 (2:29–30); 4:109–110 (2:30); 4:266 (2:31).
19. Al-Āmidī, *Abkār*, 2:27.
20. The arguments found here under Aspects 5 and 6 are also in *Minhāj*, 1:372.
21. For variations of this argument, see al-Rāzī, *Arbaʿīn*, 1:171–72; *Maṭālib*, 2:108–110.
22. See al-Rāzī, *Maṭālib*, 2:110–11, and al-Āmidī, *Abkār*, 2:26.
23. Bukhārī 986, al-Jumʿa, al-Ṣadaqa fī al-kasūf/Khān, trans., *Ṣaḥīḥ al-Bukhārī*, 2:85.
24. The portion of Ibn Taymiyya's text quoted here is found in slightly different form in Bukhārī, 4268 and 4271, Tafsīr al-Qurʾān, Qawluhu wa lā taqrabū al-fawāḥish mā ẓahara minhā wa mā baṭana/Khān, trans., *Ṣaḥīḥ al-Bukhārī*, 6:124. The latter part of the Hadith is drawn from Q. 6:151.
25. Bukhārī 6340, Al-Ḥudūd, Man raʾā maʿa imraʾatihi rajulan fa-qatalahu/Khān, trans., *Ṣaḥīḥ al-Bukhārī*, 8:553–54.

26. Al-Rāzī relates this argument in *Arbaʿīn*, 1:172, and al-Āmidī in *Abkār*, 2:26. There is a problem with Ibn Taymiyya's text in that the fourth event-denier argument appears on p. 252, lines 13–15 before his discussion of "change" in God ends on p. 253, line 7; p. 253, line 8, picks up with his response to the fourth event-denier argument.
27. Abū Bakr b. ʿAbd Allāh b. al-Dawādārī, *Kanz al-durar wa jāmiʿ al-ghurar*, vol. 9, *al-Durr al-fākhir fī sīrat al-Malik al-Nāṣir*, ed. Hans Robert Roemer (Cairo: Qism al-Dirāsāt al-Islāmiyya bi-al-Maʿhad al-almānī li-al-Āthār bi-al-Qāhira, 1960), 143. This passage is also translated somewhat more freely in Alexander Knysh, *Ibn ʿArabi in the Later Islamic Tradition: The Making of a Polemical Image in Medieval Islam* (Albany, NY: State University of New York, 1999), 96–97.
28. Ibn al-Dawādārī, *Kanz*, 9:143–44.
29. "Fī risālatihi ilā Naṣr al-Manbijī," *MF* 2:452–79.
30. *MF* 2:464–65.
31. Knysh, *Ibn ʿArabi in the Later Islamic Tradition*, 87–111, surveys Ibn Taymiyya's polemic against Ibn al-ʿArabī. See also my review of Knysh in *Islam and Christian-Muslim Relations* 10, 3 (Oct. 1999): 392–94, for corrections to his analysis of Ibn Taymiyya. While Ibn Taymiyya's antipathy for Ibn al-ʿArabī is well known, the roots of his initial appreciation for the Sufi theosophist and the affinities between the two have not been adequately explored.
32. Bukhārī 6998, al-Tawḥīd, Qawl Allāh taʿālā bal huwa Qurʾān majīd fī lawḥ maḥfūẓ.

The Qur'ānic Rational Theology of Ibn Taymiyya and his Criticism of the *Mutakallimūn*

*M. Sait Özervarli**

"Reason with faith and the Qur'ān
is like eyes with light and the Sun."[1]

The characteristics of Ibn Taymiyya's theology, particularly his understanding of rationality based on revelation, have not yet been fully explored. Biographers, as well as historians of Islamic thought, highlight Ibn Taymiyya's traditionalism and his influence on contemporary Salafism, and generally neglect the critical and rational aspects of his thought. In addition, he is charged with being the main source of Islamic radicalism or modern fundamentalism.[2] However, as a reviver of the traditionalist school (*aṣḥāb al-ḥadīth*), and a critic of al-Ghazālī (d. 505/1111), Ibn al-ʿArabī (d. 638/1240), and Fakhr al-Dīn al-Rāzī (d. 606/1209), the scope of Ibn Taymiyya's rationalist project deserves more attention. The complexity of his critique, and especially his view on the agreement of reason and revelation, is only beginning to be acknowledged.[3] Among other original contributions, it is particularly his defense of what may be called "Qur'ānic rational theology" that merits him a special place in Islamic intellectual history. This essay aims to explore the foundations and the methodological distinctiveness of Ibn Taymiyya's theology, through an examination of his critique of the *mutakallimūn*, or classical Muslim theologians.

The debate about the use of reason in understanding the Qur'ān began in the 8th and 9th centuries, with the emergence of early Muʿtazilite theologians and their traditionalist rivals. In these early theological debates, Muʿtazilite scholars employed rational methods and discussed philosophical, logical, cosmological, and ethical questions, without restricting themselves to the subjects and terms of the revealed text. The main critics of the early Muʿtazilites' use of reason were the followers of the traditionalist school, such as Aḥmad Ibn Ḥanbal (d. 241/855), al-Bukhārī (d. 256/870), Ibn Qutayba

(d. 276/889) and Abū Saʿīd al-Dārimī (d. 280/894). For them, evidence in religious matters could only be established on the basis of the Qur'ān and the Hadith.

The theological school formed by Abū al-Ḥasan al-Ashʿarī (d. 324/935-6), once a Muʿtazilite, offered a synthesis that was closer in its substance to the traditionalist views, but which continued to rely on philosophical terminology borrowed from the Muʿtazilites. These Ashʿarī theologians were therefore criticized by traditionalist scholars, such as Abū Sulaymān al-Khaṭṭābī (d. 388/998), ʿAbd Allāh al-Harawī (d. 481/1089), and the later Ibn Qudāma al-Maqdisī (d. 620/1223). They argued that the *mutakallimūn* interpreted the Qur'ān according to their pre-conceived theological views, that they inappropriately used the method of disputation (*jadal*) in matters of theology, and that they introduced foreign terminology into the fundamentals of Islamic creeds (*ʿaqā'id*). At the same time, the *mutakallimūn* were also subject to a challenge from Ibn Rushd (d. 595/1198), who revived the peripatetic tradition in Islamic thought. This philosophical challenge led Ashʿarī theologians such as Fakhr al-Dīn al-Rāzī and Sayf al-Dīn al-Āmidī (d. 631/1233) to develop *kalām* into a more theoretical discipline.[4]

Ibn Taymiyya's scholarship should be seen against this backdrop of the emergence of philosophically-oriented *kalām*. His polemics with the Ashʿarī theologians and peripatetic philosophers were means of reformulating traditionalist doctrines in a rationalist framework.[5] The traditionalist school had already been reinforced in Syria after the emigration of some established Ḥanbalī families from Iraq, Palestine, and Northern Mesopotamia to Damascus. Among them, the Banū Munajjā and Banū Qudāma families were of special importance.[6] Ibn Taymiyya, although a member of the Ḥanbalī scholarly community and a traditionalist by education, was well aware of wider intellectual trends in Islamic thought. In particular, he seems to have been influenced by al-Ashʿarī's critique of the Muʿtazilites, al-Ghazālī's of the philosophers, and Ibn Rushd's of the Ashʿarites.

The following pages will focus on Ibn Taymiyya's analysis of the Sunni *mutakallimūn* of the later period. Ibn Taymiyya was aware of the methodological shift in Sunni theology and of the influence of Avicennan philosophy on mainstream *kalām* works. He therefore sought to present an alternative theology based on the Qur'ān and the Sunna while engaging with the discourse of philosophical theology, unlike earlier traditionalist scholars. His focus on philosophical debates provided him with a deeper rationalistic approach despite his traditionalist background, as well as a more critical perspective towards inherited knowledge and revered intellectual figures. This has earned him criticism from within traditionalist circles. The Ḥanbalī scholar and biographer Ibn Rajab (d. 795/1393) points out that some of the leading traditionalists of the time, though respectful of Ibn Taymiyya as a scholar, were unhappy with his indulging in *kalām* and philosophy.[7]

Ibn Taymiyya's rational approach is evident not only in his theology, but also in his legal thought, as he often went against the dominant Ḥanbalī position of his time, following his own *ijtihād*.[8] Moreover, the range of his students, coming from different schools and backgrounds, is another indication of his intellectual flexibility. Among the students who attended Ibn Taymiyya's lectures were the renowned Shāfiʿī historians al-Dhahabī (d. 748/1348) and Ibn Kathīr (d. 774/1373), the Sufi Shaykh ʿImad al-Dīn al-Wāsiṭī (d. 711/1311), as well as moderate Ḥanbalīs, such as al-Ṭūfī (d. 716/1316) and Ibn Mufliḥ (d. 763/1362).

Questioning the Legitimacy of kalām: What are the *ʿUṣūl al-dīn*'?

One of the key aspects of Ibn Taymiyya's theology is his definition and understanding of the term *uṣūl al-dīn*, which literally means "principles of religion". This was the term used by the *mutakallimūn* to describe the subject matter of their discipline. Al-Ashʿarī, for example, uses this term in his defense of *kalām*,[9] and other Ashʿarite or Maturidite theologians, such as ʿAbd al-Qāhir al-Baghdādī (d. 429/1038) and Abū al-Yusr al-Bazdawī (or al-Pazdavī, d. 493/1100), chose it as the title of their major books.[10]

Ibn Taymiyya, however, believed that the rationalist theology of the *mutakallimūn* is quite different from the true "*uṣūl al-dīn*". When asked about the permissibility of studying the "*uṣūl al-dīn*" which are not grounded in a revealed text, i.e., *kalām* theology, Ibn Taymiyya rejects the premise of the question. *Uṣūl al-dīn* come from God and include all the necessary rational foundations. Had it been otherwise, the Prophet would be in the impossible position of neglecting an essential aspect of Islam.[11] The Qur'ān and the Sunna provide superior and sufficient rational proofs, which make the philosophical proofs of the theologians redundant. On the other hand, subjects considered by the *mutakallimūn* as *uṣūl al-dīn*, such as philosophical explanations of the attributes of God, or the cosmological argument as a proof for the existence of God, are without grounding in the revealed sources and have nothing to do with the true *uṣūl al-dīn*. Neither the Qur'ān nor the Prophet called humanity to Islam by means of these theories, which have only caused errors and corruption.[12]

Ibn Taymiyya's critique of the *mutakallimūn*'s definition of *uṣūl al-dīn* relates to their neglect of the Qur'ānic method in dealing with theological issues, as well as their use of technical terms such as material body (*jism*), substance (*jawhar*), accident (*'araḍ*), and attribute (*ṣifa*), in a manner that has no basis in the Qur'ān.[13] He says:

> These [principles] which they call *uṣūl al-dīn* are in reality not part of the *uṣūl al-dīn* that God prescribed for his servants.... When it is understood that what is called *uṣūl al-dīn* in the usage of those who employ this term, consists of indeterminacy and ambiguity caused by equivocal coinage and technical terms (*li-mā fī-hi min al-ishtirāk bi-ḥasab al-awḍā' wa-al-iṣṭilāḥāt*), it becomes evident that the *uṣūl al-dīn* accepted by God, His Messenger, and His believers, are that which was transmitted from the Prophet.
>
> As for anyone who establishes a religion without permission from God, the requisite *uṣūl al-dīn* could not be transmitted from the Prophet. Since such a religion is invalid, [the principles] required by it are also invalid.[14]

Ibn Taymiyya also accuses them of broadening the meaning of certain Qur'ānic terms in order to make them more generally applicable. He discusses at great length the terms "coming into being" (*ḥudūth*) and "divine unity" (*tawḥīd*) to demonstrate the differences between their original meanings and their meanings in theological and philosophical writings.[15] The revealed text, he argues, employs such words in accordance with the way they were understood by the Arabs, with the aim of conveying a clear message. Neither the Arabs nor the revealed sources use these terms in the technical manner of the *mutakallimūn* or the philosophers. Since so much Qur'ānic terminology has been subjected to this kind of abuse, their interpretation by the *mutakallimūn* has nothing to do with the *uṣūl al-dīn* sent down by God through the Prophet.[16]

Ibn Taymiyya argues, furthermore, that the methods of the *mutakallimūn* caused chaos in religious discourses, as each theological school or individual scholar introduced different subjects into the realm of *uṣūl al-dīn*, reaching opposite conclusions and engaging in endless theological debates. Given so many conflicting views, the *mutakallimūn*'s claim of certainty is very peculiar, not least because their discourse is so far from the truth:

> Some *kalām* theologians claim that matters of theological information (*al-masā'il al-khabariyya*),[17] which they may call matters of the principles [of religion], must all be proved with certainty. They therefore claim that it is not permissible to reason in these questions without a proof that brings certainty, and they require everyone to reach certainty in all of these questions. But what they say in such absolute and comprehensive terms is false, counter to the Book, the Sunna, and the consensus of the *salaf* and the Imams. Moreover, it is they who are the furthest from what they require, because the proofs many of them believe to be certain are wrong, let alone conjectural.[18]

When their views contradict the Qur'ān, he continues, they call the relevant verses ambiguous (*mujmal* or *mutashābih*), and try to interpret them according to their pre-conceived theories, or just cast these verses aside without considering their content. Thus, he says in the harshest terms, their *uṣūl al-dīn* deserves to be called the *uṣūl dīn al-shayṭān*, "the principles of Satanic religion," since their arguments either add something to, or effectively alter the proper principles of religion.[19]

Among the inconsistencies of the *mutakallimūn*, Ibn Taymiyya points out their habit of leveling the accusation of disbelief (*takfīr*) at their intellectual rivals. Although they regard their methodology as based on reason, they employ the term *takfīr*, which belongs to the realm of revelation. In other words, they distinguish between the domains of *'aql* and *naql*, of reason and authority received through Prophetic transmission, and consider their works to belong to the first domain; but then, by accusing their rivals of heresy, they employ a norm that belongs to the second. The *mutakallimūn*, who claim to apply a rationalistic methodology, nevertheless use the terms and concepts of religious law to silence their opponents; and they do so in the context of a debate over details of rational proof to which the accusation of unbelief does not properly apply. Disputing and rejecting the fruits of reason through the terms that religion has reserved for revelation is therefore an example of the confusion of the *mutakallimūn*:

> It is amazing that the *kalām* theologians say that the *uṣūl al-dīn*, the denial of which implies unbelief, are known solely on the basis of reason; while whatever is not known by reason alone they consider divine law (*al-shar'iyyāt*). This is the method of the Mu'tazilites, Jahmites, and those who follow them, like the disciples of the author of *al-Irshād* [al-Juwaynī] and their ilk.
>
> It should be said to them that this argument consists of two parts: First, *uṣūl al-dīn* are known through reason alone, not divine law; second, anyone who denies these principles is an unbeliever. These premises, while invalid in themselves, are also contradictory. If something is known only through reason, its denial does not consist of unbelief in religious terms. This is because there is nothing in the divine law that stipulates that the rejection of something that is known only through reason amounts to unbelief. The only causes of unbelief are a denial of what was transmitted by the Prophet, or a refusal to follow him while knowing his truthfulness.[20]

The point of Ibn Taymiyya's argument is that the rational elements of theology must remain close to the revealed sources in order not to be reduced to a natural theology. While Ibn Taymiyya criticizes the *mutakallimūn* for their "self-contained" rationalism, he is open to what he considers to be the true *uṣūl al-dīn*, which is rationalism based on the Qur'ān and the Sunna. It is indeed a folly, he argues, to oppose *uṣūl al-dīn* inherent in the revealed and transmitted sources.[21]

The Rejection of Disagreement between Reason and Revealed Knowledge

As is evident not only from the previous discussion, but also from the title and content of his *Dar' ta'āruḍ al-'aql wa-al-naql* ('The prevention of conflict between reason and revealed knowledge'), one of the central issues in Ibn Taymiyya's thought is the relation between reason and the authoritative transmitted sources.[22] The position of the *mutakallimūn* on this problem, described by Ibn

Taymiyya as the general law or governing principle (*al-qānūn al-kullī*) of al-Rāzī and his followers, is the following: The validity of revelation must be based on rational principles, since the contents of revealed knowledge, as found in the Qur'ān and Prophetic traditions, cannot be proven by reason alone. Its validity therefore depends *a priori* on a definite certainty that the Prophet was indeed sent by God, and that the Prophet and the knowledge he transmitted are entirely trustworthy. This being so, one has to use reasoning (*naẓar*) and argumentation (*istidlāl*) in order to establish revelation as a source of knowledge that is as certain and reliable as that obtained by reason.[23] The use of philosophical and logical argumentation in order to ground religious belief in reason was not seen as problematic by al-Rāzī and other theologians.

The general rule of the *mutakallimūn* applies to cases of conflict between reason and revealed knowledge, i.e., the occurrence of a rational counter-argument (*mu'āriḍ 'aqlī*) that contradicts the literal meaning of the authoritative texts. Since it is impossible either to accept or reject the conflicting proofs of both reason and revealed knowledge, then in a case of conflict the rational proof should be admitted, and the transmitted text interpreted metaphorically. Giving priority to evidence from revelation and rejecting the rational counter-argument would undermine the rational foundation for the validity of revelation as a source of knowledge—it will be groundless and therefore invalid.[24]

In other words, the *mutakallimūn* argue that what is known by revelation cannot in itself be confirmed by reason, and one must draw on reason in order to ascertain the validity of revealed knowledge. The truthfulness of the Prophet and his message is extrinsic to the content of revelation. Since rational proofs are necessary preliminaries to the authority of revealed knowledge, it must be the case that reason is primary, limiting the range of possible meanings of the content of revelation. When the sense of the transmitted texts conflicts with the dictates of reason, reason should be given precedence, and the text subjected to metaphorical yet rational interpretation (*ta'wīl* or *tafsīr*).[25]

Ibn Taymiyya, however, rejects the possibility of conflict between reason and revealed knowledge, primarily because human knowledge could not contradict the absolute truth of divine revelation. Rational proofs do not oppose religious ones, he suggests; the two should rather be seen as complementary. What Ibn

Taymiyya proposes is a rationality based on revelation and tradition. In his epistemology, all proofs are either canonical (*al-adilla al-shar'iyya*) or innovative, i.e., non-canonical (*al-adilla al-bid'iyya*). The canonical, correct proofs may be rational (*al-'aqliyya*), transmitted (*al-naqliyya*), or both.[26] As an example of the latter category, Ibn Taymiyya says that the Qur'ān (41:53) points to "signs in the horizons and in human souls"; in other words, it uses proofs taken from observation of the universe and of human nature. There is no doubt, according to Ibn Taymiyya, that these proofs derived from observing creation are rational.

Ibn Taymiyya then examines the possible counter-arguments against the rationality of the Qur'ānic proofs. Some deny the presence of this sort of proof in the Qur'ān. The *mutakallimūn* and the philosophers read the authoritative transmitted sources restrictively, as a collection of reports (sing. *khabar*). For this reason they believe it could not demonstrate and defend a rational argument.[27] Others, while accepting that the Qur'ān does indeed present proofs from creation, nevertheless interpret them erroneously. But, Ibn Taymiyya argues, those who understand these proofs reject any possible conflict between such proofs and rationality.[28] There is no sharp distinction between rational and traditional proofs in Ibn Taymiyya's classification. They exist together as two complementary components of knowledge, which are not truly separate from each other.

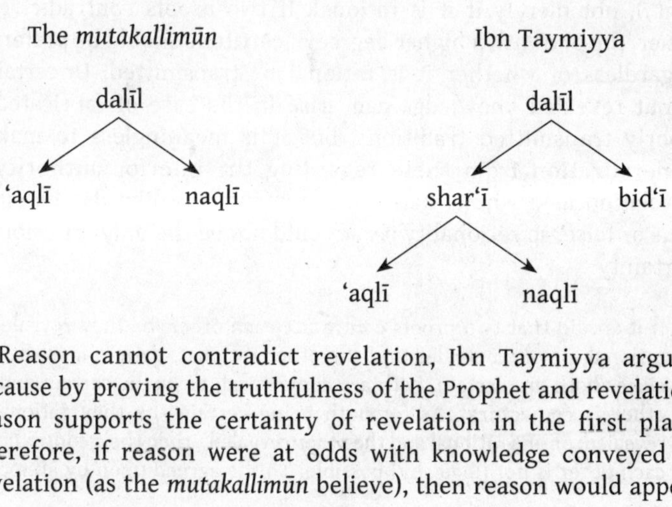

Reason cannot contradict revelation, Ibn Taymiyya argues, because by proving the truthfulness of the Prophet and revelation, reason supports the certainty of revelation in the first place. Therefore, if reason were at odds with knowledge conveyed by revelation (as the *mutakallimūn* believe), then reason would appear to negate its own conclusion, i.e., the trustworthiness and truthfulness of revelation. In other words, it is logically inconsistent to claim that reason can support the reliability of all revelation, and yet contradict specific parts of it. Doing so invalidates the status of reason as a source of knowledge, and simultaneously undermines our confidence in revelation.[29] Moreover, in his opinion, denying any part of the content of revelation is also an indirect rejection of the authority of reason, as many clear and certain rational proofs corroborate the content of the revealed and transmitted sources.[30]

Ibn Taymiyya also raises doubts regarding the *mutakallimūn*'s argument for the certainty of rational proofs and reason in general. In fact, he argues, the arguments of the practitioners of the rational sciences too often contradict each other, and the methods adopted by the *mutakallimūn* are so ill-defined as to constantly produce conflicting results.[31] Why, Ibn Taymiyya asks, do such highly regarded methods of intellectual argumentation lead to so many mutually contradictory theological views? The variety of their conclusions can readily be seen in their difference of opinion regarding the attributes of God. The level of ambiguity brought about by the *kalām* use of reason is greater than that of revelation and tradition. A methodology of argumentation that leads scholars to contradictory and therefore uncertain results should not be regarded as the best way of reaching the truth.[32]

Ibn Taymiyya insists that a proof has precedence if it is certain (*qaṭʿī*), not merely if it is rational. If two proofs contradict each other, the one with a higher degree of certitude should be preferred, regardless of whether it is rational or transmitted. Uncertainty about revealed knowledge can arise in the case of fabricated or poorly transmitted traditions, but it is meaningless to make a generalization from these regarding the inferior authority of revelation as a whole. Rational arguments can likewise be either true or false, so rationality *per se* could not be the only criterion for certainty:

> If it is said that two proofs contradict each other, be they revealed or rational, or one revealed and the other rational, then it must be that either both are certain, both are conjectural, or one is certain and the other is conjectural. As for both being certain—be they rational or revealed, or one rational and the other revealed—then their contradicting each other is not [logically] possible. This is agreed upon by all men of

> reason, because a certain proof yields the validity of what it indicates, and makes its invalidity impossible. Therefore, if two certain proofs contradicted each other, and one contradicted what is indicated by the other, this would require the combining of two opposites, which is [logically] impossible. Whenever one finds a seeming contradiction between two proofs that are thought to be certain, then it necessarily follows that both proofs or at least one of them, are not certain; or that the two indicated matters do not contradict each other. ...However, if [only] one of the contradicting proofs yields certainty, then according to the consensus of men of reason, its priority is necessary regardless of whether the proof is revealed or rational, since conjecture does not override certainty.[33]

The contents of revelation, as transmitted by the prophets, do not lack rational basis, even if revelation does provide humanity with knowledge which is otherwise unattainable. Contradictions arise when the rational argument is not sound, or when uncertain and doubtful traditions are invoked.[34] In the case of the Qur'ān and the authentic Sunna such a problem will not occur at all, whereas rational arguments need to be examined and may be found to be ambiguous, controversial, or incomplete. Despite his criticism of the *mutakallimūn*'s doctrine on the absolute priority of reason, Ibn Taymiyya emphasizes that he does not deny the authority of reason and its role in demonstrating the truthfulness of revealed and transmitted sources. He summarizes his method of combining them by stating that "reason with faith and the Qur'ān is like eyes with light and the Sun".[35]

While expounding his views on the limits of the authority of reason in religion, Ibn Taymiyya also explains his approach towards the theologians' interpretation (*ta'wīl*) of the revealed and transmitted texts. For Ibn Taymiyya, the definition of *ta'wīl* as "the employment of a secondary meaning for a better understanding of a text," is at odds with its original meaning.[36] The Qur'ānic term *ta'wīl* is misused by the *mutakallimūn*, since the *salaf* and the early exegetes understood it as explaining the text and clarifying its meaning (*tafsīr al-kalām wa-bayān ma'nā-hu*), aiming merely at better understanding. This, in Ibn Taymiyya's view, is not problematic. The later scholars, however, use the term to denote the substitution for the common meaning of a word of a less common one (*ṣarf al-lafẓ min al-iḥtimāl al-rājiḥ ilā al-iḥtimāl al-marjūḥ*) when the primary meaning raises difficulties. For Ibn Taymiyya, this moving away from the common sense meaning of the text, a method employed in *kalām* and jurisprudence, is not the true meaning of *ta'wīl*.

Ibn Taymiyya accepts that *ta'wīl* could also mean the indication of a divine truth (*al-ḥaqīqa allatī yu'awwal al-kalām ilayhā*), and in this sense applies to Qur'ānic descriptions of life after death, where the *ta'wīl* is known only to God and those whom He chose to inform. But it is not for the *mutakallimūn* to adopt this kind of interpretation by claiming to know the hidden sense behind the literal meanings, for they ascribe to the text meanings that may not reflect divine intent. Their approach, Ibn Taymiyya argues, is bound to produce a range of false interpretations and confusion. An interpretation that does not reflect the Divine intention, he reminds the *mutakallimūn*, should be regarded as alteration (*taḥrīf*).[37]

Ibn Taymiyya goes on to argue that the attributes of God mentioned in the Qur'ān should not be interpreted at all, even though some of them bear a resemblance to human qualities. The divine attributes are utterly different from human qualities, and so the use of these terms to describe God, required by the constraints of human language, is not anthropomorphic. To speak of the metaphysical world through the language of this world does not suggest similarity between the two. We can only describe the character of divine qualities with the words God mentioned in the Qur'ān, without any further evaluation or different interpretation. All the divine attributes that appear in the Qur'ān, such as hearing, seeing, sitting on the throne, or descending (*sam'*, *baṣar*, *istiwā'*, or *nuzūl*) must be treated in the same way, contrary to the practice of the *mutakallimūn*, who interpret some and accept the others literally.[38]

Nevertheless, Ibn Taymiyya does not call for an absolute rejection of interpretation. He makes an exception for those verses mentioned in Surat Āl 'Imrān (3:7) as ambiguous, obscure, or equivocal (*mutashābihāt*), while not regarding all Qur'ānic verses as belonging to this category. These verses should not be subject to the method of *tafwīḍ*, as suggested by some members of the traditionalist school, such as al-Qāḍī Abū Ya'lā (d. 1066). According to the *tafwīḍ* doctrine, knowledge of the meanings of the ambiguous verses of the Qur'ān is consigned to God alone. However, since the Qur'ān was sent by God to be understood and practiced, its content must be knowable to the reader, with the exception of ambiguous verses that require a degree of scholarship and an expertise in the sciences of the

Qur'ān. Ibn Taymiyya commends, therefore, exertion of effort in comprehending and explaining the Qur'ān, as long as the meanings of the Book are not altered.[39]

Systematizing a Qur'ānic Theology: Rationality within Tradition

As Ibn Taymiyya distanced himself from the *kalām* methods of reasoning, he tried to construct an alternative rational theology based on the revealed sources and the traditions of the *salaf*. The Qur'ān and the Sunna, Ibn Taymiyya argues, offer a cognitive unity through both knowledge and practice, while the *kalām* method leads only to abstract knowledge. Moreover, the divine message is indicated in a manner which is harmonious with innate human reality, and offers a direct method of proof. The *kalām* method, on the other hand, uses only the tools of deductive or analogical reasoning, and therefore their efforts do not lead to the true goal of religion. As he explains:

> The distinction between the Qur'ānic and the *kalām* theological methods is that God commands worship of Him, a worship which is the perfection of the soul, its prosperity, and its ultimate goal. He did not limit it to mere affirmation of Him, as is the purpose of the *kalām* method. These two [methods] do not correspond to each other, neither in methods nor in objectives. Indeed the Qur'ānic method, as we have noted, is intuitive and direct (*fiṭriyya qarība*), leading to the essence of the objective. [In contrast] the other is analogical and circuitous (*qīyasiyya ba'īda*), leading only to [a knowledge] of the form of the objective, not its essence.
>
> As for the goals, the Qur'ān relates knowledge of Him and service to Him. It thus combines the two human faculties of knowledge and practice; or sensation and motion; or perceptive volition and operation; or verbal and practical. As God says, 'Worship your Lord'. Worship necessarily entails knowledge of Him, having penitence and humility before Him, and a need for Him. This is the goal. The *kalām* method secures only the benefit of affirmation and admission of God's existence.[40]

The revealed and transmitted sources contain their own rational foundations, which are suitable for the logic of their message, and satisfy people of different educational backgrounds. They also contain within them the evidence required to substantiate the principles of religion, and therefore have no need for extraneous theories, whether by theologians or philosophers.

For example, rational proofs of the existence of God and of resurrection after death, which are based on observation of the natural world, can be found in some Qur'ānic verses. The *mutakallimūn* use abstract methods to reach a conclusion that could have been taken directly from the revealed text. Moreover, they prove the existence of God in a way that tests human rationality beyond its bounds, speculating by means of a complicated cosmological argument (*dalīl al-ḥudūth*). This argument is based on proving the changing reality of substances (*jawāhir*) and bodies (*ajsām*) in the physical world through the motions of accidents (*a'rāḍ*), in order to demonstrate the existence of a Creator. Simply put, the cause and effect chain of changing physical existence cannot go backward indefinitely, and therefore requires a beginning found only through divine creation. This proof, however, raises difficulties in reconciling the eternity of God with His creation in time. The Muslim peripatetic philosophers tried to solve the problem by proposing the eternity of the universe in time but not in essence. Ibn Taymiyya completely rejects the eternity of the universe in any form, but also criticizes the *mutakallimūn* for denying any cause or purpose in creation. In his view, God brings things into existence purposefully, through His absolute will and power, as observed in the physical world. Therefore, while rejecting the possibility of eternity for any created being, Ibn Taymiyya accepts the eternity of creation, which does not mean in his opinion an endless chain of causes, but rather the continuity of God's perpetual acting and creating.[41]

The *ḥudūth* argument may demonstrate the need for a Creator, but it does not prove it in reality. In the Qur'ān, however, the existence of God is firmly grounded in the creation of concrete and visible entities (*a'yān*) by God. The continuous creation of the universe, humans, animals, and other physical beings in a perfect way is there for all to see. It constitutes a more direct proof of the existence of God than philosophical theories.[42] The cosmological argument in fact makes the issue of divine existence more muddled and less grounded in reality.[43] Ibn Taymiyya emphasizes the importance of the signs (*āyāt*) of God in the universe. These signs are found everywhere in nature, can be observed by anyone and comprehended with no difficulty. The proof of the *mutakallimūn*, in comparison, is like a meager scrap of camel meat beyond a hill, the hill unreachable, the meat not worthwhile.[44]

For Ibn Taymiyya, moreover, our knowledge of the existence of God comes through our inner nature (*fiṭra*), and it is a knowledge that makes the theologians' proofs and argumentation redundant. Without prior knowledge and belief in God, it is impossible to take the theoretical proofs of the theologians as pointing to God. Rather, knowledge of God without these abstract proofs is like being familiar with a person without knowing his name, or understanding and manipulating objects without knowing the rules of their operation.[45] "The essence of acknowledging God and recognizing Him", he states, "is placed in the hearts of all humans and jinn" (*anna aṣl al-iqrār bi-al-ṣāni' wa-al-i'tirāf bi-hi mustaqarrun fī qulūb jamī' al-ins wa-al-jinn).*[46]

Ibn Taymiyya gives another example to support this point. Those who go to visit the Ka'ba for pilgrimage already know that it exists and may be familiar with some of its attributes through descriptions given by previous visitors and confirmed by guidebooks. Similarly, the believers' faith is satisfied by means of information transmitted by various channels and through the guidance of the Qur'ān. As the immediate relation between daylight and the Sun, or smoke and fire is perceived immediately without need for philosophical propositions or logical analogies, a similar relation can be easily set up between created and Creator.[47]

The term *fiṭra* is derived from the Qur'ānic phrase "the patterns of God according to which He has made mankind" (*fiṭrat Allāh allati faṭara al-nās 'alayhā*, Q 30:30), and is explained as the pure and primal human nature created by God to distinguish human beings from other creatures. The tradition saying that "All children are born on the *fiṭra*" (*kull mawlūd yūlad 'ala al-fiṭra*)[48] is linked to this inborn purity of human nature, which may subsequently be corrupted during one's lifetime. The *mutakallimūn* did not include the *fiṭra* argument among their proofs for the existence of God, though they paid some attention to the argument from design (*niẓām*), which emphasizes the perfect harmony within the natural world as the best evidence for God's existence. A few independent minded scholars prior to Ibn Taymiyya, such as Muṭahhar b. Ṭāhir al-Maqdisī and al-Ghazālī, touched upon the *fiṭra* in this context without discussing it in detail.[49] Al-Ghazālī's argument in the 'Revival of the Religious Sciences' that human *fiṭra*, together with

Qur'ānic examples, has no need of further proofs seems to be developed by Ibn Taymiyya as an alternative to the cosmological argument.[50]

As a point of comparison, it is interesting that in the history of Christian thought, some reformist theologians, such as Martin Luther (1483–1546) and John Calvin (1509–1564), emphasized the innate ability of human nature to recognize divine existence. Luther suggested that God rightly situated beliefs in human hearts, and there was no need for further rational activities and logical deductions in order to prove His existence, since they would not provide additional strength to religious faith.[51] Similarly, Calvin in a chapter entitled "The Knowledge of God Has Been Naturally Implanted in the Minds of Men," writes:

> There is within the human mind, and indeed by natural instinct, an awareness of divinity. This we take to be beyond controversy. To prevent anyone from taking refuge in the pretence of ignorance, God himself has implanted in all men a certain understanding of his divine majesty. Ever renewing its memory, he repeatedly shed fresh drops.[52]

The challenge to ontological and cosmological proofs of the existence of God has been taken up by modern philosophers, including Immanuel Kant. Theist thinkers, who are not in favor of using philosophical argumentation in matters of faith, suggest that religious texts do not emphasize the issue of evidence for God's existence, but rather underline the significance of firm conviction of the heart through divine guidance. They point out that philosophical arguments prove only the existence of God as a theoretical conception in mind. Moreover, the logical necessity of His existence may hinder the freedom of belief, which is offered by God to everyone.[53] Others suggest a view that believing in God is "properly basic" in human beings and does not require proving.[54] Similarities between those views and Ibn Taymiyya's approach are quite remarkable and deserve further studies and comparative analysis.

Ibn Taymiyya also points out the close relationship between belief and action, which provides a connection between the physical and metaphysical worlds. The *mutakallimūn*, who discuss faith in abstract terms, miss the practical elements, which form part of religion. It is not a coincidence, he argues, that the prophets began their call to religion through worship and love of God rather than through rational proofs.[55] The roots of religious belief, in Ibn Taymiyya's approach, are the acceptance of the fundamentals of the faith, as well as a strong commitment to act on those principles in daily life through the language and the practices of heart. Technical and abstract definitions of faith will not satisfy the expectations of the believer.[56]

For Ibn Taymiyya, another example of the difference between the works of *kalām* and the methods of the Qur'ān is the resurrection of the body on the Day of Judgment, or life after death in general. The *mutakallimūn*, Ibn Taymiyya says, try to demonstrate the theoretical possibility of resurrection, while the Qur'ān compares it to the concrete act of creation, bringing proofs from the physical world as against the speculative hypotheses of the *mutakallimūn*.[57] If something becomes possible in your mind, it means that you rule out its impossibility (*imtināʿ*), without necessarily being able to prove its existence in the world. The possible becomes real once you demonstrate it or its equivalent in the real world. The Qur'ān, by comparing the creation of the Hereafter to the creation of the temporal world, demonstrates the actual existence of the Hereafter more convincingly than the speculations of the *mutakallimūn*.[58]

Finally, Ibn Taymiyya's position on the subject of divine actions is again critical of the doctrines of the Ashʿarite theologians, offering an alternative reasoning. The Ashʿarites are reluctant to link divine actions, such as creating or providing sustenance (*tawḍīʿ al-rizq*), to some ultimate cause (*ʿilla*) or wisdom (*ḥikma*), and wary of making God dependent upon something other then Himself. God's self-perfection, the Ashʿarites argue, requires direct action, excluding any kind of intermediary. They also point out that a created cause would necessitate infinite regress (*tasalsul*).[59] The Muslim philosophers, in contrast, described divine actions as progressing deterministically through necessary causes. Ibn Taymiyya, however, suggests that God acts wisely in accordance with His aims and causes, but through absolute will and power, and therefore He is not deterministically in need of such aims and causes. Divine actions and their causes are not eternal, since they are applied to created beings. Since divine actions are not eternal, there is no theological problem for them to have causes.[60] The Ashʿarite reservations are therefore unwarranted, and their excessive attempt to defend divine perfection leads them away from the Qur'ān and the Sunna.[61]

In Ibn Taymiyya's approach, the Ash'arites are also mistaken in their deterministic understanding of human actions (*af'āl al-'ibād*) and the theory of acquisition (*kasb*), which he considers to be very close to the view of Jabrites. According to Ibn Taymiyya, although God is the creator (*khāliq*), humans are true actors (*fā'il*) of their actions. God is the creator of human actions by providing the causes and power of acting, but humans are the sole agents of their acts through their free will.[62] Therefore, his approach on human acts and predestination, as explained by Gimaret, is more rationalistic than the views of earlier Ḥanbalīs and Ash'arites, and rather similar to the position of Maturidites and the Mu'tazilite Abū al-Ḥusayn al-Baṣrī.[63]

Conclusion

Ibn Taymiyya was able to cross entrenched divisions amongst Islamic theologians, philosophers, and mystics in order to solve what he perceived to be the intellectual crisis of his time. His attempt to revive traditional views in a philosophical manner should be seen against the background of the political and social situation of his lifetime. His critical examination of Islamic intellectual history was an effort to demonstrate the shortcomings of the dominant schools of thought in order to unify the community under a religious philosophy grounded in the Qur'ān and the Sunna. Ultimately, despite his return to the Qur'ān and to the views of the *salaf*, "his ideas came to be fundamentally philosophical in their method", as Alousi put it, or "a philosophical interpretation and defense of tradition" as Hoover suggested.[64]

As a critic, Ibn Taymiyya makes insightful comparisons and highlights contradictions in the works of philosophers and theologians, undermining their reputation as systematic and consistent. His distinction between the true *uṣūl al-dīn*, or principles of religion (based on rational understanding of the Qur'ān) and *kalām* (based on mainly philosophical theories) parallels the modern distinction between religion and philosophy of religion. Like the *mutakallimūn* before him, Ibn Taymiyya was forced to import new terms and methods from his opponents. Much in the same way as those he attacks for their use of non-Qur'ānic rationalism, Ibn Taymiyya too uses several philosophical arguments when formulating his critique of the *mutakallimūn*. Indeed, Ibn Taymiyya was accused during his lifetime of applying foreign terminology. In his defense, he argued that his incorporation of foreign terms is permitted as a matter of necessity, making an analogy to someone who has to communicate with others in their native language.[65] In some ways, Ibn Taymiyya's effort to articulate a critical approach within the traditional school is in itself more significant than his specific conclusions. He may be sometimes wrong, such as when accusing the *mutakallimūn* of holding contradictory theological positions, or inclement in his condemnations of members of other schools, but his commitment to a reconstruction of an alternative to contemporary *kalām* in the form of Qur'ānic rationalism is beyond doubt.

Ibn Taymiyya's insistence on drawing attention to Qur'ānic rationality, with its reliance on direct experience rather than on intellectual theorizing, has not been taken up by his followers, with the exception of his close student Ibn Qayyim al-Jawziyya (d. 751/1350). Mention should be made of Ibn al-Wazīr (d. 840/1436) of Yemen, who was converted from Zaydism and whose arguments for rational traditionalism and Qur'ānic theology were heavily influenced by Ibn Taymiyya.[66] In the nineteenth century another Yemenite scholar, Muḥammad al-Shawkānī (1760–1834), attempted to revive traditionalism in jurisprudence.[67] At the beginning of the 20th century, the Indian Muslim Muhammad Iqbal (1876–1938) revived the idea of Qur'ānic rationality based on experience.[68]

Among modern Muslim thinkers, the true heir of Ibn Taymiyya's traditionalist rationalism is Musa Jarullah Bigiev (1875–1949) of Kazan. While most 19th-century Muslim modernists turned to Western philosophy in order to reform Islam, Jarullah opposed this importation of philosophy. For him, philosophy corrupted the purity and clarity of Islamic thought in the past, and would cause even more confusions and divisions among Muslims in the future. The *mutakallimūn* mixed their so-called rational arguments with the true principles of belief, and their internal disagreements obscured the fundamentals of Islam. Moreover, the theologians obstructed freedom of thought by accusing each other of disbelief (*kufr*). The *mutakallimūn*, Jarullah argues, usually hold a preconceived notion grounded in their system of thought, and then use all means, including false interpretations (*ta'wīl*) of the revealed texts in order to defend that view. The truths of faith cannot be discovered through the complicated logical theories in *kalām* books, but through the simple proofs presented in the Qur'ān. The similarities with Ibn Taymiyya's thought are striking. Jarullah mentions Ibn Taymiyya several times and it is obvious that he read his works and was influenced by him.[69]

It is unfortunate that Ibn Taymiyya's works are so often relegated to the bin of strict conservatism when his approach is actually multi-layered and philosophically interesting. We should attempt to look past his harsh language and to read his works more deeply, in order to discover the contribution he made to the various disciplines of Islamic thought. It is my belief that in doing so, we will open the door for novel directions in the study of Islamic philosophical thought, and shed light on the lively intellectual environment of an age that is often regarded as a period of decline. On a final note, Ibn Taymiyya's disorganized writing style, length, verbosity, and propensity for digression and repetition probably contributed to the neglect of his philosophical thought; a clearer picture of Taymiyyan theology would only come once his encyclopaedic works have been fully edited, and thematic compilations of his writings have been produced.

Notes

* The author thanks Richard Wittmann, Nicolas Trepanier, Rachel Ghoshgarian, and Ibrahim Kalin for reading parts of the earlier draft of this chapter and offering suggestions, and is grateful to Yusuf Walsh and Khalil Abdur-Rashid for their contributions and comments. He is also thankful to Yossef Rapoport for editing the final version.

1. Ibn Taymiyya, *Majmū' fatāwā shaykh al-Islām Aḥmad b. Taymiyya*, ed. 'Abd al-Raḥmān b. Muḥammad b. Qāsim and Muḥammad b. 'Abd al-Raḥmān b. Muḥammad (Beirut: Dār 'Ālam al-Kutub, 1983), 3:339.
2. See Emmanuel Sivan, *Radical Islam: Medieval Theology and Modern Politics* (New Haven: Yale University Press, 1990).
3. See Binyamin Abrahamov, "Ibn Taymiyya on the Agreement of Reason with Tradition," *The Muslim World*, 82.3–4 (1992): 256–72; Nicholas Heer, "The Priority of Reason in the Interpretation of Scripture: Ibn Taymiyah and the Mutakallimūn," in Mustansir Mir (ed.), *Literary Heritage of Classical Islam: Arabic and Islamic Studies in Honor of James A. Bellamy* (Princeton: The Darwin Press, 1993), 181–95; Mustafa Çağrıcı, "İbn Teymiyye'nin Bakışıyla Gazzâlî-İbn Rüşd Tartışması", *İslâm Tetkikleri Dergisi*, 9 (1995): 77–126; Yahya Michot, "Vanités

intellectuelles...L'impasse des rationalisms selon le *Rejet de la contradiction* d'Ibn Taymiyyah", *Oriente Moderno*, 19.3 (2000): 597–617; idem, "A Mamluk Theologian's Commentary on Avicenna's *Risāla Adḥawiyya*", Parts I and II, *Journal of Islamic Studies* 14.2 (2003): 149–203, and 14.3 (2003): 309–63. Jon Hoover's recent study of Ibn Taymiyya's views on creation within God's perfection is a fine example of how to deal with neglected aspects of Taymiyyan thought. See Jon Hoover, "Perpetual Creativity in the Perfection of God: Ibn Taymiyya's Hadith Commentary on God's Creation of this World," *Journal of Islamic Studies* 15/3 (Sept. 2004): 287–329. More recently, see his *Ibn Taymiyya's Theodicy of Perpetual Optimism* (Leiden: Brill, 2007), and the present author's *İbn Teymiyye'nin Düşünce Metodolojisi ve Kelâmcılara Eleştirisi* (*Ibn Taymiyya's Methodology of Thought and His Criticisms of the Mutakallimun*) (Istanbul: ISAM, 2008).

4. According to Ibn Khaldūn, philosophy had become so well absorbed within *kalām* that it became impossible to differentiate between the two genres (*al-Muqaddima* ([Beirut: Dār Iḥyā' al-Turāth al-'Arabī, n.d.], 466). Cf. also A. I. Sabra, "Science and Philosophy in Medieval Islamic Theology: The Evidence of the Fourteenth Century", *Zeitschrift für Geschichte der Arabisch-Islamischen Wissenschaften*, 9 (1994): 11–23; Robert Wisnovsky, "One Aspect of the Avicennian Turn in Sunnî Theology", *Arabic Sciences and Philosophy*, 14.1 (2004): 65–100; idem, "The Nature and Scope of Arabic Philosophical Commentary in Post-classical (ca. 1100–1900 AD) Islamic Intellectual History: Some Preliminary Observations", in P. Adamson, H. Baltussen and M.W.F. Stone (eds.), *Philosophy, Science and Exegesis in Greek, Arabic and Latin Commentaries*, Vol. 2, Supplement to the Bulletin of the Institute of Classical Studies 83/1–2 (London: Institute of Classical Studies 2004), 149–191.
5. See M. Sait Özervarli, "Ibn Teymiyye", *Türkiye Diyanet Vakfi Islam Ansiklopedisi* (Istanbul: Türkiye Diyanet Vakfi, 1999), 20:405–13.
6. Ibn Rajab al-Ḥanbalī, *Kitāb dhayl 'alā ṭabaqāt al-ḥanābila*, 2 vols., ed. M. Ḥ. Fiqī (Cairo: Maṭba'at al-Sunna al-Muḥammadiyya, 1952–53), 2:133–49; 332–3. Cf. also Nicola Ziyada, *Dimashq fī 'aṣr al-Mamālīk* (Beirut: Maktabat Lubnān, 1966), 201–2; and Joseph Drory, "Ḥanbalīs of the Nablus Region in the Eleventh and Twelfth Centuries", *Asian and African Studies*, 22 (1988): 93–112.
7. Ibn Rajab, *Dhayl 'alā ṭabaqāt al-ḥanābila*, 2:394.
8. Ibn Rajab lists quite a few of Ibn Taymiyya's opinions that contradicted dominant Ḥanbalī doctrine (Ibid., 2:394, 404–5).
9. Abū al-Ḥasan al-Ash'arī, *Risāla fī istiḥsān al-khawḍ fī 'ilm al-kalām*, ed. Richard J. McCarthy (Beirut: al-Maṭba'a al-Katulikiyya, 1952), 83–4.
10. See 'Abd al-Qāhir al-Baghdādī, *Uṣūl al-dīn* (Istanbul: Maṭba'at al-dawla, 1346/1928); Abū al-Yusr al-Bazdawī, *Uṣūl al-dīn*, ed. Hans Peter Lins (Cairo: Dār Iḥyā' al-Kutub al-'Arabiyya, 1963).
11. Ibn Taymiyya, *Majmū' fatāwā*, 3:294–6.
12. See Taqī al-Dīn Ibn Taymiyya, *Dar' ta'āruḍ al-'aql wa al-naql* (hereafter *Dar'*), ed. Muḥammad Rashād Sālim, 11 vols. (Riyadh: Dār al-Kunūz al-Adabiyya, 1979), 1:159–65. For French translation of this part of Ibn Taymiyya's *Dar' ta'āruḍ*, see Yahya Michot, "Vanités intellectuelles".
13. *Majmū' fatāwā*, 3:307–8.
14. *Dar' ta'āruḍ*, 1:41. The passage refers to Q 42:21, 'Have they partners (in Godhead) who have established for them some religion without the permission of God'.
15. Abrahamov, "Ibn Taymiyya on the Agreement of Reason with Tradition," 262–3.

16. *Dar' ta'āruḍ*, 1: 41; *Majmū' fatāwā*, 3: 308–9.
17. Ibn Taymiyya uses this term here in order to distinguish theology from law, or *khabar* (report) from *'amal* (practice). See Jon Hoover, *Ibn Taymiyya's Theodicy of Perpetual Optimism* (Leiden: Brill, 2007), 24.
18. *Dar' ta'āruḍ*, 1:52.
19. Taqī al-Dīn Ibn Taymiyya, *Majmū'at tafsīr Shaykh al-islām Ibn Taymiyya*, ed. 'Abd al-Ṣamad Sharaf al-Dīn (Bombay: al-Dār al-Qayyima, 1954), 370.
20. *Dar' ta'āruḍ*, 1:242. Also see 1:276.
21. *Dar' ta'āruḍ*, 1:46–51; *Majmū' fatāwā*, 3:308–9.
22. The word *naql* is usually translated into English as tradition or scripture, but in this context it must refer to both the Qur'ān and the authentic traditions, the authoritative transmitted sources of knowledge in Islam. For the sake of convenience, it will be translated here as 'revealed knowledge'.
23. For the *mutakallimūn*'s view on the possibility of discussing theological subjects through rational methods and the necessity of reasoning to prove religious principles, see Fakhr al-Dīn al-Rāzī, *Al-Maṭālib al-'āliyya min al-'ilm al-ilāhī*, ed. Aḥmad Ḥijāzī al-Saqqā, 9 parts in 5 vols. (Beirut: Dār al-Kitāb al-'Arabī, 1407/1987), 41–52; 'Aḍud al-Dīn al-Ījī, *al-Mawāqif fī 'ilm al-kalām* (Beirut: 'Ālam al-Kutub, n.d.), 21–34; Sa'd al-Dīn al-Taftāzānī, *Sharḥ al-Maqāṣid*, ed. 'Abd al-Raḥmān 'Umayra (Beirut: 'Ālam al-Kutub, 1998), 262–70.
24. For quotations from various *kalām* books pertaining to the priority of reason in case of a possible conflict with scripture, together with some of Ibn Taymiyya's responses, see Nicholas Heer, "The Priority of Reason in the Interpretation of Scripture", 181–7.
25. Outlining the above approach of the *mutakallimūn* that was formulated by al-Rāzī, Ibn Taymiyya claims that earlier scholars, such as al-Ghazālī and Abū Bakr Ibn al-'Arabī, applied a similar rule, following the example of al-Juwaynī and al-Bāqillānī (*Dar' ta'āruḍ*, 1:4–6). Ibn Taymiyya also mentions one of his earliest (now lost) books on the same subject written as a critical commentary of al-Rāzī's *Muḥaṣṣal* (Ibid., 1: 22).
26. *Dar' ta'āruḍ*, 1: 198–200.
27. *Dar' ta'āruḍ*, 1: 28.
28. *Majmū' fatāwā*, 16: 470–1.
29. *Dar' ta'āruḍ*, 1: 170–1; cf. Heer, "The Priority of Reason", 191.
30. *Dar' ta'āruḍ*, 1: 100 and 133.
31. Taqī al-Dīn Ibn Taymiyya, *al-Istiqāma*, ed. M. Rashād Sālim (Riyadh: Jāmi'at al-Imām Muḥammad Su'ūd, 1983), 1: 47 ff.
32. *Dar' ta'āruḍ*, 1: 52–3, 192–4, 229.
33. *Dar' ta'āruḍ*, 1:79. See also 1:90–1.
34. *Dar' ta'āruḍ*, 1:147–8, 155–6.
35. *Majmū' fatāwā*, 3:339.
36. *Majmū' fatāwā*, 13:277.
37. *Majmū' fatāwā*, 5:35–7 and 17:361–70; *Dar' ta'āruḍ*, 1:14–20 and 5:380–4. Also see Muḥammad al-Sayyid al-Jalayand, *al-Imām Ibn Taymiyya wa-mawqifuhu min qaḍiyyat al-ta'wīl* (Cairo: Dār al-Qibā', 2000), 137–211.
38. *Majmū' fatāwā*, 3:3–4, 25–7.
39. *Dar' ta'āruḍ*, 1:201–8.
40. *Majmū' fatāwā*, 2: 12.
41. *Dar' ta'āruḍ*, 1: 354–67; *Majmū' fatāwā*, 18: 222–30. On the differences between Ibn Taymiyya's views on creation and those of the philosophers and theologians, see

also Hoover, "Perpetual Creativity on the Perfection of God", 293–5; Husâm Muhî Eldîn al-Alousi, *The Problem of Creation in Islamic Thought: Qur'ān, Hadith, Commentaries, and Kalām* (Baghdad: The National Printing and Publishing Co., 1968), 95–6, 185–6.

42. *Majmū'at tafsīr*, 210–2.
43. *Dar' ta'āruḍ*, 1:38–9; *Majmū' fatāwā*, 3:303–4. For detailed discussion of the *ḥudūth* argument see William Lane Craig, *The Kalām Cosmological Argument* (New York: Barnes and Noble Books, 1979).
44. *Majmū' fatāwā*, 2:22.
45. *Majmū' fatāwā*, 1:48–9.
46. *Dar' ta'āruḍ*, 8:482.
47. *Majmū' fatāwā*, 2:70–4.
48. For the various versions of the tradition see Bukhārī 1270, al-Janā'iz: idhā aslama al-ṣabī wa-māta; Bukhārī 1296, al-Janā'iz: mā qīla fī awlād al-mushrikīn; Muslim 4803, al-Qadar: ma'nā kull mawlūd yūlad 'alā al-fiṭra; Abu Da'ūd 4091, al-Sunna: fī dharārī al-mushrikīn; Ahmad b. Ḥanbal 8949. Hadith references are given according to the *tarqīm al-'ālamiyya* system used at http:/hadith.al-islam.com/.
49. Muṭahhar b. Ṭāhir al-Maqdisī, *al-Bad' wa-al-ta'rīkh*, ed. Clément Huart (Baghdad, Maktabat al-Muthannā, nd.), 1: 59–60; Abū Ḥāmid al-Ghazālī, *Iḥyā' 'ulūm al-dīn* (Cairo: al-Maṭba'a al-'Uthmāniyya al-Miṣriyya, 1933), 1: 93–4. On the use of *fiṭra* as alternative to rational proofs for the existence of God see also Muḥammed Ḥasan Āl Yāsīn, *Allāh bayna al-fiṭra wa-al-dalīl* (Beirut: Dār al-Maktabat al-Ḥayāt, 1972).
50. Henri Laoust refers to Ibn Taymiyya's use of *fiṭra* as our innate and universal belief in Him ("l'innéisme et l'universalité de notre croyance en lui"). See Henri Laoust, *Essai sur les doctrines sociales et politiques de Taḳī-d-Dīn Aḥmad b. Taimīya, canoniste ḥanbalite né à Ḥarrān en 661/1262, mort à Damas en 728/1328* (Cairo: Imprimerie de l'institut français d'archéologie orientale, 1939), 153 n1. See also, in a reference to Laoust, Ssekamanya Siraje Abdullah, "Ibn Taymiyya's Theological Approach Illustrated: On the Essence (Dhāt) and the Attributes (Ṣifāt) of Allah", *al-Shajarah* 9.1 (2004): 50–1. For a comprehensive study on the concept of *fiṭra* among Muslim thinkers, see G. Gobillot, *La fitra- La conception originelle- ses interpretations et functions chez les penseurs musulmans* (Le Caire: Institut français d'archeologie orientale, 2000); and idem., "L'épitre du discours sur la fitra (Risala fi-l-kalam 'ala-l-fitra) de Taqi-l-din Ahmad ibn Taymiya (661/1262–728/1328)", *Annales Islamologiques*, 20 (1984):29ff. See also Livnat Holtzman, "Human Choice, Divine Guidance and the Fiṭra Tradition: The Use of Hadith in Theological Treatises by Ibn Taymiyya and Ibn Qayyim al-Jawziyya", in this volume.
51. Timothy F. Lull (ed.), *Martin Luther's Basic Theological Writings* (Minneapolis: Fortress Press, 1989), 13–20. For another comparison between Ibn Taymiyya and Martin Luther, focusing on their similar views on the place of saints in religion, see Niels Henrik Olesen, "Etude comparée des idées d'Ibn Taymiyya (1263–1328) et de Martin Luther (1483–1546) sur le culte des saints", *Revue des études islamiques* 50 (1982): 175–206.
52. See John Calvin, *Institutes of the Christian Religion*, tr. Ford Lewis Battles (Philadelphia: The Westminster Press, 1975), 1: 43–4.
53. For discussions on the topic see John Hick, *Arguments for the Existence of God* (London Macmillan, 1970), 101–5. And for the details of the same debate between

R. Swinburne and D. Z. Phillips, see Richard Messer, *Does God's Existence Need Proof?* (Oxford: Oxford University Press, 1993).

54. On this view and various approaches regarding the issue of reason and belief in contemporary discussions in philosophy of religion, see Alvin Plantinga, "Reason and Belief in God", in Alvin Plantinga and Nicholas Wolterstorff (eds.), *Faith and Rationality* (Notre Dame, Ind.: University of Notre Dame Press, 1991), 16–93.
55. *Majmūʿat tafsīr*, 269 and 277.
56. *Majmūʿ fatāwā*, 2: 39–40; Ibn Taymiyya, *Kitāb al-Īmān*, ed. Muḥammad Zabīdī (Beirut: Dār al-Kitāb al-ʿArabī, 1414/1993), 126–7, 370–1.
57. See for example Q 17: 99; Q 36: 78–82; Q 22: 5.
58. *Dar' taʿāruḍ*, 1: 30–5; *Majmūʿ fatāwā*, 3: 298–9.
59. For the Ashʿarite view see al-Qāḍī Abū Bakr al-Bāqillānī, *Kitāb Tamhīd al-awā'il wa-talkhīṣ al-dalā'il*, ed. ʿImad al-Dīn Aḥmad Ḥaydar (Beirut: Mu'assasat al-Kutub al-Thaqāfiyya, 1987), 50–2; Fakhr al-Dīn al-Rāzī, *Al-Arbaʿīn fī uṣūl al-dīn*, ed. Aḥmad Ḥijāzī al-Saqqā, 2 parts in 1 vol. (Cairo: Maktabat al-Kulliyāt al-Azhariyya, 1986), 1: 350–4; Saʿd al-Dīn al-Taftāzānī, *Sharḥ al-Maqāṣid*, 4: 301–2.
60. Ibn Taymiyya, *Majmūʿat al-rasā'il al-kubrā*, 5 vols. (Beirut: Dār al-Kutub al-ʿIlmiyya, 1403/1983), 5: 337, 343–4; *Minhāj al-sunna*, 1: 145–6.
61. *Majmūʿat tafsīr*, 235–8; *Majmūʿat al-rasā'il*, 5: 286–8; See a similar view in Ibn Qayyim al-Jawziyya, *Shifā' al-ʿalīl fī masā'il al-qaḍā' wa-al-qadar wa-al-ḥikma wa-al-taʿlīl* (Beirut: Dār al-Fikr, 1988), 206–16.
62. *Dar' taʿāruḍ*, 1: 81–6; *Minhāj al-sunna*, 2: 294–302.
63. Daniel Gimaret, "Théories de l'acte humain dans l'école Ḥanbalite," *Bulletin d'études orientales* 29 (1977): 156–178. For Ibn al Qayyim's similar approach see Irmeli Perho, "Man Chooses his Destiny: Ibn Qayyim al-Jawziyya's Views on Predestination", *Islam and Christian-Muslim Relations*, 12.1 (2001): 61–70. Another example of Ibn Taymiyya's original views and disagreement with the majority of scholars is his approach towards the doctrine of *ʿiṣma*, which is dealt by Shahab Ahmed in "Ibn Taymiyyah and the Satanic Verses", *Studia Islamica* 87.2 (1998): 86–90.
64. Alousi, *The Problem of Creation*, 85; Hoover, "Perpetual Creativity," 194.
65. *Dar' taʿāruḍ*, 1: 43.
66. See Ibn al-Wazīr, *Īthār al-ḥaqq ʿalā al-khalq* (Beirut: Dār al-Kutub al-ʿIlmiyya, 1983) and idem., *Tarjīḥ asālīb al-Qur'ān ʿalā asālīb al-Yūnān* (Beirut: Dār al-Kutub al-ʿIlmiyya, 1984).
67. See Bernard Haykel, *Revival and Reform in Islam: The Legacy of Muhammad al-Shawkani* (Cambridge: Cambridge University Press, 2003).
68. Muhammad Iqbal, *The Reconstruction of Religious Thought in Islam*, ed. M. Saeed Sheikh (Lahore: Iqbal Academy, 1989), 11–12.
69. For the life and works of Jarullah see Mehmet Görmez, *Musa Carullah Bigiyef* (Ankara: Türkiye Diyanet Vakfi, 1994); Ahmet Kanlidere, *Reform within Islam: the Tajdid and Jadid Movement among the Kazan Tatars (1809–1917). Conciliation or Conflict?* (Istanbul: Eren Yayıncılık, 1997); idem., *Kadimle Cedit Arasında Musa Carullah: Hayatı, Eserleri, Fikirleri* (Istanbul: Dergah Yayınları, 2005).

Ibn Taymiyya's 'Theology of the Sunna' and his Polemics with the Ash'arites*

Racha el Omari

Introduction

Henri Laoust characterized Ibn Taymiyya's theology as one of conciliation, in so far as it was proclaimed by Ibn Taymiyya himself to be in the just middle between extreme theological positions, such as *ta'ṭīl*, divesting God of his attributes, and *tashbīh*, anthropomorphism.[1] Ibn Taymiyya constantly formulated this theology of the middle ground in relation to other theological schools, and indeed it is through Ibn Taymiyya's polemics with his opponents among the *mutakallimūn* that his own theological positions are articulated.[2] Examination of Ibn Taymiyya's polemics is thus instrumental in deciphering the very formulation of what he held to be the correct way, namely for understanding what I would call his 'theology of the Sunna.'[3] Crucial to this theology is Ibn Taymiyya's definition of the Sunna and his treatment of the *salaf*, which are topics for future investigation both with regard to his relationship to modern Salafi scholarship as well as with regard to classical Ḥanbalism.[4]

The present paper examines Ibn Taymiyya's theology of the Sunna through his polemics with the Ash'arites in his work *Dar' ta'āruḍ al-'aql wa-al-naql* ("Averting the Contention between Reason and Scripture").[5] *Dar' ta'āruḍ* was composed some years after his Damascus trial (705/1306),[6] probably between 713–717/1313–1317.[7] Ibn Taymiyya wrote this work to refute a later Ash'arite[8] principle governing the relationship between reason and scripture which gives reason precedence over scripture. Focusing on Ibn Taymiyya's polemics with the Ash'arites, and in particular on his presentation of al-Ash'arī himself, I will proceed to identify first what constitutes the Sunna for Ibn Taymiyya, then his principles of hermeneutics, and finally his position on the proof for the existence of God and the divine attributes.[9]

The polemics with the Ash'arites, rather than other opponents, are especially conducive to an understanding of Ibn Taymiyya's theology. Ibn Taymiyya's theological opponents included the Mu'tazilites, the Jahmites and the Twelver Shi'a, to name but a few, but it was the Ash'arites who were his most immediate intellectual and political opponents. Unlike the Mu'tazilites, whose doctrines represented a threat to Ibn Taymiyya only in so far as they survived among the Twelver Shi'a, most importantly in the works of al-Ḥillī (d. 726/1325), the Ash'arites were the most vibrant, independent, and influential theological school in 13th and 14th-century Egypt and Syria.[10] They included followers of the prominent late Ash'arite Fakhr al-Dīn al-Rāzī (d. 606/1209), as well as of the monist Ibn al-'Arabī (d. 638/1240), and were among the members of the tribunal assigned to conduct the Damascus trial. The most noteworthy of the Ash'arites on this tribunal was Najm al-Dīn Ibn Ṣaṣrā (d. 723/1323), who studied under Maḥmūd al-Iṣfahānī (d. 688/1289), himself a student of Fakhr al-Dīn al-Rāzī.[11] The Ash'arites were not only powerful opponents, but they also made equal claims to orthodoxy, namely to being themselves *ahl al-sunna*.

However, for Ibn Taymiyya the theologies of al-Ash'arī and of his followers were separate and distinct. This distinction was highlighted by Ibn Taymiyya during his Damascus trial, which was in many ways the defining moment of his theological and political career. In this trial, Ibn Taymiyya was accused of upholding anthropomorphism (*tajsīm*) and rejecting Ash'arite interpretation (*ta'wīl*) of scriptural divine attributes. In defence of the orthodoxy of his position on divine attributes, which rejects both divesting God of his attributes (*ta'ṭīl*) and anthropomorphism (*tashbīh*), Ibn Taymiyya appealed to the authority of al-Ash'arī as a representative of the *salaf*. He denied that al-Ash'arī ever accepted the interpretation (*ta'wīl*) of verses on divine attributes and states that it was only his followers who embraced that position.[12] To make his point, he refers to al-Ash'arī's *al-Ibāna 'an uṣūl al-diyāna* as quoted in Ibn 'Asākir's (d. 571/1176) *Tabyīn kadhib al-muftarī fīmā nusiba ilā Abī al-Ḥasan al-Ash'arī*, written in vindication of al-Ash'arī's orthodoxy against Ibn 'Asākir's non-Ash'arite Shāfi'ī contemporaries.[13] In making his case before his Ash'arite audience, Ibn Taymiyya selectively cites the works that emphasize the traditionalist side of al-Ash'arī, ignoring the works in which he applies *kalām*, as in the *Kitāb al-luma'*.[14] By doing so, Ibn Taymiyya claims al-Ash'arī's legacy for himself, denying his Ash'arite adversaries their generally accepted theological lineage.

This was not the only occasion in which Ibn Taymiyya resorted to the authority of al-Ash'arī to counter the Ash'arite position. He makes similar use of al-Ash'arī in his refutation of the Ash'arite conception of divine attributes in *al-Ḥamawiyya al-kubrā*, *'Arsh al-Raḥmān*, *al-Qā'ida al-Marākishiyya*, and *Sharḥ al-'aqīda al-Isfahāniyya*.[15] However, Ibn Taymiyya's characterization of al-Ash'arī as a traditionalist is not his final word on al-Ash'arī. While in his trial we see Ibn Taymiyya referring only to al-Ash'arī's *al-Ibāna*, in which al-Ash'arī sought to win the approval of the Ḥanbalīs by attacking the Mu'tazilites and Jahmites, Ibn Taymiyya was also well aware of his *kalām* oriented works, such as *al-Luma' fī al-radd 'alā ahl al-bida'* and *Risāla ilā ahl al-thaghr*. In different contexts, Ibn Taymiyya cites these works too, fully acknowledging, and capitalizing on, the tension between al-Ash'arī's traditionalism and his *kalām* methodology.

Al-Ash'arī and the Sunna

For Ibn Taymiyya, the right path, the path of *ahl al-sunna*, is not the monopoly of Aḥmad b. Ḥanbal (d. 241/855); Ibn Ḥanbal is only as significant as any other figure among the *salaf* whose profession of faith is based on the Book and the Hadith. It was the political context in which Ibn Ḥanbal expressed his faith, as well as his trial during the episode later to be known as the *miḥna* (833–849), which made Ibn Ḥanbal, in Ibn Taymiyya's view, a leading Imam of *ahl al-sunna*.[16] Because of the trial by which Ibn Ḥanbal was tested, his prevalence (*ẓuhūr*) remains essential for any polemical presentation of the doctrine of *ahl al-sunna*. As Ibn Taymiyya sees it, the way of the *salaf* was not created by Ibn Ḥanbal but was exemplified by his enactment of its ideals through the circumstances of his life. After Ibn Ḥanbal *ahl al-sunna* split into two groups, thereby adding to the old polarized world of *ahl al-sunna* and their Jahmite opponents a third group, one led by Ibn Kullāb (d. 241/855). Ibn Kullāb relied on both scripture and the Jahmite-Mu'tazilite method of reasoning.[17] This third path, Ibn Taymiyya adds, was rejected and criticized by Ibn Ḥanbal.[18]

In attempting to identify the elements of al-Ash'arī's system that are from the Sunna and those that are not, Ibn Taymiyya often calls attention to elements from Ibn Kullāb's theology in al-Ash'arī's system. In part, Ibn Taymiyya presents the similarities between al-Ashʿarī and Ibn Kullāb in order to taint the former by his association with the latter. For example, Ibn Taymiyya points out their common view that God's volition (*mashīʾa*) and power to act (*qudra*) are not attributes of His essence but of His deeds.[19] But Ibn Taymiyya is also concerned with isolating the elements of the Sunna in al-Ashʿarī's thought, and recognizes the differences in their doctrines, particularly on the nature of the Qurʾān. While Ibn Kullāb upholds that the Qurʾān is a reproduction (*ḥikāya*), for al-Ashʿarī it is an entity (*maʿnā*) that is subsistent (*qāʾim*) in God's essence;[20] clearly in this case al-Ashʿarī's view on the Qurʾān is closer to the *ahl al-sunna* position as understood by Ibn Taymiyya. Ibn Taymiyya's presentation of their doctrines does not lead us to think that he saw an actual historical affiliation between the two figures. What counts for Ibn Taymiyya is the doctrinal similarity, which is enough to make an association between two figures despite the lack of actual direct contact between them.

Although highlighting affinities between al-Ashʿarī and Ibn Kullāb, Ibn Taymiyya also acknowledges al-Ashʿarī's self-identification as a follower of Ibn Ḥanbal. This association is so real for Ibn Taymiyya that he adds that Abū Bakr al-Bāqillānī (d. 403/1013), one of the leading disciples of al-Ashʿarī, would sometimes sign with the *nisba* "al-Ḥanbalī" in his correspondence.[21] Clearly this remark is mentioned for its dramatic resonance, since actual affiliation with a specific school, in this case Ḥanbalī versus Ashʿarite, is not what matters for Ibn Taymiyya; what carries weight are the doctrinal similarities. Ibn Taymiyya also refers to al-Ashʿarī's statements in *al-Ibāna*, *al-Maqālāt*, and his no longer extant *Mūjaz*, in which al-Ashʿarī relates how he gave up the way of the Muʿtazilites and affiliated himself with Ibn Ḥanbal.[22] The quotations are carefully chosen, since in *al-Ibāna* al-Ashʿarī strives to convince the staunch Ḥanbalī leader al-Barbahārī (d. 329/941) of his orthodoxy.[23] Ibn Taymiyya intends here to impress on his audience (including his contemporary Ashʿarite opponents) the importance of Ibn Ḥanbal as the representative figure of the doctrine of the *salaf*. By implication, Ibn Taymiyya also recognizes al-Ashʿarī as an important figure of the *ahl al-sunna*, whose support of Ibn Ḥanbal is valuable in its own right.

To consolidate al-Ashʿarī's credentials as a man of the Sunna, and specifically as a follower of Ibn Ḥanbal, Ibn Taymiyya enlists the evidence of early followers of Ibn Ḥanbal who praise al-Ashʿarī in their works. These figures include Abū Bakr b. ʿAbd al-ʿAzīz, better known as Ghulām al-Khallāl (d. 363/974), a contemporary of al-Barbahārī whose work did not survive:

> Some of the earliest followers (*al-qudamāʾ min aṣḥāb*) of Aḥmad, such as Abū Bakr b. ʿAbd al-ʿAzīz, Abū al-Ḥasan al-Tamīmī and their likes, used to mention him [al-Ashʿarī] in their books in the way they would mention someone who agreed with the Sunna on the whole (*fī al-jumla*). They also noted what he had mentioned about the incoherence of the Muʿtazilites.[24]

Ibn Taymiyya does not provide any detail on the context or the titles of the works in which this praise is reported. But he clearly goes out of his way to rehabilitate al-Ashʿarī's reception among the early Ḥanbalīs and remains silent about al-Barbahārī's antagonism to al-Ashʿarī.[25] Al-Barbahārī's disciple Ibn Baṭṭa (d. 387/997), known for his stance against al-Ashʿarī, is only mentioned by Ibn Taymiyya for contradicting the principles of the Kullābiyya, with no reference to his specific opposition to al-Ashʿarī.[26]

In other words, despite pointing out some characteristics of al-Ashʿarī as a follower of Ibn Kullāb, Ibn Taymiyya acknowledges al-Ashʿarī's claim to be a follower of Ibn Ḥanbal. No doubt, in Ibn Taymiyya's eyes, al-Ashʿarī's affiliation with *ahl al-sunna* was compromised by his practice of *kalām* methods, but this does not hinder Ibn Taymiyya from considering him to be closer to the path of Ibn Ḥanbal than some later Ḥanbalīs, including Ibn ʿAqīl (d. 513/1119) and Ibn al-Jawzī (d. 597/1200).[27] Al-Ashʿarī's relationship to the Sunna is set along a scale for evaluating the closeness of any particular thinker or group to the Sunna. Despite its hierarchy and its positing of an absolute Sunna, this scale also allows some of Ibn Taymiyya's opponents into the camp of the Sunna, at least to a degree:

> Whoever is closer to the path of the message and the *salaf* is also closer to accepting the commensurability of purely rational knowledge with the correctly transmitted one (*muwāfaqāt ṣarīḥ al-maʿqūl li ṣarīḥ al-manqūl*). Therefore, although Abū Bakr [al-Bāqillānī] is closer to accepting the commensurability of purely rational knowledge with the correctly transmitted in matters of the principles of religion (*uṣūl al-dīn*)—not in the principles of jurisprudence—than Abū al-Maʿālī [al-

> Juwaynī] and his followers, al-Ashʿarī is closer to that than him. Abū Muḥammad Ibn Kullāb is closer to that [the commensurability of rational and transmitted knowledge] than Abū al-Ḥasan [al-Ashʿarī].[28] The *salaf* and the Imams are closer to that than Ibn Kullāb. Thus, whoever is closer to the Prophet would be more worthy of rational and transmitted knowledge. Because the speech of the infallible [the Prophet] is the truth in which there is no falsehood.[29]

In this passage Ibn Taymiyya's two essential premises are made explicit: One, reason is commensurable with revealed truth, which includes the Qur'ān and the Sunna. Second, the *salaf* understand the commensurability of reason and revelation better than anyone else. Hence it follows that whoever is closer to the path of the *salaf* is also closer to the recognition of the commensurability of reason and revealed truth. Ibn Taymiyya provides no justification for his two premises, or for the way he takes them to be the yardstick by which to judge any Muslim's correct belief. At the same time, he does show some flexibility in his willingness to include "degrees" of proximity to the path of the *salaf*. In other words, while this scale reflects Ibn Taymiyya's certainty of the commensurate nature of reason and scripture, it also offers his opponents a place among *ahl al-sunna*. They are judged by their distance from the *salaf*, by how much of the Sunna they preserve and how much *bidʿa* (innovation) they introduce.

Ibn Taymiyya's manner of categorizing theologians does not reflect a historical lineage between them, as has been noted by van Ess in his work on Ibn Kullāb.[30] This illustrates a crucial point about how Ibn Taymiyya's polemical method is grounded in his theology. For Ibn Taymiyya the ideal of all theology is to reflect the Sunna, hence any theological system is measured by the extent to which it reflects the Sunna. This also entails acknowledging whatever element of the Sunna this theology preserves. Proximity to the Sunna, especially among non-Ḥanbalīs, is both a tribute and a polemical tool. Thus Ibn Taymiyya's recognition of al-Ashʿarī's closeness to the Sunna provides Ibn Taymiyya a weapon with which he demonstrates the differences that separate his contemporary Ashʿarite opponents from al-Ashʿarī himself. It should be pointed out, however, that by accepting al-Ashʿarī's self-identification as a follower of the Sunna, Ibn Taymiyya was more generous towards him than other Ḥanbalīs had been, even if this generosity had ulterior polemical purposes.

Ibn Taymiyya was not only more charitable towards al-Ash'arī than earlier Ḥanbalīs, but also more than some Shāfi'īs. He refers in several instances to passages from Ibn 'Asākir's *Tabyīn kadhib al-muftarī*, which was written in order to defend al-Ash'arī against those Shāfi'īs who argued that *kalām* theology was condemned by the founder of their school. Ibn Taymiyya concurs with Ibn 'Asākir, adding that al-Shāfi'ī condemned the Jahmite and Mu'tazilite *kalām*, the kind that existed during al-Shāfi'ī's lifetime, not the one practiced by al-Ash'arī.[31]

Reason and Scripture

We have seen how for Ibn Taymiyya the path of the Sunna entails accepting the commensurability of reason-verified knowledge (*ma'qūl*) with correctly transmitted religious knowledge (*manqūl*). One important consequence of Ibn Taymiyya's doctrine of the commensurability of rational and transmitted knowledge is his objection to any hierarchy of knowledge that would put reason ahead of scripture. He objects to the possibility of a conflict between reason and scripture and of the superiority of the former over the latter. Indeed, this objection lies at the heart of his disagreement with the later Ash'arites, and it prompted him to write *Dar' ta'āruḍ al-'aql wa-al-naql*, dedicated to refuting the general law (*al-qānūn al-kullī*) of Fakhr al-Dīn al-Rāzī.

Ibn Taymiyya perceived this law as underlying the methodology of many of his opponents—not only of al-Rāzī, who was the first to formulate it—but also of the earlier al-Ghazālī (d. 505/1111).[32] It not only places reason ahead of scripture as a source for religious knowledge but also at its foundation, so that whenever there is conflict between the former and the latter, reason must have the upper hand and scripture has to be interpreted allegorically so as to correspond to it. According to this law, scripture has its foundation in reason ("*al-'aql aṣl al-naql*"). The premises of this law are laid out at the beginning of *Dar' ta'āruḍ*[33], proceeding as follows: When rational and scriptural proofs conflict, there are three options. One, both proofs are accepted, but that is impossible because two contradictions cannot co-exist. Second, scriptural proofs are given priority, but that is impossible because reason is the principle (*aṣl*) of scripture. If we doubt the principle of something, then that of which it is the principle also becomes uncertain. Finally, this is resolved by acknowledging that reason should be given priority over scripture, since it is the foundation of scripture. Thus, an ambiguous verse would be either interpreted metaphorically or entrusted (*yufawwaḍ*) to God. According to Ibn Taymiyya, this principle is formulated and explicitly adhered to by later Ashʿarites, and is also followed by philosophers and monist (*ittiḥādī*) Sufis. In other words, as far as Ibn Taymiyya is concerned, whoever assumes that "true" reason can contradict scripture, and then gives precedence to what he mistakenly believes to be reason ahead of scripture, is a follower of this law.

It is important to note how Ibn Taymiyya posits that his opponents are not only the later Ashʿarites but everyone whose method abides by this general law, even without explicitly invoking it. He divides those who give priority to reason over scripture into two groups. The first group is that of *ahl al-tabdīl*, those who substitute a false meaning for the true meaning, and they include the philosophers, the *mutakallimūn* in general and the Ashʿarites in particular. As an example, Ibn Taymiyya introduces their views on the metaphorical interpretation of divine attributes, which he had already rejected in his earlier works, arguing that they are known solely through scripture (Qur'ān and Hadith).[34] The second group is the *ahl al-tajhīl*, who deems the prophets ignorant of the true nature of divine attributes. Ibn Taymiyya does not name proponents of this latter group, but it is clear that he is referring to anyone who subscribes to an esoteric interpretation of the text.[35]

Ibn Taymiyya rejects the claim that reason should be given priority over scripture and anything coming from the Prophet.[36] In order to do so, he sets out to deny the possibility of *al-muʿāriḍ al-ʿaqlī* (rational objection) to scripture, and he does so in two ways. First, he states that he who believes in God is also certain of what God relates in scripture and that anything that contradicts what is related by God could not be a real proof.[37] Second, he argues that the rational objection must be invalid, since it requires interpreting the verses of the Qur'ān metaphorically. Such interpretation (*ta'wīl*) is invalid since any ambiguous verse was made clear by the Prophet, as God would not neglect to provide his servants with an explanation of these verses.[38]

The Proof of the Existence of God and the Divine Attributes

As we turn to Ibn Taymiyya's polemical debates with the Ash'arites regarding the proof of the existence of God and the nature of the divine attributes, we see him apply his two essential premises regarding the concept of the Sunna and the commensurability of reason and revelation. In both cases, the figure of al-Ash'arī plays an important role in Ibn Taymiyya's refutation of the later Ash'arite positions.

In the introduction to *Dar' ta'āruḍ*, after laying out the two categories of opponents who use *al-qānūn al-kullī* (as outlined above), Ibn Taymiyya digresses to answer an inquiry from Egypt. This inquiry is about whether it is permissible to engage in theological reasoning regarding the principles of religion when those principles have not been handed down by the Prophet.[39] Ibn Taymiyya rejects the premise of this inquiry, namely, that a principle of religion that is not addressed by the Prophet can *exist* at all,[40] indicating that such an assumption had only come about because heresy has flourished.[41] Like al-Rāzī's *al-qānūn al-kullī*, such assumption presupposes a rational principle that does not overlap with the sayings of the Prophet. Ibn Taymiyya then gives examples of false principles of religion, including Mu'tazilite and Ash'arite doctrines, such as the denial of divine attributes, God's decree, and the proof for the temporal creation of the world by means of the temporal creation of accidents.[42]

It is here that Ibn Taymiyya quotes al-Ash'arī again in his capacity as a *mutakallim* in order to refute *kalām*'s false principles of religion in general, and to criticize the *kalām* proof for the existence of God in particular. Ibn Taymiyya describes al-Ash'arī as one of the skilful (*ḥudhdhāq*) among *ahl al-kalām*,[43] precisely because he acknowledges that the method of this proof is not that of the prophets and their followers, and that it is a false method (*bāṭila*).[44] The *kalām* method that Ibn Taymiyya has in mind, and which he refutes elsewhere, is the one adopted by later Ash'arites starting with al-Juwaynī (d. 478/1085). Ibn Taymiyya briefly summarizes it as follows: First, a body is never exempt (*la yakhlū*) from accidents which are attributes. Second, whatever is not free from attributes, which are temporally created (*muḥdath*), is itself temporally created, since the attributes that are accidents have to be temporally created. That which is not exempt from the genus (*jins*) of temporal createdness is temporally created because it is impossible to have an infinite regress of temporally created bodies.[45] However, this Ash'arite argument that Ibn Taymiyya relates and argues against here and in other works is *not* identical with the Mu'tazilite version of the argument from accidents that al-Ash'arī refutes in his *Kitāb al-Ibāna*.[46] Specifically, the Mu'tazilite argument refuted by al-Ash'arī does not have a final part, which was later introduced by al-Juwaynī in refutation of the philosophers' doctrine of the eternity of the world.[47] The blurring of the distinction between the early and later Ash'arite argument here is clearly polemical. Ibn Taymiyya was well aware of their difference, since he quotes al-Juwaynī's critique of this early Mu'tazilite argument in his *al-Irshād ilā qawāṭi' al-adilla*.[48] But in his polemics against the *kalām* proof for the existence of God, Ibn Taymiyya prefers to isolate al-Ash'arī in one camp, and to group the Ash'arite Juwaynī and the Mu'tazilites in another.

When using al-Ash'arī's authority to refute the *kalām* argument for the existence of God, Ibn Taymiyya not only blurs the difference between the proof of the Mu'tazilites and that of later Ash'arites, but also fails to present al-Ash'arī's full position. In fact, al-Ash'arī does not always condemn the early *kalām* argument, namely the Mu'tazilite argument from accidents. Although Ibn Taymiyya cites al-Ash'arī as criticizing this proof, his citation of al-Ash'arī's statement is only part of al-Ash'arī's entire position. In a more comprehensive passage, al-Ash'arī does not dismiss the *kalām* proof categorically, but rather recognizes its validity, with the qualification that it does not represent the method used by the prophets to prove the existence of God.[49] This additional information, namely al-Ash'arī's recognition of the validity of the *kalām* proof despite its absence from scripture, is not cited here. Clearly, Ibn Taymiyya is citing al-Ash'arī selectively as part of his polemics with his immediate Ash'arite audience.

In a later passage of *Dar' ta'āruḍ*, however, Ibn Taymiyya does quote al-Ash'arī's complete stance on the Mu'tazilite proof for the existence of God, referring to his *Risāla ilā ahl al-thaghr*.[50] Here al-Ash'arī is described as holding two separate positions on this proof. On the one hand, he condemns *ahl al-kalām*'s proof of the existence of God as contrary to the method of the Prophet and the *salaf*, and even pronounces it a prohibited innovation (*bid'a muḥarrama*). On the other hand, al-Ash'arī is listed among a group who hold that this proof is unnecessary and its adoption prohibited because it leads to pitfalls, while still accepting it to be valid in itself. It is noteworthy that Ibn Taymiyya refrains from commenting on al-Ash'arī's double position here; he limits himself to presenting these two views of al-Ash'arī among other theological positions on the *kalām* proof of the existence of God. Thus, al-Ash'arī appears both under the category of "the generality of scholars" (*'āmmat ahl al-'ilm*) and under that of "those who consider this method unnecessary" (*al-qā'ilūna bi-anna hādhihi al-ṭarīqa laysat wājiba*). In this heresiographical context, Ibn Taymiyya does not mind presenting the double position of al-Ash'arī as it is, without any direct criticism, since here al-Ash'arī's views have no immediate bearing on his polemics. It is only in the polemical context that Ibn Taymiyya chooses to refer to the insider authority of al-Ash'arī as a *mutakallim* to refute the *kalām* argument for the existence of God.

Similar use of al- Ash'arī's authority can be seen in Ibn Taymiyya's discussion of the Qur'ānic divine attributes of elevation (*'uluww*) and resting on the throne (*istiwā'*). Here, again, Ibn Taymiyya differentiates between the position of al-Ash'arī, along with Ibn Kullāb and his follower al-Ḥārith al-Muḥāsibī (d. 243/857), and that of the later Ash'arites, specifically the followers of al-Juwaynī's doctrine as developed in his *al-Irshād*.[51] Al-Ash'arī still distinguishes between the two attributes of elevation (*'uluww*) and resting on the throne (*istiwā'*), considering the first to be knowable through both reason and scripture while the second is knowable only through scripture. For Ibn Taymiyya, al-Ash'arī's position on divine attributes sets him apart from the Mu'tazilites, who deny knowing scriptural attributes except through a rational, metaphorical interpretation. Ibn Taymiyya explicitly equates this Mu'tazilite divestment of divine attributes (*ta'ṭīl*) with al-Juwaynī's position on divine attributes in his *al-Irshād*. Al-Juwaynī, in Ibn Taymiyya's account, was lured by the Mu'tazilite position and distanced himself from the path of al-Ash'arī and the leaders of his immediate followers (*a'immat aṣḥābihi*).[52]

Moreover, Ibn Taymiyya recognizes another position by al-Juwaynī on this same doctrinal question in his *al-Risāla al-Niẓāmiyya*, a position which Ibn Taymiyya considers to be close to the views of al-Ash'arī and the *salaf*. While in *al-Irshād* al-Juwaynī deems the interpretation of anthropomorphic verses in the Qur'ān necessary, in his *al-Risāla al-Niẓāmiyya* he holds it reprehensible and adopts the consensus of the *salaf* who accept these verses without interpretation.[53] For Ibn Taymiyya, al-Juwaynī follows in this instance al-Ashʿarī and his immediate followers, whose method is summarized as follows:

> They [al-Ashʿarī and his followers] adduce arguments by way of reason to support what is already confirmed by scripture. [For them] scripture is what is to be relied upon in matters of the principles of religion, while reason is only a supporter and helper to scripture.[54]

Al-Ashʿarī and his followers accept the attributes describing God's hands and face as they are presented in the Qur'ān without interpretation. Ibn Taymiyya wishes to absolve al-Ashʿarī of any ambiguity on this critical question, and points out that the double position on metaphorical interpretation originated only with al-Juwaynī. It was al-Juwaynī 's position in *al-Irshād* that influenced later Ashʿarites, such as al-Rāzī.[55] Ibn Taymiyya takes this opportunity to highlight again the distance between al-Ashʿarī and later Ashʿārism, as represented in al-Juwaynī and al-Rāzī's works. He considers the latter in particular to be uninformed of al-Ashʿarī's writings and considers his education to be based on readings of the Muʿtazilite Abū al-Ḥusayn al-Baṣrī (d. 436/1044), later Ashʿarites like al-Juwaynī, and the philosophers.

But, although Ibn Taymiyya clearly recognizes a difference between the theology of al-Ashʿarī and that of the later Ashʿarites, and, as we saw earlier, also acknowledges al-Ashʿarī's self-declared association with Ibn Ḥanbal, he remains far from completely admitting al-Ashʿarī as a follower of the Sunna, both with respect to his proof of the existence of God and to his position on divine attributes. When Ibn Taymiyya assesses al-Ashʿarī's position on these two defining theological questions independently from his immediate polemics with later Ashʿarites, we get a different perspective on al-Ashʿarī's orthodoxy from the one we have seen so far.

We have seen how Ibn Taymiyya distinguishes two positions held by al-Ashʿarī, one in which he considers the *kalām*'s proof of the existence of God invalid and in opposition to the Sunna, and the other in which he accepts its validity yet adds that it leads people astray. In another passage, which is not directly related to his polemics against the *kalām* proof of the existence of God, Ibn Taymiyya does go on to accuse al-Ash'arī of holding contradictory views on this question.[56] Moreover, Ibn Taymiyya also finds that al-Ash'arī's method of proving the existence of God—in his *Risāla ilā ahl al-thaghr*—is also nothing less than a "brief version" (*ṭarīqa mukhtaṣara*) of the very same *kalām* argument which al-Ash'arī had refuted elsewhere:

> In his *Risāla ilā ahl al-thaghr*, al-Ash'arī declared that this method is not the method of the prophets and the prophets' followers, and that it is prohibited in their religion. However, al-Ash'arī does not declare these methods false; rather, he states: "They [the methods] are judged blameworthy by scripture (*shar'*) although they are sound according to reason." He [al-Ash'arī] pursued a shorter version of the same *kalām* proof, namely consisting of proving the temporal creation of man by his necessitation of temporal creation and that whatever is not free from what is temporally created (*ḥawādith*) has to be temporally created. He agreed with them [Mu'tazilites and later Ash'arites] that what are known to be temporally created are accidents, like composition (*ijtimā'*) and separation (*iftirāq*), and that it is the accidents of animals, plants, and minerals that are created in time and not their atoms.[57]

In order to demonstrate that al-Ash'arī's proof of the existence of God is a brief version of the *kalām* argument, Ibn Taymiyya then quotes the full text of al-Ash'arī's *Risāla*. According to Ibn Taymiyya, al-Ash'arī's method contradicts the scriptural argument for the existence of God, because it relies on *kalām* atomism that is nowhere to be found in scripture.[58] In scripture, according to Ibn Taymiyya, the proof for the existence of God consists of observing the temporal creation of man and other creatures which leads to the realization that there is a Creator. The *kalām* argument used by al-Ash'arī, however, necessitates *kalām* atomism.[59] According to al-Ash'arī's version of atomism, accidents are temporally created in atoms and these accidents change; it is the observation of these changes that leads us to the knowledge of the temporal creation of things and the deduction of the existence of a temporal Creator. Ibn Taymiyya, like the philosophers, does not accept atomism, and in his refutation he appeals to the philosophers' authority as "people of speculative inquiry" (*ahl al-naẓar wa-al-falsafa*). Ibn Taymiyya also appeals to those whom he labels as the majority of rational people (*jumhūr al-*

ʿuqalāʾ) to demonstrate that he is not alone in rejecting the atomism of the *mutakallimūn*.[60]

In another passage and in reference to another work of al-Ashʿarī, *al-Lumaʿ fī al-radd ʿalā aṣḥāb al-bidaʿ*, Ibn Taymiyya speaks of the proximity of al-Ashʿarī's proof of the existence of God to that of the Qurʾān.[61] Ibn Taymiyya distinguishes two premises in al-Ashʿarī's argument: First, man changes from one state to another; second, this change has to have a cause. Here, Ibn Taymiyya acknowledges a similarity between the argument from the temporal creation of attributes and the proof of the Qurʾān. He adds, however, that the second premise of this argument resembles the atomism of the Muʿtazilite proof, as admitted by later Ashʿarites.[62] Although he admits the similarity of the Qurʾānic method to al-Ashʿarī's proof of God's existence in his *Lumaʿ*, Ibn Taymiyya concludes that al-Ashʿarī's method does not correspond to scripture.[63]

Ibn Taymiyya's assessment of al-Ashʿarī's position on scriptural attributes (*ʿuluww* and *istiwāʾ*) is similarly equivocal. While Ibn Taymiyya absolves al-Ashʿarī of any ambiguity on the interpretation of these attributes, a fault he attributes to al-Juwaynī and his followers,[64] he is critical of other aspects of his doctrine. He criticizes al-Ashʿarī for denying, like Ibn Kullāb, the subsistence (*qiyām*) of these attributes in God; this denial leads al-Ashʿarī away from *ahl al-sunna*'s view of the Qurʾān as part of God's essence.[65] This position of his, Ibn Taymiyya adds, brought upon him the scorn of the *ahl al-sunna* and tainted him with the methods of the Muʿtazilites. Al-Ashʿarī is also judged here as being culpable of bringing about a heresy by calling the letters of the Qurʾān temporally created (*ḥudūth al-ḥurūf*) and by breaking away from the consensus of the community when he considered the speech of God to be metaphorical (*majāz*).[66] Ibn Taymiyya's disagreement with al-Ashʿarī's doctrine on the nature of the Qurʾān is clearly more than a minor detail. It illustrates his contempt for al-Ashʿarī's *kalām* method, which overrides what in Ibn Taymiyya's mind is a faithful reading of scripture. Therefore, even if Ibn Taymiyya never explicitly accuses him of subscribing to the general law of preferring reason over scripture,[67] he holds him responsible in some cases for mistakes of a similar nature.

Conclusion

In what has preceded we have seen how Ibn Taymiyya rejected the late Ash'arite principle of the precedence of reason over scripture and, moreover, of the mere possibility of reason being ever in real conflict with the content of revealed knowledge. He identifies this premise as the understanding handed down from the *salaf*, who are self-sufficient in explaining scripture. This framework allowed him to accept al-Ash'arī's doctrine when it reinforced his own. As a result, Ibn Taymiyya's accepts al-Ash'arī's declared allegiance to the Sunna insofar as he sought to ground his theology in scripture, and insofar as he was critical of the *mutakallimūn* when they derived their theology from rational principles. Specifically, Ibn Taymiyya commends al-Ash'arī for refuting the *mutakallimūn*'s argument for temporal creation of the world based on atomism, and for rejecting the *kalām* view that the scriptural attributes of God, such as God's sitting on the throne, cannot be understood literally and have to be interpreted metaphorically. But Ibn Taymiyya's acceptance of al-Ash'arī, whom he distinguished from the later Ash'arites, had its limits. Al-Ash'arī was not considered a faithful follower of the Sunna when he accepted the *kalām* proof of the existence of God as a valid rational, though non-scriptural, proof, or when he denied the subsistence of the divine attributes, including God's speech.

In Ibn Taymiyya's definition of the Sunna as applied through his polemics with the Ash'arites, we can distinguish characteristics of his theology and methodology that are peculiar to him and set him apart from his Ḥanbalī school. Despite Ibn Taymiyya's awareness of the limitations of al-Ash'arī's project insofar as it claimed to be both part of the *kalām* tradition and in accordance with the Sunna, Ibn Taymiyya does not dismiss it entirely. He seems to be always willing to acknowledge elements of the Sunna in al-Ash'arī's statements, and then use them in his polemics with his contemporary Ash'arite adversaries. Thus, Ibn Taymiyya neither demonizes al-Ash'arī nor redeems him in absolute terms. He uses what can be called a "relative language" to measure the orthodoxy of al-Ash'arī's system. Nonetheless, al-Ash'arī's knowledge of the prophetic tradition remains, for Ibn Taymiyya, a "general" (*mujmal*) one, while his expertise in *kalām* is a detailed one, retaining some of the principles dear to the Mu'tazilites.[68] Ibn Taymiyya consistently wishes to prove to his contemporary Ash'arite opponents that, not only as a follower of Ibn Ḥanbal but also as a *mutakallim*, al-Ashʿarī did not share their theological outlook.

Compared to previous Ḥanbalī critics of al-Ashʿarī, Ibn Taymiyya's critique of al-Ashʿarī is unprecedented, as it is grounded in a methodology and theology that are distinct from those of earlier Ḥanbalīs. Ibn Taymiyya was not concerned with the classical classification of schools; his category of the Sunna was a broader category inclusive of any figure in Muslim history regardless of school affiliation. In this respect, Ibn Taymiyya ushered in a new category, a theology of the *salaf*, which did not correspond to any of the schools of theology of the classical period. Given the polemics over orthodoxy between the traditionalists and the rationalists among the Shāfiʿīs of his time, Ibn Taymiyya's treatment of a figure such as al-Ashʿarī, who was similarly torn between rationalism and traditionalism, provides an important case study of Ibn Taymiyya's formulation of a theology of the Sunna that strove to override the classical school divisions of medieval Islam.

Notes

* I would like to thank Yossef Rapoport and Shahab Ahmed for their comments that helped improve this paper. I also would like to thank Alexander Treiger for his feedback on an early draft.

1. See Henri Laoust, "Quelques opinions sur la théodicée d'Ibn Taymiyya," *Mélanges Maspero*, vol. 3: Orient Islamique (Cairo, 1940), 433.
2. Throughout this paper, I use the term *mutakallim* (and its plural *mutakallimūn*) to refer to dialectical theologians and *kalām* to refer to dialectical theology. The connection between Ibn Taymiyya's polemics with the *mutakallimūn* and his formulation of his own theology partially explains why scholarship on Ibn Taymiyya's criticism of *kalām* has always been part of more general studies on his theology. See, for example, ʿAbd al-Fattāḥ Muḥammad Fu'ād, *Ibn Taymiyya wa-mawqifuhu min al-fikr al-falsafī* (Alexandria: al-Hay'a al-Miṣriyya al-ʿĀmma li-al-Kitāb, 1980).
3. The term 'theology of the Sunna' is used here to denote a theology that is based on the Sunna, and that takes the Sunna as its principal criterion for what constitutes orthodox belief.
4. Modern Salafis assume an uncontested identification between their own theology and that of Ibn Taymiyya. For an example, see ʿAbd al-Raḥmān b. Ṣāliḥ b. Ṣāliḥ al-Maḥmūd, *Mawqif Ibn Taymiyya min al-Ashāʿira*, 3 vols. (Riyadh: Maktabat al-Rushd, 1995).
5. Ibn Taymiyya, *Dar' taʿāruḍ al-ʿaql wa-al-naql*, ed. Muḥammad Rashād Sālim (Riyadh: Dār al-Kunūz al-Adabiyya, 1990).

6. On Ibn Taymiyya's trial in Damascus, see Sherman A. Jackson's "Ibn Taymiyya on Trial in Damascus," *Journal of Semitic Studies* 39 (1994): 41–85.
7. Muḥammad Rashād Sālim's preface to *Dar' ta'āruḍ*, 1:9.
8. I use the term "later Ash'arites" to express the distinction Ibn Taymiyya consistently makes between the early followers of al-Ash'arī, up to Abū Bakr al-Bāqillānī (d. 403/1013), and the "later" followers starting with Imām al-Ḥaramayn al-Juwaynī (d. 478/1085).
9. I do not address in this paper brief quotations of al-Ash'arī on a few other theological questions. They are mentioned by Ibn Taymiyya in the context of a refutation of the philosophers. These doctrinal questions are al-Ash'arī's doctrine of acquisition (*kasb*) (Only God creates deeds since creating requires a comprehensive knowledge possible for God alone) (*Dar' ta'āruḍ*, 8:143, 9:167, 10:114–115); al-Ash'arī's two proofs of prophecy (9:159); and al-Ash'arī's atomism and occasionalism (4:134).
10. On the Ash'arites as a source of opposition to Ibn Taymiyya, see Laoust, "La Biographie d'Ibn Taimiya d'après Ibn Kathīr", *Bulletin d'études orientales* 9 (1943): 115–162.
11. See Henri Laoust's introduction to *La profession de Foi d'Ibn Taymiyya: Texte, traduction et commentaire de la Wāṣitiyya* (Paris: Librairie Orientaliste Paul Geuthner, 1986), 17. Ḥanafīs and Malikīs were also included. See Sherman Jackson, "Ibn Taymiyya on Trial in Damascus," 46–49.
12. Sherman A. Jackson, "Ibn Taymiyya on Trial," 82.
13. Ibid., 75, 82.
14. George Makdisi's work remains invaluable for our understanding of the polemics between Ash'arite Shāfi'īs and traditionist Shāfi'īs which formed the background to Ibn 'Asākir's *Tabyīn kadhib al-muftarī* ("Ash'arī and the Ash'arites in Islamic Religious History," parts 1 and 2, *Studia Islamica* 17 [1962]: 37–89; 18 [1963]: 19–39). However, Makdisi's conclusion that al-Ash'arī may have never practiced *'ilm al-kalām* after his turn away from Mu'tazilism has been proven untenable by Richard Frank through a textual analysis of al-Ash'arī's theological language. See R. Frank, "al-Ash'arī's Conception of the Nature and Role of Speculative Reasoning in Theology," in *Proceedings of the VIth Congress of Arabic and Islamic Studies* (Uppsala, 1975), 137–154; idem., "al-Ash'arī's 'Kitāb al-Ḥathth 'alā l-baḥth'", *Mélanges Institut Dominicain d'études orientales* 18 (1988): 83–152; and idem, "Elements in the Development of the Teachings of al-Ash'arī," *Muséon* 104 (1991): 141–190.
15. See *al-Fatwā al-ḥamawiyya al-kubrā* (Cairo: al-Maṭba'a al-Salafiyya, 1967), 61–67; *'Arsh al-Raḥmān*, ed. 'Abd al-'Azīz al-Sayrawān (Beirut: Dār al-'Ulūm al-'Arabiyya, 1995), 16–17; and *al-Qā'ida al-marākishiyya*, ed. Nādir al-Rashīd and Riḍā Mu'ṭī (Riyadh: Dār Ṭība, 1981), 69–71.
16. *Dar' ta'āruḍ*, 5:5.
17. Ibid., 2:6.
18. Ibid., 2:6, 12, 16, 98.
19. Ibid., 2:6.
20. Ibid., 2:107.
21. Ibid., 1:270.
22. Ibid., 2:16–17.
23. Ibid., 5:6–7.
24. Ibid., 2:16.

25. See Michel Allard, "En quoi consiste l'opposition faite à al-Ash'arī par ses contemporains ḥanbalites?," *Revue des études Islamiques* 28 (1960): 94–96.
26. *Dar' ta'āruḍ*, 2:17. Ghulām al-Khallāl is mentioned as both praising al-Ash'arī and standing against the principles of the Kullābiyya. The two positions are only separated by a paragraph and appear irreconcilable.
27. Ibid., 2:16.
28. This statement of Ibn Taymiyya posits Ibn Kullāb's superiority to al-Ash'arī with respect to the observance of the Sunna. As noted earlier, however, in his conception of the attribute of the divine speech, Ibn Kullāb's position was further away from the affirmative position of the Sunna on the attributes as understood by Ibn Taymiyya.
29. Ibid., 8:91.
30. Josef van Ess, "Ibn Kullāb et la miḥna", tr. Claude Gilliot, *Arabica* (1990): 188.
31. *Dar' ta'āruḍ*, 7:244–246.
32. Nicholas Heer traces the genealogy of this question back to al-Juwaynī and follows its development and influence among Ash'arites after al-Rāzī, up to al-Taftāzānī (d. 793/1390) and al-Jurjānī (d. 816/1413) ("The Priority of Reason in the Interpretation of Scripture: Ibn Taymiyyah and the *mutakallimūn*," in Mustansir Mir (ed.), *Arabic and Islamic Studies in Honor of James A. Bellamy* [Princeton: Darwin Press, 1993], 181–195). According to Heer, it was al-Rāzī who first connected the question of the contradiction of reason and scripture to a "set of conditions which must be met if scripture is to yield certain knowledge" (183). This may explain why Ibn Taymiyya chose to refute al-Rāzī's formulation of this law in particular. Ibn Taymiyya traces this law back to al-Ghazālī and not to al-Juwaynī. This, however, does not necessarily imply that he was not aware of its existence in al-Juwaynī's work (*Dar' ta'āruḍ*, 1:4–6).
33. Ibid., 1:4–5.
34. For a summary and relatively comprehensive discussion of Ibn Taymiyya's response to the *mutakallimūn*, see Thomas Michel, *A Muslim Theologian's Response to Christianity: Ibn Taymiyya's al-Jawāb al-Ṣaḥīḥ* (Delmar, N.Y.: Caravan Books, 1984), chapter 4 (pp. 40–55).
35. *Dar' ta'āruḍ*, 1:8–20.
36. Ibid., 1:20–21.
37. Ibid., 1:21.
38. Ibid., 1:21–23.
39. Ibid., 1:25–78.
40. Ibid., 1:26.
41. Ibid., 1:26–27.
42. Ibid., 1:38.
43. Ibid., 1:38.
44. Ibid., 1:39.
45. Ibid., 1:38–39.
46. Jon Hoover explains that Ibn Taymiyya objected to the *kalām* argument for God's creation from nothing, an argument the theologians had developed to reject the possibility of the eternity of matter. This *kalām* argument was rejected by Ibn Taymiyya because it assumes a change in God's state from one of not creating to one of creating. What Ibn Taymiyya proposes in response is a perpetually creating God. See Jon Hoover, "Perpetual Creativity in the Perfection of God: Ibn Taymiyya's Hadith Commentary on God's Creation of This World," *Journal of Islamic Studies* 15 (2004): 295–296.

47. On al-Juwaynī's reformulation of the Muʿtazilite proof for the existence of God, see Herbert Davidson, *Proofs for Eternity, Creation and the Existence of God in Medieval Islamic and Jewish Philosophy* (Oxford: Oxford University Press, 1987), 144–145.
48. *Dar' taʿāruḍ*, 2:188–190.
49. Ibid., 1:309.
50. Ibid., 1:308–309.
51. Ibid., 2:12–13.
52. Ibid., 2:13. "*A'immat aṣḥābihi*" is used by Ibn Taymiyya to designate the earliest followers of al-Ashʿarī, about some of whom we know very little, up to al-Bāqillānī.
53. Ibid., 2:18.
54. Ibid., 2:13.
55. Ibid., 2:159.
56. Ibid., 5:290–291.
57. Ibid., 5:291.
58. Ibid., 7:186–219.
59. Ibid., 7:221.
60. Ibid., 7:221.
61. Ibid., 8:70–73.
62. Ibid., 8:73.
63. Ibid., 8:306.
64. Ibid., 3:381.
65. Ibid., 2:18.
66. Ibid., 2:317.
67. Ibn Taymiyya also levels another kind of criticism against al-Ashʿarī's theology that I do not address in this paper, as it is only brought up twice and briefly. He targets the failure of any theology, including al-Ashʿarī's, that seeks to prove the existence of God without understanding the foremost meaning of proclaiming God's oneness (*tawḥīd*), which consists for Ibn Taymiyya of *tawḥīd al-ulūhiyya*. It is a proclamation of God's oneness that can be described as ethical rather than epistemic in that it focuses on worship. Ibn Taymiyya may have not addressed this critique at length because it is not immediately connected with the main aim of *Dar' taʿāruḍ*, namely the refutation of *al-qānūn al-kullī*. See Ibid., 1:226 and 9:377.
68. Ibid., 7:462.

III
Hermeneutics

Ibn Taymiyya and the Rise of Radical Hermeneutics: An Analysis of *An Introduction to the Foundations of Qur'ānic Exegesis**

Walid A. Saleh

When he first encountered Ibn Taymiyya, Abū Ḥayyān al-Andalusī (d. 745/1344), the leading grammarian and Qur'ān exegete of Mamluk Cairo, could hardly contain his praise for the newly arrived Damascene. Abū Ḥayyān had never seen the likes of this man (*mā ra'at 'aynāya mithl hādhā al-rajul*): he refused money from the sultan, berated the Mamluks for their impieties, and urged the community to fight. What courage, what disregard for wealth and authority! Abū Ḥayyān even wrote a few lines of poetry in praise of his new hero. True, he went over the top in these verses, claiming that Ibn Taymiyya was the awaited Messiah (*al-imām alladhī qad kāna yuntaẓar*); but then again Ibn Taymiyya was known to engender such adoration in his followers. Leave it, however, to Ibn Taymiyya to turn an ardent admirer into a determined foe. Soon enough, in one of their meetings, while disputing a grammatical point, Ibn Taymiyya heaped insults on Sībawayh, the father of Arabic grammar, even deriding Abū Ḥayyān's deference to his authority. After all, Sībawayh was not the prophet of grammar, Ibn Taymiyya mockingly growled (*mā kāna Sībaywayhi nabīya al-naḥw*); nor was he infallible (*wa-lā kāna ma'ṣūman*). Any other insult would have been forgiven, but not an insult against Sībawayh. Abū Ḥayyān not only removed the piece of poetry from his *dīwān* (it was preserved for us by the historian Ibn Ḥajar), but later returned the favor and heaped insults on Ibn Taymiyya in his major work, the Qur'ān commentary *al-Baḥr al-muḥīṭ*.[1] This anecdote shows the degree to which Ibn Taymiyya's conservatism was directly linked to his iconoclasm. By confining his respect to the early generations of Islam he was free to escape the binding authority of any other figure in subsequent Islamic intellectual history, no matter how highly regarded such a figure might be amongst his contemporaries. Ibn Taymiyya would soon take the tradition of Qur'ānic exegesis to task and show his utter disregard for the whole outlook that was at the basis of Abū Ḥayyān's academic work.

The small treatise *Muqaddima fī uṣūl al-tafsīr* (*An Introduction to the Foundations of Qur'ānic Exegesis*) by Ibn Taymiyya has had a remarkable influence on the history of Qur'ānic exegesis. Barely 15 folios, it not only proclaims a new hermeneutical program that became the foundation for a subgenre of *tafsīr* that would generate several major Qur'ānic commentaries, but it boldly attempts to overhaul the entire history of Qur'ānic exegesis. The treatise, as Ibn Taymiyya makes clear in its preface, was dictated from memory, probably during his last stint in jail, without access to his notes or books, and as such it shows a slight degree of disorganization and some fluidity in its composition.[2] This makes it sometimes difficult to comprehend fully what Ibn Taymiyya was attempting to say. Yet the author was successful in conveying to a number of influential medieval readers a systematic program of interpreting the Qur'ān and assessing the merit of any Qur'ānic commentary. Ibn Taymiyya was offering more than just a method of interpretation; he was also offering a judgment upon the collective literature of the Qur'ānic commentary tradition.

The final two chapters of this treatise, in which Ibn Taymiyya adumbrated his new theory, were incorporated *in toto* in the introduction of Ibn Kathīr's (d. 774/1373) Qur'ān commentary, the first major commentary to put into practice the theory of Ibn Taymiyya (or at least attempt to do so).[3] The verbatim quotation of these two chapters at the beginning of what proved to be the prime example of this new type of Qur'ān commentary is a strong indication of Ibn Taymiyya's influence in reshaping the exegetical tradition.[4] Ibn Taymiyya's treatise was thus influential in its own right, and because of the incorporation of its most important section in Ibn Kathīr's Qur'ān commentary. This article will offer a detailed analysis of Ibn Taymiyya's *Introduction*, an account of its background, and the reasons for its influence and continued relevance.

Given that Ibn Taymiyya left no substantial work on *tafsīr*, his influence in this field is all the more in need of explication.[5] It is a testament to the intellectual breadth of Ibn Taymiyya that it should leave such a lasting imprint on an already well established field. By the time Ibn Taymiyya wrote his treatise the field was already replete with illustrious exegetes, the likes of al-Ṭabarī, al-Tha'labī, al-Wāḥidī, al-Baghawī, al-Zamakhsharī, Ibn 'Aṭiyya, and al-Rāzī, to name some whose works have been published so far. There were several reasons for the success of this treatise in influencing the genre of Qur'ānic exegesis, but perhaps the most obvious is that Ibn Taymiyya was the first to offer a systematically articulated prescriptive theory of Qur'ānic interpretation in a pure form—that is, as a separate treatise; his work was thus assured a precedence and as such an influence that were never matched.[6] It is not that scriptural exegesis was lacking in theorizing about hermeneutics, and one could hardly speak of an intellectual vacuum in the field; indeed the opposite was true. The fact is, however, that commentators were more willing to offer their interpretation than their theoretical hermeneutical position. When such theories were presented they were usually part of introductions to Qur'ān commentaries, and as such, their impact was limited by their being part of a far more important composition.[7]

But even if one wrote a Qur'ān commentary it was no guarantee of influence in the field, and it is even more unlikely that one stood a chance to influence the field if one were to theorize about *tafsīr* without leaving a commentary. Ibn Taymiyya's theory itself must have reflected a close affinity with certain intellectual currents in late medieval Islam for it to secure such a lasting influence for itself. Ibn Taymiyya couched his theory within an ideological framework that was difficult to unseat or refute. Subsequently, the effect of Ibn Taymiyya's theory was not only that it generated a new form of Qur'ānic commentary writing—or, to be more accurate, saved an existing form from its internal contradictions—rather, his theory would also offer a formidable challenge to medieval hermeneutics that proved insurmountable in the long run. The road to prominence took some centuries, yet one can speak of a steady increase in the influence of this treatise. Indeed, there is hardly another comparable work in the history of Qur'ānic hermeneutics. It single-handedly provided the basis for the consolidation of what I have termed radical hermeneutics, which would culminate with the publication of *al-Durr al-manthūr fī al-tafsīr bi-al-ma'thūr* by al-Suyūṭī.[8] The repercussions of this treatise can be observed across the intellectual history of the Islamic world, and they were not confined to late medieval Islamic intellectual history; in fact, the triumph of this mode of hermeneutics, radical hermeneutics, was assured only in the latter part of the 20th century. Ibn Taymiyya's treatise has now become the basis for how modern conservative Muslim intellectuals conceive of Qur'ānic exegesis.

The Organization and the Introduction of the Treatise

The popularity of Ibn Taymiyya's treatise and its small size means that there exists a rather large number of editions and reprints.[9] The so-called Salafī edition was published in 1936 (Taraqqī publishers) and reprinted with corrections in 1965 (Salafī press, hence the name).[10] The one used for this study (and the only critical edition) is by ʿAdnān Zarzūr. It is based on one manuscript and the earlier edition, which itself was based on two different manuscripts; thus Zarzūr's edition utilized three manuscripts in all. All other reprints and "editions" are pirated copies of these three earlier publications (mostly of the Salafī 1965 reprint, which became the most widely used). It is important to emphasize, however, that there has not been an exhaustive study of the manuscript tradition of this treatise.[11]

Ibn Taymiyya claims in his preface to the treatise that he was asked by some colleagues to write them an introduction "which contains general rules (*qawāʿid kulliyya*) that can be used to understand the Qur'ān and enable one to know its interpretations and meanings, and enable the reader, when examining interpretations that are based on tradition (*manqūl*) and those which are based on reason (*maʿqūl*), to distinguish between the truth and the falsehood therein. Moreover, the introduction should also supply a guide for how to judge between interpretations."[12] The urgency for such a work is necessitated, according to Ibn Taymiyya, because "the books written on *tafsīr* are full of worthy and unworthy material; some of the material is manifestly false while some self-evidently true."[13] Ibn Taymiyya then offers a succinct definition of what constitutes knowledge: "Knowledge is that which is truthfully transmitted from an infallible [individual] or a statement that can be defended by an accepted [logical] proof. Anything else is either a fabrication [attributed to an infallible source] to be rejected, or a statement that is impossible to verify [logically], either positively or negatively."[14] Ibn Taymiyya is, therefore, stating that there exist two kinds of knowledge: divine, whose source is from an infallible informer (usually a prophet) and which can be verified through ascertaining the degree of the reliability of the transmission route it has traversed; and rational knowledge, which has to be verified through logical proofs. This epistemological definition will undergird the whole theory offered in Ibn Taymiyya's introduction. For *tafsīr* to have any claim to authority and to be a truthful representation of what the Word of God means, one should be able to prove that it is knowledge. Interpretations of the Qur'ān can only be treated as knowledge in so far as one can show they belong to one of the two types Ibn Taymiyya defines; only then can one be certain of their veracity. Ibn Taymiyya makes clear to his readers which kinds of *tafsīr* have the status of knowledge and what the grounds are for such a claim.

As a way of final justification for writing his *Muqaddima,* Ibn Taymiyya states that "the Muslim community (*umma*) is in dire need of understanding the Qur'ān," for it is, among other things, the sure way to salvation. This point is supported by a string of citations from Hadith and the Qur'ān all emphasizing the central role of the Qur'ān in the life of the Muslim community.[15] Ibn Taymiyya finishes his preface by informing the reader that he wrote this introduction in a summary form (*mukhtaṣara*) from memory (*min imlā' al-fu'ād*).[16]

The *Muqaddima* is divided into six chapters, the first four of which are offered as preliminary groundwork and justification for the theory of interpretation that is elaborated in the final two chapters.[17] The *Muqaddima* can thus be divided into two major parts. Yet it is not clear at first what the relationship is between the first four chapters and the final two, and it is only by making explicit this relationship that we are able to comprehend fully the scope and the ambition of Ibn Taymiyya's treatise. The definition of knowledge given at the introduction is the key to clarifying the relationship between the two parts of the treatise; it is the only thread that can string together its disparate elements. I will offer first an analysis of the content of the first four chapters (which are usually overlooked when dealing with this treatise) and then show in what way they are related to what follows them.[18] It will become evident that these preliminary four chapters are the foundation of Ibn Taymiyya's theory of hermeneutics.

Chapter One

In this chapter Ibn Taymiyya raises the issues that will form the backbone of his treatise, and statements made here will become the basis for the next three chapters. He declares in this chapter that Muḥammad, or the Prophet, as Ibn Taymiyya refers to him, clarified (*bayyana*) to his Companions the meanings of the Qur'ān (*ma'ānī*), just as he delivered to them its wording (*alfāẓahu*).[19] What Ibn Taymiyya is implying is that Muḥammad not only proclaimed the Qur'ān to the Muslims, but also its meaning, and apparently this "meaning" of the Qur'ān was something distinct from the Sunna as generally understood. Sunni jurisprudence had already posited the Sunna of Muḥammad as the interpreter of the Qur'ān, but only in a loose sense of "interpretation," that is, not as commentary but as clarification of obscure rules in the Qur'ān. Thus the transformation here, though subtle, is nonetheless profound: the Prophet is presented as having commented on the Qur'ān, in the manner of an exegete, to his Companions and hence there is another corpus of prophetic material that is, strictly speaking, not part of the traditional understanding of the Sunna. The Sunna in turn is understood by Ibn Taymiyya to include a prophetic commentary on the Qur'ān. Granted he does not explicitly make this point, yet it is an inescapable conclusion that follows from the import of his statements in this chapter.[20] Ibn Taymiyya's aim is thus to turn the commentary literature into prophetic knowledge, and as such interpretation itself, as issuing from an infallible individual, becomes a type of knowledge that is in agreement with his definition of what constitutes knowledge. One needs only to verify that it is indeed from Muḥammad for it to become authoritative. Hence inherited interpretations are to be assessed in the same way as one assesses Hadith, using the customary tools of the science of Hadith.[21]

This is a rather radical redefinition of Qur'ānic exegesis—elevating it to the level of prophetic knowledge. It raises the stakes considerably and brings with it immediate counter-arguments, which Ibn Taymiyya sets out to demolish in the subsequent chapters. The first question (or at least the one that Ibn Taymiyya attempts to circumvent) is this: if *tafsīr* is knowledge, and hence has a degree of certitude that is accorded prophetic knowledge, how do we account for the differences among the interpretations given to a particular Qur'ānic verse, since this would mean that knowledge is contradictory, which should be impossible. To this unstated objection Ibn Taymiyya will devote considerable attention, both in this first chapter and in subsequent chapters.

Having stated his thesis, that Muḥammad taught the meaning of the Qur'ān with its wording, Ibn Taymiyya then cites proofs for the validity of the thesis. First he cites a prophetic tradition that states that the companions of Muḥammad used to learn ten verses of the Qur'ān at one time, and then learn what these verses teach of "knowledge and praxis"; they thus "learned the Qur'ān, knowledge and praxis, all together."[22] The implication here is clear: the Qur'ān was not received in a vacuum; rather it was received with its "knowledge and praxis." Indeed such was the case that the Companions took a long time learning parts of the Qur'ān, an indication that memorizing it was not the only issue at hand.[23]

The second proof is based on the Qur'ān. Ibn Taymiyya cites three phrases from three verses (38:29, 4:28, 23:6) which use the Arabic root *d-b-r* (to reflect, consider, contemplate) in various forms; these verses command the believers to reflect on the Qur'ān. Ibn Taymiyya denies that reflection on a certain verse could take place without first understanding the verse. The unstated conclusion is that God could not have imposed a duty that cannot be fulfilled, and hence understanding the meaning of the Qur'ān was a given.[24] Ibn Taymiyya then cites verse 12:2 ("We have sent it down as an Arabic Qur'ān so that you may understand"); the verb used here is the Arabic *ta'qilūn* (to comprehend, understand), and Ibn Taymiyya affirms that "comprehending speech presupposes understanding it."[25] He then sums up this section by stating a truism: the aim of speech is to understand its meaning, and not merely its individual word components; as such, the Qur'ān as speech falls under this rule.[26] Clearly Ibn Taymiyya has no clear-cut proof for his assertions that Muḥammad commented on the entire Qur'ān, or else he would have produced it. The claim that Muḥammad interpreted the entire Qur'ān was not found as such anywhere in the tradition, and the contrary was actually always asserted: Muḥammad was not in need of interpreting the Qur'ān. It was in the language of the Arabs precisely so that they should have no excuse if they did not get the message of God. Indeed, the mainstream argument for the justification of the craft of commentary was that unlike the Companions, whose Arabic was impeccable and who therefore understood the Qur'ān with no mediation, later Muslims were in need of interpretation because they did not have such perfect Arabic.

Ibn Taymiyya then adduces a proof from the practice of the colleges of his time, projecting onto the past the state of contemporary scholastic methods of reading texts. Custom prevents specialists, he asserts, when they read a book in their corresponding art, like medicine and arithmetic, from reading it without its explication (*yastashriḥūhu*). The case should be more so with the Qur'ān, since it is "their protector and in it exists their salvation and their happiness, and the rectitude of their religion and the functioning of their worldly affairs."[27] The Companions must have learned the Qur'ān with its interpretation; this is the only sensible way to behave.

Suddenly, Ibn Taymiyya offers a conclusion that does not seem to follow from what has preceded so far. He states that disagreement (*nizā'*) between the Companions regarding the interpretation of the Qur'ān is rare; its occurrence among the Successors is a bit more common. The incidence of disagreement among these two generations, Ibn Taymiyya adds, is, however, far less than the differences among the subsequent generations. As I have indicated earlier, this concluding paragraph both anticipates an objection to Ibn Taymiyya's paradigm and removes a contradiction from this paradigm. The objection would be against his raising the status of interpretations of the Qur'ān to the level of prophetic knowledge, since as truthful knowledge it should not admit contradiction, but we do know that there are contradictions; hence his insistence that there is little or no contradictions in the *tafsīr* that comes from the two early generations of Muslims. The paradoxical inconsistencies inherent in Ibn Taymiyya's redefinition of *tafsīr* are thus removed, since the contradictions and differences that exist in *tafsīr* are really not part of what he would consider *tafsīr* and belong to later generations of exegetes.

As usual with Ibn Taymiyya, he then offers a catchy statement intended to summarize what he has said thus far: "The nobler the age the more consensus and agreement there is, and the more knowledge."[28] What is the import of such a statement? We should not discount a circular argument here, which can be stated as follows: since Muslims agree that the most noble of generations to ever live was that of the Companions and the Successors, it then follows that they left us with less discord and more knowledge than any other generation. Granted this is an argument not stated explicitly in this treatise, but it underlies its rationale. As we can see, Ibn Taymiyya is vacillating between two stratagems to uphold the supremacy of the interpretations of the *salaf*. One is to imply (sometimes clearly, sometimes obliquely) that the *salaf* were simply transmitting prophetic lore that Muḥammad taught about the meaning of the Qur'ān; the other is that the *salaf* as the most pious and most learned of Islam were the font of knowledge. These two rationales are both offered, and Ibn Taymiyya seems to be of two minds as to which one to choose.

Finally Ibn Taymiyya comes clean and states his *maqṣūd*, or aim in this chapter: the Successors received Qur'ānic interpretations from the Companions, just as they received from them the Sunna. They might have discussed these interpretations, but if so, it was in the same manner as they did with the Sunna, by way of using *tafsīr* as a guide for discovering (*istidlāl*) or deducing rules (*istinbāṭ*).[29] It is here that we see Ibn Taymiyya implying that *tafsīr* is a prophetic Sunna that is distinct from *the Sunna*, yet Sunna all the same. Having been received from the Companions, who, we were told, received it from the prophet, Qur'ānic interpretation has its origin with Muḥammad.[30] Ibn Taymiyya has thus offered the rationale as to why precedence should be ascribed to the interpretations of the Companions and Successors, namely because these interpretations are a part of prophetic knowledge. Having now laid the foundation and provided the general outline of his preliminaries, he proceeds to explain and elaborate on these foundations before offering his theory of interpretation.

Chapter Two

The aim of this chapter is to explain why there is disagreement among the *salaf* regarding the meaning of the Qur'ān or, more accurately, to explain away the existence of such differences or disagreements. Calling the first two Muslim generations "ancestors" (*salaf*) at this stage in the treatise is a rhetorical shift meant to make an emotional effect in what so far has been a dry argumentative treatise. Ibn Taymiyya's success can in part be attributed to his rallying of his followers behind an emotional concept, *al-salaf al-ṣāliḥ* (pious ancestors), the equivalent of the Shiʿis' *Ahl al-bayt* (Household of Muḥammad) shibboleth. Ibn Taymiyya begins this chapter by stating that "disagreement in *tafsīr* among the ancestors is miniscule (*qalīl*), while their disagreement on judicial rules is greater than their disagreement on *tafsīr*."[31] This is a most fascinating statement, for Ibn Taymiyya is in effect willing to admit to the inconsequentiality of disagreement in matters of law—the kind of legal pluralism which Sunnism enshrines as a sign of the merciful God—while he seems to think that much more hangs on a harmonious or concordant interpretation of the Qur'ān. When push comes to shove, Ibn Taymiyya is even willing to side with Shiʿi jurisprudence in certain matters, without that affecting his Sunni standing in his eyes;[32] but he seems to think that how one interprets the Qur'ān is far more indicative of one's true leanings. He does have a point. What makes a Sunni Sunni is not law, for a Muʿtazilite, an Ashʿarite, or a philosopher can be Sunni in his legal affiliation and still not be of the "people of the Sunna" according to Ibn Taymiyya. A proper theological position is the principle of discrimination. The theological, and hence the hermeneutical, in Ibn Taymiyya's worldview is thus paramount. It is no wonder that most of his production was theological or polemical in nature. The man could hardly muster the composure to write dispassionately.[33]

Ibn Taymiyya then states that what has indeed been documented to be true (*mā yaṣiḥḥu*) regarding matters of disagreement in *tafsīr* which has come down to us from the *salaf* can be understood as the result of "variations on the same theme" rather than real "contradictory disagreements."[34] What Ibn Taymiyya means by contradictory disagreements is self evident, and he will devote Chapters Three and Four to these kinds of differences and their significance—a kind of disagreement that was not present in the Companion-Successor corpus, according to Ibn Taymiyya. It is his phrase "variations on a same theme" (*ikhtilāf tanawwuʿ*) that will be elaborated in this chapter.

Although Ibn Taymiyya starts by stating that there are two kinds of disagreement that are the result of variations on a theme, he in fact gives four kinds.[35] The first is the result of each exegete using a different expression (*ʿibāra*) to describe different aspects of a term that is being explained, all of which aspects (or meanings) that the term can be said to contain. Despite the fact that one is giving two different words to explain a term, the nature of the thing being interpreted is still the same [in the minds of the readers].[36] What Ibn Taymiyya is saying is that the exegetes are not disputing the nature of the thing referred to by a word, rather the quality described by this term. Luckily, he does supply examples of what he means by this. Ibn Taymiyya uses a philological explanation: it is like the use of descriptive terms that are neither synonyms nor antonyms but rather similar. Thus the sword can be called *al-ṣārim* (the cutter) and *al-muhannad* (of Indian iron), just as the many names of God, the names of the Qur'ān, or the names of Muḥammad, all signify (*tadullu*) one thing.[37] To use one name of God (out of the 99 names) is not to negate the other terms, for each of the names of God points to the attribute being described and the essence of God; thus calling Him Mighty signifies His might and His essence, calling Him the Merciful signifies His mercy and His essence.

Ibn Taymiyya gives a concrete example from the Qur'ān of how early exegetes (and the term exegete here is used according to this new theory of Ibn Taymiyya's) "differed" with the difference in their interpretations being a variation on a theme. Verse 20:124, "and who ever turns away from my *dhikr*," raises the question of what *dhikr* is here. Some said it is the Qur'ān, or other Divine books; others said it could be the remembrance of God, that is the uttering of benedictions like "Glory to God, God is great, etc," or, that it might be God's guidance. Thus, Ibn Taymiyya concludes, *dhikr* here can mean all these since it is still referring to the same thing. Ibn Taymiyya asserts that these are not interpretations that are contradictory, as some people might think (*kamā yaẓunnuhu ba'ḍ al-nās*). He then brings along another Qur'ānic example, the famous Straight Path (*al-ṣirāṭ al-mustaqīm*). Some said it is the Qur'ān (that is following it), others said it is Islam. Ibn Taymiyya then comments:

> These two interpretations are congruent (*muttafiqān*) because Islam is nothing but following the Qur'ān, but each interpretation points to a description (*waṣf*) that is different from the other. Indeed, the term "*ṣirāṭ*" indicates other meanings, like *Sunna* and *Jamā'a* (the famous phrase for Sunnism); it is also the path of servitude, and it is obedience to God and his Prophet, and many other things. All of these explanations are pointing to one essence, yet each is using a different attribute out of the many attributes that the explained term contains.[38]

The second kind of "variations on a theme" difference is the kind that results from:

> Each exegete naming (for the sake of giving an example) a particular species as an example for a general term (or, genus); exegetes explain by examples (*tamthīl*) [what a term means] in order to alert the reader to the nature of the genus; and this method is not meant to give the definition of the term such that it includes all the instances of the term in general and specific ways.[39]

Ibn Taymiyya is using an explanation from logic to argue that the early exegetes have similar methods. The first Qur'ānic example he gives is of verse 35:32, and he is especially concerned with the terms "*ẓālim li-nafsihi*" (sinning against oneself) and "*muqtaṣid*" (follow a middle road). The term "sinning against oneself" is a general term that includes those who disobey religious injunctions and commit transgressions, while the term "following a middle road" refers to those who obey all religious injunctions. Thus when an exegete gives one instance of sinning against oneself (which we mistakenly have taken to be the only interpretation), like not praying the five prayers, while another says the sinner is one who does not pay his alms, the exegetes are giving examples of such a general term and they are not giving a full definition of the term in question. This is so since it is much easier to comprehend the meaning of a term by way of an example than by way of a dry comprehensive logical definition (*al-ḥadd al-muṭābiq*).[40]

Ibn Taymiyya also includes in this type the differences that come from stating the reasons why a verse was revealed (the occasions of revelation, or what is known in Arabic as *asbāb al-nuzūl*).[41] This is a dilemma that has to be faced squarely if one is to claim that there is no contradiction in the Companions' exegetical lore. It is no secret that many verses in the Qur'ān have more than one story as to why they were revealed. Is that a contradiction (or rather an inconsistency that borders on the contradictory) ? Before addressing this issue Ibn Taymiyya sees fit to dispose of the view that since these verses were revealed regarding a certain individual, the rule of such a verse should be restricted to this individual. It is not clear what the importance is of this point for the general argument, given that Ibn Taymiyya is arguing here for an elementary and fundamental premise of Sunni jurisprudence. I am of the opinion that this is simply a digression meant to state the obvious and hence solidify the thrust of Ibn Taymiyya's arguments in general. This digression aside, he then returns to his main argument and offers a resolution for the co-existence of different reasons for the revelation of a certain verse: the verse in question might simply have been revealed many times, in each instance for a different reason![42]

There is a paragraph in the digressive part of this section that is worth discussing, for it reveals the extent of Ibn Taymiyya's awareness of what he was attempting to change.[43] This paragraph addresses the status of the reports about the reasons for revelation. Scholars, Ibn Taymiyya informs us, are in disagreement as to how to assess these reports. Some believe they are Hadith, hence part of the *musnad* material, that is, inherited knowledge transmitted from the prophet by reliable chains of authority, while others believe they are part of the *tafsīr*, which is not part of the *musnad*. Ibn Taymiyya is here admitting that *tafsīr*, up to his time, was not considered part of the prophetic lore as such (the *musnad* material). This digression demonstrates that Ibn Taymiyya was consciously attempting to elevate *tafsīr* to the status of inherited prophetic knowledge; he was all too aware of the traditional understanding of the genre.

Ibn Taymiyya then gives a third kind of "variation on a theme" differences: differences that are the result of the nature of the term which can itself accommodate contradictory meanings, terms which he calls *mushtarak* in Arabic. He gives the word *qaswara* of verse 74:51, as an example, which could mean the hunter and the hunted, and the term *'as'as* of verse 81:17, which means the coming and going of the night.[44]

The fourth kind of variation given by Ibn Taymiyya is more or less the same as the first kind, and it is not clear to me what the difference is between the two, apart from splitting hairs. Here he claims that some differences between exegetes are the result of their giving similar terms (*mutaqāriba*) as meanings of a certain word. Thus an example of this kind is to interpret the verb *awḥā* (to reveal) in a Qur'ānic verse, as *anzala* (to make come down to you).[45]

Ibn Taymiyya sums up the issue presented in this chapter as follows: the plurality of phrases and expressions of the *salaf* in their interpretation of a certain phrase of the Qur'ān is very beneficial, for the sum total of the different interpretations given to a certain verse is more revealing of its meaning than any single one. Ibn Taymiyya admits all the same that there are mild differences (*ikhtilāf mukhaffaf*) between the *salaf*, just as there are in the juristic material.[46] This is the extent of what he is willing to concede as to the existence of any differences among the *salaf*. Ibn Taymiyya concludes the passage by giving a host of other reasons for the existence of differences among the *salaf* in their interpretation, thus admitting that his treatment is not exhaustive, but rather illustrative: "what we aim here is to give a general sense of the matter and not an exhaustive treatment."[47] What he is arguing is thus not a complete explanation for what appear to be differences among the *salaf* but rather an axiomatic new principle: the *salaf* did not disagree on the meaning of the Qur'ān.

Chapter Three

Having argued against the existence of real or contradictory differences among the *salaf*, Ibn Taymiyya turns his attention to the contradictory differences that do exist in *tafsīr* (or at least the differences he is willing to admit to) and to the question of their origin and significance. Ibn Taymiyya does after all recognize the existence of contradictory differences in *musnad* material, which until now he seemed to have denied, and he will now deal with these differences and their nature. Although Ibn Taymiyya does not mention the word contradictory (*taḍādd*) here, it is clear that it is this sort of difference that he has in mind, the kind that he has not discussed so far.[48] He begins by stating that the (contradictory) differences in *tafsīr* are of two kinds: differences that are part of the transmitted lore, and differences that are not part of the transmitted lore but come out of human activity.[49] The current chapter is dedicated to the differences that are part of the transmitted lore, while the next is devoted to the second type. Ibn Taymiyya repeats here his definition of knowledge that was given at the beginning of the treatise, thus leaving no doubt that this definition is his guiding principle.

Transmitted exegetical lore, whether transmitted from an infallible or a fallible source, comes in three varieties, according to Ibn Taymiyya: one that can be verified as truthful, *ṣaḥīḥ* (if we can prove that it was faithfully transmitted from an infallible source);

another *ḍaʿīf* (if we can ascertain the invalidity of its transmission); and a third that cannot be verified and hence of an indeterminate veracity. Since Ibn Taymiyya groups the first two kinds as one, the implication is that cases of genuine contradictory differences rather than merely apparent ones in transmitted lore are to be found in the third group.[50]

This third group of transmitted material—which contains all the contradictory material in the *musnad* exegetical lore, the one whose veracity is impossible to verify—is material that does not constitute an essential part of Islamic knowledge according to Ibn Taymiyya. To discourse and quibble on these matters is useless and redundant. Ibn Taymiyya gives us examples of these materials: the color of the dog which accompanied the Sleepers of Ephesus (different colors were given by exegetes), the part of the cow which was used in the ritual mentioned in the second Sura of the Qur'ān (different parts were named), the length of the ark of Noah, and the name of the child killed by the companion of Moses in Sura 18.[51] The only way this kind of detail could be known is if it had been transmitted from a divinely inspired source, and only the details that are verifiable and certain that were transmitted from the Prophet, like the name of the companion of Moses in Sura 18, are knowable matters (*maʿlūm*).

Material of this kind that has been transmitted by the Successors from the People of the Book (*ahl al-kitāb*) cannot be accepted or rejected unless we have proof of its veracity. Ibn Taymiyya is raising the issue of what is known as the *isrāʾīlīyāt*, material transmitted from Jewish converts to Islam (early converts who were themselves from the Successors' generation) and mostly available in *tafsīr*.[52] Ibn Taymiyya states that material of this kind transmitted from the Companions is, however, much more acceptable since the possibility that they could have heard it from the Prophet is too high to discount. Ibn Taymiyya sums up his *maqṣūd*, or aim, here: contradictory differences (like the giving of different colors to the dog of the Sleepers of Ephesus), whose veracity (*ṣaḥīḥuhu*) cannot be verified, are like Hadith material that cannot be judged and therefore inconsequential on the religious plane. God, in his wisdom, had ensured that the material necessary for salvation could be verified by the scholars of Islam.[53]

Ibn Taymiyya then moves to an important matter in transmitted *tafsīr* lore, the issue of reports attributed by a Successor to the

Prophet directly without the authority of a Companion, what is known as *marāsīl* in the parlance of Hadith science. In the previous passage he argued that interpretations from the Companions, even if not attributed directly to Muḥammad, might as well be, in so far as Muḥammad taught his Companions the meaning of the Qur'ān in addition to its wording. He is now tackling the interpretations of the Successors that are attributed indirectly to Muḥammad (omitting the Companion link in the chain of transmission). Ibn Taymiyya accepts the validity and veracity of such traditions as long as they come from different transmission lines and a conspiracy of collusion among the Successors or the transmitters cannot be proven.[54] Why is Ibn Taymiyya raising this issue here? To defend this type of Hadith is not only perplexing here but hardly worth the spilled ink. His position on this matter is neither new nor controversial among Sunni scholars. However, since most of the inherited interpretations from the Successors in the *tafsīr* material are not attributed to Muḥammad, I believe the aim is to raise the whole lore of Successor traditions to the level of prophetic lore. Ibn Taymiyya effectively implies that the material from the Successors which is not attributed to Muḥammad at all is still valid. Ibn Taymiyya does not state this directly, but it is clearly his aim; for later he will accord the interpretations from the Successors as a whole a high rank in the order of knowledge that he considers worthy of following. What I am saying is that Ibn Taymiyya is accepting the collective interpretive material from the Successors as valid by claiming that part of it could be argued to belong to the Prophetic lore.[55]

It is in this chapter that Ibn Taymiyya offers us his first assessment of the merit of previous exegetes. In the process of decrying the existence of fabricated Hadith in *tafsīr* works, especially those which belong to the Sura-merit traditions (prophetic traditions that promise rewards for reading different Suras of the Qur'ān), he mentions authors who have included such material in their works,[56] issuing judgments on al-Tha'labī (d. 427/1035) and his student al-Wāḥidī (d. 468/1076), al-Baghawī (d. 516/1122), and al-Zamakhsharī (d. 538/1144).[57] Ibn Taymiyya was not without a sense of humour; he heaps praise only to cut people down. He sums up al-Tha'labī's worth as follows: he was a man of righteous conduct; unfortunately he collected anything and everything that came his way in previous *tafsīr* works, just like a nocturnal wood gatherer unable to distinguish between the good and the bad. Ibn Taymiyya implies that al-Thaʿlabī inadvertently gathered these fabricated Hadiths because he did not know better. This is, needless to say, an unfair evaluation of one of the leading figures of classical *tafsīr*, but the last word was indeed Ibn Taymiyya's in this regard.

His assessment of al-Wāḥidī is even harsher: Ibn Taymiyya admits that al-Wāḥidī was far more knowledgeable in philology than his teacher al-Thaʿlabī, but al-Wāḥidī was less sound in his theological outlook and more unlike the *salaf*. Finally, Ibn Taymiyya offers his assessment of al-Baghawī, who, though his *tafsīr* was a summary and a reworking of the work of al-Thaʿlabī, was one of the people of sound religion and theological outlook. By going after al-Thaʿlabī, al-Wāḥidī, al-Zamakhsharī, and al-Baghawī, Ibn Taymiyya was targeting one of the most important schools in medieval *tafsīr*. Only an incisively clever mind like Ibn Taymiyya's could cut through the mountains of detail and group together the ultra-Sunni al-Baghawī, the Muʿtazilite al-Zamakhsharī, the philologist al-Wāḥidī, and the encyclopedic al-Thaʿlabī. Different as they were in their approaches, they all shared the same Sunni medieval hermeneutical theory: that the word of God was interpretable by everyone and one did not need divine knowledge to do exegesis; nor, for that matter, did one need to be correct in the interpretations offered, since one was indulging in a quasi-*ijtihād* process. Sunni medieval hermeneutics was premised on the impossibility of ever exhausting the meanings of the divine word, and contradictory interpretations were not a sign of religious heresy.

Chapter Four

This chapter is devoted to a discussion of the differences that arise from using *istidlāl* or reasoning to interpret the Qur'ān, i.e. *tafsīr* which is based not on tradition (*naql*) but on reason, or human agency.[58] Ibn Taymiyya asserts that these differences appeared only after the interpretations of the Companions, the Successors and the successors of the Successors (*tābiʿ al-tābiʿīn*). The exegetical works that mention the interpretations of the *salaf* without editorializing or comments from later generations (*fa-inna al-tafāsīr allatī yudhkar fīhā kalām hā'ulā' ṣarfan*) are the best exegetical works available and are free of disagreements. Ibn Taymiyya here is rejecting even tradition-based commentaries that see fit to add their own assessment of this material since, Ibn Taymiyya argues, the views of the early generations are sufficient on their own. Ibn Taymiyya then offers a list of the authors whom he considers to belong to this Sunni school of exegesis. He endorses the names of fifteen traditional Hadith-based exegetes, including Baqī b. Makhlad (d. 276/889), al-Ṭabarī (d. 311/923), Ibn Abī Ḥātim (d. 327/938), and Ibn Mardawayh (d. 401/1010).[59]

Ibn Taymiyya then divides the contradictory differences in this category into two kinds. The first results from the activities of exegetes who already have a meaning that they want to impute to the Qur'ān and in order to do that they force the words of the Qur'ān to give that meaning.[60] This group does not take into consideration what the words of the Qur'ān are actually saying. The second results from the activities of "the exegetes who interpret the Qur'ān according to the rules of what the speakers of the Arabic language would allow, without taking into consideration the speaker of the Qur'ān (i.e. God), the person to whom it was delivered and the audience to whom it was addressed."[61] This second group will not be discussed again in this chapter, or for that matter in the rest of the treatise, and it is not clear who Ibn Taymiyya has in mind when he speaks of this group. The most probable explanation is that he is after some pro-philological authors of Sunni and Mu'tazilite encyclopaedic *tafsīrs*, namely al-Wāḥidī and al-Zamakhsharī—and possibly also Abū Ḥayyān al-Andalusī, his foe, whom he refuses to mention.

The first kind of this new division of exegetes, the one that imputes meanings to the Qur'ān, is furthermore divided into two camps, one that robs the words of the Qur'ān of the meaning they have, and another that forces a meaning that the words do not contain.[62] In both cases, the fact is that the meanings these exegetes are trying to force upon the Qur'ān are mostly wrong and thus these exegetes are doubly wrong: they did not get the meaning right (in the spirit of the Qur'ān), and they are forcing the words to carry a meaning which they do not have (the method of interpretation is wrong). Hence, they are wrong about both the language of the Qur'ān (*al-dalīl*) and its meaning (*al-madlūl*). This being Ibn Taymiyya, he does concede the other possibility, namely that sometimes the meanings these exegetes are trying to foist on the words of the Qur'ān might be a correct interpretation (in the sense of the totality of the message of the Qur'ān), while the words of the Qur'ān to which they are imputing these correct meanings do not in reality give such meanings. They might be right about what the Qur'ān could be saying but not right about the meaning of the particular words they are interpreting.[63]

Ibn Taymiyya then gives us examples of these two groups. The ones who have it both wrong, that is both the meaning of the text and the interpretation of individual words, include groups like al-Khawārij, al-Rawāfiḍ, al-Jahmiyya, al-Mu'tazila, al-Qadariyya and al-Murji'a.[64] He then singles out the Mu'tazilites and their Qur'ān commentaries, mentioning their leading authorities in the field. The list is significant since it points to the richness of the Mu'tazilite Qur'ān commentary literature that was still available at the time.[65] Ibn Taymiyya then groups the late Shi'i commentators such as al-Ṭūsī (d. 460/1067) with the Mu'tazilites.[66] It is clear that he had read al-Ṭūsī's work since he offers an assessment of it.

Ibn Taymiyya then offers his summary (*maqṣūd*): "These exegetes had already formed opinions or doctrines and they made the Qur'ān conform to these opinions; they do not have a precedent (*salaf*) to support their claims from the Companions and the Successors, nor from the leading scholars of Islam. They lack support for their doctrines and for their interpretations."[67] Then he adds one of his penetrating observations about the influence of Mu'tazilite *tafsīrs* on the Sunni tradition: "Some of these exegetes have a nice turn of phrase, and are possessed of eloquence, and they insinuate their heretical views in their writing imperceptibly, such that most of the readers are unaware of this. An example of this is the author of *al-Kashshāf* (al-Zamakhsharī) and people of his ilk."[68] He then adds that many of those who are of sound belief fall victim to these commentaries and use them without knowing that they are copying heretical ideas. It is clear that Ibn Taymiyya was dismayed that the Sunni scholars were very receptive to al-Zamakhsharī's Qur'ān commentary, and may have even incorporated it into their scholastic curriculum.[69]

Ibn Taymiyya then gives examples of such reprehensible interpretations. The Shi'is (or, as he likes to call them, al-Rāfiḍa) interpret verse 111:1 as a curse on Abū Bakr and 'Umar. Of the string of examples that he cites, the most colourful is the interpretation given to verse 2:67 (God commands you to slaughter a cow); apparently it meant to slaughter 'Ā'isha, the wife of Muḥammad.

Yet, Ibn Taymiyya is no cheap polemicist, and he takes a swing at the pietistic Sunni interpretations of the Qur'ān that mimic the Shi'i method. Thus Sunni interpretations of certain verses as laudatory tributes to Abū Bakr, 'Umar and 'Uthmān are all wrong. Ibn Taymiyya calls them *khurāfāt*, superstitions or yarn tales.[70]

Ibn Taymiyya then returns to discussing exegetical works, and he mentions the commentary of Ibn 'Aṭiyya (d. 542/1148). He declares him to be a more consistent follower of the Sunna and far less heretical than al-Zamakhsharī.[71] Ibn Taymiyya then registers a complaint against the Sunni authors of *tafsīr*: if only they stuck to the words of the early generations and did not go beyond them, it would have been more beneficial (*wa-law dhakara kalām al-salaf al-mawjūd fī al-tafāsīr al-ma'thūra 'anhum 'alā wajhihi la-kāna aḥsan wa-ajmal*).[72] Ibn Taymiyya complains that Ibn 'Aṭiyya, although claiming to copy from al-Ṭabarī, leaves out what al-Ṭabari cited of the statements of the early generations and instead fills his commentary with what he says are the opinions of the people of scholarship (*ahl al-taḥqīq*). Ibn Taymiyya informs his readers who those "people of scholarship" really are: Sunni Ash'arite theologians who used the same methods as the Mu'tazilite theologians to argue for the Sunni viewpoint—something Ibn Taymiyya is not thrilled about.[73]

Ibn Taymiyya then states his view that anyone (and he means here the people who consider themselves part of the Sunni fold) who diverges from the opinion of the Companions and the Successors and their interpretation is wrong, an innovator even (*mubtadi'*), although he might be a *mujtahid* and if so, his mistake is forgiven.[74] Ibn Taymiyya then states his *maqṣūd* again: one has to know the methods of attaining knowledge and how to prove the validity of our knowledge (*bayān ṭuruq al-'ilm wa-adillatihi wa-ṭuruq al-ṣawāb*).[75] He states that:

> We know that the Qur'ān was read by the Companions and the Successors and their Successors and that they were the most informed about its meanings and interpretation. They were also fully aware of the truth that Muḥammad was given. Whoever disagrees with their views and contradicts their interpretation is wrong both in his new interpretation and the meaning he gives to the words themselves (the *madlūl* and *dalīl*).[76]

Ibn Taymiyya has thus made clear his approach to the problem of interpreting the Qur'ān: it is mainly centred on epistemology and not hermeneutics. The question that Ibn Taymiyya has raised so far is how we know that *tafsīr* is part of the knowledge that one can verify—the corpus of *tafsīr* is thus already a given, it is already there. He is raising the possibility that part of the *tafsīr* lore belongs to the prophetic lore. Once we realize that Ibn Taymiyya is offering a method of evaluating the interpretive tradition, rather than a method of arriving at meanings, it then makes sense that most of the treatise is a defense of the interpretations of the Companions and Successors *qua* interpretations of the Companions and the Successors. He is hardly concerned with the method by which the Companions or the Successors arrived at their interpretations. His main aim is to prove that *tafsīr* is knowledge, in the sense of transmitted, valid information, and the first part of the treatise is an attempt to prove this point. Ibn Taymiyya seems, however, to be of two minds on how to go about this, hinting on the one hand that *tafsīr*'s origins are prophetic, while on the other hand arguing that the *salaf* were the most knowledgeable and therefore are the only individuals entitled to give us back the meaning of the Qur'ān. In the final analysis hermeneutics to Ibn Taymiyya is not a repeatable process or approach; one cannot fathom the method used by the Companions and the Successors and use the same method to arrive at the truth again and independently.

This epistemological twist that Ibn Taymiyya employs also helps to explain why, for example, he does not care to mention or discuss the word *ta'wīl* or *tafsīr*, the two words that are always discussed when theorizing about hermeneutics (although he has done so in other parts of his writings). The complete absence of such a discussion in what is supposed to be a hermeneutical tractate is remarkable; it only confirms the intellectual acumen of his polemical mind. By refusing to engage directly with the usual terminology one expects to find in any theoretical hermeneutical discussion, he makes it impossible for his foes to pursue the debate on their own terms. To mention philology, the foundation of traditional *tafsīr*, let alone side with it, is to lose the battle with the Muʿtazilites and other Sunnis, including the Ashʿarite theologians. It is better to disregard philology altogether here.[77]

Ibn Taymiyya ends this chapter by stating that his aim was to draw attention to the reasons behind the contradictory differences in *tafsīr*.[78] The main reason for differences in *tafsīr*, according to him, was baseless innovations (*al-bida' al-bāṭila*), which prompted their advocates to distort and manipulate the word of God and the word of his Messenger to suit their aims.[79] Thus it is incumbent on the believers to know what the Qur'ān and the Prophet said, and to know that the interpretation of the *salaf* was different from the interpretation of the heretics. One should know, Ibn Taymiyya asserts, that the interpretations of the ones who disagree with the interpretation of the *salaf* are an innovation and a heresy.[80]

Almost as an afterthought Ibn Taymiyya gives us an example of the second group of interpreters—those who make mistakes regarding the words of the Qur'ān (*al-dalīl*) while giving right meanings all the same (*al-madlūl*). These include the Sufis, the preachers (*wu''āẓ*) and jurists (*fuqahā'*), and people like them. These groups impute the Qur'ān with interpretations that are in themselves valid but which have no basis in the wording of the Qur'ān that supposedly supports such interpretations.[81] Ibn Taymiyya mentions al-Sulamī's (d. 412/1021) *Ḥaqā'iq al-tafsīr* as an example that contains such interpretations.

This brings the first section of the treatise to an end. The main aim of this section, as I have stated, was to establish the proposition that *tafsīr* is knowledge. Ibn Taymiyya's most important claim is that Muḥammad taught the interpretation of the Qur'ān to the Companions and that they taught it to the Successors. Since such interpretations constitute part of the knowledge that can be traced back to an infallible source, it has a claim to veracity that is not accorded to other interpretations. Indeed, the main aim of Ibn Taymiyya was to indirectly imply that even if the interpretations of the Companions and more importantly, of the Successors, were not known to come directly from Muḥammad, there is enough reason to think that they might be. This in itself raises the level of these interpretations to a different order of things, since they could be theoretically part of prophetic knowledge.

Chapter Five[82]

This chapter starts with a hypothetical question: What is the best way to interpret the Qur'ān? To this question Ibn Taymiyya says: "The best way to interpret the Qur'ān is by the Qur'ān. For what is elliptical (*ujmila*) in one place is explained more fully in another and what is in summary form in one place is expounded in another. If one cannot find the interpretation through this method then one can have recourse to the Sunna, for the Sunna expounds the Qur'ān and clarifies it."[83] Explaining the Qur'ān with the Sunna is a common enough hermeneutical Sunni strategy that is not surprising here. It is the notion of interpreting the Qur'ān with the Qur'ān that seems to be the novelty. This hermeneutical device is not unknown in the tradition; many examples from the interpretive tradition show that the exegetes were well aware of this possibility as a method of interpreting the Qur'ān.[84] It is Ibn Taymiyya's placing it at the top of a hierarchical order of interpretation that is the interesting development here. One could argue that Ibn Taymiyya was admitting philology through such a formulation. This is not so. In so far as Ibn Taymiyya does not give any examples of how one interprets the Qur'ān with the Qur'ān this rule is rather ineffectual and vague. Indeed it should not be confused with our modern notions of textual criticism where it is the norm to analyze a certain text by using the text itself to explain its own usage. The rule as given here is rather a point of departure for construing the hermeneutical exercise as a juristic exercise. What Ibn Taymiyya was doing was replicating in the interpretation of the Qur'ān the same steps one followed in the discovery of God's law, as formulated by the Sunni jurists. According to Sunni legal theory, the sources of the Sharī'a are the Qur'ān, the Sunna, the consensus of the community and juristic analogy; the first two elements in both theories are thus the same. The brilliant stroke on the part of Ibn Taymiyya is to draw this parallel between the two systems. He makes his theory almost impossible to unseat as long as one also upholds the rules of the Sunni juristic practices as outlined in *uṣūl al-fiqh* manuals.[85]

That Ibn Taymiyya was presenting a reformulation of Qur'ānic *tafsīr* along the lines of Sunni juristic theory becomes evidently clear when he goes on to quote from the famous Epistle of al-Shāfi'ī, *al-Risāla*. Ibn Taymiyya quotes al-Shāfi'ī's understanding of the role of the Sunna in relationship with the Qur'ān, thus summarizing what is by then the standard position of Sunni *uṣūl al-fiqh*.[86] He then quotes the prophetic tradition of Mu'ādh, who was sent to Yemen to proselytize for Islam. Muḥammad is supposed to have asked Mu'ādh how he would make legal rulings. To this question Mu'ādh answered "by the Book of God (i.e. the Qur'ān)." If he could not find the ruling there, then he would consult the Sunna of the Messenger of God, and if not he could not find the ruling there then he would use *ijtihād*.[87] Ibn Taymiyya does not bother to explain how the *ijtihād* used in this Hadith fits with the new hermeneutical theory he is proposing, especially since he is not advocating the notion of finding the meaning of the Qur'ān through an exercise of *ijtihād*. But then he was not constructing the theory according to this Hadith or, for that matter, the principles of jurisprudence; rather he was pointing to a semblance of similarity between the two fields. It is as if *tafsīr* had the same rules as *fiqh*. Ibn Taymiyya devotes only a few lines to a discussion about the use of the Qur'ān and the Sunna in interpreting the Qur'ān. He could afford to do so because he was relying on an already well formulated theory of hierarchy that was available in jurisprudence, and thus the reader would be able to connect the two and assent to the construction of a hermeneutical theory in the image of the legal one.

The third level of interpreting the Qur'ān is through the interpretations of the Companions. If one fails to find the meaning of a certain verse in the Qur'ān itself or the prophetic Sunna, then one looks to the interpretations of the Companions. Here Ibn Taymiyya gives a more elaborate justification for such a path: "The Companions were more knowledgeable about *tafsīr*, since they witnessed the revelation of the Qur'ān and they were privileged with their close proximity. They were also more knowledgeable because they had perfect understanding, and correct knowledge, especially the scholars among them, like the four Guided Caliphs and Ibn Mas'ūd."[88] Ibn Taymiyya then brings testimonies to attest to the worth of Ibn Mas'ūd. He then mentions Ibn 'Abbās, and we are treated to long testimonies about his worth as a Qur'ān exegete. Ibn Taymiyya highlights the standard appellation for Ibn 'Abbās, "Translator of the Qur'ān," *turjumān al-Qur'ān*.

The fourth and final source for interpretation is the interpretations of the Successors. If one fails to find the meaning of a certain verse in the above-mentioned three sources then one looks for it in the interpretations from the Successors, since many of the scholars (*kathīr min al-a'imma*) followed the Successors in this matter.[89] Among the Successors Ibn Taymiyya names and praises the credentials of Mujāhid b. Jabr (d. 104/722). Then he mentions a list of Successors who were famous exegetes.[90] Again, the fact that these Successors gave multiple meanings to certain verses does not mean that they had contradictory interpretations; only the ignorant, he believes, would hold such an opinion. But Ibn Taymiyya does admit the possibility of real differences among the Successors in their interpretations. To the question of how one can follow their opinions when it is not a *ḥujja*, a proof, not even in legal matters, Ibn Taymiyya offers a resolution. If they agree on a meaning then that meaning is irrefutable. If they are in disagreement then one cannot use one Successor as an authority against another (all being equal), and must have recourse to the language of the Qur'ān, or the Sunna, or the usage of the Arabic language or the opinions of the Companions.[91] This is the only instance where the Arabic language is allowed a role in the hermeneutical theory of Ibn Taymiyya. But such is the restriction that it is never conceived of as an independent authority.

The final part of the treatise is reserved for an attack on what is known as "*tafsīr al-Qur'ān bi-al-ra'y*" or interpretation based on personal opinion.[92] A string of prophetic traditions that warn against such a practice are produced, all with the aim of showing that no one has the right to expound freely on the Qur'ān. Indeed, Ibn Taymiyya is categorically against such a method even if it reproduces the true and valid meaning of the Qur'ān! This is because the method itself is wrong (*fa-law annahu aṣāba al-ma'nā fī nafs al-amr la-kāna qad akhṭa'a li-annahu lam ya'tī al-amra min bābihi*).[93] It is precisely such statements that suggest that Ibn Taymiyya's method is a study of the value of inherited interpretations and not of hermeneutics. Even if one arrives at the true and divine meaning of the Qur'ān, the interpretation is rejected if done through the wrong method. Yet the correct method is simply impossible to replicate; one simply conveys the meaning according to the *salaf*—one cannot discover the meaning on one's own. Ibn Taymiyya argues from the traditions he cites that the *salaf* did not like to expound on topics in *tafsīr* that they did not know about; that in itself is no indication, Ibn Taymiyya adds, that they did not expound on things they did know about. On the contrary, we have a large amount of *tafsīr* material from them.[94] There is no inconsistency here, since Ibn Taymiyya was not defending the right of exegetes to interpret so much as the right of the first three generations to interpret.

Ibn Taymiyya concludes his treatise with a tradition on the authority of al-Ṭabarī stating that Ibn 'Abbās said: "*Tafsīr* is of four kinds: a kind that can be known from the language of the Arabs, a kind that every Muslim should know, a kind that only the scholars know, and a kind that only God knows."[95] One should not make much of the quotation of this Hadith here. Ibn Taymiyya has already given his theory, and these traditions add little in the way of clarification.[96]

The Significance of Ibn Taymiyya's Treatise

I have already referred to the method resulting from following the principles put forth by Ibn Taymiyya "radical hermeneutics" because it claims to take *tafsīr* back to its roots in the *salaf*.[97] Ibn Taymiyya was effectively binding the divine word with the prophetic word (newly redefined to encompass early *tafsīr* material) in ways that had never been seen before in the Sunni tradition. One understood the divine *only* through the prophetic. The binding of the two kinds of revelation had revolutionary consequences for Sunni hermeneutics. Implicit in this method was a full capitulation to the prophetic Hadith and the interpretations of the first generations as the decipherers of divine speech. Before the advent of Ibn Taymiyya, the prophetic interpretive method—that is using the Hadith and the opinions of early authorities as a commentary on the Qur'ān—was embedded in an encyclopaedic approach that was guided by philology, and thus was always a controllable method. The danger posed by Ibn Taymiyya's new hermeneutical approach was that the exegete was compelled to follow through with the governing principle of the method: the equating of the meaning of the Word of God with the prophetic word *to the exclusion of any other possible hermeneutical approach to the Qur'ān*. Given the continued growth of prophetic logia across the centuries, it was only a matter of time before the prophetic inundated the divine word. This "radical hermeneutics" approach did not see its full articulation prior to Ibn Taymiyya.[98] It was definitely Ibn Taymiyya who gave this method its theoretical foundation. His ability to create a genealogy of Qur'ānic exegetes down from Muḥammad, passing through Ibn Abī Ḥātim and Ibn Mardawayh, is testimony to his polemical ingenuity.

At the heart of this radical hermeneutics is a restriction on the ability of exegetes to say anything by way of interpreting the Qur'ān that has not been believed to have been said by authorities in the first three generations of Islam.[99] This was not only a restriction of options, but a reformulation of what exegesis is and is not. The exegete was made into a reporter of what has already been said about the Qur'ān, more in the nature of a *muḥaddith* (a transmitter of traditions or *ḥadīth*). Ibn Taymiyya repeatedly complains in this treatise that most *tafsīr* works are not pure, *ṣarfan* or *'alā wajhihi*, as he puts it;[100] they should have simply quoted the interpretations of the *salaf* without any commentary or editorial interference.[101] What he is implying is that the craft of *tafsīr* should simply be the recording of the material coming from the early generations without any additions or commentary. The final aim of these newly formulated rules of exegesis was to undermine the previous consensus among Sunni commentators that philology should be the foundation of the *tafsīr* enterprise (regardless of what may, in practice, have been the case). The dismantling of this consensus is the main achievement of Ibn Taymiyya's treatise, and it was done in an indirect method. Philology was dethroned not by a direct attack but by omission. Ibn Taymiyya did not attack the method itself inasmuch as disregard it. Reading his treatise, one is hardly aware that by consenting to what appears to be an innocuous, no-frills approach to the Qur'ān, one has discarded philology.

The Qur'ān according to Ibn Taymiyya is to be interpreted by the Qur'ān itself. Thus, what is obscure, elliptical, or unclear in one part of the Qur'ān is usually clarified in other parts of the Qur'ān. In cases where one cannot find an interpretation using this method, then one can move on to the second step: checking the interpretations of Muḥammad himself regarding obscure passages that could not be made clear in the first step. If these two ways fail to offer a meaning for a difficult passage, then one can move to the third level, the interpretations offered by the Companions of Muḥammad; and finally, failing that, one can move to the interpretations of the Successors (*tābi'ūn*). The first remark to make is that the first two steps in this process are rather inconsequential: Ibn Taymiyya does not tell us how the Qur'ān interprets the Qur'ān, and he fails to mention that there is precious little from Muḥammad in the way of direct interpretation of the Qur'ān—even if we include the non-exegetical Hadith that had been introduced to the Qur'ānic commentary tradition. The second is that this is a hierarchical method and, as such, an interpretation of the fourth level is less authoritative than an interpretation coming from the third or the second level. But since the first two levels have no practical impact on the meaning of any verse, then what we have is the privileging of the interpretations of the Companions and the Successors over and above any other. This tradition-centered approach to the exegesis of the Qur'ān is deceptively consistent with the Sunni methodology of formulating the content and the reach of the Sharī'a (the four *uṣūl* of the Sunni school). Moreover, it places Hadith methodology and mentality at the centre of the task of deciding the meaning of the Qur'ān. What Ibn Taymiyya offers is an epistemological method to decide what of the *tafsīr* material was authentic and hence part of the accepted knowledge for the Muslims; this was a hermeneutical method by default. One consented to an interpretation, one did not arrive at it.

But to submit to Ibn Taymiyya's method is to discard not only the non-Sunni exegetical tradition but most of the Sunni exegetical tradition as well. Thus, it would be a mistake to think that Ibn Taymiyya was attempting merely to disprove or dismantle the foundations of non-Sunni methods of approaching the Qur'ān (although these do get disproved in the process). Rather, he was going after the most mainstream of the Sunni schools of interpreting the Qur'ān, the encyclopaedic method which has at its basis the catholic spirit of *ijmā'* theology.[102] I am referring here to what would become the monumental works of the Sunni tradition—works by al-Tha'labī, al-Wāḥidī, and Ibn 'Aṭiyya, al-Rāzī and even al-Ṭabarī. Ibn Taymiyya found fault with most of the foundational exegetes of the medieval Sunni tradition and called into question their relevance and validity, while constantly drawing attention to other exegetes who were, though known, not of central significance. Ibn Taymiyya thus was taking issue with the Sunni hermeneutical formulation itself and in the process re-evaluating the whole output of *tafsīr*. In so doing he attempted to reposition the tradition-based current in Sunni exegesis, which had been until then on the margins of the Sunni tradition, and to place it at the centre of this newly redefined and reformed tradition.

It is impossible to understand the reasons behind such a radical redefinition of the method of exegesis in Sunnism on the part of Ibn Taymiyya without taking into consideration several factors that are not apparent in the *Muqaddima*. Three factors are at the background of Ibn Taymiyya's reformulation of Sunni hermeneutics, and also facilitated the acceptance of his radical hermeneutics by a large number of later commentators. The first is the paradoxical nature of the medieval Sunni hermeneutical enterprise itself. The encyclopedic Sunni hermeneutics was based on an internal contradiction: philology was proclaimed the tool needed to understand the Qur'ān, yet philology was not allowed to be the final arbiter of any interpretation. Sunni hermeneutics, in order to save its own theological reading of the Qur'ān and present a coherent interpretation, was ultimately willing to discard philology (which it had always maintained was the way to understand the Qur'ān) when it undermined a Sunni theological reading. To encyclopaedic Sunni hermeneutics, philology was thus only a tool, and literally so. In the last resort, what decided the meaning was the Sunni theological outlook. There lurked, however, within mainstream Sunni hermeneutics both a paradox and the danger of philology leading to a theological disaster should an exegete submit fully to the dictates of this tool. Ibn Taymiyya sought to rid the classical Sunni hermeneutics of this paradoxical dilemma. Moreover, while the position of the Sunni hermeneutical method—that philology was the handmaid of Sunnism—was superbly suited to counter a Shi'i *bāṭinī* (esoteric) reading of the Qur'ānic text, it had difficulties withstanding a Mu'tazilite challenge. What would Sunnism have to say if a philological reading of a certain verse in the Qur'ān supported a Mu'tazilite position and not its own? As philology was not a loyal servant, Mu'tazilite hermeneutics must not be given the opportunity to use philology against Sunni theology. Thus, Ibn Taymiyya was willing to discard philology altogether in his effort to undermine any Mu'tazilite and Shi'i danger to a proper Sunni explanation of the Qur'ān.

The second factor adding to the necessity of overhauling the Sunni hermeneutics was the rise of aggressive Shi'ism. By Ibn Taymiyya's time, Shi'i intellectuals were boldly publishing anti-Sunni polemical tracts that were causing serious consternation in Sunni intellectual circles. In order to combat this new trend, Ibn Taymiyya sought to make the Sunni theological outlook immune from Shi'i attacks. The main drawback of Sunni encyclopedic hermeneutics, according to Ibn Taymiyya, was its lax attitude to the Hadith corpus. It incorporated many pro-Shi'i materials without any apparent discomfort. These pro-Shi'i materials could be accommodated as long as they were not part of a polemical tug-of-war. The moment the Shi'is started pointing to this material as a proof of the validity of their religious claims, however, the Sunnis were hard pressed to disavow them altogether. Ibn Taymiyya was willing to discard the whole encyclopaedic approach if it meant getting rid of this pro-Shiʿi material.[103] And he did.

The final factor that enabled Ibn Taymiyya's brand of radical hermeneutics was the growth and consolidation of tradition-based material. The growth of exegetical material that purported to go back to the earliest generations was such that one could offer a continuous running interpretation of the Qur'ān without having to resort to any non-tradition based material. Ibn Taymiyya thus came at the cusp of a growing movement that was on the margins of the Sunni encyclopedic tradition. The *Muqaddima,* which I consider a manifesto, paved the way for the coming into being of truly monumental commentaries which were tradition-based and were capable of vying with encyclopedic commentaries.

The Influence of Ibn Taymiyya's Treatise[104]

The influence of Ibn Taymiyya's method in the medieval period was never sweeping. The medieval exegetical tradition was too polyphonic, too encyclopedic to allow his theory to triumph. A devastating response from the camp of traditional Sunni exegetes came even before the *Muqaddima* was published, from no less than Abū Ḥayyān, the exegete whom I mentioned at the beginning of this article. Abū Ḥayyān had received from Ibn Taymiyya a summary of his views before the two had their falling-out, and would later dismiss the foundations and arguments of Ibn Taymiyya's hermeneutical outlook in less than a page in his monumental *al-Baḥr al-Muḥīṭ*.[105] Indeed, Ibn Taymiyya was most probably responding to the critique of Abū Ḥayyān when he wrote the first four chapters of his treatise. Abū Ḥayyān raised the issue of contradictory interpretations in the corpus of the *salaf* as a clear proof that they were not divinely inspired. The medieval exegetical tradition simply refused to succumb to such a radical restriction on the authority of the exegete.

Ibn Taymiyya articulated and promoted a marginal, if influential, current in the medieval exegetical tradition. Only two medieval authors implemented Ibn Taymiyya's theory in the centuries after his death, namely his student Ibn Kathīr and the later al-Suyūṭī

(d. 911/1505). The earlier commentaries he has championed, like those of Baqī b. Makhlad, Ibn Abī Ḥātim, and Ibn Mardawayh, have now all been lost. The victory of Ibn Taymiyya's theory was only assured in the 20th century, and there is a danger of projecting this state of affairs back onto the medieval period. Since his treatise is one of the few available articulations of what *tafsīr* is about, some scholars have taken it to reflect the status of hermeneutical thinking prevalent in medieval tradition.[106] Ibn Taymiyya's theory was anything but representative. It was revolutionary and innovative.

Yet it would also be a misrepresentation to underestimate the influence of Ibn Taymiyya's theory. His arguments were not so much new as a forceful restatement of the supremacy of the Sunna in the hermeneutical realm. The moment a Hadith-centered approach to *tafsīr* was articulated theoretically it became impossible to reject out of hand: one could only submit to the fundamental validity of this approach, in so far as it places the Hadith (loosely redefined by Ibn Taymiyya to include all *tafsīr* material from the *salaf* generations) at the centre of how one interprets the Qur'ān. The hermeneutical theory of medieval Islam could choose not to follow this articulation but it could not dismiss it altogether.[107]

The first evidence we have of the influence of the treatise is the Qur'ān commentary of Ibn Kathīr, the student of Ibn Taymiyya. The incorporation of the second part of Ibn Taymiyya's treatise in the introduction of Ibn Kathīr's commentary is an indication of how seriously the student took this new formulation. This is not the place for a full analysis of Ibn Kathīr's commentary, but suffice it to say that the implementation of the new theory was incomplete. Ibn Kathīr was unable to break away fully from the established rules of the encyclopedic paradigm of *tafsīr*, and the work can be only described as a transitional work between the encyclopedic method and the new radical hermeneutical method. Despite the heavy emphasis on inherited interpretations Ibn Kathīr was still bound to the traditional method of philology, relying heavily as he did on al-Ṭabarī's insights and philological discussions. Ibn Kathīr was thus turning al-Ṭabarī into a figure of the *salaf*, which is hardly what Ibn Taymiyya would have wanted.

Less than two centuries later Ibn Taymiyya's theory would be implemented by no less a figure than al-Suyūṭī. In his monumental commentary *al-Durr al-Manthūr fī al-tafsīr al-ma'thūr* we have the only surviving articulation of a newly assertive type of commentary, a commentary where only inherited interpretations from the *salaf* are recorded, with no additions, no editorial comments, and no philological explanations.[108] This work is radically different from any other Qur'ān commentary (apart from Ibn Abī Ḥātim's work). The *tafsīr bi-al-ma'thūr* had now produced its classic work.

Daniel Brown has called the modern scriptural exegesis current in many parts of the Muslim world scripturalism.[109] His analysis is one of the few that has so far attempted to give us an account of the radicalization of scriptural exegesis among some modern Muslim exegetes. Brown, a historian of modern Islamic religious thought, is unaware that the current has a medieval antecedent in the theory of Ibn Taymiyya. Indeed, the main point to emphasize about this kind of scripturalism is that it is heavily indebted to Ibn Taymiyya's radicalization. The influence of Ibn Taymiyya's articulation of how to approach the Qur'ān is pervasive among modern Muslim exegetes. Unless the connection is made between Ibn Taymiyya and many modern Muslim exegetes, we will be missing an important part of the story.

Notes

* "*Tafsīr*" in this article refers both to Qur'ānic interpretation as a genre or craft and to individual Qur'ān commentaries, depending on the context. "Companions" with capital C refers to the generation of Muḥammad as understood by the Sunni Hadith criteria. "Successors" with capital S refers to the second generation of Muslims, those who came after the Companions. "*Salaf*" is the term used by Ibn Taymiyya to refer to the first three generations of Muslims.

1. The anecdote is related in Ibn Ḥajar al-'Asqalānī, *al-Durar al-kāmina fī a'yān al-mi'a al-thāmina* (Cairo, 1966), 1: 162–163. Professor Donald Little drew my attention to this anecdote.
2. For Ibn Taymiyya's life see Donald P. Little, "The Historical and Historiographical Significance of the Detention of Ibn Taymiyya," *International Journal of Middle East Studies* 4 (1973): 311–327; idem, "Did Ibn Taymiyya Have a Screw Loose?" *Studia Islamica* 41 (1975): 93–111; idem, "Religion under the Mamluks," *The Muslim World* LXXIII (1983): 165–181. For an analysis of the historical sources on Ibn Taymiyya see the little used M.A. dissertation of Ḥasan Qāsim Murād, *Miḥan of Ibn Taymiyya: A Narrative Account based on a Comparative Analysis of the Sources* (Montreal: Institute of Islamic Studies, McGill, 1968). For a narrative of the trials of Ibn Taymiyya see idem., "Ibn Taymiya on Trial: A Narrative Account of His Miḥan" *Islamic Studies* (Islamabad) 18 (1979): 1–32. For primary sources on the life of Ibn Taymiyya see Ibn 'Abd al-Hādī (d. 744/1344), *al-'Uqūd al-durriyya min manāqib Shaykh al-Islām Ibn Taymiyya*, ed. M. Ḥ. Fiqī (Beirut: Dār al-Kitāb al-'Arabī, 1970, reprint of Cairo 1938 edition); see also the new edition

of *al-'Uqūd* by Ṭal'at al-Ḥalawānī (Cairo: al-Fārūq al-Haditha, 2001). References in this article to *al-'Uqūd* are to the 1938 Cairo edition.

3. See Ibn Kathīr, *Tafsīr al-Qur'ān al-'aẓīm*, ed. M. Muḥammad et al. (Cairo: Maktabat Awlād al-Shaykh li-al-Turāth, 2000), 1: 6–19. See also the Ph.D. dissertation of Roy Young Muḥammad Mukhtar Curtis, *Authentic Interpretation of Classical Islamic Texts: An Analysis of the Introduction of Ibn Kathīr's "Tafsīr al-Qur'ān al-'Aẓīm"* (The University of Michigan, 1989). On Ibn Kathīr's use of Ibn Taymiyya see later in this article.
4. I am discounting here two Qur'ān commentaries, the partially preserved work of Ibn Abī Ḥātim (d. 327/938), and the lost work of Ibn Mardawayh (d. 410/1019)—extensive quotations of which survive in al-Suyūṭī's *Naẓm al-Durar*. Although these two commentaries follow the method prescribed by Ibn Taymiyya, they were not written as counterpoints to the traditional exegetical tradition but as part of it. They did not aim to replace *tafsīr* or redefine it in so much as to emphasize a certain aspect of it.
5. One might argue that it is precisely because he did not leave a complete, continuous Qur'ān commentary that his theory was to have such influence. When Ibn Taymiyya wrote *tafsīr*, he wrote it more in the manner of Fakhr al-Dīn al-Rāzī and not in the manner he was preaching. In recent decades two compilations of Qur'ānic exegesis from Ibn Taymiyya have been published—one under the title *al-Tafsīr al-kabīr*, ed. 'Abd al-Raḥmān 'Umayra (Beirut: Dār al-Kutub al-'Ilmiyya, 1988), the second under the title *Daqā'iq al-tafsīr* (Jedda, 1986). It is not clear to what degree the two new collections are any different from what has been available in his other writings which dealt with certain aspects of the Qur'ān (see his *Tafsīr Sūrat al-Nūr* [Beirut, 1983] as an example of his exegetical writings). These two collections simply gather Ibn Taymiyya's different pronouncements on the Qur'ān from his already published works, which are then presented as "interpretation." The present article is not a study of such material. There is, however, some confusion in the biographical dictionaries as to whether Ibn Taymiyya wrote a Qur'ān commentary or not. Ibn 'Abd al-Hādī, on the one hand, mentions that Ibn Taymiyya left a Qur'ān commentary in thirty volumes, which was never published in full during his lifetime. A closer look at Ibn 'Abd al-Hādī's statement reveals that Ibn Taymiyya did not write a commentary but gathered all the *isnād* material on the Qur'ān into a collection (*al-'Uqūd*, 42). Other evidence, however, makes it most unlikely that he wrote a full Qur'ān commentary. According to some accounts, towards the end of his life he regretted not writing one, although these should be taken with a grain of salt since they conform to a topos in the literature of Qur'ānic lore. For all the references to Ibn Taymiyya's exegetical activities see *al-'Uqūd*, pp. 19, 21, 26, 28, 29, 39, 41, 42, 43, 44, and 377. The clearest statement that he refused to write a Qur'ān commentary is found on page 43; the clearest statement that he wished he had written one is found on page 44. Ibn Baṭṭūṭa states in his *Riḥla* that while in jail Ibn Taymiyya "wrote a book of Qur'ān commentary which he entitled *al-Baḥr al-Muḥīṭ* in almost forty volumes" (see Little, "Screw loose", 96). Ibrahīm Baraka, the author of an extensive study of Ibn Taymiyya's exegetical activities, is clear about the matter: Ibn Taymiyya wrote no complete Qur'ān commentary. See his *Ibn Taymiyya wa-juhūduhu fī al-tafsīr* (Beirut: al-Maktaba al-Islāmiyya, 1984), 71–76.
6. The current state of *tafsīr* studies does not allow for certainty when making generalizations such as this, but I am not aware of any comparable treatise

prior to Ibn Taymiyya. For a possible connection, though remote, with Avicenna's philosophy and his theory of hermeneutics (*qānūn al-ta'wīl*) see Yahya J. Michot "A Mamlūk Theologian's Commentary on Avicenna's *Risāla Aḍhawiyya*: Being a Translation of a Part of *Dar' al-ta'āruḍ* of Ibn Taymiyya, with Introduction, Annotation, and Appendices," *Journal of Islamic Studies* 14 (2003): 149–203, 309–363. It is possible that Ibn Taymiyya wanted, among other things, to clarify what is the Sunni, or better, Salafi way of hermeneutics and he wrote this treatise as an indirect response to the hermeneutical paradigm of the philosophers and the Ash'arites. Ibn Taymiyya could also be responding to al-Ghazālī's formulation of hermeneutics in his *Qānūn al-ta'wīl* (Cairo, 1940).

7. The study of the introductions of Qur'ān commentaries has barely begun. The natural dependence and interplay between these introductions has not been studied yet. See Walid Saleh, *The Formation of Classical Tafsīr Tradition: The Qur'ān Commentary of al-Tha'labī* (Leiden: Brill, 2004), 78, for bibliography on studies of the introductions of Qur'ān commentaries.
8. See Saleh, *Formation*, 215–221. I will discuss the term "radical hermeneutics" later in this article.
9. It is not clear who gave the current title, *Muqaddima fī uṣūl al-tafsīr*, to this treatise. Zarzūr thinks that it was given by the first editor, the Grand Muftī of the Ḥanbalīs in Damascus. The manuscript title as shown in Zarzūr's edition simply paraphrases the beginning statement of the treatise and gives it as a title: *Qā'ida 'aẓīmat al-qadr sharīfatun fī tabyīn mā yu'īn 'alā fahm al-Qur'ān wa-tafsīrihi wa-ma'rifat ma'ānīhi.* There is something to be said for the insight of the Grand Muftī which, by giving it this title, summed up the significance of this document. It draws an unavoidable parallel with *uṣūl* treatises on jurisprudence, an association to which I shall return later. See *Muqaddima*, 22 (note 13).
10. *Muqaddima fī uṣūl al-tafsīr, Ibn Taymiyya*, ed. 'Adnān Zarzūr (Kuwait: Dār al-Qur'ān al-Karīm, 1971). I will refer to this edition simply as *Muqaddima* in this article. For the information on manuscripts used and a brief history of the publication history of this treatise see pages 21–24 of this edition. I have also consulted the second Salafī edition of Muḥibb al-Dīn al-Khaṭīb (Cairo: al-Maṭba'a al-Salafiyya, 1385/1965). I did not consult the 1936 edition. To the list of corrections given by Zarzūr for his edition add this: p. 47 line 2 insert the word *dhālika* after the second word (correction from the 1965 edition). The text of the treatise is also included in *Majmū' fatāwā shaykh al-Islām Aḥmad b. Taymiyya*, ed. 'Abd al-Raḥmān b. Muḥammad b. Qāsim and Muḥammad b. 'Abd al-Raḥmān b. Muḥammad (Riyadh, 1964), 13: 329–375.
11. For an example of other editions see the one published by Fawwāz Zamlī (Cairo: Dār Ibn Ḥazm, 1997) and the one by Maḥmūd Naṣṣār (Cairo: Maktabat al-Turāth al-Islāmī, 1988). There is a Salafi English translation by Muḥammad 'Abdul Haq Ansari (Birmingham: Al-Hidaayah Publishing, 1993). Excerpts of the treatise have been translated by Jane McAullife in *Windows on the House of Islam: Muslim Sources on Spirituality and Religious Life*, ed. John Renard (Berkeley: University of California Press, 1998), 35–43.
12. *Muqaddima*, 33.
13. Ibid.
14. Ibid.
15. Ibid., 34.
16. Ibid., 35.

17. Zarzūr only claims that the *Muqaddima* has five chapters; see his remarks, *Muqaddima*, 15.
18. The first to overlook them was of course the student of Ibn Taymiyya, Ibn Kathīr.
19. Ibid., 35. Ibn Taymiyya is rather categorical in the way he expresses this idea: "It should be known (*yajibu an yu'lam*) that the Prophet...".
20. Cf. his statements in his treatise *Tafsīr Sūrat al-Ikhlāṣ* (Beirut: Dār al-Kitāb al-'Arabī, 1993), 107: "*fa-inna al-rasūl lammā khāṭabahum bi-al-kitāb wa-al-sunna 'arrafahum mā arāda bi-tilka al-alfāẓ, wa-kānat ma'rifat al-ṣaḥābah li-ma'ānī al-Qur'ān akmal min ḥufẓihim li-ḥurūfihi. Wa-qad ballaghū tilka al-ma'ānī ilā al-tābi'īn a'ẓam mimmā ballaghū ḥurūfahu. Fa-inna al-ma'ānī al-'āmah allatī yaḥtāj ilayhā 'umūm al-muslimīn, mithl ma'nā al-tawḥīd wa-ma'nā al-wāḥid wa-al-aḥad wa-al-īmān wa-al-islām wa-naḥw dhālika kāna jamī' al-ṣaḥāba ya'rifūn mā aḥabba rasūl Allāh min ma'rifatihi, wa-lā yaḥfaẓ al-Qur'ān kullahu illā qalīlun minhum.*" This is typical of Ibn Taymiyya: Having made a point he pushes it to its natural conclusion: the Companions knew what Muḥammad meant by his religion more than they could be expected to have memorized the Qur'ān.
21. For an introduction to the science of Hadith see John Burton, *An Introduction to the Hadith* (Edinburgh: Edinburgh University Press, 1994).
22. *Muqaddima*, 35–36. This tradition is an old one, cited by al-Ṭabarī and al-Tha'labī in the introductions to their Qur'ān commentaries. The tradition as cited by these two commentators is not used to argue the same point as that made by Ibn Taymiyya, but to argue for the necessity of interpreting and the merit of doing so. The wording of the tradition does not clearly support the contention that it was Muḥammad who taught them the interpretation. Both early commentators, al-Ṭabarī and al-Tha'labī, understood the tradition to mean that the Companions of Muḥammad were the ones doing the interpretation and not Muḥammad himself. See al-Ṭabarī, *Jāmi' al-bayān 'an tafsīr al-Qur'ān*, ed. Maḥmūd Shākir (Cairo, 1961), 1:80; and al-Tha'labī, *al-Kashf wa-al-bayān 'an tafsīr al-Qur'ān*, Veliyuddin Efendi ms. 130, f. 8b.
23. *Muqaddima*, 36.
24. There seems to be evidence to indicate that Ibn Taymiyya viewed interpretation as an intuitive act, or at least manifestly accessible to everyone. At the end of his life when he was asked to write a "continuous running commentary on the Qur'ān" he answered by saying: "Parts of the Qur'ān are self-evidently clear, and others have been explained by the commentators in their commentaries. A few verses (*ba'ḍ al-āyāt*), however, have appeared problematic to some scholars. Perhaps one would read many a book searching for a solution for the meaning to no avail. An exegete might even write a whole book on one verse. So I tried to interpret these verses with demonstrative proof (the Arabic is *bi-al-dalīl*), since addressing these verses is far more urgent than attending to the others." *Al-'Uqūd*, 43.
25. *Muqaddima*, 37: "*wa-'aql al-kalām mutaḍammin li-fahmihi*".
26. Ibid., 37.
27. Ibid. The form of the verb *yastashriḥ* implies that one has to go to the source of knowledge and demand an interpretation in addition to transmission.
28. Ibid.
29. Ibid., 37–38: "What I mean (*wa-al-maqṣūd*) is that the Successors received *tafsīr* from the Companions, just as they received from them the Sunna (more exact:

the knowledge of the Sunna); granted they did discuss [the *tafsīr*] when drawing deductions and proofs, just as they discussed the Sunna."

30. The old view that *tafsīr* was not "prophetic" per se does actually make an appearance in the *Muqaddima*. See below where I discuss this paragraph, which appears on p. 48 of the *Muqaddima*.
31. Ibid., 38.
32. See Muḥammad Abū Zahra, *Ibn Taymiyya: Ḥayātuhu wa-'aṣruhu—ārā'uhu wa-fiqhuhu* (Cairo: Dār al-Fikr al-'Arabī, 2000), 334–336, for an example of legal ruling that agrees with the Shi'i legal tradition.
33. Cf. Thomas F. Michel's remark in his *A Muslim Theologian's Response to Christianity* (Delmar: Caravan Books, 1985), vii: "Ibn Taymiyya was essentially a dialogical type of thinker; among his voluminous writings there exists hardly any extended work in which the polemical element is missing. He seemed best able to say what Islam is (or should be) by pointing up its contradistinction to what Islam is not (or must not become)."
34. *Muqaddima*, 38. The Arabic phrase for what I translate as "variations on the same theme" is *ikhtilāf tanawwu'*, literally "disagreement of varieties." The Arabic for "contradictory disagreement" is *ikhtilāf taḍādd*. See Henri Laoust, *Essai sur les doctrines sociales et politiques de Taḳī-d-Dīn Aḥmad b. Taimīya, canoniste ḥanbalite né à Ḥarrān en 661/1262, mort à Damas en 728/1328* (Cairo: Imprimerie de l'institut français d'archéologie orientale, 1939), 231, where he gives an example of Ibn Taymiyya using the two terms in a different context. Laoust translates *ikhtilāf taḍādd* as "divergences contradictoires" while he gives "différenciations logiques" for *ikhtilāf tanawwu'*. I of course do not agree with his translation of the second term.
35. The editor, Zarzūr, points out the remaining two in the footnotes, see, p. 49 note 4, and p. 51 note 2.
36. *Muqaddima*, 38: "*an yu'abbira kull wāḥid minhumā 'an al-murād bi-'ibāratin ghayr 'ibārat ṣāḥibihi, tadullu 'alā ma'nān fī al-musammā ghayr al-ma'nā al-ākhar, ma'a ittiḥād al-musammā*."
37. What Ibn Taymiyya is implying is that if one were to explain the word "sword" (*sayf*) by the two terms quoted above, one is not giving contradictory explanations of the term, but rather similar variants.
38. Ibid., 42.
39. Ibid., 43.
40. Ibid., 44. He does give an example from logic. If a non-Arab were to ask what the word "bread" means, and someone pointed to a particular loaf of bread, it should not be understood that the interpreter is defining "bread-ness" in general terms but rather giving a particular example to illustrate a point.
41. On *asbāb al-nuzūl* literature see Andrew Rippin, "The Function of asbāb al-nuzūl in Qur'ānic Exegesis," *Bulletin of the School of Oriental and African Studies*, 51 (1988): 1–20.
42. *Muqaddima*, 49.
43. Ibid., 48: "*wa-qad tanāza'a al-'ulamā' fī qawl al-ṣāḥib nazalat hādhihi al-āya fī kadhā hal yajrī majrā al-musnad—ka-mā yudhkar al-sabab alladhī unzila li-ajlihi aw yajrī majrā al-tafsīr minhu alladhī laysa bi-musnad? Fa-al-Bukhārī yudkhiluhu fī al-musnad wa-ghayruhu lā yudkhiluhu fī al-musnad. Wa-akthar al-masānīd 'alā hādhā al-iṣṭilāḥ, ka-musnad Aḥmad wa-ghayrihi, bi-khilāf mā idhā dhukira sababan nazalat 'aqbahu, fa-innahum kulluhum yudkhilūn hādhā fī al-musnad*."
44. Ibid., 49–50.

45. Ibid., 51.
46. Ibid., 54. The editor is not happy with the word *mukhaffaf*, and he suggests an emendation in a footnote. His first instinct to leave the term as it is in the manuscript is right. There is no need to emend the term here. Ibn Taymiyya himself was on thin ice—hence the almost comical oxymoron. See *Muqaddima*, p. 54 note 1.
47. Ibid., 55: "*al-maqṣūd hunā al-ta'rīf bi-mujmal al-amr dūna tafāṣīlihi*"
48. The structure of the treatise is not fully articulated by Ibn Taymiyya. Zarzūr, the editor, has made it much more accessible by his editorial divisions, which are supplied with titles, although these are not part of the original text.
49. There is rather an impossible infelicity with the Arabic here, and one could only guess at what Ibn Taymiyya is aiming at after reading these chapters as a whole, and bringing their content to bear on the incomprehensible Arabic of this first paragraph of the chapter. This is another indication that he may not have had a chance to polish this treatise. There are reports in his biography that he was forced to smuggle his writings from jail without being able to revise them. I will transliterate here the Arabic for the benefit of the reader: "*al-ikhtilāf fī al-tafsīr 'alā naw'ayn: minhu mā mustanaduhu al-naql faqaṭ wa-minhu mā yu'lam bi-ghayr dhālika, idh al-'ilm immā naql muṣaddaq wa-immā istidlāl muḥaqqaq. Wa-al-manqūl immā 'an ma'ṣūm wa-immā 'an ghayr ma'ṣūm.*" (Ibid., 55).
50. Ibid., 55.
51. Ibid., 56.
52. Ibid., 56–57. For the debate on the *isrā'īlīyāt* see Roberto Tottoli, "Origin and Use of the Term Isrā'īliyyāt in Muslim Literature," *Arabica* XLVI (1999): 193–210, esp. 201–202.
53. *Muqaddima*, 58.
54. Ibid., 58–74.
55. For a different understanding of the significance of Ibn Taymiyya's arguments here see Shahab Ahmed, "Ibn Taymiyyah and the Satanic Verses," *Studia Islamica* 87 (1998), 78–86.
56. For a discussion of this type of material see Saleh, *Formation*, 103–108. A Hadith of this sort usually states that reading Sura x from the Qurān will bring such and such benefits to the reader.
57. *Muqaddima*, 76. He fails to mention Ibn Mardawayh who reported the same traditions; I have already discussed the reasons behind this leniency (Saleh, *Formation*, 218).
58. *Muqaddima*, 79. I have taken Ibn Taymiyya to say that *ikhtilāf* (contradictory differences) are the result of interpretations that are based on opinion (or *istidlāl*, or reasoning) and not *naql* (transmission). The grammatical structure of the sentence suggests a different reading, which is that some differences can be detected by *istidlāl* and not by *naql*. However, such a reading does not make sense either with what follows or with the whole drift of the treatise. The Arabic reads: *ammā al-naw' al-thānī min sababay al-ikhtilāf wa-huwa mā yu'lam bi-al-istidlāl lā bi-al-naql.*
59. Ibid., 79–80. Most of these works are lost. The authors mentioned are: 'Abd al-Razzāq al-Ṣan'ānī, Wakī' b. al-Jarrāḥ, 'Abd b. Ḥamīd, 'Abd al-Raḥmān b. Ibrāhīm Duḥaym, Aḥmad b. Ḥanbal, Isḥāq b. Rāhawayh, Baqqī b. Makhlad, Abī Bakr b. al-Mundhir, Sufyān b. 'Uyaynah, Sunayd (al-Ḥusayn b. Dāwūd), Ibn

Jarīr al-Ṭabarī, Ibn Abī Ḥātim, Abū Sa'īd al-Ashaj, Abū 'Abd Allāh b. Mājah, and Ibn Mardawayh.

60. Ibid., 81: "*qawm i'taqadū ma'āniya thumma arādū ḥaml alfāẓ al-Qur'ān 'alayhā.*"
61. Ibid.
62. Ibid., 82.
63. Ibn Taymiyya is envisioning here a scenario where the meaning an exegete ascribes to a given verse is in agreement with the spirit of the Qur'ān (hence a "right" meaning, in so far as it can be defended by the Qur'ān), but this particular meaning is not precisely the meaning of the verse in question. Hence, the exegete is misconstruing the words of the verse to mean something right (in a religious sense), but the words themselves cannot entertain such a meaning.
64. Ibid., 82.
65. Ibid., 82. Ibn Taymiyya mentions the great Qur'ān commentary of al-Qāḍī 'Abd al-Jabbār (d. 415/1025), among others, and of course, al-Zamakhsharī.
66. Ibid., 84.
67. Ibid., 85–86.
68. Ibid., 86.
69. The presence of *ḥawāshī* commentary on al-Kashshāf is my only evidence so far that it was part of the curriculum in the Mamluk era.
70. Ibid., 88.
71. Ibid., 90.
72. Ibid.
73. Ibid.
74. Ibid., 91.
75. Ibid.
76. Ibid.
77. For a detailed discussion of Ibn Taymiyya's theory of interpretation as offered in his other writings see Mohamed Mohamed Yunis Ali, *Medieval Islamic Pragmatics: Sunni Legal Theorists' Models of Textual Communication* (Surrey: Curzon, 2000), 87–140. Since it was his *Muqaddima* that ended up influencing scriptural exegesis and not his other writings, it is not necessary here to summarize Ali's analysis.
78. *Muqaddima*, 91.
79. Ibid., 91.
80. Ibid., 91–92.
81. Ibid., 92.
82. Jane Dammen McAuliffe has already analyzed this chapter of the *Muqaddima* as part of her study of Ibn Kathīr's introduction to his Qur'ān commentary. See her "Qur'ānic Hermeneutics: The Views of al-Ṭabarī and Ibn Kathīr," in Andrew Rippin (ed.), *Approaches to the History of the Interpretation of the Qur'ān*, (Oxford: Clarendon Press, 1988), 46–62, esp. 56–62. See also the analysis by Muḥammad Abū Zahra, *Ibn Taymiyya*, 178–190.
83. *Muqaddima*, 93.
84. Al-Wāḥidī for example gives a new meaning to the word *al-ghayb* of verse 2:3 which is different from the traditional interpretations given by previous exegetes. This new meaning is based on an examination of the use of the root *gh-y-b* in the Qur'ān. See *al-Basīṭ*, Nurosmaniye 236 *tafsīr*, ff. 38 a-b.
85. For *uṣūl al-fiqh* see Wael Hallaq, *A History of Islamic Legal Theories: An Introduction to Sunnī uṣūl al-fiqh* (Cambridge: Cambridge University Press, 1997).

86. *Muqaddima*, 93–94. See editor's footnotes for reference to Shāfiʿī's *Risāla*.
87. Ibid., 94.
88. Ibid., 95.
89. Ibid., 102.
90. The list includes: Saʿīd b. Jubayr, ʿIkrima, ʿAṭā' b. Abī Rabāḥ, al-Ḥasan al-Baṣrī, Masrūq b. al-Ajdaʿ, Saʿīd b. al-Musayyab, Abū ʿĀliyah, al-Rabīʿ b. Anas, Qatāda, and al-Ḍaḥḥāk b. Muzāḥim. See Ibid., 104.
91. Ibid., 105.
92. Ibid.
93. Ibid., 108.
94. Ibid., 114.
95. Ibid., 115.
96. The edition of the *Muqaddima* by al-Khaṭīb appends a *fatwā* from Ibn Taymiyya in response to this question: "Which of these Qur'ān commentaries is more in accordance with the Book of God and the Sunna of his Prophet: al-Zamakhsharī's, al-Qurṭubī's, al-Baghawī's, or some other?" Ibn Taymiyya states that the best of commentaries is the one by al-Ṭabarī; though he recommends the work of al-Baghawī, he does point out that it is a summary of the work al-Thaʿlabī, a work he is not too pleased with. He is not happy either with al-Wāḥidī, and seems to offer the same opinion about him that he gives in the *Muqaddima*. Al-Zamakhsharī gets the harshest criticism. Ibn ʿAṭiyya gets hesitant praise, at first preferring him to al-Ṭabarī, only to reaffirm the opposite. Ibn Taymiyya finally mentions the works of Ibn al-Jawzī and al-Māwardī, but he fails to issue a verdict on either. See *Muqaddima* (Damascus, 1965), 56–58. This fatwā is included in *Majmūʿ Fatāwā*, 13:385–8.
97. Also because it was a break with the traditional exegetical tradition and a repudiation of its foundations.
98. A possible earlier candidate might well be Ibn Abī Ḥātim, although the evidence we have is incomplete. On Ibn Abī Ḥātim Qur'ān's commentary see Eerik Dickinson, *The Development of Early Sunnite Hadith Criticism: The Taqdima of Ibn Abī Ḥātim al-Rāzī* (240/854–327/938) (Leiden: Brill, 2001), 36–37. Yet, not even Ibn Abī Ḥātim was calling for other ways of doing *tafsīr* to be discarded. He was simply offering the Hadiths without the other forms of interpretations. In this sense, Ibn Taymiyya was radicalizing a marginal current in *tafsīr* tradition.
99. Ibn Taymiyya is scandalized by the assertion of many exegetes that a latter commentator can come up with a new meaning for a verse if there were disagreements as to the meaning of the verse among the early generations. This implies, Ibn Taymiyya points out, that God has revealed verses whose meanings were not apparent to the early generation, which is blasphemy. See *Majmūʿ fatāwā*, 13: 59. Ibn Taymiyya discounts the possibility of finding a new meaning to a verse, a meaning that was not transmitted by the first generations of Muslims.
100. *Muqaddima*, 79 (for *ṣarfan*), 90 (for *ʿalā wajhihi*). Cf. Ibn Abī Ḥātim's remarks in his *Tafsīr Ibn Abī Ḥātim*, ed. Aḥmad al-Zahrānī (Medina: Maktabat al-Dār, 1408 AH), 1: 9. The program of interpretation as offered in Ibn Abī Ḥātim's introduction could have been the starting point of Ibn Taymiyya's theory.
101. From the little that survives of his exegetical works one could hardly guess that this is his position. Ibn Taymiyya's approach can only be compared to the master whom he rarely mentions, al-Rāzī. A fuller study of Ibn Taymiyya's exegetical works is needed to clarify the relationship between his conceptual

understanding of exegesis and his real practice. For a cautionary advice about taking the theoretical pronouncement alone without concrete examples of interpretation, see my remarks, *Formation*, 101.

102. Saleh, *Formation*, 17–22.
103. For the details of Ibn Taymiyya's attempt to purge the *tafsīr* of pro-Shi'i material see Saleh, *Formation*, 215–222.
104. Henri Laoust, "L'Influence d'Ibn Taymiyya," in Alford T. Welch and Pierre Cachia (eds.) *Islam: Past Influence and Present Challenge* (Edinburgh: Edinburgh University Press, 1979), 15–33. See also the assessment of Ibrāhīm Baraka in his *Ibn Taymiyya wa-juhūduhu fī al-tafsīr*, 181–184.
105. Abū Ḥayyān al-Andalusī, *al-Baḥr al-Muḥīṭ*, ed. 'Ādil Aḥmad 'Abd al-Mawjūd et al. (Beirut: Dār al-Kutub al-'Ilmiyya, 1993), 1: 104. Abū Ḥayyān does not name Ibn Taymiyya but refers to him as "one of our contemporaries." There is no doubt, however, that he means Ibn Taymiyya, since he gives a summary of his views as later formulated in the *Muqaddima*. Moreover, Abū Ḥayyān raises the issue of *ikhtilāf* between the interpretations of the *salaf* as a sure sign of their human origins.
106. Mustansir Mir remarks that: "The *Muqaddima fī Uṣūl at-Tafsīr* of Taqī ad-Dīn Aḥmad ibn 'Abd al-Ḥalīm ibn Taymiyyah (662–728/1262–1327) is a representative work in the field of Qur'ānic exegetical theory" in his *Coherence in the Qur'ān: A Study of Iṣlāḥī's Concept of Naẓm in Tadabbur-i Qur'ān* (Indianapolis: American Trust Publication, 1986), 28.
107. Despite the fact that we do not have a complete picture of the hermeneutical literature of the medieval period, we can still gather much from two medieval summations of Qur'ānic hermeneutical studies. These are al-Zarkashı, *al-Burhān fī 'ulūm al-Qur'ān*, ed. M. Ibrāhīm (Beirut: Dār al-Ma'rifa, reprint of 1972 Cairo edition) and al-Suyūṭī, *al-Itqān fī 'ulūm al-Qur'ān*, ed. Muḥammad Abū al-Faḍl Ibrāhīm (Beirut: Dār al-Turāth, reprint of 1967 Cairo edition). Both make clear that they knew about Ibn Taymiyya's theory and both quote it extensively, yet subsume Ibn Taymiyya's theory under the philological medieval paradigm. For details, see the index of both editions for references to Ibn Taymiyya.
108. Al-Suyūṭī, *al-Durr al-Manthūr fī al-tafsīr al-ma'thūr* (Beirut: Dār al-Kutub al-'Ilmiyya, 1990), 7 vols.
109. Daniel Brown, "The Triumph of Scripturalism: The Doctrine of Naskh and Its Modern Critics," in Earle H. Waugh (ed.), *The Shaping of an American Islamic Discourse: A Memorial to Fazlur Rahman* (Atlanta: Scholars Press, 1998), 51.

Human Choice, Divine Guidance and the *Fiṭra* Tradition: The Use of Hadith in Theological Treatises by Ibn Taymiyya and Ibn Qayyim al-Jawziyya*

Livnat Holtzman

Introduction

A major article of faith, the concept of predetermination (*al-qaḍā' wa-al-qadar*, henceforth: *qadar*) appears in every Islamic traditionalist creed and theological manual. Like other articles of faith, the concept of *qadar* has its origins in the Qur'ān and especially in Hadith material, but is also discussed in a rationalistic framework, regardless of scriptural proofs. As a key tenet of Islamic thought, it attracted the attention of both scholars and laymen, probably because it lies at the juncture of metaphysical notions, such as God's attributes, and ethical notions, such as the human being's responsibility for his actions, thus establishing a connection between the divine and the worldly. This very connection enables the Muslim theologian to address the discussion on *qadar* to the believer himself, as the person who is required to transcend from the highly philosophical debate into everyday religious practice. This transition from the metaphysical to the practical provides answers to the believer who seeks advice and comfort in his hour of need.

The problem of *qadar* constitutes a cluster of interrelated questions. Does God create the human action? Does God create in the human being the power to perform his action? Is the human being given a choice (*ikhtiyār*) whether to perform his action? Does God coerce the human being to perform an action, even a forbidden one? Does God know beforehand that an action is going to take place? These questions, which mostly fall under the category of "the creation of human actions" (*khalq al-af'āl*), emphasize the affinity between God and the human being as established in the *qadar* sections of many theological works.[1]

Some of these questions, such as "When exactly is the human being's fate determined?", or "How is the human being's fate determined?", are drawn exclusively from the Hadith, and are developed only by traditionalist thinkers. In *kalām* manuals, however, attention is mostly given to two issues: God's attributes and God's retribution. Therefore, the most frequent questions about predetermination in the theology of *kalām* are: "What is God's foreknowledge of human actions?", "What is the human being's responsibility for his actions?", and of course the cardinal question, "Is it fair to punish the human being or reward him for predetermined and foreknown actions?". Although the last question is central to the Mu'tazilī dogma of divine justice (*al-'adl*), it certainly preoccupies a great deal of the discourse of various thinkers, even those from the traditionalist wing of the Islamic theological spectrum.

Answers to these questions are usually treated in one of two ways. A solution based purely on the human intellect, associated with Mu'tazilī rationalism, leads to the conclusion that the human being has the ability to choose his actions and is the sole creator of his actions. A solution based solely on Hadith, including the teachings of the *salaf*, usually leads to the conclusion that God is the sole creator of human actions and hence the human being has no ability to choose.[2] These determinist answers are associated with the traditionalist trend of Sunni Islam. In between, Ash'arī theology aims at proving the traditionalist determinist dogma, which is based on Hadith, through the rational tools first developed by the Mu'tazila. In this way, Abū al-Ḥasan al-Ash'arī (d. 324/935) and later theologians attempted to reconcile the highly deterministic and even fatalistic Hadith material with the religious conviction of human moral responsibility. The Ash'arī solution is the *kasb* theory, which raises many difficulties,[3] and is not focused on the interpretation of Hadith. In that respect, the Ash'arī method of dealing with the issue of human choice resembles the Mu'tazilī one, even though it arrives at the opposite conclusion.

Like the Ash'arīs, Ibn Taymiyya (d. 728/1328) and his steadfast disciple, Ibn Qayyim al-Jawziyya (d. 751/1350), seek to defend the traditional interpretation of *qadar*. Their conclusions, however, are hardly similar to that of the Ash'arīs. Although drawing inspiration from Ash'arī thinkers like Fakhr al-Dīn al-Rāzī (d. 604/1209),[4] Ibn Taymiyya and his student strive to mould formulae which are very different, especially with regard to the nature and range of human choice. Ibn Taymiyya's and Ibn Qayyim al-Jawziyya's doctrines, while relying on the largely deterministic Hadith material, negate the Ash'arī *kasb* solution and assert the existence of free will. The novelty in their approach is their application of rationalist methods of Hadith interpretation in a manner that goes against the literal, common sense reading of those sacred texts. Instead of preaching fatalistic acceptance of one's destiny with humility and gratitude, they reinterpret the content of the traditions as an explicit command for the believers to take their fate in their own hands and acknowledge responsibility for their actions.

In this paper I present Ibn Taymiyya and Ibn Qayyim al-Jawziyya's understandings of one of the *fiṭra* traditions, the one which is most frequently quoted on the subject of predetermination. This tradition is the focus of a discussion in Ibn Taymiyya's theological treatise *Dar' ta'āruḍ al-'aql wa-al-naql* (*The preventing of contradiction between reason and revelation*), which Ibn Qayyim al-Jawziyya substantially copied in the thirtieth and final chapter of his magnum opus on predetermination, *Shifā' al-'alīl fī masā'il al-qaḍā' wa-al-qadar wa-al-ḥikma wa-al-ta'līl* (*Healing the person with wrong concepts about predetermination and causality*; henceforth, *Shifā' al-'alīl*).[5]

Through a close reading of a text originally written by Ibn Taymiyya and copied and edited by Ibn Qayyim al-Jawziyya, I will argue that the *fiṭra* tradition is used by Ibn Taymiyya to assert the existence of human free will when it comes to the matter of belief and unbelief. Ibn Taymiyya refers to this concept as *al-hudā wa-al-ḍalāl* (the right guidance and going astray), a concept which will be elaborated below. His goal is to interweave the belief in predetermination with the explicit assertion that matters of faith are entirely in the hands of the individual and his choice (*ikhtiyār*), a term not found in the Taymiyyan text, but nonetheless used by Ibn Qayyim al-Jawziyya.

Ibn Qayyim al-Jawziyya's role here is twofold. First, he offers an almost necessary elucidation of the unwieldy Taymiyyan style, which on its own requires a high degree of cautious reading. A parallel text by Ibn Qayyim al-Jawziyya almost always clarifies the meaning of Ibn Taymiyya's texts.[6] Second, apart from being an editor and an interpreter of Ibn Taymiyya, Ibn Qayyim al-Jawziyya also acts as an independent scholar with his own contribution to make. In a sense, Ibn Qayyim al-Jawziyya takes Ibn Taymiyya's interpretation of the *fiṭra* tradition a step further, and he offers not only a refinement of Ibn Taymiyya's approach, but also a novel contribution of his own. A comparative reading of Ibn Taymiyya's work and Ibn Qayyim al-Jawziyya's rendition of that text offers insights into Ibn Qayyim al-Jawziyya's editorial choices, and explains his decision to conclude his otherwise nuanced and elaborate *Shifā' al-'alīl* with what seems, at first sight, to be a mere reproduction.

Hermeneutical Approaches to the *Fiṭra* Tradition

The familiar and often quoted *fiṭra* tradition is attributed to the Companion Abū Hurayra (d. 58/678) who quoted the Prophet as saying:

> Every child is born with the *fiṭra* (*mā min mawlūdin yūladu illā 'alā al-fiṭrati*); it is his parents who make him a Jew or a Christian or *Majūs*, the same way as animals give birth to non-mutilated cubs. Do you think that they are mutilated before you mutilate their noses? [The Companions said]: Oh, Messenger of God, what do you think about those of them who die young? He said: God knows what they would have done [had they lived].[7]

The tradition, in its various versions, is a reference to Qur'ān 30:30 "So set thy face to the religion, a man of pure faith- the *fiṭra* of God with which He created humankind. There is no changing God's creation (*lā tabdīla li-khalqi Allāhi*). That is the right religion; but most men know it not- turning to Him."[8] In one of the versions the link with the Qur'ān is made explicit, as Abū Hurayra quotes the verse after transmitting the tradition. Another version links the *fiṭra* with God's predetermination of misery and happiness, which is said to occur either at the time of the creation of humankind or at the time of the creation of the embryo in its mother's womb. This version of the tradition opens with the phrase "Every child is born" but continues with the variation "...and on his neck there is a piece of paper which says whether he is miserable or happy."[9]

The theological and legal discussion regarding *fiṭra* also refers to Qur'ān 7:172, "And when thy Lord took from the Children of Adam, from their loins, their seed, and made them testify touching themselves, 'Am I not your Lord? ' They said, 'Yes, we testify'."

Although the term *fiṭra* is not explicitly used, this verse also suggests that the monotheistic faith is the primordial state of humankind.

As is borne out of the title of the thirtieth chapter of *Shifāʾ al-ʿalīl*, ("The first *fiṭra*, its meaning, the dispute among people about what is meant by it, and [asserting] that it does not contradict the predetermination of misery and going astray"),[10] the *fiṭra* tradition poses some difficulty for deterministic doctrines. Going astray (*al-ḍalāl*), which is described in the Qurʾānic text as well as in deterministic traditions, is interpreted as conducting a life of apostasy. The *fiṭra* tradition, however, suggests that all members of humankind are born as believers—most likely as Muslims—and only the education they get from their immediate environment leads them astray or causes them to stray to other religions, as is specifically stated in the tradition.

Ibn Taymiyya approaches the *fiṭra* tradition on two levels, in line with earlier Muslim tradition. The first level is an exploration of the different possible meanings of the term *fiṭra*, in order to elucidate practical, and mainly legal, implications. While early Islamic thinkers rarely go beyond this traditional exegetic approach, for Ibn Taymiyya the traditional approach serves as a springboard to the second level, in which the Hadith material, including the *fiṭra* tradition, is used in order to define the terminology and boundaries of theological discussion. In Ibn Taymiyya's hands, a terminology based on motifs and symbols drawn mainly from the Hadith material offers a theological alternative to the *kalām* lexicon.

On the first level, Ibn Taymiyya's discussion of *fiṭra* revolves around the exact meaning of the word, and whether it indicates an inborn tendency towards monotheism, Islam, or the predetermined happiness or misery of the human being. Recent studies have already explored the various interpretations of the term as they appear in traditionalist and theological works, indicating the legal implications of the various meanings of *fiṭra*, and they need not be repeated here.[11] In his discussion in *Darʾ al-taʿāruḍ* Ibn Taymiyya presents the familiar exegetical controversy between traditionists on the issue of *fiṭra*, whether it should be understood as the natural instinct of monotheism or specifically as Islam.[12] Elsewhere he specifies the relevant legal aspects and tries to settle apparent contradictions between various scholars.[13] His discussion revolves around the opinions attributed to Ibn Ḥanbal (d. 241/855), the eponym of the Ḥanbalī school:

> There are two reports attributed to Aḥmad [ibn Ḥanbal]. The first one states that [*fiṭra* is] recognizing [the existence] of God.... The second states that *fiṭra* is the creation of the foetus in its mother's womb, since he (i.e. the foetus) is led to the pact which He obliged them to make, that is the recognition of His [existence], as *fiṭra* leads to Islam.[14]

Ibn Taymiyya's conclusion is that *fiṭra* equals Islam:

> Aḥmad [ibn Ḥanbal] did not mention the first pact (i.e., the pact between humankind and God, taken at the time of the creation of humankind). He only said: "The first *fiṭra* according to which he created humankind is religion." He said in several places: "when the parents or one parent of an apostate [child] are dead, it is decided that he should be a Muslim." Then he mentioned this Hadith, and this proves that his interpretation of the Hadith is as follows: he [the child] is born in the state of the *fiṭra* of Islam.[15]

Ibn Taymiyya also examines a second opinion attributed to Aḥmad Ibn Ḥanbal, according to which *fiṭra* equals misery and happiness, and integrates it into the association between *fiṭra* and Islam. Thus he refutes those who argue that Aḥmad Ibn Ḥanbal gave contradictory opinions on *fiṭra*. Furthermore, he adds a novel dimension to Ibn Ḥanbal's interpretation, an element of causality which could not have been brought up by Ibn Ḥanbal himself. He does so by giving the *fiṭra* tradition, which usually carries a deterministic meaning, an additional meaning that reminds us of Mu'tazilī theodicy:

> The things that he [Aḥmad ibn Ḥanbal] said elsewhere, that this [*fiṭra*] means misery and happiness, do not contradict it [being equal to Islam], since God is the one who predetermined and ordained misery and happiness. [He] predetermined that they will be originated through means (*asbāb*), like the act of the parents, and that they will occur through these means. And so, the conversion of [the newborn] to Judaism, Christianity and Mazdaism by the parents is a part of what God has predetermined for the child.[16]

The use of the *asbāb* in this context indicates Ibn Taymiyya's causative point of view. Ibn Taymiyya uses the two opinions attributed to Ibn Ḥanbal as a raw material and moulds them into a coherent statement, which probably goes far beyond the traditionalist, and hence early Ḥanbalī, approach to this tradition.

He also refines the traditional approach to misery and happiness: while misery is straying from the route of Islam to apostasy, happiness is the convictions of Islam.

At the second level, Ibn Taymiyya draws theological conclusions from the *fiṭra* tradition, as demonstrated by the following formulation, which appears in one of Ibn Taymiyya's epistles: "Every child [is born] with what is known according to God's foreknowledge of what he is going to become [lit., that he goes to]."[17] This formulation directly connects the term *fiṭra* with predetermination. It explicitly invokes divine knowledge (*'ilm Allāh*), while the concept of *fiṭra* is suggested by the phrase "every child" (*kull mawlūd*), which is associated with the familiar version of the *fiṭra* tradition. The term *qadar* is not mentioned as such, but the phrase *sā'ir ilayhi,*"he goes to", which should most certainly read *ṣā'ir ilayhi,*"he has reached his destination" is connected with the concept of *maṣīr*, preordained fate.[18] This assertion reflects the affinity between three concepts: *'ilm* (Divine knowledge), *qadar* and *fiṭra*, as demonstrated below:

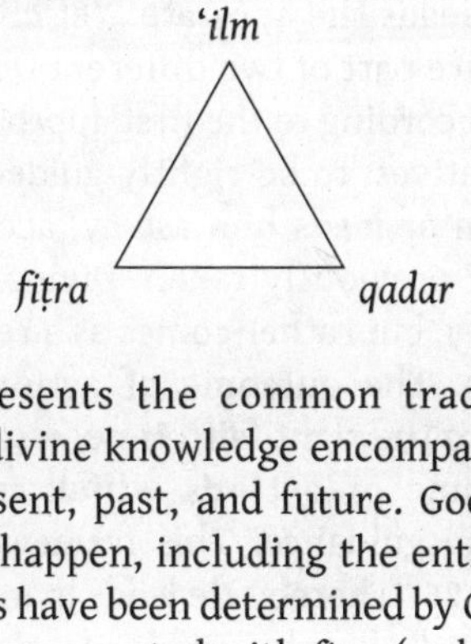

This diagram presents the common traditionalist concept, according to which divine knowledge encompasses everything that happens, in the present, past, and future. God knows in advance everything that will happen, including the entire course of human actions, and all events have been determined by God's foreknowledge. While human beings are created with *fiṭra* (or belief), some of them turn to apostasy, since that is the fate which was predetermined for them. Finally, God knows in advance that some human beings will turn to apostasy, even though they are created with *fiṭra*.

The following passage by Ibn Taymiyya, reproduced by Ibn Qayyim al-Jawziyya, summarizes this view:

> The consensus (*ijmā'*) and traditions (*al-āthār*) transmitted by the *salaf* only prove the following idea, to which we gave preference: human beings [are created] with *fiṭra*, and they meet happiness and misery,

> which were ordained according to God's foreknowledge. That does not indicate that they are without a complete *fiṭra* at birth, [a *fiṭra*] which would have led to belief, were it not for the obstacle (that is, the conversion of newborns to Judaism and Christianity by their parents).[19]

Yet, while in the above passage Ibn Taymiyya merely affirms the traditional framework of *'ilm—qadar- fiṭra*, he then moves away from predetermination and interprets the *fiṭra* tradition in light of the Qur'ānic concept of divine guidance.

Fiṭra and Divine Guidance

At the background of Ibn Taymiyya's interpretation of the *fiṭra* tradition is the concept of *al-hudā wa-al-ḍalāl.*[20] The term *al-hudā wa-al-ḍalāl* appears throughout the Qur'ān, always in the context of the right faith, to which God guides the believer, and the wrong faith, to which God leads the apostate. Yet *al-hudā wa-al-ḍalāl* (and equivalent terms)[21] are part of two different Qur'ānic approaches to predetermination. According to the first approach, every person has two opposite alternatives: to be rightly guided by God or to stray. God then guides him or leads him astray, according to the choice that the person had previously taken. Divine guidance or leading astray is not arbitrary, but rather comes as a result of human choice and human actions. The outcome of actions which indicate a person's adherence to the right faith is necessarily divine guidance, whereas the outcome of actions which indicate apostasy is necessarily divine misguidance. This framework is expressed for instance in Qur'ān 2: 26 "Thereby He leads many astray, and thereby He guides many; and thereby He leads none astray save the ungodly".[22]

The second framework, on the other hand, parallels the traditional concept of *qadar*. Here the guided person walks in the right path whereas the person being led astray walks in the wrong path. In this framework, there is no one starting point from which there is a split into two alternatives, but rather two parallel lines of existence. This is expressed, for example, in Qur'ān 6: 125, "Whomsoever God desires to guide, He expands his breast to Islam;

whomsoever He desires to lead astray, He makes his breast narrow, tight."[23]

Although this verse can be also be taken to mean that divine guidance and leading astray are outcomes of human actions, it is usually cited in connection with the vast majority of the *qadar* traditions, in which humankind was being divided into two groups prior to its creation, before people had the chance to perform righteous or else sinful deeds.[24] A representative *qadar* tradition is the following, often cited as 'Umar ibn al-Khṭṭāb's (d. 23/644) interpretation of Q 7:172, "And when thy Lord took from the Children of Adam, from their loins, their seed, and made them testify touching themselves, 'Am I not your Lord? ' They said, 'Yes, we testify'." 'Umar says that the Prophet was asked about this verse, and told his audience about an event which had occurred after the creation of Adam: "When God created Adam, He rubbed his (i.e. Adam's) back with His right hand, and pulled out his offspring. And then He said: I have created these for Paradise. Then He rubbed his back again, and pulled out his offspring. And then He said: I have created these for Hell."[25]

Diagram A

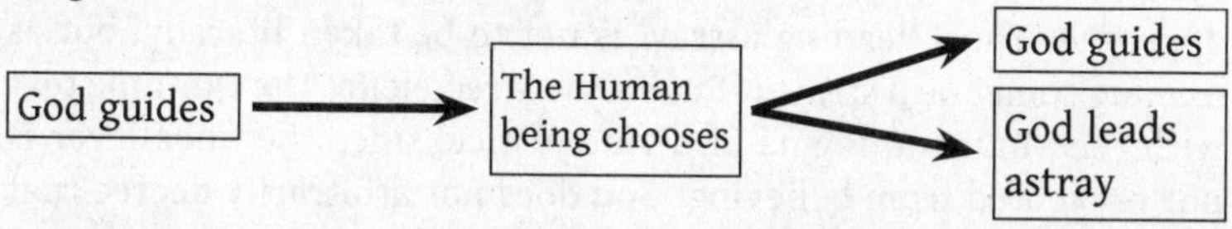

Diagram B

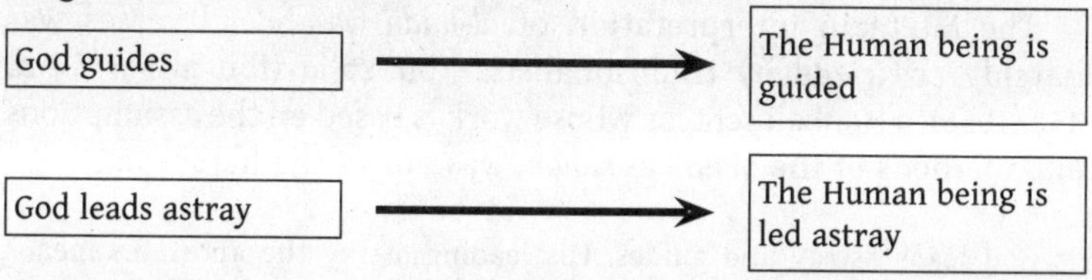

Diagram B describes an unchangeable predetermined reality, whereas diagram A expresses a dynamic and changeable reality, in which human actions have an effect on the course of events. While the majority of the Hadith material fits in with the determinist model (Diagram B), the *fiṭra* tradition is unique in emphasizing the effects of human free will (Diagram A).

The Qur'ānic verses expressing the concept of *al-hudā wa-al-ḍalāl* in various versions drew the attention of Mu'tazilī scholars. Verses expressing the idea of God sealing or imprinting (*khatama, ṭaba'a*) the hearts of some people, thus preventing them from receiving the divine deliverance, such as Q 2:7 ("God has set a seal on their hearts and on their hearing, and on their eyes there is covering") are central to Mu'tazilī discussions of divine guidance and leading astray. In Abū al-Ḥasan al-Ash'arī's heresiographic treatise *Maqālāt al-islāmiyyīn* there is a long account of Mu'tazilī scholars arguing about the interpretation of these verses. What comes out of this description is that the Mu'tazilī theologians saw the action of leading astray as a result of apostasy, not as a cause of it: "A few of [the Mu'tazila] claimed that the seal comes from God and that the imprint [which God puts] on the hearts of the apostates as a sign and a judgment that they do not believe [in God], and that [this imprint] does not prevent them from believing."[26] The anonymous Mu'tazilī thinkers quoted in *Maqālāt al-islāmiyyīn* believe that divine guidance, *al-hudā*, is actually a declaration that one is a believer, as much as divine leading astray, *al-ḍulūl* or *al iḍlāl*, is actually a declaration that one is an apostate. This typical Mu'tazilī view is meant to sterilize the traditional vocabulary of its deterministic approach. Thus, 'leading astray' is not to be taken literally, but as naming someone a strayer. Such a view reconciles the Qur'ānic text with the Mu'tazilī dogma of divine justice, since the unbeliever is not prevented from believing. God does not arbitrarily decree that someone should be an unbeliever, therefore He acts in a just manner and no evil or injustice can be ascribed to him.

The Mu'tazilī interpretation of *al-hudā wa-al-ḍalāl* verses was harshly criticized by traditionalists. Abū Ya'lā (Ibn al-Farrā', d. 458/1066), a Ḥanbalī scholar whose work is based on the assumptions and methods of the classical *kalām*, was one of the harshest:

> God leads astray and guides. His leading astray the apostates means creating the apostasy, the deviation, and the acts of disobedience in them [the apostates], as well as [creating] the ability to perform the above in them. Guiding the believers means foreordaining faith in their hearts, as well as the ability [to believe], and granting them the ability to successfully perform the acts of obedience. God's guidance indeed can be an appeal addressed to the one, whom God guides, to believe. It can be [an appeal] to obey, addressed to he, who knows how to accept this appeal and obey it.[27]

Abū Yaʿlā also twice refutes the Muʿtazilī view, that leading astray is merely calling one a strayer and guiding is merely calling one a believer, as an interpretation remote from the traditional use of *al-hudā wa-al-ḍalāl*.[28]

Ibn Taymiyya, on the other hand, uses the *fiṭra* tradition to support the non-deterministic interpretation of *al-hudā wa-al-ḍalāl*. His goal in his discussion of *fiṭra* is to remove the question of faith and apostasy from the domain of *qadar*, or predetermination, in order to establish a clear framework of human choice. The concept of *fiṭra*, like that of *al-hudā wa-al-ḍalāl*, deals exclusively with faith. The question of divine guidance poses the question whether true faith in one God can be affected by human choice or whether it is predetermined; likewise, the *fiṭra* tradition deals with the effect of the parents' choice on the faith of their child. Therefore, both intellectual frameworks leave out the typical *kalām* discussion of the overall range of voluntary or involuntary human actions, whether neutral or having moral implications, and rather focus on a dichotomy of two "actions": the action of faith and the action of apostasy.[29] Unlike other *qadar* traditions, the *fiṭra* tradition is not one-dimensional: on the one hand, it describes a situation in which the initial variables are already determined. Faith is not a matter of choice, since the newborn is born with the *fiṭra* of Islam. On the other hand, the non-Muslim parents have no real choice, since they always choose the religion which is not Islam. The alternative of choosing faith may appear theoretical, but the tradition does raise the possibility of non-Muslim parents choosing Islam for their newborn, that is, choosing to leave him with the *fiṭra*, or in the state of *fiṭra*. Leaving the newborn as he or she is, in the state of pure belief, is an action of choice. This possibility, however, is not actually pursued within the framework of Ibn Taymiyya's interpretation of the *fiṭra* tradition.

The non-deterministic interpretation of *al-hudā wa-al-ḍalāl* applies to the third human agent in the *fiṭra* tradition, that is the child. As a child he does not have a choice at all. The child, says Ibn Taymiyya, follows his parents in their unbelief, "because of his need to survive. He must have someone who educates him, and only his parents had taken the task, so he follows them because he has to."[30] However, as an adult he might come across the dilemma whether to believe in the Prophet and follow his way, or not. The *fiṭra* tradition, which presumably presents two choices, complements the adult's dilemma in the following manner:

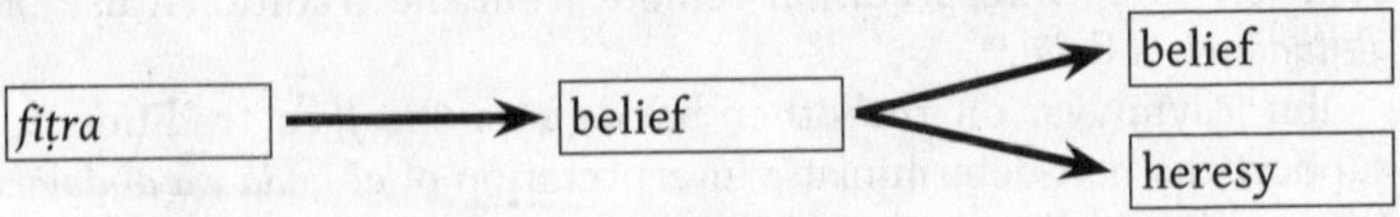

The overall framework which combines both concepts is as follows: All humans are born as Muslims; the newborns of unbelievers become unbelievers because of the way their parents educate them; an adult who hears the divine message or command can accede to it and become a believer, or ignore it, and continue to stray. Such a non-deterministic framework is generally not supported by the main body of *qadar* traditions, with the exception of the one on *fiṭra*. The *fiṭra* tradition singularly describes human ability to change the newborn's constitution, which is imprinted in every human being and whose essence is the belief in one God as the creator of humankind.

Ibn Taymiyya specifically rejects the notion that people are born *tabula rasa*, an approach attributed to the Mālikī scholar Ibn 'Abd al-Barr of Cordoba (d. 463/1070). Ibn 'Abd al-Barr interprets the concept of *fiṭra* not as Islam or faith, but rather as wholeness in creation, both physically and mentally. His approach severs the link between *fiṭra* and faith, because he assumes that faith is the outcome of an intellectual process: "It is inconceivable that the newborns understand what are unbelief and faith, because God has taken them out of the wombs of their mothers, when they know absolutely nothing."[31]

Ibn Taymiyya, however, argues that faith must have superiority over unbelief and that the choice of Islam is not one of two equal alternatives.[32] The *fiṭra* tradition gives precedence to Islam as it is the natural state of humanity, whereas other religions are deviations. He clarifies that the newborn could not be born without knowledge of the true faith:

> Since if it were, then when it comes to the *fiṭra*, there would be no difference between knowing and denying, and all the differences between conversion to Judaism, Christianity or Islam would be merely circumstantial. According to this concept it would have been more

> appropriate to say: his parents Islamize him, or Christianize him or convert him to Judaism or Mazdaism.[33]

Ibn Taymiyya thus argues that, were Ibn ʿAbd al-Barr's interpretation correct, the text of the tradition would have been different. He also adds that to be born *tabula rasa* is neither praiseworthy nor condemnable, while Islam of course is worthy of every praise.[34]

Ibn Taymiyya then strives to establish his view that faith and unbelief are not predetermined but are rather a matter for human choice. The way in which he proves his point demonstrates the distinctiveness of his exegetical and critical approach, even towards the early traditionists of the Muslim community. Ibn Taymiyya begins his argument by citing the *salaf*'s interpretation of Q 30:30, "the *fiṭra* of God with which He created humankind. There is no changing God's creation." Ibn Taymiyya sees this verse as a positive sentence, describing a fact, that is, people are always created with the *fiṭra*, as Muslims. The *salaf*, however—and Abū Hurayra, the immediate transmitter of the *fiṭra* tradition is no exception—interpreted Q 30:30 and the *fiṭra* tradition in a manner which assumes that individuals were divided into believers and unbelievers at time of the creation of humankind. Their conclusion was that the *fiṭra* constitutes a predetermined dichotomy of faith and unbelief. Their view was supported by the corpus of traditions on *qadar*, expanding the domain of predetermination, until it covered every aspect in human life. The most familiar tradition is the following, attributed to ʿĀʾisha: "A child of the *anṣār*, whose parents were Muslims, has died. I said: 'How happy he is, [being] one of the birds of Paradise! ' For that the Messenger of God replied: 'Do you not know that God created Paradise and its dwellers, and created Hell and its dwellers? '"[35] The immediate conclusion from this tradition is that faith and unbelief are implanted in men since the creation of humankind. This deterministic concept asserts that the arrival of an individual at either Paradise or Hell is predetermined, as much as his being guided or led astray. This tradition, or at least the approach it represents, inspired Abū Hurayra's interpretation of Q 30:30: "[Abū Hurayra] said: There is no changing God's creation (*khilqa*) with which He created all the children of Adam, that is, apostasy and faith, recognition [of the existence of God] and denial."[36] Accordingly, Abū Hurayra posits that faith and unbelief do not depend on divine guidance and leading astray, and certainly not on human choice, but that they are—both—the *fiṭra* with which humans are created.

Ibn Taymiyya, however, considers this rigid deterministic approach as misguided. The *salaf* meant well, says Ibn Taymiyya, as they did not want the Mu'tazila to use the *fiṭra* tradition to negate predetermination. However, they wrongly concluded that humankind was divided into believers and apostates at the moment of its creation.[37] It is while discussing the *salaf*'s interpretation of Qur'ān 7:172 that Ibn Taymiyya reaches his axial point. As mentioned previously, this verse has inspired several versions of the 'Umar ibn al-Khaṭṭāb tradition about the division of humankind from the time of creation to believers and unbelievers. Ibn Taymiyya refutes the common understanding of the verse, and by doing so ignores the entire corpus of deterministic traditions.[38] Rather, he views Q 7:172 as being unrelated to the tradition of 'Umar ibn al-Khaṭṭāb. According to him, during the making of the covenant between God and humankind, God already knew who would become a believer and who would become an unbeliever. That is the divine knowledge. But at the moment of their creation it was only a sense of recognition and faith in God, that is, the *fiṭra*, which existed in people's hearts. Ibn Taymiyya is willing to interpret the sayings of the *salaf* in the following manner:

> As for what they (the *salaf*) have said that God created them [humankind] with unbelief, faith, recognition [of His existence] and denial [of it]. If what they meant was, that God knew beforehand and predetermined that they will believe or not, recognize Him or deny Him, and that all exists through the will of God, His predetermination and creation, then that is the truth, which the Mu'tazila deny, since the exaggerators amongst them deny the existence of divine knowledge, and all of them deny His creation, will and omnipotence altogether. But if they [the *salaf*] meant, that the recognition [of God] and the denial [of God] existed while the covenant was made, then there are two [possibilities] regarding this [interpretation]: the first one is that during that time, their knowledge [of God] and belief existed in them [humankind], and this is what many of the *salaf* say.... This does not contradict what is said in the Hadith, that he [the child] is born with a religion, and that God has created His creation as monotheists (*ḥunafā'*). Moreover, it corroborates it. As of the view that while acknowledging [the existence of God], they [humankind] were actually divided into obedient and reluctant (*ṭā'i' wa-kārih*), then according to my knowledge, there is no report about it, which was transmitted by any of the *salaf*.[39]

What Ibn Taymiyya effectively says is that if the *salaf* meant that humankind is divided into unbelievers and believers at the time of creation, they were mistaken. As he subtly puts it: "The Qur'ān and the Hadith should be interpreted according to the original intention of God and His messenger."[40] In order to exonerate the *salaf* as a whole from this interpretation, he claims that only the exegete al-Suddī (d. 127/745) was guilty of making this incorrect assertion.[41] Ibn Taymiyya then condemns the way al-Suddī utilizes Hadith in his exegesis, specifically his use of a tradition which expresses a clear-cut division of humankind into unbelievers and believers at the time of creation.[42] Rather, he suggests, divine knowledge has no causal effect on human choice in matters of faith and disbelief. Divine knowledge does not predetermine who would be a believer and who would be an unbeliever. It is only the divine will which has a causal effect on the course of events.

By using the *fiṭra* tradition Ibn Taymiyya promotes the non-deterministic concept of *al-hudā wa-al-ḍalāl*. He emphasizes the ability of man to transform himself from an unbeliever to a believer and vice versa:

> God has given all human beings the ability to change that in which He has created them, through His power and will....[43] As for the opinion of he who says: There is no changing God's creation (*khilqa*) with which He created all the children of Adam, that is, apostasy and faith.[44] If he means that since apostasy and faith are predetermined, and their opposite cannot materialize, then he is right. However, this [view] does not necessarily mean that it is impossible to substitute unbelief with belief and vice versa. Nor does it necessarily mean that this is beyond human power. On the contrary, the human being has the ability to accept the faith that God has ordered him to accept, and to abandon unbelief He has prohibited him to embrace. He (i.e., the human being) can also substitute his good deeds with his bad ones and vice versa, according to the words of the Lord 'save him who has done evil, then, after evil, has changed into good' (Q 27:11), since all this substitution (*tabdīl*) is predetermined by God.[45]

In other words, Ibn Taymiyya says that the human being is ordered to embrace faith and to abandon unbelief, and that the power to do both is granted to him by God. On the other hand, the actual materialization of both opposing human acts, that is embracing faith or unbelief, is predetermined by God. What echoes in this paragraph is the difference between God's normative or religious will, as expressed by His commands and prohibitions, and God's creative will, whose outcome—the created beings—may disobey the divine command. This dichotomous view allows Ibn Taymiyya to reconcile the supposed contradiction between the injunction of Q 30:30 as an explicit divine command not to change what God has created, and the reality, in which changes indeed take place, and are, as Ibn Taymiyya says, an outcome of God's predetermination, hence God's (creative) will.

Ibn Qayyim al-Jawziyya on *Fiṭra* and Human Choice

The text that Ibn Qayyim al-Jawziyya copied from *Dar' al-ta'āruḍ* is one of the most elaborate texts written about the *fiṭra*, certainly when compared with Ibn Taymiyya's three other works dealing with the subject.[46] As opposed to the indirect manner which brings Ibn Taymiyya to the *fiṭra* tradition, Ibn Qayyim al-Jawziyya devotes a separate chapter to it, and rightly so. Ibn Taymiyya begins his discussion by citing views attributed to Abū Ya'lā, and then refuting them at length. In the course of this refutation, Ibn Taymiyya attributes to Abū Ya'lā the position that the recognition of the existence of God (*al-iqrār bi-ma'rifat Allāh*) is imprinted in humankind since creation, which then prompts Ibn Taymiyya to offer his interpretation of the *fiṭra* tradition.[47] The beginning of this refutation is not quoted in *Shifā' al-'alīl*.[48] Ibn Qayyim al-Jawziyya seems to have omitted this part since it relates to Ibn Taymiyya's use of the term *fiṭra* in his discourse on epistemology. *Fiṭra* in this Taymiyyan context is "the faculty of natural intelligence",[49] which has affinity with the term "necessary knowledge" (*'ilm ḍarūrī*).[50] The omitted part deals with ways of gaining the knowledge of God, and does not contribute to the discussion on *fiṭra* and predetermination.

Ibn Qayyim al-Jawziyya similarly omits the discussion of the legal implications of the *fiṭra* tradition with regard to the fate of the children of apostates. Ibn Taymiyya breaks this question into sub-questions: Should those children be treated as Muslims, if their parents are dead? Is it allowed to convert the child of an infidel to Islam? Is it allowed to kill a child of an infidel at wartime? For Ibn Qayyim al-Jawziyya, this discussion is largely irrelevant to the main theme of *Shifā' al-'alīl* as a theological work. The question of converting the child of infidels, which is thoroughly discussed in *Dar' al-ta'āruḍ*,[51] does not appear at all in *Shifā' al-'alīl*. These omissions are evident throughout the chapter, and suggest Ibn Qayyim al-Jawziyya's well calculated action of editing.[52]

Even with regard to the theological aspects of *fiṭra*, Ibn Qayyim al-Jawziyya does not merely reproduce the text from *Dar' al-ta'āruḍ*, even if he remains very faithful to the original. He applies his typical method of presentation, which is to describe a difficulty arising from the interpretation of a certain Qur'ānic verse or Prophetic tradition, and then to unravel the exegetical controversy about it. In this case, he also parcels the original text and shuffles its paragraphs.[53] Ibn Qayyim al-Jawziyya takes his master's text, which was part of a very long argument in *Dar' al-ta'āruḍ*, and adjusts it so that it would introduce the discussion of *fiṭra* in his *Shifā' al-'alīl*. When necessary, he also borrows sentences from other parts of Ibn Taymiyya's work. As an example of Ibn Qayyim al-Jawziyya's method of editing, the opening part of the chapter on *fiṭra* in *Shifā' al-'alīl* begins with a full citation of the relevant Qur'ānic verse (Q 30: 30) and two versions of the *fiṭra* tradition. The scriptural foundation is followed by the teachings of the next authority, i.e. Aḥmad Ibn Ḥanbal.[54] This order of authorities (Qur'ān—Hadith—*salaf*) undoubtedly meant for didactic purposes, does not appear in the original section of Ibn Taymiyya's *Dar'*.

Ibn Qayyim al-Jawziyya also contributes an occasional insight that seeks to clarify the original text. For example, Ibn Taymiyya compares *fiṭra* to milk, which is healthy to the body, and for which the newborn yearns. God, says Ibn Taymiyya, creates the newborn, human as well as animal, with instincts that protect it from potential harm. Only later in life does a human being corrupt his taste, and so he yearns for what may harm his body.[55] Ibn Qayyim al-Jawziyya then develops this metaphor further, and integrates it to the equation of *fiṭra* with Islam:

> When milk and wine were presented to the Prophet in his nocturnal journey (*al-isrā'*), he took the milk. Then he was told: `You have taken the *fiṭra*. Had you taken the wine, your people would have strayed. Milk befits the body and benefits it like nothing else, just as the *fiṭra* befits the heart and benefits man like nothing else.[56]

Ibn Qayyim al-Jawziyya's additions are sometimes more than mere elucidations of the Taymiyyan text. After establishing the connection between *fiṭra* and *qadar*, Ibn Taymiyya continues with a discussion of Qur'ān 7: 29–30 "...As He created you so will you return; a part guided, and a part justly disposed to error...". But, unlike Ibn Taymiyya who quotes a sequence of deterministic *qadar* traditions,[57] Ibn Qayyim al-Jawziyya ignores this familiar cycle in favour of five Qur'ānic verses whose theme is the creation of humankind.[58] He then uses these verses in order to interpret Qur'ān 7: 29–30. His analysis relates in fact to the first part of verse 29, "Say, my Lord has commanded justice (*qisṭ*)", which is not quoted at all by Ibn Taymiyya. Ibn Qayyim al-Jawziyya states:

> In this verse, God has commanded justice (*qisṭ*), which is the true meaning of His laws and religion. Justice includes the concept of *tawḥīd* (unity), which is the most just form of justice: justice when it comes to the right way to treat your fellow humans and justice when it comes to the worship of God. That is the golden mean of the *Sunna*.[59]

Ibn Qayyim al-Jawziyya goes here beyond the traditionalist framework of *'ilm—qadar- fiṭra*, and by doing so he reveals his ambitious aim of reconciling the concept of predetermining belief and disbelief with the principle of divine Justice. The question that Ibn Qayyim al-Jawziyya poses here is as follows: Is the punishment, which God gives the infidel after He Himself predetermined the latter's apostasy and led him astray, just? Although Ibn Qayyim al-Jawziyya draws this question, in which the old Mu'tazilī approach to the question of *qadar* echoes, from Ibn Taymiyya's text, he formulates it differently and in an original way.[60]

Finally, how then can we explain Ibn Qayyim al-Jawziyya's decision to close his monumental *Shifā' al-'alīl* with a derivative quotation from Ibn Taymiyya's work? One can put forth both aesthetic and substantive reasons. First, in terms of structure, *Shifā' al-'alīl* opens with an analysis of a tradition which bears a very clear deterministic message, that of Adam and Moses. In the tradition, Adam, whose destiny was determined years before his creation, wins an argument by using an explanation based on *qadar*: "Do you blame me for something God has predetermined forty years before He created me?"[61] Set against this initial deterministic message, the closing chapter of *Shifā' al-'alīl*, on the *fiṭra* tradition, acts as an anti-deterministic rejoinder, also based on an interpretation of tradition. *Shifāʾ al-ʿalīl* comes full circle in its discussion of *qadar*, starting with a deterministic concept and ending with a clear statement of freedom of choice coming from Ibn Taymiyya.

The second, substantive reason relates to Ibn Qayyim al-Jawziyya's actual interpretation of the *fiṭra* tradition. While Ibn Taymiyya strives to prove that the human being is responsible for his choices, Ibn Qayyim al-Jawziyya goes a step further: he uses the word "choice" (*ikhtiyār*). The use of this term is not unusual in *Shifāʾ al-ʿalīl*, and is applied to Pharaoh who brings up Moses "of his own choice" (*bi-ikhtiyārihi*).[62] Ibn Qayyim al-Jawziyya also argues that human action, while motivated by divine power, is still within the domain of choice (*ikhtiyār*) and not within the domain of compulsion (*jabr*).[63] Regarding the *fiṭra* tradition, Ibn Qayyim al-Jawziyya adds to Ibn Taymiyya's text another passage in which he claims that a child of unbelievers who chooses unbelief upon reaching adulthood does so "of his own choice" (*bi-ikhtiyārihi*).[64] This is not merely an interpretation of Ibn Taymiyya, but in fact an expansion of the domain of free will, at least in terminology.[65]

Conclusion

Unlike Ibn Qayyim al-Jawziyya, Ibn Taymiyya does not use the word "choice" (*ikhtiyār*) but the word "substitution" (*tabdīl*). Yet he is evidently preoccupied by the concept of free choice and seeks a mode of expressing it. The essence of choice is very clear. The *fiṭra* tradition completes this model, by describing the primordial state of humankind:

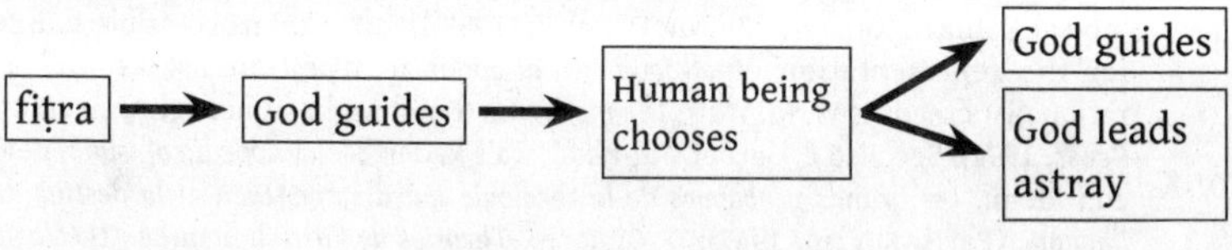

We must bear in mind that the whole process represented in this diagram is orchestrated by God's predetermination. Hence, the choice of belief or unbelief is included in God's foreknowledge, leaving the meaning of human choice somewhat vague. Nevertheless, as a whole, Ibn Taymiyya almost embraces the Muʿtazilī interpretation of this tradition.[66] With this exception of God's foreknowledge, Ibn Taymiyya's interpretation of the *fiṭra* tradition is a vigorous invitation to believe in the existence of human will, power, and choice.

Ibn Taymiyya's argument in favour of freedom of choice stands in contrast to the way the *fiṭra* tradition was interpreted by the early generations. This tradition presents two basic assumptions. One is that human beings are created with the *fiṭra*; the other is that human beings can also change or corrupt the *fiṭra*. For Ibn Taymiyya, the *fiṭra* is the pure and right way, in which humankind is created. Nevertheless, the *fiṭra* tradition itself, through several examples (parents converting the newborn child into their own religion; people mutilating their cubs' noses), states that people have the ability to change the *fiṭra*, that is to contaminate the pure state in which human beings and other creatures are created. The starting point of the *fiṭra* tradition, as opposed to other *qadar* traditions, is that human existence is dynamic. Ibn Taymiyya expresses this dynamism through an emphasis on the human ability to affect change, focusing on the journey from unbelief to faith and vice versa.

Notes

* I would like to thank Binyamin Abrahamov, Tzvi Langermann and Geneviève Gobillot for their valuable insights on the earliest version of this article. I am also very grateful to Yossef Rapoport and Shahab Ahmed for their patience and commendable professional help.

1. For a classical account, see Abū Muḥammad ʿAlī ibn Aḥmad Ibn Ḥazm (d. 457/1064), *al-Faṣl fī al-milal wa-al-ahwāʾ*, eds. Muḥammad Ibrāhīm Naṣr and ʿAbd al-Raḥmān ʿUmayra (Beirut: Dār al-Jīl [1985]), 3:33–62. An accessible source for the representation of *al-qaḍāʾ wa-al-qadar* in traditionalist as well as rationalist creeds is W. M. Watt, *Islamic Creeds* (Edinburgh: Edinburgh University Press, 1994). See also L. Gardet, "al-ḳaḍāʾ wa'l-ḳadar", *Encyclopedia of Islam*, new ed.; idem., *Les grands problèmes de la théologie musulmane: Dieu et la destine de l'homme* (Paris: J. Vrin, 1967); D. Gimaret, *Theories de l'acte humain en théologie musulmane* (Paris: J. Vrin, 1980).
2. For an analysis of the content of Hadith material on *qadar*, see A. J. Wensinck, *The Muslim Creed*, 2nd edition (London: Frank Cass, 1965), 51–57; W. M. Watt, *Free Will and Predestination in Early Islam* (London: Luzac and Company, 1948), 12–19; H. Ringgren, *Studies in Arabic Fatalism* (Uppsala: Lundequistska

bokhandeln, 1955), 86–126; J. van Ess, *Zwischen Ḥadit und Theologie. Studien zur Entstehen prädestinatianischer Überlieferung* (Berlin: de Gruyter, 1975).

3. *Kasb*, lit. acquisition, a doctrine whose roots are traced to the 2nd/8th century. It roughly expresses the idea that God creates the human action, and that the human being acquires that action. Thus, the human being is responsible for his action, although he is not the creator of it. See R. M. Frank, "The Structure of Created Causality according to Al-Aš'arî," *Studia Islamica* 25 (1966): 13–75; M. Schwarz, "Acquisition (*kasb*) in Early Kalām," in S.M. Stern, A. Hourani and V. Brown (eds.), *Islamic Philosophy and the Classical Tradition: Essays Presented by His Friends and Pupils to Richard Walzer on his Seventieth Birthday* (Columbia: University of South Carolina Press, 1972), 355–387; B. Abrahamov, "A Re-examination of al-Ash'arī's Theory of *Kasb* according to *Kitāb al-Luma'*," *Journal of the Royal Asiatic Society* 1.2 (1989): 210–221.
4. The influence of Fakhr al-Dīn al-Rāzī on Ibn Taymiyya is well demonstrated in D. Gimaret, "Theories de l'acte humain dans l'école Ḥanbalite," *Bulletin d'Études Orientales* 29 (1977):157–178.
5. I refer here to two Cairo editions of *Shifā' al-'alīl*: Ibn Qayyim al-Jawziyya, *Shifā' al-'alīl fī masā'il al-qaḍā' wa-al-qadar wa-al-ḥikma wa-al-ta'līl*, ed. Muḥammad Badr al-Dīn Abū Firās al-Na'sānī al-Ḥalabī (Cairo: al-Maṭba'a al-Ḥusayniyya al-Miṣriyya, 1323/1903) [henceforth: *Shifā'* (1903)]; and Ibn Qayyim al-Jawziyya, *Shifā' al-'alīl fī masā'il al-qaḍā' wa-al-qadar wa-al-ḥikma wa-al-ta'līl*, eds. al-Sayyid Muḥammad al-Sayyid and Sa'īd Maḥmūd (Cairo: Dār al-Ḥadīth, 1414/1994) [henceforth: *Shifā'* (1994)]. The 1903 edition, which is the first printed edition of *Shifā' al-'alīl*, is more reliable. The parallel text of Ibn Taymiyya is also found in two editions: *Dar' ta'āruḍ al-'aql wa-al-naql aw muwāfaqat ṣaḥīḥ al-manqūl li-ṣarīḥ al-ma'qūl*, ed. 'Abd al-Laṭīf 'Abd al-Raḥmān (Beirut: Dār al-Kutub al-'Ilmiyya, 1417/1997), 4:281–334 [henceforth *Dar'* (Beirut)]; and *Dar' ta'āruḍ al-'aql wa-al-naql aw muwāfaqat ṣaḥīḥ al-manqūl li-ṣarīḥ al-ma'qūl*, ed. Muḥammad Rashād Sālim (Cairo: Dār al-Kunūz al-Adabiyya, [1979]), 8:365–468 [henceforth *Dar'* (Cairo)]. Ibn Qayyim al-Jawziyya copied the same text into his jurisprudential-theological work *Aḥkām ahl al-dhimma* (*The laws regarding the non-Muslim subjects living in Muslim lands*). Ṣubḥī al-Ṣāliḥ, who edited *Aḥkām ahl al-dhimma*, noticed the similarity with the thirtieth chapter of *Shifā' al-'alīl*, but did not recognize *Dar' al-ta'āruḍ* as a common source. Ibn Qayyim al-Jawziyya, *Aḥkām ahl al-dhimma*, ed. Ṣubḥī al-Ṣāliḥ (Beirut: Dār al-'Ilm li-al-Malāyīn, 1401/1981), 2:491.
6. Ibn Qayyim al-Jawziyya's theological thought is rarely studied for its own sake, but rather in connection with Ibn Taymiyya's theology. That is the case in D. Gimaret, "Theories de l'acte humain dans l'école Ḥanbalite". A remarkable exception is J.N. Bell, *Love Theory in Later Ḥanbalite Islam* (Albany: State University of New York Press, 1979), who dedicates a whole chapter to Ibn Qayyim al-Jawziyya's theory of divine love. Irmeli Perho, "Man Chooses his Destiny: Ibn Qayyim al-Jawziyya's Views on Predestination," *Islam and Christian-Muslim Relations* 12 (Jan. 2001):61–70, is a general summary of *Shifā' al-'alīl*.
7. *Shifā'* (1994), 607; *Shifā'* (1903), 283. See also references to major Hadith compilations in C. Adang, "Islam as the Inborn Religion of Mankind: The Concept of Fiṭra in the works of Ibn Ḥazm," *Al-Qanṭara: Revista de Estudios Arabes* 21.2 (2000):394 n11.
8. Translations of Qur'ānic verses in this paper are taken from A. J. Arberry, *The Koran Interpreted* (London: Oxford University Press, 1964). The phrase "*lā tabdīla*

li-khalqi Allāhi" can also be taken as a prohibition, and translated as "Do not change God's creation". Both Ibn Taymiyya and Ibn Qayyim al-Jawziyya reject this alternative reading. See *Dar'* (Beirut), 4:309; *Dar'* (Cairo), 8:425; *Shifā'* (1994), 630; *Shifā'* (1903), 295.

9. *Shifā'* (1994), 56; *Shifā'* (1903), 22.
10. This title does not appear in *Dar' al-ta'āruḍ*, and is penned by Ibn Qayyim al-Jawziyya. In the beginning of *Shifā' al-'alīl*, Ibn Qayyim al-Jawziyya gives this chapter a slightly different title: "The first *fiṭra*, with which God has created His servants, and a clarification that it does not contradict the Divine decree and justice, rather agrees with them" (*Shifā'* [1994], 16; *Shifā'* [1903], 6). The use of the terms *qaḍā'* (divine Decree) on the one hand and *'adl* (justice), on the other, suggests the eclectic nature of the work, which appeals to both the traditionalist doctrine of predetermination and the rationalist doctrine of divine justice.
11. G. Gobillot, *La fiṭra. La conception originelle- ses interprétations et fonctions chez les penseurs musulmans* (Cairo: Institut français d`archéologie orientale, 2000), sums up the views of traditionalists as well as rationalists. Gobillot also discusses the thirtieth chapter of *Shifā' al-'alīl*, although she attributes the text solely to Ibn Qayyim al-Jawziyya. See also Y. Mohamed, *Fitrah: the Islamic Concept of Human Nature* (London: Ta Ha Publishers, 1996), 41–44, 63; C. Adang, "Islam as the Inborn Religion of Mankind". The complexity of the term *fiṭra* is demonstrated by the various ways in which it was translated into European languages. MacDonald, for example, understands this term as "Allah's kind or way of creating" ("Fiṭra", *Encyclopedia of Islam*, new ed.) Wensinck alternates between "the natural basis of the true religion" (*The Muslim Creed: Its Genesis and Historical Development* [London: Frank Cass, 1965], 42), a "predisposition towards Islam" (ibid., 43) and "man's nature" (ibid., 214). Finally van Ess regards *fiṭra* as a status of religious innocence ("Stande der religiösen 'Unschuld'", in *Zwischen Ḥadit und Theologie*, 101, 103), and Gardet as the inborn religion (*Les grands problèmes de la théologie musulmane*, 301). For legal implications of *fiṭra* see Gobillot, *La fiṭra*, 18–31; Adang, "Islam as the Inborn Religion of Mankind", 403ff.
12. *Dar'* (Beirut), 4:277–279; *Dar'* (Cairo), 8:359–361. See also Ibn Taymiyya, *Majmū'at al-fatāwā*, eds. 'Āmir al-Jazzār and Anwar al-Bāz (Riyadh and al-Mansura: Dār al-Wafā' and Maktabat al-'Abīkān 1419/1998), 4:150 (untitled epistle).
13. *Dar'* (Beirut), 4:286–287; *Dar'* (Cairo), 8:377–379; *Shifā'* (1994), 615–616; *Shifā'* (1903), 287.
14. *Shifā'* (1994), 607–608; *Shifā'* (1903), 283; *Dar'* (Beirut), 4: 277–278; *Dar'* (Cairo), 8:359–360.
15. *Shifā'* (1994), 608–609; *Shifā'* (1903), 284; *Dar'* (Beirut), 4:279; *Dar'* (Cairo), 8:361–362. Against this position, Abū Ya'lā (Ibn al-Farrā', d. 458/1066) argues that if *fiṭra* equals Islam, then the child of the apostates has no right to inherit his parents. *Shifā'* (1994), 608; *Shifā'* (1903), 284 *Dar'* (Beirut), 4:278; *Dar'* (Cairo), 8:360.
16. *Shifā'* (1994), 609; *Shifā'* (1903), 284 *Dar'* (Beirut), 4:279; *Dar'* (Cairo), 8:361.
17. Ibn Taymiyya, *Majmū'at al-fatāwā*, 4:149 (untitled epistle).
18. The phrase *ṣā'ir ilayhi* appears in the same context in *Dar'* (Beirut), 4: 291; *Dar'* (Cairo), 8:387, where Ibn Taymiyya interprets a saying attributed to 'Alī ibn Abī Ṭālib: "The true meaning of this saying [of 'Alī] is that every child is born according to God's foreknowledge of the destination he is going to reach (*Kullu mawlūdin 'alā mā sabaqa lahu fī 'ilmi Allāhi annahu ṣā'irun ilayhi*)". See also

al-Ṭabarī's interpretation of Q 17:13 ("And every man- We have fastened to him his bird of omen upon his neck; and We shall bring forth for him, on the Day of Resurrection, a book he shall find spread wide open"). According to al-Ṭabarī's interpretation, "And every man, we have forced upon him what had been predetermined that he would perform and the destination he was going to reach (*ṣā'irun ilayhi*), whether misery or sadness." Muḥammad Ibn Jarīr al-Ṭabarī (d. 320/923), *Tafsīr al-Ṭabarī Jāmi' al-bayān 'an ta'wīl āy al-Qur'ān*, ed. 'Abdallah 'Abd al-Muḥsin al-Turkī (Cairo, 1422/2001), 14: 518.

19. *Shifā'* (1994), 625; *Shifā'* (1903), 292; *Dar'* (Beirut), 4:302; *Dar'* (Cairo), 8:410. The version in *Dar' al-ta'āruḍ* begins with "the traditions" (*al-āthār*) and does not mention "the consensus" (*al-ijmā'*).
20. T. Izutsu, *God and Man in the Koran: Semantics of the Koranic Weltanschuung* (Tokyo: Keio Institute of Cultural and Linguistic Studies, 1964), 32–33, 139–147.
21. Such as *hidāya, ni'ma, tawfīq* and *khidhlān* (Izutsu, *God and Man in the Koran*, 32–33, 139–147).
22. Note Watt's indication that the leading astray is a punishment for lack of belief (*Predestination*, 15; see also H. A. Wolfson, *The Philosophy of the Kalam* [Cambridge MA: Harvard University Press, 1976], 602).
23. See also Wensinck, *Muslim Creed*, 51; Watt, *Predestination*, 14–15; Wolfson, The *Philosophy of the Kalam*, 601; *Shifā'* (1994), 192–194; *Shifā'* (1903), 80–82.
24. The division of humankind into righteous and unrighteous at the time of creation is reflected in a number of traditions, most of which are found in all the major Hadith compilations. For a nice variety, see Abū Bakr al-Ājurrī (a Ḥanbalī scholar, d. 390/971), *Kitāb al-Sharī'a* (Beirut: Mu'assasat al-Rayyān, 1421/2000), 153ff.
25. The Hadith interprets the event described in Q 7: 172 as a one-time event, which took place during the creation of Adam. Ibn Kathīr relates the *fiṭra* tradition to Q 7:172, and indicates that this is an event which takes place "every hundred years, a generation after a generation". Ibn Kathīr, *Tafsīr al-Qur'ān al-karīm* (n.p.: Dār al-Turāth al-'Arabī, n.d.), 2:264. According to Ibn Kathīr, exegetes who restrict Q 7:172 to a one-time event were wrong. The above tradition also has a second part (see Al-Ājurrī, *Kitāb al-Sharī'a*, 174–175), in which someone asks the prophet what is the purpose of human deeds, i.e., if the lot of humankind is predetermined, what is the value of human actions? See van Ess, *Zwischen Ḥadit und Theologie*, 32–36; and E. Kohlberg, "Muwāfāt Doctrines in Muslim Theology", *Studia Islamica* 57 (1983):47–66.
26. Abū al-Ḥasan al-Ash'arī, *Kitāb maqālāt al-islāmiyyīn wa-ikhtilāf al-muṣallīn*, ed. H. Ritter, 2nd edition (Wiesbaden: Franz Steiner, 1963), 259.
27. Abū Ya'lā, *Kitāb al-mu'tamad fī uṣūl al-dīn*, ed. Wadi Z. Haddad (Beirut: Dār al-Mashriq, 1974), 133.
28. Abū Ya'lā, *Kitāb al-mu'tamad*, 133–134.
29. The Sunni definition of faith actually breaks it down into several components (speech, acceptance, performing works, etc.), but for the sake of convenience I refer to belief as one action.
30. *Shifā'* (1994), 634; *Shifā'* (1903), 296; *Dar'* (Beirut), 4:311–312; *Dar'* (Cairo), 8:430.
31. *Dar'* (Beirut), 4:318; *Dar'* (Cairo), 8:442–443; *Shifā'* (1994), 638; *Shifā'* (1903), 299. Ibn 'Abd al-Barr's position is quoted by al-Qurṭūbī (d. 671/1273) in connection with Q 30:30 (*al-Jāmi' li-aḥkām al-Qur'ān*, ed. Sālim Muṣṭafā al-Badrī [Beirut: Dār al-Kutub al-'Ilmiyya, 1420/2000], 14:12). Ibn 'Abd al-Barr actually refers to Q 16:78, "And it is God who brought you forth, knowing nothing, from your

mothers' wombs." On Ibn 'Abd al-Barr's views on the subject, see Adang, "Islam as the Inborn Religion of Mankind", 408, n52, and Mohamed, *Fitrah*, 38–41.

32. *Dar'* (Beirut), 4:319; *Dar'* (Cairo), 8:443; *Shifā'* (1994), 639; *Shifā'* (1903), 299.
33. *Dar'* (Beirut), 4:319; *Dār'* (Cairo), 8:443; *Shifā'* (1994), 639; *Shifā'* (1903), 299.
34. *Dar'* (Beirut), 4:319; *Dār'* (Cairo), 8:443; *Shifā'* (1994), 639; *Shifā'* (1903), 299–300.
35. *Dar'* (Beirut), 4:304; *Dar'* (Cairo), 8:417; *Shifā'* (1994), 628–629; *Shifā'* (1903), 294. The tradition has several versions. See Yaḥyā ibn Sharaf al-Nawawī (d. 676/1277), *Muslim bi-Sharḥ al-Nawawī*, ed. Muḥammad Fu'ād 'Abd al-Bāqī (Beirut: Dār al-Kutub al-'Ilmyya, 1421/2000), 16, 173.
36. *Dar'* (Beirut), 4:304; *Dar'* (Cairo), 8:414; *Shifā'* (1994), 628; *Shifā'* (1903), 293.
37. *Dar'* (Beirut), 4:305; *Dar'* (Cairo), 8:417; *Shifā'* (1994), 629; *Shifā'* (1903), 294.
38. For a collection of the deterministic traditions connected with Q 7:172, see al-Ṭabarī's interpretation of the verse. Al-Ṭabarī himself accepts these traditions, and has no problem with their deterministic content. Ṭabarī, *Tafsīr*, 10:547- 565.
39. *Dar'* (Beirut), 4:307; *Dar'* (Cairo), 8:422; *Shifā'* (1994), 629; *Shifā'* (1903), 294.
40. *Dar'* (Beirut), 4:307; *Dar'* (Cairo), 8:422; *Shifā'* (1994), 629; *Shifā'* (1903), 294.
41. *Dar'* (Beirut), 4:307; *Dar'* (Cairo), 8:422; *Shifā'* (1994), 629; *Shifā'* (1903), 294.
42. Al-Suddī and others discuss the following tradition: "And when God took Adam out of Paradise, before He threw him down from Heaven, He wiped the right side of his back and pulled out of it pearly-white offspring, tiny as seeds, and He said to them: Come into Heaven with my mercy. Then He wiped the left side of Adam's back and pulled out black offspring, tiny as seeds, and He said to them: Come into Hell, for I do not care." Al-Suddī explains that God made a pact with those worthy of Him only after humankind had been divided into the People of Paradise and the People of Hell. The tradition is used by al-Suddī to interpret Q 7:172, "And when thy Lord took from the children of Adam, from their loins, their seed, and made them testify touching themselves." See *Dar'* (Beirut), 4:307–308; *Dar'* (Cairo), 8:422–423; *Shifā'* (1994), 629–630; *Shifā'* (1903), 294. Al-Suddī's interpretation is quoted in Ṭabarī, *Bayān*, 10:560.
43. I omit here Ibn Taymiyya's discussion of the semantics of *tabdīl* (substitution), a term which appears in Q 30:30. In brief, Ibn Taymiyya rejects the possibility that *taghyīr* (change) is a synonym for *tabdīl*. See *Dar'* (Beirut), 4:309; *Dar'* (Cairo), 8:425; *Shifā'* (1994), 631; *Shifā'* (1903), 295.
44. This view is attributed to Abū Hurayra. *Dar'* (Beirut), 4:304; *Dar'* ed. Sālim, 8:414; *Shifā'* (1994), 628; *Shifā'* (1903), 293.
45. *Dar'* (Beirut), 4:309; *Dar'* (Cairo), 8:425; *Shifā'* (1994), 631; *Shifā'* (1903), 295.
46. For a translation of one of Ibn Taymiyya's epistles on *fiṭra*, see G. Gobillot, "L`épître du discours sur la *fiṭra* (*Risāla fī-l-kalām 'alā-l-fiṭra*) de Taqī-i-Dīn Aḥmad ibn Taymīya (661/1262–728/1328). Présentation et traduction annotée," *Annales Islamologiques* XX (1984):29–53. The epistle was also published as "The Dispute about the *Fiṭra*" (*Risāla fī al-kalām 'alā al-fiṭra*), in Ibn Taymiyya, *Majmū'at al-rasā'il al-kubrā*, ed. Rashīd Riḍā (Cairo: Maktabat wa-Maṭba'at Muḥammad 'Alī Ṣubayḥ wa-Awlādihi, 1385–1386/1966), 2:333–349. The other two untitled epistles are rather short and uncomplicated. Ibn Taymiyya, *Majmū'at al-fatāwā*, 4:149–152.
47. *Dar'* (Beirut), 4:277; *Dar'* (Cairo), 8:357. This statement does not appear in Abū Ya'lā's published works. A modern editor of Abū Ya'lā's works, 'Abdallāh ibn Salmān al-Aḥmadī, notes that Abū Ya'lā discusses *fiṭra* in a manuscript of *Kitāb al-riwāyatayn wa al-wajhayn* that was unavailable to me (Abū Ya'lā, *al-Masā'il wa*

al-rasā'il al-marwiyya 'an al-imām Aḥmad ibn Ḥanbal, ed. 'Abdallāh ibn Salmān al-Aḥmadī [Riyadh: Dār Ṭayba, 1412/1991], 1:184 n2). The printed edition of this work does not include such a discussion. See Abū Ya'lā, *Al-Masā'il al-uṣūliyya min kitāb al-riwāyatayn wa al-wajhayn*, ed. 'Abd al-Karīm Muḥammad al-Lāḥim (Riyadh: Maktabat al-Ma'ārif, 1985).

48. However, it is quoted in *Aḥkām ahl al-dhimma*, 2:529–534; *Dar'* (Beirut), 4:272-281; *Dar'* (Cairo), 8:348–365.
49. W.B. Hallaq, "Ibn Taymiyya on the Existence of God", *Acta Orientalia* 52 (1991): 55.
50. A useful summary on *fiṭra* as the basis of human knowledge appears in N. Madjid, "Ibn Taymiyya on Kalam and Falsafa", PhD dissertation (University of Chicago, 1984), 65–77.
51. *Dar'* (Beirut), 4:295–302; *Dar'* (Cairo), 8:397–410. Cf. *Aḥkām ahl al-dhimma*, 2:609–619.
52. Ibn Qayyim al-Jawziyya declares that he will not deal with the legal status of the orphan child of infidels, since he dealt with it thoroughly in his *Aḥkām ahl al-milal*, surely referring here to his *Aḥkām ahl al-dhimma. Shifā'* (1994), 637; *Shifā'* (1903), 299. Thus he omits a major part of Ibn Taymiyya's discussion, which appears in *Dar'* (Beirut), 4:315–318; *Dar'* (Cairo), 8:436–442.
53. The same method is used in the corresponding passage of *Aḥkām ahl al-dhimma*, where Ibn al-Qayyim also adds his own preface (*Aḥkām ahl al-dhimma*, 2:523–528), and then continues with citation from *Dar' al-ta'āruḍ*.
54. *Shifā'* (1994), 607–608; *Shifā'* (1903), 283. Aḥmad Ibn Ḥanbal's interpretation of *fiṭra* appears in *Dar'* (Beirut), 4: 277; *Dar'* (Cairo), 8: 359–360, while the Qur'ānic verse and the *fiṭra* tradition appear in *Dar'* (Beirut), 4: 281; *Dar'* (Cairo), 8:365.
55. *Shifā'* (1994), 618; *Shifā'* (1903), 289; *Dar'* (Beirut), 4:289; *Dar'* (Cairo), 8:383–384.
56. *Shifā'* (1994), 619; *Shifā'* (1903), 289. The story of the wine and the milk (and in another version the water, the wine, and the milk) appears in the biography of the Prophet. Ibn Hishām (d. 218/833), *al-Sīra al-nabawaiyya*, eds. Jamāl Thābit et. al. (Cairo: Dār al-Ḥadīth, 1416/1996), 2:6.
57. *Dar'* (Beirut), 4:303–306; *Dar'* (Cairo), 8:413–419.
58. *Shifā'* (1994), 625–626; *Shifā'* (1903), 292–293. The verses are: "If you are in doubt as to the Uprising, surely We created you of dust" (Q 22:5); "And he has struck for Us a similitude and forgotten his creation" (Q 36:78); "What, does man reckon he shall be left to roam at will? Was he not a sperm-drop spilled? Then he was a blood-clot, and He created and formed" (Q 75:36–38), "Cannot He bring the dead to life?" (Q 75:40, my translation), "So let man consider of what he was created; he was created of gushing water issuing between the loins and the breast-bones. Surely He is able to bring him back" (Q 86:5–8).
59. *Shifā'* (1994), 626–627; *Shifā'* (1903), 293.
60. Ibn Qayyim al-Jawziyya's discussion of Hell's perdition reflects his commitment to a concept that resembles the Mu'tazilī principle of God's justice. See B. Abrahamov, "The Creation and Duration of Paradise and Hell in Islamic Theology", *Der Islam* 79.1 (2002):87–102.
61. *Shifā'* (1994), 35; *Shifā'* (1903), 13. The tradition of Adam and Moses, which appears in all major Hadith compilations, posits two diametrically opposite views on the human being's responsibility for his actions. Moses apparently conveys the Qadarī view, while Adam adheres to the traditional concept. See van Ess, *Zwischen Ḥadīt und Theologie*, 161–167. The role of this tradition in the thought of Ibn Taymiyya is mentioned by Fazlur Rahman, *Revival and Reform in*

Islam: A Study of Islamic Fundamentalism, ed. E. Moosa (Oxford: Oneworld, 2000), 155.

62. *Shifāʾ* (1994), 422; *Shifāʾ* (1903), 191.
63. *Shifāʾ* (1994), 341; *Shifāʾ* (1903), 151–152.
64. The context of the passage is the treatment of children of unbelievers. *Shifāʾ* (1994), 633; *Shifāʾ* (1903), 297.
65. Ibn Qayyim al-Jawziyya's concept of *ikhtiyār* in this context needs a further investigation, especially since it appears in other works, such as *Miftāḥ dār al-saʿāda*.
66. D. B. MacDonald, "Fiṭra", *Encyclopedia of Islam*, new ed.

IV
Law

Ibn Taymiyya's Radical Legal Thought: Rationalism, Pluralism and the Primacy of Intention

*Yossef Rapoport**

Taqī al-Dīn al-Subkī (d. 756/1355), the most prominent Shāfiʿī adversary of Ibn Taymiyya, opened one of his polemical refutations with a list of his opponent's theological errors. On matters of creed, Ibn Taymiyya had contradicted the consensus of the Muslims by his anthropomorphism, by his claims that accidents subsist in God, by suggesting that God was speaking in time, and by his alleged belief in the eternity of the world. Yet, in spite of the gravity of Ibn Taymiyya's theological errors, they did less harm than his innovations in the legal domain, which were also a source of his popular appeal:

> Although they [i.e., his theological doctrines] represent an abominable heresy whose totality far outweighs his innovation in the details of law (*furūʿ*), there are but a few who listen to his theology (*al-uṣūl*) and comprehend it.... However, his innovations in matters of law are something which has caused widespread confusion. These include his legal opinions that declare conditional divorce to be an oath that can be atoned for when breached. The common people had sought refuge in his opinion, rushed to endorse it, and lost sight of the [divine] law of divorce...I have been informed that he sent his propagandists (*duʿātihi*) to the corners of the Earth in order to spread his vile message, and he thus led astray, in the matter of divorce oaths, commoners, Arab nomads, fellahs, and the people of the foreign lands.[1]

In spite of al-Subkī's observation, Ibn Taymiyya the jurist has received far less attention in modern Western scholarship than Ibn Taymiyya the theologian and polemicist. This goes back to Henri Laoust's decision to virtually exclude jurisprudence from his seminal *Essai sur les doctrines sociales et politiques de Takī-d-Dīn Aḥmad b. Taimīya*. He relegated the subject to a companion volume, which includes a French translation of two legal treatises (*Maʿārij al-wuṣūl ilā ʿilm al-rasūl* and *Risāla fī al-qiyās*).[2] Laoust had an intimate understanding of Ibn Taymiyya's idiosyncratic style, but he was not a legal historian, and his introduction to the volume does little more than to summarize the treatises. It is mainly over the last decade that Western scholarship revived its interest in Ibn Taymiyya's jurisprudence, with several studies dealing with his contributions to the Islamic law of contracts, oaths, testimony and rebellion.[3] A major step forward has been the recent publication of Abdul Hakim I. al-Matroudi's *The Ḥanbalī School of Law and Ibn Taymiyyah. Conflict or conciliation.*[4] Al-Matroudi provides a reliable comprehensive survey of Ibn Taymiyya's views on a very diverse range of legal topics. His erudition, however, is aimed primarily at practitioners. While Arabic readers can enjoy the rich and influential monographs of M. Abu Zahra and S. al-ʿAṭīshān, among others[5], there is still a need for a concise thematic overview of the Ibn Taymiyya's legal thought in a European language.

In what follows, I attempt to delineate the outlines of a 'Taymiyyan' legal methodology, on par with the 'Taymiyyan' theological approach explored in other papers in this volume. This is not a comprehensive survey of all the points of law discussed by Ibn Taymiyya, a task too large for this volume and, besides, one that has already been accomplished by al-Matroudi and others. Rather, my aim is to highlight what I consider to be the underlying themes of Ibn Taymiyya's approach to Islamic legal theory, to sources of authority in Islamic law, and to questions of legal detail (*furūʿ*). I will suggest that in spite of his convoluted and digressive style, Ibn Taymiyya's legal thought can be framed in terms of a few general principles, which he systematically applied throughout his legal writings. I will also argue that Ibn Taymiyya's legal thought is closely linked to the wider framework of his intellectual output, and even, as in the case of his approach to legal theory, implies a transposition of a theological principle to the field of jurisprudence. Finally, I will present Ibn Taymiyya's approach to questions of social practice, specifically with regard to land tenure and family structure.

The fundamentals of Ibn Taymiyya's legal thought are analysed here under four headings. The first section deals with the impossibility of contradiction between revealed and rational knowledge. This theological principle, when transposed into legal theory, means that the primary tool of legal rationalism, i.e., analogy, can never contradict a revealed text; if it does, it means that the assumed analogy is necessarily incorrect. Furthermore, the impossibility of contradiction between rational and revealed knowledge affects other tools of legal rationalism, like *istiḥsān* (legal preference), or *maṣlaḥa*. The second section highlights Ibn Taymiyya's undermining of the authority of the school of law and of the consensus of the jurists (*ijmā'*) in favour of independent *ijtihād*. Ibn Taymiyya's rejection of the dominant forms of legal authority implies legal pluralism: if a solution to a legal question is subject to *ijtihād*, then each knowledgeable Muslim is allowed to form and voice his own opinion, without being silenced either by the legal professionals or by the political authorities.

Ibn Taymiyya's radical approach to legal theory went hand in hand with, and provided the justification for, a series of innovative opinions on matters of legal detail. Underlying most of Ibn Taymiyya's innovative legal opinions is the principle of the primacy of intention, discussed in the third section. For Ibn Taymiyya, an act is considered permissible or prohibited according to the intention, or objective, of the agent. The primacy of intention means that contracting parties can choose any means to indicate their objective (*maqṣūd*), and as long as their objective is legal, the contract is valid, regardless of the utterance of specific formulae. The fourth section demonstrates that Ibn Taymiyya's legal thought is also governed by a pervasive pragmatism. Far from being an idealist or a rigid purist, Ibn Taymiyya is ever attentive to the needs of the ordinary believer. When his legal opinions are set in their historical context, it becomes clear that Ibn Taymiyya often lends a stamp of legitimacy to widely used agricultural transactions and ritual practices that were prohibited by the majority of contemporary jurists.

Legal Theory:
Correct Analogy and Qur'ānic Rationalism

The central premise of Ibn Taymiyya's legal theory, like that of his theology, is the impossibility of contradiction between revealed and rational knowledge. In response to a question about jurists who declare some Qur'ānic verses or Prophetic traditions to be contrary to analogy, Ibn Taymiyya explains that the term 'analogy' is an equivocal term, referring to both correct and incorrect analogy. The correct forms of analogy are the ones provided by divine law, which are either equating similar cases or distinguishing between dissimilar cases. He continues:

> It is not a necessary condition of correct and valid analogy (*al-qiyās al-ṣaḥīḥ al-muʿtadal*) that everybody should know its correctness. If anyone sees a ruling in divine law that contradicts analogy, it only means that this ruling contradicts the subjective analogy that he has made up for himself; the ruling does not contradict the correct analogy that invariably lies at the heart of the matter.
>
> When we are told that a revealed text is in opposition to analogy, we know for certain that this is an invalid analogy (*qiyās fāsid*), in the sense that the revealed text refers to a case which has a distinctive feature distinguishing it from other cases that are wrongly thought to be analogous. This distinguishing feature requires the limitation of the ruling to the case (referred to by revelation). Nothing in divine law contradicts a correct analogy; the divine law can only be in opposition to an invalid analogy, even if some do not recognize it as invalid.[6]

Far from rejecting the use of rational proofs, Ibn Taymiyya argues that correct rational proofs are in complete accordance with the revealed sources. When transposed into Sunni legal theory, this principle means that the primary tool of legal reasoning, i.e. analogy, can never contradict a revealed text; if it does, it means that the analogy is null and void. Therefore, when we learn that the revealed sources contradict analogy, we know categorically that this analogy itself is invalid.

This argument bears remarkable similarity to the argument made in Ibn Taymiyya's *Dar' taʿāruḍ al-ʿaql wa'l-naql* (*Prevention of Conflict between Reason and Revelation*) with regard to the interpretation of divine attributes. This connection between theology and legal theory is made explicit in the following excerpt from his short treatise on analogy (*Risāla fī al-qiyās*). It is only false reasoning and invalid analogies that lead to apparent contradictions between revealed and rational proofs, writes Ibn Taymiyya. False reasoning in matters of law and false reasoning in matters of theology also share the tendency to apply analogies where only partial similarities exist:

> He who does not object to invalid analogies, but rather equates two things on the basis of their partial similarity (*bi-ishtirākihimā fī amr min*

> *al-umūr*), is logically bound to equate any two existing things on the basis of their sharing the mere denotation (*musammā*) of existence. He is thus led to equating God with any one of his creatures, becoming one of those who consider God to have equals and associates. This is one of the worst forms of incorrect analogy.... Anyone who acquaints himself with rational proofs can see the general misguidance of the philosophers and theologians who erred by applying invalid analogies between two things on the basis of their partial similarity, while the differences between these two things require them to be markedly distinguished from each other. You can observe this in their discussion of the existence of God and the existence of created things. Their discussion in this matter is thoroughly confused, as we have explained elsewhere.[7]

The correct methods of analogical reasoning are the inductive methods indicated in the revealed sources. This means for Ibn Taymiyya that the Qur'ān and the Sunna are not merely a repository of reports, or positive knowledge, but also a guide to correct reason. The Qur'ān and the Prophets provide the proverbial examples (*al-amthāl al-maḍrūba*) that instruct a rational argumentation based on analogy.[8] The Prophets provided mankind with the means by which to distinguish similarity and difference, and through them we know the way of equating things that are similar and distinguishing things that are dissimilar.[9] Thus, all valid rational proofs supposedly brought forward by the theologians and the philosophers are already indicated in the Qur'ān.[10]

This Qur'ānic method of reasoning was best understood by the Companions, whose ability to construct correct analogies was far superior to that of later jurists. Ibn Taymiyya takes as an example a ruling of the caliph 'Umar ibn al-Khaṭṭāb with regard to a grass widow, who was married off after her husband was absent for four years. When the first husband came back to find that his wife had married another man, 'Umar ruled that the first husband could choose to take the wife back (although she was now married to another man), or to accept as compensation the marriage-gift he had given her at marriage. Later scholars declared that this ruling goes against analogy, since the woman should be considered to be married either to the first husband or to the second. Some even proclaimed that 'Umar's ruling was so far away from the principles of analogy, that if a *qāḍī* would make a judgment in accordance with 'Umar's opinion, his judgment would be null and void. Ibn Taymiyya argues, however, that it is 'Umar who made the correct analogy, which is based on the suspension of contracts in case of need. 'Umar's understanding of valid analogies is far superior to that of later scholars, argues Ibn Taymiyya, who adds that "to this hour I have never learned of a saying of the Companions, over which they have agreed, that did not conform to correct analogy".[11]

For Ibn Taymiyya, questions of practice often lie just below the surface of his theoretical discussions. His theory of analogy is put to use through his re-interpretation and legitimization of sharecropping contracts in Islamic law (*muzāra'a* and *musāqāt*). Although most of the agricultural land in Egypt and Syria was cultivated under these types of contracts, jurists viewed sharecropping as a legal anomaly that should be accepted only out of necessity. Their objection was based on an analogy between sharecropping and rent (or hire) contracts, in which both the amount of work and the remuneration must be known in advance in order for the contract to be valid—conditions which cannot possibly be met in sharecropping. Ibn Taymiyya, however, regards sharecropping contracts as contracts of partnership. In a contract of sharecropping, as in partnership, the object is not performance of a specific task but an increase in capital. The landowner, like investors of capital in partnerships, is not interested in cultivation for its own sake, but rather in the profit that may result from the cultivation of the land. While those who equate sharecropping with hire contracts view these contracts as being tainted by injustice and uncertainty, Ibn Taymiyya argues that the opposite is true. In a sharecropping contract one of the partners provides labor, the other capital, and they share whatever profits God has decreed for them. It is not fair for the cultivator to pay for the use of the land were his cultivation to bear no fruit.[12]

The impossibility of contradiction between rational and revealed proofs requires Ibn Taymiyya to consider other tools of legal rationalism, such as *istiḥsān* (legal preference) and *maṣlaḥa* (utility), and to invest them with new meanings. In the terminology of the jurists, *istiḥsān* is defined as a ruling that goes against a relevant analogy, usually on the basis of counter-evidence from the revealed sources. Ibn Taymiyya finds this definition unacceptable, as he fundamentally rejects any possibility of contradiction between a correct analogy and scripture. However, rather than denying the validity of *istiḥsān* altogether, he prefers to invest the term with a different meaning through re-interpretation. According to Ibn

Taymiyya, when Ibn Ḥanbal used *istiḥsān* to arrive at a ruling, he was not contradicting analogy but rather perfecting it, through the limitation of the *ratio legis* (*takhṣīṣ al-'illa*). Limitation of the *ratio legis* was a concept used to describe a situation in which the cause of a legal ruling would exist, but its effect would not, as a result of an effective differentiating factor. According to Ibn Taymiyya, the wisdom of the Lawgiver means that He would never order two different rulings for two similar situations; rather, if the Lawgiver has ordained two different rulings, it must necessarily mean that the situations are dissimilar. Therefore, *istiḥsān* and *takhṣīṣ al-'illa* are two terms denoting the same process of finding the relevant difference between two otherwise similar cases, a difference that invalidates a full analogy.[13]

An example of Ibn Taymiyya's re-interpretation is the case of usurped land, to which Ibn Ḥanbal is said to have applied *istiḥsān*. According to an authentic Hadith, the produce of usurped land belongs to the landowner, who is required to pay the expenses of the usurping cultivator. Jurists have argued that the correct analogy would suggest that the produce should belong to the cultivator, but this analogy was rejected through *istiḥsān* in favour of the indicant from Hadith. Ibn Taymiyya, however, offers an alternative analogy, equating the planting of seeds in the land with the insemination of an animal's womb. Since the product of a union between two animals belongs to the owner of the female animal, the correct analogy is that the produce of usurped land should belong to the landowner and not to the cultivator. If unlawful insemination of a female animal and unauthorized cultivation of land are fully analogous cases, then the cultivator, like the owner of the male animal, should receive no remuneration at all. It is here that Ibn Taymiyya introduces the limitation of the *ratio legis* (*takhsīs al-'illa*). Although the *ratio legis* is common in cultivation of land and insemination of female animals, it is limited by a relevant difference, which is that the semen in the womb doesn't need tending to, while the seeds in the land do. As a result of this relevant difference, the usurping cultivator has a right to receive expenses for the work he has put into the cultivation. According to Ibn Taymiyya, this limitation of the *ratio legis* is the true meaning of *istiḥsān* applied by Ibn Ḥanbal and others. Therefore, contrary to the traditional legal discourse on usurpation of land, Ibn Taymiyya finds here no contradiction between the Sunna and correct analogy, merely a case of a Hadith limiting the applicability of the analogy.[14]

Ibn Taymiyya's short discussion of the concept of *maṣlaḥa* (utility), another vehicle of legal rationalism, is again closely related to his ideas about the complete congruence between rational and revealed knowledge.[15] On the one hand, Ibn Taymiyya regards the concept of *maṣlaḥa* with suspicion, for it is often used to permit innovations, as "the rulings supported by *maṣāliḥ mursala* quite often make legal what God has not given license to."[16] Many of the innovations in Islam were introduced by people who thought they were *maṣlaḥa*, or beneficial. This was true of many of the theologians and the Sufis who introduced their innovations because they truly thought them to be beneficial, even though they were not actually so. This misinterpretation of *maṣlaḥa* has happened because the notion was not used in reference to the revealed sources. In fact, all possible valid benefits that fall under the category of *maṣlaḥa* have been indicated by the Prophet. In Ibn Taymiyya's words:

> The overall principle is that the divine law never neglects a benefit (*maṣlaḥa*); rather, God has perfected the religion for us, and completed His grace in our respect. Therefore, the Prophet has informed us of everything that may bring us closer to paradise. He caused us to see the clear way, whether by day or by night, and anyone who later deviates from this path shall surely perish.
>
> If the intellect suggests something to be a *maṣlaḥa*, then one of two possibilities becomes necessary: It is either indicated in the law without the person being cognizant of it, or it is not really a *maṣlaḥa*, even if that person considers it to be one. This is because the *maṣlaḥa* is the preponderant or accruing benefit, and it often happens that people imagine something to bring benefit in religious and worldly matters, when in fact its benefit is overridden by harm.[17]

As with analogy, if one recognizes a benefit by rational means, and this benefit is not indicated by the revealed sources, this could mean one of two possibilities: either that the revealed sources do provide it, but the jurist is not aware of that; or that the perceived benefit is not really a benefit, as it often happens that perceived benefit is outweighed by harm.[18] Again, Ibn Taymiyya systematically applies the general theological principle, i.e., the impossibility of contradiction between reason and revelation, to the theory of the sources of Islamic law.

Finally, it also follows that Ibn Taymiyya's definition of *maṣlaḥa* is more general than the technical and restrictive definitions of other scholars. Jurists commonly limit *al-maṣāliḥ al-mursala* to the preservation of life, property, honour, mind and religion. But Ibn Taymiyya argues that this is not so:

> Rather, *al-maṣāliḥ al-mursala* are those matters that bring about benefit and prevent harm. Preventing harm in the above mentioned five categories is merely one of the two aspects. [They also include] things that bring about benefit, whether in worldly affairs or in religious affairs. In worldly affairs these could be transactions or acts that are said to be in the interest of the people, and that are not legally prohibited. In religious affairs these include many of the Gnostic insights and mystical experiences (*al-ma'ārif wa-al-aḥwāl*), acts of worship and asceticism that are said to bring about *maṣlaḥa* without any legal hindrance. Limiting the *maṣāliḥ* to [deterring] punishments that serve to prevent harm in these matters, in order to preserve the corporeal body alone, is too restrictive.[19]

Anything that brings about a benefit and prevents harm could be viewed as *maṣlaḥa*. Ibn Taymiyya includes both material aspects, such as social interactions that bring about benefit to humanity and aspects of worship and asceticism that are beneficial without anything in the law to oppose them. Thus, although he is keen to point the dangers inherent in undiscerning application, his definition of *maṣlaḥa* can potentially encompass all that is beneficial to human society; as long as it can be supported by an indicant from the revealed sources.

Challenging Legal Authority: *Ijtihād* and *ijmā'*

In his *Encyclopaedia of Islam* article, Henri Laoust remarks that Ibn Taymiyya could not have announced the re-opening of the gates of *ijtihād* because he did not consider these gates to have closed.[20] Subsequent scholarship, especially the works of Wael Hallaq, has conclusively shown that most medieval jurists saw a continuous need for independent legal reasoning. That being said, Ibn Taymiyya does stand apart from his contemporaries, both in terms of his theoretical justification for *ijtihād* and in terms of his independent reasoning on specific questions of law. As is well known, Ibn

Taymiyya's legal opinions, especially towards the end of his life, often went against the dominant doctrine in the Ḥanbalī school of law, and even against the views of the three other Sunni schools. Al-Dhahabī (d. 748/1348) famously noted that, "for several years now [Ibn Taymiyya] has been giving legal opinions not according to any particular legal school, but according to what evidence he finds convincing."[21]

Did Ibn Taymiyya view himself as a member of the Ḥanbalī school of law? There is no doubt that his legal education was formed by Ḥanbalī texts, including the legal works of his grandfather Majd al-Dīn. He is intimately familiar with the works of Abū Ya'lā (d. 458/1066), Ibn 'Aqīl (d. 513/1119) and other Ḥanbalī jurists, and his attention to legal variants within the Ḥanbalī school far exceeds his familiarity with the nuances within the other Sunni schools. Although he often finds faults either with the opinions of prominent Ḥanbalī jurists or with their transmission of the views of Ibn Ḥanbal, Ibn Taymiyya does acknowledge the validity of a legal methodology based on Ibn Ḥanbal's principles and statements. The eponym of the school is generally, if not completely, beyond reproach, and Ibn Taymiyya would often attempt to interpret the founder's words in a way that corresponded with his own view.[22]

Still, Ibn Taymiyya is adamant that the dominant opinion in the Ḥanbalī school, derived from Aḥmad's reported rulings and methodology, is not necessarily the same as the correct ruling in God's law. Because the Ḥanbalī school is closest to the revealed sources, there is benefit in being affiliated with it:

> Aḥmad was more knowledgeable than others with regard to the Qur'ān and the Sunna, the sayings of the Companions and the righteous Successors. For this reason he has almost no ruling that contradicts a revealed text, unlike other (school founders). Most often, even when the ruling cited from him is weak, there is another ruling in the Ḥanbalī school that corresponds with the stronger opinion.[23]

However, direct examination of the sources of Islamic law is always preferable:

> Those who are knowledgeable in the legal methodology (*uṣūl*) of Aḥmad and the rulings reported from him (*nuṣūṣihi*) can ascertain the preponderant ruling (*rājiḥ*) of his school regarding all legal questions.

> But those who can comprehend the legal indicants (*al-adilla al-shar'iyya*) would ascertain the preponderant ruling in the Divine law.[24]

Ibn Taymiyya views his attachment to the Ḥanbalī school as one of choice, based on independent criteria of legal methodology, rather than on mere imitation (*taqlīd*). Ibn Taymiyya further plays down strict affiliation to legal schools by suggesting that very few doctrines are unique to any one school. When it comes to the legal issues that most preoccupy Ibn Taymiyya, such as the prohibition of legal stratagems, consideration of intention and custom in contracts and the use of circumstantial evidence, he finds the views of Mālik to be very similar to those of Ibn Ḥanbal.[25] For Ibn Taymiyya, allegiance is owed to the revealed sources and the ways of the first generations, not to a particular school of law or Sufi brotherhood: "Whoever considers the doctrines of an individual scholar or jurist, or one of the mystics and the ascetics, to be above those of the Companions, is an innovator who is leading people astray."[26]

Ibn Taymiyya does not reject *taqlīd* as such, certainly not for laymen, and even jurists are allowed attachment to a school of law in all legal questions or in a particular one, as long as the jurist is not aware of evidence to the contrary. Ibn Taymiyya, always conscious of the limitations of the human mind, grants that most people are incapable of deriving the law from its sources. He affirms—as he does in many of his legal writings—that God does not burden men with more than they are capable of undertaking.[27] But school affiliation is not obligatory. The opinions of the school founders, or of any jurist after them, are opinions and not proofs. Ibn Taymiyya objects to any manifestation of school fanaticism,[28] and laments the current practice of legal writing, where jurists limit themselves to citing the opinions of the founders of the schools, without mentioning the proofs from the revealed sources.[29]

Ultimately, the fact that someone else may have a superior overall knowledge and understanding of the law is irrelevant. He writes:

> *Ijtihād* is not one whole that cannot be subject to division and partition. A man could be a *mujtahid* in one discipline or one field (*bāb*) or an individual legal question, without being a *mujtahid* in all other disciplines, or books, or questions. Everyone can practice *ijtihād* according to his

> abilities. When one observes a legal question that has been subject to a dispute among the scholars, and then one finds revealed texts in support of one of the opinions, with no known counter-evidence (*mu'āriḍ*), then there are two choices. One is to follow another opinion simply because it was the opinion of the founder of the legal school in which he was trained. This is, however, not a legal proof, but rather merely a custom (*'āda*), which can be contradicted by the custom of others, who were trained in the legal school of another Imam. The second option is to follow the opinion that he, in his own judgment, finds preponderant by the indicants from the revealed texts. He is then in agreement with the founder of a different school, yet for him the revealed texts remain uncorrupted, as they are not contradicted by his actions. And this is the right thing to do.[30]

Once a jurist has exerted himself to the best of his ability in studying a point of law, and then reached a certain conclusion, he is not allowed to follow an opposite point of view merely because it is cited from the school founders. As long as one is capable, one should study the evidence and form one's own opinion rather than merely imitate past authorities, who are in any case prone to disagree with each other.[31]

It also follows that a jurist should not incur blame for reaching the wrong conclusions, as long as he acted in good faith. The dictum that 'every *mujtahid* is correct' is often quoted by Ibn Taymiyya, and does not contradict his belief in the comprehensive nature of the Prophetic message.[32] The Lawgiver does provide all the necessary legal proofs, so that it is potentially possible to reach the one correct legal ruling in every single legal question. But God also recognizes the shortcomings of individual human minds. Although every legal question has only one correct solution, the *mujtahid* may or may not find it. But a jurist should never be deterred from pursuing *ijtihād*, as only those who knowingly act against God's command shall be punished. A *mujtahid* is like a person who inadvertently prays in an incorrect direction, and who, as long as he exerted an effort to find the correct direction, has fulfilled the duty of prayer. Both are acting in obedience to God, and in that respect they are correct (*muṣīb*) and deserve a reward. A *mujtahid* who exerted his full efforts and reached an incorrect ruling has not committed a sin, nor does he incur blame:

> Any *mujtahid*, whether it be a ruler or judge or scholar or mufti or any other person, who substantiates his legal reasoning with proof, and obeys God as much as he can, has fulfilled what God has entrusted him with. He acts in obedience to God, and deserves a reward for having acted with piety to the utmost of his ability, and God never punishes him.[33]

For Ibn Taymiyya, this principle has implications not only for legal questions, but, mainly, in theological matters, where it was often claimed that incorrect *ijtihād* could incur sin.[34]

Ibn Taymiyya's support for direct engagement with the revealed sources at the expense of rigid school doctrines finds an ingenious rhetorical expression in his *Raf' al-malām 'an al-a'imma al-a'lām* (*Absolving the Glorious School Founders from Reproach*).[35] As the title indicates, the treatise ostensibly sets out to absolve the school founders from the accusation of proclaiming legal rulings that go against authentic Hadith. But (not unlike Mark Antony's 'Honourable Men'), this argument is a double-edged sword, as the main purpose of the treatise is actually to undermine the authority of the schools. Ibn Taymiyya opens the treatise by praising the Imams as the best of the community and the heirs of the Prophet. Therefore, he argues, they could never have intended to contradict anything in the revealed sources. How come then, he asks, one finds that they sometimes formulated a legal doctrine that goes against a valid Hadith? The answer is that the school founders, who were by necessity well-intentioned scholars, must have committed an honest mistake. It is either that the particular tradition has not reached them, or that they did not accept the reliability of the tradition, or that they could not see the relevance of the tradition to the question at hand, or that they believed the particular tradition to have been abrogated.

Therefore, any of the school founders who appear to have put aside a valid tradition is excused, for they acted in good faith and exerted their utmost effort to reach the truth. If every *mujtahid* receives a reward even when he issues an incorrect ruling, then surely the school founders did not incur sin by their mistakes. But these are mistakes nonetheless. Ibn Taymiyya's discourse here in fact closely parallels sections of Ibn Ḥazm's major legal treatise *al-Iḥkām*, without ever acknowledging his debt to the Ẓāhirī scholar.[36] Ibn Taymiyya's generosity in forgiving the mistakes of the school founders should not obscure the main objective of the treatise, which is to demonstrate that the school founders were not infallible. Indeed, the conclusion of the treatise is that it is not allowed for a jurist to turn away an opinion indicated by the Sunna in favour of an opinion of a scholar, as knowledgeable as he may be, for that scholar may or may not have had the evidence to support this view. The valid tradition is a legal proof, the view of a scholar—even that of Aḥmad Ibn Ḥanbal—is not:

> In the case of many traditions it is possible that the scholar (i.e., one of the school founders) had a valid proof (*ḥujja*) for setting aside a tradition, and this proof is unknown to us. The paths (*madārik*) of knowledge are many, and we cannot know all of the scholars' hidden thoughts. Some of them make their proof explicit and some do not; and even if they make it explicit, it may have reached us and it may have not; and even if it had reached us we may understand this proof and we may not, regardless of whether the proof is actually correct. However, even if we allow for all that, we are still not allowed to deviate from an opinion whose proof (*ḥujja*) comes from an authentic tradition, supported by a group of scholars, in favour of another opinion of a scholar, as knowledgeable as he may be, who may or may not have had a reason to reject this proof. This is because a mistake creeps into the opinions of scholars far more easily than it does into the legal sources (*adilla*). The legal sources, unlike the opinion of a scholar, are the proof of God over all his servants.[37]

Not only does Ibn Taymiyya reject the individual schools of law as sources of legal authority, but he also rejects the authority of a consensus (*ijmāʿ*) formed in any generation after that of the Companions. Thus, even the claim for the collective agreement of all the jurists can never provide certainty. This is so, primarily, for practical reasons. There are so many jurists in the Islamic world, spread all over the Islamic realms, that it is simply impossible to know with certainty that they have all agreed on any single issue. Therefore, claims for binding consensus are quite often based on flimsy evidence. Here the influence of Ibn Ḥazm is directly acknowledged. In a commentary on a work of the Ẓāhirī scholar, itself a critique of excessive claims of consensus made by jurists, Ibn Taymiyya criticizes Ibn Ḥazm for being still too permissive, and accepting claims for consensus without the necessary requirement of widespread undeniable knowledge.[38] That kind of knowledge, Ibn

Taymiyya argues, is not possible after the generation of the Companions, and therefore consensus is by definition limited to the early generations of Islam. Any other claim to consensus is rejected, allowing Ibn Taymiyya the freedom to tackle afresh a wide variety of legal questions that other scholars of his time regarded as settled forever.[39]

Ibn Taymiyya views consensus as a secondary source, inasmuch as the Prophet had clarified every question on which a consensus was later established. Consensus, like analogy, could never be used as a proof without an indicant from revelation, nor could it ever contradict revelation. When jurists claim that some rulings, such as the rulings of the *muḍāraba* partnership contract, are based only on consensus, they do so because of their ignorance of the revealed sources, or because they interpret the Prophetic material too restrictively:

> Some have said that there are legal questions in which the ruling is derived from consensus, with no revealed text, such as the *muḍāraba* [partnership] contract. This is not so, because the *muḍāraba* contract was known in the period of the Jāhiliyya, especially among the Quraysh. Most of them were merchants, and those who owned property sent it with their agents. The Prophet (pbuh) had traveled with the property entrusted to him by others before the beginning of his Prophethood, as well as with the property of Khadija. The caravan in which Abū Sufyān was traveling was mostly subject to *muḍāraba* contracts with Abū Sufyān and others. With the advent of Islam the Prophet (pbuh) affirmed these contracts, and his Companions were traveling with goods that were not owned by them and were subject to *muḍāraba* contracts, and he did not forbid them from doing so. The Sunna of the Prophet consists of his words, deeds and affirmation (*iqrār*), so when he affirmed the [*muḍāraba* contract] it has become solidly lodged in the Sunna.[40]

In his treatise on the *Correctness of the Principles of the Medinese*, Ibn Taymiyya elaborates his theory of consensus as limited to the first generations of the Muslim community.[41] During the first three generations, the people of Medina followed the footsteps of the Prophet more than the people of any other city, as they possessed a living record of the Prophet, which other cities did not have. For this reason, as Mālik claimed in his *Muwaṭṭā'*, the consensus of the people of Medina in this period is a proof that must be followed. The consensus of the Medinese was based on direct transmission from the Prophet, either through widespread oral transmission in Medina, or through a unanimous practice of the Medinese that shows direct continuity with the practice of the Prophet. As Ibn Taymiyya says, "the practice of the Medinese, when it runs the same course as oral transmission, is considered a proof by all Muslims".[42] A second degree of consensus is the ancient practice in Medina before the murder of 'Uthmān, including the normative practice of the Medinese rightly-guided caliphs.[43] The practices of the early generations are thus elevated to the rank of binding proofs, resulting in a remarkable expansion of the Sunnaic material that could be used in jurisprudence.

Ibn Taymiyya effectively turned the notion of consensus on its head. Instead of a tool of legal conservatism defending dominant doctrine, Ibn Taymiyya uses the consensus of the Medinese (or the early generations) in order to undermine these same doctrines. Again, this position had practical implications, as is evident in his legal opinion permitting the lease of orchards, a contract of considerable economic importance in Damascus and its environs.[44] On the basis of a Prophetic tradition prohibiting the sale of fruits before they have ripened, almost all Sunni jurists see contracts for the lease of orchards as invalid. The lease of orchards for a fixed sum was considered unfair, as the landowner leases his orchard trees and their eventual produce to a cultivator for a secured annual rent while the cultivator's remuneration is in the form of fruits that may or may not ripen. This prohibition was widely accepted, and was even considered a matter of consensus. Against this prohibition Ibn Taymiyya adduces a ruling by 'Umar ibn al-Khaṭṭāb, who is said to have rented out an orchard belonging to Usayd ibn Khuḍayr in order to pay the debts on Usayd's estate. Ibn Taymiyya argues that this decision by 'Umar must have become widely known in the Muslim community, and that since none of the Companions objected to it, their silence should be considered as a binding consensus.[45] Thus, Ibn Taymiyya's theory of consensus allows him to reject the preponderant opinion of the later schools of law in favor of a single uncontested ruling by 'Umar.

Ibn Taymiyya's rejection of legal authority, whether it is the legal school or the consensus of the scholars, leads him to adopt a remarkably pluralist position with regard to freedom of legal interpretation. A judge could, of course, impose a judgment on litigants in a specific trial case. But with regard to legal opinions that are subject to *ijtihād*, each knowledgeable Muslim is allowed to form, and express, his own opinion:

> In these general matters [i.e., not a specific trial case] no judge, whoever he may be—even if he was one of the Companions—can impose his view on another person who does not share his opinion by declaring: 'I obliged him (*alzamtuhu*) not to act and not to issue legal opinions unless they are according to the view of my legal school.'
>
> In these matters, judgment is reserved for God and His messenger. A judge is merely one of the Muslims. If he possesses knowledge, he should express his opinion in accordance with that knowledge. In the same way, if his adversary has a different view, he should also express his opinion accordingly. If then the truth becomes apparent, and the judgment of God and His messenger becomes known, it is obligatory for all to follow that opinion. But, as long as the judgment of God is concealed, each of them is allowed to hold his opinion—the one saying 'this is my opinion' while the other says 'this is my opinion.' They are not allowed to prevent each other from expressing his opinion, except through the vehicles of knowledge, proof (*ḥujja*) and evidence (*bayān*), so that each speaks on the basis of the knowledge that he has.[46]

Ibn Taymiyya's insistence on the freedom of all Muslims to practice *ijtihād* was somewhat self-serving. Ibn Taymiyya himself was ordered to stop issuing legal opinions that went against the Ḥanbalī doctrine, specifically in the matter of divorce. To a degree, one feels that Ibn Taymiyya was trying to claim immunity from prosecution under his 'inviolable right for *ijtihād*'. But the insistence on the freedom of legal interpretation vis-à-vis the state authorities was also a natural extension of Ibn Taymiyya's challenge to the schools of law and the authority of consensus. Throughout his writings, Ibn Taymiyya systematically supports the right of the individual believer to form and express an independent and critical opinion, and this position has implications that, so far, have not been fully explored.

Law and Practice: The Primacy of Intention

Ibn Taymiyya's re-interpretation of the sources of Islamic law, especially analogy and consensus, allowed him to consider practical questions of legal detail (*furū'*) from fresh perspectives. A central principle governing his approach to most legal questions brought before him is the primacy of intention, which, for Ibn Taymiyya, determines the permissibility or impermissibility of the act. The Prophetic dictum 'The reward for deeds is dependent upon the intention and every person will be rewarded according to what he has intended' is one of the most oft-quoted traditions in his corpus. Ibn Taymiyya's emphasis on intention has strong roots in traditionalist attitudes to law in general, and in the Ḥanbalī school of law in particular.[47] The primacy of intention is also a common theme of late medieval moralist literature, the so-called 'anti-*bid'a* literature', such as the well-known *al-Madkhal ilā tanmiyat al-a'māl bi-taḥsīn al-niyyāt* (*The Path to the Perfection of Deeds through Good Intentions*) by the Egyptian Mālikī scholar Ibn al-Ḥājj (d. 1336).[48] Ibn Taymiyya's emphasis on intention and motive lies within this moralist context, but he is more daring and radical in taking the approach to its logical conclusions.

Ibn Taymiyya formulates the primacy of intention as a principle (*qā'ida*) of the Islamic law of contracts.[49] Against the Shāfi'ī view that places emphasis on correct formulae, and the Ḥanafī emphasis on the actions of the parties, Ibn Taymiyya argues that contracts are concluded through any means—action or word—that indicate intent. When the baker says 'this bread is for so-and-so dirhams', and the buyer takes the bread, we know that the parties have the intention of concluding a contract and therefore the contract is valid even though the offer was verbal and acceptance was not. Similarly, when a buyer hands over the money and takes a bundle of vegetables or sweets, without any verbal interaction, we consider this a valid contract because we understand the actions of the parties as indications of intention. Ibn Taymiyya turns these observations into a general principle:

> Contracts are concluded by any means that indicate the intention or objective (*maqṣūd*) of the contracting parties, whether it is through word or deed. Everything that the people consider sale and rent is a sale and a rent. As the language and practice of people differ, every nation concludes contracts by the formulae and actions that they mutually agree upon, and these have no fixed definition (*ḥadd mustamirr*), neither in law nor in language. What constitutes a contract varies according to the variety in the expressions (*iṣṭilāḥ*) of the people, in the same way their languages differ from each other. For it is known that the terms used for sale and rent in Arabic are not the ones used in Persian, Greek, Turkish, Berber or Ethiopian. There are even differences in the dialects

> of a single language. Therefore, people are under no obligation to follow a particular expression in their exchange, nor are they prohibited from concluding contracts in ways that are unique to them, as long as the means by which they contracted indicate their objective.[50]

If contracts are valid so long as their objectives are valid, it also follows that contracts that aim to achieve an illegal objective are invalid, even if they are concluded in an outwardly legal manner. Such contracts constitute the legal stratagems (*ḥiyal*), which form the butt of many of Ibn Taymiyya's attacks on contemporary mores, and are the subject of the extensive treatise *Iqāmat al-dalīl fī buṭlān al-taḥlīl* (*Furnishing of the Proof on the Invalidity of Legal Stratagems*).[51] The objection to legal stratagems flows from the ethical position of the Ḥanbalī school, and Ibn Taymiyya is therefore in line with a traditional Ḥanbalī position when he declares legal subterfuges as nothing but an attempt to decieve God. The Lawgiver would not have prohibited something only to allow it through trickery and mockery of His laws. The argument is supported by a systematic application of the concept of intention. Actions in the sphere of human relations are judged by the intention of the man taking the action, in the same way acts of devotion to God are judged by the existence of a pious intention behind the act.[52]

Ibn Taymiyya identifies and attacks legal subterfuges common in his time, like fictitious sales with the purpose of circumventing the prohibition of usury, or, most importantly for Ibn Taymiyya, *taḥlīl* marriages. A *taḥlīl* marriage is one in which a woman who has been triply divorced by her husband contracts a marriage with another man with the sole purpose of allowing her to re-marry the husband who had previously divorced her. Here Ibn Taymiyya considers not the direct intention but the goal or aim (*maqṣūd*) of an action. In a *taḥlīl* marriage the bride and groom do have the intention of contracting a valid marriage. But the aim of the groom is to dissolve the marriage and make the bride lawful to another man, i.e., her first husband. This aim contradicts the permissible aim of the institution of marriage.[53] As usual in Ibn Taymiyya's polemics, the attack on *taḥlīl* marriages is accompanied by social observations. *Taḥlīl* marriages have a corrupting effect on society, as they are usually performed by a 'professional' *muḥallil*, who would become so busy as to contract simultaneous marriages with more than four women, the maximum number permitted by law; the *muḥallil* would even marry a woman, and later would go on to contract incestuous marriages with her daughter or her mother.[54]

The primacy of intention is not limited to contracts, but is also applied by Ibn Taymiyya to acts of worship. An interesting example is his opposition to the proclamation of intent before prayer.[55] While all jurists agree that intention must accompany an act of worship in order to make it valid, the dominant Sunni position is that it is also recommended to verbalize this intention. In practice, it had become common at the time to precede every prayer with a declaration of an intention of worship. Ibn Taymiyya, however, argues that this verbal pronouncement of intention is an innovation, and was never practiced by the Prophet or the Companions. The main issue here, however, is not the practice of the Prophet but the link between intentions and actions. Since the intention is located in the heart, the oral utterance is superfluous:

> The proclamation of intention is a defect in religion and in reason. It is a defect in religion as it is an innovation. It is a defect in reason because it is like someone who is about to eat and then proclaims: 'By putting my hand into this vessel I intend to take a morsel, put it in my mouth, then chew upon it, then swallow it, so that I satiate my hunger.' The same is true for someone who proclaims: 'I intend to pray this obligatory prayer now, four *rak'as*, in a group, fulfilling God's command.' All this is stupidity and ignorance, because the intention is a necessary corollary (*balīgh*) of knowledge. If the person knows what is it he is about to do, by necessity he has the intention of doing it. As long as the knowledge exists in the mind, it is not possible to act without intention, and when there is no knowledge, there cannot be an intention.[56]

Thus, it is precisely Ibn Taymiyya's emphasis on intention that leads him to reject the verbalization of intention in prayer as a superfluous formalization that casts doubt over the sincerity of the act.

Ibn Taymiyya's legal opinion regarding the visitation of tombs, leading to his final imprisonment, is another matter of worship in which he considered intention as paramount. The background to Ibn Taymiyya's polemics against visitation is undoubtedly theological, emanating from a doctrine of direct and unmediated relationship between God and man. However, the polemics took the form of a legal debate, and, expressed in legal terminology, Ibn Taymiyya's objection to visitation revolved around the intention of the worshippers. In his writings, Ibn Taymiyya is careful not to object to the visitation of tombs or cemeteries in and of themselves, but rather to journeys made with the sole purpose, or intention, of visiting a grave. Ibn Taymiyya's argument hinges on the tradition "Do not make a journey except to three mosques: the Mosque of al-Ḥarrām (in Mecca), my mosque (the mosque of the Prophet) and al-Aqṣā mosque", which he interprets as prohibiting visitation of all other mosques, let alone cemeteries. It appears—at least this is the version that we have from Ibn Taymiyya's disciples—that the Mamluk authorities misinterpreted his opinion as an all-inclusive ban on visitation of graves, including the tomb of the Prophet in Medina. In his reply to these accusations, entitled *al-Jawāb al-bāhir*, Ibn Taymiyya is at pains to argue that he does not object to visitation of cemeteries in general or to visitation that does not involve a journey made for that purpose. His objection relates only to visitation made with the wrong intention.[57]

Finally, the primacy of intention over legal formalism leads Ibn Taymiyya to advocate the use of circumstantial evidence in criminal cases.[58] A central feature of classical Sunni doctrine was a formalistic attitude to proof and evidence, limiting the admissible evidence to verbal utterances such as depositions by witnesses. While the formalism of the judicial procedure protected the position of the judge, it also allowed little use of circumstantial evidence and made criminal convictions difficult to obtain. To counter the excesses of this formalistic attitude, criminal cases were usually brought before the court of a Mamluk military officer, also known as a *siyāsa* court, where the judges were not bound by strict procedure and were able to exercise discretion with regard to circumstantial evidence and the range of corporal punishments.[59] Ibn Taymiyya, however, calls on *qāḍīs* to relax their laws of procedure in order to respond to the needs of society. According to Ibn Taymiyya, the judge is capable of establishing the truth by his ability to read signs and interpret them as proofs. In this context, circumstantial evidence should play a much more prominent role in trial procedures. Judges should be able to read all the available signs—such as physical signs in things and property, known social hierarchies, and prevailing customs—rather than depend solely on depositions of witnesses. Thus, proof for adultery can come from pregnancy, and the punishment for drinking wine can be imposed when someone is found drunk or vomiting from it.

Since the divine law is one, the duality of *siyāsa* and *sharīʿa* with regard to criminal law could be avoided if *qāḍīs* applied the law in a non-formalist way that takes account of circumstantial evidence, while military courts grounded their judgment in the revealed sources. The prevailing narrow formalism of the *qāḍī* courts was behind the unwelcome judicial reality, where the courts of the *Sharīʿa* are too weak, and the *siyāsa* courts of the military officials too arbitrary:

> The reason for that is that those who claim to judge by divine law are in fact lacking in the knowledge of the Sunna. So when they give judgments in many matters, they deprive people of their rights and fail to uphold the limits set by God (*ʿaṭṭalu al-ḥudūd*), so that blood is shed, property is usurped illegally and prohibited activities become accepted as licit. On the other hand, those who judge by *siyāsa* resort to a kind of personal opinion without reliance on the Qur'ān and the Sunna. The best of them would pass judgments with no bias and seek justice, but many are biased and give preference to the strong, those who give them bribes and the like.[60]

Law and Practice: Ibn Taymiyya's Legal Pragmatism

Ibn Taymiyya is sometimes maligned as a strict purist, preaching unattainable ideals. Yet, alongside Ibn Taymiyya's unabashed opposition to certain social and religious practices, his legal thought is governed by a pervasive pragmatism. Ibn Taymiyya's legal thought is distinguished by an ingenious ability to combine his intention-based morality with pragmatic consideration for the application of the law in society. He is consistently attentive to the needs of the ordinary believer, and, fearful that religion will become a dead letter, he is constantly striving to make Islamic law relevant to everyday life. Because Ibn Taymiyya is seeking practical solutions to the dilemmas facing ordinary Muslims by constantly weighing the scales of benefits and harms, we often find him lending a stamp of legitimacy to transactions and practices prohibited by the majority of his contemporary jurists.

When applied to contracts, Ibn Taymiyya formulates this permissive approach as a principle (*qāʿida*) of a general presumption of permission in contracts. Arguing from the Qur'ānic verses that call for the fulfilment of contracts and commitments, Ibn Taymiyya reasons that all contracts and the clauses they contain should be presumed to be permissible, unless specifically prohibited by the Lawgiver. The argument is also one of necessity, as contracts of sale, gifts, and rent are necessary for human sustenance—just like food, drink and clothes. Since men are allowed to eat and drink whatever they like as long as not specifically forbidden, they are also allowed to buy and sell as they like, as long as not forbidden by the law. This leads Ibn Taymiyya to argue that the parties to a contract are free to stipulate whatever terms they judge to be in their interest, as long as these stipulations are not specifically prohibited. While Ḥanbalī doctrine recognizes the validity of many individual stipulations, and is more permissive in this respect than other Sunni schools, Ibn Taymiyya was the first one to formalize this approach as a legal principle. As Oussama Arabi has recently shown, his formulation, with its corollary freedom of the contracting parties to set any clauses they wish, set an important precedent in Sunni legal thought.[61]

This permissive approach is in direct opposition to what Ibn Taymiyya considers to be the contemporary malaise of excessive *wara*ʿ, i.e., pious caution in cases of disagreement or doubt. The concept of *wara*ʿ, argues Ibn Taymiyya, has been subject to debilitating misinterpretations that have caused considerable hardship to the believers. One common mistake is to apply *wara*ʿ only passively, leading the excessively pious to abstain from doing what may be hypothetically prohibited, while at the same time not fulfilling their certain active duties, such as charity or holy war. This passive piety goes against the declared activism of Ibn Taymiyya, who formulates the principle that acting in fulfilment of God's command is greater than abstaining from what God has forbidden (*jins fiʿl al-maʾmūr bi-hi aʿẓam min jins tark al-manhī ʿanhu*).[62] Another common mistake is excessive prohibition, which is based on social customs rather than on the revealed sources. Finally, some rightly observe a reason for prohibition, but fail to observe an overriding and preponderant reason for permissibility. Excessive piety creates unbearable hardship, and is usually counter-productive, as it may result in a wholesale acceptance of all illegal practices. Ibn Taymiyya is here weighing considerations of caution against the resulting harm: If the scale shows that the harm is preponderant, the excessive piety should be set aside.[63]

An example explored at length by Ibn Taymiyya is the application of excessive piety in ritual purity. Most scholars agreed that if a minimal amount of impurity falls into a body of standing water, the water as a whole becomes impure and cannot be used for ablution. Against this view, and against the dominant view in the Ḥanbalī school, Ibn Taymiyya supported an opinion attributed to the early Medinese. According to this position, water remains in a state of purity if the impurity has dissolved in it. This is because the water has not changed and still retains its distinctive attributes, such as taste, color and smell. Therefore, such water still falls under the general permission to use water for ablution. Ibn Taymiyya adduces evidence from Hadith and from analogy, but adds that this option is also easier for the believers. It does seem likely that, compared with the severe and cumbersome school doctrines on this matter, ordinary believers with scarce access to water found his ruling to be simple and easy to follow.[64]

Even when prohibitions appear to be based on solid foundations in the Sunna and in analogy, Ibn Taymiyya argues for leniency on the basis of necessity (*ḍarūra*). In an interesting example, Ibn Taymiyya allowed menstruating women to perform the circumambulation of the Kaʿba (*ṭawāf*) during the pilgrimage to Mecca.[65] The vast majority of scholars argued, on the basis of an authentic Prophetic tradition, that menstruating woman can perform all the rites of the pilgrimage except the *ṭawāf*. Ibn Taymiyya, however, opposes this prohibition with arguments based on necessity. The principle in this matter and in others, says Ibn Taymiyya, 'is that one should not only take into consideration the severity of the impediment (*mafsada*) that requires prohibition, but one should also consider the need (*ḥāja*) that leads to permission".[66] Need exists in this case, because menstruating women cannot purify themselves through ablution, nor are they in a position to repeat the pilgrimage at a later time:

> If the woman is in a state of need, i.e., she is unable to complete the pilgrimage unless she performs the circumambulation while menstruating, and since she cannot remain in Mecca until she becomes pure, then there are two possibilities. One is that she will perform the circumambulation while menstruating. The other option brings a harm that contradicts the divine law. The law does not require her to remain in Mecca if that would put her under threat to herself and her property, or if she will not be able to travel back to her family, or if she does not

> have the financial ability to reside in Mecca.... Now, many women will not be able to return to their families if they do not go back with those who accompanied them on the pilgrimage journey. Moreover, even if she was able to return later to her family, she will still be prohibited from having sexual intercourse until she goes back to Mecca (to complete the pilgrimage rites). This is a most dire situation, which God would not have made obligatory. It is worse than an obligation to perform two pilgrimages, and God has made obligatory only one.[67]

During the pilgrimage, a menstruating woman is in need of permission to perform the circumambulation because she is not likely to have a second chance. She cannot stay in Mecca and wait for the end of her period, because the caravans embark on the journey back immediately after the rites of the pilgrimage are over, and women do not make the journey unaccompanied. On the other hand, without performing the *ṭawāf* her entire journey was in vain, as her pilgrimage was not complete. Furthermore, she will remain in a state of *iḥrām* and not be allowed to have sexual intercourse until she comes back and completes her pilgrimage in another year. For Ibn Taymiyya, this practical argument from necessity serves to refute the overwhelming prohibition based on Sunna, analogy, and an apparent consensus.

Ibn Taymiyya did not always adopt the more lenient, permissive opinion in every legal question. As we have seen, he wrote extensively against what he saw as the scourge of legal stratagems prevalent in his society. In the case of *taḥlīl* marriages, or in the matter of usury disguised as fictitious sales, Ibn Taymiyya's absolute prohibition is in direct opposition to popular practice. But even in these cases, he argued, the need for legal stratagems only arose when jurists adopted rigid views, based on formalistic interpretation and excessive, unnecessary piety. Ibn Taymiyya is never satisfied with mere criticism of social practices. He is committed to the active implementation of the law, and often seeks innovative legal doctrines aimed at obviating the need for legal stratagems.

This Taymiyyan pattern of simultaneously rejecting legal subterfuges while also tackling the root causes of their popularity can be demonstrated by two examples. First is Ibn Taymiyya's solution to the pervasive social problem of *taḥlīl* marriages, a legal position which eventually led to his arrest in 1319.[68] As we have seen, Ibn Taymiyya regarded *taḥlīl* marriages as one of the worst forms of legal subterfuges. But Ibn Taymiyya also observed that these marriages were usually a result of triple divorces issued by husbands who did not have a real intention to divorce their wives, but rather violated oaths undertaken on the pain of triple divorce (such as 'May my wife be divorced three times if I fail to pay my debt'). After he had identified divorce oaths as the root cause of *taḥlīl* marriages, Ibn Taymiyya then applied his intention-based, non-formalist methodology, and argued that when a man says 'May my wife be divorced three times if I do not pay my debt', he does not intend to divorce his wife but only to incite himself to a certain action, in the manner of oaths. God has commanded men to respect valid oaths to the utmost of ability, but if a man has no choice but to violate his oath, he should provide expiation, by fasting, feeding or clothing the poor, or manumitting a slave. This interpretation of divorce oaths ran against the dominant interpretation of all Sunni schools of law, bolstered by occasional claims to consensus.[69]

The second example is the lease of orchards. As noted above, most jurists regarded the lease of orchards for a fixed sum as an invalid contract because of its element of uncertainty. However, jurists have also come up with legal stratagems to allow the practice.[70] The most common method was to lease the land, but not the trees, for an agreed sum that was the de facto annual rent. The landowner and the cultivator would also draw up an additional, fictitious sharecropping agreement for the yield of the trees (*musāqāt*), in which the cultivator had to pay only a token share of the produce, usually 1/1000. This method was so prevalent that even some Ḥanbalī jurists accepted it as permissible stratagem, owing to the practical necessity of the transaction. True to principle, Ibn Taymiyya does not take this option and rejects the circumvention of God's law through a stratagem or a subterfuge. But he is also aware of the practical implications, as prohibiting the transaction altogether would bring about harm for the entire community, something that God could not have wanted. Therefore, he argues, it must mean that God did not prohibit the lease of orchards in the first place:

> Those who do not accept legal subterfuges understand that this stratagem is invalid. They are then faced with two choices. One is to still resort to this legal stratagem due to the need for it. Then they are convinced that they are doing something unlawful, and this applies to most people. The other option is to abstain from doing it, and then

> abstain from tending to the fruits that are the subject of this transaction. This would then cause damage and harm, the extent of which only God knows. It may be possible for one or two persons to abide by this prohibition, but it is not possible for the Muslims as a whole to abide by it without such a loss of property not brought about by any law, let alone the divine law regarding which God said 'and He imposed no difficulties on you in religion'.[71] When something is essential for sustenance, then its prohibition brings about difficulties, and this is legally impossible.
>
> The point is this: the community could not abide by a prohibition of something like that [i.e., the lease of orchards], as it brings about intolerable harm. It is therefore known that it is not prohibited, but rather worse than the heavy burdens and yokes (*al-aghlāl wa-al-āṣār*)[72] that bound the Israelites, yet were removed from our necks by the word of Muḥammad (pbuh).... Whatever people need for their sustenance, and is not caused by sin, i.e., abstaining from a duty or doing what is forbidden, then this is not prohibited for them, because they are like the one who is in need.[73]

Again, Ibn Taymiyya applies the concept of need extensively, and is here generalizing it into a legal principle. When the need for something is so great as to make sustenance impossible, the jurist should take it as an indication of permission.

The questions of divorce oaths and the lease of orchards bring together Ibn Taymiyya's morality and pragmatism, and also a sense of his lightly condescending, but nonetheless real, tolerance. At the time of the Prophet, he argues, divine law must have been interpreted correctly. Divine Clemency was apparent, and the true believers were free from the shackles and fetters that bound followers of other religions. However, when the interpreters of the divine law started following rigid and formalistic doctrines, swaying from the correct path, they burdened the believers with intolerable yokes. It was then that well-meaning jurists introduced legal subterfuges in order to relieve the believers from these burdens. But, since God could not have prohibited something and then allowed it through trickery and deceit, these legal subterfuges are of no use, adding to the sources of corruption rather than reducing them. Legal subterfuges would not have—indeed, could not have—been introduced to Muslim society if God's laws had been interpreted correctly. Legal subterfuges are thus symptoms of the real disease, which is the misinterpretation of God's word through formalistic and overly severe interpretations.[74]

Conclusion

In some ways, Ibn Taymiyya's legal thought should not hold much interest to modern Muslims. The questions of agricultural law with which he has been predominantly occupied, such as sharecropping agreements and the lease of orchards, are of very marginal relevance to increasingly urbanized Muslim societies, where the economic settings bear little resemblance to that of the predominantly rural economy of Mamluk Syria. *Taḥlīl* marriages are hardly common any longer, quickly disappearing together with the family structures and codes of honour in which they were embedded and in whose framework they made cultural sense. The *siyāsa* justice and its arbitrariness disappeared, replaced by modern codes of law. To a modern reader the subject matter is likely to appear otiose, and often altogether incomprehensible. In the case of some modern radical activists, such misreading of the historical and legal background can prove deadly.[75] And yet, Ibn Taymiyya has had a significant influence on the development of Islamic law in the modern period. This is obviously the case in Saudi Arabia, where Ibn Taymiyya's influence is well documented.[76] More fascinating perhaps is the appeal of elements of his legal thought to reformist thinkers in quite disparate contemporary Muslim communities.

One such element is Ibn Taymiyya's systematic challenge to traditional sources of legal authority, be they the schools of law or the consensus of the legal practitioners. While the gates of *ijtihād* were never closed, Ibn Taymiyya's emphasis on the right of individual Muslims to engage directly with the sources of the law has made him the adopted champion of the Salafi movement of the 19th and 20th centuries. However, to describe Ibn Taymiyya's legal thought as "Salafi", in the sense of strict accordance with the practice of the first generations, is to reduce his legal thought to only one of its components. For Ibn Taymiyya, the reliance on the *salaf* (or the school of the Medinese) serves to dislodge established legal authority. Emulating the ways of the first generations was not necessarily an aim in and of itself, but often a means of legitimating a challenge to the legal and theological orthodoxy of his time. That challenge, it should be pointed out, also encapsulated an emphatic call for intellectual pluralism.

As expected, modern Salafi writers seek to demonstrate that Ibn Taymiyya's legal rulings are the closest to the Sunna and the practice of the first generations. They take their cue, of course, from Ibn Taymiyya himself, and in particular from his *The Correctness of the Principles of the Medinese.* But, taking a bird's-eye view of Ibn Taymiyya's writings as I have done here, it is quite possible to understand Ibn Taymiyya's legal thought without much reference to the evidence from the Hadith, but rather with due consideration of the historical practices and circumstances of his day. It is sufficient to note here that the same legal questions discussed in detail in *The Correctness of the Principles of the Medinese*, such as the purity of water for ablution and the legality of the sharecropping contracts, recur also in the *Treatise on Analogy*, in his *Legal Principles* and in isolated legal opinions, where the emphasis is not on the central authority of the first generations. Furthermore, Ibn Taymiyya's central legal principles, i.e., the impossibility of contradiction between analogy and revealed sources, the primacy of intention, the presumption of permissibility—go far beyond what could be attributed directly to the Companions. These principles can be seen as free standing and independent of any precedent in the early Islamic generations.

In fact, the influence of Ibn Taymiyya's legal principles on modern Islamic law goes far beyond the Salafi movement. On a few specific legal questions, modern Sunni legislators have directly adopted the legal opinions of Ibn Taymiyya against the dominant opinions of all four schools. One example is Ibn Taymiyya's rulings on divorce oaths and triple divorces. Modern laws in Arab nation states, beginning with the Egyptian Family Law of 1929, all maintain that a proclamation of an oath on pain of divorce is null and void. Similarly, most Arab countries (again following the Egyptian example) have legislated that a triple divorce pronounced in one utterance shall always be counted as a single repudiation. Both these views take their inspiration from the legal opinions of Ibn Taymiyya, while standing in direct opposition to the view of the vast majority of past Sunni jurists.[77] In a more general way, the Egyptian jurist al-Sanhūrī found the ethical, intention-based position of the Ḥanbalīs to be attractive because of its similarity to modern French law, where the legality of a transaction is also determined by the legality of its underlying motives.[78]

Another example of Ibn Taymiyya's influence on modern codification is the incorporation of his presumption of permissibility into a 1922 amendment to the Ottoman *Majalla*, as studied by

O. Arabi. The Ottoman *Majalla* of 1877 codified the Ḥanafī presumption of invalidity of clauses in contracts unless explicitly allowed by the Lawgiver. Therefore, the section on stipulations in the 1877 *Majalla* only lists permissible clauses, such as clauses inherent in the nature of the transaction, or customary clauses. It excludes all clauses that are meant to benefit one party over the other, which were considered illegal in Ḥanafī doctrine. In 1922, however, a suggested amendment explicitly allowed for such clauses, and presumed their validity unless otherwise indicated: "A sale contract containing a stipulation which benefits one of the contracting parties is valid, and the transaction is binding." The explanatory memorandum says that the change was required in order to legalize the present practice of the community as much as possible, and in response to its economic needs. It claims to adopt the Ḥanbalī position on contracts, but, as shown by O. Arabi, such a sweeping acceptance of stipulations in contracts was only formalized by Ibn Taymiyya, and it was his distinct contribution that the legislators chose here to adopt. The amendment, however, was never turned into law, as the Turkish legal reforms of 1926 replaced the entire *Majalla*.[79]

The primacy of intention in Ibn Taymiyya's thought has found a resonance with the agendas of modernist reformers, as far away as the Gayo highlands of Sumatra.[80] The common practice in Gayo, as in Mamluk Damascus, was to precede prayer with a short statement like "I worship at daybreak with two cycles on account of God, may He be exalted". In the mid-1930s, however, a group of reformist religious teachers began to urge their fellow Muslims to purify their religious life of non-Islamic elements. Consciously influenced by the Salafi movements in other parts of the Islamic world, they triggered a divisive debate over this statement of intent to worship, which then became a focal point of reformist and traditionalist identities up until the 1980s. The reformist argument, like Ibn Taymiyya's, was that verbalization of intent was not part of the practice of the Prophet, but also, and more emphatically, that the addition of the intention formula implies that intent is not already part of the ritual act. In modernist argumentation, the issue was closely linked to rejection of ignorance and *taqlīd*—blindly following the authority of others, which in the Sumatran context also meant following local norms rather than universal Islamic norms. The similarities with the reasoning of Ibn Taymiyya are striking, although it is not known whether the Gayo reformists were aware of his legacy.

As the preceding examples suggest, Ibn Taymiyya's legal thought has had a certain affinity with the sensibilities of the past century, and its appeal will probably continue in the present one. Ibn Taymiyya's ideas about Qur'ānic rationality, and his corollary critique of Greek philosophy, could be used as a platform for a postmodernist critique of modern science as an instrument of power, an interpretation recently suggested by Sherman Jackson.[81] Ibn Taymiyya's emphasis on the right of the individual believer to exercise his own *ijtihād* against the prevailing orthodoxy and its ancillary political structures should, and does, appeal to Muslims living in the age of the World Wide Web. Finally, Ibn Taymiyya's distinctive commitment to the actual implementation of the law in society will probably continue to attract new generations of activists seeking medieval validation for their modern agendas. It is merely hoped that they will explore Ibn Taymiyya's legal thought in a fuller and richer intellectual framework, and will eventually save him from the Salafi strait-jacket to which he has been so often subjected.

Notes

* I would like to thank Caterina Bori, John-Paul Ghobrial and Christopher Melchert for reading through versions of this paper prior to its publication. I am also indebted to Yahya Michot for sharing with me his vast knowledge of the Taymiyyan corpus.

1. Taqī al-Dīn Subkī, *al-Rasā'il al-Subkiyya fī al-radd 'alā Ibn Taymiyya wa-tilmīdhi-hi Ibn Qayyim al-Jawziyya* (Beirut: 'Ālam al-Kutub, 1983), "al-durra al-muḍiyya fī al-radd 'alā Ibn Taymiyya", 151–2.
2. Henri Laoust, *Contribution à une étude de la méthodologie canonique de Taki-d-din Ahmad b. Taimiya* (Cairo: Institut français d'archéologie orientale, 1939). Laoust also translated Ibn Taymiyya's treatise on divorce oaths in a separate study ("Une risāla d'Ibn Taimīya sur le serment de répudiation", *Bulletin d'études orientales* 7–8 [1937–8]:215–36).
3. George Makdisi, "Ibn Taimiya's Autograph Manuscript on Istihsān: Materials for the Study of Islamic Legal Thought", in G. Makdisi (ed.), *Arabic and Islamic Studies in Honor of Hamilton A. R. Gibb* (Leiden: E. J. Brill, 1965), 446–479; Oussama Arabi, "Contract Stipulations (*shurūṭ*) in Islamic Law: The Ottoman Majalla and Ibn Taymiyya", in *Studies in Modern Islamic Law and Jurisprudence* (The Hague; London: Kluwer Law International, 2001), 39- 62 (reprint of *International Journal of Middle Eastern Studies* 30.1 [1998]: 29–50); Baber Johansen, "Signs as Evidence: the Doctrine of Ibn Taymiyya (1263–1328) and Ibn Qayyim al-Jawziyya (d. 1351) on Proof", *Islamic Law and Society*, 9.2 (2002): 168–193; Yossef Rapoport, "Ibn

Taymiyya on Divorce Oaths", in A. Levanoni and M. Winter (eds.), *The Mamluks in Egyptian and Syrian Politics and Society* (Leiden: Brill, 2004), 191–217; Khaled Abou el Fadl, *Rebellion and Violence in Islamic Law* (Cambridge: Cambridge University Press, 2001), 271–9; Benjamin Jokisch, *Islamisches Recht in Theorie und Praxis: Analyse einiger kaufrechtlicher Fatwas von Taqi'd-Din Ahmad b. Taymiyya* (Berlin: Klaus Schwarz Verlag, 1996); and idem., "*Ijtihād* in Ibn Taymiyya's *Fatāwā*", in Robert Gleave and Eugenia Kermeli (eds.), *Islamic Law: Theory and Practice* (London and New York: I.B. Tauris, 1997), 119–137; Felicitas Opwis, "The Construction of *Madhhab* Authority: Ibn Taymiyya's Interpretation of Juristic Preference (*Istiḥsān*)", *Islamic Law and Society* 15.2 (2008): 219–49. See also the discussion of legal thought in Victor E. Makari, *Ibn Taymiyyah's Ethics: The Social Factor*, American Academy of Religion, Academy series, vol. 34 (Atlanta, GA: Scholars Press, 1983).

4. Abdul Hakim I. Al-Matroudi, *The Ḥanbalī School of Law and Ibn Taymiyyah. Conflict or conciliation*, Culture and Civilization in the Middle East series (London and New York: Routledge, 2006).
5. Muḥammad Abu Zahra, *Ibn Taymiyya: ḥayātuhu wa 'aṣruhu—ārā'uhu wa-fiqhuhu* (Cairo: Dār al-Fikr al-'Arabī, 1952); Sa'ūd al-'Aṭīshān (or al-'Uṭayshān), *Manhaj Ibn Taymiyya fī al-fiqh* (Riyadh: Maktabat al-'Ubaykān, 1999); Isma'īl ibn Ḥasan ibn Muḥammad 'Ulwān, *al-Qawā'id al-fiqhiyya al-Khams al-Kubrā wa-al-Qawā'id al-Mundarija taḥtaha: Jam' wa-dirāsa min Majmū' Fatāwā Shaykh al-Islām Ibn Taymiyya* (al-Dammam: Dār Ibn al-Jawzī, 2000).
6. *Majmū' fatāwā shaykh al-Islām Aḥmad ibn Taymiyya* [hereafter *MF*], ed. 'Abd al-Raḥmān b. Muḥammad b. Qāsim and Muḥammad b. 'Abd al-Raḥmān b. Muḥammad al-'Āṣimī al-Najdī al-Ḥanbalī (Riyadh: Maṭābi' al-Riyāḍ, 1961–6), 20:505 (*Risāla fī al-qiyās*). Translated in Laoust, *Contribution*, 114–5; see also Matroudi, *Ibn Taymiyyah*, 72–4.
7. *MF* 20:541–2 (*Risāla fī al-qiyās*); translated in Laoust, *Contribution*, 163–4. In fact, as Jon Hoover demonstrates, Ibn Taymiyya does not permit the univocal use of analogy with respect to God at all, but only permits its use in *a fortiori* mode (*Ibn Taymiyya's Theodicy of Perpetual Optimism* [Leiden: Brill, 2007], 58–9). I thank Anke von Kügelgen for drawing my attention to this distinction. See also her "'The poison of philosophy'—Ibn Taymiyya's struggle for and against reason", in Birgit Krawietz and Georges Tamer (eds.), *Proceedings of the Workshop "Neo-Hanbalism Reconsidered: The Impact of Ibn Taymiyya and Ibn Qayyim al-Jawziyya" (Berlin, 23.-25. October 2007)*, (Berlin: de Gruyter Verlag [Beiheft to Der Islam], forthcoming).
8. *MF* 2:61 (*Tawḥīd al-rubūbiyya*).
9. *MF* 9:242–3 (*al-Radd 'alā al-Manṭiqiyīn*).
10. See also Wael B. Hallaq, *A history of Islamic legal theories. An introduction to Sunnī* uṣūl al-fiqh (Cambridge: Cambridge University Press, 1997), 140.
11. *MF* 20:576–82 (*Risāla fī al-qiyās*), quotation from p. 583.
12. *MF* 20:506–11 (*Risāla fī al-qiyās*). Translated in Laoust, *Contribution*, 116ff; see also Matroudi, *Ibn Taymiyyah*, 75.
13. Makdisi, "Ibn Taimiya's Autograph Manuscript on *Istihsān*"; Opwis, "The Construction of *Madhhab* Authority".
14. Makdisi, "Ibn Taimiya's Autograph Manuscript on *Istihsān*", 475–6; Opwis, "The Construction of *Madhhab* Authority".
15. *MF* 11:343–9 (*al-Mu'jizāt wa-al-karāmāt*). See also Matroudi, *Ibn Taymiyyah*, 78–80; 'Aṭīshān, *Manhaj*, 96.
16. *MF* 11:344.

17. *MF* 11:344–5.
18. *MF* 11:343–4.
19. *MF* 11:343.
20. H. Laoust, "Ibn Taymiyya", *Encyclopaedia of Islam*, 2nd ed.
21. Ibn ʿAbd al-Hādī (d. 744/1343), *al-ʿUqūd al-durriyya min manāqib Shaykh al-Islām Ibn Taymiyya*, ed. Muḥammad Ḥāmid al-Fiqī (Cairo: Maṭbaʿat al-Ḥijāzī, 1938), 117. See also Caterina Bori, "A new source for the biography of Ibn Taymiyya," *Bulletin of the School of Oriental and African Studies* 67.3 (2004):321–48.
22. See the discussion in Matroudi, *Ibn Taymiyyah*, 56–7, 107–110.
23. *MF* 20:229.
24. *MF* 20:228–9.
25. *MF* 20:228–31.
26. MF 11:15 (Risālat al-ṣūfiyya wa-al-fuqarāʾ).
27. *MF* 20:212.
28. *MF* 22:254, where the reference is to the situation in the eastern and western regions of Islam, not in the central Islamic lands under Mamluk control.
29. *MF* 10:367.
30. *MF* 20:212–3.
31. *MF* 20:208–26. On *ijtihād* in Ibn Taymiyya's thought, see also Matroudi, *Ibn Taymiyyah*, 84–9; ʿAṭīshān, *Manhaj*, 320ff.
32. *MF* 20:19–33, for full discussion. See also *MF* 10:477–8; 13:121 (*al-Furqān bayna al-ḥaqq wa-al-bāṭil*).
33. *MF* 19:216–7 (*Maʿārij al-wuṣūl*).
34. *MF* 19:203–17 (*Maʿārij al-wuṣūl*). See also Matroudi, *Ibn Taymiyyah*, 67–9; ʿAṭīshān, *Manhaj*, 296.
35. The treatise is published as *MF* 20:231–290, and in several separate publications.
36. Compare Ibn Ḥazm, *al-Iḥkām fī uṣūl al-Aḥkām* (Cairo, 1978), 2:301–7; translated in *Classical Islam. A sourcebook of religious literature*, edited and translated by Norman Calder, Jawid Mojaddedi and Andrew Rippin (London; New York: Routledge, 2003), 202–6. For a discussion of Ibn Ḥazm's critique of the schools of law, see A. Sabra, "Ibn Ḥazm's literalism: A critique of Islamic legal theory", *Al-Qanṭara* 28.1 (2007): 7–40.
37. *MF* 20:250 (*Rafʿ al-malām*).
38. *Naqḍ marātib al-ijmāʿ*, on the margins of Ibn Ḥazm, *Marātib al-ijmāʿ fī al-ʿibādāt*, 3rd edition (Cairo: Dār Zāhid al-Qudsī, 1986).
39. On Ibn Taymiyya's view of consensus, see also Matroudi, *Ibn Taymiyyah*, 58–9; ʿAṭīshān, *Manhaj*, 83.
40. *MF* 19:195 (*Maʿārij al-wuṣūl*). Translated in Laoust, *Contribution*, 103–4.
41. Published as *MF* 20:294–396, and in several separate editions. Translated by Aisha Bewley, *The Madinan way: the soundness of the basic premises of the school of the people of Madina* (Norwich: Bookwork, 2000)
42. *MF* 20:304 (*Ṣiḥḥat madhhab ahl al-Madīna*).
43. Ibn Taymiyya's position on the consensus of the Medinese runs against the dominant position in the Ḥanbalī school (Matroudi, *Ibn Taymiyyah*, 89–91).
44. This legal question is studied in detail by Jokisch, "*Ijtihād* in Ibn Taymiyya's *Fatāwā*", 125–9.
45. *MF* 29:65 (*Qawāʿid jāmiʿa fī ʿuqūd al-muʿāmalāt al-māliyya wa-al-nikāḥiyya*). The work has been edited by Muḥammad Ḥāmid al-Fiqī as *al-Qawāʿid al-nūrāniyya al-fiqhiyya*

(Cairo: Maṭbaʻat al-Sunna al-Muḥammadiyya, 1951), and in several other more recent editions.

46. Ibn Taymiyya, *Majmūʻ Fatāwā Shaykh al-Islām Ibn Taymiyya*, ed. Muṣṭafā ʻAbd al-Qādir ʻAṭā (Beirut: Dār al-Kutub al-ʻIlmiyya, 2000), 35:360. Translated in Yahya Michot, *Le pouvoir et le religion* (Paris: Albouraq, forthcoming). I am grateful to Professor Michot for both drawing my attention to this passage and allowing me to read his translation prior to publication. See also ʻAṭīshān, *Manhaj*, 328–9.
47. See Paul R. Powers, *Intent in Islamic Law. Motive and Meaning in Medieval Sunnī Fiqh* (Leiden: Brill, 2006), 205; Noel J. Coulson, "Doctrine and Practice in Islamic Law: One aspect of the Problem", *Bulletin of the School of Oriental and African Studies* 18.2 (1956): 211–226.
48. Ibn al-Ḥājj, *al-Madkhal ilā tanmiyat al-aʻmāl bi-taḥsīn al-niyyāt*, ed. Tawfīq Ḥamdān (Beirut: Dār al-Kutub al-ʻIlmiyya, 1995). For discussion of the work, see Huda Lutfi, "Manners and Customs of Fourteenth- Century Cairene Women: Female Anarchy versus Male Sharʻi Order in Muslim Prescriptive Treatises," in N. Keddie & B. Baron (eds.), *Women in Middle Eastern History: Shifting Boundaries in Sex and Gender* (New Haven: Yale University Press, 1991). On the genre, see also Maribel Fierro, "The treatises against innovations (*kutub al-bidaʻ*)", *Der Islam* 69 (1992): 204–46.
49. *MF* 29:5ff (*Qawāʻid jāmiʻa fī ʻuqūd al-muʻāmalāt*). See ʻAṭīshān, *Manhaj*, 286–93.
50. *MF* 29:7 (*Qawāʻid jāmiʻa*).
51. First published in Ibn Taymiyya, *Majmūʻat Fatāwā Ibn Taymiyya* (Cairo, 1326–9/1908–11), vol. 3. For a recent edition, see *Kitāb Bayān al-dalīl ʻalā buṭlān al-taḥlīl*, ed. Ḥamdī ʻAbd al-Majīd al-Salafī (Beirut: al-Maktab al-Islāmī, 1998).
52. For Ibn Taymiyya's view on legal subterfuges, see also Matroudi, *Ibn Taymiyyah*, 98–10; Abū Zahra, *Ibn Taymiyya*, 352. On the place of legal subterfuges in Islamic law in general, see Joseph Schacht, *An Introduction to Islamic Law* (Oxford: Oxford University Press, 1964), 78–82.
53. The permissible goal (*maqṣūd*) of a marriage contract, according to Ibn Taymiyya, is a long-term commitment emanating from mutual desire. Ibn Taymiyya acknowledges that some men contract marriages in order to become in-laws of the bride's family, while others marry in order to have someone to manage the household or to take care of daughters and sisters. Ibn Taymiyya insists, however, that these secondary goals associated with marriage not only do not contradict its primary and essential goal, but rather bring it about (*Iqāmat al-Dalīl*, 87, 91).
54. Ibn Taymiyya, *Iqāmat al-Dalīl*, 216–18.
55. *MF*, 22:219–21; Powers, *Intent in Islamic Law*, 37–9; Matroudi, *Ibn Taymiyyah*, 95–6.
56. *MF* 22:231–2.
57. *MF* 27:214ff. See also Matroudi, *Ibn Taymiyyah*, 96–8. For a study of the visitation polemics in its historical and intellectual context, see Christopher S. Taylor, *In the vicinity of the righteous. Ziyāra and the veneration of Muslim saints in late medieval Egypt* (Leiden: Brill, 1999).
58. For full discussion, see Johansen, "Signs as Evidence".
59. On the parallel jurisdiction of the courts of military officers, see Emile Tyan, *Histoire de l'organisation judiciare en pays d'Islam*, 2nd edition (Leiden: Brill, 1960), 490–92, 539–45.
60. *MF* 20:392–3 (*Ṣiḥḥat madhhab ahl al-Madīna*). Translated in Bewley, *The Madinan Way*, 87. The attitude of the scholarly elite to the courts of military officers was

not always as favourable as Ibn Taymiyya's. See the criticism of the *siyāsa* courts by Taqī al-Dīn al-Maqrīzī, *Kitāb al-mawāʿiẓ wa-al-iʿtibār fī dhikr al-khiṭaṭ wa-al-āthār al-maʿrūf bi-al-khiṭaṭ al-Maqrīziyya*, ed. M. Zaynhum and M. al-Sharqāwī, 3 vols. (Cairo: Maktabat al-Madbūlī, 1998), 3:80, 88.

61. Oussama Arabi, "Contract Stipulations (*shurūṭ*) in Islamic Law"; Matroudi, *Ibn Taymiyyah*, 123–4. Al-Matroudi also discusses some interesting applications of this principle by Ibn Taymiyya, such as clauses in marriage contracts or in truces agreed with unbelievers (ibid., 111–113).
62. *MF* 20: 85ff.
63. *MF* 20:137–44. See also Matroudi, *Ibn Taymiyyah*, 103–7. Ibn Taymiyya's position may appear to conflict with Ibn Ḥanbal's legacy of asceticism. See Nimrod Hurvitz, *The Formation of Ḥanbalism: Piety into Power* (London: Routledge Curzon, 2002), 91–102; Christopher Melchert, *Ahmad ibn Hanbal* (Oxford: Oneworld Publications, 2006), 103–20.
64. *MF* 21:24ff, 20:516 (*Risāla fī al-qiyās*) (discussed in Laoust, *Contribution*, 16–25), 20:337 (*Ṣiḥḥat madhhab ahl al-Madīna*) (translated in Bewley, *Madinan Way*, 38–40). See also Matroudi, *Ibn Taymiyyah*, 120–1; Aṭīshān, *Manhaj*, 512–7.
65. *MF* 26:177. See ʿAṭīshān, *Manhaj*, 517–30.
66. *MF* 26:181.
67. *MF* 26:185–6.
68. I discuss this controversy in more detail in my "Ibn Taymiyya on Divorce Oaths". See Ibn Taymiyya, *Al-ijtimāʿ wa-al-iftirāq fī al-ḥilf bi'l-ṭalāq*, ed. Muḥammad ʿAbd al-Razzāq Ḥamza (Cairo: al-Manār press, 1346/1926–7). H. Laoust translated this epistle into French in "Une risāla", 221–36. See also Abū Zahra, *Ibn Taymiyya*, 79–82, 437–8, 451; Matroudi, *Ibn Taymiyyah*, 181–3
69. In another attempt to remove the root causes of *taḥlīl* marriages, Ibn Taymiyya declared the utterance of triple divorces to be an invalid form of divorce. While Sunni schools of law agreed that the pronunciation of three repudiations in one utterance is a reprehensible innovation, Ibn Taymiyya now argued that the utterance of a triple divorce should be considered not only reprehensible, but also invalid. See Abū Zahra, *Ibn Taymiyya*, 414–27; Matroudi, *Ibn Taymiyyah*, 171–81, and ʿAṭīshān, *Manhaj*, 545–68, for a detailed discussion of the legal proofs adduced by Ibn Taymiyya.
70. *MF* 29:61–4. See also Jokisch, "*Ijtihād* in Ibn Taymiyya's *Fatāwā*", 125–9.
71. Q 22:78 (trans. Yusuf ʿAli).
72. Reference to Q 7:15: "He releases them from their heavy burdens and from the yokes that are upon them."
73. *MF* 29:63–4.
74. See, for example, Ibn Taymiyya's discussion of divorce oaths in *Majmūʿat Fatāwā*, 3:54–5.
75. As demonstrated by Yahya Michot in Ibn Taymiyya, *Mardin: Hégire, fuite du péché et "demeure de l'Islam"*, textes traduits de l'arabe, annotés et présentés en relation à certains textes modernes par Yahya Michot (Beirut: Albouraq, 1425 [2004]). See also Mona Hassan, "Modern Interpretations and Misinterpretations of a Medieval Scholar: Apprehending the Political Thought of Ibn Taymiyya", in this volume.
76. Frank E. Voğel, *Islamic Law and Legal System. Studies of Saudi Arabia* (Leiden: Brill, 2000), 12–13, and passim; Matroudi, *Ibn Taymiyyah*, 159–68.
77. Jamal J. Nasir, *The Islamic law of personal status*, 3rd ed. (The Hague; London: Kluwer Law International, 2002), 110–2. An interesting exception is the Saudi

state, where, in spite of the avowed influence of Ibn Taymiyya, his views on divorce are applied by only a minority of the courts (Vogel, *Islamic Law*, 5–14. esp. p. 6).

78. Oussama Arabi, "Intention and Method in Sanhūrī's *Fiqh*: Cause as Ulterior Motive," *Islamic Law and Society* 4.2 (1997): 200–223.
79. Idem., "Contract Stipulations (*shurūṭ*) in Islamic Law".
80. John R. Bowen, "Modern Intentions: Reshaping subjectivities in an Indonesian Muslim society", in Robert W. Hefner and Patricia Horvatich (eds.), *Islam in an era of nation-states* (Honolulu: University of Hawai'i Press, 1999), 157–82; Powers, *Intent in Islamic Law*, 208–9.
81. Sherman Jackson, *Islam and the Blackamerican* (New York: Oxford University Press, 2005), 9–13. Jackson is citing Ibn Taymiyya's treatise against the syllogism, on which see Wael B. Hallaq, *Ibn Taymīyya Against the Greek Logicians* (Oxford: Clarendon Press, 1993).

V
Shi'i and Christian Polemics

Ibn Taymiyya and Ibn al-Muṭahhar al-Ḥillī: Shiʿi Polemics and the Struggle for Religious Authority in Medieval Islam

Tariq al-Jamil

Ibn Taymiyya's most scathing critique of Imāmī Shiʿa, *Minhāj al-sunna al-nabawiyya fī naqḍ kalām al-Shīʿa al-Qadariyya*, was written in response to *Minhāj al-karāma fī maʿrifat al-imāma* by the prominent Shiʿi scholar, Ḥasan ibn Yūsuf ibn al-Muṭahhar al-ʿAllāma al-Ḥillī (d. 726/1325). Ibn Taymiyya's extended response highlights the contested nature of religious authority and the dynamic relationships of power between Sunni and Shiʿi scholars during this period, a time when Shiʿi scholars participated in Syrian scholarly circles and authored works that would provide the foundations for later Shiʿi intellectual history. While this was Ibn Taymiyya's first direct response to a work by a Shiʿi *ʿālim*, it was not the only treatise in which he attempted to counteract what he perceived to be a Shiʿi threat to the purity of Islam. Ibn Taymiyya's opposition to the Shiʿa was not only part of his lifelong crusade against *bidʿa* (innovation), but also a response to specific historical circumstances and, in particular, to the Īlkhānid sponsorship of the Shiʿa. Furthermore, the refutation of al-ʿAllāma al-Ḥillī by Ibn Taymiyya reflects the accessibility and availability of Shiʿi works within the medieval Sunni scholarly community.

Shiʿi Scholarship and its Intellectual Context

Although Ibn Taymiyya was born in the small Mesopotamian town of Ḥarrān, his intellectual and political life was formed in Damascus. The city had been a centre of scholastic activity from the earliest Islamic centuries, and during Ibn Taymiyya's lifetime scholars who travelled to the city enjoyed a wealth of opportunities. New religious institutions continued to be established and salaried posts for teachers and stipends for students were widely available.[1] The long-standing tradition of travel in search of learning remained a dominant educational and career pattern of the *'ulamā'* during the thirteenth and fourteenth centuries, resulting in a network of scholarly contacts across the Islamic world. These networks brought together Sunni and Shi'i scholars, who participated side by side in a host of professional, social, and religious settings.

A growing body of evidence indicates the degree to which Shi'i scholars were actively engaged in the transmission of knowledge during Ibn Taymiyya's lifetime. Stefan H. Winter describes the presence of Shi'i scholars in Syria as a constant feature of the Mamluk period. Moreover, Winter argues that the apparently regular inclusion of Shi'i scholars in Syrian scholarly circles illustrates their ambivalent social position. While some Shi'i scholars studied alongside their Sunni counterparts, other individuals and groups were subject to persecution. Violence against individual Shi'is tended to come in the form of spontaneous and "populist" outbreaks rather than as systematic inquisition, although a few Shi'i scholars were put on trial for vituperation of the Companions of the Prophet, an offence which was vaguely defined.[2] Nevertheless, Shi'i-Sunni mutual engagement, whether polemic or dialogic, corresponded to, and in many ways produced, a shift in the scholarship of both communities during the period.

As Shi'i scholars participated as teachers, students, and colleagues in shared academic circles with their Sunni counterparts, new trends developed within Shi'i scholarship. It was during this period that Najm al-Dīn Ja'far ibn al-Ḥasan al-Ḥillī (al-Muḥaqqiq) introduced into Shi'i jurisprudence reformulated theories of *ijtihād* and *taqlīd*, which he borrowed from Sunni works. Shi'i legal works written during the period were modelled on Sunni antecedents, but they also challenged and reinterpreted Sunni legal presuppositions in light of Shi'i doctrines.[3] The Sunni science of Hadith criticism was adopted by Jamāl al-Dīn Aḥmad Ibn Ṭāwūs and al-Muḥaqqiq, despite the differences between the Shi'i Hadith corpus and the Sunni one.[4] Al-'Allāma al-Ḥillī later expanded and elaborated on the work of al-Muḥaqqiq and Ibn Ṭāwūs, and this system of Hadith classification became widely identified with his name in subsequent generations.[5] Shi'i scholars, alongside Sunni scholars, made significant contributions to the so-called rational sciences (*'ulūm 'aqliyya*), as can be seen in the large number of scholars attracted to Naṣīr al-Dīn al-Ṭūsī's observatory at Marāgha, and the volume of works produced there.[6] Writing from Ibn Taymiyya's home city of Damascus in the last decades of the eighth/fourteenth century, Shams al-Dīn Muḥammad Ibn Makkī produced one of the most influential works of jurisprudence in Shiʿi intellectual history, *al-Lumʿa al-Dimashqiyya fī fiqh al-Imāmiyya*. Muḥammad ibn Mukarram Ibn Manẓūr, who served as *qāḍī* of Tripoli in North Africa and was later employed in the chancery of Sultan Qalāwūn, completed his famous dictionary, *Lisān al-ʿArab*, in 689/1290.[7] According to Sunni biographers, Ibn Manẓūr is said to have maintained certain moderate Shiʿi proclivities (*wa kāna fāḍilan wa ʿindahu tashayyuʿ bi-lā rafḍ*).[8] Later Shiʿi biographers present him as a Shiʿi, citing his work as an important contribution to the Shiʿi intellectual tradition.[9] Taken as a whole, these centuries witnessed Shiʿi scholars employing a similar vocabulary, and engaging in the same intellectual disciplines as their Sunni counterparts.

However, rather than merely signifying accommodation and acceptance of Sunni dominance, adoption of Sunni methodological frameworks allowed Shiʿi scholars to both participate in, and to some degree transform, the intellectual world of their time. Sunni-Shiʿi polemics challenge the image, commonly found in modern historiography about the period, of Shiʿi scholars subjugated to the coercive power of exclusionary Sunni norms. In fact, the consolidation of a unified Sunni identity was a discursive process that continued well into the seventh/thirteenth and eighth/fourteenth centuries, as Sunni scholars sought to refine and assert their theological positions. At the same time, Shiʿi *ʿulamāʾ* were equally engaged in the articulation of foundational theological and legal doctrines. Shiʿi-Sunni polemical discourse demonstrates that the process of theological and legal formation was for both communities informed by mutual engagement. In fact, although polemical writings are explicitly concerned with points of divergence between Shiʿi and Sunni scholars, they are at the same time indicative of academic exchange and of the degree of diversity present and tolerated among medieval Sunni scholars.

Al-ʿAllāma al-Ḥillī's *Minhāj al-karāma fī maʿrifat al-imāma* [also known as *Minhāj al-karāma fī ithbāt al-imāma*], is a fine example of the vigour of contemporary Shiʿi scholarship. It was probably composed in 710/1311 at the request of the Mongol Īlkhān Öljeitü with the aim of elucidating of the Imāmī Shiʿi doctrine of the imamate while refuting the Sunni theory of the caliphate. Al-ʿAllāma al-Ḥillī's *Minhaj al-karāma* directly challenged the Sunni concept of legitimate leadership and its related theological constructions by asserting the divine election and superiority of the Shi'i Imams. Moreover, *Minhāj al-karāma* was not the first attempt by al-'Allāma al-Ḥillī to formulate systematic refutations of Sunni doctrine. During his stay at the court of Öljeitü, al-'Allāma al-Ḥillī composed several other polemical works dedicated to the Īlkhān. These include *Nahj al-ḥaqq wa-kashf al-ṣidq* which addresses the views of the Ash'arites, and *Istiqsā' al-naẓar fī baḥth 'an al-qaḍā' wa-al-qadar*, where he defends the Mu'tazilite view of free choice in human action. It was also during this period that al-Ḥillī composed *Kashf al-yaqīn fī faḍā'il amīr al-mu'minīn*, which praises the virtues of 'Alī and his superiority over the first three Sunni caliphs.[10] All in all, however, al-'Allāma al-Ḥillī's polemical or apologetic writings directed against Sunni theology and jurisprudence are not of major importance within the corpus of his scholarly output, and *Minhaj al-karāma* stands out as his most extensive polemical work.

Ibn Taymiyya's Opposition to the Shi'a

Minhāj al-Karāma, with its articulation of Shi'i claims to religious authority, provoked Ibn Taymiyya to produce his *Mihnāj al-sunna*, his most extensive attack on the Shi'a.[11] The anti-Shi'i polemics of Ibn Taymiyya, self-appointed defender of Sunni traditionalism, formed part of his broader condemnation of innovations in beliefs, customs, and religious practices. In his writings, as well as in other contemporary treatises on innovations (*bida'*), society appears to be thoroughly corrupted at the hands of Shi'is, Christians, Jews, Mongols and nominally Islamized converts, all of whom challenged the established patterns of leadership and the social and political authority of the Sunni *'ulamā'*.[12] A persistent theme in these articulations of Sunni traditionalism is the corrupting influence that non-Muslims, as well as recent converts to Islam, have on the Muslim community. Indeed, the process of Islamization was gathering pace in the seventh/thirteenth and eighth/fourteenth centuries, and Egypt in particular experienced large-scale forced conversions of Copts to Islam.[13] Ibn Taymiyya and others argued that converts carried over remnants of their pre-existing spiritual and ritual practices into their new religion, and in various ways brought to their new community deviant practices, customs, beliefs or "innovations". Ibn Baydakīn al-Turkumānī specifically claims that the popularity of certain festivals of Coptic Christian origin among Muslims was a consequence of their practice by Christian converts to Islam.[14]

For Ibn Taymiyya, heterodox groups within Islam were the most vulnerable to the threat posed by non-Muslim minorities. He dedicates one of the early sections of *Minhāj al-sunna* to pointing out the similarities between Shi'is, Jews, and Christians.[15] In particular, Ibn Taymiyya argues that Shi'is share with Christians indeterminate prayer times, and maintain dietary regulations that are comparable to those of the Jews. He also argues that the Imāmī Shi'i insistence on relegating the proclamation of jihad to the exclusive authority of the Imam is of Jewish and Christian origin.

Jonathan Berkey, commenting on these treatises against innovation, draws attention to contemporary changes in social, political, cultural, and religious institutions that may have formed the backdrop to the genre:

> Might we see the polemics of men such as Ibn al-Ḥājj and Ibn Taymiyya, not so much as rearguard actions to defend an Islam they inherited intact from earlier generations, but rather as an attempt to assert control, to define authoritatively a cultural complex which had always been fluid and dynamic, but which through a variety of external and internal pressures, looked to their eyes to be on the verge of spiralling out of control.[16]

It is this sense of decay and uncertainty, as well as the overall contested nature of scholarly and political authority, that fuelled Ibn Taymiyya's attacks on Shi'i scholarship and religious practice. Whether or not one accepts the complaint about 'the corruption of the time' as a reflection of social reality or as an anxious response to cultural change, it is a frequent *topos* of historical writing from the period.[17]

Ibn Taymiyya's opposition to Shi'a went beyond his use of the pen. On two separate occasions he participated in military campaigns against Shi'is. In 700/1300, he took part in an expedition undertaken by the Mamluk authorities against the Shi'is in Kasrawān, a highland region to the north-east of Beirut, where the local community was accused of cooperating with the Franks and the Mongols. Ibn Taymiyya then participated in a second military campaign to the same region in 704/1305. In connection with these campaigns, Ibn Taymiyya also produced a *fatwā* condemning the *rāfiḍa*, or Shiʿa of Kasrawān, in order to justify fighting against them. The precise identity of these Shiʿa communities has been a subject of debate. Druze chieftains, possibly assisted by Nuṣayrī Shiʿis and Maronite Christians, led resistance to the Mamluk invasion of the region, but Ibn Taymiyya's *fatwā* denounced a generalized amalgam of doctrines held by various Shiʿi groups.[18]

Ibn Taymiyya was also concerned about the influence of Shiʿi scholars and local rulers in Medina. In his treatise on the precedence and superiority of Hadith scholarship in Medina during the first three centuries of Islam, *Ṣiḥḥat uṣūl madhhab ahl al-Madīna*, he attempts to explain why the prestige of the Medinese school had gradually declined.[19] He argues that beginning in the fourth/tenth century, other cities could boast of scholars superior to those of Medina, as Shiʿi heresy (*rafḍ*) had taken root in the city of the Prophet.[20] Ibn Taymiyya argues that the majority of the inhabitants of Medina continued to adhere to the Mālikī school of law until around the beginning of the sixth/twelfth century, when the religious life of the city became corrupted by the immigration of heretics from the East (*rāfiḍat al-mashriq*).[21] According to Ibn Taymiyya, many of these Shiʿis came from Qāshān, and were descendants of the family of the Prophet. Heretical works incompatible with the Qur'ān and Sunna circulated among the Medinese, and a great deal of money was spent on them. Consequently, innovations (*bidaʿ*) increased in Medina from that time onward.[22]

During Ibn Taymiyya's lifetime, the Mamluk regime took concrete steps to curb the power and influence of the Shiʿi ruling elite of Medina. Following his pilgrimage of 1269, Sultan Baybars initiated a policy of sending Sunni scholars to Medina in order to challenge the authority of both the local Shiʿi rulers and the still dominant Shiʿi *ʿulamāʾ*. The contemporary *amīrs* of Medina, the Āl Shīhā, and their allies tried to resist this policy by different means, including the mobilization of their supporters against the Sunni immigrants whom they considered to be agents of forced "sunnification".[23]

One could view Ibn Taymiyya's anti-Shiʿi polemical writing as a complement to the political and military policies of the Mamluk sultans against the influence of Shiʿi political, military and scholarly groups. In this sense, Ibn Taymiyya's work is part of a struggle for hegemony over religious discourse, itself reflecting a struggle for social position and status across sectarian boundaries. This struggle also had, perhaps, a personal dimension. Al-ʻAllāma al-Ḥillī was one of the most accomplished Shiʻi scholar of the seventh/thirteenth and early eighth/fourteenth centuries, a figure of towering importance in the development of the Shiʻi intellectual tradition, composing numerous works in a range of disciplines including theology, philosophy, logic, law, grammar, Hadith, and exegesis. He was a well-known public Shiʻi figure, whose career path could serve as a model for both Shiʻi and Sunni scholars. Thus, in the context of competition for social position and academic prestige, Ibn Taymiyya's polemical refutation may have had both personal and doctrinal dimensions.

The Texts of *Minhāj al-karāma* and *Minhāj al-sunna*

It is relatively certain that *Minhāj al-karāma* was written shortly after 709/1310 when al-Ḥillī, together with the Shiʻi theologian Tāj al-Dīn Muḥammad ibn ʻAlī Āwī, were appointed as advisors to the court of the Īlkhānid ruler, Muḥammad Khudābandah Öljeitü. Their influence may have ultimately led to Öljeitü's conversion to Shiʻa in that same year. *Minhāj al-karāma* was subsequently written at the request of the newly converted ruler.[24] In contrast to al-Ḥillī's work, it is difficult to identify with precision *Minhāj al-sunna*'s date of composition. Muḥammad Rashād Sālim, the editor of the 1962 Cairo edition of *Minhāj al-sunna*, dates it as early as 710/1310, placing it during Ibn Taymiyya's stay in Egypt.[25] However, in the introduction to his later edition of Ibn Taymiyya's *Dar' taʻāruḍ al-ʻaql wa-al-naql*, Sālim dates the work to sometime between 713/1313 and 717/1317. Since *Minhāj* mentions *Dar' taʻāruḍ al-ʻaql wa-al-naql* several times, it could not have been written before 713/1313.[26] Henri Laoust states that *Minhāj al-sunna* was written in 716/1317, following Ibn Taymiyya's involvement in the opposition to Ḥumayḍa, the *amīr* of Mecca who had formed an alliance with Öljeitü and who was favourable to the Shiʻa in the holy city.[27]

Ibn Taymiyya's refutation closely follows al-ʻAllāma al-Ḥillī's text. He first quotes the Shiʻi author before beginning his counter-argument, responding point by point to each of the seven chapters of *Minhāj al-karāma*. At times, however, Ibn Taymiyya shifts course and directs his attacks against a variety of antinomian Islamic sects, abandoning his doctrinal preoccupation with Imāmī Shiʿa to focus on manifestations of popular Sunnism, including popular festivals and the visitation of shrines. As a result of Ibn Taymiyya's lengthy digressions, *Minhāj al-sunna* is an exponentially larger work than al-ʿAllāma al-Ḥillī's *Minhāj al-karāma*.[28] Yet, despite its length, Ibn Taymiyya's criticism often ignores important doctrinal and ritual differences between various Shiʿi groups, and he generalizes about Shiʿi practices, perhaps as a rhetorical strategy. Nonetheless, in the opening pages of *Minhāj al-sunna*, Ibn Taymiyya makes a fundamental distinction between the Imāmī Shiʿis whom he regards as misguided Muslims, and the Ismāʿīlīs (*Qarāmiṭa*)[29] whom he considers to be outright hypocrites (*munāfiqūn*) and no better than people of the *jāhiliyya*.[30]

Turning now to the details of the refutation and counter-refutation, one can highlight a few main areas of contention. One was al-ʿAllāma al-Ḥillī's claim that the imamate is one of the pillars of faith (*arkān al-īmān*), to which Ibn Taymiyya countered by arguing that there is nothing in the Qur'ān and the Sunna to support this Shiʿi claim.[31] Ibn Taymiyya further argues that the imamate cannot be a pillar of faith when the Imam's disappearance has in practice reduced him to an ineffectual being, unable to respond to any of the temporal or spiritual needs of the believers. According to Ibn Taymiyya, the hidden Imam's absence of over four centuries and the anticipation of his return produced nothing but false hopes, sedition, and corrupt practices in the community.[32] For Ibn Taymiyya, Islamic belief and piety are embodied by moral and ethical practices, and he cites several Qur'ānic verses as proof.[33] Obedience to God and the Prophet is in itself sufficient, and it entitles every Muslim to paradise, without an intercession by the Imam.[34] According to Ibn Taymiyya, by requiring obedience to a hidden Imam who cannot be seen, heard, or communicated with, the Shiʿa impose a duty which is beyond the capacity of the believers, and this fundamentally conflicts with the nature of God's justice. The doctrine of the imamate thus aims at creating a human order that is impossible to attain, a purpose that negates the Sunna of the Prophet.[35]

Throughout the text, Ibn Taymiyya broaches wider aspects of Shiʿi scholarship and methodology, and he comments on what he sees as the potentially dangerous implications of Shiʿi theological interpretations and religious practices. Ibn Taymiyya's comments are not merely polemical abstractions, but rather demonstrate a familiarity with the theological and legal debates that emerged from Shi'i intellectual discourses. His acquaintance with Shi'i scholars may have extended well beyond reading and responding to Shi'i polemical works. According to Ibn Ḥajar al-'Asqalānī, Ibn Taymiyya met and had discussions with al-'Allāma al-Ḥillī while on pilgrimage to Mecca, during the last years of al-Ḥillī's life.[36]

Another major point of contention, and one of the central points of Ibn Taymiyya's critique, concerns the ontological status of the Imam that allows him to assume certain divine prerogatives, such as an ability to foretell future events, communication with divine beings, and knowledge of the unseen (*'ilm al-ghayb*).[37] Al-'Allāma al-Ḥillī argues that all of the Imams were *muḥaddathūn*, meaning that they possessed the prophetic ability to communicate with celestial beings.[38] He argues that God's justice, majesty, and benevolence dictate that in the absence of the infallible prophets, who were protected from error, forgetfulness, and disobedience, it is now the Imams who must continue to possess this infallibility in order to safeguard the community from error.[39] He therefore argues that the Sunni failure to recognize that God appointed a successor is to attribute to Him a repulsive act and a failure to discharge His responsibility (*fi'l al-qabīḥ wa-al-ikhlāl bi-al-wājib*).[40] Ibn Taymiyya responds that the argument is rooted in an impermissible analogy between God and his creation, that is, it draws an improper comparison between the acts of human beings and God's essence and attributes.[41] He then invokes historical anecdotes and Hadith that emphasize God's transcendence and his incomparability to inherently fallible human beings.[42]

Throughout the text, al-'Allāma al-Ḥillī associates injustice and error with the actions of the Sunni caliphs, and he provides several examples of the transgressions of the caliphs, such as the killing of al-Ḥusayn. In this regard he quotes a number of prominent scholars, such as the Ḥanbalī jurist Abū al-Faraj Ibn al-Jawzī (d. 597/1200), who cursed those who took part in al-Ḥusayn's murder.[43] Each of al-'Allāma al-Ḥillī's criticisms of the caliphs are subsequently taken up by Ibn Taymiyya in his refutation.[44]

The next portion of al-'Allāma al-Ḥillī's text is a commentary on the Qur'ānic and Hadith-based justifications for the imamate, emphasizing the necessity of the kind of prophetic knowledge and guidance which can only be provided by the Imams.[45] Al-ʿAllāma al-Ḥillī cites in defence of his position the well-known, "to split into many groups (*sataftariq*)" tradition.[46] He comments that when Naṣīr al-Dīn al-Ṭūsī was asked about the different paths within Islam (*madhāhib*) he would quote the Prophet as saying: "My community will be divided into seventy-three groups and only one of them will be saved, and the rest will be in the hellfire." Naṣīr al- Dīn al-Ṭūsī would go on to explain that the Prophet identified those who will be saved when he said: "The likeness of my family (*ahl al-bayt*) is similar to Noah's Ark: those who rode it were saved and those who were left behind drowned."[47] Al-ʿAllāma al-Ḥillī concludes this portion of his disputation with the definitive statement that indeed the saved group (*al-firqa al-nājiyya*) will be those who support the imamate.[48]

One of the central points of contention in the polemical discourse between Ibn Taymiyya and al-ʿAllāma al-Ḥillī is the authoritative power of knowledge (*ʿilm*). Al-ʿAllāma al-Ḥillī bases his claims for the necessity of the imamate on the Imam's command of the so-called transmitted intellectual disciplines and, perhaps more importantly, his ability to approach these disciplines with divine perfection. He turns to historical evidence demonstrating that all the Imams were regarded as the most competent scholars, teachers, and individuals of their respective generations. Al-ʿAllāma al-Ḥillī also includes a short excursus on the supernatural qualities of the Imams, which is mostly focused on ʿAlī. ʿAlī's highest virtue, he writes, was that he was infallible (*maʿṣūm*).[49] This divine gift manifested itself in ʿAlī's intellectual superiority, and made him incapable of even an inadvertent error (*sahw*), in contrast to the Sunni caliphs who are defined not only by such inadvertent errors but also by conscious acts of injustice.[50] ʿAlī was granted a divine dispensation of exceptional knowledge, which guaranteed him perfect use of his intellectual faculties as well as complete esoteric knowledge.[51] This esoteric knowledge included the ability to intuitively grasp the underlying cause of events in human history as well as foresee the future. Al-ʿAllāma al-Ḥillī argues that ʿAlī had prior knowledge of his own death and the martyrdom of al-Ḥusayn.[52] In addition to his supernatural abilities, ʿAlī founded and developed virtually all intellectual disciplines, including Arabic grammar, *kalām*, jurisprudence, and *tafsīr*.[53] Even when an explicit link between ʿAlī and the origins of any discipline could not be identified, al-ʿAllāma al-Ḥillī argues that it can still be circuitously traced back to ʿAlī through a chain of disciples.[54] In his refutation, Ibn Taymiyya argues that there were others who excelled over ʿAlī in some disciplines; moreover, not all the disciplines mentioned by al-ʿAllāma al-Ḥillī are relevant for justifying ʿAlī's claim to the imamate.[55]

Al-ʿAllāma al-Ḥillī also points out that ʿAlī's knowledge leads to a deeper intimation of religious practice and, therefore, he is the most perfect model of piety after the Prophet Muḥammad. According to al-ʿAllāma al-Ḥillī, ʿAlī's piety was manifested by his asceticism (*zuhd*), his coarse robes, simple food and modest lodgings.[56] His poverty was not for selfish reasons; rather he accepted poverty in order to help others by giving his material possessions away as charity. Al-ʿAllāma al-Ḥillī argues that the following Qur'ānic verse was revealed as a recognition of ʿAlī's generosity: "Your guardian is God alone, as well as His Messenger and those who believe, those who establish prayer and give in charity while bowing down [in prayer]" (Q 5:55).[57] According to al-ʿAllāma al-Ḥillī, "Indeed ʿAlī was the most ascetic (*azhad*) human being after the Prophet Muḥammad."[58] Ibn Taymiyya refutes this claim by arguing that it was Abū Bakr who was the most exemplar model of *zuhd*.[59]

Another point of contention between the two scholars revolves around ʿAlī's bravery and courage. Al-ʿAllāma al-Ḥillī contends that ʿAlī was the most courageous of human beings.[60] Al-ʿAllāma al-Ḥillī cites a number of traditions to assert ʿAlī's superior bravery and military acumen, including a Hadith in which the Prophet praises ʿAlī's slaying of the Meccan warrior ʿAmr ibn ʿAbd Wudd ibn Abī Qays during the Battle of the Trench (al-Khandaq): "Truly ʿAli's killing ʿAmr ibn ʿAbd Wudd on the day of al-Khandaq is the most excellent act of my community until the Day of Judgment."[61] He maintains that ʿAlī was the bravest warrior in several other military battles, such as Badr, Banū Nadīr, al-Silsila, Khaybar, and Ḥunayn.[62] For al-ʿAllāma al-Ḥillī, ʿAlī's unequalled bravery on the battlefield demonstrates both his exalted position relative to the caliphs and his dedication to implementing God's command. In his response, Ibn Taymiyya is careful to avoid denigrating ʿAlī's distinguished military performance. However, Ibn Taymiyya argues that others, in particular Abū Bakr, had equal claim to military achievements.

Al-ʿAllāma al-Ḥillī goes on to examine one of the defining events in early Shiʿi history, the contested designation of ʿAlī as the

Prophet's successor at Ghadīr Khumm, drawing his evidence from a wealth of Sunni sources describing the event.[63] In particular, he frequently cites the Qur'ān commentary of Abū Isḥāq al-Tha'labī (d. 427/1035), *al-Kashf wa-al-bayān 'an tafsīr al-Qur'ān* [*Tafsīr al-Tha'labī*].[64] Ibn Taymiyya strongly denies the historicity of the Shi'i narrative and counters that it was Abū Bakr, rather than 'Alī, who had in fact received the designation (*naṣṣ*) of the Prophet.[65]

Al-'Allāma al-Ḥillī concludes his discussion of 'Alī's designation as the Prophet's successor by offering further Qur'ānic and Hadith evidence pointing to 'Alī's superiority over the caliphs, supported by sayings attributed to the founders of the four Sunni legal schools. One important example is his invocation of the Qur'ānic passage, "God only desires to keep away uncleanness from you, O People of the House (*ahl al-bayt*) and to purify you a [thorough] purification" (Q 33:33). Al-'Allāma then quotes a tradition found in Ibn Ḥanbal's *Musnad* in order to argue that the verse applies only to the Prophet Muḥammad, al-Ḥasan, al-Ḥusayn, 'Alī, and Fāṭima.[66]

The use of Sunni Hadith and Sunni Qur'ānic exegesis is one of the primary literary strategies employed by Shi'i scholars in polemical debates. While Ibn Taymiyya exclusively relies on Sunni materials in support of his arguments, al-'Allāma al-Ḥillī freely appropriates Sunni sources in addition to the Shi'i material. The use of a wide range of Sunni texts to bolster Shi'i doctrinal claims developed long before the exchanges between al-'Allāma al-Ḥillī and Ibn Taymiyya.[67] It served Shi'i scholars as they confronted Sunni hostility to foundational Shi'i doctrines and practices, including temporary marriage (*zawāj al-mut'a*), the conception of dissimulation (*taqiyya*), and intercession (*tawassul*, *istighātha*, *shafā'a*). Selective appropriation of Sunni materials as part of Shi'i polemics and apologetics was an effective way of asserting intellectual opposition from a social position of weakness, while at the same time reinforcing a sense of communal solidarity through shared respect for the revealed sources.

Conclusion

This examination of the competing claims set forth by two of the most prominent Shi'i and Sunni scholars of the seventh/thirteenth and eighth/fourteenth centuries does not purport to represent the general pattern of Shiʿi-Sunni polemics, or to exhaust the diverse range of arguments within the texts. The aim of the preceding analysis was to frame the polemical and apologetic writings of al-ʿAllāma al-Ḥillī and Ibn Taymiyya within the contested nature of religious authority that characterized the social contexts in which they were produced.

In this context, one of the functions of Ibn Taymiyya's text can be seen as negotiating authority through polemical discourse. There is little doubt that Ibn Taymiyya was aware of patronage enjoyed by al-ʿAllāma al-Ḥillī in the Īlkhānid court. Although this political dimension is not explicitly mentioned in *Minhāj al-sunna*, Ibn Taymiyya's counter-arguments cannot be disconnected from their historical context. Shiʿi-Sunni polemics served an important social function of defining Sunni and Shiʿi identities through dialogue across sectarian lines. In this sense, the polemics of al-ʿAllāma al-Ḥillī and Ibn Taymiyya are an attempt to define the orthodox beliefs of each community and to delineate Sunni and Shiʿi group membership and affiliation, as the boundaries between the communities continued to be negotiated well into the eighth/fourteenth century.

The Mamluk period witnessed the development of new intellectual approaches, especially among the Shiʿa. Rather than signifying accommodation to the dominant claims of the majority community, the literary debates between Shiʿi and Sunni scholars reflect power relations as complex as the social and political order. The arguments elaborated by al-ʿAllāma al-Ḥillī and Ibn Taymiyya have influenced contemporary polemical works, and modern Shiʿi refutations of *Minhāj al-sunna* have provoked a number of Sunni counter-refutations.[68] In fact, it is reported that al-ʿAllāma al-Ḥillī himself considered continuing the cycle of refutations and counter-refutations, but for his adversary's lack of discernment. When al-ʿAllāma al-Ḥillī learned of Ibn Taymiyya's response, he remarked, "Had he understood what I said, I would have replied to him (*law kāna yafham mā aqūl la-ajabtuhu*)."[69]

Notes

1. Michael Chamberlain, *Knowledge and Social Practice in Medieval Damascus, 1190–1350* (Cambridge: Cambridge University Press, 1994), 37–43, 47–66; Joan E. Gilbert, "Institutionalization of Muslim Scholarship and Professionalization of the 'Ulamā' in Medieval Damascus," *Studia Islamica* 52 (1980): 106–107.
2. Stefan H. Winter, "Shams al-Dīn Muḥammad ibn Makkī 'al-Shahīd al-Awwal' (d. 1384) and the Shi'ah of Syria", *Mamluk Studies Review* 3 (2000): 149–182.
3. Hossein Modarressi Tabātabā'ī, *An Introduction to Shī'ī Law: A Bibliographical Study* (London: Ithaca Press, 1984), 47–48; Wilferd Madelung, "Authority in the Absence of the Imam," in W. Madelung, *Religious Schools and Sects in Medieval Islam* (Aldershot, Great Britian: Variorum, 1985), 168. See also Devin J. Stewart, *Islamic Legal Orthodoxy: Twelver Shiite Responses to the Sunni Legal System* (Salt Lake City: University of Utah Press, 1998), 111–173.
4. Asma Afsaruddin, "An Insight into the Ḥadith Methodology of Jamāl al-Dīn Aḥmad b. Ṭāwūs," *Der Islam* 72 (1995): 24–46; Etan Kohlberg, *A Medieval Muslim Scholar at Work: Ibn Ṭāwūs and His Library* (Leiden: E. J. Brill, 1992), 17.
5. Shi'i biographers have often credited al-'Allāma al-Ḥillī with the introduction of the quadripartite system of Hadith classification (sound, good, reliable, and weak) into Shi'i literature. See Muḥammad Bāqir al-Khwānsārī, *Rawḍat al-jannāt fī aḥwāl al-'ulamā' wa-al-sādāt*, 8 vols. (Tehran: Maktabat Ismā'īlīyān, n.d.), 2:266, 271–272; Muḥammad Mahdī ibn Murtaḍā Baḥr al-'Ulūm al-Ṭabāṭabā'ī, *al-'Ulūm [al Fawā'id al-rijāliyya]*, 4 vols. (Najaf: Maṭba'at al-Ādāb, 1965–1967), 2:260; Muḥsin al-Amīn, *A'yān al-shī'a*, 11 vols. (Beirut: Dār al-Ta'āruf, 1986), 9:15, 22; 'Abd Allāh al-Māmaqānī, *Miqbās al-hidaya fī 'ilm al-dirāya*, 7 vols. (Qum: Mu'assasat Āl al-Bayt li-Iḥyā' al-Turāth), 1411/1990, 1:137–140.
6. On the importance of Marāgha and the scholarship produced there see Bar Hebraeus (Abū al-Faraj ibn al-'Ibrī), *Tārīkh mukhtasar al-duwal* (Beirut: al-Maṭba'a al-Kāthūlīkiyya li-al-Ābā' al-Yasū'īyīn, 1890), 500–501; 'Abd Allāh al-Ni'ma, *Falāsifat al-shī'a: ḥayātuhum wa-ārā'uhum* (Beirut: Dār Maktabat al-Ḥayāt, 1961), 484; E.S. Kennedy, "The Exact Sciences in Iran under the Saljuqs and Mongols," in *The Cambridge History of Iran* (Cambridge: Cambridge University Press, 1968), 5: 558ff; Sabine Schmidtke, *Theology of al-'Allāma al-Ḥillī (d. 725/1325)* (Berlin: Klaus Schwarz Verlag, 1991), 13–14.
7. Ibn Ḥajar, *al-Durar al-kāmina fī a'yān al-mi'a al-thāmina*, ed. 'Abd al-Wārith Muḥammad 'Alī (Beirut: Dār al-Kutub al-'Ilmiyya, 1997), 4:262–264, no. 725.
8. al-Ṣafadī, *A'yān al-'aṣr wa-a'wān al-naṣr* (Beirut: Dār al-Fikr al-Mu'āsir, 1418/1998), 5:270; al-Suyūṭī, *Bughyat al-wu''āh fī ṭabaqāt al-lughawiyyīn wa-al-nuḥāh* (Cairo: Maṭba'at 'Isa al-Bābī al-Ḥalabī, 1964–1965), 1:106; Muḥammad ibn Mukarram ibn 'Alī ibn Aḥmad ibn Manẓūr, *Lisān al-'Arab* (Beirut: Dār Iḥyā' al-Turāth al-'Arabī, 1968/1417), 1:9–10. It is not clear what his Sunni biographers meant by *tashayyu' bi-lā rafḍ*. However, it reflects the fluidity of religious affiliations and the indeterminate nomenclature used to refer to the varieties of Shi'a during the period. See Etan Kohlberg, "Early Attestations of the Term 'Ithnā 'Ashariyya'", *Jerusalem Studies in Arabic and Islam* 24 (2000): 343–357.
9. Al-Khwānsārī, *Rawḍat al-jannāt*, 8:79, no. 693; Aghā Buzurg al-Ṭihrānī, *Ṭabaqāt a'lām al-shī'a*, 6 vols. (Qum: Maktabat Ismā'īlīyān, n.d.), 3:204–205; idem.,

al-Dharī'a ilā taṣānīf al-shī'a, 26 vols. (Najaf: Maṭba'at al-Gharā, 1936-), 18:308, no. 234; Muḥsin al-Amīn, *A'yān al-shī'a*, 14:370, no. 10133.

10. Aghā Buzurg al-Ṭihrānī, *al-Dharī'a ilā taṣānīf al-shī'a*, 2:32, 18:69–70, 24:416; Muḥsin al-Amīn, *A'yān al-shī'a*, 9:23–32; Muḥammad ibn al-Ḥasan al-Ḥurr al-'Āmilī, *Amal al-āmil fī 'ulamā' Jabal 'Āmil* (Qum: Dār al-Kitāb al-Islāmī, 1965–1966), 2:82–85; Sabine Schmidtke, *The Theology of al-'Allāma al-Ḥillī*, 27–34.
11. Ibn Taymiyya explains his decision to respond to al-'Allāma al-Ḥillī at the beginning of his work. See Ibn Taymiyya, *Kitāb minhāj al-sunna al-nabawiyya fī naqḍ kalām al-Shī'a wa-al-Qadariyya,* 2 vols. (Cairo: Maktabat Dār al-'Urūba, 1962), 1:15–16. I have also used the Beirut edition of the work: *Kitāb minhāj al-sunna* (Beirut: Dār al-Kutub al-'Ilmiyya, 1420/1999). On Ibn Taymiyya's reaction to al-'Allāma al-Ḥillī's work, see also Ibn 'Abd al-Hādī, *al-'Uqūd al-durrīya min manāqib Shaykh al-Islām Aḥmad ibn Taymiyya*, ed. Muḥammad Ḥāmīd al-Fiqī (Beirut: Dār al-Kutub al-'Ilmiyya, 1938), 28.
12. See Maribel Fierro, "The Treatises against Innovations (*kutub al-bida'*)", *Der Islam*, 69 (1992): 204–46; Vardit Rispler, "Towards a New Understanding of the Term *bid'a*", *Der Islam* 68 (1991): 320–328. Well known *bida'* treatises produced in the Mamlūk period include Ibn Taymiyya, *Iqtiḍā' al-ṣirāṭ al-mustaqīm mukhālafat aṣḥāb al-jaḥīm* (Cairo, 1950), trans. Muḥammad Umar Memon as *Ibn Taymīya's Struggle against Popular Religion* (Paris: Mouton & Co., 1976); Idrīs Ibn Baydakīn, *Kitāb al-luma' fī al-ḥawādith wa-al-bida'*, 2 vols., ed. Ṣubḥī Labīb (Cairo: Qism al-Dirāsāt al-Islāmiyya, al-Ma'had al-Almānī li-al-Āthār bi-al-Qāhira, 1986), and Ibn al-Ḥājj al-'Abdarī, *al-Madkhal* (Cairo, 1960).
13. Tamer el-Leithy, "Coptic Culture and Conversion in Medieval Cairo, 1293–1524 A.D." (Ph.D. diss., Princeton University, 2004); Donald Little, "Coptic Conversion to Islam Under the Baḥrī Mamlūks, 692–755/1293–1354," *Bulletin of the School of Oriental and African Studies* 39 (1976): 552–669; Ira Marvin Lapidus, *Muslim Cities in the Later Middle Ages* (Cambridge, MA: Harvard University Press, 1967), 86, 143–184, 266, 288–292; Moshe Perlmann, "Notes on Anti-Christian Propaganda in the Mamluk Empire," *Bulletin of the School of Oriental and African Studies* 10.4 (1942): 843–861. In the case of Jews, see for example, Mark R. Cohen, *Under Crescent & Cross: The Jews in the Middle Ages* (Princeton: Princeton University Press, 1994), 28–29, 174–177; Mark R. Cohen, "Jews in the Mamluk Environment: The Crisis of 1442 (A Geniza Study)," *Bulletin of the School of Oriental and African Studies* 47 (1984):425–448.
14. Subhi Labib, "The Problem of *Bida'* in the Light of an Arabic Manuscript of the 14th Century", in *Proceedings of the 26th International Congress of Orientalists, 4-10th January 1964*, 4 vols. (Poona: Bhandarkar Oriental Research Institute, 1966–1970), 4:277.
15. Ibn Taymiyya, *Kitāb minhāj al-sunna*, 1:13–24.
16. Jonathan P. Berkey, "The Mamluks as Muslims: the Military Elite and the Construction of Islam in Medieval Egypt", in Thomas Philipp and Ulrich Haarmann (eds.), *The Mamluks in Egyptian Politics and Society* (Cambridge: Cambridge University Press, 1998), 168.
17. Ibid.
18. Ibn Kathīr, *al-Bidāya wa al-nihāya*, 14:12, 25; Ibn Taymiyya, *Majmū' fatāwā Shaykh al-Islām Aḥmad ibn Taymiyya* (Riyadh, 1962–66), 5:149–160. See also the following studies: Yaron Friedman, 'Ibn Taymiyya's Fatāwā against the Nuṣayrī-'Alawī Sect', *Der Islam* 82.2 (2005): 349–363; Niels Henrik Olesen, *Culte des saints et pélerinages chez Ibn Taymiyya* (Paris: Libraire Orientaliste Paul Geuthner S.A.,

1991), 13–14; Henri Laoust, "Remarques sur les expéditions du Kasrawān sous les premiers Mamluks," *Bulletin du Musée de Beyrouth* 4 (1940): 93–115; Robert Irwin, *The Middle East in the Middle Ages: The Early Mamluk Sultanate 1250–1352* (Beckenham, Kent: Croon Helm, 1986), 101–102; Kamal Salibi, "Mount Lebanon Under the Mamluks", in Samir Seikaly et al. (eds.), *Quest for Understanding: Arabic and Islamic Studies in Memory of Malcolm Kerr* (Beirut: American University of Beirut, 1991), 15–32.

19. Werner Ende, "The Nakhāwila, A Shiite Community in Medina Past and Present", *Die Welt des Islams*, 37.3 (1997): 274–275.
20. From the context, it appears that Ibn Taymiyya was referring to Mongol domains in Iraq and Iran. Ibn Taymiyya, *Ṣiḥḥat uṣūl madhhab ahl al-Madīna*, ed. Zakarīyā 'Alī Yūsuf (Cairo: Maṭba'at al-Imām, n.d.), 20–22.
21. Ibid., 21.
22. Ibid.
23. Shaun E. Marmon, *Eunuchs and Sacred Boundaries in Islamic Society* (Oxford and New York: Oxford University Press, 1995), 56–60, 138 n159; Other scholars have also concurred with Marmon's observation that Shi'i *'ulamā'* and rulers remained dominant in Medina while subject to increasing pressure from the Mamluk regime. See Ende, "The Nakhāwila", 276; and Richard T. Mortel, "The Ḥusaynid Amirate of Madīna during the Mamlūk Period", *Studia Islamica* 80 (1994): 100–102.
24. Muḥammad Bāqir Majlisī, *Biḥār al-anwār*, 110 vols. (Tehran: Dār al-Kutub al-Islāmiyya, 1956–1972), 107:138–42; 'Alī al-Ḥusaynī al-Mīlānī, *Dirāsāt fī Minhāj al-sunna li-ma'rifat Ibn Taymiyya: Madkhal li-sharḥ Minhāj al-karāma* (Iran: 'Alī al-Ḥusaynī al-Mīlānī, 1419/1998 or 1999), 36–38; Sabine Schmidtke, *Theology of al-'Allāma al-Ḥillī*, 23–34.
25. Ibn Taymiyya, *Kitāb minhāj al-sunna*, 1:15.
26. Jon Hoover, *Ibn Taymiyya's Theodicy of Perpetual Optimism* (Leiden: E.J. Brill, 2007), 10–11.
27. H. Laoust, "Ibn Taymiyya," *Encyclopedia of Islam*, new ed., 3:952. In an earlier work, Laoust put the date of composition of *Minhāj al-Sunna* to no earlier than 721/1321, as he believed *Minhāj al-karāma* was written in that year (H. Laoust, "La biographie d'Ibn Taimīya d'apres Ibn Kathīr," *Bulletin d'études orientales* 9 [1942], 155). However, it is unlikely that *Minhāj al-karāma* would have been written at such a late date since Öljeitü, who commissioned the work, died in 716/1316.
28. In the 1962 Cairo edition of *Minhāj al-sunna*, which includes the text of al-'Allāma al-Ḥillī's *Minhāj al-karāma fī ma'rifat al-imāma*, al-'Allāma al-Ḥillī's work occupies less than a quarter of the published text.
29. At various times in the text Ibn Taymiyya uses the pejorative term *qarāmiṭa* to refer to all Ismā'īlīs. The term originally referred to the followers of Ḥamdān Qarmaṭ, an Ismā'īlī leader in the *sawād* of al-Kūfa during the later part of the third/ninth century. Although the *qarāmiṭa* in al-Bahrayn were rivals of the Fatimids, the term was also pejoratively applied to all Ismā'īlīs. See Abū Muḥammad al-Ḥasan ibn Mūsā al-Nawbakhtī, *Kitāb firaq al-shī'a* (Istanbul: Maṭba'at al-Dawla, 1931), 61–64; Wilferd Madelung, "ḳarmaṭī", *Encyclopedia of Islam*, new ed.
30. Ibn Taymiyya, *Kitāb minhāj al-sunna*, 1:2–4.
31. Ibid., 1:70–72.
32. Ibid.

33. Ibid., 1:71.
34. Ibid., 1:72.
35. Ibid.
36. Ibn Ḥajar, *al-Durar al-kāmina*, 2:159. This account is mentioned by Schmidtke, who acknowledges that it is not confirmed by any other source (*The Theology of al-'Allāma al-Ḥillī*, 34).
37. Ibn Taymiyya, *Kitāb minhāj al-sunna*, 1:47–60. On the development of these views in Shi'i theology see, Hossein Modarressi, *Crisis and Consolidation in the Formative Period of Shi'ite Islam* (Princeton: Darwin Press, 1993), 19–51; Mohammad Ali Amir-Moezzi, *The Divine Guide in Early Shi'ism: The Sources of Esotericism in Islam* (Albany: State University of New York Press, 1994), 70–97.
38. The common Twelver Shi'a view was that the Imāms were given the ability to hear and understand celestial beings without seeing their forms, while prophets were endowed with the ability of both hearing and seeing these beings. However, the extent of the Imam's knowledge was a matter of debate among Shi'i scholars. See Muḥammad ibn Ya'qūb al-Kulaynī, *Uṣūl min al-kāfī* (Beirut: Dār al-Ta'ārif, 1401/1980), 1:271; Amir-Moezzi, *The Divine Guide in Early Shi'ism*, 70, 190ff, 191ff.
39. Al-'Allāma al-Ḥillī, *Minhāj al-karāma* (printed in volume 1 of Ibn Taymiyya, *Kitāb minhāj al-sunna* [Cairo, 1962]), 78.
40. Ibid.
41. Ibn Taymiyya, *Kitāb minhāj al-sunna*, 1:315.
42. Ibid.
43. Al-'Allāma al-Ḥillī, *Minhāj al-karāma*, 85–89.
44. For Ibn Taymiyya's responses, see *Kitāb minhāj al-sunna*, 1:261–286, 1:378, 2:1–28.
45. Al-'Allāma al-Ḥillī, *Minhāj al-karāma*, 89–144.
46. Ibid., 95.
47. Ibid.
48. Ibid. For Ibn Taymiyya's response, see *Kitāb minhāj al-sunna*, 2:99–108.
49. Al-'Allāma al-Ḥillī, *Minhāj al-karāma*, 145.
50. Ibid., 146.
51. Ibid., 131–135. Ibn Taymiyya takes up the refutation of these points by criticizing the authenticity of the traditions used as proof texts. See *Kitāb minhāj al-sunna*, 3:122–128.
52. Al-'Allāma al-Ḥillī, *Minhāj al-karāma*, 186–189.
53. Ibid., 177–180.
54. Ibid.
55. Ibn Taymiyya, *Kitāb minhāj al-sunna* (Beirut: Dār al-Kutub al-'Ilmiyya, 1420/1999), 4:132–135.
56. Al-'Allāma al-Ḥillī, *Minhāj al-karāma*, 145–148, 174–177.
57. Ibid., 148.
58. Ibid., 174–177.
59. Ibn Taymiyya, *Kitāb minhāj al-sunna* (Beirut), 4:129–131.
60. al-'Allāma al-Ḥillī, *Minhāj al-karāma*, 179.
61. Ibid., 126.
62. Ibid., 181–186,
63. Ibid., 149–150.
64. On al-Tha'labī, see al-Khwānsārī, *Rawḍat al-jannāt*, 1:245–246; Ibn Khallikān, *Wayfayāt al-a'yān wa-anbā' abnā' al-zamān*, ed. Iḥsān 'Abbās (Beirut: Dār al-Sādir,

n.d.), 1:79–80; Walid A. Saleh, *The Formation of the Classical Tafsīr Tradition: The Qur'ān Commentary of al-Tha'labī (d. 427/1035)*, (Leiden; Boston: Brill, 2004).

65. Ibn Taymiyya, *Kitāb minhāj al-sunna*, 1:343–375.
66. Al-'Allāma al-Ḥillī, *Minhāj al-karāma*, 151.
67. The approach has endured in modern popular Shi'i polemical works. See al-Sayyid Muḥammad al-Mūsawī Sulṭān al-Wā'iẓīn al-Shīrāzī, *Shabhā-yi Pīshāvar: dar difā' az harīm-i Tashayyu'* (Tehran: Dār al-Kutub al-Islāmiyya, 1343/1964); Muḥammad al-Tījānī al-Samāwī, *Thumma ihtadayt* (Beirut: Mu'assasat al-Fajr, 1980); Muḥammad al-Tījānī al-Samāwī, *Fa-is'alū ahl al-dhikr* (Beirut: Mu'assasat al-Fajr, 1991); Muḥammad al-Tījānī al-Samāwī, *al-Shī'a hum ahl al-Sunna* (Beirut: Shams al-Mashriq, 1993); 'Abd al-Ḥusayn Sharaf al-Dīn al-Musawī, *al-Murāja'āt* (Beirut: al-Dār al-Islāmiyya, 1986).
68. Sabine Schmidtke lists a number of these books (*Theology of al-'Allāma al-Ḥillī*, 95–96).
69. Ibn Ḥajar al-'Asqalānī, *Lisān al-mīzān*, 7 vols. (Beirut: Mu'assasat al-A'lamī li-al-Maṭbū'āt, 1390/1971), 2:317; Also see Ṣā'ib 'Abd al-Ḥamīd, *Ibn Taymiyya: ḥayātuhu, 'aqā'iduhu, mawqifuhu min al-Shī'a wa-Ahl al-Bayt* (Qum: Markaz al-Ghadīr li-al-Dirāsāt al-Islāmiyya, 1994), 220.

Apologetic and Polemic in the *Letter from Cyprus* and Ibn Taymiyya's *Jawāb al-ṣaḥīḥ li-man baddala dīn al-Masīḥ*

David Thomas

Responses to Christianity feature prominently among the many polemical works of Ibn Taymiyya. These range from relatively brief *fatwās* to exhaustive examinations and rebuttals of the faith, and include as many as seven major works in addition to briefer pieces written throughout Ibn Taymiyya's lifetime, the first datable to 694/1293 and the last to 721/1321.[1] Without doubt, the voluminous *Jawāb al-ṣaḥīḥ li-man baddala dīn al-Masīḥ* (*The correct reply to those who have altered Christ's religion*) is both the longest and most detailed of these. It sums up its author's attitude towards Christianity and, when placed in the controversialist setting in which it was composed, eloquently details the Islamic rejection of Christian beliefs and its understanding of the right relationship between the two faiths. Therefore, an examination of this work and the Christian letter to which it forms a response affords an instructive insight into the assumptions typical of the warlike age in which both letters originated and provides salutary lessons for Christian-Muslim relations today.

Paul of Antioch and the *Letter from Cyprus*

The *Jawāb al-ṣaḥīḥ* is part of the most protracted and detailed correspondence in the history of Christian-Muslim relations. It was initiated by a letter from the Melkite Bishop of Sidon, Paul of Antioch, written probably towards the end of the twelfth century. This letter was supposedly sent to a Muslim friend who wanted to know about the trip the Bishop had made to Byzantium, Italy, and other parts of Europe.[2] Paul relates that on his journey he met Christian scholars who had read the Qur'ān and knew it. But rather than accepting Islam, they had felt strengthened in their own beliefs by what they had encountered. He goes on to show how these scholars found in the Qur'ān not only clear statements that it was intended for pagan Arabs alone, but also attestations to all the main teachings of Christianity, including the divinity of Christ, the Trinity, the establishing of the faith by the apostles and aspects of Christian worship.

The letter purports to present a view, very unsettling from a Muslim perspective, of the Qur'ān as a crypto-Christian document. By careful selection of isolated verses or parts of verses, it claims to demonstrate that Christianity is the supreme faith and that the Prophet Muḥammad had never contested this, but had in fact supported it. A few examples will illustrate Paul's technique. When arguing that the Qur'ān supports the doctrine of Christ's two natures, Paul writes:

> In the book [Qur'ān] there appears what accords with our teaching, for it calls Christ "the word and spirit of God" and calls him "Jesus son of Mary" as it says, "Christ Jesus, son of Mary, was only the messenger of God and his word which he cast into Mary and a spirit from him" [Q 4:171].[3] And in another place in the book it says, "This is (*dhālika*) the word of truth about which they doubt" [Q 19.34].[4]

The two quotations appear solidly to support belief in the humanity and divinity of Christ, by explicitly referring to him as son of Mary and as word and spirit of God, and by calling him the universal word of truth, *qawl al-ḥaqq*. The verses, however, are of course taken out of their original context: Q 4:171 goes on to warn against belief in Trinity, and insists that it is far "removed from [God's] transcendent majesty that he should have a son". Q 19:34 is followed by an even more direct denial: "It befits not Allah that he should take to himself a son. Glory be to him! When he decrees a thing, he says to it only: Be! And it is!" (Q 19:35). Only by carefully omitting these elements of context is Paul able to make his point at all.

Another example of Paul's selective reading of the Qur'ān is his identification of a reference to Jesus and the Gospel in the obscure letters opening *Sūrat al-Baqara*. This identification bolsters his argument for Qur'ānic validation of Christian scripture:

> It [the Qur'ān] witnesses that it [the Gospel] is guidance for the God-fearing, when it says: "A.L.M. That is the book (*dhālika al-kitāb*) in which is no doubt, guidance for the God-fearing" [Q 2:1–2]. ALM are part of '*al-Masīḥ*'. And "that is the book" refers to the Gospel, because it [the

> Qur'ān] says, "If they deny you, even so did they deny messengers who were before you, who came with clear proofs, with the Psalms and with the book giving light" [Q 3:184]. This is the Gospel, which apostles before him brought, together with clear proofs. [Also], "that is the book" [refers to the Gospel] because 'that' is not 'this'.[5]

This ingenious exegesis identifies the three letters at the start of *Sūrat al-Baqara* as a partial reference to Christ in his Arabic title *al-Masīḥ*, and interprets the opening words *dhālika al-kitāb* literally, as an obvious reference to something outside the Qur'ān rather than the Qur'ān itself. In this latter case, Paul might have been aware of support from exegetes early in the Islamic tradition,[6] but the identification of the mysterious letters seems to be his own.

Paul's epistle must have been put into circulation almost immediately after its composition. Ibn Taymiyya says he knows of old copies of it and also that Christians have made polemical use of it a number of times. He refers to its title as "The Most Eloquent Treatise of Weighty Authority which proves Sound Belief and Correct Discernment".[7] It also comes to the notice of the Egyptian jurist Aḥmad b. Idrīs al-Qarāfī (d. 684/1285), who refutes its arguments in his *Al-ajwiba al-fākhira 'an al-as'ila al-fājira* (*Excellent answers to execrable enquiries*), although without explicitly referring to it.

Ibn Taymiyya's *Jawāb*, however, is not directed at Paul's original letter but rather is formulated as a response to a later version sent to him from Cyprus by an unnamed Christian. The identity of the author of this 'Letter from Cyprus' remains unknown, but his work makes it clear that he intended to convey a more conciliatory approach to Muslims than that offered by Paul. A brief examination of the changes he made to Paul's treatise will give some impression of the change in tone introduced by this second, Cypriot author.

The first noticeable change is that of tone. Whereas Paul of Antioch places himself at the centre of his narrative and becomes the interrogator of European scholars, thus making his letter quite explicitly a dialogue between Christians about the Qur'ān, the anonymous Cypriot author is much less definite. He places his dialogue in Cyprus, in the context of his landing there, meeting with the local population and their leaders, and conferring with their scholars about "their faith, what they believed and the arguments they set out in defence of themselves".[8] There is nothing to suggest that he himself is a Christian, and a reader might actually be given the impression that he is Muslim. The matter of faith is left open, maybe as an invitation to Muslims to read on.

The structure of this second letter is more or less the same as Paul's. Thus, the author explains how his Cypriot informants do not accept that the Qur'ān or the Prophet Muḥammad were sent to them, and they demonstrate how the Qur'ān supports Christian faith by specifying belief in the divinity of Christ, the Trinity, and so on. But the author frames his discourse so as to offer an invitation to his Muslim readers to agree and acknowledge that there is truth in Christianity, just as they affirm there is in Islam.

The changes to Paul's letter include additions, deletions, and alterations.[9] The additions are the most evident feature and have led some scholars to observe that the author was no more than an editor of Paul's original letter.[10] They comprise, in the main, new arguments against the notion that Christian scripture has been corrupted; a series of quotations from the Old Testament to prove that the Jews, rather than the Christians, are those whom the Qur'ān condemns as wrongdoers; a series of Old Testament quotations that prove the Christian liturgy is authentic; and further quotations to prove that Christ was foretold by the Jewish prophets, and that the Jews ignored these because they corrupted their own religion. The author makes a strong case for the authenticity of the biblical books, and on that builds an equally strong case for the correctness of Christianity and the deviance of Judaism.

The argument he makes for the incorruptness of the Bible is worth quoting in full, since it demonstrates an unusual intensity of feeling about the points being made:

> I said to them [the Cypriot scholars]: "What if someone should say that substitution and alteration [of Christian scripture] could have taken place after [the revelation of] this teaching [in the Qur'ān]?" They said: "We would be amazed at how these people [the Muslims], despite their knowledge, intelligence and perceptiveness, could confront us with such a remark. For if we were to argue with them in the same way, and say that they had made alterations and substitutions in the book which they possess today, and had written in it what they wanted and desired, would they tolerate our words?" I said to them, "This would not be tolerated, nor could anyone ever say it. It is impossible for a single jot of it to have been altered."

> So they said, "If the book which they have in the one language of Arabic and is in one location cannot have been altered and not one letter of it substituted, how can our books, which are written in seventy-two languages, be altered?[11] In each one of them there are thousands of copies, which were accepted for six hundred years before the coming of Muḥammad. They came into people's hands, and they read them in their different languages despite the size of their countries and the distance between them. Who can speak seventy-two languages? Or who could take the decision to collect them from the four corners of the earth in order to change them? If some of them were changed and some were left—this was not possible because they are all one message, all the languages. So such a thing cannot ever be said."[12]

Clearly, the author is keen to drive home his point about the uncorrupted nature of the Christian scriptures.

The author also omits some of the more contentious arguments found in Paul's letter, and whereas Paul is not slow to capitalise on any possible approval of Christianity in the Qur'ān, the second author is more judicious. For example, he completely removes Paul's ingenious exegesis of Q 2:1–2 about *al-Masīḥ* and "that is the book". He also shows more respect to the Qur'ānic text. Where Paul subtly alters the meaning of Q 57:25 by quoting only the first part of the verse ("We sent our apostles with clear proofs, and with them the book"), in order to deduce a reference to the disciples of Christ,[13] the Cypriot author quotes the full and correct Qur'ānic text. To make his point, he prefers to quote Q 2:213 ("God sent the prophets as bearers of good news and as warners, and revealed with them the book with truth so that it might judge between people concerning what they differ over"), in which he identifies "the prophets as bearers of good news" as the apostles sent out by Jesus. Regardless of whether the Qur'ānic text can actually be understood here to allude to the Gospel not as a book but as *evangelion* ('godspell', or good news), the author's care in respecting the text of Muslim scripture is clear.

Comparison of the two letters shows that the Cypriot author takes considerable trouble to remove from Paul's original work those instances of usage of the Qur'ān that might offend Muslims, or might appear as manipulation or misunderstanding of the Qur'ān. This second author, therefore, was refashioning the text with a view to excluding any obstacles that would impede a Muslim reader from accepting two main points. The first is that the Bible is textually sound and has suffered no disruption throughout its history. He argues this with unusual vehemence on the grounds that the geographical distribution of the text is so widespread that any form of concerted alteration of passages is inconceivable. Second, the doctrines and practices of Christianity are based upon the injunctions of the Bible and sanctioned by it. He argues this point both by showing that Christians have adhered to the teachings of the Bible more faithfully than the Jews, who are condemned for their aberrances, and, significantly, by showing that the Qur'ān also refers with approval to Christian doctrines and practices. The end result of his revised work is that Christianity can be shown to be firmly based upon the divine word of both the Bible and the Qur'ān.

The use the author makes of the Qur'ān calls for further comment. By employing it to support his case he tacitly acknowledges that it has authority as a divinely-inspired text. This, of course, would have helped him gain acceptance by Muslim readers. However, it is also a logical consequence of the point he makes right at the beginning of the letter, which is that Muḥammad was, indeed, a messenger sent from God. The Cypriot Christians excuse themselves from accepting Islam by arguing that the Qur'ān explicitly and repeatedly says that Muḥammad was sent not to them, nor to humanity in general, but only to the people of Arabia.[14] In this view, Muḥammad is an authentic prophet, but one sent as a messenger only to a local community, rough pagan Arabs who required some pre-evangelisation before they could accept the full Trinitarian monotheism of Christianity.

The full thrust of this letter is, then, that Christianity is an authentic God-given religion that has been passed down from the earliest times in full and unaltered form. It is based upon the teachings of the Bible, which has been transmitted without change or blemish, and, significantly, it is supported by the Qur'ān, a later revelation handed down by a local prophet to one pagan nation. Against the common Muslim accusation that the Bible had long ago been altered or neglected, the letter asserts its uncorrupted status; it argues that Christian beliefs and practices are authenticated by both the Bible and the Qur'ān; and it finds a place for the latter-day prophet Muḥammad within a divine economy in which Christianity remains supreme.

These are remarkably unprecedented features, which suggest a unique historical context. We know that the letter was sent to Ibn Taymiyya in 716/1316, and later to his Damascene contemporary Muḥammad Ibn Abī Ṭālib al-Dimashqī in 721/1321.[15] It is therefore likely that it was written around 715/1315. Such a date would place the letter at a period when active crusading efforts had more or less ceased, but when plans for new military expeditions were announced almost by the year, with the aim of reclaiming for Christendom the areas so recently taken by Egyptian Muslims. It was still a time when many European Christians put faith in rumours that Islam was on the brink of collapse, thanks to predictions said to come from the Prophet himself, and when the invading Mongols were still thought to be the ultimate nemesis of Islam.[16] The Cypriot author must have been aware of these plans and expectations, and may well have regarded his work as part of the crusading effort.

It is clear from the letter that the author wrote Arabic with ease and knew the Qur'ān so well he could make good the omissions left in Paul's quotations. He was also, unlike Paul, able to cite the name of the relevant Sura for each verse cited, and could at will quote additional verses to support his argument. He also seems to have known the leading Muslim scholars of Damascus in his day, the fiery Ibn Taymiyya and less celebrated though still prominent Ibn Abī Ṭālib al-Dimaṣhqī, who was renowned as a wide-ranging polymath.[17] It is therefore possible that the author was Syrian in origin, and may even have been a convert from Islam (his Biblical knowledge is nothing like his mastery of the Qur'ān). If so, he could have been one of the many refugees who fled the mainland to Cyprus at the end of the thirteenth century, after the fall of the last Crusader enclaves on the Syro-Palestinian littoral.

The question that remains is that of audience. As we have said, it was sent to at least two celebrated Damascene scholars at an interval of five years, and the author, or those who had sponsored him, seemed to expect a considered response. Several indications suggest that the anonymous author was indeed attempting to open a dialogue with leading Muslims, in what may have been his former homeland. The *Letter from Cyprus* can be seen as a robust but fair attempt to argue before Muslims the validity of Christianity on the basis of an unsullied authoritative Bible and of the Qur'ān. Muslims reading the letter, the author hoped, would not be able to deny the strength of its arguments, and might be enticed by its careful use of the Qur'ān in support of its points to give it a sympathetic reading. That he anticipated Muslims to accept the contents of the letter is borne out by the concluding prayer:

> Praise and blessing be to God, for he has brought unanimity of view and put an end to suspicion between his servants the Christians and Muslims, may God protect them all! If he [the Muslim scholar] has found anything different from this, may our master the revered teacher (may God eternally protect him and prolong his existence) point it out so that I may inform them [the Cypriot scholars] about it and determine what views they have on it.[18]

Did the author sincerely hope to open avenues of dialogue with Muslims by laying out his arguments so carefully? It would have been naïve to imagine that Muslims would agree that Muḥammad and the Qur'ān were sent to the Arabs alone, or that the Qur'ān confirms the integrity and finality of Christianity.

Another possible audience may have been Christians who continued to live under Muslim rule in Damascus and its environs. They are not the immediate addressees of the letter, but would presumably have heard of it and its contents and they would have been encouraged by it to persevere in their faith. Its central message would have suggested to subjected Christians that Islam is part of God's overall plan to bring all creatures under his rule, and is specifically directed at the Arabs as a means of bringing them to believe in one God, and thus closer to faith in the three-in-one God. If this was the author's intention, it is not surprising that he should end the main argument of his letter with the message:

> If the rank of the complete man born from Mary outstrips the ranks of all humans in exaltedness, including the prophets, the blessed and the angels, to the limit I have described of the creative Word of God and his Spirit uniting with him, then he must be perfection. After such perfection there was nothing left to institute, because everything that preceded it necessitated it, and there was no need for what came after it. For nothing can come after perfection and be superior, but it will be inferior or derivative from it, and there is no need for what is derivative. This statement is final, so peace be upon those who follow guidance.[19]

Here he offers support to Christians who may read the Letter, and offers what may be regarded as an appropriate invitation to Muslims to accept that Christ represents the fullness of God's communicative intention, in the process somewhat revealing his ecumenical openness.

Ibn Taymiyya's *al-Jawāb al-ṣaḥīḥ*

The two known Muslim recipients of the 'Letter from Cyprus' countered in treatises of their own. Muḥammad Ibn Abī Ṭālib composed his response immediately after receiving a copy of the letter, sometime between March and June 1321. It is a forceful diatribe, which draws on the long tradition of Muslim anti-Christian polemic to refute each of the points made by the Christian author. Ibn Taymiyya's response, *al-Jawāb al-ṣaḥīḥ li-man baddala dīn al-Masīḥ*, is the longest and most elaborate anti-Christian polemic known from any Muslim author. It seems obvious that both respondents did not buy into the letter's conciliatory tone, but rather saw it as a threat. As al-Dimashqī says, it is "a letter exemplary in politeness but alien in intention and shocking in purpose".[20]

Ibn Taymiyya does not give any information about when he wrote his response, though his remarks in the introduction of the *Jawāb* about the arrival of the letter from Cyprus suggest that he was so unsettled by its contents as to start writing almost immediately.[21] However, he also indicates in the introduction that his purpose is not merely to respond to the Cypriot author, unlike Muḥammad Ibn Abī Ṭālib a few years later. In fact, the *Jawāb* is as much an exposition and defence of correct Islamic belief as it is a response and refutation. Rather than being regarded simply as a polemical rejoinder in a tradition of Christian-Muslim debate, it has some claim to be compared with the tradition of Islamic theological treatises, with their blend of positive exposition of the teachings of the faith and of negative polemics.

The structure of the *Jawāb* is based upon the *Letter from Cyprus*, with quotations from the Christian author followed by Ibn Taymiyya's commentary and refutation. However, the responses to each section of the Christian work are so varied and elaborate as to go far beyond the immediate argument, and rather constitute a wide-ranging survey of correct and incorrect theological doctrines. In his introduction to the *Jawāb*, Ibn Taymiyya argues that there are right and wrong forms of religion. The right form is manifested in self-evident proofs and conviction of heart and mind, while the wrong form is manifested in contentiousness and all manner of heretical invention.[22] God in the Qur'ān condemned the Jews and Christians for their erroneous religion, and, as he says, "made what happened to them an example for those with understanding". By this he appears to imply that the demise of both faiths, and maybe the overthrow of the Crusader kingdoms on the Syro-Palestinian littoral within his own lifetime, are directly related to their corruptness of belief. Yet this also serves as an example for perceptive Muslims. As he goes on to say:

> The Prophet disclosed that these things [deviations from Islam] must occur in part of this [Muslim] community, although he had disclosed that there would always be within his community a community established on truth whose enemies and deserters would never harm them until the arrival of the Hour, and that his community would not agree on error nor would the communities outside it defeat it, but it would always remain prominent and triumphant, following its guided, triumphant Prophet.[23]

Ibn Taymiyya conveys here a sense of a beleaguered community of the righteous within Islam, a community whose cause he is supporting by demonstrating the errors of Christianity as a cautionary example. It is through an understanding of the real nature of Christianity and its fallacy that one can also know the fallacy of those views which resemble it—that is the views of the perpetrators of apostasy and innovation.[24]

Ibn Taymiyya does not so much refute the *Letter from Cyprus* point by point, in the way that Muḥammad Ibn Abī Ṭālib later did, but rather uses it to demonstrate to his fellow Muslims the consequences of abandoning the pure form of Islam.[25] Whereas Ibn Abī Ṭālib addresses the Christians directly, Ibn Taymiyya addresses Muslims, referring to the Christians in the third person, and holding up each of their arguments for refutation. His purpose is to demonstrate the erroneous belief of the Christians to his own fellow believers. As he says:

> We will show—to God be praise and strength—that all that they adduce as religious argument, whether from the Qur'ān or from the books preceding the Qur'ān, as well as reason itself, does not contain any argument in their favour. All the books which they adduce besides the

> Qur'ān, as well as reason, are proof against them not for them. Everything they adduce from the prophetic texts and from what is reasonable is in itself a proof against them and manifests the corrupt nature of their teaching.[26]

Ibn Taymiyya identifies six main themes in the Cypriot letter, and, quoting the letter *seriatim*, demonstrates the errors of each of them.[27] As mentioned above, his discussion constantly ranges beyond the arguments presented by the Cypriot author, bringing in a variety of related, and some only tenuously connected, points. He also refers liberally to parallel heterodoxies in Islam and beyond, and sometimes incorporates long passages from earlier authors when it suits his case.[28] A brief examination of the manner Ibn Taymiyya confronts the Cypriot author's argument for belief in the Trinity will demonstrate his method.

This section[29] begins with a quoted passage from the *Letter from Cyprus* in which the Christians argue from first principles as follows: all temporal things must have been brought into being by an agent who is not temporal; since creatures are either living or dead, this agent must be living; since living creatures are either articulate (*nāṭiq*) or not, he must be articulate; thus he is a thing, living and articulate, essence, speech and life, or Father, Son and Spirit—"we have not named these names ourselves".[30]

This argument, which can be traced back to the early Islamic period, is in tune with the methodology of contemporary Muslim theology. Ibn Taymiyya, however, offers an array of counter-arguments. First, he points out, the Christians' argument is inconsistent. On the one hand they claim to establish their doctrine by rational means, while on the other they claim to derive it from scripture. But neither reason nor revelation support what they state. The true relationship between the two is that revelation never contradicts human reason, but only provides knowledge which reason cannot attain.[31] The point he makes is that Christians have misapplied both reason and scripture, since their rational arguments are spurious (God has many more qualities than simply being living and articulate) and their interpretation of scripture eccentric.

Ibn Taymiyya's main point follows, as he goes on to mention people and groups within Islam who commit the same errors:

> The innovators and the wayward among those who associate themselves with Islam resemble the Christians in this matter.... Whoever claims pantheism (*al-waḥda*) and divine indwelling as a specified particular divine union like that held by the Christians is in this category—thus the view of Shiʿi extremists on ʿAlī, that of a sect like the Nusayrīs concerning the family of the Prophet and those like them who claim divinity for ʿAlī, or like the claim of some Ismāʿīlīs of divinity for al-Ḥākim or another of the Fāṭimids who affiliate themselves with Muḥammad b. Ismāʿīl b. Jaʿfar.[32]

Ibn Taymiyya expands upon this by complaining how such sects often claim that their beliefs cannot be investigated by reason, or that they have been handed down from venerable masters whose authority cannot be questioned. The *Jawāb* repeatedly draws comparisons between these sects and the Christians, and suggests such a close resemblance as to infer that the heterodox Muslim groups were not only culpable of the same fundamental errors, but also directly tainted by Christian teachings. The Muslim heresies are condemned by association with the Christians, who manifestly err in failing to safeguard the absolute oneness of God.

Ibn Taymiyya goes on from this to demonstrate that the Cypriot author fails to employ reason properly and misinterprets his own scripture. These errors are not limited to Christians, but are shared by all those who disagree with Ibn Taymiyya's strict understanding of the oneness of God.

This pairing of aberrant Muslim groups with Christians is repeated throughout the *Jawāb*. Ibn Taymiyya's main purpose is as much to demonstrate the consequences of abandoning strict monotheism as to expose Christian errors in order to warn fellow Muslims; the *Jawāb al-ṣaḥīḥ* is as much a work of Muslim apologetic as of anti-Christian polemic. He is not truly engaging with the Cypriot letter, but rather taking the opportunity to set out the fundamental errors of Christianity as detailed in the Qur'ān and in the Islamic tradition of anti-Christian polemic, and then to show how some Muslims have fallen into the same errors. Ibn Taymiyya resists close discussion of the arguments raised in the letter from Cyprus, perhaps sensing that these are traps that would only land him in a muddle. The Cypriot author's invitation to a dialogue, and his unrealistic and cunning attempt to make Christianity palatable to Muslims, are duly disregarded.[33]

As was suggested earlier, the Christian author was writing at a time when predictions of the impeding end of Islam were widespread. Thus, his letter invited Muslims to see the truth of Christianity endorsed in their own scripture, and encouraged Christians to see that their faith had not been superseded by Islam. However, nothing of the kind can be seen in Ibn Taymiyya's response. It may be that his insistence upon the plain truths of Islam arose out of a sense of siege, with external enemies encroaching upon Muslim territory, and internal heretics challenging the supremacy of the Qur'ān and associating God with created beings. But the *Jawāb* gives no indication that he was in fact responding to acute difficulties. Rather, his main concerns were threats to Islamic orthodoxy which had been endemic since the early period of Islamic thought.

The *Jawāb* and the Anti-Christian Polemical Tradition

Ibn Taymiyya's *Jawāb* should be viewed against the background of a long tradition in which anti-Christian polemics had often been a means to promote Islamic orthodoxy. The earliest extant substantial anti-Christian treatises, dating from the early third/ninth century, demonstrate extensive bodies of knowledge about the beliefs of the other. In what may be the earliest, the brief work simply called *Radd 'alā al-Naṣārā* (*Refutation of the Christians*) by the Zaydī Imām al-Qāsim b. Ibrāhīm al-Rassī (d. 246/860), can be found a wide-ranging description of Christian doctrines that includes a full account of the Trinity as it was explained by the Church Fathers, an explanation of the Incarnation, and the Christological teachings of the main denominations within the Islamic empire, the Melkites, Nestorians and Jacobites.[34] In another, the exhaustive *Radd 'alā al-thalāth firaq min al-Naṣārā* (*Refutation of the three Christian sects*) of the mid third/ninth century independent monotheistic thinker Abū 'Īsā Muḥammad b. Hārūn al-Warrāq (d. after 250/864) there is an even fuller description of Christian doctrines that contains a variety of models of the Trinity, a series of metaphorical explanations of the Incarnation, the Christologies of the main denominations, a version of the Creed and a brief outline of doctrinal development, along with strong hints that the author knew about a great number of heterodox Christian sects.[35]

Yet, for all their intimate knowledge of the range of Christian beliefs, when al-Qāsim b. Ibrāhīm and Abū ʿĪsā al-Warrāq begin their own counter arguments they ignore these beliefs almost entirely. Instead of attacking a whole set of doctrines, as might be expected after such descriptions, they focus only on two, the Trinity and the Incarnation. The Muslim authors demonstrate that these two doctrines respectively introduce plurality into the being of God and associate Him with created beings, and that both are incoherent in the very terms in which Christians themselves express them. The reason for choosing these two doctrines at the expense of all others is clear—it is because both question the doctrine of the absolute oneness of God in different ways, and hence challenge Islamic orthodoxy. In refuting these doctrines, the Muslim authors are not only proving the fallacy of the Christians, but also proving to Muslims that deviation from the norm of Islam leads to incoherence and inconsistencies. In this respect, these early polemical works are not directed at Christianity as an assemblage of beliefs as such, or as a faith in its own right, but at particular beliefs that deviate from a norm, and they are as much assertions of orthodox Islam as refutations of beliefs outside it.

The same pattern can be seen in other works from the later third/ninth and fourth/tenth centuries. The work known as *Kitāb al-awsaṭ fī al-maqālāt* (*The middle way among the teachings*) of the Baghdad Muʿtazilī al-Nāshiʾ al-Akbar (d. 293/906) includes an elaborate list of the beliefs held by more than twenty heterodox Christian sects, but completely ignores them in its refutation of the two central doctrines.[36] And the *Radd ʿalā al-Naṣārā* (*Refutation of the Christians*) of his younger Basran contemporary Abū ʿAlī al-Jubbāʾī (d. 303/915–16) focuses entirely upon these two doctrines in both its initial description of Christian beliefs and the arguments that follow.[37]

A final example comes in the form of the mammoth *al-Mughnī fī abwāb al-tawḥīd wa-al-ʿadl* (*The* Summa *on topics of divine unity and justice*), composed by the Muʿtazilī theologian ʿAbd al-Jabbār b. Aḥmad al-Hamadhānī (d. 415/1025) between 360/971 and 380/990.[38] It is a multi-volume encyclopaedic digest of contemporary theology covering epistemology, the oneness of God (*tawḥīd*) and God's justice in His relationship with the world (*ʿadl*). Interestingly, the work occasionally digresses to refutations of non-Islamic beliefs, which, at first glance, seem randomly scattered. Close examination, however, shows that each refutation follows an aspect of Islamic belief to which it corresponds: thus, the refutation of Judaism follows the exposition of the doctrine of the prophethood of Muḥammad, since while the Jews accept the oneness of God and the general principle of prophethood they deny Muḥammad's status as a prophet. Similarly, 'Abd al-Jabbār's refutation of Christianity follows his exposition of the absolute oneness of God, is linked to an account of dualist religions, and focuses on the doctrines of a triune God and of a union of the divine and human in Christ. Here 'Abd al-Jabbār follows earlier anti-Christian polemicists in attacks on the Trinity and Incarnation without reference to other Christian doctrines.

This organization of the *Mughnī* presents an eloquent example of Muslim attitudes towards Christianity in the early Islamic centuries. First, the main focus is on those doctrines that relate most closely to Islamic equivalents—there is little, if anything, on the doctrine of the atonement, for example. The refutation demonstrates that these doctrines are contrary to reason and suffer from incoherence and inconsistency, and that there is no rational alternative to *tawḥīd*, and no right-minded believer would embrace any other form of belief. Second, Christian beliefs are held up as counter examples to Muslim beliefs, placed together with explicitly dualist beliefs after the exposition of the logical doctrine of the oneness of God. They function as a warning against deviating from the sound, rationally defensible norm.

The dual aim of confronting the rival faith and demonstrating the uprightness and correctness of Islam, shared by 'Abd al-Jabbār and the early Muslim authors was, of course, grounded in the teachings of the Qur'ān. They accepted that the original revelation given to the human prophet Jesus had concurred with earlier revelations and the revelation of the Qur'ān, and that through distortion of the *Injīl* (Gospel) this teaching had also become distorted. So the logic of their approach to Christianity was that the distortion must be exposed for what it was in order to restore the faith to its pristine monotheism, in reality to show the way to Islam.

Conclusion

Seen within this polemical tradition, it is evident that Ibn Taymiyya's *al-Jawāb al-ṣaḥīḥ* shares a similar theological outlook. As a work of detailed refutation of Christian doctrines, the *Jawāb* refers to the arguments present in the *Letter from Cyprus*, while also going beyond them in order to demonstrate the incoherence at the core of Christian doctrines. But as a work of theology it uses Christianity as an example to illustrate the danger of these errors to Muslims. In this respect, Ibn Taymiyya's response is not so much a refutation of the Christian arguments as a defence of Islam and a call for vigilance against unorthodox beliefs. Ibn Taymiyya resists any direct engagement with the Cypriot author, refusing to be tempted by the invitation to examine Christianity through biblical and Qur'ānic teachings.

Strangely, both the Christian and Muslim theologians involved in this correspondence share a similar attitude, which is that the faith of the other is an incomplete version of their own. The Cypriot author, as we have said, accepts the Qur'ān as divinely inspired revelation handed down by Muḥammad, a true prophet, which was sent only to the pagan Arabs. Its limited message is a first step in wresting its inhabitants from their ignorance on the way to the full Trinitarian faith of Christianity. Thus, the Qur'ān is an authentic attestation of Christian truth, but its full meaning can only emerge in the light of Christian scripture itself. It contains confirmations of Christianity, but these have to be separated from other elements in order to become truly comprehensible. Once they have, the Qur'ān and the Islamic religion that follows from it can be shown to be congruent with Christianity and completed by it.

In a similar way, though more centrally to his own tradition, Ibn Taymiyya views Christianity as an earlier form of monotheism founded on the authentic basis of the *Injīl* as preached by Jesus, but sadly corrupted through the centuries, and now requiring correction and normalisation by having its incidental errors and methodological incoherence pointed out and rectified. While Ibn Taymiyya refutes the arguments in the *Letter from Cyprus*, and thereby undermines Christian doctrines and beliefs, he also appears to give Christianity scant regard in his concern to defend Islamic orthodoxy as he sees it and to warn against deviations from the straight path of strict monotheism.

As might have been assumed at the start, this correspondence was doomed to fail, because of the historical context of military confrontation, the authorial strategies employed in the letters, and the set attitudes of its participants. Can there be a more constructive way forward for Christians and Muslims, which preserves respect and sincerity while remaining true to the truth as it is claimed by either side? If so, it cannot rest on the attitude or strategy adopted by either of these diatribes.

Notes

1. Thomas Michel, *A Muslim Theologian's Response to Christianity. Ibn Taymiyya's* Al-Jawab al-Sahih (Delmar NY: Caravan Books, 1984), 68–86.
2. 'Lettre aux Musulmans', in Paul Khoury, ed. and trans., *Paul d'Antioche, évêque melkite de Sidon (XIIe s.)* (Beirut: Imprimerie Catholique, 1964), 59–83 Arabic, 169–87 French.
3. In this essay, translations of the Qur'ān are taken from M.M. Pickthall, *The Meaning of the Glorious Koran* (New York: Mentor Books, 1953).
4. Khoury, *Paul d'Antioche*, §40 (74 Arabic, 180 French).
5. Khoury, *Paul d'Antioche*, § 16 (65 Arabic, 173 French).
6. Cf. Herbert Berg, "Tabarī's Exegesis of the Qur'ānic Term *al-Kitāb*", *Journal of the American Academy of Religion* 63 (1995): 761–74, esp. 767–8.
7. Ibn Taymiyya, *Al-jawāb al-ṣaḥīḥ li-man baddala dīn al-Masīḥ*, 4 vols (Cairo: Maṭba'at al-Nīl, 1905), 1:19–20.
8. Bibliothèque Nationale, MS arabe 214, f. 48r. Cf. n. 9 below.
9. The following analysis of the letter is based upon David Thomas, "Paul of Antioch's *Letter to a Muslim Friend* and *The Letter from Cyprus*", in D. Thomas (ed.), *Syrian Christians under Islam, the first thousand years* (Leiden: Brill, 2001), [203–21] 213–21, and in Rifaat Ebied and David Thomas (eds.), *Muslim-Christian Polemic during the Crusades. The Letter from the People of Cyprus and Ibn Abī Ṭālib al-Dimashqī's Response* (Leiden: Brill, 2005), 6–19.
10. Erdman Fritsch, *Islam und Christentum im Mittelalter* (Breslau: Verlag Müller und Seiffert, 1930), 30; Khoury, *Paul d'Antioche*, 10, n. 9.
11. For a discussion of the origin of this number, cf. Ebied and Thomas, *Muslim-Christian Polemic during the Crusades*, 255.
12. Ebied and Thomas, *Muslim-Christian Polemic during the Crusades*, 71–3.
13. Khoury, *Paul d'Antioche*, § 13 (63 Arabic, 172 French).
14. Ebied and Thomas, *Muslim-Christian Polemic during the Crusades*, 57–9.
15. Al-Dimashqī himself says that he received his copy in 721/1321 and that a copy had already been sent to Ibn Taymiyya (Ebied and Thomas, *Muslim-Christian Polemic during the Crusades*, 155–7). The date of Ibn Taymiyya's copy is given in Bibliothèque Nationale, MS arabe 215, f. 203r (*c.* 15th century). The letter is extant in three manuscripts in the Bibliothèque Nationale: MS arabe 204 ff. 49v–66r (AD 1336), MS arabe 214 ff. 48r–65r (AD 1538), and MS arabe 215 ff. 203r–28r (AD 1590). Another copy is found in Bibliothèque de l'Université Saint Joseph (Beirut) 946, pp. 303–32 (AD 1856). On the manuscripts, see S. K. Samir,

'Notes sure la "Lettre à un Musulman de Sidon" de Paul d'Antioche', *Orientalia Lovaniensia Periodica* 24 (1993): 179–95, esp. 191–2. Together with the quotations given in the refutations of Ibn Taymiyya and al-Dimashqī, these offer six versions with clear, though minor, differences between them. Two of the Paris manuscripts (MS arabe 214 and 215), as well as the Beirut manuscript, openly state that they contain the version sent to Ibn Taymiyya.

16. For a fuller account of these circumstances, cf. Ebied and Thomas, *Muslim-Christian Polemic during the Crusades*, 13–16.
17. For a biographical account of al-Dimashqī, cf. Ebied and Thomas, *Muslim-Christian Polemic during the Crusades*, 23–5.
18. Ibid., 147.
19. Ibid., 145–7.
20. Ibid., 155.
21. Ibn Taymiyya, *Jawāb*, 1:19 (Michel, *A Muslim Theologian's Response*, 140). Ibn Taymiyya appears to suggest that he received the letter written by Paul of Antioch rather than that of the anonymous Cypriot editor, but his quotations throughout the *Jawāb* make it clear that he had the latter text before him.
22. Ibn Taymiyya, *Jawāb*, 1:16.
23. Ibn Taymiyya, *Jawāb*, 1:16–17 (Michel, *A Muslim Theologian's Response*, 138–9).
24. Ibn Taymiyya, *Jawāb*, 1:19 (Michel, *A Muslim Theologian's Response*, 140).
25. Cf. Michel, *A Muslim Theologian's Response*, 100: "The principal motive for [Ibn Taymiyya] writing the work was not to buttress the faith of the Muslims by supplying them with polemical argumentation, but rather to let the Christian experience of *kufr* serve as a warning to tendencies within the Islamic *umma* that could lead Muslims to the same type of unbelief."
26. Ibn Taymiyya, *Jawāb*, 1: 20–1 (Michel, *A Muslim Theologian's Response*, 141–2).
27. Ibn Taymiyya, *Jawāb*, 1: 20 (Michel, *A Muslim Theologian's Response*, 141).
28. The published text of the letter incorporates what Thomas Michel has suggested is an unrelated work of Ibn Taymiyya on prophethood (*A Muslim Theologian's Response*, 370–82). This work is found in the 1905 edition of the *Jawāb*, from 3:243 (3:275 in the 1964 edition which Michel uses) to the end of volume 4. Michel's arguments in support of this suggestion are persuasive, not least because this final section of the published work makes no reference to the *Letter from Cyprus*, which has been dealt with fully in the early parts. Mark Swanson, "Ibn Taymiyya and the *Kitāb al-Burhān*: A Muslim Controversialist responds to a Ninth-Century Arabic Christian Apology", in Yvonne Y. Haddad and Wadi Z. Haddad (eds.), *Christian-Muslim Encounters* (Gainsville: University Press of Florida, 1995), 95–107, discusses some of the Muslim and Christian works mentioned by Ibn Taymiyya.
29. Ibn Taymiyya, *Jawāb*, 2:87ff. (Michel, *A Muslim Theologian's Response*, 255ff). Its main arguments are outlined in Michel, *A Muslim Theologian's Response*, 120–7. Other criticisms of the doctrine to be found in various parts of the *Jawāb* and in other writings of Ibn Taymiyya are discussed by Nancy Roberts, "Reopening the Muslim-Christian Dialogue of the 13th–14th Centuries: Critical Reflections on Ibn Taymiyyah's Response to Christianity in *Al-Jawāb al-Ṣaḥīḥ li man baddala Dīn al-Masīḥ*", *Muslim World* 86 (1996):342–66.
30. Ibn Taymiyya, *Jawāb*, 2:87 (Michel, *A Muslim Theologian's Response*, 255); cf. Ebied and Thomas, *Muslim-Christian Polemic during the Crusades*, 91–3.

31. On Ibn Taymiyya's understanding of the relationship between reason and revelation, see also the contributions of M. Sait Özervarli and Racha el-Omari in this volume.
32. Ibn Taymiyya, *Jawāb*, 2:89 (Michel, *A Muslim Theologian's Response*, 256–7).
33. Roberts, "Reopening the Muslim-Christian Dialogue", reaches a similar conclusion on the basis of an examination of further anti-Trinitarian arguments found in the third volume of the printed text of the *Jawāb*. For example, Ibn Taymiyya makes a *reductio ad absurdum* argument that if Christ was incarnate by the Holy Spirit (the Life of God, according to Arab Christian elucidations) and the Virgin Mary, he must have been both the Word of God (i.e. the Son of the Father) and the Life of God (i.e. the offspring of the Spirit). Roberts observes that this inference reflects neither the Christian doctrine which Ibn Taymiyya attacks nor the Qur'ānic teaching that Jesus was created by God's command 'Be! ' ("Reopening the Muslim-Christian Dialogue", 354–5). Elsewhere Roberts' criticisms of Ibn Taymiyya's approach are sometimes harsh: for example, Ibn Taymiyya presents models of the Trinity which present the Father as source and Son and Holy Spirit proceeding from Him, and of the three Persons as attributes of the essence. Roberts argues that Ibn Taymiyya's presentation of Christian doctrine is unfounded (Ibid., 356); however, Christians under Muslim rule offered exactly these models in their apologies to Muslims (reported, for example, by al-Nāshi' al-Akbar, *Kitāb al-awsaṭ fī al-maqālāt*, in J. van Ess, *Frühe Mu'tazilitische Häresiographie* [Beirut: Dar al-Machreq Éditeurs, 1971], 76, and Abū Bakr al-Bāqillānī, *Kitāb al-tamhīd*, ed. R.J. McCarthy [Beirut: al-Maktaba al-Sharqiyya, 1957], 79). Nevertheless, the general point of her article, that there is a measure of inconsistency in Ibn Taymiyya's approach, is borne out by her examination and supports the contention of this paper.
34. I. di Matteo, "Confutazione contro i Cristiani dello zaydita al-Qāsim b. Ibrāhīm", *Rivista degli Studi Orientali* 9 (1921–2):301–64, esp. 314–18.
35. *Anti-Christian Polemic in Early Islam. Abū 'Īsā al-Warrāq's "Against the Trinity"*, ed. and trans. by David Thomas (Cambridge: Cambridge University Press, 1992), 66–77.
36. Van Ess, *Frühe Mu'tazilitische Häresiographie*, 76–87.
37. Cf. David Thomas, "A Mu'tazilī response to Christianity: Abu 'Alī al-Jubbā'ī's Attack on the Trinity and Incarnation", in Rifaat Ebied and Herman Teule (eds.), *Studies on the Christian Arabic Heritage in honour of Father Prof Dr Samir Khalil Samir* (Leuven: Peeters, 2004), 279–313.
38. The author himself gives these dates in *al-Mughnī*, vol. 16, part 20/2, ed. M. M. al-Khuḍayrī (Cairo: Al-Dār al-Miṣriyya li-al-Ta'līf wa-al-Tarjama, 1958), 257.

VI
Legacy

From Ibn Ḥajar al-Haytamī (d. 1566) to Khayr al-Dīn al-Ālūsī (d. 1899): Changing views of Ibn Taymiyya among non-Ḥanbalī Sunni scholars*

Khaled El-Rouayheb

Ibn Taymiyya is the one Arab-Islamic religious thinker from the so-called "post-classical" period (1258–1798) whose views have received sustained scholarly interest from modern Arab and Western historians. There has accordingly been a marked tendency to cast him as a major figure in Islamic religious history. Thus, in the index to Jonathan Berkey's recent—and in my opinion commendable—overview of the history of Islam, Ibn Taymiyya has more entries than any other Islamic religious thinker—almost twice as many as the runner-up Abū Ḥāmid al-Ghazālī.[1] The non-specialist or undergraduate reader for whom the book is intended can hardly fail to conclude that Ibn Taymiyya was one of the most influential Islamic thinkers, though Berkey is careful not to state so explicitly. Other scholarly works reinforce this impression. Majid Fakhry's influential history of Islamic philosophy, for instance, informs the reader that Ibn Taymiyya and his fourteenth-century followers "insured the victory of neo-Ḥanbalism over scholastic theology and philosophy."[2] Alexander Knysh's recent study of attitudes to Ibn 'Arabī in the Islamic religious tradition similarly states that Ibn Taymiyya "dealt monistic Sufism a devastating blow, which made him undoubtedly the most implacable and consequential opponent of Ibn 'Arabī and his followers."[3]

Such statements are, I believe, based on an exaggerated sense of the influence of Ibn Taymiyya in subsequent centuries. In fact, Ibn Taymiyya had very little influence on mainstream Sunni, non-Ḥanbalī Islam until the nineteenth century. There is for example no evidence that the influence of Sunni *kalām* abated after Ibn Taymiyya's criticisms. On the contrary, the immensely influential theological works of 'Aḍud al-Dīn al-Ījī (d. 1355), Sa'd al-Dīn al-Taftāzānī (d. 1390), al-Sayyid al-Sharīf al-Jurjānī (d. 1413),

Muḥammad ibn Yūsuf al-Sanūsī (d. 1490), Jalāl al-Dīn al-Dawānī (d. 1502), and Ibrāhīm al-Laqānī (d. 1631)—works that bio-bibliographic evidence suggests were read by almost every Sunni student from Morocco to India until at least the nineteenth century—postdate Ibn Taymiyya. Logic too continued to be a standard part of the education of Sunni scholars until modern times, and there is no evidence that Ibn Taymiyya's attacks on the discipline had any effect.[4] During the period from the fifteenth to the eighteenth centuries, the influence of Ibn 'Arabī was probably at its height in Sunni scholarly circles. Prominent and widely respected Sunni scholars such as Jalāl al-Dīn al-Suyūṭī (d. 1505), Zakariyā al-Anṣārī (d. 1519), Kemālpāşāzāde (d. 1534), 'Abd al-Wahhāb al-Sha'rānī (d. 1565), Ibn Ḥajar al-Haytamī (d. 1566), 'Abd al-Ra'ūf al-Munāwī (d. 1622), Ibrāhīm al-Kūrānī (d. 1690), 'Abd al-Ghanī al-Nābulusī (d. 1731), and Abū Sa'īd al-Khādimī (d. 1763) all defended Ibn 'Arabī, and some of them openly espoused the monist doctrine of *waḥdat al-wujūd*. Significantly, the later apologists for *waḥdat al-wujūd* seem simply to have ignored Ibn Taymiyya's criticisms of the idea, and focused on rebutting the independent and much more "consequential" criticisms of Sa'd al-Dīn al-Taftāzānī and 'Alā' al-Dīn al-Bukhārī (d. 1438).[5] The idea that Ibn Taymiyya had an immediate and significant impact on the course of Sunni Islamic religious history simply does not cohere with the evidence that we have from the five centuries that elapsed between his death and the rise of Sunni revivalism in the modern period.

What follows is an attempt to elaborate and defend this point. I will discuss in turn the verdict of mainstream non-Ḥanbalī Sunni scholars on the two issues for which Ibn Taymiyya got into trouble in his own lifetime: his literal interpretation of apparently anthropomorphic passages in the Qur'ān and Sunna, and his position on visiting the tombs of prophets and saints. I will then go on to consider bio-bibliographic evidence suggesting that Ibn Taymiyya's works were little read in the period between the fifteenth and eighteenth centuries. Finally, I will briefly discuss the nineteenth century "rediscovery" of Ibn Taymiyya.

I

> Ibn Taymiyya is a servant whom God has forsaken, led astray, made blind and deaf, and degraded. Such is the explicit verdict of the leading scholars who have exposed the rottenness of his ways and the errors of his statements. He who is interested may consult the words of the *imām* and *mujtahid*, whose status, loftiness and rank is agreed upon, Abū al-Ḥasan al-Subkī (d. 1355) and his son Tāj al-Dīn (d. 1370) and Shaykh ʿIzz al-Dīn ibn Jamāʿa (d. 1333) and their contemporaries from amongst Shāfiʿīs, Mālikīs and Ḥanafīs. He did not confine his objections to the later Sufis, but objected to the likes of ʿUmar ibn al-Khaṭṭāb and ʿAlī ibn Abī Ṭālib, may God be pleased with them. The upshot is that his words are not to be taken seriously, but should be tossed aside, and it should be believed that he is a wayward innovator and an ignorant and extremist deceiver. May God treat him to His justice, and protect us from the likes of his way, doctrine and acts. Amen.[6]

Thus starts a *fatwā* by the prominent sixteenth-century Shāfiʿī jurist Ibn Ḥajar al-Haytamī. Born and educated in Egypt, Ibn Ḥajar eventually settled in Mecca, where he died.[7] His works include an esteemed commentary on the standard handbook of Shāfiʿī law, the *Minhāj* of al-Nawawī (d. 1277)—a commentary that continued to be regarded as one of the most authoritative expressions of Shāfiʿī law well into the twentieth century.[8] He also left behind a host of other influential works, including two collections of *fatāwā*, one on strictly juridical matters (*al-Fatāwā al-fiqhiyya*), and the other on more broadly religious topics (*al-Fatāwā al-ḥadithiyya*). The condemnation of Ibn Taymiyya is in the latter collection.

Ibn Ḥajar al-Haytamī was not the first Shāfiʿī jurist to condemn Ibn Taymiyya. As indicated by Ibn Ḥajar himself, Taqī al-Dīn al-Subkī and his son Tāj al-Dīn had penned similar condemnations in the fourteenth century. The Damascene jurist Taqī al-Dīn al-Ḥisnī (d. 1426) had also condemned Ibn Taymiyya in even stronger terms, inveighing against the "heretic from Harran" (*zindīq ḥarrān*) who had appeared from the "rear end of time" (*fī ṭīz al-zamān*).[9] For these jurists as well as for Ibn Ḥajar al-Haytamī, it was particularly Ibn Taymiyya's literalist interpretation of the passages in the Qur'ān and Sunna that apply anthropomorphic and spatial descriptions to God, as well as his proscriptions against travelling to visit the grave of the Prophet and asking for his intercession that caused offence. Indeed, amongst Sunni scholars from the fifteenth to the nineteenth century, it would appear that Ibn Taymiyya's position on these matters was widely considered to be very close to the bounds of acceptability. For some scholars, such as Ibn Ḥajar al-Haytamī, Ibn Taymiyya had actually transgressed these bounds. As will be shown below, other scholars disagreed, but even they do not seem to have shared Ibn Taymiyya's general outlook.

Asked specifically about Ibn Taymiyya's objections to the later Sufis, Ibn Ḥajar summarised some of what Ibn Taymiyya had said about them—particularly his claim that they had absorbed some of the heretical doctrines of the Islamic philosophers. It was obviously of some irritation to Ibn Ḥajar that one of those whom Ibn Taymiyya had criticised was the venerable founder of the Shādhilī order:

> One of the many whom he has pursued with criticism is the Saint, the Pole, the Gnostic Abū al-Ḥasan al-Shādhilī (d. 1258)—may God make us benefit from his knowledge and insights...just as he pursued Ibn 'Arabī and Ibn al-Fāriḍ and Ibn Sab'īn, and pursued al-Ḥallāj al-Ḥusayn ibn Manṣūr. He continued to pursue the greats with his criticism, until the people of his age united against him and declared him a sinner and an innovator—indeed many of them declared him an unbeliever.[10]

Ibn Ḥajar went on to list a number of juridical and theological points on which he believed that Ibn Taymiyya had broken with the established consensus of Sunni scholars. Some of these relate to details of religious law, such as the idiosyncratic position that declaring a wife divorced three times in one declaration amounted to a single divorce, or that a menstruating woman could perform the circumambulation of the Ka'ba. Other issues relate to more general theological positions taken by Ibn Taymiyya: for example the position that God is in the direction (*jiha*) of "above" and that he sometimes descends down to the lower heavens; or the position that it is not permitted to travel to visit the grave of the Prophet, or to entreat him (*tawassul*) for intercession with God. The list also includes a number of other points that would seem to be somewhat garbled versions of the historical Ibn Taymiyya's views, such as the purported claim that the Prophet was not infallible, or that the world is eternal in kind. Ibn Ḥajar was obviously not well-versed in the writings of Ibn Taymiyya, and ended his *fatwā* with the caveat that some who have read Ibn Taymiyya's works hesitate to attribute some of the listed positions to him. However, Ibn Ḥajar added, there is little doubt that Ibn Taymiyya did defend the view that God is in the direction of "above", and this view, even if not beyond the pale of belief, was unacceptable.[11]

Ibn Ḥajar reiterated the point in another *fatwā*.[12] Asked if it is permissible to say that God is in heaven (*fī al-samā'*), he replied that spatial expressions ought not to be applied to God since they imply that He is a body and is in space and has spatial relations to other things, all of which are unacceptable. He then went on to state that the scholars who agreed on this principle differed in the way they dealt with the Qur'ānic verses and Hadith that suggested the contrary. Some of the early Sunni scholars (*al-salaf*) suspended judgement (*waqf*) with regard to the meaning of the passages, and simply accepted them as part of divine revelation, while refraining from interpretation: "They say: one must believe in them as they have appeared (*kamā waradat*) and we do not presume to explain them (*lā nata'addā ilā tafsīrihā*)." Ibn Ḥajar deemed the position unsatisfying, since there was—or so he claimed—a consensus to the effect that the relevant expressions should not be understood in accordance with the conventional, everyday meaning of words. Hence, refraining from giving an alternative interpretation would give "false impressions to commoners and an opportunity for the ignorant." The position of the majority (*al-jumhūr*) of Sunni theologians, which was also favoured by Ibn Ḥajar, was that one ought to provide non-literal interpretations of the problematic expressions, in accordance with what language and religious law permits. "This is laid down", Ibn Ḥajar added, "by Imām al-Ḥaramayn [al-Juwaynī (d. 1085)] and the astute among the *mutakallimūn*."

Opposed to these two acceptable positions, was the position that spatial expressions may be used of God "without adding how" (*min ghayr takyīf*). Ibn Ḥajar attributed the position to heretical groups such as the early Karrāmiyya and the "Ḥashwiyya"—a term commonly applied by later Ash'arīs to the literalist position of some Ḥanbalīs (Ibn Qayyim al-Jawziyya, for example, was well aware that he was considered to be one of the Ḥashwiyya by his opponents).[13] Ibn Ḥajar was careful to point out that upholders of this literalist position should not be considered unbelievers. However, this did not mean that he found their position acceptable. A person who claimed that God is in heaven should, he stated, be queried: if he accepted the implications of the position, i.e. that God is confined in space, then he should be considered an apostate and treated accordingly. If his view was akin to that of the Karrāmiyya and Ḥashwiyya, then one should take into account whether he believed so privately or actively sought to convince others. In the former case, he should be reprimanded and chastised. In the later case, he should be fought as an enemy. Ibn Ḥajar presumably considered Ibn Taymiyya to belong to the latter category.

In yet a third *fatwā*, Ibn Ḥajar asserted that the position of the venerable Aḥmad Ibn Ḥanbal himself was perfectly in accordance with that of the Sunnis in divesting the conception of God from any anthropomorphic or corporeal element (*tanzīh*). The idea that Ibn Ḥanbal had himself been a proponent of the view that God is in the direction of above was, according to Ibn Ḥajar, foisted upon him by ignorant elements within his school:

> Make sure you do not listen to what is in the books of Ibn Taymiyya and his student Ibn Qayyim al-Jawziyya and other such people who have taken their own whim as their God, and who have been led astray by God, and whose hearts and ears have been sealed, and whose eyes have been covered by Him. And who will help them if not God? How these heretics (*mulḥidūn*) have crossed the lines and broken the fences of the Sharīʿa and the Ḥaqīqa, thinking that they are on the right path, and they are not! Rather they are in the worst of errors, the foulest of qualities, the most odious loss, and the utmost falsity. May God forsake the one who follows them, and purify the earth of their likes.[14]

In his commentary on *al-Shamā'il al-Nabawiyya* of al-Tirmidhī (d. 892), Ibn Ḥajar had yet another opportunity to denounce Ibn Taymiyya's literalism. He cited—apparently at second-hand—Ibn Qayyim al-Jawziyya to the effect that Ibn Taymiyya had suggested that the Prophet Muḥammad had let down a part of his turban to mark the spot between his shoulders that God had touched with His hand. This provoked the following response by Ibn Ḥajar:

> This is among their repulsive opinions and their waywardness, since it is based on their claim, which they argued for at length and castigated Sunnis for rejecting, that God is in a direction and is a body, may He be exalted above what the unjust and stubborn say! They have in this regard abominations and heresies to which the ear cannot listen, and one cannot but adjudge them a falsity, a slander and a lie. May God shame them and those who say that. The Imam Aḥmad and the

distinguished among his school are innocent of this ugly stain. How could it be otherwise, and it is unbelief according to many?![15]

Ibn Ḥajar's view on the correct interpretation of the seemingly anthropomorphic and spatial expressions used of God was widely shared amongst his Sunni contemporaries. The standard handbooks on *'aqā'id* and *kalām* used in Sunni schools from the Maghrib to India in the post-classical age (1258–1798) propounded the view that there were two acceptable ways of understanding the problematic expressions in the Qur'ān and Sunna. The first way, corresponding to the first option mentioned by Ibn Ḥajar, was to leave knowledge of the meaning of the expressions to God. This was stated to have been the way of the early scholars—*al-salaf*—and called the position of *tafwīḍ*. The second way, corresponding to the second and preferred option mentioned by Ibn Ḥajar, was to find theologically and linguistically acceptable non-literal meanings of the problematic expressions. This was called the position of *ta'wīl*, and associated with "the later scholars" (*al-khalaf*).

The two options were clearly presented in the widely studied commentary of Sa'd al-Dīn al-Taftāzānī on *al-'Aqā'id al-Nasafiyya*. Having expounded the doctrine that God is not a body and is not in space or time, he noted that some opponents (*al-mukhālifūn*) denied this, and that they appealed to certain passages in the Qur'ān or Hadith in support of their anthropomorphic and spatial conception of God. To this al-Taftāzānī replied:

There is unassailable evidence for divesting the conception of God from any anthropomorphic or corporeal element (*tanzīh*). It is therefore imperative either to leave (*tafwīḍ*) the knowledge of these passages to God, as was the habit of the *salaf* who preferred the safest option (*al-ṭarīq al-aslam*), or to give correct, non-literal interpretations (*ta'wīlāt ṣaḥīḥa*) of the passages, as the *khalaf* have chosen to do, thus warding off the stabs of the ignorant.[16]

Both options were acceptable. What was not acceptable was to accept the problematic passages at face value (*'alā ẓāhirihā*), since that would lead to the heresies of anthropomorphism (*tajsīm* or *tashbīh*) or believing that God is in space or a direction (*mutaḥayyiz* or *fī jiha*).

Al-Taftāzānī listed the seven traditionally recognised essential attributes of God: knowledge, power, life, hearing, sight, will, and speech. In his longer work *Sharḥ al-Maqāṣid*, he considered the view that one should add other attributes suggested by a literal understanding of the Qur'ān, such as "being seated on the throne" or having a "face" or "hand." However, he rejected the view, arguing instead that these expressions were plausibly seen as figurative expressions (*majāzāt*), referring the reader to his commentary on the standard manual of semantics and rhetoric *Talkhīṣ al-miftāḥ*.[17]

A similar distinction between *tafwīḍ* and *ta'wīl* was enunciated in *Jam' al-jawāmi'* by Tāj al-Dīn al-Subkī and its commentary by Jalāl al-Dīn al-Maḥallī (d. 1459), which became a standard handbook on the principles of jurisprudence (*uṣūl al-fiqh*) for Shāfi'īs and Mālikīs:

> We divest of anthropomorphism (*nunazzihu*) when we hear the problematic passages such as His statement "sat Himself upon the throne" and "still abides the face of thy Lord" and "to be formed in view of my eye" and "God's hand is over their hands" and such as [the Prophet's] statement—may God bless him and grant him salvation—"The hearts of Adam's progeny are all between two fingers of the Raḥmān..." and "He opens His hand during the night for the repentance of those who sin during the day...". And our Imams have differed as to whether we give a non-literal interpretation (*nu'awwil*) of the problematic passages or leave (*nufawwiḍ*) knowledge of its meaning to Him while divesting the conception of Him from what the literal meaning suggests (*munazzihīn lahu 'an ẓāhirihi*)...*Tafwīḍ* is the way of the *salaf*, which is safest, and *ta'wīl* is the way of the *khalaf*, which requires more knowledge. Thus in the Qur'ānic verses *istawā* is interpreted as dominion (*istīlā'*) and the face as self (*dhāt*) and the eye as sight and the hand as power. The two traditions mentioned above are examples of figurative speech mentioned in rhetoric, as when we say to someone who is in two minds about something, "I see you're putting one foot forward and another backward."[18]

In his super-commentary to the work, the Rector of the Azhar Ḥasan al-'Aṭṭār (d. 1834) pointed out that the position of *tafwīḍ* was also to reject the literal sense (*ẓāhir*). Insofar as *ta'wīl* is to reject the literal sense, both the *salaf* and the *khalaf* practiced *ta'wīl*. However, whereas the *khalaf* were prepared to suggest an alternative interpretation, the former were not. The distinction between *tafwīḍ* and *ta'wīl* was thus more appropriately described as one between the *salaf*'s non-specific reinterpretation (*ta'wīl ijmālī*) and the *khalaf*'s specific reinterpretation (*ta'wīl tafṣīlī*). The point was also made in the commentary of the Egyptian Mālikī scholar ʻAbd al-Salām al-Laqānī (d. 1668) on his father Ibrāhīm's didactic creedal poem *Jawharat al-tawḥīd*—a handbook on theology widely used in al-Azhar from the seventeenth century until the present day:

> Since as has been mentioned both reason and revelation dictate that He is utterly different from anything created, and since there occurs in the Qur'ān and Sunna what may suggest that He is in a direction or has a body, it is the position of the people of truth, both *salaf* and *khalaf*, to reinterpret these apparent meanings (*ta'wīl tilka al-ẓawāhir*), since it is imperative, by the agreement of the people of truth, and others besides, to divest the conception of Him from what a literal understanding indicates. Hence he [the author of *Jawharat al-tawḥīd*, i.e. Ibrāhīm al-Laqānī] refers to this, mentioning the position of the *khalaf* first since it is the preferable.
>
> Interpret every passage that may suggest *tashbīh* in a non-literal way, i.e., it is imperative that you do this by understanding it in a non-literal sense. The meaning is that you must reinterpret it in a definite way involving a specific meaning ...as is the chosen position of the *khalaf* or later theologians. Thus you understand "above" as exalted greatness and not with reference to space, and the "face" as self or existence, and the hand as power ...Or leave (*fawwiḍ*) knowledge of the intended meaning of the passage in its details to Him, and reinterpret it generally (*awwilhu ijmālan*) as is the way of the *salaf*... For the *salaf* divest the conception of Him from any impossible meanings that the passages literally suggest, and leave the knowledge of the specific meaning to Him.[19]

The longer creed (*al-'Aqīda al-kubrā*) of Muḥammad ibn Yūsuf al-Sanūsī, which for centuries was a standard handbook on theology in North Africa, also outlined these two approaches. Al-Sanūsī, however, was not convinced that the way of the *khalaf* was always preferable. He wrote:

> As for that which cannot literally be true [of God] such as "sat Himself upon the throne", we do not accept the literal meaning (*naṣrifahu 'an ẓāhirihi*) by common agreement. If it has [no more than] one appropriate non-literal interpretation, then it is incumbent to understand it in that way. Otherwise, one must leave the specific interpretation to God (*tafwīḍ*) while divesting the conception of God of anthropomorphisms. This is the way of the early theologians, in contrast to Imām al-Ḥaramayn [al-Juwaynī].[20]

In his own commentary on the passage, al-Sanūsī explained that the term *istawā* had more than one acceptable non-literal meaning, and to prefer one to the other without any grounds was both innovative and presumptuous.

Yet, al-Sanūsī also did not believe that the position of the *salaf* was a literalist one. They denied the literal meaning just as much as the *khalaf*, but merely refrained from specifying which of the many possible non-literal options was correct. Insisting on a literal interpretation was for al-Sanūsī, as for Ibn Ḥajar, the hallmark of heretical groups such as the Karrāmiyya and Ḥashwiyya. According to al-Sanūsī, the latter group refused to abandon the literal meaning (*imtana'at 'an al-ta'wīl*) in the case of passages stating, for example, that God is seated on His throne, and they accordingly accepted that God is in the direction of "above." They also insisted that God's eternal speech consists of letters and sounds, again basing their view on a literalist understanding of Qur'ānic passages stating that God had spoken to Moses. Such claims were vehemently rejected by al-Sanūsī:

> The Ḥashwiyya, who uphold the literal meaning, claim that God's self-subsistent speech consists of letters and sounds, and though it consists of letters and sounds is eternal. These people are the ultimate in waywardness and immersion in luxuriant ignorance! Other heretical sects may raise a problem that is not refuted from the very first by self-evident principles, but these people ignore the necessary truths of reason and do not stay within its bounds for an instant—may God protect us from abandonment! They believe that God is a body sitting on the Throne, touching it and resting on it, and then moves down every Friday night during the last third of the night to the heavens, and then goes back to His place at dawn.[21]

There is an element of caricature in the portrait, but nevertheless there can be little doubt that al-Sanūsī would have dismissed Ibn Taymiyya's position as *Ḥashwī*. Ibn Taymiyya and his followers defended the view that God is literally on the throne, in the direction of "above", and that His speech consists of letters and sounds. Ibn Taymiyya had also gained notoriety for his literal interpretation of the *ḥadīth al-nuzūl* to which Sanūsī alluded, i.e. the tradition stating that God descends to the lowest heaven during the last third of the night (or according to a variant, on the night of mid-Sha'bān). The later North African scholar Aḥmad Bābā al-

Tunbuktī (d. 1624), author of a popular biographical dictionary of Mālikī scholars, referred precisely to Ibn Taymiyya's literal interpretation of this Hadith. Al-Tunbuktī noted that the scholar Abū Zayd ibn al-Imām al-Tilimsānī (d. 1342) had gone to Egypt and while there had disputed successfully with Taqī al-Dīn Ibn Taymiyya. He added that:

> The mentioned Taqī al-Dīn had some repugnant claims, such as taking literally the Hadith *al-nuzūl*, saying: "like I descend now".... May God protect us from this claim! And someone has said that the attribution of this to him is not certain, and God knows best.[22]

The anecdote about Ibn Taymiyya saying "like I descend now" may or may not be true, but it does capture an important point. Ibn Taymiyya insisted that we know what the word "descend" means, and that it was wrong to suspend judgement about its meaning, or leave its meaning to God. He thus rejected *tafwīḍ* as well as *ta'wīl*, and disputed the claim that the former approach was indeed the position of the venerable *salaf*. In one of his *fatāwā* he wrote:

> The unacceptable *ta'wīl* is not to understand the words in their apparent sense but in another sense. If it is said...that only God knows its *ta'wīl* then we concede to the Jahmiyya that the Qur'ānic verse has a true *ta'wīl* that is other than the apparent, but that it is known only to God. This is not the position of the *salaf* and the Imams. Rather, their position is to deny and reject *ta'wīl*, not to suspend judgement.[23]

We do, Ibn Taymiyya insisted, know the meaning of words such as *yad* or *wajh* or *istawā* or *yanzilu*. What we do not know is what it is like for God to have a hand or face, or to sit or descend. In other words, his position corresponded to the third option cited by Ibn Ḥajar al-Haytamī: one should accept that the anthropomorphic and spatial expressions are literally true of God. One should thus accept at face-value—and without asking how—the passages in the Qur'ān and Sunna that suggested that God is in the direction of above, and that He is seated on His throne, and that He on occasion descends to the lower heavens.

For post-classical Sunni theologians, *tafwīḍ* and *ta'wīl* were the two ways of warding off the literalist interpretations that they attributed to heretical corporealist (*mujassima*) groups such as the Karrāmiyya and Ḥashwiyya. Ibn Taymiyya rejected both options, and it is thus not surprising that a scholar such as Ibn Ḥajar al-Haytamī should have castigated him for having the same heretical views. Already the theologian and heresiographer al-Shahrastānī (d. 1153) had expressed the view that the origins of all shades of heretical anthropomorphism (*tashbīh*) lay in the insistence on going beyond the *tafwīḍ* of the *salaf*:

> A group of later people added to what the *salaf* have said. They said: It is imperative to keep to the literal sense and to understand it as it appears, without presuming to reinterpret or suspend judgement as regards the literal meaning (*lā budda min ijrā'ihā 'ala ẓāhirihā wa-al-qawl bi-tafsīrihā kamā waradat min ghayr ta'arruḍ li-al-ta'wīl wa la tawaqquf fī al-ẓāhir*). Hence they fell into pure anthropomorphism (*tashbīh*). This is contrary to what the *salaf* believed.[24]

Shahrastānī went on to divide the anthropomorphists into extremist Shi'is and Ḥashwiyya. The views he attributed to the latter makes it understandable why Ibn Taymiyya and his followers were often thought to belong to this group: they claim that God is a body, though unlike any other body (*lā ka-al-ajsām*). The passages of the Qur'ān that speak of God's being seated or having a hand or coming and going and being in the direction of above were understood literally: "what is understood by these words when they are applied to bodies (*mā yufham 'inda al-iṭlāq 'alā al-ajsām*)." They also invented spurious Hadith such as: "My Lord met me and shook my hand and faced me and placed His hand between my shoulders so that I could feel the coldness of His fingers." They also believe that the letters and sounds of which the Qur'ān consists are eternal.[25]

The accusation that some corporealist groups hid behind the caveat *bi-lā kayfa*—an accusation originally levied by Mu'tazilites against the early Ash'arites—reappears in the context of the later Sunni theologians' condemnations of corporealism. In the *Sharḥ al-'Aqā'id al-'Aḍudiyya* of Jalāl al-Dīn al-Dawānī it is stated that corporealists are of two kinds. The first are blatantly corporealist and should be regarded as unbelievers. The latter, who are wayward but not unbelievers, "hide behind the caveat *bi-lā kayfa*", saying that God had a body "unlike any other body (*lā ka-al-ajsām*), and position unlike any position, and a relation to this spatial position that was unlike any other relation to a spatial position." He apparently classified Ibn Taymiyya as belonging to the latter group:

> Most of the corporealists are the literalists who follow the literal meaning of the Book and Sunna, and most of them are people of Hadith. Ibn Taymiyya Abū al-'Abbās Aḥmad and his followers strongly incline to affirm that He is in a direction, and go to extremes in attacking those who deny this. I have seen in one of his books that according to reason there is no difference between saying 'He does not exist' and saying 'I looked for Him everywhere and did not find Him', and he accused those who disagreed on this point of denying the divine attributes (*ta'ṭīl*). And this despite his proficiency in the rational and traditional sciences, as can be seen by anyone who reads his works.[26]

In the influential *al-Mawāqif fī 'ilm al-kalām* by 'Aḍud al-Dīn al-Ījī (d. 1355), the belief that God is a body unlike any other body, and that he has bodily organs, and that it is possible to touch and be touched by him, and that he moves and descends, is held to be characteristic of the Ḥashwiyya and Karrāmiyya, who are declared to be two of the many errant sects that, according to a well-known Hadith, are destined for hell-fire.[27]

The idea that God is in a direction (*fī jiha*) was routinely declared to be very close to unbelief (*kufr*). For example, the prominent Egyptian Shāfi'ī jurist Shihāb al-Dīn Aḥmad al-Ramlī (d. 1550) was asked for a *fatwā* concerning those who claim that God is in the direction of "above" *bi-lā kayf*, and who supported their position by quoting early Sunni authorities such as Abū Ḥanīfa (in the apocryphal *al-Fiqh al-akbar*), al-Ash'arī (in his *al-Ibāna*), and the Mālikī jurist Ibn Abī Zayd al-Qayrawānī (d. 998). Al-Ramlī replied that the position was wrong. He cited the arguments of later Sunni theologians such as al-Ghazālī, al-Bayḍāwī, al-Ījī, and al-Taftāzānī in support of the view that it is rationally impossible that God should be in a direction, and he argued that therefore passages from Scripture or from early venerable Sunni authorities that suggested otherwise should not be accepted at face value. Those who persisted in attributing directionality to God should be chastised by the authorities and punished, especially if there was a danger that their heretical innovation (*bid'a*) would spread.[28]

The Egyptian Mālikī jurist Aḥmad al-Nafarāwī (d. 1713), in his commentary on the *Risāla* of Ibn Abī Zayd al-Qayrawānī, discussed the latter's apparent claim that God's Self is above the throne (*fawq al-'arsh al-majīd bi-dhātihi*). His handling of the phrase is instructive and shows clearly that commentators often did more than merely explain texts. He argued that the phrase should be understood as follows: God is "above" the throne that is glorious in itself. The perhaps more natural reading was, Nafarāwī pointed out, theologically unacceptable since it implied that God is confined in space and is in a direction—a position that, even if not tantamount to unbelief (*kufr*), was still theologically erroneous (Sunni scholars tended to class the errors of the Muʿtazila and the non-extremist Shiʿis in this category). To say that God is "above" the throne was acceptable as long as one did not qualify this with the phrase "in Himself" (*bi-dhātihi*), and as long as one realized that the word "above" was understood not in a physical or spatial sense (*fawqiyyat al-ḥayz wa-al-makān*) but in the spiritual (*maʿnawī*) sense of being more honourable and majestic (*fawqiyyat al-sharaf wa-al-jalāl*)—just as a sultan could be said to be "above" his vizier. This interpretative strategy, Nafarāwī added, was that of the later theologians. The earliest generations confined themselves to denying that "above" should be understood in the physical or spatial sense and abstained from further discussion of the matter. This, he added, was because they had a solid grasp of Arabic and were not liable to misunderstand such expressions as implying that God is in a direction. This was, however, no longer the case, and hence there was a need for the later theologians' further specification of the acceptable meaning. Nafarāwī concluded his discussion by citing the previously quoted passage from al-Laqānī's *Jawharat al-tawḥīd* on the two ways of understanding the "problematic" expressions in the Qur'ān and Sunna.[29]

The difference between the position of *tafwīḍ* and the position of literalists such as Ibn Taymiyya may be formulated somewhat schematically as follows: the former is that we do not know the meaning of a word such as *istawā* or *yad* when used of God, but know that it does not mean "to sit" or "hand", while the latter is that we do know what the expressions mean, but do not know what it is like for God to be seated or have a hand. The former agnostic approach leaves it open whether the terms *yad* and *istawā* denote additional unknown attributes of God or can be reduced to the other acknowledged attributes of God.[30] The latter literalist approach insists on the former option, argues that all divine attributes should be treated on a par, and hence decisively rejects the mainstream theological tendency to confine the attributes of the divine Self to seven or eight. Some scholars nevertheless tended to conflate the two positions. After all, both positions invoked the *bi-lā kayfa* statements attributed to venerable early Sunni figures such as Mālik and Abū Ḥanīfa, and both could gloss a Qur'ānic statement such as "seated Himself on the throne" by "in a manner appropriate to him" (*istiwā'un yaliqu bihi*).[31] From this perspective, the position of Ibn Taymiyya was simply that of the *salaf*, and Ibn Ḥajar's condemnation was inappropriate. Ironically, this meant that Ibn Taymiyya was defended from the charge of heresy only by ignoring a distinction that he had himself stressed.

For example, the Egyptian Shāfi'ī scholar and mystic 'Abd al-Ra'ūf al-Munāwī (d. 1622), in his commentary on al-Tirmidhī's *Shamā'il*, cited Ibn Ḥajar's condemnation of Ibn Taymiyya's suggestion that the Prophet Muḥammad had let down a part of his turban to mark the spot between his shoulders that God had touched with His hand. Though al-Munāwī's overall assessment of Ibn Taymiyya and Ibn Qayyim al-Jawziyya was anything but positive, he did not believe that this particular proposition of theirs was beyond the pale:

> I say: As to them [Ibn Taymiyya and Ibn Qayyim al-Jawziyya] being reprehensible innovators, there is no disagreement (*ammā kawnahumā min al-mubtadi'a fa-musallam*). As to this particular claim being based on corporealism, this is not correct. First, because they said that the mentioned seeing was during sleep.... Second, because we believe that He has a hand unlike the hand of a created being, and hence there is nothing to prevent placing It in a manner that does not resemble the placing of a created being.[32]

The point that God has a hand unlike any created hand, and that He can place it in a manner unlike the placing of any created hand, is of course one that Ibn Taymiyya often reiterated in his polemics against *ta'wīl*. Unlike Ibn Taymiyya, however, al-Munāwī apparently did not think that this point was incompatible with *tafwīḍ*, or that it implied that the attribution of hands (and feet and fingers and being seated on the throne) to God was on a par with attributing to Him Knowledge and Speech and Sight. An Ash'arī theologian could assert that God has a hand and mean by this that the term "hand" is used of God in Scripture and that one should not inquire any further about this while denying that the term "hand" in this context meant what it meant in ordinary language (the *tafwīḍ* position), or alternatively that the term "hand" is a metaphorical reference to one of the acknowledged attributes of the divine Self or Acts (the *ta'wīl* position). Al-Munāwī's own view seems to have been in line with the prevalent opinion that these two possibilities were exhaustive and were both legitimate. For example, when commenting on the Hadith that urges believers to have mercy on those on earth so that they would in turn be treated mercifully by "he who is in heaven", al-Munāwī engaged in *ta'wīl*:

> There is disagreement concerning the "he" who is in heaven. It has been said that it is God, in which case...the meaning is that they would be treated mercifully by Him whose will is done in heaven, or Him whose power and capacity and rule is there, or Him who is high and majestic and elevated. For God does not take up a space.... Rather He is related to heaven because it is greater and vaster than the earth, or because of its being higher and more elevated, or the *qibla* of supplication, or the place of the pure and holy spirits.[33]

Commenting on the Hadith that human hearts were tossed and turned by two fingers of God, al-Munawi again engaged in *ta'wīl:*

> The two fingers mean the appearance (*ẓuhūr*) of divine power in the appearance of good and evil in the heart of the servant. It is not that God has limbs, may He be exalted above this!

Al-Munāwī then quoted in support of his reinterpretation the prominent Ash'arī theologian Kamāl al-Dīn Ibn Abī al-Sharīf (d. 1500):

> This is among the Hadiths concerning the attributes, and people deal with it in two ways: The first is that belief in it is obligatory just as the problematic passages of the Qur'ān are obligatory and that enquiring into it is an innovation. This is the view of the majority of the *salaf*. The second is that enquiring into it is obligatory and its reinterpretation (*ta'wīl*) as above is incumbent.... For God the Exalted has only revealed the problematic passages to be known, and His messenger has only said what he has said to be understood. By knowing the meaning of the problematic passages the more eminent is distinguished from the less eminent, and the learned from the learner, and the wise from the presumptuous.[34]

The Meccan Ḥanafī scholar 'Ali al-Qāri' al-Harawī (d. 1614) also discussed the claim of Ibn Taymiyya that God had laid His hands between the shoulder-blades of His Prophet. He too dissented from the view that this suggestion marked Ibn Taymiyya off as a corporealist. In his own commentary on the *Shamā'il*, he cited Ibn Ḥajar's condemnation of Ibn Taymiyya's and Ibn Qayyim al-Jawziyya's suggestion and added:

> I say: God protect them from this ugly accusation and horrendous attribution! He who reads *Sharḥ Manāzil al-sā'irīn* [by Ibn al-Qayyim] will see that they were amongst the prominent Sunnis and the saints of this community.[35]

Al-Qāri' went on to cite a lengthy passage from Ibn al-Qayyim's work, after which he wrote:

> It is clear that his creed is identical to the correct creed of the *salaf* and the majority of the *khalaf*, and hence defamation and denunciation is not appropriate. His words correspond to those of the great Imam and first *mujtahid* [Abū Ḥanīfa] in his *al-Fiqh al-akbar*, which are: "He—may He be exalted—has a hand and a face and a breath, and what He—may He be exalted—has mentioned in the Qur'ān of a hand and face and breath are attributes of His, *bi-lā kayfa*. It should not be said that his hand is his power or his blessing, for this is to nullify the attribute, and this is the position of the Qadarīs and Mu'tazilīs".... Once the accusation of corporealism has been rebutted, his [Ibn Taymiyya] explanation of the Hadith has an obvious and clear plausibility, whether the Prophet saw his Lord during sleep, or God manifested Himself to him in a sensible form (*tajallī ṣuwarī*), as is known amongst the people of spiritual stations and rank (*arbāb al-ḥāl wa-al-maqām*).[36]

The rejection of allegorical interpretation in *al-Fiqh al-akbar*, and the endorsement of the *bi-lā kayfa* formulation would at first sight seem to be in line with Ibn Taymiyya's position on the matter, and al-Qāri' al-Harawī believed that this was the case. However, he may not have read the works of Ibn Taymiyya (why else would he cite a work by Ibn al-Qayyim?) and may not have realized the radical character of his hermeneutics. Certainly, Maturidi commentators of *al-Fiqh al-akbar* seem to have understood the work as affirming *tafwīḍ* and *ta'wīl ijmālī*. Ahmet Mağnisāvī (d. 1539), for example, glossed the *bi-lā kayfa* qualification in this manner: "i.e. this should not be understood in its literal sense but is among the problematic expressions (*ay laysa hadhā 'alā ma'nāhu al-ẓāhir bal min al-mutashābihāt*)."[37] Later Ottoman scholars such as Ahmet Beyâzî (d. 1687) and Eyyüp Kefevî (d. 1684) explicitly stated that the relevant passage from *al-Fiqh al-akbar* should be understood as endorsing *ta'wīl ijmālī.*[38] Neither the work nor its commentators treated the attribution of "hand" and "face" to God to be on a par with attributing Knowledge and Power to Him. In contrast to Ḥanbalī dogmatic works, *al-Fiqh al-akbar* listed only seven attributes of the Divine Self—the seven mentioned by al-Taftāzānī above.[39] Al-Qāri' al-Harawī thus elided, consciously or unconsciously, a distinction that had long been a source of controversy between Ash'arī-Maturidi theologians and their Ḥanbalī critics.

Al-Qāri' al-Harawī's final remarks in the just-quoted lemma, in which he speaks of God manifesting Himself to the people of elevated spiritual rank, suggest that he was giving a mystical interpretation to the seemingly anthropomorphic Hadith. Commenting on another purported Hadith according to which Muḥammad had said that he had seen his Lord in a woollen garment and seated on a camel (or according to variants: in the shape of a young man with thick hair or a beardless youth), al-Qāri' al-Harawī wrote:

> God may He be exalted may manifest Himself in many ways, both with respect to his Self and His Attributes. Furthermore, He has the full power and ability, even more than the angels, to assume forms and shapes while being in Himself free of corporeality and shape and directionality. In this way, many of the problems that arise from verses and Hadith that suggest corporeality are resolved.[40]

As will be seen below, this was not the last time that a mystically motivated literal approach to anthropomorphic passages was seen as coinciding with the approach of Ibn Taymiyya and Ibn al-Qayyim. This ought to alert us to the possibility that the scholars who defended Ibn Taymiyya on this particular point were doing so, not because they were "influenced" by him, but because of agendas of their own—agendas with which the historical Ibn Taymiyya may not have had much sympathy.

In any case, al-Qāri' al-Harawī was far from being a "Taymiyyan." His own theological works show this clearly. In his *Sharḥ Bad' al-amālī*, completed towards the end of his life, Al-Qāri' al-Harawī showed little or no traces of being influenced by Ibn Taymiyya. God, he wrote, is not in any direction, in explicit contrast to the claims of the *mushabbiha* and Karrāmiyya who claim that he is above His throne. God's speech, he wrote, does not consist of words and sounds, in explicit contrast to the Karrāmiyya and Ḥanbalīs.[41] Literalist interpretation was rejected in favour of the two options of *tafwīḍ* and *ta'wīl*. Al-Qārī' al-Harawī preferred the option of *tafwīḍ*, and his justification of this preference again took on a mystical tone:

> To leave the meaning (*tafwīḍ*) to God and believe in the truth of what He says without knowing its meaning is the ultimate servitude. This is the reason it was the chosen option of the *salaf*. To explain the problematic passages and reinterpret it as the *khalaf* do, while not insisting that this is what He means, is an act of worship (*'ibāda*) on the part of the servant. However, servitude is more elevated than worship, for servitude is contentment with what the Lord does, while worship is to do what pleases the Lord. Contentment is more elevated than action, so that not being content is unbelief, while not doing is sin.[42]

As in the case of al-Sanūsī, the preference for the option of *tafwīḍ* meant suspension of judgement, not literalism. Against the Karrāmiyya and the *mujassima* who appealed to the literal sense of the Qur'ānic verses stating that God is on the throne, al-Qārī' al-Harawī wrote: "they have no argument here, for *istawā* has many meanings such as *istīlā'*...and there can be no argument when the possibilities are many."[43] It is hard to imagine the historical Ibn Taymiyya agreeing to all of this.

II

In one of his legal *fatāwā*, Ibn Ḥajar al-Haytamī defended the commendable status of visiting the tombs of saints (*ziyārat qubūr al-awliyā'*).[44] "They are a pious and commendable deed," he stated, "as is travelling to them." He noted that some early jurists had prohibited the practice, on the basis of the Hadith: "There should be no travelling except to three mosques: the mosque of the Haram, my mosque here [in Medina], and the al-Aqsa mosque." However, he rejected the view that the Hadith ruled out such practices:

> For mosques other than the three mentioned are of the same rank, and there is nothing to be gained from travelling to them. As for the saints, they are of different degrees of closeness to God, and the benefits that accrue to those who visit them by virtue of their gnosis and esoteric

> knowledge differs. Hence, travelling to them is beneficial, and what benefits!

Ibn Ḥajar conceded that inappropriate practices such as the mixing of women and men occurred at shrines and tombs. However, he added: "pious deeds should not be abandoned because of such things." Rather, one ought to condemn inappropriate practices and prevent them if possible. If this was not possible, one should choose to go to the tombs at times when such practices did not occur. If inappropriate mixing of men and women were a reason to stop visiting tombs, then they would also be a reason to stop performing many of the rites of the Hajj. After all, the latter rites were also associated with the mixing of men and women, "and what mixing!".

In a work dedicated specifically to the visiting of the Prophet's tomb, Ibn Ḥajar upheld the principle that it was "permissible and commendable by the Book, the Sunna, the consensus of the community, and by analogy."[45] What was debatable was merely whether it was obligatory or, as the majority of scholars believed, merely commendable. He then went on to state a possible objection to this position:

> If you say: How can you relate that there is a consensus on the permissible and commendable status of visiting and travelling to it [the Prophet's tomb] when Ibn Taymiyya among the later Ḥanbalīs deems all of this inappropriate?

Ibn Ḥajar answered the objection thus:

> I say: Who is Ibn Taymiyya so that one takes his words into consideration or relies on them in any religious matter? Is he anything but—in the words of the leading scholars who have followed his rotten statements and unsalable arguments...—a servant whom God has forsaken and led astray and clothed in the garments of ignominy.... The Shaykh al-Islam, the scholar of the world, concerning whose status, *ijtihād*, rectitude and prominence there is a consensus, Taqī al-Dīn al-Subkī—may God sanctify his soul and cast light on his grave—has dedicated himself to answering him in a separate work [*Shifā' al-saqām fi ziyārat khayr al-anām*] in which he has done a great service and shown with dazzling arguments the correct path.[46]

Ibn Ḥajar noted that Ibn Taymiyya had appealed to the above-mentioned Hadith "There should be no travelling except to three mosques", but argued—as in his *Fatāwā*—that he misconstrued its meaning. The Hadith stated that one ought not to travel to any other mosque, and did not rule out travel to what was not a mosque. The trip to 'Arafa during the Hajj was obligatory by consensus, as was travelling to obtain knowledge or for holy war. Travelling for trade and worldly interests was also permissible.[47] Ibn Ḥajar further stated that Ibn Taymiyya had also appealed to the Hadith "Do not make my grave into a festival", but countered that it was far from obvious that this Hadith should be understood in the way that Ibn Taymiyya understood it. It could mean, for example, that one should visit the grave, not on specified occasions, but at all times of the year. If it had been the Prophet's intention to prohibit people from visiting his grave, why did he not simply say: "Do not visit my grave"?[48] Why had he rather ordered—as even Ibn Taymiyya had to admit—his followers to visit graves? And if it was commendable to visit graves, then it was commendable to travel to visit graves—the truth of this conditional was evident to all but the "obstinate."[49]

Ibn Ḥajar's view on this matter was entirely mainstream. Already al-Ghazālī had assumed that travelling to visit the tombs of prophets was legitimate, and argued for the permissibility of travelling to visit the tombs of saints by analogy. In his monumental *Iḥyā' 'ulūm al-dīn* he discussed the Hadith: "There should be no travelling except to three mosques." Al-Ghazālī noted that some scholars had used this Hadith to rule out travelling to the tombs of saints, but argued this was not correct. The Hadith ruled out travelling for the purpose of praying in any other mosque, since all mosques other than the three mentioned were of equal rank. The tombs of saints, on the other hand, were not of equal rank, and the *baraka* that accrued from visiting them differed accordingly. In what seemed to al-Ghazālī to be a *reductio ad absurdum*, he asked:

> Would he who says this also prohibit travel to the tombs of prophets, such as the tomb of Abraham and Moses and John and others—may God bless them!? Prohibiting this is the ultimate absurdity (*fī ghāyat al-iḥāla*), and if one permits it then the tombs of saints and scholars and good people are analogous to it. Hence it is not unreasonable to say that this is one of the commendable motives for travelling, just as travelling to visit scholars while they are alive.[50]

The Cairo-based scholar Muḥammad Murtaḍā al-Zabīdī (d. 1790), in his voluminous commentary on the *Iḥyā'*, had nothing substantial to add to al-Ghazālī's discussion. He supplied the names of scholars who had appealed to this Hadith when prohibiting travel to visit shrines and tombs, including Ibn Taymiyya. He also supplied a few more names of prophets and the location of their tombs. There is nothing to suggest that he disagreed with the text he was commenting upon, or believed that al-Ghazālī's view was controversial amongst the Sunni scholars of his time.

Indeed, the kind of interpretation of the Hadith favoured by Ibn Taymiyya had been routinely dismissed by influential Sunni jurists such as Yaḥyā al-Nawawī and Taqī al-Dīn al-Subkī.[51] Their dismissal came to be enshrined in widely read Hadith commentaries of subsequent centuries. For example, in his monumental commentary on the *Saḥīḥ* of al-Bukhārī, Ibn Ḥajar al-'Asqalānī (d. 1449) wrote:

> There has been disagreement concerning travelling to other places such as visiting good people, alive and dead, and shrines for obtaining *baraka* and praying. The Shaykh Abū Muḥammad [al-Juwaynī the father (d. 1046)] has said: it is prohibited to travel to other places in accordance with the literal sense of the Hadith.... The correct position according to Imām al-Ḥaramayn [al-Juwaynī the son] and other Shāfi'īs is that it is not prohibited, and they respond to the Hadith in many ways.... One of these is that the intention only pertains to mosques, and that one should not travel to any mosque other than these three to pray. As for travelling to what is not a mosque, such as to visit a good person or relative or friend or to seek knowledge or to trade or just for recreation, this is not included in the prohibition.[52]

Ibn Ḥajar al-'Asqalānī went on to note that this particular Hadith had given rise to much discussion in recent times:

> Al-Kirmānī [d. 1384] has said: On this issue there has been much discussion in our Syrian lands, and many treatises have been written by both parties. I say: He is referring to Shaykh Taqī al-Dīn al-Subkī and others' responses to Shaykh Taqī al-Dīn Ibn Taymiyya...and the crux of the matter is that they have pointed out that his position implies that it is prohibited to travel to visit the tomb of the Prophet.... This is one of the ugliest positions that has been reported of Ibn Taymiyya. One of the things he has adduced to deny the claim that there is a consensus on the matter is the report that Mālik disliked people saying: I have visited the tomb of the Prophet. The discerning scholars of the [Mālikī]

> school have replied that he disliked the phrase out of politeness, and not the visiting itself, for it is one of the best of actions and the noblest of pious deeds with which one draws near to God the Majestic, and its legitimacy is a matter of consensus without any doubt, and God is the One who leads to truth.[53]

The position of al-Ghazālī, al-Nawawī, and al-Subkī that the Hadith did not rule out travelling to visit the graves of prophets and saints was also reiterated by later Hadith scholars such as Jalāl al-Dīn al-Suyūṭī, Aḥmad al-Qaṣtallānī (d. 1517), ʻAlī al-Qāri' al-Harawī, ʻAbd al-Ra'ūf al-Munāwī, ʻAlī al-ʻAzīzī al-Būlāqī (d. 1658) and Abū al-Ḥasan ibn ʻAbd al-Hādī al-Sindī (d. 1726).[54]

Ibn Ḥajar al-ʻAsqalānī's statement that travelling to visit the tomb of the Prophet was "one of the best of actions and the noblest of pious deeds with which one draws near to God, and its legitimacy is a matter of consensus" reflects the position of the immensely influential work on the virtues of Muḥammad entitled *al-Shifā' fī ta'rīf ḥuqūq al-Muṣṭafā* by the Mālikī scholar al-Qāḍī ʻIyāḍ (d. 1159). This work was so highly esteemed that the prominent Yemeni Shāfiʻī jurist Ismāʻīl Ibn al-Muqri' (d. 1434) reported that nothing bad would occur to a place with a copy of the book, nor would a ship sink if a copy of the work was on it. He reported that he had himself been cured from illness after reading it.[55]

Al-Qāḍī ʻIyāḍ wrote that visiting the tomb of the Prophet was "a *sunna* of the Muslims on which there was consensus, and a good and desirable deed." After relating a series of traditions to this effect, al-Qāḍī ʻIyāḍ noted that Imam Mālik had reportedly disliked people saying they had visited the tomb of the Prophet. He mentioned various suggestions as to why he did so, all of which assume that Mālik had no problem with visiting the tomb as such. Some had suggested that the problem had been with the verb "visited", which could connote a familiarity and lack of respect, or that the act was something one chose to do, whereas travelling to visit the tomb of the Prophet was an obligation (*wājib*). Al-Qāḍī ʻIyāḍ himself suggested that the problem was with the word "tomb", and that Mālik preferred people to say that they had visited the Prophet. This, al-Qāḍī ʻIyāḍ suggested, was because of the Hadith according to which Muḥammad had implored God that his tomb not become an idol that is worshipped.[56] In his commentary on *al-Shifā'*, the

Egyptian scholar, belletrist and judge Aḥmad al-Khafājī (d. 1658) wrote concerning the latter Hadith:

> Know that this is the Hadith that led Ibn Taymiyya and those who follow him, such as Ibn al-Qayyim, to the despicable statement due to which he was declared an unbeliever, and against which al-Subkī devoted a separate work, and this is his prohibiting the visit to the tomb of the Prophet—may God bless him and grant him salvation—and travelling to it.... He imagined that he protected monotheism (*tawḥīd*) on the basis of drivel that should not be mentioned, for they do not come from a rational, let alone an eminent, person, may God the Exalted forgive him.[57]

In his commentary on the same work, ʿAlī al-Qāriʾ al-Harawī was almost as unsympathetic to the claims of Ibn Taymiyya:

> Amongst the Ḥanbalīs Ibn Taymiyya has gone to an extreme by prohibiting travelling to visit the Prophet—may God bless him and grant him salvation—just as others have gone to the opposite extreme in saying: the fact that the visiting is a pious deed is known with certainty and he who denies this is an unbeliever. Perhaps the second position is closer to the truth, for to prohibit something that scholars by consensus deem commendable is unbelief, since it is worse than prohibiting what is [merely] permissible, in regards to which there is agreement [i.e. there is agreement that the prohibition of what is permissible by consensus is unbelief].[58]

The position that al-Qāriʾ al-Harawī considered to be at the opposite extreme from that of Ibn Taymiyya had been expressed in another popular work on the virtues of the Prophet, *al-Mawāhib al-laduniyya* by Aḥmad al-Qaṣṭallānī. Writing in the early seventeenth century, the Damascene scholar Najm al-Dīn al-Ghazzī (d. 1651) wrote that his contemporaries valued al-Qaṣṭallānī's work highly, and that demand pushed up the prices of copies of it.[59] The contemporary Turkish bibliographer Kâtip Çelebi (d. 1657) also praised the work, and noted that the famous poet and judge Bâki (d. 1600) had translated it into Turkish.[60] Al-Qaṣṭallānī stated the mainstream position on visiting the tomb of the Prophet in uncompromising terms:

> Know that visiting his noble tomb is one of the greatest of pious deeds and one of the most desired acts of obedience and one of the ways of

obtaining the highest ranks. He who believes otherwise has discarded the noose of Islam and disobeyed God and His prophet and the community of learned scholars.[61]

After adducing a number of relevant Hadith underlying the judgement, al-Qaṣtallānī went on to express his outrage at the position of Ibn Taymiyya:

> The Shaykh Taqī al-Dīn Ibn Taymiyya has abominable and odd statements on this issue to the effect that travelling to visit the Prophet is prohibited and is not a pious deed but the contrary. Shaykh Taqī al-Dīn al-Subkī has replied to him in *Shifā' al-saqām* and has gratified the hearts of the believers.[62]

In his commentary on *al-Mawāhib*, the Egyptian Mālikī scholar Muḥammad al-Zurqānī (d. 1720) mentioned that Subkī's work had elicited a reply by Ibn Taymiyya's student Ibn 'Abd al-Hādī (d. 1343), who had adduced the Hadith stating that one should only travel to one of three mosques and claimed that the venerable Imam Mālik had taken a position identical to that of Ibn Taymiyya. Al-Zurqānī rejected the argument:

> What he has reported of Mālik is not known to be an opinion of his, and he has no support in the Hadith, for its meaning is that one should not travel to pray in a mosque [other than the three mentioned mosques].[63]

Al-Zurqānī's verdict that Mālik had not been known to disapprove of visiting the tomb of the Prophet was entirely in line with the position of Mālikī jurists of the post-classical age. As suggested by al-Qāḍī 'Iyāḍ and Ibn Ḥajar al-'Asqalānī, jurists of the school agreed that Mālik had disapproved of someone saying "I have visited the tomb of the Prophet" because he deemed the wording to be problematic, and not because he disapproved of the underlying action.[64]

Al-Qaṣtallānī went on to cite a story involving the prominent Hadith scholar Zayn al-Dīn al-'Irāqī (d. 1404) and the Ḥanbalī scholar Ibn Rajab (d. 1393) who were related through marriage. While on a trip to Jericho together, the latter reportedly declared that he was travelling, not to visit Abraham's grave there, but to pray in

Abraham's mosque, so as to conform to the position of Ibn Taymiyya on this issue. To this al-ʿIrāqī replied:

> My intention is to visit the grave of Abraham—peace be upon him. You have disobeyed the Prophet—may God bless him and grant him salvation—for he has said: "There should be no travelling except to three mosques", and you have travelled to a fourth mosque. As for me, I follow the Prophet—may God bless him and grant him salvation—for he has said "Visit graves." Did he say, "except the graves of Prophets?"[65]

Al-Qaṣtallānī also affirmed that the visitor to the tomb of the Prophet should "engage in much supplication and imploring and asking and entreating him—may God bless him and grant him salvation—for help and intercession, for it befits the one who seeks his intercession that God should accept it." In his commentary, al-Zurqānī expanded on the point by quoting from a work by Khalīl Ibn Iṣḥāq (d. 1365), author of the standard epitome of Mālikī law, *al-Mukhtaṣar*:

> Let him [the visitor to the tomb of the Prophet] entreat him—may God bless him and grant him salvation—and ask God by the standing of the Prophet, since he will bear the weighty faults and heavy sins. The *baraka* and greatness of his intercession is such that no sin is too great. He who believes otherwise is the one who is debarred [from blessing], whose eyes have been sealed and heart led astray by God.

Al-Zurqānī suggested that the last words were aimed at Ibn Taymiyya.[66]

The position that it was permissible to ask the Prophet for his intercession with God was enshrined in a Hadith according to which Muḥammad had instructed a blind man to ask God to restore his sight "by your Prophet, the Prophet of mercy." This Hadith was mentioned in the esteemed collections of al-Tirmidhī and Ibn Māja, and made its way into later influential compilations such as *Mishkat al-maṣābiḥ* by Walī al-Dīn al-Qazwīnī (fl.1337) and *al-Jāmiʿ al-ṣaghīr* by Jalāl al-Dīn al-Suyūṭī. In his commentary on the later compilation, the Egyptian scholar and mystic ʿAbd al-Raʾūf al-Munāwī cited—without any comment or qualification—al-Subkī's statement:

> It is proper to entreat and ask for the help and intercession of the Prophet with God. No one from amongst the *salaf* and the *khalaf* denied

this, until Ibn Taymiyya came along and disapproved of this, and deviated from the straight path, and invented a position that no scholar has said before, and he became a deterrent example for Muslims.[67]

III

The idea that Ibn Taymiyya was a central figure whose appearance marked the decisive victory of so-called "traditionalist" Islam within Sunni scholarly circles was explicitly defended by George Makdisi in a series of influential articles published in the 1960s and 1970s.[68] Makdisi argued that though the Ḥanbalī school constituted a small minority within Sunnism, its thinkers spearheaded a traditionalist revival between the eleventh and thirteenth centuries. This revival resulted in the decisive defeat of Ashʿarism and its efforts to gain a substantial following amongst Sunni scholars. Earlier Orientalist scholars such as Goldziher had, Makdisi argued, mistakenly believed that Ashʿarism had managed to establish itself as Sunni orthodoxy from the eleventh century onwards, and confined its opponents, including Ibn Taymiyya, to marginality. Makdisi suggested that Goldziher had been seriously misled on this point. This was partly because Goldziher had relied on biased, pro-Ashʿarī and anti-Ḥanbalī sources such as Tāj al-Dīn al-Subkī's *Ṭabaqāt al-Shāfiʿīyya*. It was also partly because Goldziher had looked at the Islamic world through the distorted lenses of a nineteenth-century European who unwittingly saw the position of Ashʿarism within Islam as analogous to that of Thomism within nineteenth-century Catholicism, and who tended to view Islam from the perspective of the Ottomans, for whom the Wahhabis were heretical enemies.

To my mind there is little doubt that Goldziher was right and Makdisi wrong.[69] Already Taqī al-Dīn al-Subkī noted that he had never met a Mālikī who was not an Ashʿarī, and that the great majority of Shāfiʿīs in his day were Ashʿarī, and that the great majority of Ḥanafīs were in substantial agreement with the Ashʿarīs, though differing on certain minor points.[70] Al-Subkī's testimony could perhaps be dismissed as biased, but it is difficult to see how he could have made such claims if they were wildly off the mark. In any case, his statement had been made in the context of supporting a similar claim made by the earlier Shāfiʿī jurist ʿIzz al-Dīn ibn ʿAbd al-Salām (d. 1262). Al-Subkī's statement about the Ash'arī leanings of all Mālikīs was cited with approval and pride by the later North African Mālikī scholar 'Abdallāh al-'Ayyāshī (d. 1680).[71] The idea that the phrase *Ahl al-Sunna wa-al-jamā'a* meant those who were either Ash'arī or Maturidi in creed was reiterated by al-Taftāzānī in the second half of the fourteenth century and by the fifteenth-century Ottoman scholars Ahmet Hayâlî (d. 1460) and Muslihüddin Kastalî (d. 1495).[72] The above-mentioned Egyptian-based scholar Muḥammad Murtaḍā al-Zabīdī also propounded the view that when the phrase *ahl al-sunna wa-al-jamā'a* was used it meant the Ash'arīs and Māturidis.[73] He cited, without comment or qualification, a long passage by al-Subkī expanding on the point. After dividing the *mutakallimūn* into three groups: the Mu'tazila, the Ash'ariyya and the Ḥashwiyya, al-Subkī went on to discuss the latter group in the following words:

> As for the Ḥashwiyya, they are a despicable and ignorant lot who claim to belong to the school of Aḥmad [ibn Ḥanbal].... They have corrupted the creed of a few isolated Shāfi'īs, especially some of the Hadith scholars among them who are lacking in reason.... They were held in utmost contempt, and then towards the end of the seventh century [AH, thirteenth century AD] a man appeared who was diligent, intelligent and well-read and did not find a Shaykh to guide him, and he is of their creed and is brazen and dedicated to teaching his ideas.... He said that non-eternal attributes can subsist in God, and that God is ever acting, and that an infinite chain of events is not impossible either in the past or the future. He split the ranks and cast doubts on the creed of the Muṣlims and incited dissension amongst them. He did not confine himself to creedal matters of theology, but transgressed the bounds and said that travelling to visit the tomb of the Prophet is a sin.... The scholars agreed to imprison him for a long time, and the Sultan imprisoned him...and he died in prison. Then some of his followers started to promulgate his ideas and teach them to people in secret while keeping quiet in public, and great harm came from this.[74]

Al-Subkī's portrayal of Ibn Taymiyya's anti-Ash'arī followers as forming a clandestine minority, rather than—as Makdisi would have it—"the main current" of Muslim religious thought, is supported by the later polemics of Taqī al-Dīn al-Ḥisnī and Ibn Ḥajar al-Haytamī. The former wrote of Ibn Taymiyya's followers:

> Discretionary punishment and floggings and imprisonment and beheadings have not ceased to be their lot, despite their concealing what they believe and their utmost secrecy in not expressing their foul beliefs except in hidden places after taking care, and locking the doors, and speaking softly, saying that the walls have ears.[75]

Ibn Ḥajar wrote:

> The scholars of his age rose against him [Ibn Taymiyya] and impelled the Sultan to either kill or imprison him, so he imprisoned him until he died and his innovations died out and his darkness disappeared. Then he was supported by followers whose heads God has not raised, nor has He granted them power or strength; rather they were afflicted with humiliation and remained under God's wrath, due to their disobedience and their beliefs.[76]

A concrete example of the discretion forced upon followers of Ibn Taymiyya is given by a story related by the Damascene Shāfiʿī scholar Najm al-Dīn al-Ghazzī (d. 1651). In a biographical notice on a contemporary Ḥanbalī scholar, Aḥmad al-Shuwaykī (d. 1598), al-Ghazzī mentioned that he would secretly return a woman to her husband after the latter had divorced her three times in a single declaration, in accordance with the view of Ibn Taymiyya. When word got out about this, he was widely condemned, even by his Ḥanbalī colleagues. Al-Ghazzī wrote that he himself publicly reprimanded al-Shuwaykī for this, saying to him:

> It is not permissible for a man to take back his wife after the three divorces according to the doctrine of the Muslims, except for Ibn Taymiyya's view, which it is not permitted to imitate in this matter due to its deviance (*li-shudhūdhihi*). What has been established on this matter is that he who follows the view of Ibn Taymiyya must be chastised, and the doubt (*shubha*) constituted by his [Ibn Taymiyya's] disagreement does not cancel the prescribed punishment (*ḥadd*) of the man who has intercourse with the woman after she is returned to him, nor [the punishment] of her.

In other words, al-Ghazzī emphasized that the severe (capital) punishments for adultery would be applicable in a case in which a man took back his wife after divorcing her three times in a single declaration. The "deviant" opinion of Ibn Taymiyya did not even constitute a legal shade of doubt that could be argued to ameliorate or suspend this punishment. Such a public reprimand by a scholar who was forty years younger than himself must have been particularly humiliating to al-Shuwaykī. Al-Ghazzī added that some of the people present started insulting outright the Ḥanbalī scholar.[77]

Bio-bibliographical sources provide yet further support for the view that Ibn Taymiyya's influence in subsequent centuries can easily be exaggerated. The just-mentioned Damascene scholar Najm al-Dīn al-Ghazzī wrote a biographical dictionary of Sunni scholars and notables who died in the tenth century of the Hijra (1492–1588), a work that incorporates material from biographical dictionaries by the Ottoman scholar Ahmet Ṭāşköprüzāde (d. 1568), the Aleppine scholar Raḍī al-Dīn Ibn al-Ḥanbalī (d. 1563), the Egyptian scholar 'Abd al-Wahhāb al-Sha'rānī (d. 1565), and the Damascene scholar Ibn Ṭūlūn (d. 1546). Al-Ghazzī's compilation has been edited and thoroughly indexed by Jibrā'īl Jabbur. The index of titles mentioned by al-Ghazzī provides for an interesting contrast with the index to a contemporary introduction to Islamic religious history such as Berkey's *The Formation of Islam*. Al-Ghazzī's text does not mention a single work by Ibn Taymiyya or Ibn Qayyim al-Jawziyya. By contrast, the *kalām* works of al-Taftāzānī are mentioned ten times; the semantic-rhetorical works of al-Taftāzānī ten times; the *kalām* works of al-Jurjānī fourteen times; books on logic thirteen times; Ibn 'Arabī's works seven times; the *Jam' al-Jawāmi'* of al-Subkī twenty-seven times (mostly along with the commentary of al-Maḥallī); the *Shifā'* of al-Qāḍī 'Iyāḍ ten times; and the *Mawāhib* of al-Qasṭallānī four times.[78]

The more detailed obituaries of scholars in 'Abd al-Raḥmān al-Jabartī's well-known chronicle of eighteenth-century Egypt also provides valuable information on the books studied by prominent Egyptian scholars. Again, there are no references to the works of Ibn Taymiyya or Ibn Qayyim al-Jawziyya, while the theological works of al-Taftāzānī, al-Sanūsī, and al-Laqānī appear regularly, as does the *Shifā'* of al-Qāḍī 'Iyāḍ and the *Mawāhib* of al-Qasṭallānī.[79]

The *athbāt*—i.e. works listing the books one had a certificate to teach—by prominent seventeenth- and eighteenth-century scholars in the Hijaz tend to reinforce the impression obtained from biographical entries. The *thabat* of the Meccan Shāfi'ī scholar Aḥmad al-Nakhlī (d. 1717), for example, does not mention any works by Ibn Taymiyya or Ibn al-Qayyim, but mentions the *Sharḥ al-'Aqā'id al-*

Nasafiyya of al-Taftāzānī and the *Jawharat al-tawḥīd* of al-Laqānī, as well as Ibn ʿArabī's *Futūḥāt*, al-Maḥallī's commentary on al-Subkī's *Jamʿ al-Jawāmiʿ*, *al-Shifāʾ* of al-Qāḍī ʿIyāḍ, and *al-Mawāhib* of al-Qaṣtallānī.[80] The *thabat* of the Meccan scholar ʿAbdallāh ibn Sālim al-Baṣrī (d. 1722) likewise does not mention the works of Ibn Taymiyya and Ibn al-Qayyim, while mentioning the theological works of al-Taftāzānī, al-Jurjānī, al-Dawānī, and al-Laqānī, as well as the *Shifāʾ* of al-Qāḍī ʿIyāḍ and the works of Ibn ʿArabī.[81] Even the *thabat* of the Damascene Ḥanbalī scholar Abū al-Mawāhib al-Ḥanbalī (d. 1714) does not mention the works of Ibn Taymiyya or Ibn al-Qayyim, while mentioning the theological works of al-Taftāzānī, al-Sanūsī and al-Laqānī, as well as the *Mawāhib* of al-Qaṣtallānī, the *Shifāʾ* of al-Qāḍī ʿIyāḍ, and the works of Ibn ʿArabī.[82] To be sure, the evidence of the *athbāt* is not conclusive, partly because they sometimes mention works under a general description, such as "all the works that he is certified to teach" or "the books of the jurists of the school, both earlier and later." It is thus not unlikely that some of the mentioned scholars were acquainted with the works of Ibn Taymiyya and Ibn Qayyim al-Jawziyya. Yet, it is striking that Ibn ʿArabī, whose ideas were supposedly dealt a decisive blow by Ibn Taymiyya, and philosophical theologians such as al-Taftāzānī and al-Jurjānī, whose field was supposedly marginalized by the victory of traditionalist neo-Ḥanbalīs, appear regularly in these *athbāt* while Ibn Taymiyya does not.

The Ottoman scribe and polymath Kâtip Çelebi, author of the well-known bibliographic compilation *Kashf al-ẓunūn ʿan asāmī al-kutub wa-al-funūn*, was also obviously much better acquainted with the works of Ibn Taymiyya's critics than with the works of Ibn Taymiyya himself. For example, he mentioned Ibn Taymiyya's *Minhāj al-sunna*, but did not give the incipit, presumably because he had not actually seen a copy of the work. Instead, he quoted Ibn Taymiyya's critic Taqī al-Dīn al-Subkī to the effect that it was a powerful response to a Shiʿi polemical work by Ibn Muṭahhar al-Ḥillī (d. 1326), but also expounded the heretical views that created things need not have a beginning in time, and that non-eternal attributes subsist in God.[83] After mentioning Ibn Taymiyya's *Kitāb al-ʿarsh*, Kâtip Çelebi again did not give an incipit, but quoted the grammarian and Qurʾān commentator Abū Ḥayyān al-Andalusī (d. 1344) as stating that he had seen this work, and that Ibn Taymiyya had written there that God is literally seated on the throne, and had left a place on it for the Prophet Muḥammad to sit next to him.[84] After mentioning Ibn Taymiyya's work *[Iqtiḍā'] al-ṣirāṭ al-mustaqīm*, Kâtip Çelebi yet again did not give an incipit, and merely wrote that this was the work in which Ibn Taymiyya, according to Taqī al-Dīn al-Ḥisnī, expressed the outrageous view that the venerable Companion and transmitter of Hadith Ibn 'Abbās was an unbeliever.[85]

An exception to this trend is the *thabat* of the Kurdish-born Medinan-based Ibrāhīm al-Kūrānī (d. 1690), a Shāfi'ī scholar and mystic of the Ibn 'Arabī school, who listed the works of Ibn Taymiyya and Ibn Qayyim al-Jawziyya alongside the other more widely-studied works mentioned above.[86] This unusual appearance is explained by the Maghribi scholar 'Abdallāh al-'Ayyāshī (d. 1680), who studied with al-Kūrānī in Medina. While listing the works of al-Kūrānī, al-'Ayyashī mentioned a work devoted to the question of God's speech, and went on to describe it as follows:

> The aim of the work is to verify the reason for the dispute between the Ash'arīs and the Ḥanbalīs regarding God's speech, and the Ḥanbalīs' position that it consists of letters and sounds...without regard to what this implies of its non-eternity and its passing away. Many words have been exchanged between the later Ash'arīs and the Ḥanbalīs, leading the parties to accuse one another of waywardness in doctrine. Because of this issue and others in which the Ḥanbalīs have adhered to the literal meaning of the Qur'ān and Sunna in the matters of *istiwā'* and *nuzūl* and the foot and eyes and hands, contemporary Shāfi'īs such as the Subkīs and others declared that Shaykh al-Islam Ibn Taymiyya and his followers such as Ibn al-Qayyim were wayward in doctrine, and they were prejudiced against him and attributed cardinal errors to him. The Shaykh [i.e. al-Kūrānī] did well to investigate these allegations, and did not imitate the people of his school, the Shāfi'īs, since he knows what can happen between disputants.... He started reading the works of Ibn Taymiyya and his followers...and then started to write the work.[87]

Al-'Ayyāshī went on to quote at some length from al-Kūrānī's work:

> He said: when I read carefully the works of these people I found that they were innocent of many of the accusations levelled at them by the people of our Shāfi'ī school, such as anthropomorphism (*tajsīm wa tashbīh*). Rather, they adhere to the position of the great Hadith scholars of the past, as is known from the case of their Imam Aḥmad, which is to hold on to the literal meaning of the Qur'ānic verses and Hadith and

> believe in them as they appear, while adhering to *tafwīḍ* with regard to the passages with a problematic meaning. This is not condemned by any Ash'arī.[88]

In other words, al-Kūrānī reduced the position of Ibn Taymiyya and Ibn al-Qayyim on the anthropomorphic passages of the Qur'ān and Sunna to the perfectly respectable position of *tafwīḍ* preferred by the *salaf*. What was distinctive about their position was, according to al-Kūrānī, that they argued fiercely and at length against the *ta'wīl* preferred by the *khalaf*. Though al-Kūrānī himself, as was typical of Sufis of the Ibn 'Arabī school, preferred the position of the *salaf*, he took exception to the tone of these arguments. "Ibn al-Qayyim", he wrote, "has exceeded the limits in responding to the Ash'arīs on this issue, until it led him to calumny." Al-Kūrānī then quoted Ibn al-Qayyim as comparing the Ash'arīs' understanding of *istawā* as *istawlā* (i.e. with a *lam* added) to the Jews falsifying (*taḥrīf*) the words of God. This was too much for al-Kūrānī, who wrote:

> He has spoken ill, may God forgive him, and strayed from the truth out of mere partisanship. The Ash'arīs—may God be pleased with them—do not reject the word *istawā*, and do not stop saying it. This is what they recite and how they draw near to Him, but some of them reinterpret the meaning since they see that the literal meaning is impossible of God, and say that the meaning of *istawā* is *istawlā* since the two words are synonyms in the Arabic language.... This is the kind of fanatical partisanship that has led the two groups to where they are, though both of them are, if God wills, on the right path. The one who leaves interpretation to God (*al-mufawwiḍ*) accepts whatever God may mean, and merely desists from what he is not charged to do. The one who reinterprets (*al-muta'awwil*) follows what he knows to be true of the Qur'ān and Sunna, and understands that which has an unclear meaning in the light of these, so that the creed is homogenous and so that those lacking in discernment should not understand something that is not proper to God and attribute this to Him. Reinterpretation for this aim is good since it is a safeguard against believing what it is not permitted to believe. If the imperfect of understanding hears *istawā* only the impossible meaning will occur to him, and if he hears the scholar saying: "It means *istawlā* by force and overpowering" this problematic understanding will be erased from his heart. And this reinterpretation, even if it were not to accord with the intentions of God and His Prophet, is without doubt something that is truc of God and does not contradict whatever God's meaning is. Hence there is no great damage done, and no arbitrary decision, since we do not say: it has no meaning except the

> one we offer, but rather that it is possible that this is its meaning—and this is true, since it is possible [that this is the meaning].[89]

Al-Kūrānī's defence of Ibn Taymiyya has led some modern historians to believe that he was a proto-revivalist prefiguring the more famous Sunni revivalist thinkers of the eighteenth century.[90] In light of this it bears emphasis that al-Kūrānī, far from being a latter-day follower of Ibn Taymiyya, was a mystic of the Ibn 'Arabī school and an apologist for the idea of *waḥdat al-wujūd*.[91] Al-Kūrānī's preference for *tafwīḍ* over *ta'wīl* was fully in line with the position of the Greatest Master himself, who had little sympathy with rationalist reinterpretations of the problematic passages of the Qur'ān and Sunna.[92] According to Ibn 'Arabī and his followers, the tension between the *tanzīh* demanded by theology and the *tashbīh* suggested by certain passages in the Qur'ān and Sunna was ultimately resolved by invoking the notion of divine epiphany or manifestation (*tajallī*). God is in Himself radically different from anything created, but He can manifest Himself in the world of created phenomena. All references to God's anthropomorphic and spatial attributes should be understood to refer to the divine epiphanies, and not to the divine Self. This line of thought was expressed clearly by al-Kūrānī in a treatise written towards the end of his life, *Tanbīh al-'uqūl 'alā tanzīh al-ṣūfiyya 'an i'tiqād al-tajsīd wa-al-'ayniyya wa-al-ittiḥād wa-al-ḥulūl*.[93] Al-Kūrānī's works are a testimony to the influence, not of Ibn Taymiyya, but of Ibn 'Arabī.[94] It should also be added that al-Kūrānī's theological positions were far from uncontroversial. They provoked a virulent response from a contemporary Ash'arī theologian, the Maghribi scholar Yaḥyā al-Shāwī (d. 1685), who condemned him as a heretic (*zindīq*), primarily for his acceptance of the historicity of the story of the Satanic verses incident, but also for his defence of *waḥdat al-wujūd*, his "corporealism", and his rehabilitation of Ibn Taymiyya.[95]

The well-known Indian Naqshbandi mystic Shāh Walī Allāh al-Dihlawī (d. 1762), who was strongly influenced by his studies with al-Kūrānī's son Abū al-Ṭahir Muḥammad (d. 1733) in Medina, also combined an adherence to the metaphysics of Ibn 'Arabī with admiration for Ibn Taymiyya.[96] This combination of attitudes on the part of al-Kūrānī and Shāh Walī Allāh is somewhat curious and deserves further exploration, which would have first to establish which works of Ibn Taymiyya they read. It is possible that they were not acquainted with his condemnations of Ibn 'Arabī and his followers, and thought of him primarily as an opponent of *kalām* and the *khalaf's* position regarding anthropomorphic expressions in the Qur'ān and Sunna. Sufis tended to share this opposition, and like many Ḥanbalīs often clothed it in a rhetoric that emphasized revelation over mere "opinion", and hence extolled disciplines such as Hadith at the expense of scholastic jurisprudence and theology.

It is important to remember that Ibn 'Arabī himself was a member of the Ẓāhirī school of law and no friend of scholastic jurisprudence and theology. In the eighteenth century, there seems to have been a marked rise in attacks on the established tradition of jurisprudence and theology by scholars with Sufi affiliations who called for an approach that was more directly based on Hadith.[97] Some of these Sufi critics of scholasticism found aspects of the thought of Ibn Taymiyya and Ibn al-Qayyim congenial, and adduced them in their polemical writings without abandoning their positive view of Ibn 'Arabī.[98] It is perhaps ironic that seventeenth- and eighteenth-century Sufis should have played this role in the rehabilitation of Ibn Taymiyya, given that he has become an icon of modern movements that are aggressively opposed to Sufism and that have to some extent been successful in putting it on the defensive in the contemporary Sunni world.

Another thinker who is often stated to have fallen under the influence of Ibn Taymiyya is the Turkish scholar Mehmet Birgiwî (d. 1573) who inspired the violently puritan Kadizadeli movement within the Ottoman Empire in the seventeenth and eighteenth centuries. A treatise on *ziyārat al-qubūr* that has been attributed to Birgiwî is explicitly indebted to Ibn Qayyim al-Jawziyya's *Ighāthat al-lahfān*.[99] If the attribution is reliable, then some sort of influence is undeniable. However, it is important to stress that in other areas Birgiwî showed little traces of being influenced by Ibn Taymiyya or Ibn al-Qayyim. In his main work *al-Ṭarīqa al-Muḥammadiyya*, for example, he wrote that studying disciplines such as *kalām* and logic is a collective duty of the Muslim community (*farḍ kifāya*)—a view vehemently denied by Ibn al-Qayyim.[100] Birgiwî also followed mainstream Maturidi tradition in recognising eight essential attributes of God: the seven mentioned by al-Taftāzānī above and the attribute of "bringing into existence" (*takwīn*). This was in contrast to later Ḥanbalīs influenced by Ibn Taymiyya such as the Palestinian scholar Muḥammad al-Saffārīnī (d. 1774) who also mentioned the hands and face and being seated on the throne as additional attributes of God.[101] Birgiwî denied that God's speech consists of letters and sounds, again in contrast to Ḥanbalīs such as al-Saffārīnī.[102] He also explicitly denied that God is in space or a direction. Indeed, those who use spatial expressions of God, saying that He is in the heavens or "above" are condemned as unbelievers.[103] Birgiwî followed mainstream Sunni theologians in denying that non-eternal attributes can subsist in God, apparently ruling out the possibility that "being seated on the throne" or "descending on the night of mid-Sha'bān" can be thought of as attributes of the divine Self. While Ash'arī theologians held that those who believed that non-eternal attributes subsist in God were wayward but not unbelievers, Birgiwî characteristically adopted the strict Maturidi view that they are unbelievers.[104] Ibn Taymiyya was accused by al-Subkī and Ibn Ḥajar al-Haytamī of precisely that which Birgiwî claimed was tantamount to *kufr*, namely believing that non-eternal attributes can subsist in the divine Self, and apparently with some reason. In one of his lengthier *fatāwā* Ibn Taymiyya stated that "the position of the Imāms of the Sunna and the Hadith from amongst the *salaf*" was that "created attributes subsist in Him and cease to do so (*taqūmu bihi al-ḥawādith wa tazūl*)."[105] Davûd Karsî, an eighteenth century Turkish scholar who was explicitly inspired by Birgiwî, mentioned the Ḥanbalīs along with the Mu'tazilīs and the Karrāmiyya as one of the wayward, non-Sunni sects (*min al-firaq al-ḍālla*).[106] The views of Birgiwî and his Kadizadeli followers may have been rooted, not in the thought of Ibn Taymiyya, but in an intolerant current within the Ḥanafi-Maturidi school, represented by such scholars as 'Alā' al-Dīn al-Bukhārī (d. 1438), who famously declared both Ibn 'Arabī and Ibn Taymiyya unbelievers.

More akin to the overall tenor of Ibn Taymiyya's views was a current of thought amongst some Yemeni scholars such as Muḥammad Ibn al-Wazīr (d. 1436), Ṣāliḥ al-Maqbalī (d. 1696), Muḥammad b. Ismā'īl Ibn al-Amīr (d. 1768) and Muḥammad al-Shawkānī (d. 1834). Such scholars shared Ibn Taymiyya's hostility toward *kalām*, logic, monist mysticism, and the veneration of saints and shrines.[107] Whether, and to what extent, this current of thought was influenced by Ibn Taymiyya, or merely happened to agree with him on a number of points, is not clear. Certain ideas that were quite central to these Yemeni thinkers have no parallel in Ibn Taymiyya's thought, such as their rejection—in the name of *ijtihād*—of the idea of belonging to an established school of law. On the other hand, Ibn al-Amīr and al-Shawkānī are known to have thought highly of Ibn Taymiyya and Ibn al-Qayyim, and to have been acquainted with at least some of their writings.[108] In the nineteenth century, the influence of this tradition was to extend beyond the Yemen, and leave its mark on the Salafi movement in Iraq, Syria and Egypt, and the *Ahl-i ḥadīth* movement in India.

IV

The posthumous reputation of Ibn Taymiyya amongst non-Ḥanbalī Sunni scholars was to change considerably between the eighteenth and twentieth centuries. From a little-read scholar with problematic and controversial views, he was to become for many Sunnis of the modern age one of the central figures in the Islamic religious tradition. One of the seminal works in the nineteenth-century rediscovery of Ibn Taymiyya was *Jalā' al-'aynayn fi muḥākamat al-Aḥmadayn* by the Iraqi scholar Khayr al-Dīn Nu'mān ibn Maḥmūd al-Ālūsī (d. 1899). The work takes the form of a detailed refutation of the *fatwā* against (Aḥmad) Ibn Taymiyya by (Aḥmad) Ibn Ḥajar al-Haytamī. A detailed exposition of the arguments of al-Ālūsī lies beyond the scope of this paper. In what follows, I will confine myself to a few remarks about the context of the work.

One of the first places outside Najd to be touched by the iconoclastic movement of Muḥammad ibn 'Abd al-Wahhāb (d. 1792) was southern Iraq. The historian Ibn Sanad al-Baṣrī (d. 1827) already described a movement in Baghdad that seemed to him to be at one with the Wahhabis of Najd, and which called itself the "*salaf*" and its opponents the "*khalaf*."[109] The Baghdadi scholar 'Alī al-Suwaydī (d. 1822)—who was suspected of harbouring Wahhabi sympathies—wrote an influential creedal work entitled *al-'Iqd al-thamīn fi masā'il al-dīn* that embodied some of the sentiments of the new self-styled Salafi movement.[110]

At around the same time, the Kurdish Naqshbandi mystic Shaykh Khālid al-Shahrazūrī (d. 1827) was gaining supporters amongst Iraqi scholars. Shaykh Khālid belonged to the so-called Mujaddidi branch of the Naqshbandi order, i.e. the branch of the order influenced by the Indian Naqshbandi Aḥmad al-Sirhindī (d. 1624) and characterised by revivalist and politically activist sentiments and by a lukewarm attitude towards the metaphysics of Ibn ʿArabī, and opposition to aspects of popular religion that smacked of syncretism and innovation.[111] Shaykh Khālid and his followers also adopted the characteristic Sufi rejection of allegorical interpretation of the seemingly anthropomorphic passages of the Qur'ān and Sunna, and upholding the position of the *salaf* on this issue.[112] The exact relationship between the pro-Wahhabi Salafism described by Ibn Sanad al-Baṣrī and that of the followers of Shaykh Khālid is not clear. In the later part of the nineteenth century, the followers of Shaykh Khālid and the Salafis were to become inveterate opponents, but it is not clear that this was so from the beginning. For instance, ʿAlī al-Suwaydī's son Muḥammad Amīn, who wrote a commentary on his father's Salafi creedal work, was initiated into the Naqshbandi order by Shaykh Khālid. The Baghdadi scholar and Ḥanafī Mufti Maḥmūd al-Ālūsī (d. 1854), who was also initiated by Shaykh Khālid, found nothing objectionable in the creedal work of ʿAlī al-Suwaydī.[113]

Whatever the relationship between pro-Wahhabi Salafism and the Salafism of Khālid al-Naqshbandi, it is clear that the terms "Salafi" and "Khalafi" were being used in early nineteenth-century Iraq to identify supporters and opponents of a movement. As has been shown above, the terms had appeared in earlier creedal works to distinguish between two approaches to the seemingly anthropomorphic passages in the Qur'ān and Sunna. However, the use of the terms in biographical entries as a way of classifying contemporary scholars is absent from the biographical works of Egyptian and Syrian scholars from the sixteenth, seventeenth and eighteenth centuries.

The new Salafi movement met with resistance, and there is reason to believe that this resistance was especially powerful amongst Shāfiʿī scholars. Thus the later Salafi Maḥmūd Shukrī al-Ālūsī (d. 1924) described a contemporary Shāfiʿī scholar as being "weak in the way of the *salaf*, as is the case with all those who belong to the Shāfiʿī school (*qaṣīr al-bāʿ fī madhhab al-salaf kamā sha'n sā'ir al-muntasibīn li-al-Shāfiʿī*)."[114] It is also clear that Ibn Ḥajar al-Haytamī's writings continued to enjoy prestige amongst Iraqi Shāfiʿīs in the nineteenth century. The chronicler Ibn Sanad al-Baṣrī, after mentioning Ibn Ḥajar in passing in his chronicle, interrupted his narrative to heap lavish praises on him:

> He who looks at his works will be dazzled and say: Praise God who has allowed the minds of man to reach its subtle depths! He is the Shāfiʿī who mediated between the finer points of law and the subtleties of the discipline of tradition. He did not treat any discipline without reaching depths that his contemporaries never hoped to reach. No one disputed with him without finding him an abounding sea of knowledge. He was firm in matters of religion while being high-minded, composed and intelligent.... Those who came after him have depended on what he has chosen, and thus his works are the standard references for *fatāwā*, and no Shāfiʿī will give a *fatwā* that is not in accordance with what he has considered. The prominent scholars esteem his works, and give it the foremost rating.[115]

Khayr al-Dīn al-Ālūsī's work also testifies to the continued influence of Ibn Ḥajar's condemnation of Ibn Taymiyya. "Many students", he noted, "who have little acquaintance with the detailed evidence of the Qur'ān and Sunna hear the words, and are unable to distinguish the husk [of truth] from the kernel."[116]

A look at some of the main sources on which al-Ālūsī drew in his apology may also throw some light on the intellectual forces underlying his work. Al-Ālūsī seems, unlike Ibn Ḥajar, to have read some of Ibn Taymiyya's works. He could thus draw attention to the points on which Ibn Taymiyya had not actually said what Ibn Ḥajar had condemned him for saying. Al-Ālūsī was also acquainted with the works of the Palestinian Ḥanbalī scholar Muḥammad al-Saffārīnī, many of which feature extensive quotations from Ibn Taymiyya and Ibn al-Qayyim.[117] Similarly, al-Ālūsī also read the works of Ibrāhīm al-Kūrānī and Shāh Walī Allāh al-Dihlawī. Though he had no sympathy with the theory of *waḥdat al-wujūd*, he invoked their writings in support of the view that Ibn Taymiyya's position on seemingly anthropomorphic passages in the Qur'ān and Sunna was the same as the view of the *salaf*—thus glossing over the difference between Ibn Taymiyya's literalism and the position of *tafwīḍ*.[118]

A more pervasive influence on al-Ālūsī seems to have come from two sources: First, the writings of his father Maḥmūd al-Ālūsī, a disciple of Shaykh Khālid, in whom Salafism in theology was combined with opposition to the veneration of tombs and other "innovations" of popular religion.[119] Maḥmud al-Ālūsī had already started the process of rehabilitating Ibn Taymiyya before his son. During a visit to Istanbul, he got involved in a debate on Ibn Taymiyya with the Ottoman Grand Mufti ʿArif Ḥikmet (d. 1859): ʿArif

Ḥikmet charged, and al-Ālūsī denied, that Ibn Taymiyya was a corporealist (*mujassim*) and that his idiosyncratic deviations on points of law from the four established schools were not tolerable.[120] An interesting aspect of the debate is that al-Ālūsī reported a few pages earlier that the Grand Mufti "inclined to the position of the *salaf* concerning the problematic expressions".[121] Obviously, 'Arif Ḥikmet did not see any contradiction between preferring the "*salaf*" approach in theology and believing that Ibn Taymiyya was a heretic. The term "Salafi" had not yet acquired, in Istanbul at least, the connotation of a religious reform movement with Ibn Taymiyya as iconic hero.

A second important influence on Khayr al-Dīn al-Ālūsī came from the Yemeni scholar Muḥammad al-Shawkānī and his second-generation Indian student Muḥammad Ṣiddiq ibn Ḥasan Khān al-Qannawjī (d. 1889)—the latter being Khayr al-Dīn al-Ālūsī's own teacher.[122] As stated above, a central theme in the writings of al-Shawkānī was the necessity of exercising *ijtihād* based on the Qur'ān and Hadith, rather than the precedent-based reasoning of the established schools of law. He was of course not merely stressing an abstract, formal principle of jurisprudence. Emphasis on the Qur'ān and Sunna would, he believed, cleanse the law and creed from later innovations and accretions such as tomb veneration, philosophy and logic, and most aspects of Sufism. From this perspective, Ibn Taymiyya's opposition to Ash'arī *kalām*, Greek logic, tomb veneration, and most manifestations of Sufism was welcome. The fact that his ideas were considered idiosyncratic and opposed by most of his contemporary colleagues merely underlined his exalted status as a *mujtahid* who refused the straitjacket of *taqlīd*.

Al-Ālūsī also drew on the above-mentioned *al-'Iqd al-thamīn* of 'Alī al-Suwaydī.[123] This work would seem to betray Wahhabi influence in its expressed worry that contemporary Muslims are actually practicing *shirk* by visiting tombs and shrines, seeking *baraka*, and entreating prophets and saints for intercession with God. The polytheist Arabs had not, Suwaydī stressed, denied the existence and power of Allah. Their *shirk* had rather consisted in invoking and venerating other gods and shrines.

The worry that the great majority of nominally Sunni Muslims may actually be hypocrites or polytheists had surfaced on previous occasions—for example in the Turkish Kadizadeli movement inspired by Birgiwî. However, it had previously been counterbalanced by the widespread belief that the community could not agree on error, and that "what Muslims saw as good is good in the eyes of God." Already al-Subkī had urged against Ibn Taymiyya and Ibn al-Qayyim that an implication of their view was that the great majority of Sunni Muslim scholars were heretics, and this had to be wrong. We know for certain, al-Sukbī argued, that the majority of Ḥanafī, Mālikī and Shāfi'ī scholars are on the right path, and ideas that implied that this was not so could be rejected out of hand.[124] A similar argument was invoked by Ibn Ḥajar al-Haytamī in his work on visiting the tomb of the Prophet:

> Just as there is a consensus among scholars that *ziyāra* and travelling to perform it are legitimate, so there is a consensus amongst Muslims, scholars and others, in actually doing this. People have continuously come from all corners to visit him, may God bless him and grant him salvation, since the time of the Companions—may God be pleased with them—until this day, before the Hajj and after, and they traverse long distances and spend their money and their energy thinking that this is one of the greatest of deeds. He who claims that this great multitude of people through the ages is wrong is himself wrong and deprived of truth.[125]

A similar line of reasoning was sometimes used to buttress widespread practices that contravened a Hadith of impeccable *isnād*. For example, the practice of writing names on tombs was expressly prohibited by one Hadith, but scholars who insisted on the permissibility of the practice replied that the Hadith had no legal force, since "the Imams of the Muslims from the east to the west had their names written on graves, and this is something that the *khalaf* has taken from the *salaf*."[126] The eminent Damascene jurist Muḥammad Amīn ibn 'Ābidīn (d. 1836) also overruled a Hadith that prohibited practices such as plastering tombs, writing the names of the deceased on them, and building cupolas on them, by appealing to another Hadith according to which "what Muslims see as good is good in the eyes of God."[127] Ibn Ḥajar al-Haytamī was not willing to go as far in this direction as others, but he too explicitly stated that even if one supposed that the Prophet had explicitly said "Do not visit my grave", it would have been necessary to reinterpret this saying since it contradicted a scholarly consensus (*ijmā'*) on the permissibility of visiting graves.[128] He also argued that even if it were the case—and he believed that it was not—that visiting the graves of saints was an innovation unknown to the earliest generations of Muslims, then it would still be permissible for later generations to visit them, since not all innovations were reprehensible. Some innovations were obligatory (*wājiba*) or commendable (*mandūba*) let alone permissible; examples would be studying grammar or founding a *madrasa* or collectively performing *ṣalāt al-tarāwīḥ*—the supererogatory night-prayers of Ramadan.[129]

Ibn Taymiyya's rejection of *all* innovations, even of such popular expressions of piety as litanies (*awrād* and *aḥzāb*), was widely rejected as idiosyncratic. For example, the prominent Maghribi-born Medinan-based scholar Muḥammad Ibn al-Ṭayyib al-Fāsī (d. 1756/7), one of the teachers of the famous scholar and lexicographer Muḥammad Murtaḍā al-Zabīdī, conceded in his commentary on the popular litany (*ḥizb*) of al-Nawawī that litanies did not exist in the first centuries of Islam, but he nevertheless defended them as commendable expressions of piety. He went on to briefly consider and reject Ibn Taymiyya's position on the matter:

> Ibn Taymiyya criticized *aḥzāb* and rejected them in a most inappropriate manner, and went to extremes in undermining it. They have responded to him, and gone to extremes in criticizing him, and have stated that his abilities are conceded as far as memory is concerned, but that he is unreliable in matters of dogma, and that he is deficient in reason, let alone mystical gnosis (*'irfān*). Some have even gone to the extent of attributing to him not only heresy (*zandaqa*) but unbelief. The Imam of Imams, Taqī al-Dīn al-Subkī was asked about him and said: He is a man whose knowledge is greater than his reason. Shaykh Zarrūq [al-Burnusī (d. 1493)] has said: The upshot of this is that consideration is given to items of knowledge that he relates, but not to his handling of this knowledge. Hence no heed is given to his rejection, and no consideration given to his analysis and judgement. And God knows best.[130]

Such tolerance of "commendable innovation" (*bid'a ḥasana*) and emphasis on an *evolving* consensus stands in stark contrast to the anxiety about religious decadence that is so prominent in the writings of Ibn Taymiyya. This anxiety was strengthened in the nineteenth and twentieth centuries by the increasingly widespread assumption that the political, military and technological superiority of the West had underlined the fact that the Muslim community had taken a wrong turn, and that what was needed was a reassertion of pristine, uncorrupted Islam.

V

Al-Ālūsī's apology for Ibn Taymiyya is known to have made an impact on scholars who went on to become central figures of the Salafi movement in Syria and Egypt, such as Jamāl al-Dīn al-Qāsimī (d. 1914) and Muḥammad Rashīd Riḍā (d. 1935).[131] The latter, in his annotations to *Risālat al-tawḥīd* by his one-time mentor Muḥammad 'Abduh, had the following to add to 'Abduh's brief outline of the history of *kalām:*

> The author has failed to mention in his historical survey that after the power of the Ash'arīs reigned supreme in the Middle Ages (*al-qurūn al-wusṭā*) and the *ahl al-ḥadīth* and the followers of the *salaf* were weakened, there appeared in the eighth century [AH, fourteenth century AD] the great *mujaddid*, Shaykh al-Islam Aḥmad Taqī al-Dīn Ibn Taymiyya, whose like has not been seen in mastery of both the traditional and rational sciences and in the power of argument. Egypt and India have revived his books and the books of his student Ibn Qayyim al-Jawziyya, after a time when they were only available in Najd. Now, they have spread to both east and west, and will become the main support of the Muslims of the earth.[132]

'Abduh's outline of the history of *kalām* highlighted the emergence of Ash'arism as a commendable mean between naïve literalism and unbridled rationalism, and the later incorporation of a fair share of philosophy by Ash'arī theologians after al-Ghazālī. To this traditional account (found for example in Ibn Khaldūn), 'Abduh added the novel nineteenth-century view, which he may have derived from Ernest Renan, that not long after al-Ghazālī Muslim theology entered a period of prolonged stagnation. There is no hint that 'Abduh thought of Ibn Taymiyya as a major figure in the history of Sunni Islam.[133] Riḍā supplemented 'Abduh's narrative by introducing Ibn Taymiyya as a central and heroic character, whose appearance and power of argument had a dramatic and corrective impact on the course of Muslim religious thought. However, he was only able to create this impression by jumping from the career of Ibn Taymiyya in the fourteenth century to the recovery of his books in Egypt and India in his own time. During the intervening five centuries, Ibn Taymiya's views had found little resonance amongst mainstream Sunni scholars. In order to impart momentous significance to the appearance of Ibn Taymiyya, these centuries had to be ignored.

Notes

* I would like to thank Michael Cook, Yossi Rapoport, Shahab Ahmad, Recep Goktas, Tim Winter and an anonymous reviewer for their helpful comments on earlier drafts of this paper.

1. Jonathan Berkey, *The Formation of Islam: Religion and Society in the Near East, 600–1800* (Cambridge: Cambridge University Press, 2003), 276–286.
2. Majid Fakhry, *A History of Islamic Philosophy*, 3rd edition (New York: Columbia University Press, 2004), 334.
3. Alexander Knysh, *Ibn ʻArabi in the Later Islamic Tradition: The Making of a Polemical Image in Medieval Islam* (Albany, NY: State University of New York, 1999), 87.
4. I present the evidence for this in my "Sunni Muslim Scholars on the Status of Logic, 1500–1800", *Islamic Law and Society* 11 (2004): 213–232.
5. See Bakrī ʻAlāʼ al-Dīn's introduction to his edition of ʻAbd al-Ghanī al-Nābulusī, *al-Wujūd al-ḥaqq* (Damascus: Institut Français de Damas, 1995).
6. Ibn Ḥajar al-Haytamī, *al-Fatāwā al-ḥadīthiyya* (Cairo: Muṣṭafā al-Bābī al-Ḥalabī, 1970), 114–115.
7. For biographical entries on Ibn Ḥajar al-Haytamī, see Najm al-Dīn al-Ghazzī, *al-Kawākib al-sāʼira fī aʻyān al-miʼa al-ʻāshira*, ed. J. Jabbour (Beirut: American University of Beirut Press, 1958), 3:111–113; Ibn al-ʻImād al-Ḥanbalī, *Shadharāt al-dhahab fī akhbār man dhahab* (Cairo: Maktabat al-Qudsī, 1351H), 8:370–372; ʻAbd al-Qādir al-ʻAydarūsī, *al-Nūr al-sāfir ʻan akhbār al-qarn al-ʻāshir* (Baghdad: al-Maktaba al-ʻArabiyya, 1934), 287–292.
8. C. Brockelmann, *Geschichte der Arabischen Literatur* (Leiden: Brill, 1937–49), 2:321; J. Schacht, *An Introduction to Islamic Law* (Oxford: Clarendon Press, 1964), 262.
9. Taqī al-Dīn al-Ḥisnī, *Dafʻ shubah man shabbaha wa tamarrada*, ed. by ʻAbd al-Wāḥid Muṣṭafā (Amman: Dār al-Razī, 2003).
10. Ibn Ḥajar, *al-Fatāwā al-ḥadīthiyya*, 115.
11. Ibn Ḥajar, *al-Fatāwā al-ḥadīthiyya*, 116–117. Ibn Ḥajar would seem to be relying on the account of Ibn Taymiyya's idiosyncrasies given by Salāḥ al-Dīn Khalīl ibn Kaykaldī al-ʻAlāʼī (d. 1359), the teacher of the prominent Hadith scholar Zayn al-Dīn al-ʻIrāqī (d. 1404). See the account by al-ʻAlāʼī reproduced in the editor's introduction to *al-Rasāʼil al-Subkiyya fī al-radd ʻalā Ibn Taymiyya* (Beirut: ʻĀlam al-Kutub, 1983), 69–70. For clarification of the actual position of Ibn Taymiyya on some of the issues mentioned here, see Y. Rapoport, "Ibn Taymiyya on Divorce Oaths", in M. Winter & A. Levnoni (eds.), *The Mamluks in Egyptian and Syrian Politics and Society* (Leiden: E. J. Brill, 2004): 191–217; Shahab Ahmed, "Ibn Taymiyyah and the Satanic verses," *Studia Islamica* 87 (1998): 67–124; J. Hoover, "Perpetual Creativity in the Perfection of God", *Journal of Islamic Studies* 15 (2004): 287–330.
12. Ibn Ḥajar, *al-Fatāwā al-ḥadīthiyya*, 110–113.
13. See for example the passages from Ibn al-Qayyim quoted in Khayr al-Dīn al-Ālūsī, *Jalāʼ al-ʻaynayn fī muḥākamat al-Aḥmadayn* (Beirut: Dār al-Kutub al-ʻIlmiyya, n.d. [reprint]), 297, 379–380.
14. Ibn Ḥajar, *al-Fatāwā al-ḥadīthiyya*, 203–204.
15. Ibn Ḥajar al-Haytamī, *Ashraf al-wasāʼil ilā fahm al-shamāʼil*, ed. Aḥmad al-Mazīdī (Beirut: Dār al-Kutub al-ʻIlmiyya, 1998), 172–173.
16. Saʻd al-Dīn al-Taftāzānī, *Sharḥ al-ʻAqāʼid al-Nasafiyya* (Istanbul: Dār Saʻādet, 1326AH), 72.

17. Sa'd al-Dīn al-Taftāzānī, *Sharḥ al-Maqāṣid*, ed. 'Abd al-Raḥmān 'Umayra (Beirut: 'Ālam al-Kutub, 1998), 4:174–175.
18. Ḥasan al-'Aṭṭār, *Ḥāshiya 'alā sharḥ Jam' al-jawāmi'* (Beirut: Dār al-Kutub al-'Ilmiyya, n.d. [reprint]), 2:461–462.
19. 'Abd al-Salām al-Laqānī, *Itḥāf al-murīd sharḥ Jawharat al-tawḥīd* (Beirut: Dār al-Kutub al-'Ilmiyya, 2001), 181–183.
20. Muḥammad ibn Yūsuf al-Sanūsī, *'Umdat ahl al-tawfīq fī sharḥ 'Aqīdat ahl al-tawḥīd* (Cairo: Jarīdat al-Islām, 1316AH), 276.
21. Sanūsī, *'Umdat ahl al-tawfīq*, 140.
22. Aḥmad Bābā al-Tunbuktī, *Nayl al-ibtihāj bi-taṭrīz al-Dībāj*. Printed on the margins of Ibn Farḥūn, *al-Dībāj al-mudhahhab fī ma'rifat a'yān al-madhhab* (Cairo: Maṭba'at al-Sa'āda, 1329AH), 166.
23. Ibn Taymiyya, *al-Iklīl fī al-mutashābah wa-al-ta'wīl*, in *Majmū' fatāwā Shaykh al-Islām Aḥmad Ibn Taymiyya* (Beirut: Mu'assasat al-Risāla, 1997), 13: 296.
24. Muḥammad al-Shahrastānī, *Kitāb al-milal wa-al-niḥal*, ed. by W. Cureton (Leipzig: Otto Harrassowitz, 1923 [reprint of 1846 edition]), 64.
25. Shahrastānī, *Kitāb al-milal wa-al-niḥal*, 77–79.
26. Jalāl al-Dīn al-Dawānī, *Sharḥ al-'Aqā'id al-'Aḍudiyya* (Istanbul: 'Arif Efendi, 1316H), 43.
27. Al-Sayyid al-Sharīf al-Jurjānī, *Sharḥ al-Mawāqif* (Cairo: al-Maṭba'a al-'Āmira al-Sharafiyya, 1292AH), 2: 492.
28. Aḥmad al-Ramlī, *Fatāwā* [printed on the margins of Ibn Ḥajar al-Haytamī, *al-Fatāwā al-kubrā al-fiqhiyya* (Cairo: al-Maṭba'a al-Muyammaniyya, 1308H)], 4:263–284. Interestingly, though al-Ramlī cited the *kalām* works of al-Bayḍāwī, al-Ījī and al-Taftāzānī, he explicitly stated that he had not read Ash'arī's *al-Ibāna* (p.269).
29. Aḥmad al-Nafarāwī, *al-Fawākih al-dawānī 'alā Risālat Ibn Abī Zayd al-Qayrawānī* (Beirut: Dār al-Ma'rifa, n.d. [reprint]), 1:55–56.
30. This is stated clearly in *al-Mawāqif* by 'Aḍud al-Dīn al-Ījī. see Jurjānī, *Sharḥ al-Mawāqif*, 2:366.
31. For the difference between early Ash'arī and Ḥanbalī construals of *bi-la kayfa*, see R. Frank, "Elements in the Development of the Teachings of al-Ash'arī", *Le Museon* 104 (1991): 154–168.
32. 'Abd al-Ra'ūf al-Munāwī, *Sharḥ al-Shamā'il* (MS British Library; Or. 12522), fol. 148a. The passage is quoted in al-Ālūsī, *Jalā' al-'aynayn*, 569, though al-Ālūsī left out the first sentence in which al-Munāwī agreed that Ibn Taymiyya and Ibn Qayyim al-Jawziyya were innovators (*mubtadi'a*). The British Library manuscript from which I have quoted was written in 999/1590–1, 32 years before the death of al-Munāwī, and may be an autograph.
33. 'Abd al-Ra'ūf al-Munāwī, *al-Fayḍ al-qadīr sharḥ al-Jāmi' al-ṣaghīr* (Beirut: Dār al-Kutub al-'Ilmiyya, 2001), 1:605 (Hadīth no. 941)
34. Ibid., 2:481 (Hadith no. 2086).
35. 'Alī al-Qāri' al-Harawī, *Jam' al-wasā'il fī sharḥ al-Shamā'il* (Istanbul: Maṭba'at Shaykh Yaḥyā, 1290AH), 200.
36. Harawī, *Jam' al-wasā'il*, 201.
37. Ahmet Mağnisāvī, *Sharḥ al-Fiqh al-akbar*, in *al-Rasā'il al-sab'a fī al-'aqā'id* (Hyderabad: Jam'iyyat Dā'irat al-Ma'ārif al-'Uthmāniyya, 1948), 68.
38. Ahmet Beyâzî, *Ishārat al-marām min 'ibārat al-imām*, ed. by Y. 'Abd al-Razzāq (Cairo: Muṣṭafā al-Bābī al-Ḥalabī, 1949), 186–187; Eyyüp Kefevî, *al-Kulliyyāt*, ed. by 'A. Darwish & M. al-Miṣrī (Damascus: Wizārat al-Thaqāfa, 1974), 3: 97–99.

39. *Al-Fiqh al-akbar* [printed with Maghnīsāwī's *Sharḥ*], 34.
40. 'Alī al-Qārī' al-Harawī, *al-Asrār al-marfū'a fī al-akhbār al-mawḍū'a*, ed. M. Ṣabbāgh (Beirut: Mu'assasat al-Risāla, 1971), 205.
41. 'Alī al-Qārī' al-Harawī, *Sharḥ bad' al-amālī* (Istanbul: Maṭba'at al-Ḥaydarī, 1295AH), 7–9.
42. Ibid., 11.
43. Ibid., 11.
44. Ibn Ḥajar al-Haytamī, *al-Fatāwā al-kubrā al-fiqhiyya* (Cairo: al-Maṭba'a al-Muyammaniyya, 1308AH), 2: 24.
45. Ibn Ḥajar al-Haytamī, *al-Jawhar al-munaẓẓam fī ziyārat al-qabr al-sharīf al-nabawī al-mukarram*, ed. M. Zaynhum (Cairo: Maktabat Madbūlī, 2000), 17.
46. Ibid., 29–30.
47. Ibid., 31.
48. Ibid., 35–36.
49. Ibid., 31.
50. Abū Ḥāmid al-Ghazālī, *Iḥyā' 'ulūm al-dīn*, printed on the margins of Muḥammad Murtaḍā al-Zabīdī, *Itḥāf al-sāda al-muttaqīn bi-sharḥ Iḥyā' 'ulūm al-dīn* (Cairo: al-Maṭba'a al-Muyammaniyya, 1311AH), 4:286.
51. C.S. Taylor, *In the Vicinity of the Righteous: Ziyāra and the Veneration of Muslim Saints in Late Medieval Egypt* (Leiden: Brill, 1999), chapter 5 (especially pp. 203–204).
52. Ibn Ḥajar al-'Asqalānī, *Fatḥ al-bārī sharḥ Ṣaḥīḥ al-Bukhārī* (Cairo: Muṣṭafā al-Bābī al-Ḥalabī, 1959), 3:307.
53. Ibid., 3:308.
54. *Sunan al-Nasā'ī bi-sharḥ al-Suyūṭī wa-ḥāshiyat al-Sindī* (Cairo: al-Maktaba al-Tijāriyya, 1930), 2:37–38; Aḥmad al-Qasṭallānī, *Irshād al-sārī ilā sharḥ Ṣaḥīḥ al-Bukhārī* (Bulaq: Dār al-Ṭibā'a, 1285H), 2:390; 'Alī al-Qārī' al-Harawī, *Mirqāt al-mafātīḥ sharḥ Mishkāt al-maṣābīḥ* (Beirut: Dār al-Fikr, 1992), 2:397; 'Abd al-Ra'ūf al-Munāwī, *al-Fayḍ al-qadīr*, 6:523–524; 'Alī al-'Azīzī al-Būlāqī, *al-Sirāj al-munīr sharḥ al-Jāmi' al-ṣaghīr* (Cairo: 'Isā al-Bābī al-Ḥalabī, 1939), 3:462.
55. Aḥmad al-Khafājī, *Nasīm al-riyāḍ fī sharḥ Shifā' al-Qāḍī 'Iyāḍ* (Beirut: Dār al-Kutub al-'Ilmiyya, 2001), 1:14.
56. Khafājī, *Nasīm al-riyāḍ*, 5:96–100.
57. Ibid., 5:100–101.
58. 'Alī al-Qārī' al-Harawī, *Sharḥ al-Shifā'* (Beirut: Dār al-Kutub al-'Ilmiyya, 2001), 2:152.
59. Najm al-Dīn al-Ghazzī, *al-Kawākib al-sā'ira*, 1:127.
60. Ḥājjī Khalīfa, *Kashf al-ẓunūn 'an asāmī al-kutub wa-al-funūn* (Istanbul: Wikālat al-Ma'ārif al-Jalīla, 1941–43), 2:1896–1897.
61. Muḥammad ibn 'Abd al-Bāqī al-Zurqānī, *Sharḥ al-Mawāhib al-laduniyya* (Cairo, 1291AH), 8:340.
62. Ibid., 8:343.
63. Ibid., 8:343.
64. Al-Ḥaṭṭāb (d. 1547), *Sharḥ Mukhtaṣar Khalīl* (printed along with the commentary of al-Mawwāq [d. 1492] on the same work on the margins) (Cairo: Maṭba'at al-Sa'āda, 1328AH), 3:139; Muḥammad al-Kharashī (d. 1689), *Sharḥ Mukhtaṣar Khalīl* (with the glosses of 'Alī al-'Adawī al-Sa'īdī [d. 1775]) (Cairo: al-Maṭba'a al-'Āmira al-Sharafiyya, 1316AH), 2:248; Aḥmad al-Dardīr (d. 1786), *al-Sharḥ al-kabīr 'alā Mukhtaṣar Khalīl* (with the glosses of Muḥammad ibn 'Arafa al-Dasūqī [d. 1815]) (Cairo: Maṭba'at Dār al-Sa'āda, 1911), 2:55.

65. Al-Zurqānī, *Sharḥ al-Mawāhib al-laduniyya*, 8:343–4.
66. Ibid., 8: 361. Khalīl would seem to be quoting from Ibn al-Ḥājj (d. 1336), *al-Madkhal* (Beirut: Dār al-Kitāb al-ʿArabī, 1972), 1: 253.
67. Al-Munāwī, *Fayḍ al-qadīr*, 2:170.
68. See in particular G. Makdisi, "Hanbalite Islam", in M. Swartz (ed. and trans.), *Studies in Islam* (New York & London: Oxford University Press, 1981), 216–274; G. Makdisi, "Ashʿarī and the Ashʿarites in Islamic Religious History", *Studia Islamica* 17 (1962):37–80 and 18 (1963):19–39; G. Makdisi, "The Sunni Revival", in D.S. Richards (ed.), *Islamic Civilization, 950–1150* (Oxford: Cassirer, 1973), 155–168.
69. Makdisi's claims have already been rejected by W. Madelung in his "The Spread of Maturidism and the Turks", reprinted in W. Madelung, *Religious Schools and Sects in Medieval Islam* (Ashgate: Variorum Reprints, 1985), p.110n3. Madelung cites pre-thirteenth-century material in support of the view that Ashʿarism was predominant amongst Shāfiʿīs and Mālikīs by the thirteenth century at the latest.
70. Quoted in Zabīdī, *Itḥāf al-sāda al-muttaqīn*, 2:7–8.
71. ʿAbdallāh al-ʿAyyāshī, *al-Riḥla al-ʿAyyāshiyya* (Rabat: Dār al-Maghrib, 1977 [reprint]), 1:402–403.
72. Taftāzānī, *Sharḥ al-ʿAqāʾid al-Nasafiyya*, 16–17. The glosses of Kastalî are printed on the margins of the edition. The glosses of Hayâlî are printed in an appendix with independent pagination.
73. Zabīdī, *Itḥāf al-sāda al-muttaqīn*, 2:6ff.
74. Ibid., 2:11. Zabīdī is quoting from al-Subkī's *al-Sayf al-ṣaqīl fī al-radd ʿalā Ibn Zafil*, see *al-Rasāʾil al-Subkiyya*, 84–85.
75. Ḥisnī, *Dafʾ shubah man shabbaha wa tamarrada*, 236–7.
76. Ibn Ḥajar al-Haytamī, *al-Jawhar al-munaẓẓam*, 31.
77. Najm al-Dīn al-Ghazzī, *Luṭf al-samar wa qaṭf al-thamar min tarājim aʿyān al-ṭabaqa al-ūlā min al-qarn al-ḥādī ʿashar*, ed. Maḥmūd al-Shaykh (Damascus: Manshūrāt Wizārat al-Thaqāfa, 1981), 1:268.
78. Al-Ghazzi, *al-Kawākib al-sāʾira*, 3: 314–346. Al-Ghazzi mentions one work by Ibn Taymiyya's grandfather Majd al-Dīn ibn Taymiyya (d. 1254)—a handbook on Ḥanbalī law entitled *al-Muḥarrar*.
79. ʿAbd al-Raḥmān al-Jabartī, *ʿAjāʾib al-āthār fī al-tarājim wa-al-akhbār* (Cairo: al-Maṭbaʿa al-ʿĀmira, 1297AH), 1:309–310, 1:390–391, 2:25–26, 2:227–228, 4:185–186.
80. Aḥmad al-Nakhlī, *Bughyat al-ṭālibīn li-bayān al-mashāyikh al-muḥaqqiqīn al-muʿtamadīn* (Hyderabad: Dāʾirat al-Maʿārif al-ʿUthmāniyya, 1328AH).
81. Sālim ibn ʿAbdallāh al-Baṣrī, *al-Imdād bi-maʿrifat ʿuluww al-isnād* (Hyderabad: Dāʾirat al-Maʿārif al-ʿUthmāniyya, 1328AH).
82. Abū al-Mawāhib al-Ḥanbalī, *Mashyakha*, ed. Muḥammad Muṭīʿ Ḥāfiẓ (Damascus & Beirut: Dār al-Fikr, 1990).
83. Ḥājjī Khalīfa, *Kashf al-ẓunūn*, 2:1872.
84. Ibid., 2:1438.
85. Ibid., 2:1078.
86. Ibrāhīm al-Kūrānī, *al-Amam li-īqāẓ al-himam* (Hyderabad: Dāʾirat al-Maʿārif al-ʿUthmāniyya, 1328 [1910]), 100.
87. ʿAyyāshī, *Riḥla*, 1:399.
88. Ibid., 1:399.
89. Ibid., 1:401.

90. B. Nafi, "Tasawwuf and Reform in Pre-Modern Islamic Culture: In Search of Ibrahim al-Kūrānī", *Die Welt des Islams* 42 (2003): 307–355.
91. See A.H. Jones, "al-Kūrānī, Ibrāhīm", *Encyclopedia of Islam*, new ed.; and A. Knysh, "Ibrāhīm al-Kūrānī (d. 1101/1690): An Apologist for *waḥdat al-wujūd*", *Journal of the Royal Asiatic Society* 5 (1995): 39–47.
92. W.C. Chittick, *The Sufi Path of Knowledge: Ibn 'Arabī's Metaphysics of Imagination* (New York: SUNY Press, 1989), chapter 5 (especially pp. 199–202).
93. MS Chester Beatty 4443, fols. 42–54.
94. Al-Kūrānī repeatedly cited Ibn 'Arabī in all his major works, and never with any suggestion of disagreement. His citations from Ibn Taymiyya and Ibn Qayyim al-Jawziyya are much less regular, and his agreement with them often qualified.
95. Yaḥyā al-Shāwī, *al-Nabl al-raqīq fī ḥulqum al-sābb al-zindīq* (MS Süleymaniye: Laleli 3744), fol. 71b-72a.
96. See J.M.S. Baljon, *Religion and Thought of Shāh Walī Allāh al-Dihlawī* (Leiden: Brill, 1986), 200ff.
97. See Muḥammad Ḥayāt al-Sindī (d. 1750), *Tuḥfat al-anām fī al-'amal bi-ḥadīth al-nabī 'alayhi al-ṣalāt wa al-salām* (Beirut: Dār Ibn Ḥazm, 1993); Muḥammad Mu'īn al-Thattawī (d. 1748), *Dirāsat al-labīb fī al-uswa al-ḥasana bi-al-ḥabīb* (Karachi: Sindhi Adabi Board, 1957) and Ṣāliḥ al-Fūlānī (d. 1803), *Īqāẓ himam ūlī al-abṣār li-al-iqtidā' bi-sayyid al-muhājirīn wa al-anṣār* (printed with no date and place of publication in the series *al-Salafiyyūn yataḥaddathūn*, vol. 6). The first of these works has been discussed in B. Nafi, "A Teacher of Ibn 'Abd al-Wahhāb: Muḥammad Ḥayāt al-Sindī and the Revival of Aṣḥāb al-Ḥadīth's Methodology", *Islamic Law & Society* 13 (2006): 208–241.
98. It may be noted in this context that Ṣafī al-Dīn al-Bukhārī (d. 1786), who wrote perhaps the first book-length apology for Ibn Taymiyya by a non-Ḥanbalī scholar since the early fifteenth century, was both a Hadith scholar and a Khalwatī Sufi initiated by the prominent Medinan mystic Muḥammad ibn 'Abd al-Karīm al-Sammān (d. 1776), who in turn was a disciple of the Damascene Muṣṭafā al-Bakrī (d. 1749)—an influential adherent of the ideas of Ibn 'Arabī. Bukhārī disagreed with Ibn Taymiyya's position on *ziyāra* and on divorce, and explicitly defended the view that Ibn 'Arabī was a saint. (See his *al-Qawl al-jalī fī tarjamat Taqī al-Dīn Ibn Taymiyya al-Ḥanbalī*, ed. by S. al-Dakhīl [Riyad: Dār al-Waṭan, 1999]. Note however that the Saudi editors of the work have carefully omitted any reference to Bukhārī's Sufi affiliations in their introduction. For these, see the introduction to Bukhārī's *Mu'jam*, edited by M. M. Ḥāfiẓ [Damascus: Dār al-Bashā'ir, 1999].) It is interesting and revealing that a person with such affiliations and views should have gone out of his way to defend Ibn Taymiyya. Presumably, what was at stake was not just an academic question about the orthodoxy or otherwise of a long dead fourteenth-century scholar. The issue clearly had a contemporary relevance in the eighteenth century, and was a part of broader polemical struggle between established jurisprudence and Hadith-oriented scholars with Sufi affiliations.
99. Mehmet Birgiwî, *Risāla fī ziyārat al-qubūr*, printed under the title *Ziyārat al-qubūr al-shar'iyya wa al-shirkiyya* (Cairo: Maṭba'at al-Imām, no date). However, there are manuscripts of this work that attribute it to either Sinân Yûsuf Amâsî (d. 1591) or Ahmet Rûmî Akhisârî (d. 1631/2). See R. Mach, *Catalogue of the Arabic Manuscripts (Yahuda Section) in the Garrett Collection, Princeton University Library* (Princeton: Princeton University Press, 1977), nos. 2471 and 2543.

100. Abū Saʻīd al-Khādimī, *al-Barīqa maḥmūdiyya bi-sharḥ al-Ṭarīqa al-Muḥammadiyya* (Cairo: Dār al-Ṭibaʻa al-Bāhira, 1257AH), 1: 176. Ibn al-Qayyim's vehement denial of the position that studying logic is a *farḍ kifāya* is quoted in Zabīdī, *Itḥāf al-sāda al-muttaqīn*, 1: 176.
101. Abū Saʻīd al-Khādimī, *al-Barīqa maḥmūdiyya*, 1:115–116. Compare Muḥammad al-Saffārīnī, *Lawā'iḥ al-anwār al-saniyya wa lawāqiḥ al-afkār al-sunniya*, ed. ʻAbd Allāh al-Basīrī (Riyadh: Maktabat al-Rushd, 2000), 1: 299ff.
102. Ibid., 1:117. Compare Saffārīnī, *Lawā'iḥ al-anwār al-saniyya*, 1: 1:232ff
103. Ibid., 1:113, 1:152–153.
104. Ibid., 1:151–152. This view is expressed in *al-Fiqh al-akbar* attributed to Abū Ḥanīfa, see *al-Rasā'il al-sabʻ fī al-ʻaqā'id*, 36.
105. Ibn Taymiyya, *al-Furqān bayna al-ḥaqq wa-al-bāṭil*, in *Majmūʻ Fatāwā* 13:156. The affinity between Ibn Taymiyya's views on this point and that of the Karrāmiyya (against whom the severe Maturidi position was presumably aimed) is noted in W. Madelung, *Religious Sects in Early Islamic Iran* Bibliothecia Persica, (Albany, NY: Persian Heritage Foundation, 1988), 43.
106. Davûd Karsî, *Sharḥ al-Nūniyya* (Istanbul: Mehmet Tâlib, 1318AH), 41. Karsî's affiliation with Birgiwî is apparent in his denunciation of monist mystics (*al-wujūdiyya al-malāḥida al-kafara*) on p. 17, and his statement that he composed the work in the city of Birgi "blessed by the presence of the deceased and the students there, and not by most of its inhabitants who are hypocrites (*munāfiqūn*)" on p. 131. Karsî also wrote an influential commentary on Birgiwî's *Uṣūl al-ḥadīth* (printed in Istanbul in 1275H, 1288H and 1326H).
107. On Shawkānī's religious thought, see B. Haykal, *Revival and Reform in Islam: The Legacy of Muḥammad al-Shawkānī* (Cambridge: Cambridge University Press, 2003), 76–108.
108. Ibn al-Amīr al-Ṣanʻānī, *Dīwān* (Medina: Manshūrāt al-Madīna, 1986), 108–109, 171–2; Muḥammad al-Shawkānī, *al-Badr al-ṭāliʻ bi-maḥāsin man baʻd al-qarn al-sābiʻ* (Cairo: Maṭbaʻat al-Saʻāda, 1348AH), 1: 63–72; 2: 143–146.
109. Ibn Sanad al-Baṣrī, *Maṭāliʻ al-Suʻūd*, ed. by Ra'ūf & Qaysī (Baghdad: al-Dār al-Waṭaniyya, 1991), 250.
110. B. Abu Manneh, "Salafiyya and the Rise of the Khālidiyya in Baghdad in the early nineteenth century", *Die Welt des Islams* 43 (2003): 354–361.
111. B. Abu Manneh, "The Naqshbandiyya-Mujaddidiyya in the Ottoman Lands in the Early 19th Century", *Die Welt des Islams* 22 (1982): 12–17.
112. See the quotation from Shaykh Khālid in al-Ālūsī, *Jalā' al-ʻaynayn*, 134–135.
113. Abu Manneh, "Salafiyya and the Rise of the Khālidiyya", 371. I am indebted to Abu Manneh's article, but he seems to me to be too quick to assume that the antagonism of the late nineteenth century was there from the outset.
114. Maḥmūd Shukrī al-Ālūsī, *al-Misk al-adhfar fī nashr mazāyā al-qarn al-thānī ʻashar wa-al-thālith ʻashar*, ed. ʻAbdallāh al-Jabbūrī (Riyadh: Dār al-ʻUlūm, 1982), 391.
115. Baṣrī, *Maṭāliʻ al-Suʻūd*, 133.
116. Khayr al-Dīn al-Ālūsī, *Jalā' al-ʻaynayn*, 2.
117. Ibid., 63, 111, 128, 133, 250.
118. Ibid., 16, 40–41, 339–340, 344–5, 381, 406–407, 415, 569.
119. Ibid., 220, 494–503. For Maḥmūd al-Ālūsī, see B. Nafi, "Abū'l-Thanā' Maḥmūd al-Ālūsī: an *ʻālim*, Ottoman mufti and exegete of the Qur'ān", *International Journal of Middle East Studies* 44 (2002): 465–494.
120. Maḥmūd al-Ālūsī, *Gharā'ib al-ightirāb* (Baghdad: Maṭbaʻat al-Shahbandār, 1327H), 388.

121. Ibid., 384.
122. Khayr al-Dīn al-Ālūsī, *Jalā' al-'aynayn*, 48–50, 175, 236.
123. Ibid., 442–465.
124. Al-Subkī makes the point in his *al-Sayf al-ṣaqīl*. See *al-Rasā'il al-Subkiyya*, 85. His remarks are quoted in Zabīdī, *Itḥāf al-sāda al-muttaqīn*, 2:11–12.
125. Ibn Ḥajar, *al-Jawhar al-munaẓẓam*, 38.
126. Al-Suyūṭī, *Sharḥ Sunan al-Nasā'ī*, 4:86. Al-Suyūṭī is quoting a statement from al-Ḥākim al-Nisābūrī (d. 1014), author of the influential *Mustadrak* on the *Ṣaḥīḥayn* of Bukhārī and Muslim. Ibn Ḥajar al-Haytamī himself rejected this position. See his *Tuḥfat al-muḥtāj fī sharḥ al-Minhāj* (Beirut: Dār Ṣādir [reprint of 1315H edition]), 3:197.
127. Ibn 'Ābidīn, *Radd al-muḥtār 'alā al-Durr al-mukhtār*, ed. Ḥusām al-Dīn ibn Muḥammad Ṣāliḥ Farfūr (Damascus: Dār al-Thaqāfa wa-al-Turāth, 2000), 5:350.
128. Ibn Ḥajar al-Haytamī, *al-Jawhar al-munaẓẓam*, 36.
129. Ibn Ḥajar al-Haytamī, *al-Fatāwā al-kubrā al-fiqhiyya*, 2:24; Ibn Ḥajar al-Haytamī, *al-Fatāwā al-ḥadīthiyya*, 150–1.
130. Ibn al-Ṭayyib al-Fāsī, *Sharḥ Ḥizb al-Imām al-Nawawī* (MS Princeton University Library: Yahuda 3861), fol. 135a–135b.
131. D.D. Commins, *Islamic Reform: Politics and Change in Late Ottoman Syria* (New York & Oxford: Oxford University Press, 1990), 25.
132. Muḥammad 'Abduh, *Risālat al-tawḥīd* [with annotations by Riḍā] (Beirut & Limassol: Dār Ibn Ḥazm, 2001), 78 (footnote 2).
133. In his super-commentary on al-Dawānī's *Sharḥ al-'Aqā'id al 'Aḍudiyya*, 'Abduh revealed the usual combination of unfamiliarity with the writings of Ibn Taymiyya and lack of sympathy for his reputed literalism. Al-Dawānī had mentioned that Ibn Taymiyya was one of those who had argued that the world—in this case the throne of God—was eternal in kind. 'Abduh commented that Ibn Taymiyya had been driven to this by his literal interpretation of the statement that God is on His throne, adding: "God be extolled! How ignorant is man, and how abominable is that which he finds correct! And I do not know if Ibn Taymiyya really said something like this. Often things are related of him that he has not said." As for the idea, also attributed to Ibn Taymiyya by al-Dawānī, that God is in the direction of above, 'Abduh commented: "He is most exalted above this! (*ta'alā 'an dhālika 'uluwwān kabīrān*)." See *Al-Shaykh Muḥammad 'Abduh bayna al-falāsifa wa-al-kalāmiyyīn*, ed. S. Dunyā (Cairo: Muṣṭafā al-Babī al-Ḥalabī, 1958), 1:82–83 and 1:533–4.

The Sensitive Puritan? Revisiting Ibn Taymiyya's Approach to Law and Spirituality in Light of 20th-century Debates on the Prophet's Birthday (*mawlid al-nabī*)

Raquel M. Ukeles

This paper argues that contemporary debates over Aḥmad Ibn Taymiyya's approach to the *mawlid al-nabī* festival illuminate complexities within Ibn Taymiyya's thinking regarding the relationship between law and spirituality. Ibn Taymiyya rules that the *mawlid* is a reprehensible innovation yet he also holds that certain *mawlid* practitioners deserve "a great reward (*ajr aẓīm*)."[1] Contemporary Salafis and Sufis each claim Ibn Taymiyya's support for their oppositional views by emphasizing one aspect of his position to the exclusion of the other. Salafis focus on Ibn Taymiyya's rejection of the *mawlid* while Sufis focus on Ibn Taymiyya's claim that some practitioners deserve a great reward. The first part of my paper examines these diverse and conflicting 20th century readings. Then, in the second part, I examine Ibn Taymiyya's approach to the *mawlid* in the context of medieval debates about the *mawlid* and his writings on other devotional innovations. Unlike the polarized views of contemporary Muslims, Ibn Taymiyya's narrow definition of normative devotional acts combined with his broad awareness of human spiritual needs forms a dynamically coherent religious legal perspective.

Introduction

In contemporary intra-Muslim debates played out across the pages of newspapers, in the writings of scholars and even on the Web, all groups recognize Aḥmad Ibn Taymiyya as a force to be reckoned with. Groups defining themsevles as Salafis hail Ibn Taymiyya as a heroic reformer who zealously defended the Prophet Muḥammad's way (*sunna*) and relentlessly struggled against myriad innovations (*bida'*).[2] Scholars and writers who define themselves as Sufis[3] vacillate between denouncing Ibn Taymiyya for his campaigns against traditional practices (and for his literalist theology) and valorizing him as a Sufi adorned with the cloak of the Qādiriyya Order.[4] In debates over devotional practices, Salafi writers generally downplay or ignore Ibn Taymiyya's sympathy for Sufism. Sufi polemicists, seeking to undermine the Salafi position, attempt either to marginalize Ibn Taymiyya's views or to reclaim them as pro-Sufi. Thus, the two groups, even within themselves, put forth radically different images of the medieval scholar.

Contemporary Salafi-Sufi contests over Ibn Taymiyya's legacy are clearly evident in their debates over the legal status of the Prophet's birthday festival (*mawlid al-nabī*, hereafter referred to as "the *mawlid*"). As will be discussed, most Salafis regard the *mawlid* as a reprehensible innovation, while Sufis uphold the day as one of the most important festivals in the Muslim calendar.[5] The controversial status of the *mawlid*, however, has long preceded these contemporary debates. Since the 12th century, Muslims throughout the world have celebrated the festival of the Prophet's birth, despite its universally-recognized status as a post-Prophetic innovation (*bid'a*).[6] In medieval legal debates about the status of post-Prophetic innovations, numerous jurists upheld the *mawlid* as the paradigm of the good innovation (*bid'a ḥasana*), whereas others rejected the *mawlid* as a way of demonstrating zero tolerance towards devotional innovations.[7] Among the medieval jurists, Ibn Taymiyya ruled that the *mawlid* is a reprehensible (*makrūh*) devotional innovation, since the pious ancestors (*salaf*) did not celebrate it.[8] At the same time, he recognized that some observe the Prophet's birthday out of a desire to show their love of the Prophet and thus deserve a great reward for their good intentions.[9] Ibn Taymiyya's two-part approach, i.e., his strict interpretation of Islamic devotional law and his appreciation of the intention to venerate the Prophet, renders his perspective distinct from both medieval and modern interlocutors on the *mawlid*. The subtlety of this approach is brought to the fore by the way in which each of the opponents in the contemporary *mawlid* debate claim to follow Ibn Taymiyya's position.

Contemporary (Mis) readings of Ibn Taymiyya

Most Sufi writers emphasize Ibn Taymiyya's assertion that some *mawlid* practitioners deserve a great reward and downplay or exclude his negative views on the *mawlid*. Sufi polemicists, in some cases, even turn Ibn Taymiyya's "great reward" statement into a wholehearted endorsement of the *mawlid*. For example, in an article by Hisham Kabbani, a Sufi scholar in America, the author focuses exclusively on the "great reward" statement and distorts Ibn Taymiyya's writing to claim that he approves of the *mawlid*.[10] Salafi writers, in contrast, focus only on Ibn Taymiyya's rejection of the *mawlid* as a reprehensible innovation. They acknowledge, and subsequently downplay, Ibn Taymiyya's "great reward" statement only in the context of rebutting the arguments of Sufi scholars. One can trace this pattern, for example, in the exchanges between Muḥammad b. Ibrāhīm Āl al-Shaykh, Muftī of Saudi Arabia and President of the Higher Council of *'Ulamā'*, and Muhammad Muṣṭafā al-Shanqīṭī, a Sufi-oriented writer.[11] Al-Shanqīṭī first wrote an article that appeared in the Saudi newspaper *al-Nadwa* in 1963, arguing in favor of the *mawlid* as a good innovation. Āl al-Shaykh's response to al-Shanqīṭī's article, called *Rejecting the Celebration of the Prophet's Birthday Festival* (*Fī inkār al-iḥtifāl bi-al-mawlid al-nabawī*), relied heavily on Ibn Taymiyya's rejection of devotional innovations in general and of the *mawlid* in particular. In al-Shanqīṭī's rebuttal, also published in *al-Nadwa* later that year, he challenged Āl al-Shaykh's reliance on Ibn Taymiyya, pointing to Ibn Taymiyya's position that certain *mawlid* practitioners receive a great reward. In fact, al-Shanqīṭī called his second article, "This is what Ibn Taymiyya says about the lawful celebration (*al-iḥtifāl al-mashrū'*) in commemoration of the Prophet's birthday," and argued that Ibn Taymiyya supported the observance of *mawlid* celebrations that are free of forbidden acts.[12] Only then did Āl al-Shaykh dedicate an appendix to acknowledging and then dismissing the relevance of Ibn Taymiyya's positive statements about *mawlid* given his clear ruling against the festival.[13]

Other Salafi scholars follow the pattern of ignoring Ibn Taymiyya's positive remark about the *mawlid* until they are forced to rationalize it. Ismā'īl b. Muḥammad al-Anṣārī (d. 1996), a Saudi Hadith scholar and an editor of Ibn Taymiyya's *al-'Aqīda al-Wāṣitiyya*, wrote a lengthy treatise against the *mawlid* called, *The Last Word on the Ruling*

Regarding Intercession with the Greatest of Messengers (al-Qawl al-faṣl fī ḥukm al-tawassul bi-khayr al-rusul).[14] At first, al-Anṣārī discussed only Ibn Taymiyya's negative views of the *mawlid*. He then mentioned the opposing positions of contemporary Muslim scholars, particularly that of Muḥammad 'Alawī (d. 2004), a leading Saudi scholar of Hadith and law and a member of the 'Alawī Sufi order.[15] 'Alawī, in response to an earlier *fatwā* against the *mawlid* by the previous Mufti of Saudi Arabia, 'Abd al-'Azīz b. 'Abdallāh b. Bāz (d. 1999), had written a short treatise in its favor entitled, "On celebrating the noble Prophet's birthday (*Ḥawl al-iḥtifāl bi-al-mawlid al-nabawī al-sharīf*)."[16] In his treatise, 'Alawī cited Ibn Taymiyya's praise of certain *mawlid* practitioners in defense of the *mawlid*. Unlike the other Sufi scholars mentioned, 'Alawī did not recast Ibn Taymiyya's notion of a reward awaiting some *mawlid* practitioners as a wholehearted endorsement. However, he did engage in selective reading when he included Ibn Taymiyya's words under the heading, "Shaykh Ibn Taymiyya's opinion states: some of the people might receive a reward for practicing the *mawlid*."[17] Al-Anṣārī later criticized 'Alawī for distorting Ibn Taymiyya's views.

Whereas most Salafi scholars dismiss the significance of Ibn Taymiyya's affording a great reward to some *mawlid* practitioners, Muḥammad Ḥāmid al-Fiqī (d. 1959), an Egyptian Salafi scholar and a prolific editor of Ḥanbalī texts, candidly expresses his astonishment at Ibn Taymiyya's position and asks:

> How can they receive a reward for this, when they are opposing the guidance of God's messenger (pbuh) and the guidance of his Companions? And if one said, because they exercised independent reasoning (*ijtihād*) and erred, then we say: What *ijtihād* is this? Is abandoning the authoritative texts on devotional acts (*nuṣūṣ al-'ibādāt*) a [proper] domain for *ijtihād*?[18]

Al-Fiqī thus regards the notion of rewarding *mawlid* practitioners for their intentions as implausible and irreconcilable with the legal reprehensibility of the *mawlid* practice.

Each of these contemporary readers regards Ibn Taymiyya's composite ruling—against the *mawlid* and in favor of rewarding some of its practitioners—as deeply problematic if not internally contradictory, and thus subject to distortion or emendation in one direction or another. These contemporary (mis) readings highlight an intriguing element of Ibn Taymiyya's position—one that demands further exploration.

Ibn Taymiyya, in his Own Words, on the *Mawlid*

How does Ibn Taymiyya himself reconcile these seemingly contradictory positions? Ibn Taymiyya discusses the *mawlid* festival in a legal opinion (*fatwā*) and in his polemical treatise against Muslim participation in non-Muslim festivals, *The Necessity of the Straight Path to Oppose the Followers of Hellfire* (*Iqtiḍā' al-ṣirāṭ al-mustaqīm li-mukhālafat aṣḥāb al-jaḥīm*—hereafter, *Iqtiḍā'*). The *fatwā* responds to the question, "can one recite the whole Qur'an (*khatma*) in honor of the Prophet's birthday?"[19] Rather than limiting himself to this question, Ibn Taymiyya takes the opportunity to address all innovated festivals. He writes:

> The gathering of people for a banquet during the two [canonical] festivals or the 11th–13th of Dhū al-Ḥijja (*ayyām al-tashrīq*)[20] is a normative commendable practice (*sunna*), these being among the rites of Islam that the Messenger of God (pbuh) instituted for Muslims, and [similarly] caring for the poor by feeding them during the month of Ramadan is one of the commendable norms (*sunan*) of Islam. For the Prophet (pbuh) had said: "whoever provides breakfast food for one who is fasting, he receives akin to his reward, and helping the poor [Qur'ān] reciters is a pious act (*'amal ṣāliḥ*) at any time, and whoever supports them shares in their reward. And as for the establishment of a seasonal festival (*mawsim*) that is not among the lawful (*shar'iyya*) festivals, such as one of the nights of Rabī' al-Awwal, which is said to be the night of the *mawlid*, or one of the nights of Rajab, or the 18th day of Dhū al-Ḥijja or the first Friday prayer of Rajab or the eighth of Shawwāl, which the ignorant call the festival of the righteous ones (*'īd al-abrār*), these are among the innovations (*bida'*) that the ancestors (*salaf*) did not recommend nor did they practice, and God Sublime and Exalted knows best.[21]

As a legal question, the *mawlid* is thus an innovation (*bid'a*) and, consonant with Ibn Taymiyya's general approach to *bid'a*, is reprehensible. Ibn Taymiyya was one of the most vociferous medieval proponents of realigning Muslim normative practice with the Prophet's Sunna and of censuring all *bida'*, by which he meant primarily all devotional practices that could not be traced to the Prophet or the early Muslim community.[22] Since the pious ancestors (*al-salaf al-ṣāliḥ*) of the early Muslim community did not observe the festival, which also implies that no early textual source exists condoning the practice, the festival is not lawful.

Given the simplicity of Ibn Taymiyya's legal position on the *mawlid*, his circuitous approach to answering the question is puzzling. First, Ibn Taymiyya describes the festivals that are lawful and that present opportunities for pious and righteous deeds. Then, he lists several festivals that Muslims have innovated. Among these is the Prophet's birthday, for which there is no precedent in the practice of the early ancestors. Why does Ibn Taymiyya review legally permissible festivals before addressing the *mawlid* as one example in the general category of innovated festivals? The answer, I believe, may be found by examining Ibn Taymiyya's more systematic exposition of the *mawlid* and other innovated festivals in *Iqtiḍā'*.

Ibn Taymiyya, in his treatment of the *mawlid* in *Iqtiḍā'*, first establishes his legal position by situating the festival within his typology of innovations. But he does not limit his treatment to the *mawlid*'s legal status. He chooses to expand the discussion by recognizing and addressing those psychological and spiritual aspects of devotional practice that can often stand in tension with legal norms.

Ibn Taymiyya discusses the Prophet's birthday festival within the context of his discussion of innovations of time.[23] Although he recognizes the Prophet's birthday as an actual day in Islamic history, Ibn Taymiyya rejects the festival's legitimacy since the Divine law does not identify the day as worthy of special attention.[24] The observance of the *mawlid* is a reprehensible innovation, since it lacks textual attestation or a precedent in the practice of the *salaf*. Ibn Taymiyya notes that the Prophet's Companions—who loved and venerated him best, and were the most diligent in performing good works—did not institute a celebration of the Prophet's birthday even when it would have been natural for them to do so. Therefore, he rules, the *mawlid* ought not to be celebrated.

At the same time, Ibn Taymiyya recognizes that people observe the *mawlid* for different reasons and should be recompensed according to their intentions. Some, for example, observe the *mawlid* out of a desire to imitate the Christian celebration of Jesus' birthday on Christmas. This intention is reprehensible, as Ibn Taymiyya amply demonstrates throughout his treatise. He recognizes, however, that others observe the *mawlid* out of great love and reverence for the Prophet (*maḥabbatan li-al-nabī wa-ta‘ẓīman*).[25] In his view, these people, however misguided, should be rewarded for this love as well as for their independent reasoning (*ijtihād*) in determining the *mawlid* to be lawful.[26] Still, the celebrants are not rewarded for participating in the innovated act itself. Later, he articulates this idea in stronger terms: "A person may venerate the *mawlid* and make it a seasonal festival (*mawsim*), and deserve a great reward (*ajr aẓīm*) because of his good purpose (*li-ḥusn qaṣdihi*) and his veneration of the Messenger of God".[27] Ibn Taymiyya acknowledges the pious purpose of the celebrants of the *mawlid*, and even anticipates their being rewarded. However, their good purpose does not change the status of the *mawlid* as a reprehensible innovation.

Through his discussion of the *mawlid*, Ibn Taymiyya develops a hierarchy of religious behavior by taking into account both the letter and the spirit of the law. Although Ibn Taymiyya appreciates the love of the Prophet expressed in the *mawlid* celebration, he sees it as clearly inferior to the love expressed through following the Prophet's normative way (*sunna*) as embodied in the practice of the *salaf*. The ideal Muslim, whom Ibn Taymiyya later calls the rightly-guided believer (*al-mu'min al-musaddad*), expresses his love for the Prophet by limiting his actions to the norms set out by the Prophet.[28] With a touch of sarcasm, Ibn Taymiyya notes that those who are diligent in practicing these kinds of innovations, "with the good purpose and independent reasoning that brings them reward," are often lax about obeying the Prophet's express command.[29]

Unlike the ideal of the early Muslim community, the community contemporary to Ibn Taymiyya was a composite of good and bad elements that echoed the status of the *mawlid* itself:

> Know that an act may have good (*khayr*) in it, inasmuch as it incorporates elements of the lawful (*mashrū‘*), and evil (*sharr*) in it as well, such as being an innovation (*bid‘a*); and thus the act is good according to the legally ordained elements included and evil in proportion to how much it turns away from the [normative] religion, as in the case of the hypocrites (*munāfiqūn*) and sinners (*fāsiqūn*). In later times, most of the community have fallen sway (*ubtuliya*) to this.[30]

The community of Ibn Taymiyya's time combines licit practices and pious intentions with innovated and deviant ones. Given this reality, Ibn Taymiyya suggests that the role of the scholar is first and foremost to be a model of righteous behavior, adhering to the Sunna and practicing good works.[31] Second, one should intelligently encourage others to follow the Sunna, by paying close attention to the religious and emotional background of the practitioner:

> If you see someone observing [the *mawlid*] and you know that he would only abandon it for worse (*sharr minhu*), do not summon him to abandon a detestable deed (*munkar*) for an even more detestable one, nor should you enjoin him to abandon something obligatory or recommended, which [its abandonment] would be worse than observing this reprehensible deed (*makrūh*). But if there was a good element in the innovated practice (*bid'a*), substitute it for a lawful good (*khayr mashrū'*) to the best of your ability. Since people do not relinquish something without something [to replace it], and it is not necessary to abandon something good except for something equally good or better.[32]

Although he is clear about the *mawlid*'s legal status, Ibn Taymiyya, as a pragmatist, was keenly aware of the emotional and psychological elements at play in religious practice. He urges that one should not admonish an observer of the *mawlid* to abandon his innovated practice without providing a substitute normative practice through which he could channel his piety.

Here, Ibn Taymiyya sets up two levels of religious expectations. The Muslim who engages in innovated practices out of misdirected piety may be rewarded greatly for his good purpose (as cited above), whereas the rightly-guided believer (*al-mu'min al-musaddad*) would not be rewarded, since, "what is good for some people is repugnant for the rightly-guided believer."[33] He brings a precedent from the eponym of his school, Aḥmad b. Ḥanbal, who responded to reports of a ruler spending 1, 000 dinars on a copy of the Qur'ān by saying, "Let him, for this is the best way to spend his money." As Ibn Taymiyya explains,

> This was despite his legal position that adorning Qur'ān copies is reprehensible. One of the disciples interpreted [his statement] to mean that the prince spent [money] on fine paper and calligraphy. However, this was not Aḥmad's intended [meaning], rather his intended [meaning]

was that this deed had a benefit (*maṣlaḥa*) as well as a negative element (*mafsada*) that rendered [the deed] reprehensible.[34]

Even though Ibn Ḥanbal ruled that adorning the Qur'ān is reprehensible, he recognized the positive elements in the ruler's actions in addition to the negative elements that led to the act's legal status. Just as Ibn Ḥanbal preferred the ruler spending money on a Qur'ān rather than "immoral books, such as entertainment and poetry, or Persian or Greek philosophy," so too Ibn Taymiyya develops the notion of relative goods among popular practices.[35]

It is true that Ibn Taymiyya develops this relativistic approach in his polemical treatise, designed to convince the educated Muslim public to abandon innovated practices. Yet, this approach is part of an attempt to draw the participants in devotional innovations into the circle of what he perceived as the Sunni community, rather than leave them outside. Ibn Taymiyya sifts between the positive and negative elements within popular practice without relinquishing the ideal that he strives for, both individually and communally.

We can now, perhaps, understand better the seemingly circuitous structure of Ibn Taymiyya's *fatwā* on the *mawlid*. The first half of the *fatwā*, which may have seemed like an odd digression, represents his reform program in action. That is, one should not censure a Muslim for celebrating the *mawlid* unless one recommends orthodox occasions into which the hapless celebrant can channel his pietistic urges. Ibn Taymiyya thus recommends a number of such orthodox occasions before he succinctly dismisses the whole group of innovated festivals. By identifying a number of opportunities for hosting banquets and doing good works, Ibn Taymiyya seeks to transfer the efforts exerted for the innovated festivals to legally sanctioned time periods and rituals. Pulling together Ibn Taymiyya's writings on the *mawlid*, we can begin to understand how his restrictive approach to defining normative devotional acts coheres with his more expansive recognition of pious intentions beyond the boundaries of text-based norms. Within Ibn Taymiyya's system, these two elements interact in an ongoing process of narrowing the gap between devotional norms and spiritual needs.

The *mawlid* in the Medieval Legal Context

The distinctiveness of Ibn Taymiyya's position becomes strikingly clear when juxtaposed with the opinions of other medieval jurists on the *mawlid*. Almost all other jurists regarded the *mawlid* either as a meritorious event that was legally commendable or as a hedonistic festival that was legally reprehensible or forbidden. That is, most jurists linked their legal positions on the *mawlid* as an innovation with their attitudes towards the value of the practices involved.

For many medieval jurists, the *mawlid*, which venerated the Prophet's birth and showed gratitude to God for sending him, was the most compelling of all the popular devotional innovations. For example, the Shafiʿī jurist ʿAbd al-Raḥmān Abū Shāma (d. ca. 665/1268) identified the commemoration of the Prophet's birthday festival as the example *par excellence* of a praiseworthy innovation. In his treatise on *bidʿa*, Abū Shāma writes:

> Among the most beautiful of these types of matters [i.e., good innovations], of what has been innovated (*ubtudiʿa*) during our time, is what was done in the city of Irbil—may God exalted keep it strong—every year on the day corresponding with the birthday of the Prophet, peace and blessings of God upon him, including voluntary contributions of alms (*ṣadaqāt*), good deeds (*al-maʿrūf*) and the displays of splendor and joy. For these [practices] are, together with beneficent acts toward the poor (*al-iḥsān ilā al-fuqarāʾ*), a visible expression (*mashʿar*) of love for the Prophet, out of reverence and veneration for him in the heart of the practitioner, and out of gratitude to God, may He be exalted, for the blessing that He bestowed upon [the practitioner], that is, bringing forth His messenger that He sent as a mercy for humankind and [out of gratitude] for all messengers. And the first one who practiced that was *Shaykh* ʿUmar ibn Muḥammad al-Mallāʾ, one of the famous holy men, and the Lord of Irbil and others—God's mercy be upon them—followed him in that.[36]

Abū Shāma acknowledges that the *mawlid* celebration is a *bidʿa* and even identifies the originator of the festival by name.[37] He then describes the practices that took place on this day, namely, pious works, alms-giving and regal displays; it is noteworthy that Abū Shāma only mentions acts that are universally acknowledged as meritorious. Finally, he alludes to the purpose of this festival, which is the demonstration of one's love and veneration for the Prophet as well as gratitude to God for sending this and other messengers to the world. Although Abū Shāma does not articulate what distinguishes this *bid'a* from other devotional innovations, his description suggests that its legal status is grounded in three virtuous aspects of the practice: the pious intent and status of the originator, the meritorious nature of the practices involved, and the piety of the overarching purpose of this festival. Later proponents of the *mawlid* based their legal support for the festival on these virtuous aspects as well.[38]

In sharp contrast, the Mālikī jurists Tāj al-Dīn al-Fākihānī (d. 734/1334) and Ibn al-Ḥājj al-'Abdarī (d. 737/1336) rejected the *mawlid* festival as a blameworthy innovation and saw nothing redeeming about its associated practices. Al-Fākihānī describes the *mawlid* as "an innovation that was created (*aḥdathahā*) by idlers (*al-baṭṭālūn*) and by the vain desires to which the gluttons (*al-akkālūn*) abandon themselves."[39] That is, al-Fākihānī not only rejects the *mawlid* on the basis of its being an innovation, but he also dismisses the merit of all three aspects that Abū Shāma discussed in his defense of the *mawlid*: the piety of the festival's originator, the merits of the practices involved, and the purposes of these practices. Ibn al-Ḥājj, who at least recognizes the potential merit of a day celebrating the Prophet's birth, bemoans the gap between the decadent nature of the popular *mawlid* celebration and the sacredness of the occasion:

> Among the [innovations and reprehensible deeds] are the performance of singers accompanied by percussive instruments like jingling tambourines, reed flutes and other instruments, which they use for musical sessions (*samā'*). In doing so, they carry out blameworthy customs (*'awā'id dhamīma*) because they engage in innovations and reprehensible acts during times that God has favored and venerated. If there is no doubt that musical concerts [pose numerous problems] on other nights, how much more so when [these acts] are associated with the virtue (*faḍīla*) of this great month that God—may He be exalted—venerated and favored us by this noble Prophet. For, what connection is there between percussive instruments on the one hand, and the esteem for this noble month in which God bestowed upon us the lord of the early and late [messengers] on the other hand?[40]

In Ibn al-Ḥājj's description, popular celebrations of the noble Prophet's birth teem with reprehensible acts, chief among them singing and dancing with musical instruments, which undermine the venerable status of the Prophet. Although Ibn al-Ḥājj applauds the desire to venerate the Prophet's birth, he ultimately rejects the *mawlid* festival as a day of reprehensible, if not sinful, deeds and as an innovation that deviates from the Prophet's own practice.

Unlike the Shāfiʿī proponents of the *mawlid* who declared it to be a commendable innovation (*bidʿa ḥasana*) on the basis of its virtuous purpose, Ibn Taymiyya does not allow the merit of pious intentions to affect the outcome of his legal ruling. On the other hand, unlike al-Fākihānī and Ibn al-Ḥājj who disparage *mawlid* practitioners as pleasure-seeking idlers, Ibn Taymiyya recognizes the pious intentions of some *mawlid* observers and anticipates a reward for them. Within the spectrum of juristic approaches to the *mawlid*, Ibn Taymiyya upholds a narrow conception of the scope of the law paired with a broader spiritual approach.

Ibn Taymiyya on Other Devotional Innovations

Does Ibn Taymiyya's approach to the *mawlid* stem from something exceptional about the *mawlid* or does it represent his general approach to devotional innovations? To examine this question, I turn briefly to his writings on two other controversial devotional cases, those of auditory sessions (*samāʿ*) and of supplications (*duʿāʾ*) at the Prophet's grave. In these cases, consistent with his discussions of the *mawlid*, Ibn Taymiyya asserts that although the acts are innovations, certain pious practitioners are forgiven for their transgressions, and, in some cases, are even rewarded.

In a *fatwā* on auditory sessions (*samāʿ*), Ibn Taymiyya criticizes those who attend sessions that involve singing and clapping for participating in a reprehensible practice that was invented after the time of the Prophet and his Companions.[41] Ibn Taymiyya notes that the acts of clapping and whistling are marks of infidel prayer, which the Qurʾān condemns. Singing is, furthermore, an intoxicating practice that can lead to immoral acts. Ibn Taymiyya asserts that "innovated *samāʿ*" is of the same genus (*jins*) as the *samāʿ* of polytheists, although he shies away from identifying the two as the same. However, Ibn Taymiyya concedes that certain righteous Sufi masters (*shuyūkh*) did engage in innovated *samāʿ* for sincere and pious reasons.[42] He subsequently asserts that these masters are forgiven for participating either because they were exercising their own judgment (*mujtahidīn*) or because they possessed other merits that erased this error (*li-ḥasanāt māḥiya*).[43] As in the case of the *mawlid*, Ibn Taymiyya recognizes the sincere piety that motivates certain *samāʿ* practitioners, yet rejects the form that their piety takes.

In his discussion of supplications (*duʿā'*) at the Prophet's grave, Ibn Taymiyya likewise rules that it is a reprehensible innovation, since the Prophet and his Companions did not pray at gravesites and since such prayers approximate polytheistic practices.[44] But at the same time, Ibn Taymiyya feels compelled to address the widespread popularity of these prayers, including its endorsement by early and later scholars. In particular, he cites a disagreement between the Medinan scholar Rabīʿa b. Abī ʿAbd al-Raḥmān (d. 135/753) and his companions, found in *Kitāb Akhbār al-Madīna*, regarding a man they witnessed uttering a personal prayer by the Prophet's grave. While his companions were shocked by this behavior, Rabīʿa dissuaded them from intervening by saying, "Let him be! A man receives [a reward] for his [good] intention! (*daʿūhu, fa-innamā li-al-mar' mā nawā*)."[45] Ibn Taymiyya interprets this tradition in the following way:

> Thus, there is a disagreement on that matter. But the justification of Rabīʿa for it, that every man receives [a reward] for his [good] intention, does not necessitate approval for that which he disapproved of.[46] For were [the man] to intend to pray the prayer rite there, [Rabīʿa] would have forbidden him, likewise were he to intend to pray at a[n incorrect] time, [Rabīʿa] would have forbidden him. What [Rabīʿa] meant was—and God knows best—that a person with a righteous intention can be rewarded for his intention (*man kāna lahu niyya ṣāliḥa uthība ʿalā niyyatihi*), even when he performs an act that is not lawful (*laysa bi-mashrūʿ*), as long as he did not mean to oppose the law. In other words, this supplication, even though it was not lawful, was undertaken with a righteous intention, for which the man is rewarded.[47]

Ibn Taymiyya uses this tradition first to assert that Rabīʿa's companions clearly held that such a prayer was prohibited, since they wanted to stop the man. Furthermore, Rabīʿa himself must have held that the prayer was not commendable, since he focused on the man's intention and not the status of his action; at the same time, though, Rabīʿa must have held that the act was not prohibited explicitly, otherwise Rabīʿa would have stopped the man as well. Ibn Taymiyya here distinguishes between supplicating at gravesites, which is reprehensible, and performing an obligatory prayer, which is prohibited. Thus, Ibn Taymiyya interprets Rabīʿa's statement to mean that a person with a pious intention can be rewarded for his intention even when he unwittingly performs an act that is reprehensible (*man kāna lahu niyya ṣāliḥa uthība ʿalā niyyatihi, wa-in kāna al-fiʿl alladhī faʿalahu laysa bi-mashrūʿ*).[48] Ibn Taymiyya's interpretation of Rabīʿa's statement echoes his own position on the *mawlid*, that a person can be rewarded for his intention even while his action is incorrect.

These two cases highlight Ibn Taymiyya's capacity to separate between sincere intentions and problematic actions, even if those actions lead others astray. The success of the supplicant at the Prophet's grave allows others to believe that his manner of prayer was proper, while it was actually due only to the sincerity of his heart at the moment of prayer (*bi-ṣidq qāma bi-qalb fāʿilihi ḥīn al-fiʿl*).[49] Likewise, when the students observe their Sufi masters achieving particular effects (*āthār*) from the heightened state brought out by music sessions, they mistakenly assume that this form of *samāʿ* is correct. In fact, says Ibn Taymiyya, the efficacy of their masters' states in fact derives from their exercising independent judgment (*mujtahidīn*) or from the merits of their purpose (*li-ḥasanāt qaṣdihim*).[50] Ibn Taymiyya affirms the benefits of sincerity and independent, albeit erroneous, reasoning even as he notes the resulting confusion among their followers.

Conclusion

This cursory examination of Ibn Taymiyya's treatment of *samāʿ* and *duʿāʾ* at the Prophet's grave suggests that Ibn Taymiyya generally recognizes positive elements in the performance of a devotional act that are not strictly connected to the act's legal status. His nuanced approach to the *mawlid* reflects a more general tendency to acknowledge the sincerity and righteousness of a practitioner's intentions while at the same time condemning the practice as a reprehensible innovation. Common elements in the three cases discussed underscore aspects of Ibn Taymiyya's position. In each case, Ibn Taymiyya links the practitioners' being forgiven or rewarded with (a) the piety of the person's intention or purpose (*niyya* or *qaṣd*)—distinct from the act itself; (b) his incorrect belief that the act is permissible (through exercising *ijtihād*); and (c) the subtle distinction between the reprehensible and the forbidden status of the act in question. In all three cases of devotional innovations, Ibn Taymiyya consistently recognizes the possibility of sincere and pious acts outside the boundaries of law while holding fast to his narrow definition of normative devotional behavior.

This image of Ibn Taymiyya as a firm yet sensitive pragmatist flies in the face of contemporary perceptions—both Western and Muslim—of the scholar as an intractable puritan. From a close examination of Ibn Taymiyya's writings on the *mawlid*, as well as other controversial devotional acts, we see how Ibn Taymiyya addresses the tension between grounding devotional practices in the restricted authority of the *sunna* and responding to the spiritual needs of the Muslim public in his own time. They also illuminate the ways in which contemporary Muslims are able to reinvent Ibn Taymiyya's legacy for a variety of purposes.

Notes

1. Ibn Taymiyya, *Iqtiḍā' al-ṣirāṭ al-mustaqīm li-mukhālafat ashāb al-jaḥīm*, ed. Nāṣir b. 'Abd al-Karīm al-'Aql (Riyadh: Maktabat al-Rushd, 2000), 2:123, 126.
2. The sheer number of Ibn Taymiyya's works edited and published by Saudi scholars, who identify themselves as Salafis, testifies to his central importance, as do the collections of Ibn Taymiyya's writings published together with that of Muḥammad Ibn 'Abd al-Wahhāb. See, for example, the volume of works by Ibn Taymiyya and Ibn 'Abd al-Wahhāb edited by the Mufti of Saudi Arabia, Muḥammad b. Ibrahīm Āl al-Shaykh, entitled *al-Majmū'a al-'ilmiyya al-sa'ūdiyya min durar shaykhay al-islām* (The Saudi Scientific Collection of the Pearls of the Two Masters of Islam) (Riyadh: Dār al-Ṭuwayq li-al-Nashr wal-Tawzī', 1997).
3. Yūsuf al-Rifā'ī, a contemporary Sufi scholar, defines Sufis as the great majority of Muslims in the majority of the Muslim countries who follow one of the four schools of law, uphold the doctrine of the pious ancestors (*'aqīdat al-salaf al-ṣāliḥ*)—including that of al-Ash'arī—and who practice the religious practices of their fathers such as observing the festivals of the Prophet's birthday (*mawlid*) and his night journey and ascension (*al-isrā' wa-al-mi'rāj*) in their proper times, visiting the Prophet's grave during the pilgrimage, completing the recitation of the Qur'ān on the third day after someone's death, using the prayer beads for remembering God, visiting the graves of relatives and reciting Qur'ān at their gravesites on holidays. Al-Rifā'ī refers to this group as the silent majority of Muslims whose beliefs and practices have been attacked in modern

times. Yusuf al-Sayyid Hāshim al-Rifāʿī, *al-Ṣūfiyya wa-al-taṣawwuf fī ḍawʾ al-kitāb wa-al-sunna* (Kuwait, 1999), 1–2.

4. For details on Ibn Taymiyya's affiliation with the Qādiriyya and evidence of his affirmed spiritual discipleship of Abd al-Qādir al-Jīlānī, see George Makdisi, "Ibn Taimīya: A Ṣūfi of the Qādiriya Order," *American Journal of Arabic Studies*, 1 (1973): 118–129.
5. For an extensive and colorful set of examples—modern and medieval—regarding the proponents and opponents of the *mawlid*, see Annemarie Schimmel on "The Celebration of the Prophet's Birthday," in her *And Muḥammad is His Messenger* (Chapel Hill and London: University of North Carolina Press, 1985), 144–158 and especially n. 20 on p. 148. See also Marion Katz's exhaustive treatment of *mawlid* ceremonies and the devotional literature that emerged for these celebrations, from the earliest *mawlid* texts through the contemporary period. Marion H. Katz, *The Birth of the Prophet Muḥammad: Devotional Piety in Sunni Islam* (London: Routledge, 2007).
6. For a thorough examination of the origin of the *mawlid* in Fāṭimid circles in the 11th century and its subsequent spread throughout the Sunni world in the 12th century, see Nico Kaptein, *Muḥammad's Birthday Festival* (Leiden: E.J. Brill, 1993).
7. For an extensive discussion of the medieval legal debates over devotional innovations, see Raquel Ukeles, "Innovation or Deviation: Exploring the Boundaries of Islamic Devotional Law." Ph.D. Thesis, Harvard University (May 2006).
8. Ibn Taymiyya, *Majmūʿat fatāwā shaykh al-Islām Taqī al-Dīn Ibn Taymiyya* (Cairo: Maṭbaʿat Kurdistān al-Azharī, 1910), 1:312.
9. *Iqtiḍāʾ*, 1:123, 126.
10. Muhammad Hisham Kabbani, *Encyclopedia of Islamic Doctrine* (Mountain View, CA: As-Sunnah Foundation of America, 1998), 3: 15. One of the main purposes of Kabbani's seven-volume encyclopaedia is to refute the positions of contemporary Saudi scholars, and a large section of the third volume is dedicated to defending the legality of the *mawlid*. See also, Kabbani's article on the Internet, http://www.islamic-paths.org.
11. Some of the correspondence can be found in Āl al-Shaykh's contribution to a collection of *fatāwā* against the *mawlid*, *Rasāʾil fī ḥukm al-iḥtifāl bi-al-mawlid al-nabawī* (Riyadh: *Dār al-ʿĀṣima*, 1998), 1:17–53. Muḥammad Muṣṭafā al-Shanqīṭī published the first article in the Saudi newspaper, *al-Nadwa*, no. 1112 (1383/4/7AH) and the response to Āl al-Shaykh's treatise in *al-Nadwa*, Saturday edition (1383/4/16AH). I have been unable to locate the original articles in a U.S. library and have relied instead on Āl al-Shaykh's reformulation of al-Shanqīṭī's views. Although this citation method is far from ideal, I feel confident that Āl al-Shaykh faithfully renders al-Shanqīṭī's writings on Ibn Taymiyya, since it forced Āl al-Shaykh to refine his own position. Al-Shanqīṭī's Sufi affiliation is underscored by Āl al-Shaykh's reference to him as "al-ʿAlawī," i.e., a member of the ʿAlawī Sufi order. The ʿAlawī order was founded by Muḥammad b. ʿAlī (d. 653/1255) of the Bā ʿAlawī tribe and has survived as a small independent lineage until the present day in Southern Arabia. J. Spencer Trimingham, *The Sufi Orders in Islam* (New York and Oxford: Oxford University Press, 1998), 16 n1.
12. *Rasāʾil*, 1:45.
13. Ibid., 45–53.

14. Ibid., 2:391–884. Born in Mali, W. Africa, al-Anṣārī trained first as a Mālikī scholar but later described himself either as a Ḥanbalī or as unaffiliated with any legal school, and as a Salafi. He lived for a significant portion of his life in Saudi Arabia, studying with Muhammad b. Ibrahim Āl al-Shaykh, among others. This biographical information comes from a memorial volume produced by his students entitled, *Hady al-sārī ilā asānīd al-shaykh Ismā'īl al-Anṣārī*, ed. 'Abd al-'Azīz b. Fayṣal al-Rājiḥī (Riyadh: Maktabat al-Rushd, 2001), 93–4.
15. Muḥammad 'Alawī Mālikī (also written as Muḥammad b. 'Alawī) wrote over one hundred works in the domains of Hadith, law, Sufism and theology (see a selected bibliography on a website established by one of his students, http://www.alawi.cjb.net/(Accessed, 21 July 2006)). His most famous work, *Mafāhīm yajib an tuṣaḥḥahā* (Concepts That Need to Be Corrected), is a collection of articles on theology and the Prophet in which he defends contemporary Sufism, which he says has become a term of slander and censure in contemporary Islam. Against the attacks of contemporary Saudi scholars, he defends the classical approach to *bid'a* (i.e., classifying *bid'a* into positive and negative types), the characteristics and capacities of the Prophet (including his intercession and the merits of visiting his grave) and the merits of the Prophet's birthday festival. 'Alawī argues that Ibn Taymiyya and even Ibn 'Abd al-Wahhāb permitted visiting the Prophet's grave under certain circumstances and that it is only the spiritual descendants of Wahhabism that have taken an extremist rigid view on traditional Muslim practice and thought (Muḥammad b. 'Alawī, *Mafāhīm yajib an tusaḥḥahā* [Cairo: Dār al-Insān, 1985], 35). It is noteworthy for our discussion that 'Alawī, in *Mafāhīm*, refers to Ibn Taymiyya's positions more than to those of any other jurist. See, for example, ibid., 48; 55–58; 82–3; 111–3; 121; 181–3; 195; and 200–2.
16. 'Alawī, "*Ḥawl al-iḥtifāl bil-mawlid al-nabawī al-sharīf*," in *Bāqa 'aṭira min ṣiyagh al-mawālid wa-al-madā'iḥ al-nabawiyya al-karīma* (n.p., 1983), 5–22. 'Alawī is said to have edited 'Alī al-Qārī's (d. 1013/1605) treatise in support of the *mawlid*, *al-Mawrid al-rāwī fī al-mawlid al-nabawī*, which was also published under 'Alawī's name as *Ḥāshiyat al-mawrid al-rāwī fī al-mawlid al-nabawī*. However, I have been unable to locate this edition.
17. 'Alawī, "*Ḥawl al-iḥtifāl*," 12. 'Alawī also discusses the Prophet's birthday festival in *Mafāhīm*, but there he argues that special gatherings on the Prophet's birthday are lawful solely because they fall under the category of custom (*'adāt*) and not devotional acts (*'ibādāt*). He further argues that were the *mawlid* to be considered a special day of worship, it would be an unlawful innovation (*bid'a*). 'Alawī, *Mafāhīm*, 224–6.
18. Ibn Taymiyya, *Iqtiḍā' al-ṣirāṭ al-mustaqīm li-mukhālafat asḥāb al-jaḥīm*, ed. Muḥammad Ḥāmid al-Fiqī (Lahore: Maktabat al-Salafiyya, 1977; reprint of Cairo, 1950 edition). See al-Fiqī's footnote comments on pp. 294–6. His comments are also reprinted in *Rasā'il*, 1:220–223.
19. Ibn Taymiyya, *Majmū'at fatāwā*, 1:312.
20. Lit., the days of drying strips of meat, celebrated as festive days, when the pilgrim stays in Mīna and throws pebbles at *al-jamarāt*.
21. *Majmū'at fatāwā*, 1: 312.
22. Ibn Taymiyya addresses the phenomenon of *bid'a*, in particular, in his *Iqtiḍā'*, in which he categorically rejects all devotional practices that had no precedent in the Qur'ān and Hadith and challenges the legal basis of a good innovation (*bid'a ḥasana*) (*Iqtiḍā'*, 2:82–3). He bases his legal position on the unqualified

condemnation of innovations found in numerous Prophetic traditions, chief among them, "every innovation is an error (*kull bid'a ḍalāla*)." Variants of this Hadith are found in all nine major Hadith collections except those of Bukhārī and Mālik. See, for example, *Ṣaḥīḥ Muslim*, Book of Friday Congregational Prayer (*Jum'a*), Chapter 14: Hadith No. 2042 (Vaduz, Lichtenstein: Jam'iyyat al-Maknaz al-Islamī, 2000), 1:339.

23. *Iqtiḍā'*, 2:123–128.
24. Ibn Taymiyya distinguishes between three types of time-related innovations: (1) Days that were never venerated in Islamic law (*sharī'a*) nor by the ancestors (*salaf*), and without any reason for veneration (e.g., prayer of desirable gifts (*ṣalāt al-raghā'ib*) recited on the first Thursday evening of Rajab); (2) Days that commemorate an actual event in the Prophet's life but one that was not marked as special neither by Islamic law nor by the ancestors, which Ibn Taymiyya regards as a Jewish or Christian tendency (e.g., the Prophet's birthday); and (3) Innovated practices on days venerated by the *sharī'a* (e.g., *'Ashūrā'*, celebrated on the tenth day of Muḥarram). *Iqtiḍā'*, 2:123.
25. Ibid.
26. Ibid. Ibn Taymiyya's use of the term *ijtihād* is peculiar and deserves further analysis. On the one hand, since Ibn Taymiyya addresses both scholars and laymen in his treatise, one might think that he uses it in the general sense of exerting effort or judgment, rather than in its technical jurisprudential sense of the independent analytical reasoning of the qualified jurist. On the other hand, as Memon notes in his introduction to his annotated translation of *Iqtiḍā'*, Ibn Taymiyya also uses the term in reference to the famous Hadith that a judge who exercises *ijtihād* and errs still receives a reward (Muhammad Memon, *Ibn Taimiya's Struggle against Popular Religion* (The Hague and Paris: Mouton & Co., 1976), 41; the Hadith can be found, for example, in *Ṣaḥīḥ Bukhārī*, Book of Adhering to the Book and the *Sunna*, Chapter on "the reward of a judge when he exercises *ijtihād* and is correct or errs," No. 7438, 3:1483). This tradition is generally quoted solely in relation to the independent reasoning of the jurist.
27. *Iqtiḍā'*, 2:126.
28. Ibid., 2:124.
29. Ibid.
30. Ibid., 2:124–5.
31. Ibid., 2:125.
32. Ibid.
33. Ibid., 2:126.
34. Ibid.
35. Ibid., 2:126–7.
36. 'Abd al-Raḥmān Abū Shāma, *al-Bā'ith 'alā inkār al-bida' wa al-ḥawādith*, ed. 'Ādil 'Abd al-Mun'im Abū al-'Abbās (Cairo: Maktabat Ibn Sīnā, n.d.), 38.
37. As Kaptein points out, scholarly proponents of the *mawlid* such as Abū Shāma and Jalāl al-Dīn al-Suyūṭī (d. 911/1505) both ascribed its origin to Sunni rulers of Mosul and Irbil, respectively, even though they were most likely aware of its Fāṭimid origins (Kaptein, *Muḥammad's Birthday Festival*, 67, 71). In re-ascribing the festival's originator, they thereby provided the controversial practice with what Kaptein calls "unimpeachable origins" (Ibid., 69). Abū Shāma called Shaykh 'Umar ibn Muḥammad al-Mallā', whom he considered to be the one who established the practice of the *mawlid*, "a famous holy man" (*al-Bā'ith*, 38). Al-Suyūṭī referred to the person he credited with originating the ritual,

Muẓaffar al-Dīn Kökbürī, as "a judicious and learned ruler (*malik 'ādil 'ālim*)." Jalāl al-Dīn al-Suyūṭī, "*Ḥusn al-maqṣid fī 'amal al-mawlid*" in *al-Ḥawī li-al-fatāwā* (Beirut: Dār al-Kutub al-'Ilmiyya, 1975), 1:192.

38. Other notable Shāfi'ī proponents include Ibn Ḥajar al-'Asqalānī (852/1449) and al-Suyūṭī, mentioned above. Both Ibn Ḥajar and al-Suyūṭī base their positive legal ruling both on the presence of virtuous practices and legal evidence adduced by analogy to Prophetic Hadith. See Ukeles, "Innovation or Deviation," Chapter Three, for a detailed discussion of these and other medieval positions on the legal status of the *mawlid*.
39. Tāj al-Dīn al-Fākihānī, "*al-Mawrid fī al-kalām 'alā 'amal al-mawlid*," as cited in Jalāl al-Dīn Suyūṭī's, "*Ḥusn al-maqṣid fī 'amal al-mawlid*" in *al-Ḥawī li-al-fatāwā* (Beirut: Dār al-Kutub al-'Ilmiyya, 1975), 1:191. Kaptein believed this work to be lost, as it is mentioned in later biographical dictionaries but does not appear in Brockelmann, or in Sezgin, *GAL*, 51, n. 31). Al-Fākihānī's treatise is also printed in *Rasā'il ḥukm al-iḥtifāl bi-al-mawlid al-nabawī*, 1: 7–14. Since the edition does not provide manuscript information, there is reason to believe that the editors lifted the text from Suyūṭī's treatise as it matches Suyūṭī's citation almost verbatim.
40. Ibn al-Ḥājj, *al-Madkhal ilā tanmiyat al-a'māl bi-taḥsīn al-niyyāt wa al-tanbīh 'alā ba'ḍ al-bida' wa-al-'awā'id allatī intaḥalat wa-bayān shanā'ihā*, ed. Tawfīq Ḥamdān (Beirut: Dār al-Kutub al-'Ilmiyya, 1995), 2: 229.
41. *Majmū' fatāwā Shaykh al-Islām Aḥmad Ibn Taymiyya*, ed. 'Abd al-Raḥmān ibn Muḥammad ibn Qāsim al-Najdī al-Ḥanbalī (Riyadh, 1961), 11:587–602. On the medieval debates over *samā'*, see Arthur Gribetz, "The *samā'* Controversy: Sufi vs. Legalist," *Studia Islamica* 74 (1991): 43–62.
42. *Majmū' fatāwā*, 11:597.
43. Ibid., 11:596–7. Ibn Taymiyya, here as in many other places, cites the famous Hadith that a *mujtahid* who errs receives one reward and twice the reward if he is correct (see also note 26 above).
44. *Iqtiḍā'*, 2:213–4.
45. Ibid., 2:250.
46. I have followed here Memon's translation (*Ibn Taimiya's Struggle*, 291). The Arabic in this edition appears to be corrupt. Compare Ibn Taymiyya, *Iqtiḍā' al-ṣirāṭ al-mustaqīm li-mukhālafat aṣḥāb al-jaḥīm*, ed. 'Iṣām Fāris al-Ḥarastānī and Muḥammad Ibrāhīm al-Zaghlī (Beirut: Dār al-Jīl, 1993), 393: *lā yaqtaḍī al-iqrār 'alā mā yakrahu*.
47. *Iqtiḍā'*, 2:250–251.
48. Ibid., 2:251.
49. Ibid., 2:215.
50. Ibid., 2:216.

Modern Interpretations and Misinterpretations of a Medieval Scholar: Apprehending the Political Thought of Ibn Taymiyya

Mona Hassan

"The world was bereft of a caliph for three and a half years," exclaimed Jalāl al-Dīn al-Suyūṭī (d. 911/1505) with incredulity.[1] This hitherto unprecedented absence of a caliph, as noted by al-Suyūṭī in his chronicle, had been precipitated by the Mongol destruction of Baghdad in 656/1258. Not only did the city's inhabitants and leading intellectual and political figures fall victim to the invading Mongol forces, but all members of the Abbasid family, which had assumed the symbolic position of the caliphate for centuries, were exterminated or enslaved—all, except perhaps for two. In the subsequent struggle to carve out legitimate spheres of power, those two individuals, Abū al-Qāsim Aḥmad ibn al-Ẓāhir bi-Allāh (later known as al-Mustanṣir bi-Allāh, d. 660/1261) and Abū al-ʿAbbās Aḥmad ibn Muḥammad (later known as al-Ḥākim bi-Amr Allāh, d. 701/1302), would become central figures. Most notably, both al-Mustanṣir and then al-Ḥākim would be installed as Abbasid caliphs in Cairo by the Mamluk Sultan al-Ẓāhir Baybars (d. 676/1277). However, it was soon to become clear that the newly established caliphate in Cairo, which bestowed a sense of legitimacy and grandeur on Baybars' reign, was a mere shadow of the Abbasids' legendary power and prestige.[2]

It was within this socio-political milieu that Ibn Taymiyya articulated his concepts of proper Islamic governance, and it is commonly understood that he rejected the institution of *khilāfa* (the caliphate) as being no longer necessary or obligatory. As we are repeatedly told, Ibn Taymiyya sought to do away with the fiction of a caliphate altogether. Yet does Ibn Taymiyya represent such a radical departure from traditional Islamic political theory and jurisprudence? In fact, a closer examination of Ibn Taymiyya's various intellectual contributions reveals his juristic attachment to and engagement with the concept of the caliphate as a moral and legal necessity for the Muslim community's welfare and well-being. Furthermore, the penetrating logic with which Ibn Taymiyya approaches this endeavour—in a manner tied at once to the overall aims of the Sharī'a and carefully attuned to contemporary circumstances—is one that continues to resonate within modern Islamist circles today.

Constructing Ibn Taymiyya's Rejection of the Caliphate

It is perhaps one of the greatest historiographical ironies of Islamic political thought that Ibn Taymiyya's polemics against the Shi'i conception of the imamate have been misconstrued as a rejection, on his part, of the Sunni interpretation and development of the caliphal institution. This misinterpretation originates with Henri Laoust's influential work on Ibn Taymiyya's social and political doctrines, *Essai sur les doctrines sociales et politiques de Taḳī-d-dīn Aḥmad b. Taimīya*, published in 1939. In his section on "The Imamate and the State," Laoust boldly asserts that Ibn Taymiyya rejected the obligatory status of the caliphate, which had been consecrated by Muslim jurists for centuries, and that under Khārijite influence he had also dispensed with any thought of maintaining a unitary caliphate and allowed for multiple caliphs.[3] Other scholars followed Laoust's lead.

In a 1955 article on Islamic constitutional law, Hamilton Gibb embraced Laoust's interpretations by presenting Ibn Taymiyya as a rabid figure who "in his effort to cleanse Islam of its accretions of heresy, deviations, and abuses, and to preach a return to the purity of early doctrine and practice, inevitably attacked the web of juristic argument regarding the caliphate."[4] Gibb's student Ann Lambton elaborated upon the argument of her teacher and placed Ibn Taymiyya on a downward spiralling trajectory of Muslim jurisprudence regarding the caliphate.[5] Influenced by the historical drama of the Mongol destruction of Baghdad in 1258, these authors were persuaded to read an end to the Islamic caliphate into the works of Ibn Taymiyya as the only logical stance. In this dramatic narrative, Ibn Jamā'a (d. 733/1333) represents the polar opposite to

Ibn Taymiyya, justifying sheer abuse of power in order to maintain the caliphate and thereby contributing to the disintegration of Islamic jurisprudence. In either case, scholars such as Gibb and Lambton declared a definitive end to the Islamic caliphate in the thirteenth and fourteenth centuries, based on their readings of these Muslim jurists.[6]

Other studies of Islamic political thought were similarly shaped by Laoust's authoritative work. In his *Political Thought in Medieval Islam: An Introductory Outline*, Erwin Rosenthal reiterates the view that Ibn Taymiyya "ignores the problem of the *khilāfa* altogether, denies its necessity (though for other reasons than the Khārijites) and is very critical of its theoretical foundation.... It is clear from this attitude that the centre of gravity has shifted from the *khilāfa* and the *khalīfa* to the community, whose life must be regulated by the divine law."[7] In 1968, Montgomery Watt merely refers readers of his *Islamic Political Thought: The Basic Concepts* to Laoust's "careful study of [Ibn Taymiyya's] political theories" for information on the influential writer's views.[8] Qamaruddin Khan, while expressing reservations about Laoust's tone and some of his conclusions, also acknowledges his debt to the French scholar's "scientific and methodical" study in *The Political Thought of Ibn Taymiyya*, first published in 1973. Therein, Khan too suggests that Ibn Taymiyya "abandons the thought about the Caliphate and theorising about it for good, and is not the least interested in the form or pattern of government."[9] Likewise, historians of modern Islamic political movements who seek to ground their work in the medieval tradition—such as Malcom Kerr in his monograph on modern Egyptian intellectuals, Itzchak Weismann in his work on late Ottoman Damascus, and Richard Bonney in his recent book on jihad—all refer back to Laoust (or those who cite him) in restating what has become standard knowledge through continuous repetition: that Ibn Taymiyya did not deem the caliphate to be at all necessary.[10]

Laoust's Fundamental Misreading of Ibn Taymiyya

Yet this abiding perception is ultimately rooted in a fundamental misunderstanding of Ibn Taymiyya's polemical text, *Minhāj al-sunna fī naqḍ kalām al-Shīʿa wa-al-Qadariyya*.[11] In his *Essai*, Laoust argues that

Ibn Taymiyya adopted an innovative position regarding the Sunni caliphate, which included the view, dubiously related to Khārijite doctrine, that after the Righteous Caliphs a unitary caliphate is no longer obligatory. In Laoust's words:

> From then on [after the Rightly Guided Caliphs], the unified caliphate no longer has any character of necessity [according to Ibn Taymiyya]. In this way, the last of the doctrines waiting to be situated rightly in the conciliatory synthesis of the system of Ibn Taymiyya was indeed incorporated—this doctrine being Khārijite, one of the characteristics of which is to deny the necessity of having a caliph at the head of the community, even though Ibn Taymiyya, in frequent presentations he makes about the doctrine, never presents as one of the central tenets of Khārijism the negation of the eternal quality of the caliphate.[12]

According to Laoust, Ibn Taymiyya grounds this highly unconventional view in the absence of any specific injunction in the Qur'ān regarding the obligatory form of government, Khārijite-inspired Hadiths, and the claim that the Prophet Muḥammad's Companions had never agreed on the caliphate's obligatory status in the first place. Laoust goes on to suggest that Ibn Taymiyya avoids prescribing the caliphate as a form of governance for the Muslim community and does not regard the caliphate as necessary, in order to avert legal and moral difficulties arising from the absence of the institution.[13]

Yet a careful review of the passages of *Minhāj al-sunna* referred to by Laoust reveals no correlation whatsoever between them and Laoust's interpretations of Ibn Taymiyya's views. In his passionate response to the Shi'i propositions of Ibn al-Muṭahhar al-Ḥillī (d. 726/1325), Ibn Taymiyya does not explicitly nor even implicitly broach the opinions attributed to him by Laoust regarding the Sunni caliphate, and the sources that Ibn Taymiyya utilizes to refute the Shi'i doctrines do not lend themselves to any such possible interpretation of the caliphate's loss of obligatory legal status. Rather, in the first section of *Minhāj al-sunna* to which Laoust refers in general terms, Ibn Taymiyya discusses the absurdity of the Shi'i doctrine of the Awaited Imam, whom they believe to have disappeared into minor and then major occultation in the years 260/874 and 329/940 respectively.[14] In the second section referred to by Laoust, Ibn Taymiyya addresses the issue of Shi'i enmity towards those who fought 'Alī but not towards those who killed

'Uthmān.[15] Nowhere, however, do the passages support Laoust's sweeping conclusions nor does he cite any specific text, from there or elsewhere, that could support his peculiar reading.

Such lack of foundation for Laoust's arguments is also apparent in his claim that Ibn Taymiyya allowed for the multiplicity of rulers, in lieu of the unified caliphate of the Islamic legal tradition. Laoust points to the Hadiths marshalled by Ibn Taymiyya in *Minhāj al-sunna*'s opening section on the Imamate as evidence for this interpretation, "Ibn Taymiyya considers as part of the Sunna many Hadiths of Khārijite inspiration, which are included in the orthodox collections and which do not limit the number of Imams."[16] Why Laoust considers these prophetic traditions to be of Khārijite inspiration is unclear, but, in any case, they do not indicate the permissibility of simultaneous Imams. Ibn Taymiyya cites these traditions for three purposes. First, he aims to correct a variant prophetic tradition cited by al-Ḥillī. Second, Ibn Taymiyya seeks to demonstrate the impermissibility of armed rebellion against those invested with political power. Third, Ibn Taymiyya therefore draws on this Hadith corpus to point to the known existence of these Imams, or legitimate political leaders, in contradistinction to the centuries-long absence of the Shi'a's Imam in occultation.[17] The only correlation with Laoust's argument regarding a coexisting multiplicity of Imams is that some of the Hadiths utilize the plural form of the word "imām" (*al-a'imma*) in order to describe how one should interact with Imams in general, presupposing that the existence of a leader is an essential Islamic requisite. Yet there is nothing particular to suggest that these Imams would be contemporaneous with one another as opposed to succeeding to the caliphate one after another. For example:

> In the Ṣaḥīḥ Muslim on the authority of 'Awf b. Mālik al-Ashja'ī who said, "I heard the Prophet (May God's peace and blessings be upon him) say: 'The best of your Imams are those whom you love and they love you, and you pray for them and they pray for you. And the worst of your Imams are those whom you detest and they detest you, and you curse them and they curse you.'" ['Awf b. Mālik] said, "We said, 'O Messenger of God, should we not fight them at that point?' The Prophet replied 'No, not as long as they maintain the prayer among you. Whoever has someone appointed in authority over him and then sees that leader engaged in some act (s) of disobedience to God, let him abhor whatever

> has been done in disobedience to God, but do not let that person withdraw his hand from his [promise of] obedience [to that leader].'"[18]

Furthermore, one of the Hadiths that Ibn Taymiyya cites in this section—upon which Laoust bases his claims—has been traditionally employed to substantiate the obligation of retaining only a single Imam at any particular moment in time. This tradition, in which the Prophet orders the believers to be faithful to their pledge of allegiance to the future caliphs one after the other (*al-awwal fa-al-awwal*), is understood by al-Nawawī (d. 676/1277) and Ibn Ḥajar al-'Asqalānī (d. 852/1449) to affirm that the position of retaining a single Imam is both the majority opinion of Muslim scholars and also the correct position.[19] Thus, far from demolishing classical jurisprudence on the caliphate, Ibn Taymiyya upholds Sunni sources and interpretations of the institution in his polemics against the Shi'i imamate. And as Muḥammad al-Mubārak and Bassām 'Aṭiyya Ismā'īl Faraj have demonstrated, Ibn Taymiyya's refutation of Shi'i doctrines actually provides him with the opportunity to detail and reaffirm numerous aspects of classical Sunni jurisprudence regarding the caliphate, such as stipulation of the caliph's Qurashī lineage, the possible methods of his ascension to the caliphate, and guidelines for the proper procedures for the election of the caliph.[20]

Ibn Taymiyya's Assessment of the Caliphate

Rather than seizing the Mongol destruction of Baghdad as an opportune moment to declare the end of the caliphate as it had been previously known, Ibn Taymiyya engages in a process similar to the one that Sunni jurists had been preoccupied with for centuries—namely, how to comprehend the historical position of the caliphate from a sound Islamic legal perspective. Ibn Taymiyya develops his ideas on the caliphate in a lengthy *fatwā*, in which he addresses the well-known statement of the Prophet that there would be a thirty-year period of *khilāfat al-nubuwwa* (righteous vice-regency of the Prophet after his passing away) which would be ultimately superseded by *mulk* (kingship). Historically, this Hadith provides affirmation of the righteous leadership of the first few caliphs. In terms of a juristic evaluation, however, the key question arises:

What then are the appropriate legal classifications of *khilāfat al-nubuwwa* and of *mulk*?

Ibn Taymiyya delineates four main responses among Muslims to this question; two of them he identifies as unacceptable extremes, and two as representing centrist positions.[21] The first of the two potentially acceptable middle paths is to proclaim *khilāfat al-nubuwwa*—or the highest representation and standard of the caliphate—obligatory (*wājiba*), which means that deviations from this model are only permissible by necessity of circumstance (*an yuqāl al-khilāfatu wājibatun wa-innamā yajūzu al-khurūju 'anhā bi-qadr al-ḥāja*). According to this classification, *mulk*—or political rule associated with the worldly detractions of kingship—is a case of dire need (*ḥāja*) and not inherent permissibility (*jawāz aṣlī*). The other centrist position, which Ibn Taymiyya associates at one point with Abū Ya'lā Ibn al-Farrā' (d. 458/1066), is to consider *khilāfat al-nubuwwa* meritorious (*mustaḥabba*). This position leaves slightly more conceptual room for the permissibility of *mulk* (which Ibn Taymiyya specifies as caliphal rule besmirched by elements of kingship: *shawb al-khilāfa bi-al-mulk*), so long as it facilitates the actual intent behind this Islamic public office of the caliphate (*an yuqāl yajūzu qabūluhā min al-mulk bi-mā yuyassiru fi'l al-maqṣūdi bi-al-wilāya wa-lā yu'assiruhu*).

In contradistinction to both these middle positions are the two extremes. The first is the position adopted by religious innovators like the Khārijites, Mu'tazilites, and some pious ascetics who deem *khilāfat al-nubuwwa* to be obligatory under all conditions, regardless of any extenuating circumstances, and accordingly condemn anyone who falls short of it (*yūjibu dhālika fī kulli ḥālin wa-zamānin wa-'alā kulli aḥadin wa-yadhummu man kharaja 'an dhālika muṭlaqan aw li-ḥājatin*). The other extreme, which Ibn Taymiyya identifies as the purview of oppressors, libertines, and some Murji'ites, is to declare the absolute permissibility of *mulk*, or worldly rule, without holding it to the standards of the righteous caliphs (*yubīḥu al-mulk muṭlaqan min ghayr taqayyudin bi-sunnat al-khulafā'*). A fully modern interpretation of these last two categories would identify religious extremism as the first excess and excessive secularism as the other opposing extreme. As for Ibn Taymiyya's middle path, achieving an exemplary caliphate, one which realistically embraces the guidance of the Prophet and his righteous successors, is the ideal form of Islamic governance.

In drawing this normative distinction between *khilāfat al-nubuwwa* and *mulk*, Ibn Taymiyya does not seek to negate the historical development of the caliphate. Rather he recognizes the validity of referring to rulers subsequent to the Rightly Guided Caliphs as caliphs themselves—even if the substantive character distinguishing their rule was that of kingship (*mulk*). He locates religious grounds for this position in the saying of the Prophet Muḥammad, as reported by Abū Hurayra and recorded in the two most authoritative Hadith collections of al-Bukhārī and Muslim:

> "The Israelites were led by prophets; each time a prophet passed away, he was succeeded by another prophet. Yet there will be no prophet after me; there will be vice-regents (*khulafā'* or caliphs), and they will be many." [The Companions] asked, "What do you order us to do?" He said, "Be loyal to your pledge of allegiance (*bay'a*), to one after the other, and give them their rights, for God will ask them about how they shepherded you."[22]

According to Ibn Taymiyya's analysis, the acknowledgement of a future multitude of caliphs indicates that there would be more caliphs than just the first few righteous ones (since they alone could not be considered "many"). The Prophet's instruction to be loyal to one's pledge of allegiance to whoever had assumed the caliphate first also suggested to Ibn Taymiyya that, unlike the time of the Rightly Guided Caliphs, succession would later become a matter of dispute. Ibn Taymiyya further regards the Prophet's injunction to respect the rights of those later caliphs, who would eventually be taken to task by God for their shepherding of the Muslim community, as evidence supporting the Sunni position of recognizing temporal political authority.[23] Thus, while acknowledging the oppressive character of Yazīd b. Mu'āwiya's rule in *Minhāj al-sunna* (*kāna fīhi min al-ẓulm mā kāna fīhi*),[24] Ibn Taymiyya does not hesitate to refer simultaneously to that period of rule as "the caliphate of Yazīd" (*khilāfat Yazīd*).[25] And Ibn Taymiyya more generally refers to the Umayyad and Abbasid caliphs (*khulafā' banī Umayya wa-banī 'Abbās*), while acknowledging that the word "caliph" is a common term for those entrusted with political authority among Muslims.[26]

In his legal exposition, though, Ibn Taymiyya also remains unequivocally clear that all such rulers should be held to the standards of the Righteous Caliphs in their governance. He condemns the notion that worldly rulers should not be bound to the exemplary model of the caliphs (*min ghayr taqayyudin bi-sunnat al-khulafā'*) while concomitantly recognizing the likelihood that such rulers might occasionally have to diverge from this standard of governance due to circumstances rendering it impossible (*ta'adhdhur*) or even simply difficult (*ta'assur*) to adhere to it. Wanton disregard for the noble path of caliphs, however, would be inadmissible (*ammā mā lā ta'adhdhur fīhi wa-lā ta'assur, fa-inna al-khurūj fīhi 'an sunnat al-khulafā' ittibā'un li-al-hawā*).[27] Elsewhere, Ibn Taymiyya also recalls the injunction of the Prophet Muḥammad that Muslims should follow his example and the example set by the Righteous and Rightly Guided Caliphs (*al-khulafā' al-rāshidīn al-mahdiyyīn*) who would follow him.[28] Yet Ibn Taymiyya does not lay the blame for the degeneration of political rule into worldly kingship solely at the feet of the leaders of state; for him, the metaphorical flock also shares its portion of the blame, as in the aphorism: "People will be appointed over you according to how you are" (*kamā takūnūna yuwallā 'alaykum*).[29] Therefore, in addition to people improving their own condition and maintaining political order through general yet qualified obedience, the Muslim community's duty to offer sincere advice (*naṣīḥa*) to those placed in authority over them acquires immense significance within the sphere of Ibn Taymiyya's political thought.[30]

Al-Siyāsa al-shar'iyya as Advice Literature

In light of the preceding discussion, Ibn Taymiyya's well-known treatise *al-Siyāsa al-shar'iyya fī iṣlāḥ al-rā'ī wa-al-ra'iyya*[31] can be understood as a composition designed to advise the ruling elite and elevate their moral standards of governance. As Ibn Taymiyya explains in his opening remarks, the treatise was solicited by a member of the ruling class whom God had made it obligatory to advise (*iqtaḍāhā man awjaba Allāhu nuṣḥahu min wulāt al-umūr*). He then elaborates upon this obligation by quoting the prophetic Hadith which praises the offering of sincere advice to such officials (*an tanāṣiḥū man wallāhu Allāh amra-kum*) as an act pleasing to God.[32] The absence of a detailed and legalistic discussion of the caliphate in *al-Siyāsa al-shar'iyya* cannot be construed as evidence of Ibn Taymiyya's total disregard for the institution. We have already seen how Ibn Taymiyya clearly articulates his classification of the caliphate in his *fatwā* collection as an obligatory or, at the very least, a highly commendable aspect of government as well as his reiteration of technical legal rulings about the election and qualifications of the caliph in the polemical context of *Minhāj al-sunna*. By contrast, his seeming silence in *al-Siyāsa al-shar'iyya* can be easily explained as a matter of genre. *Al-Siyāsa al-shar'iyya* is not a legal manual, a book of jurisprudence, where one would look for laboriously detailed legal rulings on all conceivably related issues. Rather, as a treatise designed to advise those already in power, the work is more significantly comparable to the genre of advice literature, typically referred to as "Mirrors for Princes," in which the state structure is a given, and the aim is to guide its leading officials to the best of practices.

Lambton offers a rich set of descriptions of these Islamic Mirrors for Princes along such lines, explaining that the authors of these works "were concerned not so much with the theory of government, as with its practice," and that "they did not seek...to justify the state, but were concerned with the need to modify the effects of its operations which altered the circumstances of the time." And they:

> ...emphasized, above all, justice. Their works were intended to edify and they pointed society to an ideal—the ideal, it is true, predominantly of the official classes. In part, their works were also a protest against the evils of contemporary society and its failure to reach that ideal. Mirrors thus, in some measure, aimed at the remedy of contemporary political evils. In a society in which power was arbitrary and flattery the common practice, short of armed rebellion, negative protest was often all that was open to the subject.[33]

Leading into these intriguing evaluations, however, Lambton also suggests a sharp distinction that separates the writers of advice literature from the jurists and philosophers of Muslim society, as if a jurist or philosopher could not also write a Mirror for Princes. Patricia Crone, who convincingly disproves al-Ghazālī's authorship of the second half of *Naṣīḥat al-mulūk*, also argues that the first half, correctly attributed to al-Ghazālī, should be considered a "Fürstenermahnung" (an admonition of princes) and not a "Fürstenspiegel" (a mirror for princes).[34] Like Lambton, Crone draws a line between the Iranian royal tradition and the social and political ideals of religious scholars—a distinction which Louise Marlow also detects but reveals to be "rather less tidy" in the thirteenth- and fourteenth-century texts that she studies. Acknowledging the complexity of this genre, Marlow observes,

> Mirrors for princes, and other works of counsel on the ethical and practical aspects of government, were written by members of several intellectual and professional groups. Advice literature consequently encompasses a great variety of perspectives and styles, and sometimes overlaps substantially with other forms of literary expression, including historiographical, philosophical and juristic writings.[35]

So what would a "Mirror for Princes" written by a jurist look like? One could take Crone's own definition as a possible starting point:

> The name of the genre is borrowed from medieval European history (Latin *specula regis*). It casts the advice as a mirror in which the prince would look at himself and try to improve his appearance, and this idea is encountered on the Muslim side too, even though the term itself is not. "A loyal man may serve one as a mirror; by regarding him one may straighten one's habits and character," as an eleventh-century Turkish work puts it.[36]

If we then translate this concept into a normative Islamic framework, where the believer is the mirror of another believer according to the moral prescription attributed to the Prophet,[37] could not jurists, such as al-Ghazālī and Ibn Taymiyya, have considered their own written reflections for rulers to be valuable contributions toward rectifying contemporary governmental affairs? As al-Ghazālī comments in his epistle advising rulers of their responsibilities and the consequences in this world and the hereafter, "Every *'ālim* [religious scholar] who meets kings should give this sort of advice, without suppressing the truth and without flattering their conceit so as to share in their tyranny."[38] And Ibn Taymiyya further widens the scope of what we would typically consider advice literature on state matters in *al-Siyāsa al-shar'iyya* by including the ruler's proverbial flock among the beneficiaries of his advice. In Ibn Taymiyya's doing so, *al-Siyāsa al-shar'iyya* even more deeply reflects a scholastic paradigm for this genre by drawing inspiration from scriptural references and ideals rooted in the Qur'ān and the Hadith that hold both the ruler and his flock responsible for the successful performance of the state.

The Caliphate in Ibn Taymiyya's *al-Siyāsa al-shar'iyya*

Though one would not expect theoretical legal explications in a work of this genre aimed at rectifying contemporary malaise, Ibn Taymiyya nevertheless firmly roots his arguments in *al-Siyāsa al-shar'iyya* within an Islamic discursive tradition that revolved around the caliphate. As Ibn Taymiyya explains in the introduction, the conceptual framework of *al-Siyāsa al-shar'iyya* springs from two Qur'ānic verses in Sūrat al-Nisā' (4: 58–59):

> God commands you to render your trusts back to those to whom they are due; And when you judge between people, that you judge with justice: Verily how excellent is the teaching with which He admonishes you! For God is He Who hears and sees all things. O you who believe! Obey God, and obey the Messenger, and those charged with authority (*ulū al-amr*) among you. And if you differ in anything among yourselves, refer it back to God and His Messenger, if you do indeed believe in God and the Last Day: That is better and more seemly in the end.[39]

In his early work of Qur'ānic exegesis, al-Ṭabarī (d. 310/923) elucidates that these verses demonstrate the Muslim community's obligation to elect and maintain a caliph, making clear his own preference for interpreting those vested with authority (*ulū al-amr*) as the community's political and military leaders (*al-umarā'*)[40]—an interpretation that was to become the majority opinion among Muslim scholars by the seventh/thirteenth century.[41] Ibn Taymiyya likewise embraced this explanation of the Qur'ān's conceptual terminology, readily interchanging the expression "those in authority" (*wulāt al-umūr*) with those for the political and military authorities (*al-umarā'*), the caliphs (*al-khulafā'*), and the Imams (*al-a'imma*) as though they were synonymous.[42] In this fashion, he embraces the lengthy trajectory of Muslim scholars' highly practical considerations regarding the caliphate.

In *al-Siyāsa al-shar'iyya*, Ibn Taymiyya also acknowledges the caliph's place at the head of the state's political and military hierarchy. While explaining the weighty responsibility of judging truthfully among people, and hence ruling over them, he addresses all key officials of the state, "whether he is caliph (*khalīfa*), sultan (*sulṭān*), vice-regent (*nā'ib*), governor (*wālī*), a Shar'ī judge, or his deputy".[43] Rather than directing specific bureaucratic advice to each of these government officials within the Mamluk system, Ibn Taymiyya begins *al-Siyāsa al-shar'iyya* by offering general advice regarding how such responsible members of state could best discharge the public duties entrusted to them.[44] And notably, Ibn Taymiyya specifically places the caliph at the head of this state bureaucracy above and before the actual sultan. Written in the context of the Mamluk state, Ibn Taymiyya's choice of words in this descending order of rank is an unmistakable reference simultaneously paralleling and legitimizing the contemporaneous bureaucratic structure. Specifically, it acknowledges the Abbasid caliph as the symbolic figurehead who transferred all of his essential functions and duties over to the Mamluk sultan for execution. Accepting the legitimacy of the Mamluk state structure for what it was, with an Abbasid caliph nominally at its pinnacle, Ibn Taymiyya thus directs most of his attention in *al-Siyāsa al-shar'iyya* towards ameliorating the actual performance and execution of Islamic governance, by addressing the administration of finances and criminal punishment[45] as well as offering essential reminders regarding the need for wise exercise of the government's resources and power.[46] All of this advice is directed towards improving the actual daily functioning of the state under which Ibn Taymiyya lived—comprised of a ceremonial Abbasid caliph, a governing Mamluk sultan, and numerous other administrative officials.

Modern Muslims and Ibn Taymiyya

Moving beyond the scope of his written corpus, Muslims of the twentieth and twenty-first centuries have admired and sought to emulate Ibn Taymiyya's active interest in ensuring the welfare of his community and society. Ibn Taymiyya is frequently ranked among those jurists of the highest caliber (*mujtahid*) for his sparkling intellect and incisive writings, while his religiously oriented social and political activism has inspired modern Muslims' recognition of Ibn Taymiyya as a revivalist of his age (*mujaddid*).[47] This model of

Ibn Taymiyya's political thought and social activism, however, has not been recalled and reconstituted in a monolithic fashion, and his precedent has been subject to multiple, and even conflicting, interpretations in the modern era. Among Egyptian Islamist groups of the twentieth century, for instance, Ibn Taymiyya's presence seems to emerge as a small, but common, denominator. Upon closer examination, however, the ends for which these Islamic groups seek to interpret and utilize Ibn Taymiyya's political thought are widely divergent. Yet, despite the dramatically different approaches of moderate and extremist Islamic groups—which we may call the accommodationists and the confrontationists[48]—each of them calls upon Ibn Taymiyya and his work to authenticate its position.

The Accommodationists and Yūsuf al-Qaraḍāwī

Emblematic of the accommodationist approach is the Society of Muslim Brothers (Jamā'at al-Ikhwān al-Muslimīn), whose legacy, as Raymond William Baker explains, has been a significant influence upon all centrist groups that "have responded with moderation to the violence of their age, drawing on the religious and cultural heritage of Islam to do so."[49] As Sana Abed-Kotob discusses in her article on the movement's goals and strategies, the Muslim Brothers have committed themselves to working within Egypt's existing political system in pursuit of democratic ideals and socioeconomic justice.[50] Likewise, in carefully documenting the Egyptian Society of Muslim Brothers' rethinking of women's rights, political pluralism, and the shared citizenship of Copts, combined with their longstanding rejection of violence, Mona El-Ghobashy further belies the criticism that the Islamist group is merely posturing in order to gain power, and she criticizes the exaggerated sense of paranoia she finds among "Western policymakers, Arab state elites, and some academics" that obfuscates how Islamist groups, like the Muslim Brothers, have been shaped by their institutional political environments.[51] In his work on the Muslim Brothers of Egypt, Jan Stark also emphasizes how "the debate on political Islam of the past 20 years has sidelined and seriously underestimated the impact of moderate Islamic groups (often deemed 'extremist' and 'deviationist' by a zealous state) on discourses of democratization and its potential to bring about social change."[52]

In this centrist vein, one of the most influential thinkers and voices of moderation has been that of Dr Yūsuf al-Qaraḍāwī, who joined the Muslim Brothers while he was still a student at al-Azhar's Religious Institute in the provincial capital of Ṭanṭā.[53] Born in one of Egypt's Western Delta villages in 1926,[54] al-Qaraḍāwī had completed memorization of the Qur'ān at a local *kuttāb* as well as his mandatory state education in the village's school, before continuing on to pursue his Islamic Studies in al-Azhar's schooling system.[55] At al-Azhar University in Cairo, al-Qaraḍāwī graduated the first in his class in 1953 and then again for his teaching specialization in 1954, receiving another advanced degree from al-Azhar in 1960, and ultimately his doctorate with highest honors in 1973.[56] Meanwhile, al-Qaraḍāwī had been appointed in 1961 to head Qatar's newly established Religious Institute, and, later on, he also established and led Qatar University's College of Islamic Law and Islamic Studies in the capital city of Doha, where he has lived ever since.[57] Through his prolific writing and engaging public appearances, however, al-Qaraḍāwī has garnered immense international prestige and prominence for his religious scholarship.[58] And even though he declined the Egyptian Muslim Brothers' chief executive office of General Guide (*al-Murshid al-'Āmm*) when it was offered to him in 2002, al-Qaraḍāwī's critically independent and outspoken writings over the decades, seeking to guide the Islamic movement aright, have greatly influenced its progressive development and have been embraced by its current leadership.[59]

In one such work, *Awlawiyyāt al-ḥaraka al-islāmiyya fi al-marḥala al-qādima*,[60] al-Qaraḍāwī explicates what he thinks should be the priorities of the Islamic movement, turning to the *fatāwā* collection of Ibn Taymiyya for support in his call for courteousness and a pluralistic civil society. In the realm of politics and broader social interaction, al-Qaraḍāwī locates the origin of the contemporary malaise of Islam in the mentalities of some Muslim groups, ranging from the constantly beseiged, the literalist, the harsh and narrow-minded, to the excessively traditionalistic. Al-Qaraḍāwī advocates instead that Muslims should develop a depth of understanding that is attuned to the ways of the world, reflects the overall aims of Sharī'a, and recognizes the importance of prioritization and balance.[61] Critically, al-Qaraḍāwī urges Islamists to break out of an isolationist mode (where they only speak and write to one another) and emphasizes the importance of engaging in sincere and productive dialogue with other groups, such as secular nationalists. He also encourages positive interfaith interaction between Muslims and Christians, emphasizing the commonalities and humanitarian concerns of both religious groups. Moreover, al-Qaraḍāwī suggests that Islamists should constructively engage with local regimes as well as with Western governments and intellectuals, in recognition of Islam's mission of mercy (*raḥma*) and not wrathful vengeance. Among fellow Muslims, he perceives the need for increased cooperation between members of the traditional religious establishment and those of popular Islamic movements, and elsewhere, al-Qaraḍāwī has written of the need to rescue passionate Muslim youth from extremism and violence.[62]

In order to supplement and bolster his argument for a more enlightened engagement with the contemporary world, al-Qaraḍāwī includes two appendices, both of which are culled from the *fatāwā* literature of Ibn Taymiyya. The first *fatwā* by Ibn Taymiyya addresses the permissibility of assuming public office in an unjust state, in order to alleviate the oppression and harm that it might otherwise inflict.[63] Specifically, Ibn Taymiyya is asked whether a government official who strives to ease some of the state's oppressive practices should remain in his post or cleanse his hands from all its potentially sinful oppression. The complicating factor is the official's inability to remove all iniquity associated with his post, despite his, or anyone else's, best efforts. Yet were he to resign and absolve himself from the system's injustice, the oppression inflicted by whoever would succeed him would only persist and increase. In his response, Ibn Taymiyya is unequivocal that such a person who strives to achieve justice and alleviate oppression as much as possible should remain in public office. It is more commendable than abandoning his position along with any attending evil, since that would only result in greater evil and harm to others. And if there is no one else capable of alleviating some of the oppression of his official post, it would even be considered obligatory for this well-intentioned individual to continue to fulfill his duties. It is not sinful for him to do so, Ibn Taymiyya assures; rather, this public official would be rewarded by God for the good he was able to achieve and not be punished for whatever ill he could not avert.[64]

In al-Qaraḍāwī's second appendix to *Awlawiyyāt al-ḥaraka al-islāmiyya*, Ibn Taymiyya attempts to resolve the moral and philosophical quandary of how to evaluate the conflicting balance of good and evil, or harm and benefit, which invariably presents itself in any number of circumstances, including those of political governance.[65] The excerpt itself is drawn from a larger section of Ibn Taymiyya's *Majmūʿ al-fatāwā* on matters related to principles of Islamic jurisprudence. Here, the overarching principle is one that Ibn Taymiyya remarks he has articulated in another treatise on government and the caliphate, namely that the purpose of Sharīʿa is to achieve and augment what is beneficial and to ward off and decrease what is harmful as well as to assess and attain the better of two good options and to avoid the greater of two evils by enduring the lesser. One example that Ibn Taymiyya adduces is the preference for the presence of a ruler (*sulṭān*) and his oppressive ways over his total absence. In support of this view, Ibn Taymiyya reiterates the saying that sixty years under an oppressive ruler is better than one night with none. Moreover, Ibn Taymiyya observes that while a ruler would be held fully accountable by God for his acts of aggression and excess if he is capable of avoiding them, it would be permissible, or even obligatory, for a ruler or lesser public official to fulfill commendable duties involving the inevitable wrongdoing of others beyond his own control, for the sake of the greater good. While pondering in further detail the possible pairings of good and evil in relation to public office, Ibn Taymiyya also points to the Qur'ānic example of the Prophet Joseph's assuming responsibility for the storage and distribution of the agricultural harvest under the King of Egypt, even though the king and his people were disbelievers. As Ibn Taymiyya observes, Joseph still strove to establish justice and beneficence while functioning within the governing system of Egypt which was based on the ways and laws of disbelief.[66]

In utilizing these two sets of juristic opinions by Ibn Taymiyya, al-Qaraḍāwī seeks to overcome some modern Muslims' puritan abhorrence for what are often perceived as corrupt state apparatuses and institutions in favor of balanced social and political involvement for the betterment of society, all the while respecting the legitimacy of the state. And in doing so, al-Qaraḍāwī utilizes the very source that is impeccably respected by the most stringent and literalist of contemporary Muslims. Yet this is not a mere manoeuvre on his part; to the contrary, in his call for moderation, al-Qaraḍāwī himself has been influenced and impressed by the vivacity of Ibn Taymiyya's thought.[67] As al-Qaraḍāwī comments, "The Imam Ibn Taymiyya is among the most beloved scholars—perhaps [he is] even the most beloved scholar—of the *umma* to my heart and the closest to my intellect" and then qualifies this statement by adding how he also can and does in fact differ with some of Ibn Taymiyya's views.[68] What is particularly noteworthy, therefore, is the contribution of Ibn Taymiyya's scholarship towards the development of a modern system of moral thought that does not rebel against the political order, but rather views itself as an integral component of the political system by representing a positive and moderate voice inspired by the Islamic tradition.

The Confrontationists and Muḥammad ʿAbd al-Salām Faraj

Far more attention, however, is typically accorded to the extremist permutations of Ibn Taymiyya's thought in the modern period, with the result that Ibn Taymiyya is invariably characterized as the evil progenitor of Islamic radicalism. In seeking an explanation for the roots of this extremism, historians and journalists have misconstrued Ibn Taymiyya's views in an attempt to make sense of the present. That is, contemporary circumstances are superimposed upon the historical past, so much so that even those positions which Ibn Taymiyya specifically argued against are attributed to him.[69] In a rare example of dissent, Johannes Jansen contradicts this predominant position by referring to Ibn Taymiyya's own "clear condemnation of tyrannicide." As he concludes, "Such short and clear remarks, one is tempted to say, do not help to establish the reputation of Ibn Taymiyya as the spiritual father of modern Muslim terrorism. It would seem obvious that religiously motivated tyrannicides can expect little help from Ibn Taymiyya."[70]

In order to isolate and examine the interpretative processes at play, I would like to turn to the so-called Mongol *fatwās*[71] of Ibn Taymiyya as a particularly salient example of extremist Muslims' readings of his work in the modern era. Ibn Taymiyya's responses at the turn of the fourteenth century to those inquiring about the permissibility of fighting the newly Islamized Mongols, who were repeatedly invading Syria-Palestine, gained substantial notoriety in 1981 for being the texts that inspired the assassins of the Egyptian

President Anwar Sadat. The group that undertook this assassination, Jamāʿat al-Jihād, was founded in 1979 by Muḥammad ʿAbd al-Salām Faraj, a recent graduate of Cairo University's Faculty of Engineering, with no formal religious training or education. His group relied heavily upon other Egyptian university students, who were recruited predominantly through existing ties of kinship and friendship.[72] As articulated in the document circulated by Faraj among his youthful cohorts, members of this Jihād group decried Egypt's rulers as apostates who were comparable to the Mongols of Ibn Taymiyya's *fatwā* for not instituting and implementing Islamic law. Therefore, in making the argument that Egypt's current rulers deserved to be fought and eliminated, Faraj drew extensively upon Ibn Taymiyya's legal rulings. As Jansen rightly observes, "No other Muslim scholar is quoted so often, or so extensively."[73] In its pastiche incorporation of Ibn Taymiyya's text, however, Faraj's work *al-Farīḍa al-ghā'iba*[74] purposefully disregards the socio-historical context of Ibn Taymiyya's *fatwā* and, even worse, distorts its juristic integrity.

Perhaps the most ironic aspect of Faraj's selective reading of Ibn Taymiyya's work is the transformation of Ibn Taymiyya's legal categories. The Mongol *fatwā*s of Ibn Taymiyya grapple with the concept of *qitāl ahl al-baghy*, conceptualizing the invading Mongol forces as a group rebelling against the Islamic state, represented by the Mamluks of Egypt and Syria-Palestine.[75] The intellectual creativity of Ibn Taymiyya's *fatwā*s lies in the way that he breaks down this category of insurgents (*ahl al-baghy*) even further into its particulars—so that there can be no question about the necessity of fighting the Mongols.[76] As the historian Ibn Kathīr (d. 774/1373) explains, when Ibn Taymiyya's *fatwā* was issued the Muslim population of the Mamluk realm had been confused over the legality of fighting the recently Islamized Mongols who invaded Syria in 702/1303. Ibn Taymiyya therefore clarified matters by comparing the Mongols to the Khawārij who had rebelled against ʿAlī and Muʿāwiya, all the while claiming to be more rightly guided than those Muslims against whom they fought (*hā'ulā' min jins al-khawārij alladhīna kharajū ʿalā ʿAlī wa-Muʿāwiya wa-ra'aw annahum aḥaqqu bi-al-amri minhumā*). As was the case with these Khārijite predecessors, continues Ibn Kathīr, the Mongols' claim for the moral upper hand and their censure of the Mamluks' wrongdoing were both ill-founded, for they had in fact committed what was many times worse. According to Ibn Kathīr, the impact of Ibn Taymiyya's assessment was profound and significantly raised the courage and resolve of the Muslims in the Mamluk domains (*quwwiyat qulūbuhum wa-niyyātuhum*) to fight against the invading Mongols, whose misguided belligerence they now understood to be similar to the errant Khawārij's armed rebellion.[77]

Indeed, when Ibn Taymiyya addresses the converted Mongols' invasion of the Mamluk realm and their atrocities committed against the local Muslim inhabitants, he turns to the juristic discourse on rebels as the guiding framework for his analysis. Within this legal framework, the measure of leniency or severity shown towards the defiant group depends on its classification, and Ibn Taymiyya delineates two main paradigms among Muslim jurists. The first, which he attributes to Shāfiʿīs, Ḥanafīs, and some Ḥanbalīs, classifies all Muslims who fight against the state as *bughāt* (rebels of the juristic discourse) who are deserving of leniency.[78] The second opinion, which Ibn Taymiyya traces back to eminent scholars of Hadith and jurisprudence like Mālik and Aḥmad Ibn Ḥanbal, draws an underlying distinction between politically motivated and religiously inspired rebels. On the one hand are those Muslims who fight against the community's leaders based on a plausible, albeit incorrect, religious interpretation and therefore should be dealt with mildly, such as the Companions who fought against ʿAlī at the battles of the Camel and of Ṣiffīn. And on the other hand are those rebels who transgress, not just against the state but even more gravely against Islam itself, by abandoning some of its essential and defining tenets, as was the case with the Khawārij during the reign of ʿAlī and the withholders of *zakāt* during the reign of Abū Bakr, and who thereby warrant harsher treatment.[79]

In support for the second juristic distinction between categories of insurgents, Ibn Taymiyya produces a long list of scriptural and historical evidence. As an example of rebels who merit leniency for their plausible yet mistaken interpretations, Ibn Taymiyya points to many Companions' reluctance to intervene in civil wars among Muslims as well as to the Prophet's laudatory prediction of his grandson al-Ḥasan's reconciling the two Muslim parties instead of using force to suppress the insurgents.[80] As an example of the other category, Ibn Taymiyya points to the Prophet Muḥammad's description and stern condemnation of the misguided Khawārij as well as the unanimous opinion of the Companions that the Khawārij should be fought with unyielding determination.[81] Another example that Ibn Taymiyya adduces of the severe treatment shown to rebels against the tenets of Islam is Abū Bakr's resolve to fight against those who withheld their *zakāt*. Abū Bakr overcame the initial hesitations of other Companions by arguing that the willful rejection of such an essential obligation could not be tolerated.[82]

When Ibn Taymiyya introduces the Mongols into this juristic framework of rebellion, he locates them within this last category of insurgents who defy not only the ruler but also Islam itself and therefore merit no reprieve. He marshals contemporary evidence of the Mongols' atrocious conduct and unacceptable beliefs to support this conclusion,[83] and he repeatedly compares the Mongols with earlier groups in the Islamic past. He finds the Mongols fitting the Prophet's worst condemnation of the Khawārij[84] and, unlike the combatants at the battles of the Camel and Ṣiffīn, there is no plausible interpretation for their misconduct.[85] Therefore, they should be denied the leniency that would be due to such insurgents. Moreover, even the profoundly misguided Khawārij and the withholders of *zakāt*, who were dealt with harshly, had more of a plausible interpretation than what the Mongols could possibly claim.[86] As rebels of this second category, the Mongols, comprising a considerable armed force in open defiance of all religiously sanctioned authority,[87] deserved to be fought with all resolve and determination—in fact, Ibn Taymiyya considered it obligatory for Muslims to do so.[88]

In contrast to Ibn Taymiyya's engagement with the laws of rebellions, the passages that Faraj isolates and selectively cites from Ibn Taymiyya's *fatwās*, address the Mongols' failure to implement central elements of the Sharīʿa despite their conversion to Islam. In Ibn Taymiyya's *fatwā*, these passages are subordinate to his overarching juristic framework, and therefore the Mongols' open deviance and defiance is sufficient to classify them as rebels of the second category, who should be fought unreservedly. Faraj, however, generalizes these statements, and uses the absence of an Islamic code of law in modern Egypt as a justification for rebellion against the State[89]—a complete corruption of Ibn Taymiyya's legal categories. Completing the irony of this transformation of Ibn Taymiyya's original paradigm is the resulting parallel between the ideology of Faraj's Jihād group and the Khawārij.[90] Ibn Taymiyya unequivocally condemns the misguided piety of the Khawārij which leads them to shed the blood of other Muslims, and, as we have seen, this rebellious group forms one of the key discursive focal points of his original legal opinions.[91]

Muslim religious scholars and moderate Islamist writers have consistently pointed to Faraj's disastrous misreading of Ibn Taymiyya's scholarship. In a four-part series of articles run by *al-Liwā' al-Islāmī* based on interviews with religious scholars, the Director of Egypt's Islamic Research Institute, Dr al-Ḥusaynī Hāshim, clarified that extremists, such as the Jihād group, had manifestly misunderstood the texts of Ibn Taymiyya's work and deviated from the medieval scholar's teachings. Ibn Taymiyya, Hāshim asserted, "made it clear and stressed that those who declare the blood of people lawful [to spill] or rebel against the ruler or fight against the populace are only rebels violating Islamic law."[92] Dr Sayyid al-Ṭawīl, a professor of Islamic Studies, further explained that Faraj's poor understanding of the texts that he had cited from Ibn Taymiyya in *al-Farīḍa al-ghā'iba* led him to misuse Ibn Taymiyya's words and employ them outside their appropriate context.[93] When assessing Faraj's interpretations of *ridda* as religious apostasy instead of political treason, the prominent Islamist intellectual Dr Muḥammad 'Imāra also exclaims that "the text and judgment of Ibn Taymiyya have been pulled out of its context and utilized in a different way that bears no relationship to the [original] subject!"[94] In his official statement, the Grand Muftī of Egypt, Shaykh Jādd al-Ḥaqq 'Alī Jādd al-Ḥaqq, elaborates on how the reality of contemporary Egypt clearly contradicts Ibn Taymiyya's descriptions of the Mongols, thereby rendering Faraj's belligerent comparisons entirely baseless.[95] And Jamāl al-Bannā, brother of the late founder of the Society of Muslim Brothers, finds the rash comparison of today's Muslim rulers with the Mongols to be so ludicrously narrow-minded and spiteful as to not warrant any further commentary.[96]

The Modern State, the Caliphate, and the Impact of Ibn Taymiyya

The concept of an Islamic caliphate is central to both strains of Egyptian Islamism discussed above—the accommodationists on the one hand and the confrontationists on the other. Among the moderate centrists, leaders of the Society of Muslim Brothers recognize the Islamic nature of the Egyptian state as declared in its constitution and therefore attempt to work within the system to implement Islamically oriented principles and policies of governance and socio-economic justice.[97] Extremists, on the other hand, reject this characterization of the state and advocate violence in order to bring about Islamic rule.[98] For both of these groups, the caliphate represents an Islamic ideal and model of governance, although they have adopted significantly different interpretations of what that legacy means for Muslims in the present. Ibn Taymiyya's writings are an inspiration to divergent visions of this ideal.

To conclude with one of the questions posed by this collection of essays: has Ibn Taymiyya dominated or been dominated by the twentieth-century? Perhaps, the answer is both. The vitality of Ibn Taymiyya's thought has certainly been a prominent contribution to modern interpretations of Islam and its role in society, and, at the same time, his work has refracted multifariously in the present, sometimes well beyond the letter, and even spirit, of his medieval scholarship.

Notes

1. Jalāl al-Dīn al-Suyūṭī, *Ḥusn al-muḥāḍara fī akhbār Miṣr wa-al-Qāhira* ([Cairo]: al-Maṭba'a al-Sharafiyya, 1909), 2:44.
2. The implications of these dramatic events are discussed in my PhD dissertation, "Loss of Caliphate: The Trauma and Aftermath of 1258 and 1924" (Princeton University, 2009).
3. Henri Laoust, *Essai sur les doctrines sociales et politiques de Taḳī-d-dīn Aḥmad b. Taimīya* (Cairo: Imprimerie de l'institut français d'archéologie orientale, 1939), 281–3.
4. Hamilton Gibb, "Constitutional Organization: The Muslim Community and the State," in *Law in the Middle East*, ed. Majid Khadduri and Herbert Liebesny (Washington, D.C.: The Middle East Institute, 1955), 23–4.
5. Ann Lambton, *State and Government in Medieval Islam: An Introduction to the Study of Islamic Political Theory* (Oxford: Oxford University Press, 1981), 143–51.
6. Gibb, "Constitutional Organization," 23; Lambton, *State and Government*, 138–43. I further discuss this misconception of Ibn Jamā'a's work in my "Loss of Caliphate."
7. Erwin Rosenthal, *Political Thought in Medieval Islam: An Introductory Outline* (Cambridge: Cambridge University Press, 1962), 52.
8. W. Montgomery Watt, *Islamic Political Thought: The Basic Concepts* (Edinburgh: Edinburgh University Press, 1968), 107.
9. Quamaruddin Khan, *The Political Thought of Ibn Taymiyya* (Lahore: Islamic Book Foundation, 1983), xvi, xix, 107. Although Khan flags Laoust's confusion over Ibn

Taymiyya's rejection of the imamate as an article of faith (38–40), he fails to develop an overall consistent and logical argument on the topic. He seems convinced of Ibn Taymiyya's decision to distance himself from Muslim jurisprudence and theology regarding the imamate and caliphate, as passionately expressed in the passage quoted here.

10. Malcolm Kerr, *Islamic Reform: The Political and Legal Theories of Muḥammad 'Abduh and Rashīd Riḍā* (Berkeley: University of California Press, 1966), 28; Itzchak Weismann, *Taste of Modernity: Sufism, Salafiyya, and Arabism in late Ottoman Damascus* (Leiden: Brill, 2001), 264; Richard Bonney, *Jihād: From Qur'ān to bin Laden* (New York: Palgrave Macmillan, 2004), 112.
11. Ibn Taymiyya, *Minhāj al-sunna fī naqḍ kalām al-Shī'a wa-al-Qadariyya* (Bulaq: al-Maṭba'a al-Kubrā al-Amīriyya, 1903).
12. Laoust, *Essai*, 282 ("Le caliphat unitaire ne présente plus, dès lors [depuis l'imāma des Rāshidūn], aucun caractère d'obligation. Ainsi se trouve incorporée au système d'ibn Taimīya la dernière des doctrines qui attendait d'être, elle aussi, justement située dans sa synthèse conciliatrice, la doctrine Ḥārijite, dont l'une des caractéristiques est de nier l'obligation pour la communauté d'avoir à sa tête un calife, bien qu'ibn Taimīya, dans les exposés fréquents qu'il en fait, ne présente jamais comme l'une des thèses maîtresses du Ḥārijisme cette négation de la pérennité califienne").
13. Ibid., 282–3.
14. Ibn Taymiyya, *Minhāj al-sunna*, 1:16–30.
15. Ibid., 2:222.
16. Laoust, *Essai*, 282 ("Ibn Taimīya considère comme appartenant à la Sunna plusiers ḥadiths, d'inspiration Ḥārijite, reproduits par les recueils orthodoxes, qui ne fixent aucun terme au nombre des imams").
17. Ibn Taymiyya, *Minhāj al-sunna*, 1:27–8.
18. Ibid., 1:28.
19. The Hadith is translated in full below, in the discussion of Ibn Taymiyya's actual attitude to the caliphate. Al-Nawawī and Ibn Ḥajar al-'Asqalānī further state that the key phrase "one after the other" (*al-awwal fa-al-awwal*) conveys that only the oath of allegiance (*bay'a*) to the first caliph is valid, even if the electors of the second caliph did not know of the first caliph's election, and regardless of the geographical distance between the two. See Ibn Taymiyya, *Minhāj al-sunna*, 1:28; Muḥyī al-Dīn Abū Zakariyyā Yaḥyā b. Sharaf al-Nawawī, *Sharḥ Ṣaḥīḥ Muslim*, ed. Khalīl al-Mays (Beirut: Dār al-Qalam, 1987), 12:473–4; Abū Faḍl Shihāb al-Dīn Aḥmad b. 'Alī Ibn Ḥajar al-'Asqalānī, *Fatḥ al-bārī bi-sharḥ Ṣaḥīḥ al-Bukhārī*, ed. Ṭāhā 'Abd al-Ra'ūf Sa'd, Muṣṭafā Muḥammad al-Hawwārī, al-Sayyid Muḥammad 'Abd al-Mu'ṭī (Cairo: Maktabat al-Kulliyāt al-Azhariyya, 1978), 13:258–9; Abū 'Abdallāh Muḥammad b. Yazīd Ibn Māja al-Qazwīnī, *Sunan Ibn Māja*, ed. Maḥmūd Muḥammad Maḥmūd Ḥasan Naṣṣār (Beirut: Dār al-Kutub al-'Ilmiyya, 1998), 3:400.
20. Muḥammad al-Mubārak, *al-Dawla wa-niẓām al-ḥisba 'inda Ibn Taymiyya* ([Damascus]: Dār al-Fikr, 1967), 34–43; Bassām 'Aṭiyya Ismā'īl Faraj, *al-Fikr al-siyāsī 'inda Ibn Taymiyya* (Amman: Dār al-Yāqūt, 2001), 144–5, 166–75; Ibn Taymiyya, *Minhāj al-sunna*, 1:135, 141–5, 3:165; Ibn Taymiyya, *Majmū' al-fatāwā*, ed. 'Abd al-Raḥmān b. Muḥammad Ibn Qāsim (Beirut: n.p., 1997), 19: 29–30. Laoust and Khan, among others, erroneously suppose that Ibn Taymiyya does not necessitate that a caliph be a descendent of Quraysh (e.g. Laoust, *Essai*, 294 and Khan, *Political Thought*, 144–5); for some of Ibn Taymiyya's emphatic remarks

to the contrary, where he necessitates the Qurashī lineage of an imam or caliph, see the passages of his *Minhāj* and *Majmūʿ* cited above.

21. Ibn Taymiyya, *Majmūʿ fatāwā shaykh al-islām Aḥmad b. Taymiyya*, ed. ʿAbd al-Raḥmān b. Muḥammad Ibn Qāsim (Cairo: Dār al-Raḥma, n.d.), 35:18–32.
22. Ironically enough, as noted above, this is precisely the prophetic Hadith that Laoust identifies as the inspiration for Ibn Taymiyya's rejection of the caliphate. For the Hadith, see al-Nawawī, *Sharḥ Ṣaḥīḥ Muslim*, 12:473–4; Ibn Ḥajar al-ʿAsqalānī, *Fatḥ al-bārī*, 13:258–9; Ibn Māja, *Sunan Ibn Māja*, 3:400.
23. Ibn Taymiyya, *Majmūʿ fatāwā* (Cairo), 35:20.
24. Ibn Taymiyya, *Minhāj al-sunna*, 1:27.
25. Ibid., 1:8.
26. Ibid., 3:131.
27. Ibn Taymiyya, *Majmūʿ fatāwā* (Cairo), 35:24–32.
28. Ibn Taymiyya, *Minhāj al-sunna*, 3:131.
29. Ibn Taymiyya, *Majmūʿ fatāwā* (Cairo), 35:20.
30. Ibid., 35:5–9, 20.
31. Ibn Taymiyya, *al-Siyāsa al-sharʿiyya fī iṣlāḥ al-rāʿī wa-al-raʿiyya* (Beirut: Dār al-Kutub al-ʿIlmiyya, n.d.). This work was translated by Omar Farrukh under the slightly misleading title *Ibn Taimiyya on Public and Private Law in Islam, or Public Policy in Islamic Jurisprudence* (Beirut: Khayats, 1966).
32. Ibn Taymiyya, *al-Siyāsa al-sharʿiyya*, 7.
33. Ann Lambton, "Islamic Mirrors for Princes," in *La Persia nel medioevo: Atti del Convegno internazionale, Roma 1970* (Rome: Accademia Nazionale dei Lincei, 1971), 419–20.
34. Patricia Crone, "Did al-Ghazālī write a Mirror for Princes?", *Jerusalem Studies in Arabic and Islam* 10 (1987): 173. Carole Hillenbrand adroitly questions the authenticity of the second part of *Naṣīḥat al-mulūk* in her article examining al-Ghazālī's major political works, "Islamic Orthodoxy or Realpolitik? Al-Ghazālī's Views on Government", *Iran: Journal of the British Institute of Persian Studies* 26 (1988): 91–3.
35. Louise Marlow, "Kings, Prophets, and the 'Ulamā' in Mediaeval Islamic Advice Literature," *Studia Islamica* 81 (1995): 102.
36. Patricia Crone, *God's Rule: Government and Islam* (New York: Columbia University Press, 2004), 149.
37. As narrated in the Hadith collections of Abū Dāwūd and al-Tirmidhī: Abū Dāwūd Sulaymān b. al-Ashʿath al-Sijistānī, *Sunan*, ed. Muḥammad ʿAbd al-ʿAzīz al-Khālidī (Beirut: Dār al-Kutub al-ʿIlmiyya, 1996), 3:285; Muḥammad Shams al-Ḥaqq ʿAẓīmābādī, *ʿAwn al-maʿbūd sharḥ Sunan Abī Dāwūd maʿa sharḥ al-ḥāfiẓ Ibn Qayyim al-Jawziyya*, ed. ʿAbd al-Raḥmān Muḥammad ʿUthmān (Medina: al-Maktaba al-Salafiyya, 1968), 13:260–1; Abū ʿĪsā Muḥammad b. ʿĪsā al-Tirmidhī, *al-Jāmiʿ al-kabīr*, ed. Bashshār ʿAwwād Maʿrūf (Beirut: Dār al-Gharb al-Islāmī, 1996); Muḥammad ʿAbd al-Raḥmān b. ʿAbd al-Raḥīm al-Mubārakfūrī, *Tuḥfat al-aḥwadhī bi-sharḥ Jāmiʿ al-Tirmidhī*, ed, ʿIṣām al-Ṣabābiṭī (Cairo: Dār al-Ḥadīth, 2001), 5:343.
38. Cited in Crone, "al-Ghazālī," 173.
39. Ibn Taymiyya, *al-Siyāsa al-sharʿiyya*, 8–9.
40. Abū Jaʿfar Muḥammad b. Jarīr al-Ṭabarī, *Jāmiʿ al-bayān fī tafsīr al-Qurʾān* [*Jāmiʿ al-bayān ʿan taʾwīl āy al-Qurʾān*] (Bulaq: al-Maṭbaʿa al-Kubrā al-Amīriyya, 1916–17), 5:93–5.

41. Abū ʿAbdallāh Muḥammad b. Aḥmad al-Anṣārī al-Qurṭubī, *al-Jāmiʿ li-aḥkām al-Qur'ān*, ed. Aḥmad ʿAbd al-ʿAlīm al-Bardūnī, 3rd ed. (Cairo: Dār al-Qalam and Dār al-Kitāb al-ʿArabī, 1966), 5:258–61.
42. Ibn Taymiyya, *Minhāj al-sunna*, 1:28 (*al-a'imma hum al-umarā' wulāt al-umūr*), 3:131 (*al-nās yusammūna wulāt umūr al-Muslimīn al-khulafā'*).
43. Ibn Taymiyya, *al-Siyāsa al-sharʿiyya*, 21–2.
44. Ibid., 13–28.
45. Ibid., 28–137.
46. Ibid., 137–43.
47. See, for example, Abul Hasan Ali Nadwi, *Saviours of Islamic Spirit*, trans. Muhiddin Ahmad, 2nd ed. (Lucknow, India: Academy of Islamic Research and Publications, 1977), 2:19–143, and S. Abul ʿAla Maududi, *A Short History of the Revivalist Movement in Islam*, trans. al-Ashʿari (Lahore: Islamic Publications Limited, 1963), 62–8.
48. These key terms "accommodationist" and "confrontationist" are adapted from Sana Abed-Kotob's article, "The Accommodationists Speak: Goals and Strategies of the Muslim Brotherhood in Egypt," *International Journal of Middle Eastern Studies* 27 (1995): 321–39. Although Abed-Kotob initially uses these terms to describe academic researchers of Islamic movements in accordance with their general attitudes towards their subject matter, the words "accommodationist" and "confrontationist" are particularly apt in describing the Islamists themselves and their views of the state. Indeed, Abed-Kotob herself evokes this set of linguistic associations when she concludes at the end of her article that "[the Muslim Brothers'] major strategy was labelled 'accommodation' with the existing political system, for the group has become totally reliant on constitutional channels for the changes they demand" (336).
49. Raymond William Baker, "Invidious Comparisons: Realism, Postmodern Globalism, and Centrist Islamic Movements in Egypt," in John L. Esposito (ed.), *Political Islam: Revolution, Radicalism, or Reform?* (Boulder, CO: Lynne Rienner Publishers, 1997), 122.
50. Abed-Kotob, "The Accommodationists Speak," 321–39.
51. Mona El-Ghobashy, "The Metamorphosis of the Egyptian Muslim Brothers," *International Journal of Middle Eastern Studies* 37 (2005): 374.
52. Jan Stark, "Beyond 'Terrorism' and 'State Hegemony': Assessing the Islamist Mainstream in Egypt and Malaysia," *Third World Quarterly* 26, no. 2 (2005): 308.
53. Yūsuf al-Qaraḍāwī, *Ibn al-qarya wa-al-kuttāb: malāmiḥ sīra wa-masīra* (Cairo: Dār al-Shurūq, 2002), 1:161, 177–8, 242; Muḥammad Akram al-Nadwī, *Kifāyat al-rāwī ʿan ʿallāmat al-shaykh Yūsuf al-Qaraḍāwī* (Damascus: Dār al-Qalam, 2001), 13.
54. al-Qaraḍāwī, *Ibn al-qarya wa-al-kuttāb*, 1:15, 104; al-Nadwī, *Kifāyat al-rāwī*, 11; ʿIṣām Talīma, *Yūsuf al-Qaraḍāwī: Faqīh al-Duʿāt wa-Dāʿiyat al-Fuqahā'* (Damascus: Dār al-Qalam, 2001), 12; *al-Shaykh Yūsuf al-Qaraḍāwī: shakhṣiyyat al-ʿām al-islamiyya 1421 A.H./2000 C.E.* (Cairo: Maktabat Wahba, 2001), 6; ʿAbd al-ʿAẓīm al-Dīb (ed.), *Yūsuf al-Qaraḍāwī: kalimāt fī takrīmihi wa-buḥūth fī fikrihi wa-fiqhihi muhdātun ilayhi bi-munāsabati bulūghihi al-sabʿīn* (Cairo: Dār al-Salām: 2004), 1:19.
55. al-Qaraḍāwī, *Ibn al-qarya wa-al-kuttāb*, 1:131–55; al-Nadwī, *Kifāyat al-rāwī*, 12; Talīma, *Yūsuf al-Qaraḍāwī*, 12–14; *al-Shaykh Yūsuf al-Qaraḍāwī*, 6; al-Dīb, *Yūsuf al-Qaraḍāwī*, 1:19.
56. al-Qaraḍāwī, *Ibn al-qarya wa-al-kuttāb*, 1:486–94, 2:13–16, 210–26, 317–8; al-Nadwī, *Kifāyat al-rāwī*, 13; Talīma, *Yūsuf al-Qaraḍāwī*, 14; *al-Shaykh Yūsuf al-Qaraḍāwī*, 6–7; al-Dīb, *Yūsuf al-Qaraḍāwī*, 1:19.

57. al-Qaraḍāwī, *Ibn al-qarya wa-al-kuttāb*, 2:318–9, 330, 333–6, 343–6; al-Nadwī, *Kifāyat al-rāwī*, 15; Talīma, *Yūsuf al-Qaraḍāwī*, 15; *al-Shaykh Yūsuf al-Qaraḍāwī*, 8; al-Dīb, *Yūsuf al-Qaraḍāwī*, 1:20–1.
58. Raymond William Baker, *Islam without Fear: Egypt and the New Islamists* (Cambridge, MA: Harvard University Press, 2003), 4, 12–13, 183, 215–16, 275; Baker, "Invidious Comparisons," 125–8; *al-Shaykh Yūsuf al-Qaraḍāwī*, 9–49. Baker even notes that al-Qaraḍāwī is "frequently identified as perhaps the most influential Islamic scholar in the Islamic world today" (Baker, *Islam without Fear*, 4), and also observes that when he "speaks publicly, he will draw crowds at times reaching over a quarter of a million" (Baker, "Invidious Comparisons," 125).
59. Baker, *Islam without Fear*, 12–13, 46–7, 95, 166–7, 170, 173, 179, 185, 192–203; El-Ghobashy, "Metamorphosis," 382–5, 386–7, 389–90; *al-Shaykh Yūsuf al-Qaraḍāwī*, 28–36.
60. Yūsuf al-Qaraḍāwī, *Awlawiyyāt al-ḥaraka al-islāmiyya fīal-marḥala al-qādima* (Cairo: Maktabat Wahba, 1991). English translation as Yousef al-Qaradawi, *Priorities of the Islamic Movement in the Coming Phase* (Cairo: Dār al-Nashr for Egyptian Universities, 1992); also revised translation under the same title by S.M. Hasan Al-Banna (Swansea: Awakening Publications, 2000).
61. Ibid., 121–2.
62. Ibid., 164–84; Yūsuf al-Qaraḍāwī, *al-Ṣaḥwa al-islāmiyya bayna al-juḥūd wa-al-taṭarruf* (Doha: al-Maḥākim al-Shar'iyya wa-al-Shu'ūn al-Dīniyya fī Dawlat Qaṭar, 1982); translated as Yusuf al-Qaradawi, *Islamic Awakening between Rejection and Extremism*, New English ed., trans. A.S. Al-Shaikh-Ali and Mohamed B.E. Wasfy (Herndon, VA: American Trust Publication and the International Institute of Islamic Thought, 1991).
63. Qaraḍāwī, *Awlawiyyāt*, 31, 199–201.
64. Ibn Taymiyya, *Majmū' al-fatāwā* (Beirut), 30: 356–60.
65. Qaraḍāwī, *Awlawiyyāt*, 31, 202–6.
66. Ibn Taymiyya, *Majmū' al-fatāwā* (Beirut), 20: 48–61.
67. Muḥammad Akram al-Nadwī, *Kifāyat al-rāwī*, 18–19; *al-Shaykh Yūsuf al-Qaraḍāwī*, 7; al-Dīb, *Yūsuf al-Qaraḍāwī*, 1:20.
68. On his regard for Ibn Taymiyya, al-Qaraḍāwī also clarifies, "I love Ibn Taymiyya, but I am not a Taymiyyan [i.e., a blind follower of him]." See Yūsuf al-Qaraḍāwī, *Kayfa nata'āmalu ma'a al-sunna al-nabawiyya: ma'ālim wa-ḍawābiṭ* (Herdon, VA: al-Ma'had al-'Ālamī li-al-Fikr al-Islāmī, 1990), 170–1.
69. See, for example, Emmanuel Sivan, "Ibn Taymiyya: Father of the Islamic Revolution, Medieval Theology & Modern Politics," *Encounter* 60, no. 3 (1983): 41–4; Emmanuel Sivan, *Radical Islam: Medieval Theology and Modern Politics* (New Haven, CT: Yale University Press, 1990), 94–101; Natana Delong-Bas, *Wahhabi Islam: From Revival and Reform to Global Jihad* (Oxford: Oxford University Press, 2004), 248–50, 253–4, 256; Johannes Jansen, "Ibn Taymiyya and the Thirteenth Century: A Formative Period of Modern Muslim Radicalism," *Quaderni di studi arabi* 5–6 (1987–88): 396; Stephen Schwartz, *The Two Faces of Islam: The House of Sa'ud from Tradition to Terror* (New York: Doubleday, 2002), 54–6, 182; Daniel Benjamin and Steven Simon, *The Age of Sacred Terror: Radical Islam's War against America* (New York: Random House, 2003), 38–52.
70. Jansen, "Ibn Taymiyya and the Thirteenth Century," 393. For additional discussion of Ibn Taymiyya's condemnation of rebellion, see Khaled Abou El Fadl, *Rebellion and Violence in Islamic Law* (Cambridge: Cambridge University Press, 2001), 273–5.

71. For a detailed discussion of these *fatwās*, see Thomas Raff, *Remarks on an Anti-Mongol Fatwā by Ibn Taymīya* (Leiden: n.p., 1973); Denise Aigle, "The Mongol invasions of Bilād al-Shām by Ghazan Khān and Ibn Taymiyya's three 'anti-Mongol' Fatwas", *Mamluk Studies Review*, 11/2 (2007): 89–120. For a critical edition and French translation, see Yahya Michot, "Mongols et Mamlūks: l'état du monde musulman vers 709/1310", *Textes spirituels d'Ibn Tayimiyya XI, XII, XII*, available online at http://www.muslimphilosophy.com/.
72. Nemat Guenena, *The 'Jihad' an 'Islamic Alternative' in Egypt*, Cairo Papers in Social Science (Cairo: The American University in Cairo Press, 1986), 50–2, 61–5.
73. Jansen, "Ibn Taymiyya and the Thirteenth Century," 391.
74. Muḥammad 'Abd al-Salām Faraj, *al-Jihād, al-farīḍa al-ghā'iba* (n.p., 1990). For an English translation, see Johannes Jansen, *The Neglected Duty: The Creed of Sadat's Assassins and Islamic Resurgence in the Middle East* (New York: Macmillan Publishing Company, 1986), 159–234, and for a partial critical French translation, see Yahya Michot, *Mardin: Hégire, fuite de péché et « demeure de l'Islam »* (Beirut: Les Éditions Albouraq, 2004), 105–11; and in English as Yahya Michot, *Muslims under non-Muslim Rule* (Oxford: Interface Publications, 2006).
75. Ibn Taymiyya, *Majmū' fatāwā* (Cairo), 28: 531–4, 552. Abou El Fadl's *Rebellion and Violence in Islamic Law* traces the development of this juristic discourse on insurrection as well as brigandage.
76. Ibid., 28: 513–19, 540–2, 548–52.
77. Abū al-Fidā' 'Imād al-Dīn Ibn Kathīr, *al-Bidāya wa-al-Nihāya*, ed. 'Alī Muḥammad Mu'awwaḍ and 'Ādil Aḥmad 'Abd al-Mawjūd (Beirut: Dār al-Kutub al-'Ilmiyya, 1994), 14:20.
78. Ibn Taymiyya, *Majmū' fatāwā* (Cairo), 28: 513–15, 548, 551.
79. Ibid., 28: 502–4, 515–16, 548–9, 551.
80. Ibid., 28: 512, 516, 549–50.
81. Ibid., 28: 512–13, 516–18, 545–6, 549, 550.
82. Ibid., 28: 519, 545.
83. Ibid., 28: 504–5, 519–28, 551.
84. Ibid., 28: 528–31, 546.
85. Ibid., 28: 541–3, 548.
86. Ibid., 28: 542. As Ibn Taymiyya exclaims, "*Fa-ayyu ta'wīlin baqiya lahum?! Thumma law quddira annahum muta'awwilūna lam yakun ta'wīluhum sā'ighan, bal ta'wīl al-khawārij wa-māni'ī al-zakāti awjahu min ta'wīlihim...*".
87. Ibid., 28: 549, 551.
88. Ibid., 28: 502–4, 510–12, 545, 546, 551.
89. Faraj, *al-Farīḍa al-ghā'iba*, 10–13, 16, 17–18, 27.
90. Indeed, Shaykh Jādd al-Ḥaqq 'Alī Jādd al-Ḥaqq discusses this peculiar similarity in his official statement, "Kutayyib al-Farīḍa al-ghā'iba wa-al-Radd 'alayhi," *al-Fatāwā al-islāmiyya min Dār al-Iftā' al-Miṣriyya*, 3 January 1982, http://www.dar-alifta.org. See also Jansen's comments in *The Neglected Duty* (59–60) and in "Ibn Taymiyya and the Thirteenth Century" (392–3).
91. Ibn Taymiyya, *Majmū' fatāwā* (Cairo), 28: 502, 512–13, 516–18, 528–31, 546, 548, 551. Delong-Bas' bold assertion that "Ibn Taymiyya drew his inspiration from the militant interpretation of Islam developed by the seventh-century extremist Kharijite movement" is untenable in this light, and she erroneously surmises that Ibn Taymiyya's utilization of the Khawārij in his anti-Mongol *fatwās* (as an analytical category representing blameworthy individuals) is somehow an endorsement of their views (*Wahhabi Islam*, 248–9).

92. "al-Liwā' al-Islāmī tunāqishu kitāb al-Farīḍa al-ghā'iba (1): Man huwa al-Imām Ibn Taymiyya alladhī akhadhū 'anhu da'wat al-ightiyāl wa-al-taṭarruf?," *al-Liwā' al-Islāmī*, Februrary 25, 1982, 8.
93. "al-Liwā' al-Islāmī tuwāṣilu munāqashat kitāb al-Farīḍa al-ghā'iba (3)," *al-Liwā' al-Islāmī*, 11 March 1982, 9.
94. Muḥammad 'Imāra, *al-Farīḍa al-ghā'iba: 'ard wa-ḥiwār wa-taqyīm* (Cairo: Dār Thābit, 1982), 44–5, 47–56.
95. Jādd al-Ḥaqq, "Kutayyib al-Farīḍa al-ghā'iba wa-al-Radd 'alayhi".
96. Jamāl al-Bannā, *al-Farīḍa al-ghā'iba: jihād al-sayf am jihād al-'aql* (Cairo: Dār Thābit, 1984), 26.
97. El-Ghobashy, "Metamorphosis," 389; Baker, "Invidious Comparisons," 126–7.
98. Abed-Kotob, "The Accommodationists Speak," 321; Tamer Moustafa, "Conflict and Cooperation between the State and Religious Institutions in Contemporary Egypt," *International Journal of Middle Eastern Studies* 32 (2000): 10–11.

BIBLIOGRAPHY

1. Works by Taqī al-Dīn Ibn Taymiyya (1263–1328)

An introduction to the principles of tafseer [*Muqaddima fī uṣūl al-tafsīr*], translated by Muḥammad 'Abdul Haq Ansari (Birmingham: Al-Hidaayah Publishing, 1993).

al-Fatwā al-ḥamawiyya al-kubrā (Cairo: al-Maṭba'a al-Salafiyya, 1967).

al-Ḥisba fī al-Islām, aw waẓīfat al-ḥukūma al-Islāmīya, ed. Muḥammad al-Mubārak (Beirut: Dār al-Kutub al-'Arabiyya, 1967).

al-Ijtimā' wa al-iftirāq fī al-ḥilf bi-al-ṭalāq, ed. Muḥammad 'Abd al-Razzāq Ḥamza (Cairo: al-Manār press, 1346/1926–7).

al-Īmān, ed. Muḥammad Zabīdī (Beirut: Dār al-Kitāb al-'Arabī, 1414/1993).

al-Istiqāma, ed. M. Rashād Sālim (Riyadh: Jāmi'at al-Imām Muḥammad Su'ūd, 1983).

al-Jawāb al-Ṣaḥīḥ li-man baddala dīn al-Masīḥ, 4 vols. (Cairo: Maṭba'at al-Nīl, 1905).

al-Nubuwwāt (Beirut: Dār al-Qalam, n.d.).

al-Qā'ida al-Marākishiyya, ed. Nādir al-Rashīd and Riḍā Mu'ṭī (Riyadh: Dār Ṭība, 1981).

al-Qawā'id al-nūrāniyya al-fiqhiyya, ed. Muḥammad Ḥāmid al-Fiqī (Cairo: Maṭba'at al-Sunna al-Muḥammadiyya, 1951).

al-Siyāsa al-shar'iyya fī iṣlāḥ al-rā'ī wa-al-ra'iyya (Beirut: Dār al-Kutub al-'Ilmiyya, n.d.).

al-Tafsīr al-kabīr, ed. 'Abd al-Raḥmān 'Umayra (Beirut: Dār al-Kutub al-'Ilmiyya, 1988).

'Arsh al-Raḥmān, ed. 'Abd al-'Azīz al-Sayrawān (Beirut: Dār al-'Ulūm al-'Arabiyya, 1995).

Bayān al-dalīl 'alā buṭlān al-taḥlīl, ed. Ḥamdī 'Abd al-Majīd al-Salafī (Beirut: al-Maktab al-Islāmī, 1998).

Bayān talbīs al-Jahmiyya fī ta'sīs bida'ihim al-kalāmiyya aw Naqḍ ta'sīs al-Jahmiyya, ed. Muḥammad b. 'Abd al-Raḥmān b. Qāsim, 2 vols. (n.pl.: Mu'assasat Qurṭuba, n.d.).

Daqā'iq al-tafsīr (Jedda, 1986).

Dar' ta'āruḍ al-'aql wa al-naql, ed. Muḥammad Rashād Sālim, 11 vols. (Cairo: Dār al-Kunūz al-Adabiyya, 1971–1979; reprinted in Riaydh, 1990).

Dar' ta'āruḍ al-'aql wa al-naql aw muwāfaqat ṣaḥīḥ al-manqūl li-ṣarīḥ al-ma'qūl, ed. 'Abd al-Laṭīf 'Abd al-Raḥmān (Beirut: Dār al-Kutub al-'Ilmiyya, 1417/1997).

Ibn Taimiyya on Public and Private Law in Islam, or Public Policy in Islamic Jurisprudence [*al-Siyāsa al-shar'iyya fī iṣlāḥ al-rā'ī wa-al-ra'iyya*], translated by Omar Farrukh (Beirut: Khayats, 1966).

Ibn Taymīya's Struggle against Popular Religion [*Iqtiḍā' al-ṣirāṭ al-mustaqīm mukhālafat aṣḥāb al-jaḥīm*], translated by Muḥammad Umar Memon (The Hague: Mouton & Co., 1976).

Iqtiḍā' al-ṣirāṭ al-mustaqīm mukhālafat aṣḥāb al-jaḥīm (Cairo: al-Maṭba'a al-Sharīfa, 1907).

Iqtiḍā' al-ṣirāṭ al-mustaqīm mukhālafat aṣḥāb al-jaḥīm, ed. Muḥammad Ḥāmid al-Fiqī (Cairo, 1950; reprint Lahore: Maktabat al-Salafiyya, 1977).

Iqtiḍā' al-ṣirāṭ al-mustaqīm li-mukhālafat aṣḥāb al-jaḥīm, ed. 'Iṣām Fāris al-Ḥarastānī and Muḥammad Ibrāhīm al-Zaghlī (Beirut: Dār al-Jīl, 1993).

Iqtiḍā' al-ṣirāṭ al-mustaqīm li-mukhālafat aṣḥāb al-jaḥīm, ed. Nāṣir b. 'Abd al-Karīm al-'Aql (Riyadh: Maktabat al-Rushd, 2000).

Majmū' fatāwā shaykh al-Islām Aḥmad b. Taymiyya, ed. 'Abd al-Raḥmān b. Muḥammad b. Qāsim and Muḥammad b. 'Abd al-Raḥmān b. Muḥammad al-'Āṣimī al-Najdī al-Ḥanbalī, 35 vols. (Riyadh: Maṭābi' al-Riyāḍ, 1961–6; reprinted in Beirut, 1983; Rabat: Maktabat al-Ma'ārif, 1981; Cairo).

Majmū' fatāwā Shaykh al-Islām Ibn Taymiyya, ed. Muṣṭafā 'Abd al-Qādir 'Aṭā, 37 vols. (Beirut: Dār al-Kutub al-'Ilmiyya, 2000).

Majmū'at al-fatāwā, ed. 'Āmir al-Jazzār and Anwar al-Bāz (Riyadh and al-Mansura: Dār al-Wafā' and Maktabat al-'Abīkān, 1419/1998).

Majmū'at al-rasā'il al-kubrā, ed. Rashīd Riḍā (Cairo: Maktabat wa-Maṭba'at Muḥammad 'Alī Ṣubayḥ wa-Awlādihi, 1385–1386/1966).

Majmū'at al-rasā'il wa al-masā'il, 5 vols. (Beirut: Dār al-Kutub al-'Ilmiyya, 1403/1983).

Majmū'at fatāwā Shaykh al-Islām Taqī al-Dīn Ibn Taymiyya, 5 vols. (Cairo: Maṭba'at Kurdistān al-Azharī, 1326–9/1908–11).

Majmū'at tafsīr Shaykh al-Islām Ibn Taymiyya, ed. 'Abd al-Ṣamad Sharaf al-Dīn (Bombay: al-Dār al-Qayyima, 1954).

Minhāj al-sunna al-nabawiyya fī naqḍ kalām al-Shī'a wa-al-Qadariyya (Bulaq: al-Maṭba'a al-Kubrā al-Amīriyya, 1903).

Minhāj al-sunna al-nabawiyya fī naqḍ kalām al-Shī'a wa-al-Qadariyya, 2 vols. (Cairo: Maktabat Dār al-'Urūba, 1962).

Minhāj al-sunna al-nabawiyya fī naqḍ kalām al-Shī'a al-Qadariyya, ed. Muḥammad Rashād Sālim, 9 vols. (Riyadh: Jāmi'at al-Imām Muḥammad b. Su'ūd al-Islāmiyya, 1406/1986).

Minhāj al-sunna (Beirut: Dār al-Kutub al-'Ilmiyya, 1420/1999).

Muqaddima fī uṣūl al-tafsīr, ed. Muḥibb al-Dīn al-Khaṭīb (Cairo: al-Maṭba'a al-Salafiyya, 1385/1965).

Muqaddima fī uṣūl al-tafsīr, ed. 'Adnān Zarzūr (Kuwait: Dār al-Qur'ān al-Karīm, 1971).

Muqaddima fī uṣūl al-tafsīr, ed. Maḥmūd Naṣṣār (Cairo: Maktabat al-Turāth al-Islāmī, 1988).

Muqaddima fī uṣūl al-tafsīr, ed. Fawwāz Zamlī (Cairo: Dār Ibn Ḥazm, 1997).

Ṣiḥḥat uṣūl madhhab ahl al-Madīna, ed. Zakarīyā 'Alī Yūsuf (Cairo: Maṭba'at al-Imām, n.d.).

Public duties in Islam: The institution of the Ḥisba [*al-Ḥisba fī al-Islām*], translated by Muhtar Holland; introduction and editorial notes by Khurshid Ahmad (Leicester: Islamic Foundation, 1982).

Tafsīr Sūrat al-Nūr (Beirut, 1983).

The Madinan way: the soundness of the basic premises of the school of the people of Madina, [*Ṣiḥḥat uṣūl madhhab ahl al-Madīna*], translated by Aisha Bewley (Norwich: Bookwork, 2000).

2. Other medieval and early modern works (pre–1800)

Abū Ḥayyān al-Andalusī al-Gharnāṭī (d. 745/1344). *Al-Baḥr al-Muḥīṭ*, ed. 'Ādil Aḥmad 'Abd al-Mawjūd et al. (Beirut: Dār al-Kutub al-'Ilmiyya, 1993).

Abū Shāma, Abd al-Raḥmān (d. 665/1267). *Al-Bāʿith ʿalā inkār al-bidaʿ wa al-ḥawādith*, ed. ʿĀdil ʿAbd al-Munʿim Abū al-ʿAbbās (Cairo: Maktabat Ibn Sīnā, n.d.).

Abū Yaʿlā ibn al-Farrāʾ (d. 458/1066). *Al-Masāʾil al-uṣūliyya min kitāb al-riwāyatayn wa al-wajhayn*, ed. ʿAbd al-Karīm Muḥammad al-Lāḥim (Riyadh: Maktabat al-Maʿārif, 1985).

———, *Al-Masāʾil wa al-rasāʾil al-marwiyya ʿan al-imām Aḥmad ibn Ḥanbal*, ed. ʿAbdallāh ibn Salmān al-Aḥmadī (Riyadh: Dār Ṭayba, 1412/1991).

———, *Kitāb al-muʿtamad fī uṣūl al-dīn*, ed. Wadi Z. Haddad (Beirut: Dār al-Mashriq, 1974).

al-Ājurrī, Abū Bakr (d. 390/971), *Kitāb al-Sharīʿa* (Beirut: Muʾassasat al-Rayyān, 1421/2000).

al-Āmidī, Sayf al-Dīn (d. 631/1233). *Abkār al-afkār fī uṣūl al-dīn*, ed. Aḥmad Muḥammad al-Mahdī, 5 vols. (Cairo: Maṭbaʿat Dār al-Kutub wa al-Wathāʾiq al-Qawmiyya, 1423/2002).

al-ʿĀmilī, Muḥammad ibn al-Ḥasan al-Ḥurr (d. 1693). *Amal al-āmil fī ʿulamāʾ Jabal ʿĀmil* (Qum: Dār al-Kitāb al-Islāmī, 1965–1966).

al-Ashʿarī, Abū al-Ḥasan (d. 935). *Kitāb maqālāt al-islāmiyyīn wa-ikhtilāf al-muṣallīn*, ed. H. Ritter, 2nd edition (Wiesbaden: Franz Steiner, 1963).

———, *Risāla fī istiḥsān al-khawḍ fī ʿilm al-kalām*, ed. Richard J. McCarthy (Beirut: al-Maṭbaʿa al-Katulikiyya, 1952).

al-ʿAynī, Badr al-Dīn (d. 855/1451). *ʿIqd al-jumān fī taʾrīkh ahl al-zamān*, ed. M. M. Amīn (Cairo: al-Hayʾa al-Miṣriyya al-ʿĀmma li-al-Kitāb, 1992).

al-ʿAyyāshī, ʿAbdallāh (d. 1680). *Al-Riḥla al-ʿAyyāshiyya* (Rabat: Dār al-Maghrib, 1977 [reprint]).

al-Baghdādī, ʿAbd al-Qāhir (d. 429/1038). *Uṣūl al-Dīn* (Istanbul: Maṭbaʿat al-dawla, 1346/1928).

al-Bakrī, Muṣṭafā (d. 1749). *Al-Qawl al-jalī fī tarjamat Taqī al-Dīn Ibn Taymiyya al-Ḥanbalī*, ed. by S. al-Dakhīl (Riyad: Dār al-Waṭan, 1999).

al-Bāqillānī, Abū Bakr (d. 403/1013). *Kitāb al-tamhīd*, ed. R.J. McCarthy (Beirut: al-Maktaba al-Sharqiyya, 1957).

———, *Kitāb Tamhīd al-awāʾil wa-talkhīṣ al-dalāʾil*, ed. ʿImad al-Dīn Aḥmad Ḥaydar (Beirut: Muʾassasat al-Kutub al-Thaqāfiyya, 1987).

al-Baṣrī, ʿAbdallāh ibn Sālim (d. 1722). *Al-Imdād bi-maʿrifat ʿuluww al-isnād* (Hyderabad: Dāʾirat al-Maʿārif al-ʿUthmāniyya, 1328AH).

al-Bazdawī, Abū al-Yusr (d. 493/1100). *Uṣūl al-Dīn*, ed. Hans Peter Lins (Cairo: Dār Iḥyāʾ al-Kutub al-ʿArabiyya, 1963).

al-Bukhārī, Ṣafī al-Dīn (d. 1786). *Muʿjam*, edited by M. M. Ḥāfiẓ (Damascus: Dār al-Bashāʾir, 1999).

al-Būlāqī, Alī al-ʿAzīzī (d. 1658). *Al-Sirāj al-munīr sharḥ al-Jāmiʿ al-ṣaghīr* (Cairo: ʿIsā al-Bābī al-Ḥalabī, 1939).

al-Dardīr, Aḥmad (d. 1786). *Al-Sharḥ al-kabīr ʿalā Mukhtaṣar Khalīl* (with the glosses of Muḥammad ibn ʿArafa al-Dasūqī [d. 1815]) (Cairo: Maṭbaʿat Dār al-Saʿāda, 1911).

al-Dawānī, Jalāl al-Dīn (d. 1502). *Sharḥ al-ʿAqāʾid al-ʿAḍudiyya* (Istanbul: ʿArif Efendi, 1316H).

al-Dhahabī, Shams al-Dīn (d. 1348). *Bayān zaghal al-ʿilm wa-al-ṭalab*, ed. M. Z. Al-Kawtharī (Damascus: Maṭbaʿat al-Tawfīq, 1928–29).

———, *Taʾrīkh al-Islām wa-wafayāt al-mashāhīr wa-al-aʿlām*, ed. ʿUmar al-Tadmurī, 52 vols. (Beirut: Dār al-Kitāb al-ʿArabī, 1987–2000).

________, *Thalāth tarājim nafīsa li-al-a'imma al-a'lām: Shaykh al-Islām Ibn Taymiyya, al-ḥāfiẓ 'Alam al-Dīn al-Birzālī, al-ḥāfiẓ Jamāl al-Dīn al-Mizzī: min kitāb Dhayl Tārīkh al-Islām*, ed. M. Nāṣir al-'Ajamī (Kuwayt: Dār Ibn al-Athīr, 1995).

al-Ghayyānī, Ibrāhīm ibn Aḥmad. *Nāḥiya min ḥayāt Shaykh al-Islām Ibn Taymiyya*, ed. Muḥibb al-Dīn al-Khaṭīb (Cairo: al-Maṭba'a al-Salafiyya, 1352H).

al-Ghazālī, Abū Ḥāmid (d. 505/1111). *Iḥyā' 'ulūm al-dīn* (Cairo: al-Maṭba'a al-'Uthmāniyya al-Miṣriyya, 1933).

________, *Qānūn al-ta'wīl* (Cairo, 1940).

al-Ghazzī, Najm al-Dīn (d. 1651). *Al-Kawākib al-sā'ira fī a'yān al-mi'a al-'āshira*, ed. J. Jabbour (Beirut: American University of Beirut Press, 1958).

________, *Luṭf al-samar wa qaṭf al-thamar min tarājim a'yān al-ṭabaqa al-ūlā min al-qarn al-ḥādī 'ashar*, ed. Maḥmūd al-Shaykh (Damascus: Manshūrāt Wizārat al-Thaqāfa, 1981).

al-Hamadhānī, 'Abd al-Jabbār b. Aḥmad (d. 415/1025). *Al-Mughnī fī abwāb al-tawḥīd wa-al-'adl*, ed. M. M. Al-Khuḍayrī (Cairo: Al-Dār al-Miṣriyya li-al-Ta'līf wa-al-Tarjama, 1958).

al-Harawī, 'Alī al-Qari' (d. 1614). *Al-Asrār al-marfū'a fī al-akhbār al-mawḍū'a*, ed. M. Ṣabbāgh (Beirut: Mu'assasat al-Risāla, 1971).

________, *Jam' al-wasā'il fī sharḥ al-Shamā'il* (Istanbul: Maṭba'at Shaykh Yaḥyā, 1290AH).

________, *Mirqāt al-mafātīḥ sharḥ Mishkāt al-maṣābīḥ* (Beirut: Dār al-Fikr, 1992).

________, *Sharḥ al-Shifā'* (Beirut: Dār al-Kutub al-'Ilmiyya, 2001).

________, *Sharḥ bad' al-amālī* (Istanbul: Maṭba'at al-Ḥaydarī, 1295AH).

al-Ḥaṭṭāb (d. 1547), *Sharḥ Mukhtaṣar Khalīl* (printed along with the commentary of al-Mawwāq [d. 1492] on the same work on the margins) (Cairo: Maṭba'at al-Sa'āda, 1328AH).

al-Ḥisnī, Taqī al-Dīn (d. 1426). *Daf' shubah man shabbaha wa tamarrada*, ed. 'Abd al-Wāḥid Muṣṭafā (Amman: Dār al-Razī, 2003).

al-Ījī, 'Aḍud al-Dīn (d. 756/1355). *Al-Mawāqif fī 'ilm al-kalām* (Beirut: 'Ālam al-Kutub, n.d.).

al-Jazarī (d. 739/1338–39). *Ta'rīkh ḥawādith al-zamān wa-anbā'i-hi wa-wafayāt al-akābir wa-al-a'yān min abnā'i-hi al-ma'rūf bi-Ta'rīkh Ibn al-Jazarī*, ed. 'Umar al-Tadmurī, 3 vols. (Beirut: al-Maktaba al-'Aṣriyya, 1998).

al-Jurjānī, al-Sayyid al-Sharīf (d. 816/1413). *Sharḥ al-Mawāqif* (Cairo: al-Maṭba'a al-'Āmira al-Sharafiyya, 1292AH).

al-Khādimī, Abū Sa'īd (d. 1762). *Al-Barīqa maḥmūdiyya bi-sharḥ al-ṭarīqa al-Muḥammadiyya* (Cairo: Dār al-Ṭiba'a al-Bāhira, 1257AH).

al-Khafājī, Aḥmad (d. 1658). *Nasīm al-riyāḍ fī sharḥ Shifā' al-Qāḍī 'Iyāḍ* (Beirut: Dār al-Kutub al-'Ilmiyya, 2001).

al-Kharashī, Muḥammad (d. 1689). *Sharḥ Mukhtaṣar Khalīl* (with the glosses of 'Alī al-'Adawī al-Sa'īdī [d. 1775]) (Cairo: al-Maṭba'a al-'Āmira al-Sharafiyya, 1316AH).

al-Kulaynī, Muḥammad ibn Ya'qūb (d. 941?). *Uṣūl min al-kāfī* (Beirut: Dār al-Ta'ārif, 1401/1980).

al-Kūrānī, Ibrāhīm (d. 1690). *Al-Amam li-īqāẓ al-himam* (Hyderabad: Dā'irat al-Ma'ārif al-'Uthmāniyya, 1328/1910).

al-Laqānī, 'Abd al-Salām (d. 1631). *Itḥāf al-murīd sharḥ Jawharat al-tawḥīd* (Beirut: Dār al-Kutub al-'Ilmiyya, 2001).

al-Mağnisāvī, Aḥmad (d. 1539). *Sharḥ al-Fiqh al-akbar*, in *al-Rasā'il al-sab'a fī al-'aqā'id* (Hyderabad: Jam'iyyat Dā'irat al-Ma'ārif al-'Uthmāniyya, 1948).

al-Maqdisī, Muṭahhar b. Ṭāhir (fl. 966). *Al-Bad' wa-al-ta'rīkh*, ed. Clément Huart (Baghdad, Maktabat al-Muthannā, n.d.).

al-Maqrīzī, Taqī al-Dīn (d. 845/1441). *Kitāb al-mawā'iẓ wa-al-i'tibār fī dhikr al-khiṭaṭ wa-al-āthār al-ma'rūf bi-al-khiṭaṭ al-Maqrīziyya*, ed. M. Zaynhum and M. Al-Sharqāwī, 3 vols. (Cairo: Maktabat al-Madbūlī, 1998).

———, *Kitāb al-muqaffā al-kabīr*, ed. M. Ya'lāwī (Beirut: Dār al-Gharb al-Islāmī, 1991).

———, *Kitāb al-sulūk li-ma'rifat duwal al-mulūk*, ed. Muṣṭafā Ziyāda, 3 vols. (Cairo: Maṭba'at al-Ta'līf wa-al-Tarjama wa-al-Nashr, 1971).

al-Munāwī, 'Abd al-Ra'ūf (d. 1621). *Sharḥ al-Shamā'il* (MS British Library, Or. 12522).

———, *al-Fayḍ al-qadīr sharḥ al-Jāmi' al-ṣaghīr* (Beirut: Dār al-Kutub al-'Ilmiyya, 2001).

al-Nābulusī, 'Abd al-Ghanī (d. 1731). *Al-Wujūd al-ḥaqq*, ed. Bakrī 'Alā' al-Dīn (Damascus: Institut Français de Damas, 1995).

al-Nafrawī, Aḥmad (d. 1714?). *Al-Fawākih al-dawānī 'alā Risālat Ibn Abī Zayd al-Qayrawānī* (Beirut: Dār al-Ma'rifa, n.d. [reprint]).

al-Nakhlī, Aḥmad (d. 1717). *Bughyat al-ṭālibīn li-bayān al-mashāyikh al-muḥaqqiqīn al-mu'tamadīn* (Hyderabad: Dā'irat al-Ma'ārif al-'Uthmāniyya, 1328AH).

al-Nawawī, Yaḥyā ibn Sharaf (d. 676/1277). *Muslim bi-Sharḥ al-Nawawī*, ed. Muḥammad Fu'ād 'Abd al-Bāqī (Beirut: Dār al-Kutub al-'Ilmyya, 1421/2000).

al-Nawbakhtī, Ḥasan ibn Mūsā (fl. 900–913). *Kitāb firaq al-shī'a* (Istanbul: Maṭba'at al-Dawla, 1931).

al-Nu'aymī, 'Abd al-Qādir ibn Muḥammad (d. 1521). *Al-Dāris fī ta'rīkh al-madāris*, ed. Ibrāhīm Shams al-Dīn (Beirut: Dār al-Kutub al-'Ilmiyya, 1990).

al-Nuwayrī, Shihāb al-Dīn (d. 733/1333). *Nihāyat al-arab fī funūn al-adab*, ed. M. 'Ulwī Shaltūt et al., 33 vols. (Cairo: Dār al-Kutub al-Miṣriyya, 1923–2002).

al-Qaṣṭallānī, Aḥmad (d. 1517). *Irshād al-sārī ilā sharḥ Ṣaḥīḥ al-Bukhārī* (Bulaq: Dār al-Ṭibā'a, 1285H).

al-Qurṭubī, Abū 'Abdallāh Muḥammad b. Aḥmad (d. 671/1273). *Al-Jāmi' li-aḥkām al-Qur'ān*, ed. Aḥmad 'Abd al-'Alīm al-Bardūnī, 3rd ed. (Cairo: Dār al-Qalam and Dār al-Kitāb al-'Arabī, 1966).

———, *al-Jāmi' li-aḥkām al-Qur'ān*, ed. Sālim Muṣṭafā al-Badrī (Beirut: Dār al-Kutub al-'Ilmiyya, 1420/2000).

al-Ramlī, Aḥmad (d. 1550). *Fatāwā* (printed on the margins of Ibn Ḥajar al-Haytamī, *al-Fatāwā al-kubrā al-fiqhiyya* [Cairo: al-Maṭba'a al-Muyammaniyya, 1308H]).

al-Rāzī, Fakhr al-Dīn (d. 606/1210). *Al-Arba'īn fī uṣūl al-dīn*, ed. Aḥmad Ḥijāzī al-Saqā, 2 parts in 1 vol. (Cairo: Maktabat al-Kulliyyāt al-Azhariyya, n.d.).

———, *al-Maṭālib al-'āliyya min al-'ilm al-ilāhī*, ed. Aḥmad Ḥijāzī al-Saqā, 9 parts in 5 vols. (Beirut: Dār al-Kitāb al-'Arabī, 1407/1987).

al-Ṣafadī, Khalīl ibn Aybak (d. 1363). *Al-Wāfī bi-al-wafayāt*, ed. H. Ritter at al. (Leipzig: Deutsche Morgenländische Gesellschaft, 1931–2004).

———, *A'yān al-'aṣr wa-a'wān al-naṣr*, ed. F. Aḥmad Bakkūr, 4 vols. (Beirut: Dār al-Fikr al-Mu'āsir, 1418/1998).

———, *A'yān al-'aṣr wa-a'wān al-naṣr*, ed. 'A. Abū Zayd et al., 6 vols. (Damascus: Dār al-Fikr, 1998).

al-Saffārīnī, Muḥammad (d. 1188/1774). *Lawā'iḥ al-anwār al-saniyya wa lawāqiḥ al-afkār al-sunniya*, ed. 'Abd Allāh al-Basīrī (Riyadh: Maktabat al-Rushd, 2000).

al-Sakhāwī, Muḥammad b. 'Abd al-Raḥmān (d. 902/1497). *Al-I'lān bi-al-tawbīkh li-man dhamma al-ta'rīkh* (Damascus: al-Maktabat al-Qudsī, 1930–31).

al-Sanūsī, Muḥammad ibn Yūsuf (d. 1490). *'Umdat ahl al-tawfīq fī sharḥ 'Aqīdat ahl al-tawḥīd* (Cairo: Jarīdat al-Islām, 1316AH).
al-Shahrastānī, Muḥammad (d. 1153). *Kitāb al-milal wa-al-niḥal*, ed. by W. Cureton (Leipzig: Otto Harrassowitz, 1923 [reprint of 1846 edition]).
al-Shāwī, Yaḥyā (d. 1685). *Al-Nabl al-raqīq fī ḥulqum al-sābb al-zindīq* (MS Süleymaniye: Laleli 3744).
al-Sindī, Ḥasan ibn 'Abd al-Hādī (d. 1726). *Sunan al-Nasā'ī bi-sharḥ al-Suyūṭī wa-ḥāshiyat al-Sindī* (Cairo: al-Maktaba al-Tijāriyya, 1930).
al-Sindī, Muḥammad Ḥayāt (d.1750). *Tuḥfat al-anām fī al-'amal bi-ḥadīth al-nabī 'alayhi al-ṣalāt wa al-salām* (Beirut: Dār Ibn Ḥazm, 1993).
al-Subkī, Tāj al-Dīn (d. 771/1369). *Al-Ṭabaqāt al-Shāfi'īyya*, 6 vols. (Cairo: al-Maṭba'a al-Ḥusayniyya, 1906).
al-Subkī, Taqī al-Dīn (d. 756/1355). *Al-Rasā'il al-subkiyya fī al-radd 'alā Ibn Taymiyya wa-tilmīdhi-hi Ibn Qayyim al-Jawziyya*, ed. K. Abū al-Mūnā (Beirut: 'Ālam al-Kutub, 1983).
al-Suyūṭī, Jalāl al-Dīn (d. 911/1505). *Al-Durr al-Manthūr fī al-tafsīr al-ma'thūr*, 7 vols. (Beirut: Dār al-Kutub al-'Ilmiyya, 1990).
———, *al-Ḥawī li-al-fatāwā* (Beirut: Dār al-Kutub al-'Ilmiyya, 1975).
———, *al-Itqān fī 'ulūm al-Qur'ān*, ed. Muḥammad Abū al-Faḍl Ibrāhīm (Beirut: Dār al-Turāth, reprint of 1967 Cairo edition).
———, *Bughyat al-wu''āh fī ṭabaqāt al-lughawiyyīn wa-al-nuḥāh* (Cairo: Maṭba'at 'Isa al-Bābī al-Ḥalabī, 1964–1965).
———, *Ḥusn al-muḥāḍara fī akhbār Miṣr wa-al-Qāhira* ([Cairo]: al-Maṭba'a al-Sharafiyya, 1909).
al-Ṭabarī, Muḥammad ibn Jarīr (d. 320/923). *Jāmi' al-bayān 'an tafsīr al-Qur'ān*, ed. Maḥmūd Shākir (Cairo, 1961).
———, *Tafsīr al-Ṭabarī Jāmi' al-bayān 'an ta'wīl āy al-Qur'ān*, ed. 'Abdallah 'Abd al-Muḥsin al-Turkī (Cairo, 1422/2001).
al-Taftāzānī, Sa'd al-Dīn (d. 1390). *Sharḥ al-'Aqā'id al-Nasafiyya* (Istanbul: Dār Sa'ādet, 1326AH).
———, *Sharḥ al-Maqāṣid*, ed. 'Abd al-Raḥmān 'Umayra (Beirut: 'Ālam al-Kutub, 1998).
al-Tha'labī (d. 427/1035). *Al-Kashf wa-al-bayān 'an tafsīr al-Qur'ān* (Veliyuddin Efendi, ms. 130).
al-Thattawī, Muḥammad Mu'īn (d. 1748). *Dirāsat al-labīb fī al-uswa al-ḥasana bi-al-ḥabīb* (Karachi: Sindhi Adabi Board, 1957).
al-Tunbuktī, Aḥmad Bābā (d. 1624). *Nayl al-ibtihāj bi-taṭrīz al-Dībāj*. Printed on the margins of Ibn Farḥūn, *al-Dībāj al-mudhahhab fī ma'rifat a'yān al-madhhab* (Cairo: Maṭba'at al-Sa'āda, 1329AH).
al-Wāsiṭi, 'Imād al-Dīn Aḥmad ibn Ibrāhīm (d. 711/1311). *Al-Naṣīḥa fī al-ṣifāt* and *Madkhal ahl al-fiqh wa-al-lisān ilā maydān al-maḥabba wa-al-'irfān*, ed. Muḥammad 'Abd Allāh al-'Alī in *Liqā' al-'ashr al-awākhir bi-al-masjid al-ḥarām* (Beirut: Shirkat Dār al-Bashā'ir al-Islāmiyya, 2005), vol. 4, no. 39.
———, *al-Tadhkira wa-al-i'tibār wa-al-intiṣār li-al-abrār fī al-thanā' 'alā Shaykh al-islām wa-al-wiṣāya bi-hi*, ed. 'Abd al-Jabbār al-Furaywā'ī (Riyadh: Dār al-'Āṣima, 1415/1994).
al-Yūnīnī, Mūsá ibn Muḥammad (d. 1325–6). *Dhayl Mir'āt al-Zamān*, ed. Li Guo, 2 vols. (Leiden: E. J. Brill, 1998).
al-Zabīdī, Muḥammad Murtaḍā (d. 1790). *Itḥāf al-sāda al-muttaqīn bi-sharḥ Iḥyā' 'ulūm al-dīn* (Cairo: al-Maṭba'a al-Muyammaniyya, 1311 AH).

al-Zarkashī, Badr al-Dīn (D. 1392). *Al-Burhān fī 'ulūm al-Qur'ān*, ed. M. Ibrāhīm (Beirut: Dār al-Ma'rifa, reprint of 1972 Cairo edition).

al-Zurqānī, Muḥammad ibn 'Abd al-Bāqī (d. 1720). *Sharḥ al-Mawāhib al-laduniyya* (Cairo, 1291 AH).

Bar Hebraeus (Abū al-Faraj ibn al-'Ibrī) (d. 1286). *Tārīkh mukhtasar al-duwal* (Beirut: al-Maṭba'a al-Kāthūlīkiyya li-al-Ābā' al-Yasū'īyīn, 1890).

Beyâzî, Ahmet (d. 1687). *Ishārat al-marām min 'ibārat al-imām*, ed. Y. 'Abd al-Razzāq (Cairo: Muṣṭafā al-Bābī al-Ḥalabī, 1949).

Birgiwî, Mehmet (d. 1573). *Risāla fi ziyārat al-qubūr*, printed under the title *Ziyārat al-qubūr al-shar'iyya wa al-shirkiyya* (Cairo: Maṭba'at al-Imām, n.d.).

Calvin, John (d. 1564). *Institutes of the Christian Religion*, tr. Ford Lewis Battles (Philadelphia: The Westminster Press, 1975).

Ibn 'Abd al-Hādī (d. 744/1343), *al-'Uqūd al-durriyya min manāqib Shaykh al-Islām Ibn Taymiyya*, ed. Muḥammad Ḥāmid al-Fiqī (Cairo: Maṭba'at Ḥijāzī, 1938).

———, *al-'Uqūd al-durriyya min manāqib Shaykh al-islām Ibn Taymiyya*, ed. Ṭal'at al-Ḥalawānī (Cairo: al-Fārūq al-Ḥadītha, 2001).

Ibn Abī Ḥātim (d. 327/938). *Tafsīr Ibn Abī Ḥātim*, ed. Aḥmad al-Zahrānī (Medina: Maktabat al-Dār, 1408 AH).

Ibn al-Amīr al-Ṣan'ānī (d. 1768). *Dīwān* (Medina: Manshūrāt al-Madīna, 1986).

Ibn al-Dawādārī, Abū Bakr b. 'Abd Allāh (fl. 1309–1335). *Kanz al-durar wa jāmi' al-ghurar*; vol. 9, *al-Durr al-fākhir fī sīrat al-Malik al-Nāṣir*, ed. Hans Robert Roemer (Cairo: Qism al-Dirāsāt al-Islāmiyya bi-al-Ma'had al-almānī li-al-Āthār bi-al-Qāhira, 1960).

Ibn al-Ḥājj, Muḥammad b. Muḥammad (d. 1336). *Al-Madkhal ilā tanmiyat al-a'māl bi-taḥsīn al-niyyāt wa al-tanbīh 'alā ba'ḍ al-bida' wa-al-'awā'id allatī intaḥalat wa-bayān shanā'ihā*, ed. Tawfīq Ḥamdān (Beirut: Dār al-Kutub al-'Ilmiyya, 1995).

———, *al-Madkhal ilā tanmiyat al-a'māl bi-taḥsīn al-niyyāt* (Cairo: Maṭba'at Muṣṭafá al-Bābī al-Ḥalabī, 1960).

Ibn al-'Imād (d. 1080/1670). *Shadharāt al-dhahab fī akhbār man dhahab* (Cairo: al-Maktaba al-Tijāriyya, 1350–51H; reprint in Beirut, 1979).

Ibn al-Jawzī (d. 597/1200). *Manāqib al-Imām Aḥmad ibn Ḥanbal*, ed. 'A. M. Al-Turkī and 'A. M. 'Umar (Cairo: Maktabat al-Khānjī, 1979).

Ibn al-Ṭayyib al-Fāsī (d. 1756/7). *Sharḥ Ḥizb al-Imām al-Nawawī* (MS Princeton University Library, Yahuda 3861).

Ibn al-Wazīr (d. 840/1436). *Īthār al-ḥaqq 'alā al-khalq* (Beirut: Dār al-Kutub al-'Ilmiyya, 1983).

———, *Tarjīḥ asālīb al-Qur'ān 'alā asālīb al-Yūnān* (Beirut: Dār al-Kutub al-'Ilmiyya, 1984).

Ibn Baydakīn, Idrīs (13th or 14th c.). *Kitāb al-luma' fī al-ḥawādith wa-al-bida'*, ed. Ṣubḥī Labīb, 2 vols. (Cairo: Qism al-Dirāsāt al-Islāmiyya, al-Ma'had al-Almānī li-al-Āthār bi-al-Qāhira, 1986).

Ibn Ḥajar al-'Asqalānī, Shihāb al-Dīn Aḥmad b. 'Alī (d. 836/1432). *Al-Durar al-kāmina fī a'yān al-mi'a al-thāmina*, ed. 'Abd al-Wārith Muḥammad 'Alī (Beirut: Dār al-Kutub al-'Ilmiyya, 1997).

———, *al-Durar al-kāmina fī a'yān al-mi'a al-thạmina*, ed. Muḥammad Sayyid Jād al-Ḥaqq, 5 vols. (Cairo, 1966).

———, *Fatḥ al-bārī sharḥ Ṣaḥīḥ al-Bukhārī* (Cairo: Muṣṭafā al-Bābī al-Ḥalabī, 1959).

———, *Fatḥ al-bārī bi-sharḥ Ṣaḥīḥ al-Bukhārī*, ed. Ṭāhā 'Abd al-Ra'ūf Sa'd, Muṣṭafā Muḥammad al-Hawwārī, al-Sayyid Muḥammad 'Abd al-Mu'ṭī (Cairo: Maktabat al-Kulliyāt al-Azhariyya, 1978).

———, *Lisān al-mīzān,* 7 vols. (Beirut: Mu'assasat al-A'lamī li-al-Maṭbū'āt, 1390/1971).

Ibn Ḥajar al-Haytamī (d. 1566). *Al-Fatāwā al-ḥadīthiyya* (Cairo: Muṣṭafā al-Bābī al-Ḥalabī, 1970).

———, *al-Fatāwā al-kubrā al-fiqhiyya* (Cairo: al-Maṭba'a al-Muyammaniyya, 1308AH).

———, *al-Jawhar al-munaẓẓam fī ziyārat al-qabr al-sharīf al-nabawī al-mukarram*, ed. M. Zaynhum (Cairo: Maktabat Madbūlī, 2000).

———, *Ashraf al-wasā'il ilā fahm al-shamā'il,* ed. Aḥmad al-Mazīdī (Beirut: Dār al-Kutub al-'Ilmiyya, 1998).

Ibn Ḥazm, Abū Muḥammad 'Alī ibn Aḥmad (d. 457/1064). *Al-Faṣl fī al-milal wa-al-ahwā'*, eds. Muḥammad Ibrāhīm Naṣr and 'Abd al-Raḥmān 'Umayra (Beirut: Dār al-Jīl, 1985).

———, *al-Iḥkām fī uṣūl al-Aḥkām* (Cairo, 1978).

———, *Marātib al-ijmā' fī al-'ibādāt* (Cairo: Dār Zāhid al-Qudsī, 1986).

Ibn Hishām (d. 218/833). *Al-Sīra al-nabawaiyya*, eds. Jamāl Thābit et. al. (Cairo: Dār al-Ḥadīth, 1416/1996).

Ibn Kathīr, 'Imād al-Dīn Ismā'īl ibn 'Umar (d. 1373). *Al-Bidāya wa-al-nihāya fī al-ta'rīkh*, ed. F.A. Al-Kurdī, 14 vols. (Cairo: Maṭba'at al-Sa'āda, 1932–39).

———, *al-Bidāya wa-al-Nihāya*, ed. 'Alī Muḥammad Mu'awwaḍ and 'Ādil Aḥmad 'Abd al-Mawjūd (Beirut: Dār al-Kutub al-'Ilmiyya, 1994).

———, *Tafsīr al-Qur'ān al-'aẓīm*, ed. M. Muḥammad et al. (Cairo: Maktabat Awlād al-Shaykh li-al-Turāth, 2000).

———, *Tafsīr al-Qur'ān al-karīm* (n.p.: Dār al-Turāth al-'Arabī, n.d.).

Ibn Khaldūn (d. 1406). *Al-Muqaddima* (Beirut: Dār Iḥyā' al-Turāth al-'Arabī, n.d.).

Ibn Khallikān (d. 1282). *Wayfayāt al-a'yān wa-anbā' abnā' al-zamān*, ed. Iḥsān 'Abbās (Beirut: Dār al-Sādir, n.d.).

Ibn Manẓūr, Muḥammad ibn Mukarram (d. 1311–2). *Lisān al-'Arab* (Beirut: Dār Iḥyā' al-Turāth al-'Arabī, 1968/1417).

Ibn Nāṣir al-Dīn (d. 842/1438). *Al-Radd al-wāfir 'alā man za'ama anna man sammā Ibn Taymiyya shaykh al-islām huwa kāfir*, ed. Z. Al-Shāwīsh (Damascus: al-Maktab al-Islāmī, 1973).

Ibn Qayyim al-Jawziyya (d. 751/1350). *Aḥkām ahl al-dhimma*, ed. Ṣubḥī al-Ṣāliḥ (Beirut: Dār al-'Ilm li-al-Malāyīn, 1401/1981).

———, *Shifā' al-'alīl fī masā'il al-qaḍā' wa-al-qadar wa-al-ḥikma wa-al-ta'līl*, ed. Muḥammad Badr al-Dīn Abū Firās al-Na'sānī al-Ḥalabī (Cairo: al-Maṭba'a al-Ḥusayniyya al-Miṣriyya, 1323/1903).

———, *Shifā' al-'alīl fī masā'il al-qaḍā' wa-al-qadar wa-al-ḥikma wa-al-ta'līl* (Beirut: Dār al-Fikr, 1988).

———, *Shifā' al-'alīl fī masā'il al-qaḍā' wa-al-qadar wa-al-ḥikma wa-al-ta'līl*, ed. Al-Sayyid Muḥammad al-Sayyid and Sa'īd Maḥmūd (Cairo: Dār al-Ḥadīth, 1414/1994).

Ibn Rajab (d. 795/1393). *Al-Radd 'alā man ittaba'a ghayr al-madhāhib al-arba'a*, printed as an introduction to Ibn Hubayra al-Baghdādī al-Ḥanbalī (d. 560/1165), *al-Fiqh 'alā madhāhib al-a'imma al-arba'a*, eds. I. I. Al-Qāḍī and 'I. Al-Mursī (Cairo: Dār al-Ḥaramayn, 2000).

———, *Kitāb al-dhayl 'alā Ṭabaqāt al-Ḥanābila*, ed. Muḥammad Ḥāmid al-Fiqī, 2 vols. (Cairo: Maṭba'at al-Sunna al-Muḥammadīya, 1952–1953).

Karsî, Davûd (18th c). *Sharḥ al-Nūniyya* (Istanbul: Mehmet Tâlib, 1318AH).

Kefevî, Eyyüp (d. 1684). *Al-Kulliyyāt*, ed. ʻA. Darwish and M. Al-Miṣrī (Damascus: Wizārat al-Thaqāfa, 1974-).
Majlisī, Muḥammad Bāqir (d. ca. 1699). *Biḥār al-anwār*, 110 vols. (Tehran: Dār al-Kutub al-Islāmiyya, 1956–1972).

3. Modern Works

ʻAbd al-Ḥamīd, Ṣāʼib. *Ibn Taymiyya: Ḥayātuhu, ʻaqāʼiduhu, mawqifuhu min al-Shīʻa wa-Ahl al-Bayt* (Qum: Markaz al-Ghadīr li-al-Dirāsāt al-Islāmiyya, 1994).
ʻAbduh, Muḥammad. *Al-Shaykh Muḥammad ʻAbduh bayna al-falāsifa wa-al-kalāmiyyīn*, ed. S. Dunyā (Cairo: Muṣṭafā al-Babī al-Ḥalabī, 1958).
———, *Risālat al-tawḥīd* [with annotations by Rashīd Riḍā] (Beirut & Limassol: Dār Ibn Ḥazm, 2001).
Abdullah, Ssekamanya Siraje. "Ibn Taymiyya's Theological Approach Illustrated: On the Essence (Dhāt) and the Attributes (Ṣifāt) of Allah", *al-Shajarah* 9.1 (2004): 50–1.
Abed-Kotob, Sana. "The Accommodationists Speak: Goals and Strategies of the Muslim Brotherhood in Egypt," *International Journal of Middle Eastern Studies* 27 (1995): 321–39.
Abou el Fadl, Khaled. *Rebellion and Violence in Islamic Law* (Cambridge: Cambridge University Press, 2001).
Abrahamov, Binyamin. "A Re-examination of al-Ashʻarī's Theory of *Kasb* according to *Kitāb al-Lumaʻ*," *Journal of the Royal Asiatic Society* 1.2 (1989): 210–221.
———, "Ibn Taymiyya on the Agreement of Reason with Tradition," *The Muslim World* 82.3–4 (1992): 256–72.
———, *Islamic Theology: Traditionalism and Rationalism* (Edinburgh: Edinburgh University Press, 1998).
———, "The Creation and Duration of Paradise and Hell in Islamic Theology", *Der Islam* 79.1 (2002):87–102.
Abu Manneh, Butrus. "Salafiyya and the Rise of the Khālidiyya in Baghdad in the early nineteenth century", *Die Welt des Islams* 43 (2003): 354–361.
———, "The Naqshbandiyya-Mujaddidiyya in the Ottoman Lands in the Early 19th Century", *Die Welt des Islams* 22 (1982): 12–17.
Abū Zahra, Muḥammad. *Ibn Taymiyya: Ḥayātuhu wa-ʻaṣruhu—ārāʼuhu wa-fiqhuhu* (Cairo: Dār al-Fikr al-ʻArabī, 2000).
Adang, Camilla. "Islam as the Inborn Religion of Mankind: The Concept of Fiṭra in the works of Ibn Ḥazm," *Al-Qanṭara: Revista de Estudios Arabes* 21.2 (2000):391–410.
Afsaruddin, Asma. "An Insight into the Ḥadith Methodology of Jamāl al-Dīn Aḥmad b. Ṭāwūs," *Der Islam* 72 (1995): 24–46.
Ahmed, Shahab. "Ibn Taymiyya and the Satanic Verses," *Studia Islamica* 87 (1998): 67–124.
Aigle, Denise. "The Mongol invasions of Bilād al-Shām by Ghazan Khān and Ibn Taymiyya's three 'anti-Mongol' Fatwas", *Mamluk Studies Review* 11/2 (2007): 89–120.
Āl al-Shaykh, Muḥammad b. Ibrahīm (edited). *Al-Majmūʻa al-ʻilmiyya al-saʻūdiyya min durar shaykhay al-islām* (The Saudi Scientific Collection of the Pearls of the Two Masters of Islam) (Riyadh: Dār al-Ṭuwayq li-al-Nashr wal-Tawzīʻ, 1997).
Āl Yāsīn, Muḥammed Ḥasan. *Allāh bayna al-fiṭra wa-al-dalīl* (Beirut: Dār al-Maktabat al-Ḥayāt, 1972).

al-Alousi, Husâm Muhî Eldîn. *The Problem of Creation in Islamic Thought: Qur'ān, Hadith, Commentaries, and Kalām* (Baghdad: The National Printing and Publishing Co., 1968).

al-Ālūsī, Khayr al-Dīn Nu'mān ibn Maḥmūd (d. 1899). *Jalā' al-'aynayn fī muḥākamat al-Aḥmadayn* (Beirut: Dār al Kutub al-'Ilmiyya, n.d. [reprint]).

al-Ālūsī, Maḥmūd (d. 1854). *Gharā'ib al-ightirāb* (Baghdad: Maṭba'at al-Shahbandār, 1327H).

al-Ālūsī, Maḥmūd Shukrī (d. 1924). *Al-Misk al-adhfar fī nashr mazāyā al-qarn al-thānī 'ashar wa-al-thālith 'ashar*, ed. 'Abdallāh al-Jabbūrī (Riyadh: Dār al-'Ulūm, 1982).

al-Amīn, Muḥsin. *A'yān al-shī'a*, 11 vols. (Beirut: Dār al-Ta'āruf, 1986).

al-'Aṭīshān (or al-'Uṭayshān), Sa'ūd. *Manhaj Ibn Taymiyya fī al-fiqh* (Riyadh: Maktabat al-'Ubaykān, 1999).

al-'Aṭṭār, Ḥasan. *Ḥāshiya 'alā sharḥ Jam' al-jawāmi'* (Beirut: Dār al-Kutub al-'Ilmiyya, n.d. [reprint]).

'Alawī, Muḥammad. "*Ḥawl al-iḥtifāl bil-mawlid al-nabawī al-sharīf*," in *Bāqa 'aṭira min ṣiyagh al-mawālid wa-al-madā'iḥ al-nabawiyya al-karīma* (n.p., 1983).

________, *Mafāhīm yajib an tusaḥḥahā* (Cairo: Dār al-Insān, 1985).

al-Bannā, Jamāl. *Al-Farīḍa al-ghā'iba: jihād al-sayf am jihād al-'aql* (Cairo: Dār Thābit, 1984).

al-Dīb, 'Abd al-'Aẓīm (edited). *Yūsuf al-Qaraḍāwī: kalimāt fī takrīmihi wa-buḥūth fī fikrihi wa-fiqhihi muhdātun ilayhi bi-munāsabati bulūghihi al-sab'īn* (Cairo: Dār al-Salām: 2004).

Ali, Mohamed Mohamed Yunis. *Medieval Islamic Pragmatics: Sunni Legal Theorists' Models of Textual Communication* (Surrey: Curzon, 2000).

al-Jabartī, 'Abd al-Raḥmān. *'Ajā'ib al-āthār fī al-tarājim wa-al-akhbār* (Cairo: al-Maṭba'a al-'Āmira, 1297AH).

al-Jalayand, Muḥammad al-Sayyid. *Al-Imām Ibn Taymiyya wa-mawqifuhu min qaḍiyyat al-ta'wīl* (Cairo: Dār al-Qibā', 2000).

al-Khwānsārī, Muḥammad Bāqir. *Rawḍat al-jannāt fī aḥwāl al-'ulamā' wa-al-sādāt*, 8 vols. (Tehran: Maktabat Ismā'īlīyān, n.d.).

Allard, Michel. "En quoi consiste l'opposition faite à al-Ash'arī par ses contemporains ḥanbalites?," *Revue des études Islamiques* 28 (1960): 94–96.

al-Maḥmūd, 'Abd al-Raḥmān b. Ṣāliḥ b. Ṣāliḥ. *Mawqif Ibn Taymiyya min al-Ashā'ira*, 3 vols. (Riyadh: Maktabat al-Rushd, 1995).

al-Māmaqānī, 'Abd Allāh. *Miqbās al-hidāya fī 'ilm al-dirāya*, 7 vols. (Qum: Mu'assasat Āl al-Bayt li-Iḥyā' al-Turāth, 1411/1990).

al-Matroudi, Abdul Hakim I. *The Ḥanbalī school of law and Ibn Taymiyyah* (London: Routledge, 2006).

al-Mīlānī, Alī al-Ḥusaynī. *Dirāsāt fī Minhāj al-Sunna li-ma'rifat Ibn Taymiyya: Madkhal li-sharḥ Minhāj al-Karāma* (Iran: 'Alī al-Ḥusaynī al-Mīlānī, 1419/1998 or 1999).

al-Mubārak, Muḥammad. *Al-Dawla wa-niẓām al-ḥisba 'inda Ibn Taymiyya* ([Damascus]: Dār al-Fikr, 1967).

al-Munajjid, Ṣalāḥ al-Dīn (edited). *Shaykh al-Islām Ibn Taymiyya: sīratu-hu wa-akhbāru-hu 'inda al-mu'arrikhīn* (Beirut: Dār al-Kutub al-'Ilmiyya, 1976).

al-Musawī, 'Abd al-Ḥusayn Sharaf al-Dīn. *Al-Murāja'āt* (Beirut: al-Dār al-Islāmiyya, 1986).

al-Nadwī, Muḥammad Akram. *Kifāyat al-rāwī 'an 'allāmat al-shaykh Yūsuf al-Qaraḍāwī* (Damascus: Dār al-Qalam, 2001).

al-Ni'ma, 'Abd Allāh. *Falāsifat al-shī'a: ḥayātuhum wa-ārā'uhum* (Beirut: Dār Maktabat al-Ḥayāt, 1961).

al-Qaraḍāwī, Yūsuf. *Al-Ṣaḥwa al-islāmiyya bayna al-juḥūd wa-al-taṭarruf* (Doha: al-Maḥākim al-Shar'iyya wa-al-Shu'ūn al-Dīniyya fī Dawlat Qaṭar, 1982); translated by A.S. Al-Shaikh-Ali and Mohamed B.E. Wasfy as *Islamic Awakening between Rejection and Extremism* (Herndon, VA: American Trust Publication and the International Institute of Islamic Thought, 1991).

_______, *Awlawiyyāt al-ḥaraka al-islāmiyya fī al-marḥala al-qādima* (Cairo: Maktabat Wahba, 1991); English translation as *Priorities of the Islamic Movement in the Coming Phase* (Cairo: Dār al-Nashr for Egyptian Universities, 1992); also revised translation under the same title by S.M. Hasan Al-Banna (Swansea: Awakening Publications, 2000).

_______, *Ibn al-qarya wa-al-Kuttāb: malāmiḥ sīra wa-masīra* (Cairo: Dār al-Shurūq, 2002).

_______, *Kayfa nata'āmalu ma'a al-sunna al-nabawiyya: ma'ālim wa-ḍawābiṭ* (Herdon, VA: al-Ma'had al-'Ālamī li-al-Fikr al-Islāmī, 1990).

al-Rājiḥī, Abd al-'Azīz b. Fayṣal (edited). *Hady al-sārī ilā asānīd al-shaykh Ismā'īl al-Anṣārī* (Riyadh: Maktabat al-Rushd, 2001).

al-Rifā'ī, Yusuf al-Sayyid Hāshim. *Al-Ṣūfiyya wa-al-taṣawwuf fī ḍaw' al-kitāb wa-al-sunna* (Kuwait, 1999).

al-Samāwī, Muḥammad al-Tījānī. *Thumma ihtadayt* (Beirut: Mu'assasat al-Fajr, 1980).

al-Shawkānī, Muḥammad. *Al-Badr al-ṭāli' bi-maḥāsin man ba'd al-qarn al-sābi'* (Cairo: Maṭba'at al-Sa'āda, 1348AH).

al-Ṭabāṭabā'ī, Muḥammad Mahdī ibn Murtaḍā Baḥr al-'Ulūm. *al-'Ulūm [al-Fawā'id al-rijāliyya]*, 4 vols. (Najaf: Maṭba'at al-Ādāb, 1965–1967).

al-Ṭihrānī, Aghā Buzurg. *Al-Dharī'a ilā taṣānīf al-shī'a*, 26 vols. (Najaf: Maṭba'at al-Gharā, 1936-).

_______, *Ṭabaqāt a'lām al-shī'a*, 6 vols. (Qum: Maktabat Ismā'īlīyān, n.d.).

al-Zarkān, Muḥammad Ṣāliḥ. *Fakhr al-Dīn al-Rāzī wa ārā'uhu al-kalāmiyya wa al-falsafiyya* (Cairo: Dār al-Fikr, 1963).

Amir-Moezzi, Mohammad Ali. *The Divine Guide in Early Shi'ism: The Sources of Esotericism in Islam* (Albany: State University of New York Press, 1994).

Amitai, Reuven. "The Mongol Occupation of Damascus in 1300: A Study of Mamluk Loyalties", in A. Levanoni and M. Winter (eds.), *The Mamluks in Egyptian and Syrian Politics and Society* (Leiden: Brill, 2004), 21–41.

Arabi, Oussama. "Contract Stipulations (*shurūṭ*) in Islamic Law: The Ottoman Majalla and Ibn Taymiyya", in idem. *Studies in Modern Islamic Law and Jurisprudence* (The Hague; London: Kluwer Law International, 2001), 39- 62 (reprint of *International Journal of Middle Eastern Studies* 30.1 [1998]: 29–50).

_______, "Intention and Method in Sanhūrī's *Fiqh*: Cause as Ulterior Motive," *Islamic Law and Society* 4.2 (1997): 200–223.

Baker, Raymond William. "Invidious Comparisons: Realism, Postmodern Globalism, and Centrist Islamic Movements in Egypt," in John L. Esposito (ed.), *Political Islam: Revolution, Radicalism, or Reform?* (Boulder, CO: Lynne Rienner Publishers, 1997), 115–133.

_______, *Islam without Fear: Egypt and the New Islamists* (Cambridge, MA: Harvard University Press, 2003).

Baljon, J.M.S. *Religion and Thought of Shāh Walī Allāh al-Dihlawī* (Leiden: Brill, 1986).

Baraka, Ibrahīm. *Ibn Taymiyya wa-juhūduhu fī al-tafsīr* (Beirut: al-Maktaba al-Islāmiyya, 1984).

Bell, Joseph N. *Love Theory in Later Ḥanbalite Islam* (Albany, NY: State University of New York, 1979).

Benjamin, Daniel and Steven Simon. *The Age of Sacred Terror* (New York: Random House, 2002).

Berg, Herbert. "Tabarī's Exegesis of the Qur'ānic Term *al-Kitāb*", *Journal of the American Academy of Religion* 63 (1995): 761–74.

Berkey, Jonathan P. *Popular Preaching and Religious Authority in the Medieval Islamic Near East* (London and Seattle: University of Washington Press, 2001).

———, "Storytelling, Preaching and Power in Mamluk Cairo", *Mamlūk Studies Review* IV (2000): 53–73.

———, *The Formation of Islam: Religion and Society in the Near East, 600–1800* (Cambridge: Cambridge University Press, 2003).

———, "The Mamluks as Muslims: the Military Elite and the Construction of Islam in Medieval Egypt", in Thomas Philipp and Ulrich Haarmann (eds.), *The Mamluks in Egyptian Politics and Society* (Cambridge: Cambridge University Press, 1998), 163–173.

———, *The Transmission of Knowledge in Medieval Cairo: a Social History of Education* (Princeton: Princeton University Press, 1992).

———, "Tradition, Innovation and the Social Construction of Knowledge in the Medieval Islamic Near East", *Past&Present* 146 (1995): 38–65.

Bonney, Richard. *Jihād: From Qur'ān to bin Laden* (New York: Palgrave Macmillan, 2004).

Bori, Caterina. "A new source for the biography of Ibn Taymiyya," *Bulletin of the School of Oriental and African Studies* 67.3 (2004):321–48.

———, *Ibn Taymiyya: una vita esemplare.* Analisi delle fonti classiche della sua biografia, Supplemento monografico n. 1 alla Rivista degli Studi Orientali LXXVI (Roma and Pisa: Istituti Poligrafici Internazionali, 2003).

Bowen, John R. "Modern Intentions: Reshaping subjectivities in an Indonesian Muslim society", in Robert W. Hefner and Patricia Horvatich (eds.), *Islam in an era of nation-states* (Honolulu: University of Hawai'i Press, 1999), 157–82.

Brown, Daniel. "The Triumph of Scripturalism: The Doctrine of Naskh and Its Modern Critics," in Earle H. Waugh (ed.), *The Shaping of an American Islamic Discourse: A Memorial to Fazlur Rahman* (Atlanta: Scholars Press, 1998).

Burton, John. *An Introduction to the Hadith* (Edinburgh: Edinburgh University Press, 1994).

Çağrıcı, Mustafa. "İbn Teymiyye'nin Bakışıyla Gazzâlî-İbn Rüşd Tartışması", *İslâm Tetkikleri Dergisi*, 9 (1995): 77–126.

Chamberlain, Michael. *Knowledge and Social Practice in Medieval Damascus, 1190–1350* (Cambridge: Cambridge University Press, 1994).

Chittick, W.C. *The Sufi Path of Knowledge: Ibn 'Arabī's Metaphysics of Imagination* (New York: SUNY Press, 1989).

Cohen, Mark R. "Jews in the Mamluk Environment: The Crisis of 1442 (A Geniza Study)," *Bulletin of the School of Oriental and African Studies* 47 (1984):425–448.

———, *Under Crescent & Cross: The Jews in the Middle Ages* (Princeton: Princeton University Press, 1994).

Commins, D.D. *Islamic Reform: Politics and Change in Late Ottoman Syria* (New York & Oxford: Oxford University Press, 1990).

Cook, Michael. *Commanding right and forbidding wrong in Islamic thought* (Cambridge: Cambridge University Press, 2000).

Cooperson, Michael. *Classical Arabic Biography. The Heirs of the Prophets in the Age of al-Ma'mūn* (Cambridge: Cambridge University Press, 2000).
Coulson, Noel J. "Doctrine and Practice in Islamic Law: One aspect of the Problem", *Bulletin of the School of Oriental and African Studies* 18.2 (1956): 211–226.
Craig, William Lane. *The Kalām Cosmological Argument* (New York: Barnes and Noble Books, 1979).
Crone, Patricia. "Did al-Ghazālī write a Mirror for Princes?", *Jerusalem Studies in Arabic and Islam* 10 (1987):167–191.
———, *God's Rule: Government and Islam* (New York: Columbia University Press, 2004).
Curtis, Young Muḥammad Mukhtar. "Authentic Interpretation of Classical Islamic Texts: An Analysis of the Introduction of Ibn Kathīr's *'Tafsīr al-Qur'ān al-'Aẓīm'*", PhD. Dissertation (The University of Michigan, 1989).
Davidson, Herbert. *Proofs for Eternity, Creation and the Existence of God in Medieval Islamic and Jewish Philosophy* (Oxford: Oxford University Press, 1987).
Delong-Bas, Natana. *Wahhabi Islam: From Revival and Reform to Global Jihad* (Oxford: Oxford University Press, 2004).
Dickinson, Eerik. *The Development of Early Sunnite Hadith Criticism: The Taqdima of Ibn Abī Ḥātim al-Rāzī* (240/854–327/938) (Leiden: Brill, 2001).
Drory, Joseph. "Ḥanbalīs of the Nablus Region in the Eleventh and Twelfth Centuries", *Asian and African Studies*, 22 (1988): 93–112.
Ebied, Rifaat and David Thomas (eds.), *Muslim-Christian Polemic during the Crusades. The Letter from the People of Cyprus and Ibn Abī Ṭālib al-Dimashqī's Response* (Leiden: Brill, 2005).
El-Ghobashy, Mona. "The Metamorphosis of the Egyptian Muslim Brothers," *International Journal of Middle Eastern Studies* 37 (2005): 373–395.
Elisséeff, Nikita. *La Description de Damas d'Ibn 'Asākir* (Damas: IFEAD, 1956).
El-Leithy, Tamer. "Coptic Culture and Conversion in Medieval Cairo, 1293–1524 A.D." (Ph.D. diss., Princeton University, 2004).
El-Rouayheb, Khaled. "Sunni Muslim Scholars on the Status of Logic, 1500–1800", *Islamic Law and Society* 11 (2004): 213–232.
Ende, Werner. "The Nakhāwila, A Shiite Community in Medina Past and Present", *Die Welt des Islams* 37.3 (1997): 263–348.
Escovitz, Josef H. *The office of qâḍî al-quḍât in Cairo under the Baḥrî Mamlûks* (Berlin: K. Schwarz, 1984).
Fakhry, Majid. *A History of Islamic Philosophy*, 2nd ed. (New York: Columbia University Press, 1983; 3rd edition, 2004).
Faraj, Bassām 'Aṭiyya Ismā'īl. *Al-Fikr al-siyāsī 'inda Ibn Taymiyya* (Amman: Dār al-Yāqūt, 2001).
Faraj, Muḥammad 'Abd al-Salām. *Al-Jihād, al-farīḍa al-ghā'iba* (n.p., 1990).
Fierro, Maribel. "The treatises against innovations (*kutub al-bida'*)", *Der Islam* 69 (1992): 204–46.
Frank, Richard M. "Al-Ash'arī's Conception of the Nature and Role of Speculative Reasoning in Theology," in *Proceedings of the VIth Congress of Arabic and Islamic Studies* (Uppsala, 1975), 137–154.
———, "Al-Ash'arī's *'Kitāb al-Ḥathth 'alā l-baḥth'*", *Mélanges Institut Dominicain d'études orientales* 18 (1988): 83–152.
———, "Elements in the Development of the Teachings of al-Ash'arī," *Muséon* 104 (1991): 141–190.

________, "The Structure of Created Causality according to al-Aš'arî," *Studia Islamica* 25 (1966): 13–75.

Friedman, Yaron. "Ibn Taymiyya's Fatāwā against the Nuṣayrī-'Alawī Sect", *Der Islam* 82.2 (2005): 349–363.

Fritsch, Erdman. *Islam und Christentum im Mittelalter* (Breslau: Verlag Müller und Seiffert, 1930).

Fu'ād, 'Abd al-Fattāḥ Muḥammad. *Ibn Taymiyya wa-mawqifuhu min al-fikr al-falsafī* (Alexandria: al-Hay'a al-Miṣriyya al-'Āmma li-al-Kitāb, 1980).

Gardet, Louis. *Les grands problèmes de la théologie musulmane: Dieu et la destine de l'homme* (Paris: J. Vrin, 1967).

Geoffroy, Eric. "Le Traité de soufisme d'un disciple d'Ibn Taymiyya: Aḥmad 'Imād al-Dīn al-Wāsiṭī (d. 711/1311)," *Studia Islamica* 82/2 (1995): 83–101.

Gibb, Hamilton. "Constitutional Organization: The Muslim Community and the State," in *Law in the Middle East*, ed. Majid Khadduri and Herbert Liebesny (Washington, D.C.: The Middle East Institute, 1955), 3–27.

Gilbert, Joan E. "Institutionalization of Muslim Scholarship and Professionalization of the 'Ulamā' in Medieval Damascus," *Studia Islamica* 52 (1980):105–134.

Gilliot, C."Al-Dhahabī contre la «pensée speculative»," *Zeitschrift der Deutschen Morgenländischen Gesellschaft* 150.1 (2000): 69–106.

Gimaret, Daniel. *Theories de l'acte humain en théologie musulmane* (Paris: J. Vrin, 1980).

________, "Théories de l'acte humain dans l'école Ḥanbalite," *Bulletin d'études orientales* 29 (1977): 156–78.

Gobillot, Geneviève. *La fitra- La conception originelle ses interprétations et functions chez les penseurs musulmans* (Le Caire: Institut français d'archeologie orientale, 2000).

________, "L`épître du discours sur la *fiṭra* (*Risāla fī-l-kalām 'alā-l-fiṭra*) de Taqī-i-Dīn Aḥmad ibn Taymīya (661/1262–728/1328). Présentation et traduction annotée," *Annales Islamologiques* XX (1984):29–53.

Goldziher, Ignaz. *Introduction to Islamic Theology and Law*, translation of *Vorlesungen über den Islam* (Heidelberg, 1910) by Andras and Ruth Hamori (Princeton, NJ: Princeton University Press, 1981).

Görmez, Mehmet. *Musa Carullah Bigiyef* (Ankara: Türkiye Diyanet Vakfi, 1994).

Gribetz, Arthur. "The *samā'* Controversy: Sufi vs. Legalist," *Studia Islamica* 74 (1991): 43–62.

Guenena, Nemat. *The 'Jihad' an 'Islamic Alternative' in Egypt*, Cairo Papers in Social Science (Cairo: The American University in Cairo Press, 1986).

Hallaq, Wael B. *A History of Islamic Legal Theories: An Introduction to Sunnī uṣūl al-fiqh* (Cambridge: Cambridge University Press, 1997).

________, *Ibn Taymīyya Against the Greek Logicians* (Oxford: Clarendon Press, 1993).

________, "Ibn Taymiyya on the Existence of God", *Acta Orientalia* 52 (1991): 49–69.

Hassan, Mona. "Loss of Caliphate: The Trauma and Aftermath of 1258 and 1924" (PhD dissertation, Princeton, 2009).

Haykel, Bernard. *Revival and Reform in Islam: The Legacy of Muḥammad al-Shawkānī* (Cambridge: Cambridge University Press, 2003).

Heer, Nicholas. "The Priority of Reason in the Interpretation of Scripture: Ibn Taymiyah and the Mutakallimūn," in Mustansir Mir (ed.), *Literary Heritage of Classical Islam: Arabic and Islamic Studies in Honor of James A. Bellamy* (Princeton: The Darwin Press, 1993), 181–95.

Hick, John. *Arguments for the Existence of God* (London Macmillan, 1970).

Hillenbrand, Carole. "Islamic Orthodoxy or Realpolitik? Al-Ghazālī's Views on Government", *Iran: Journal of the British Institute of Persian Studies* 26 (1988): 91–3.

Homerin, Th. Emil. "Ibn Taymīya's *al-Ṣūfiya wa'l-fuqarā'*," *Arabica* 32 (1985): 219–244.

Hoover, Jon. *Ibn Taymiyya's Theodicy of Perpetual Optimism* (Leiden: Brill, 2007).

———, "Perpetual Creativity in the Perfection of God: Ibn Taymiyya's Hadith Comentary on the Creation of this World," *Journal of Islamic Studies* 15.3 (Sept. 2004): 287–329.

Hourani, Albert. "Islamic History, Middle Eastern History, Modern History," in Malcolm H. Kerr (ed.), *Islamic Studies: A Tradition and its Problems* (Malibu, CA: Undena Publications, 1980), 5–26.

Hurvitz, Nimrod. "Biographies and mild asceticism: a study of Islamic moral imagination", *Studia Islamica* 85/1 (1997): 41–65.

———, *The Formation of Ḥanbalism: Piety into Power* (London: Routledge Curzon, 2002).

Ibn 'Ābidīn, Muḥammad Amīn ibn 'Umar (d. 1836). *Radd al-muḥtār 'alā al-Durr al-mukhtār*, ed. Ḥusām al-Dīn ibn Muḥammad Ṣāliḥ Farfūr (Damascus: Dār al-Thaqāfa wa-al-Turāth, 2000).

Ibn Sanad al-Baṣrī (d. 1827). *Maṭāli' al-Su'ūd*, ed. Ra'ūf and Qaysī (Baghdad: al-Dār al-Waṭaniyya, 1991).

'Imāra, Muḥammad. *al-Farīḍa al-ghā'iba: 'ard wa-ḥiwār wa-taqyīm* (Cairo: Dār Thābit, 1982).

Iqbal, Muhammad. *The Reconstruction of Religious Thought in Islam*, ed. M. Saeed Sheikh (Lahore: Iqbal Academy, 1989).

Irwin, Robert. *The Middle East in the Middle Ages: The Early Mamluk Sultanate 1250–1352* (Beckenham, Kent: Croon Helm, 1986).

Izutsu, T. *God and Man in the Koran: Semantics of the Koranic Weltanschuung* (Tokyo: Keio Institute of Cultural and Linguistic Studies, 1964).

Jackson, Sherman A. "Ibn Taymiyyah on Trial in Damascus," *Journal of Semitic Studies* 39 (1994): 41–85.

———, *Islam and the Blackamerican* (New York: Oxford University Press, 2005).

Jādd al-Ḥaqq, Shaykh Jādd al-Ḥaqq 'Alī. "Kutayyib al-Farīḍa al-ghā'iba wa-al-radd 'alayhi," *al-Fatāwā al-islāmiyya min Dār al-Iftā' al-Miṣriyya*, 3 January 1982, http://www.dar-alifta.org.

Jansen, Johannes. "Ibn Taymiyya and the Thirteenth Century: A Formative Period of Modern Muslim Radicalism," *Quaderni di studi arabi* 5–6 (1987–88): 391–396.

———, *The Neglected Duty: The Creed of Sadat's Assassins and Islamic Resurgence in the Middle East* (New York: Macmillan Publishing Company, 1986).

Johansen, Baber. "Signs as Evidence: the Doctrine of Ibn Taymiyya (1263–1328) and Ibn Qayyim al-Jawziyya (d. 1351) on Proof", *Islamic Law and Society* vol. 9.2 (2002): 168–193.

Jokisch, Benjamin. "*Ijtihād* in Ibn Taymiyya's *Fatāwā*", in Robert Gleave and Eugenia Kermeli (eds.), *Islamic Law: Theory and Practice* (London and New York: I.B. Tauris, 1997), 119–137.

———, *Islamisches Recht in Theorie und Praxis: Analyse einiger kaufrechtlicher Fatwas von Taqi'd-Din Ahmad b. Taymiyya* (Berlin: Klaus Schwarz Verlag, 1996).

Kabbani, Muhammad Hisham. *Encyclopedia of Islamic Doctrine* (Mountain View, CA: As-Sunnah Foundation of America, 1998).

Kanlidere, Ahmet. *Kadimle Cedit Arasında Musa Carullah: Hayatı, Eserleri, Fikirleri* (Istanbul: Dergah Yayınları, 2005).

———, *Reform within Islam: the Tajdid and Jadid Movement among the Kazan Tatars (1809-1917). Conciliation or Conflict?* (Istanbul: Eren Yayıncılık, 1997).

Kaptein, Nico. *Muḥammad's Birthday Festival* (Leiden: E.J. Brill, 1993).

Katz, Marion H. *The Birth of the Prophet Muhammad: Devotional Piety in Sunni Islam* (London: Routledge, 2007).

Kennedy, E.S. "The Exact Sciences in Iran under the Saljuqs and Mongols," in *The Cambridge History of Iran* (Cambridge: Cambridge University Press, 1968).

Kerr, Malcolm. *Islamic Reform: The Political and Legal Theories of Muḥammad 'Abduh and Rashīd Riḍā* (Berkeley: University of California Press, 1966).

Khan, Quamaruddin. *The Political Thought of Ibn Taymiyya* (Lahore: Islamic Book Foundation, 1983).

Khoury, Paul. *Paul d'Antioche, évêque melkite de Sidon (XIIe s.)* (Beirut: Imprimerie Catholique, 1964).

Knysh, Alexander. *Ibn 'Arabi in the Later Islamic Tradition. The Making of a Polemical Image in Medieval Islam* (Albany: State of New York Press, 1999).

———, "Ibrāhīm al-Kūrānī (d. 1101/1690): An Apologist for *waḥdat al-wujūd*", *Journal of the Royal Asiatic Society* 5 (1995): 39–47.

Kohlberg, Etan. *A Medieval Muslim Scholar at Work: Ibn Ṭāwūs and His Library* (Leiden: E. J. Brill, 1992).

———, "Early Attestations of the Term 'Ithnā 'Ashariyya'", *Jerusalem Studies in Arabic and Islam* 24 (2000): 343–357.

———, "Muwāfāt Doctrines in Muslim Theology", *Studia Islamica* 57 (1983):47–66.

Labib, Subhi. "The Problem of *Bida'* in the Light of an Arabic Manuscript of the 14th Century", in *Proceedings of the 26th International Congress of Orientalists, 4–10th January 1964*, 4 vols. (Poona: Bhandarkar Oriental Research Institute, 1966–1970), 4:277.

Lambton, Ann. "Islamic Mirrors for Princes," in *La Persia nel medioevo: Atti del Convegno internazionale, Roma 1970* (Rome: Accademia Nazionale dei Lincei, 1971), 419–442.

———, *State and Government in Medieval Islam: An Introduction to the Study of Islamic Political Theory* (Oxford: Oxford University Press, 1981).

Laoust, Henri. *Contribution à une étude de la méthodologie canonique de Taki-d-din Ahmad b. Taimiya* (Cairo: Institut français d'archéologie orientale, 1939).

———, *Essai sur les doctrines sociales et politiques de Taḳī-d-Dīn Aḥmad b. Taimīya, canoniste ḥanbalite né à Ḥarrān en 661/1262, mort à Damas en 728/1328* (Cairo: Imprimerie de l'institut français d'archéologie orientale, 1939).

———, "La Biographie d'Ibn Taimiya d'après Ibn Kathīr", *Bulletin d'études orientales* 9 (1943): 115–162.

———, *La profession de Foi d'Ibn Taymiyya: Texte, traduction et commentaire de la Wāṣitiyya* (Paris: Librairie Orientaliste Paul Geuthner, 1986).

———, "Le Hanbalisme sous les Mamlouks Bahrides (658/784–1260/1382)", *Revue des Études Islamiques* 28 (1960): 1–71.

———, "L'Influence d'Ibn Taymiyya," in Alford T. Welch and Pierre Cachia (eds.) *Islam: Past Influence and Present Challenge* (Edinburgh: Edinburgh University Press, 1979), 15–33.

———, "Quelques opinions sur la théodicée d'Ibn Taymiyya," *Mélanges Maspero*, vol. 3: Orient Islamique (Cairo, 1940).

———, "Remarques sur les expéditions du Kasrawān sous les premiers Mamluks," *Bulletin du Musée de Beyrouth* 4 (1940): 93–115.

———, "Une risāla d'Ibn Taimīya sur le serment de répudiation", *Bulletin d'études orientales* 7–8 (1937–8):215–36.

Lapidus, Ira. *Muslim Cities in the Later Middle Ages* (Cambridge, MA: Harvard University Press, 1967).

Little, Donald P. "Coptic Conversion to Islam Under the Baḥrī Mamlūks, 692–755/1293–1354," *Bulletin of the School of Oriental and African Studies* 39 (1976): 552–669.

———, "Did Ibn Taymiyya have a screw loose?," *Studia Islamica* 41 (1975), 93–111.

———, "Religion under the Mamluks," *The Muslim World* LXXIII (1983): 165–181.

———, "The Historical and Historiographical Significance of the Detention of Ibn Taymiyya," *International Journal of Middle East Studies* 4 (1973): 311–327.

Lull, Timothy F. (ed.). *Martin Luther's Basic Theological Writings* (Minneapolis: Fortress Press, 1989).

Lutfi, Huda. "Manners and Customs of Fourteenth- Century Cairene Women: Female Anarchy versus Male Shar'i Order in Muslim Prescriptive Treatises," in N. Keddie & B. Baron (eds.), *Women in Middle Eastern History: Shifting Boundaries in Sex and Gender* (New Haven: Yale University Press, 1991), 99–121.

Madelung, Wilferd. "Authority in the Absence of the Imam," in idem., *Religious Schools and Sects in Medieval Islam* (Aldershot, Great Britian: Variorum, 1985).

———, *Religious Trends in Early Islamic Iran* (Albany, NY: Persian Heritage foundation, 1988).

———, "The spread of Māturīdism and the Turks," *Actas do IV congresso de estudos árabes e Islâmicos, Biblos* 46 (1970): 109–168.

Madjid, N. "Ibn Taymiyya on Kalam and Falsafa", PhD dissertation (University of Chicago, 1984).

Makari, Victor E. *Ibn Taymiyyah's Ethics: The Social Factor* (Chico, CA: Scholars Press, 1983).

Makdisi, George. "Ash'ari and the Ash'arites in Islamic Religious History", *Studia Islamica* 17 (1962):37–80 and 18 (1963):19–39.

———, "Hanbalite Islam", in M. Swartz (ed. and trans.), *Studies in Islam* (New York & London: Oxford University Press, 1981), 216–274.

———, "Ibn Taimīya: A Ṣūfi of the Qādiriya Order," *American Journal of Arabic Studies*, 1 (1973): 118–129.

———, "Ibn Taimiya's Autograph Manuscript on Istihsān: Materials for the Study of Islamic Legal Thought", in G. Makdisi (ed.), *Arabic and Islamic Studies in Honor of Hamilton A. R. Gibb* (Leiden: E. J. Brill, 1965), 446–479.

———, "L'Islam hanbalisant", *Revue des Études Islamiques* 42 (1974): 241–44.

———, "The Hanbali school and Sufism," *Humaniora Islamica* 2 (1974): 61–72.

———, "The Sunni Revival", in D.S. Richards (ed.), *Islamic Civilization, 950–1150* (Oxford: Cassirer, 1973), 155–168.

Marlow, Louise. "Kings, Prophets, and the 'Ulamā' in Mediaeval Islamic Advice Literature," *Studia Islamica* 81 (1995):101–120.

Marmon, Shaun E. *Eunuchs and Sacred Boundaries in Islamic Society* (Oxford and New York: Oxford University Press, 1995).

Matteo, I. di. "Confutazione contro i Cristiani dello zaydita al-Qāsim b. Ibrāhīm", *Rivista degli Studi Orientali* 9 (1921–2):301–64.

Maududi, S. Abul 'Ala. *A Short History of the Revivalist Movement in Islam*, trans. al-Ash'ari (Lahore: Islamic Publications Limited, 1963).

McAuliffe, Jane Dammen. "Ibn Taymiya: Treatise on the principles of tafsir", in John Renard (ed.), *Windows on the House of Islam: Muslim Sources on Spirituality and Religious Life*, (Berkeley: University of California Press, 1998), 35–43.

________, "Qur'ānic Hermeneutics: The Views of al-Ṭabarī and Ibn Kathīr," in Andrew Rippin (ed.), *Approaches to the History of the Interpretation of the Qur'ān* (Oxford: Clarendon Press, 1988), 46–62.

Meier, Fritz."Das Sauberste über die Vorberstimmung. Ein Stuck Ibn Taymiyya," *Speculum* 32 (1981): 74–89.

Melchert, Christopher. *Ahmad ibn Hanbal* (Oxford: Oneworld Publications, 2006).

Messer, Richard. *Does God's Existence Need Proof?* (Oxford: Oxford University Press, 1993).

Michel, Thomas. *A Muslim theologian's response to Christianity: Ibn Taymiyya's* al-Jawab al-Sahih, edited and translated by Thomas F. Michel (Delmar, N.Y.: Caravan Books, 1984).

________, "Ibn Taymiyya's Sharḥ on the *Futūḥ al-Ghayb* of 'Abd al-Qādir al-Jīlānī," *Hamdard Islamicus* 4/2 (1981): 3–12.

Michot, Jean R [Yahya]. *Ibn Taymiyya: Lettre à Abû l-Fidâ'* (Louvain-la-Neuve: Institut Orientaliste de l'Université Catholique de Louvain, 1994).

Michot, Yahya. "A Mamluk Theologian's Commentary on Avicenna's *Risāla Adḥawiyya*", Parts I and II, *Journal of Islamic Studies* 14.2 (2003): 149–203, and 14.3 (2003): 309–63.

________, *Ibn Taymiyya. Les saints du Mont Liban: absence, Jihad, et spiritualité entre la montagne et la cité* (Beirut: Editions Albouraq, 2007).

________, "Je ne suis dans cette affaire qu'un musulman parmi d'autres...", Textes Spirituels d'Ibn Taymiyya, x. *Le Musulman* 23 (Mai 1994): 27–32.

________, *Le pouvoir et le religion* (Paris: Albouraq, forthcoming).

________, *Mardin: Hégire, fuite de péché et « demeure de l'Islam »* (Beirut: Les Éditions Albouraq, 2004); English translation as *Muslims under non-Muslim Rule* (Oxford: Interface Publications, 2007).

________, "Mongols et Mamlūks: l'état du monde musulman vers 709/1310", *Textes spirituels d'Ibn Tayimiyya XI, XII, XII*, available online at http://www.muslimphilosophy.com/.

________, "Vanités intellectuelles...L'impasse de rationalistes selon le *Rejet de la contradiction* d'Ibn Taymiyya," *Oriente Moderno* 19 (2000): 597–617.

Mir, Mustansir. *Coherence in the Qur'ān: A Study of Iṣlāḥī's Concept of Naẓm in Tadabbur-i Qur'ān* (Indianapolis: American Trust Publication, 1986).

Modarressi Tabātabā'ī, Hossein. *An Introduction to Shī'ī Law: A Bibliographical Study* (London: Ithaca Press, 1984).

________, *Crisis and Consolidation in the Formative Period of Shi'ite Islam* (Princeton: Darwin Press, 1993).

Mohamed, Yasien. *Fitrah: the Islamic Concept of Human Nature* (London: Ta Ha Publishers, 1996).

Mortel, Richard T. "The Ḥusaynid Amirate of Madīna during the Mamlūk Period", *Studia Islamica* 80 (1994):97–123.

Moustafa, Tamer. "Conflict and Cooperation between the State and Religious Institutions in Contemporary Egypt," *International Journal of Middle Eastern Studies* 32 (2000): 3–22.

Murad, Hasan Q. "Ibn Taymiya on Trial: A Narrative Account of his *miḥan*", *Islamic Studies* 18 (1979), 1–32.

________, "Miḥan of Ibn Taymiyya. A Narrative Account based on a Comparative Analysis of the Sources", MA dissertation (Montreal: Institute of Islamic Studies, McGill, 1968).

Nadwi, Abul Hasan Ali. *Saviours of Islamic Spirit*, trans. Muhiddin Ahmad, 2nd ed. (Lucknow, India: Academy of Islamic Research and Publications, 1977).
Nafi, Basheer M. "A Teacher of Ibn 'Abd al-Wahhāb: Muḥammad Ḥayāt al-Sindī and the Revival of Asḥāb al-Ḥadīth's Methodology", *Islamic Law & Society* 13 (2006): 208–241.
———, "Abū'l-Thanā' Maḥmūd al-Ālūsī: an *ʿālim*, Ottoman mufti and exegete of the Qur'ān", *International Journal of Middle East Studies* 44 (2002): 465–494.
———, "Tasawwuf and Reform in Pre-Modern Islamic Culture: In Search of Ibrahim al-Kūrānī", *Die Welt des Islams* 42 (2003): 307–355.
Nasir, Jamal J. *The Islamic law of personal status*, 3rd ed. (The Hague; London: Kluwer Law International, 2002).
Olesen, Niels Henrik. *Culte des saints et pélerinages chez Ibn Taymiyya* (Paris: Libraire Orientaliste Paul Geuthner S.A., 1991).
———, "Etude comparée des idées d'Ibn Taymiyya (1263–1328) et de Martin Luther (1483–1546) sur le culte des saints", *Revue des études islamiques* 50 (1982): 175–206.
Opwis, Felicitas. "The Construction of *Madhhab* Authority: Ibn Taymiyya's Interpretation of Juristic Preference (*Istiḥsān*)", *Islamic Law and Society* 15.2 (2008): 219–49.
Özervarli, M. Sait. "Ibn Teymiyye", *Türkiye Diyanet Vakfi Islam Ansiklopedisi* (Istanbul: Türkiye Diyanet Vakfi, 1999), 20:405–13.
———, *İbn Teymiyye'nin Düşünce Metodolojisi ve Kelâmcılara Eleştirisi* ("Ibn Taymiyya's Methodology of Thought and His Criticisms of the Mutakallimun") (Istanbul: ISAM, 2008).
Pagani, S. *Il rinnovamento mistico dell'Islam. Un commento di 'Abd al-Ghanī al-Nābulusī a Aḥmad Sirhindī* (Napoli: Università di Napoli l'Orientale, Disserationes 3:2003).
Perho, Irmeli. "Man Chooses his Destiny: Ibn Qayyim al-Jawziyya's Views on Predestination," *Islam and Christian-Muslim Relations* 12 (Jan. 2001):61–70.
Perlmann, Moshe. "Notes on Anti-Christian Propaganda in the Mamluk Empire," *Bulletin of the School of Oriental and African Studies* 10.4 (1942): 843–861.
Plantinga, Alvin and Nicholas Wolterstorff (eds.). *Faith and Rationality* (Notre Dame, Ind.: University of Notre Dame Press, 1991).
Pouzet, Louis. *Damas au VIIe/XIIIe s. Vie et structure religieuses dans une métropole islamique* (Beirut: Dār al-Mashriq, 1991).
Powers, Paul R. *Intent in Islamic Law. Motive and Meaning in Medieval Sunnī Fiqh* (Leiden: Brill, 2006).
Raff, Thomas. *Remarks on an Anti-Mongol Fatwā by Ibn Taymīya* (Leiden: n.p., 1973).
Rahman, Fazlur. *Revival and Reform in Islam: A Study of Islamic Fundamentalism*, ed. E. Moosa (Oxford: Oneworld, 2000).
Rapoport, Yossef. "Ibn Taymiyya on Divorce Oaths", in M. Winter and A. Levanoni (eds.), *The Mamluks in Egyptian Syrian and Society* (Leiden: Brill, 2004), 191–217.
———, "Legal diversity in the age of *taqlīd*: the four chief *qāḍīs* under the Mamlūks," *Islamic Law and Society* 10/2 (2003): 210–28.
———, *Marriage, Money and Divorce in Medieval Islamic Society* (Cambridge: Cambridge University Press, 2005).
Ringgren, H. *Studies in Arabic Fatalism* (Uppsala: Lundequistska bokhandeln, 1955).
Rippin, Andrew. "The Function of *asbāb al-nuzūl* in Qur'ānic Exegesis," *Bulletin of the School of Oriental and African Studies* 51 (1988): 1–20.
Rispler, Vardit. "Towards a New Understanding of the Term *bid'a*", *Der Islam* 68 (1991): 320–328.

Roberts, Nancy. "Reopening the Muslim-Christian Dialogue of the 13th–14th Centuries: Critical Reflections on Ibn Taymiyyah's Response to Christianity in *Al-Jawāb al-Ṣaḥīḥ li man baddala Dīn al-Masīḥ*", *Muslim World* 86 (1996):342–66.

Rosenthal, Erwin. *Political Thought in Medieval Islam: An Introductory Outline* (Cambridge: Cambridge University Press, 1962).

Rosenthal, Franz. *A History of Muslim Historiography* (Leiden: E. J. Brill, 1968).

Sabra, A. I. "Science and Philosophy in Medieval Islamic Theology: The Evidence of the Fourteenth Century", *Zeitschrift für Geschichte der Arabisch-Islamischen Wissenschaften*, 9 (1994): 11–23.

Sabra, Adam. "Ibn Ḥazm's literalism: A critique of Islamic legal theory", *Al-Qanṭara* 28.1 (2007): 7–40.

Saleh, Walid. *The Formation of Classical Tafsīr Tradition: The Qur'ān Commentary of al-Tha'labī* (Leiden: Brill, 2004).

Salibi, Kamal. "Mount Lebanon Under the Mamluks", in Samir Seikaly et al. (eds.), *Quest for Understanding: Arabic and Islamic Studies in Memory of Malcolm Kerr* (Beirut: American University of Beirut, 1991), 15–32.

Samir, S. K. "Notes sure la "Lettre à un Musulman de Sidon" de Paul d'Antioche", *Orientalia Lovaniensia Periodica* 24 (1993):179–95.

Sayeed, Asma. "Women and *Ḥadīth* Transmission. Two Case Studies from Mamlūk Damascus," *Studia Islamica* 95 (2002):71–94.

Schacht, Joseph. *An Introduction to Islamic Law* (Oxford: Oxford University Press, 1964).

Schimmel, Annemarie. "The Celebration of the Prophet's Birthday," in idem., *And Muḥammad is His Messenger* (Chapel Hill and London: University of North Carolina Press, 1985).

Schmidtke, Sabine. *Theology of al-'Allāma al-Ḥillī (d. 725/1325)* (Berlin: Klaus Schwarz Verlag, 1991).

Ṣchwartz, Stephen. *The Two Faces of Islam: The House of Sa'ud from Tradition to Terror* (New York: Doubleday, 2002).

Schwarz, M. "Acquisition (*kasb*) in Early Kalām," in S.M. Stern, A. Hourani and V. Brown (eds.), *Islamic Philosophy and the Classical Tradition: Essays Presented by His Friends and Pupils to Richard Walzer on his Seventieth Birthday* (Columbia: University of South Carolina Press, 1972), 355–387.

Shams, Muḥammad 'Uzayr and 'Alī ibn Muḥammad al-'Umrān. *Al-Jāmi' li-sīrat Shaykh al-Islām Ibn Taymiyya khilāla sab'a qurūn* (Mecca: Dār 'Ālam al-Fawā'id, 1420H).

Sivan, Emmanuel. "Ibn Taymiyya: Father of the Islamic Revolution. Medieval Theology & Modern Politics," *Encounter* 60, no. 3 (1983): 41–51.

———, *Radical Islam: Medieval Theology and Modern Politics* (New Haven: Yale University Press, 1990).

Somogyi, J. de. "Adh-Dhahabī record of the destruction of Damascus by the Mongols in 699–700/1300–1301", in S. Löwinger and J. de Somogyi (eds.), *Goldziher Memorial Volume* (Budapest, 1948): 353–386.

Sourdel, Dominique. "Deux documents relatifs à la communauté hanbalite de Damas", *Bulletin d'Etudes Orientales* 25 (1972): 141–50.

Stark, Jan. "Beyond 'Terrorism' and 'State Hegemony': Assessing the Islamist Mainstream in Egypt and Malaysia," *Third World Quarterly* 26, no. 2 (2005): 307–327.

Stewart, Devin J. *Islamic Legal Orthodoxy: Twelver Shiite Responses to the Sunni Legal System* (Salt Lake City: University of Utah Press, 1998).

Swanson, Mark. "Ibn Taymiyya and the *Kitāb al-Burhān*: A Muslim Controversialist responds to a Ninth-Century Arabic Christian Apology", in Yvonne Y. Haddad and Wadi Z. Haddad (eds.), *Christian-Muslim Encounters* (Gainsville: University Press of Florida, 1995), 95–107.

Talīma, 'Iṣām. *Yūsuf al-Qaraḍāwī: Faqīh al-Du'āt wa-Dā'iyat al-Fuqahā'* (Damascus: Dār al-Qalam, 2001).

Talmon-Heller, Daniella. "The Shaykh and the Community: Popular Hanbalite Islam in the 12th–13th Century in Nablus and Jabal Qasyūn," *Studia Islamica* 79 (1994): 103–20.

Taylor, Christopher S. *In the vicinity of the righteous. Ziyāra and the veneration of Muslim saints in late medieval Egypt* (Leiden: Brill, 1999).

Thomas, David. "A Mu'tazilī response to Christianity: Abu 'Alī al-Jubbā'ī's Attack on the Trinity and Incarnation", in Rifaat Ebied and Herman Teule (eds.), *Studies on the Christian Arabic Heritage in honour of Father Prof Dr Samir Khalil Samir* (Leuven: Peeters, 2004), 279–313.

———, (edited and translated), *Anti-Christian Polemic in Early Islam. Abū 'Īsā al-Warrāq's "Against the Trinity"*, (Cambridge: Cambridge University Press, 1992).

———, "Paul of Antioch's *Letter to a Muslim Friend* and *The Letter from Cyprus*", in D. Thomas (ed.), *Syrian Christians under Islam, the first thousand years* (Leiden: Brill, 2001), 203–21.

Tottoli, Roberto. "Origin and Use of the Term Isrā'īliyyāt in Muslim Literature," *Arabica* XLVI (1999): 193–210.

Trimingham, J. Spencer. *The Sufi Orders in Islam* (New York and Oxford: Oxford University Press, 1998).

Tyan, Emile. *Histoire de l'organisation judiciare en pays d'Islam*, 2nd edition (Leiden: Brill, 1960).

Ukeles, Raquel. "Innovation or Deviation: Exploring the Boundaries of Islamic Devotional Law," PhD. Dissertation (Harvard University, 2006).

'Ulwān, Isma'īl ibn Ḥasan ibn Muḥammad. *Al-Qawā'id al-fiqhiyya al-Khams al-Kubrā wa-al-Qawā'id al-Mundarija taḥtaha: Jam' wa-dirāsa min Majmū' Fatāwā Shaykh al-Islām Ibn Taymiyya* (al-Dammam: Dār Ibn al-Jawzī, 2000).

van Ess, J. *Frühe Mu'tazilitische Häresiographie* (Beirut: Dar al-Machreq, 1971).

———, "Ibn Kullāb et la miḥna", tr. Claude Gilliot, *Arabica* (1990): 173–233.

———, *Zwischen Ḥadit und Theologie. Studien zur Entstehen prädestinatianischer Überlieferung* (Berlin: de Gruyter, 1975).

Vogel, Frank E. *Islamic Law and Legal System. Studies of Saudi Arabia* (Leiden: Brill, 2000).

von Kügelgen, Anke. "'The poison of philosophy'—Ibn Taymiyya's struggle for and against reason", in Birgit Krawietz and Georges Tamer (eds.), *Proceedings of the Workshop "Neo-Hanbalism Reconsidered: The Impact of Ibn Taymiyya and Ibn Qayyim al-Jawziyya" (Berlin, 23.–25. October 2007)*, (Berlin: de Gruyter Verlag [Beiheft to Der Islam], forthcoming).

Watt, W. Montgomery. *Free Will and Predestination in Early Islam* (London: Luzac and Company, 1948).

———, *Islamic Creeds* (Edinburgh: Edinburgh University Press, 1994).

———, *Islamic Political Thought: The Basic Concepts* (Edinburgh: Edinburgh University Press, 1968).

———, *The Formative Period of Islam* (Edinburgh: Edinburgh University Press, 1973).

Weismann, Itzchak. *Taste of Modernity: Sufism, Salafiyya, and Arabism in late Ottoman Damascus* (Leiden: Brill, 2001).

Wensinck, J. *The Muslim Creed: Its Genesis and Historical Development* (London: Frank Cass, 1965).

Winter, Michael. "Inter-*madhhab* competition in Mamlūk Damascus: al-Ṭarsūsī's counsel for the Turkish Sultans," *Jerusalem Studies in Arabic and Islam* 25 (2001): 195–211.

Winter, Stefan H. "Shams al-Dīn Muḥammad ibn Makkī 'al-Shahīd al-Awwal' (d. 1384) and the Shi'ah of Syria", *Mamluk Studies Review* 3 (2000): 149–182.

Wisnovsky, Robert. "One Aspect of the Avicennian Turn in Sunnî Theology", *Arabic Sciences and Philosophy*, 14.1 (2004): 65–100.

———, "The Nature and Scope of Arabic Philosophical Commentary in Post-classical (ca. 1100–1900 AD) Islamic Intellectual History: Some Preliminary Observations", in P. Adamson, H. Baltussen and M.W.F. Stone (eds.), *Philosophy, Science and Exegesis in Greek, Arabic and Latin Commentaries*, Vol. 2, Supplement to the Bulletin of the Institute of Classical Studies 83/1–2 (London: Institute of Classical Studies 2004), 149–191.

Wolfson, H. A. *The Philosophy of the Kalam* (Cambridge MA: Harvard University Press, 1976).

Zaman, M. Qasim. "Death, Funeral Processions, and the Articulation of Religious Authority in Islam," *Studia Islamica* 93 (2001): 27–58.

Ziyada, Nicola. *Dimashq fī 'aṣr al-Mamālīk* (Beirut: Maktabat Lubnān, 1966).

INDEX

A. Titles of works by Ibn Taymiyya

B. General index

A

Z

Ẓāhirī (school of law), 203, 204, 303
zakāt (alms), 134, 328, 357, 358
Zarzūr, ʻAdnān, 126
ziyāra, see visitation